Dictatorship
& Politics

Dictatorship & Politics

Intrigue, Betrayal, and Survival in Venezuela, 1908–1935

University of Notre Dame Press

Notre Dame, Indiana

Copyright © 2008 by University of Notre Dame
Notre Dame, Indiana 46556
www.undpress.nd.edu
All Rights Reserved

Manufactured in the United States of America

Library of Congress Cataloging in-Publication Data

McBeth, B. S. (Brian Stuart), 1951–
   Dictatorship and politics : intrigue, betrayal, and survival in Venezuela,
1908–1935 / Brian S. McBeth.
       p. cm.
   "Recent titles from the Helen Kellogg Institute for International Studies."
   Includes bibliographical references and index.
   ISBN-13: 978-0-268-03510-5 (cloth : alk. paper)
   ISBN-10: 0-268-03510-5 (cloth : alk. paper)
 1. Venezuela—Politics and government—1908–1935.   2. Dictatorship—
Venezuela—History—20th century.   I. Helen Kellogg Institute for
International Studies.   II. Title.
   F2325.M388   2008
   987.06'313—dc22
                                                          2008000406

This book is dedicated to Ramón J. Velásquez, a man of immense personal courage and great intellectual and political powers, who has served Venezuela and his native Táchira with distinction for more than fifty years, becoming president of the country in 1993. His political career started in the 1940s, and he was later imprisoned and tortured for many long years for opposing the Pérez Jiménez dictatorship in the 1950s. He was secretary general of the presidency (1959–63) during the difficult years of Rómulo Betancourt's administration and assumed the reigns of power after Betancourt was wounded on June 24, 1960, during an attempted assassination paid for by the Dominican dictator general Rafael Leónidas Trujillo. Velásquez was first elected senior senator for his home state of Táchira in 1959 and represented the state until 1979, returning later in 1989 until 1994. While a senator he headed a number of important committees. He has written a large number of erudite and immensely readable books on modern Venezuelan history, bringing to light a period of darkness in the country's history. He was editor of *El Nacional* newspaper for many years (1964–69 and 1979–81). He saved and nurtured the *Archivo Histórico de Miraflores,* publishing a vast array of documents from the archive. He also founded FUNRES, an institution dedicated to saving historical archives on Venezuela. Velásquez is a truly modern Renaissance man.

CONTENTS

LIST OF TABLES

ACKNOWLEDGMENTS

Part of the research for this book was financed by a Foreign Area Fellowship granted by the (US) Social Science Research Council and the American Council of Learned Societies, and by grants from the Centro de Estudios Latinoamericanos Rómulo Gallegos, Fundación John Boulton, and St. Antony's College, Oxford. I am also indebted to George Philip for having read the original manuscript and for his comments. I would also like to thank the two anonymous readers for their insightful commentaries. A very special mention must be made of my wife, María Cristina, for her wise comments and general encouragement. I would also like to thank in particular the Archivo Histórico de Miraflores, the Biblioteca Nacional of Venezuela, the Public Records Office, the British Library, and the Latin American Library at the Latin American Centre, Oxford, for allowing me access to their collection. The author translated all quotations from the original Spanish. For any error of omission or commission, I alone am accountable.

AAA	Archivo del General Antonio Aranguren
AGT	Archivo particular del Dr. Gumersindo Torres
AHM	Archivo Histórico de Miraflores
AHMCOP	Archivo Histórico de Miraflores, Copiador
AHMSGPRCP	Archivo Histórico de Miraflores, Secretaría General de la Presidencia de la República, Correspondencia Presidencial
AHMSGPRCS	Archivo Histórico de Miraflores, Secretaría General de la Presidencía de la República, Correspondencia del Secretario General
AJMH	Archivo del General José Manuel Hernández
AMLR	Archivo de Manuel Landaeta Rosales
BAHM	*Boletín del Archivo Histórico de Miraflores*
BCCC	*Boletín de la Cámara de Comercio de Caracas*
Bs.	bolívares
CO	Colonial Office, Public Record Office
DDCS	*Diario de Debates de la Cámara del Senado*
DS	U.S. Department of State
FO	Foreign Office, Public Record Office
HAHR	*Hispanic American Historical Review*
MinFo	Ministerio de Fomento
MinHa	Ministerio de Hacienda

MinRelExt	Ministerio de Relaciones Exteriores
MinRelInt	Ministerio de Relaciones Interiores
MOP	Ministerio de Obras Públicas
PP	*Parliamentary Papers*
Shell	Royal Dutch–Shell Group

Introduction

General Juan Vicente Gómez came to power in a bloodless coup on December 19, 1908,[1] and died in his sleep still in power twenty-seven years later, on December 17, 1935. In 1908, Venezuela was little known to the outside world, but by the time of Gómez's death the country was of vital strategic importance to the British Empire and, in addition, a significant supplier of oil to the Atlantic seaboard of the United States.[2] During Gómez's time, Venezuela was transformed from being a predominantly agricultural country to the second largest oil producer in the world. The history of the Gómez regime has been written as though it was almost preordained that the dictator would remain in power for twenty-seven years. Such a view detracts from the political acumen that Gómez displayed in order to remain in power. Gómez was not only the undisputed leader of Venezuela from the end of 1908 until his death in December 1935, but also the second most important political figure in the country during the previous Cipriano Castro administration (1899–1908).[3]

This book is a reappraisal of the Gómez regime, which by no means was a time of inert dictatorship, and the struggle by various groups to topple the dictator. What is new in the treatment of the regime is that it departs from previous studies by demonstrating that Gómez's ability to withstand opponents' attacks resulted from more than ruthless repression. The exiles' political disagreements, personal rivalries, financial difficulties, occasional harassment by foreign powers, and at times plain bad luck were important contributing factors, together with Gómez's political acumen and repressive apparatus, that allowed the regime to survive so many plots against it. In addition, in examining the opposition to the Gómez regime I have removed oil from the center stage of the regime's foreign relations and examined instead the tolerance and intolerance by foreign governments of the exiles' activities. This book refutes the usual picture of the steadfast foreign support for Gómez from the United States and European powers interested in Venezuelan oil by focusing on the variable fortunes of the Venezuelan political exiles as they attempted to arrange anti-Gómez uprisings from foreign soil. The historiography of the period has also overlooked the internal strife that took place within the Gomecista supporters of the regime.

The Gómez dictatorship has been viewed as one long period of peace, but there was barely a year of his rule in which some kind of anti-government conspiracy was not being hatched. The permanent nature of the political threat that Gómez faced, both from inside and outside the regime, placed him in a rather embattled position. The intellectual justification for the Gómez regime was brought about by the local intelligentsia who belonged to the school of positivism such as Pedro Manuel Arcaya, José Gil Fortoul, and Laureano Vallenilla Lanz.[4] The Venezuelan intellectuals of the time were attracted to the philosophy of positivism because it helped explain and justify the country's turbulent history in a rational manner.[5] In Gómez's correspondence and actions, as we shall see, there is a strong sense of destiny, with no room for doubt or for second thoughts.

Gómez, a man of medium height and a successful agricultural businessman in his native Táchira before entering politics who is reputed to have sired seventy-four children from thirty-three women, was the largest single financial backer of Castro's successful 1899 Revolución Restauradora, which brought the Tachirenses to power. Gómez's entrepreneurial skills were put to good use during the military campaign when he was appointed quartermaster, ensuring that supplies and ammunition reached the fighting men. Gómez's own military skill was later fully tested during Manuel Antonio Matos's Libertadora revolution (1901–1903) when, as vice president and head of the army, he defeated the ablest regional enemy caudillos. From then on Gómez's military skill would be unquestioned by friend and foe, giving him the firm conviction that he would always defeat his enemies.

During the Castro administration, Gómez, together with Castro and other government officials, acquired large cattle ranches in Guayana, Apure, and the central states. Gómez, for example, when he was federal district governor from 1899 to 1900, secured the exclusive right to supply the capital city with meat, later adding the cities of Puerto Cabello, Maracay, and Valencia. In addition, Gómez controlled the lucrative cattle export trade to the West Indies, which at the time represented 10 percent of the country's total export trade of $16 million. This aspect of Gómez's activities continued on an even greater scale once he achieved power. He and his family became the main shareholders in the Compañía Venezolana de Navegación, the paper and cement factories at Maracay, the Lactuario de Maracay, C.A. Central Azucarero del Zulia, Compañía Ganadera Nacional, and the Venezuelan Tanning and Coloring Extracts Ltd. Gómez's brother, Juan Crisóstomo (Juancho) Gómez, held the monopoly and sale concession for the supply of frozen fish to Caracas together with Teodoro Arriens, for which the latter paid him $946 each month. These ventures were extremely profitable; for example, Eustoquio Gómez, a first cousin who began his political career with no real assets to his name, by 1924 had $574,713 deposited with the Banco de Venezuela, $123,165 with the Royal Bank of Canada in Maracaibo, and $400,000 in the latter's bank branch in New York.[6]

Gómez referred to his December 1908 coup as being an "evolution within the same cause,"[7] because his arrival to power only involved a change at the head of the Castroist structure of government. Although Gómez was one of the most important linchpins in Castro's administration, he intended his new government to be a breath of fresh air that revitalized the country's image, which had been thoroughly discredited during the previous regime. His underlying desire was to bring peace and prosperity to the country, encapsulated in one of the regime's mottoes of "Peace and Work." In political terms, the December coup was rationalized as abolishing "absolutism as a form of government"[8] and establishing a "genuinely democratic regime."[9] Gómez wanted to strengthen Congress by instituting a system that ensured that the democratic principles of government remained intact by preventing the executive from accumulating too much power. The new government promised to safeguard the constitutional rights of its citizens by allowing freedom of expression, respect for the sovereignty of the states, and the protection of industry from the pernicious impact of monopoly power that the previous government had pursued with a vengeance. Gómez wanted initially, above all, to reach agreement on the country's pressing international disputes to recover some sense of stability in order to live in "peace and harmony."[10]

There was, however, a need to strip Castro of his powers because he remained the nominal head of government. Gómez would do so by instituting a trial at the Federal Court and of Cassation against the former president, who was accused of conspiracy to murder Gómez. On February 27, 1909, the court unsurprisingly found Castro guilty, immediately suspending him of his presidential duties. At the same time, Héctor Luis Paredes instituted criminal charges against Castro for the murder of his brother Antonio Paredes in Barrancas in 1907. Castro's trial in absentia for crimes against the state and for the murder of Paredes allowed the government to strip Castro of his presidential title and bar him from ever holding office again. This was an eminently neat way of solving the legal problem of Gómez staying in power without the need to suspend Congress and local councils. Consequently, all executive and legislative officers remained in place, with the same congressmen, state presidents, court officers, and minor government officials appointed by Castro continuing under the new Gómez administration.

The opposition to Gómez's rule came mainly from the following groups: former members of his government exiled in Colombia, the Caribbean, Central America, Mexico, Europe, and the United States (detailed in table 1), a small dissenting group of young army officers; various left-wing groups, and from certain sectors of an incipient middle class produced by the prosperity and relative stability enjoyed by Venezuela during this period. The opposition from organized labor was minimal, as there was no real labor movement.[11] The rebels and exiles came from all walks of life. There were large landowners such as Leopoldo Baptista, José María Ortega Martínez, and Arístides Tellería; professionals (medical doctors, lawyers, engineers) such as Francisco Hermógenes Rivero, Alejandro Rivas Vásquez, Santos Aníbal Domínici, Carlos León, Néstor Luis Pérez, Rafael Ernesto López, Manuel Antonio Pulido Méndez, and Atilano Carnevali; other professionals (working in banks, industry, and commerce) such as Rodolfo Rojas, Pedro Felipe Rojas, Pedro Elías and Francisco de Paúla Aristeguieta Rojas, and Manuel Jové; and finally others, like Juan Pablo Peñaloza, Guillermo Egea Mier, Doroteo Flores, and Carlos López Bustamante, who worked in miscellaneous industries such as hotels and shipyards. As we shall see, the "caudillo-type" expeditions against Gómez such as the *Odin/Harrier, Angelita, Falke,* and *Superior* expeditions were difficult to organize owing to the logistical problems encountered and sometimes just plain bad luck. The exiles, however, showed greater political acumen than current historiography credits them with; many of the rebel expeditions were linked to simultaneous uprisings in the countryside, as well as support from nations such as Mexico that opposed Gómez.

A contemporary commentator portrayed Gómez as the "shame of America"[12] for his savage repression of his political opponents, but it is doubtful

Table 1   Cabinet Ministers and State Presidents Who Became Exiles

Name	Ministry	Period	State	Period
Alcántara, Francisco Linares	Interior	1908–12		
Baptista, Leopoldo	Secretary General	1908–1909		
Baptista, Trino	Education	1909–11	Trujillo	1909
Baptista, Víctor M.			Trujillo	1909–12
Carabaño, Rafael María	Development	1908–10		
Iturbe, Aquiles	Federal District Governor	1908–1909	Carabobo	1913
			Táchira	1909–10
	Development	1911–12		
León, Carlos	Federal District Governor	1909		
Olivares, Régulo	Defense	1908–10	Táchira	1910–11
Ortega Martínez, José María	Public Works	1909		
Rolando, Armando			Anzoátegui	1909–13
Tellería, Arístides			Bolívar	1909–11
				1912–14
Vargas, Roberto	Public Works	1908–1909	Guárico	1909

Source: Adapted from Appendix A.

whether his methods were any worse than those of his contemporaries. Moreover, with the demise of Castro (of natural causes) in 1924, Gómez was extremely confident that his enemies would be unable to topple him; he allowed thousands of Tachirenses exiled in Colombia to return to the country in 1925 and two years later released all political prisoners from the notorious La Rotunda jail in Caracas. Gómez cultivated good foreign relations with all the major foreign powers because he did not want a repeat of what happened during the Castro years, when the country was subjected to a "peaceful blockade"[13] by the British, German, and Italian navies and later the United States, France, the Netherlands, and Colombia broke off diplomatic relations. Nevertheless, the rebels almost succeeded during 1917–18 in getting the United States to sever diplomatic relations. Mexico was the only country that showed any open hostility toward Gómez, breaking off diplomatic relations for almost ten years beginning in 1923. Other Latin American countries such as Colombia, Cuba, Nicaragua, and Peru at different times also supported various exile groups in their quest to oust Gómez. The oil companies, especially the American ones, were at times suspected of financing various abortive revolutions, but their involvement with the exiled political leaders was extremely limited. Certain oil companies did help the government by providing intelligence on political activity at the various oil camps and operational centers. The one important personal and local link between the oil industry and the exiled revolutionaries was through General Antonio Aranguren, the richest man in the country, who held the oil concession operated by the Venezuelan Oil Concessions Ltd. (VOC), a Royal Dutch–Shell Group (Shell) subsidiary. In addition to being on the board of VOC, Aranguren was a director of the Venezuelan Eastern Oilfields Ltd. and the Venezuelan Consolidated Oilfields Ltd. He was also the country's most successful oil intermediary and negotiator who, together with Gil Fortoul in 1928, successfully negotiated the transfer of the national reserves acquired by the Compañía Venezolana de Petróleo, Gómez's own company, to the Creole Syndicate.[14] In the early 1920s, Aranguren became a fierce opponent of Gómez, partly financing the 1921 *Odin/Harrier* expedition, the 1924 *Angelita* expedition, the 1929 *Falke* expedition, and probably the 1931 *Superior* expedition.

There are books in Spanish that touch on certain topics included in this study, but none offers the comprehensive treatment on exile politics found in this book. Previous authors of the Gómez dictatorship, such as Brito Figueroa, Rangel, Polanco Alcántara, Betancourt, Fuenmayor, Caballero, Baptista, Brandt, and Siso, have argued that Gómez survived for so long in power because of international support for the regime, his success in building the national army, and the fierce repression of the opposition.[15] The nonrecognition or the threat of nonrecognition was one of the chief means by which the United States attempted to discourage revolutionary changes of government in the Caribbean after 1909. Although it is true that the United States left Gómez to his own devices after the development of the oil industry in the 1920s, the rebels in 1917–18 almost succeeded in getting the American government to withdraw recognition of the Gómez regime, but the entry of the United States into World War I in 1917 brought this effort to an end. Gómez was able to use the 30 percent surtax on imported goods from Curacao and Trinidad, the Dutch and British colonial islands respectively off the coast of Venezuela, to get the two European countries to keep a close check on the exiles living on those islands. Gómez saw the formation of a modern army as essential in order to defend the gains made by his government, but he ensured that he controlled the vast majority of the country's armory by only allowing his state presidents a small cache of arms.

Table 2 Distribution of State Presidents between Single, Double, and Multiple States, 1909–35

Number States Governed	Number of Presidents	%	Years in Office	%
One	65	63.7	191	35.3
Two	27	26.5	231.5	42.8
Three +	10	9.8	118.5	21.9
Total	102	100	541	100

Source: Adapted from Appendix A.

The historiography of the period asserts that Gómez rotated his state presidents periodically so that they could not gain a regional political foothold to challenge him. A detailed examination of the time spent in each state (see table 2) by state presidents reveals that out of a total of 102 state presidents during the period, only 10 percent were rotated, defined as governing in three or more states. If we broaden the definition to include governing in two states, the rotation accounts for just over 36 percent. If we look at the number of years in office by the state presidents, we find that around a third of the state presidents governed in two or more states, accounting for over 65 percent of the total period governed. Of these, a select group of ten governed in three or more states, representing just under 22 percent of the total period governed. What is more revealing from the figures is that twenty-five of the state presidents governed for periods of six or more years in a single state, accounting for 42 percent of the total period.

Moreover, a number of state presidents spent more than 10 years in one state. Amador Uzcátegui headed Mérida State for 14 years, León Jurado was president of Falcón State for 19.5 years over two periods, José Rafael Luque in Miranda State and José Domínguez in Apure State spent 12 years governing their states, and Guillermo Barreto Méndez was president of Cojedes State for 11.5 years. Many of the state presidents had long-standing connections with Gómez, such as José María García Velasco, Rafael María Velasco Bustamante, Emilio Fernández, Gumersindo Méndez, Elbano Mibelli, Eustoquio Gómez, and Pedro María Cárdenas, who were some of the young officers who accompanied Castro's invasion of Venezuela on May 23, 1899. Others, such as Félix Galavís, Aquiles Iturbe, León Jurado, and Vincencio Pérez Soto, were part of Gómez's military campaign against Matos in 1901–1903.

At the national level, Gómez surrounded himself, especially at the beginning of his rule, with intellectual and prestigious men such as Román Cárdenas, José Gil Fortoul, Samuel Dario Maldonado, and Pedro Manuel Arcaya. Gómez appointed seventy-four different ministers during his regime, with eight ministers serving six years or more, representing 25 percent of the total period. The figure would be higher if we stripped out a number of ministers at the beginning of the regime who later turned against Gómez. Some of the ministers served for long periods, in particular Pedro Itriago Chacín as foreign affairs minister for almost fourteen years, Carlos Jiménez Rebolledo as defense minister for twelve years, Juancho Gómez as federal district governor for ten years, and Román Cárdenas as finance minister for ten years. Many of the ministers were also state presidents, and in the case of Victorino Márquez Bustillos, also provisional president from 1914 to 1922 (see table 3).

The book is divided into three parts: Part I, 1908–1916, deals with the establishment of Gómez as a dictator; Part II, 1917–1928, deals with the consolidation of power and the internal and external pressure Gómez withstood to remain in power; and, finally, Part III, 1929–1935, deals with the largest filibustering expedition mounted against the regime in 1929 and the declining years of the regime until Gómez's death of natural causes while still in power on December 17, 1935. Appendix A provides a brief biographical note to some of the more important political actors of the Gómez regime and a number of tables that list the names and dates of the ministers and state presidents during the regime. It should be noted that, with minor exceptions, all currencies have been converted into US dollars for ease and consistency. The foreign exchange conversion tables are given in Appendix B, where there is also a present-day (2003) value multiplier. This allows the reader to arrive at a present-day value for a particular sum at a given date. For instance, to calculate the 2003 value of $100 in 1909 all the reader needs to do is multiply the sum by a factor of 19.5, which is found in the table, to arrive at the value of $1,950. Finally, to avoid confusion with the various surnames, "Gómez" throughout the book refers to the dictator. For other family members either their nicknames, such as Vicentico for José Vicente Gómez, or their first names, such as Eustoquio Gómez, are used. For other families the paternal and maternal surnames are used, so that José Rosario García Bustamante is referred to as García Bustamante, and José María García Velasco is referred to as García Velasco. Where there are two brothers such as Pedro César Domínici and Santos Aníbal Domínici, their first given names together with their surnames are used for the sake of clarity.

Table 3 Cabinet Ministers Who Were Also State Presidents

Name	Ministry	Period	State	Period	Provisional Presidency
Antonio Alamo	Development	1922–29	Bolívar	1933–35	
			Sucre	1929–31	
Trino Baptista	Education	1909–11	Trujillo	1909	
Manuel Díaz Rodríguez	Foreign Affairs	1914	Nueva Esparta	1925	
			Nueva Esparta	1932–34	
	Development	1916–17			
Santiago Fontiveros	Development	1914–15	Trujillo	1915–17	
			Trujillo	1921–25	
José María García Velasco	Federal District Governor	1929–31	Trujillo	1912–14	
			Zulia	1914–18	
			Carabobo	1928	
Juan Crisóstomo Gómez	Federal District Governor	1912–23	Miranda	1911–14	
Julio Hidalgo	Federal District Governor	1923–24	Aragua	1914–18	
Carlos Jiménez Rebolledo	Defense	1917–28	Barinas	1909–15	
Samuel Darío Maldonado	Education	1908–1909	Aragua	1921–23	
Victorino Márquez Bustillos	Federal District Governor	1911–12			1915–22
	Defense	1912–13			
Rafael Requena	Secretary General	1931–33	Aragua	1929–31	
Rafael María Velasco Bustamante	Federal District Governor	1925–28	Aragua	1918–20	
	Finance	1929–30			
	Federal District Governor	1931–35	Lara	1921–25	

Source: Adapted from Appendix A.

Establishment of Power, 1908 – 1916

A New Era

The arrival of Gómez at the presidential palace on December 19, 1908, was perceived by many as the dawning of a new era after the excesses of Castro's administration. A period of political liberalization developed, with the various Liberal and Conservative political factions taking advantage to reorganize themselves. The Gómez administration also instituted a series of policies across the various ministries aimed at modernizing the state apparatus. Gómez also tackled with vigor the country's finances, which were in a mess, and ended many of the monopolies that were strangling the economy. At the same time, the armed forces and the educational system were modernized, and the slow process of binding the country together was started with a large road construction program. Gómez would receive his biggest surprise when dealing with the country's pressing international problems, especially its relationship with the United States, which sent an overwhelmingly large naval force to compel the new government to accept five outstanding claims that the previous administration had rejected.

One of the first political acts by Gómez was to free the political prisoners and allow a free press. A general amnesty was decreed on April 19, 1909, for all prisoners taken during the disturbances of December 13, 14, and 19 of the previous year. Ironically, this also included Castro, the former president deposed by Gómez; all the charges against him were dropped.[1] In addition, the monopolies created during Castro's regime, such as cigarettes, explosives, and salt, were abolished. At the same time, Eustoquio Gómez, Gómez's cousin, was freed from jail after the Supreme Court reexamined his involvement in the murder of General Luis Mata Illas, the Governor of Caracas, in 1907 and found that there was not enough evidence for a conviction.[2] In order to prevent the threat of an armed uprising, Gómez ordered the collection of all the arms that had been distributed prior to the December coup.

Once in power, Gómez could pursue two possible political options. The first was to remain in power until 1914 as vice president in charge of a provisional government; alternatively he could change the constitution in order to be elected president. The former option carried the risk of allowing other people to launch their own presidential bid, with the possibility of succeeding, while the latter option allowed Gómez a quick, favorable result. Francisco Linares Alcántara, the newly appointed interior minister, revived a process that was originally initiated by the state of Lara in 1908 asking the municipalities to request congress to lengthen the presidential period. Such a maneuver was first mooted to appoint Castro president for life, but it would now be used instead to help Gómez consolidate his position. Congress was thus convened in 1909 to amend the constitution, with Gómez duly elected for a four-year period the following year, on April 19, 1910.

During 1909, there was a steady shift of the erstwhile Castro supporters to Gómez. Although Gómez was unable to change the state presidents appointed by Castro because the former presidential period had not ended, he designated the military commanders and the general secretaries to the state administration. The secretary general was of utmost importance "because he was the man who understood the law and made speeches, at a time when most of the regional leaders had scant education and paid almost no attention to legal conflicts."[3] The secretary generals, composed mainly of keen young men, would form in effect a team of foremen who managed the country for Gómez as well as alerting him of any future trouble, reporting whether his instructions had been complied with and which political factions were in the ascendancy in the various states.

The case of Zulia illustrates this point well, as it was a specially pressing problem for Gómez because there was strong opposition to the new regime. Victorino Márquez Bustillos was appointed secretary general to General José Ignacio Lares, president of Zulia, with strict instructions to increase support for the government. The result was that two political power bases developed in Zulia: one allied to the state president, who while accepting the new situation preferred to see Castro back in power, and the other to Victorino Márquez

Bustillos and his family, who "form the governing nucleus that has penetrated everything."[4] In Táchira, Gómez congratulated Pedro Murillo for bringing the state under his control because it had been the "fiefdom of Don Celestino,"[5] Castro's eldest brother. Not content with this, Gómez sent Jesús Velazco to assist Murillo while appointing Jesús Rojas Fernández secretary general, Adolfo Méndez, *jefe civil* of Santa Ana, and General Elías Amaya, *jefe de batallón* of Santa Ana, among others. Gómez also instructed Murillo to "gather all the scattered arms, leaving only enough for the heads of Districts and Parishes to maintain order."[6] Finally, Gómez reduced the presence of the army to one battalion in San Cristóbal and two companies in San Antonio because an attack from the exiles in Colombia was unlikely.

In order to govern Gómez relied heavily on a number of young state presidents such as Pérez Soto, Silverio González, Jurado, Luque, Juan Alberto Ramírez, Domínguez, Barreto Méndez, Eustoquio Gómez, and Fernández, among others. They would head one state after the other acting as regional agents of the dictator, who gave them "a guide that outlined your duties and the extent of your power."[7] They in turn had their own team of advisers and trusted associates who "were part of an interchangeable administrative force that was at home in Trujillo, Cumaná, San Cristóbal or in San Fernando de Apure, and which excluded natives of the region."[8] As a result, during the Gómez dictatorship many of the state presidents lost all regional political importance, becoming "simply local representatives of the Head of the Cause."[9] Gómez did not tolerate any sort of dissidence among his staff, making a clear statement of his intentions when he informed Alcántara, the interior minister, in September 1909 that his biggest desire was "harmony among Venezuelans, something I request and demand from my officials in government. I do not demand from the latter that they should go against their conscience but I believe that the best way of defending this principle is by maintaining discipline because anarchy among the members of the regime only serves to diminish the efforts made to improve the State."[10]

Social and Economic Objectives

During the previous government of Castro, Vice President Gómez traveled the country extensively and knew it well, having engaged militarily many of the local caudillos during the Matos Libertadora revolution between 1901 and 1903. During his travels, Gómez became painfully aware of the backward nature of the country and increasingly saw his role as that of bringing Venezuela out of the nineteenth century and into the twentieth. After 1909, Gómez laid the foundations for modernizing Venezuela by centralizing the role of government, something that Castro had started but had lacked the determination and conviction to complete. As with his state presidents, Gómez surrounded himself with a group of young and trusted ministers such as Itriago Chacín, Maldonado, Felipe Guevara Rojas, Juancho Gómez, Abel Santos, Román Cárdenas, César Zumeta, Jiménez Rebolledo, and Luis Muñoz Tébar, who were primarily interested in modernizing the country. In his first annual message to Congress, Gómez called for it to establish a system that ensured that the democratic principles of government remained intact by preventing the executive from accumulating too much power. The Consejo de Estado (Council of State), at the suggestion of Baptista[11] and Alcántara, was resurrected as a countervailing power in order to keep an eye on the executive, and would be composed by "advisors who in a certain way represent Federal autonomies."[12] The new federal entity approved all new laws concerning the development of mines, land, and credit. Gómez also wanted Congress to create an agricultural bank that ensured faster development of the country's agricultural sector, while the abolition of export taxes would stimulate demand for the country's traditional exports. Gómez saw the formation of a modern army as essential in order to defend the gains made by his government. A professional army would be established, with Gómez requesting Congress to create a military academy now that the building in which it was to be housed was completed. The Academia Militar de Venezuela and the Escuela Náutica de Venezuela were officially established on June 22, 1910.[13] Many of the items on the Gómez agenda were embodied in the new 1909 constitution. There was little doubt that when the Senate opened its sessions in 1909 there was an optimistic feeling that the country, with Gómez at its head, had "regained its freedom and rights."[14]

One of the first social areas tackled by Gómez was the improvement of the country's health and sanitary conditions. At the time, no adequate legislation nor means for coping with plague and other epidemics existed, so that Maldonado created the Comisión de Higiene Pública on March 17, 1909.[15] This was later replaced in 1910 by the Concejo Superior de Higiene y Salubridad Pública within the Interior Ministry, financed by a levy of 1 percent on annual customs receipts. Later, in November 1911, the various health dependencies were centralized in the Oficina de Sanidad Nacional, under the direct control of the president.[16] During this period the first educational reforms of José Gil Fortoul, Samuel Dario Maldonado, and Felipe Guevara Rojas were also initiated, culminating with the 1912 Código de Instrucción, which stimulated and reorganized the educational system. Carlos León, governor of the Federal District, elaborated the first draft for a comprehensive labor legislation, and Román Cárdenas presented the country's first transit plan. Cárdenas also brought some order to the chaotic government accounts inherited from Castro's administration. In addition, there were the additional fiscal and monetary reforms by Finance Minister Santos, the municipal reforms by Zumeta, and finally a plan for an integrated railway network put forward by Muñoz Tébar. Román Delgado Chalbaud's plans for the modernization of the banking system and colonization of the Territorio Amazonas were in alignment with these progressive plans.

The experience of the Venezuelan government during World War I showed that it could not depend on customs receipts, as these fell to a very low level. The government decided to create a revenue source that would equal customs receipts and not be subject to the vagaries of international trade, culminating in 1918 with the enactment of the Ley Orgánica de la Hacienda Nacional,[17] which replaced the Treasury Code. This established the country's modern financial base by creating an internal revenue source capable "of equaling by its amount the Customs Revenue."[18] The new system created a national budget and was the start of national accounts, with the compulsory declaration of taxes.

The greatest impact that Gómez made on the economy during these initial years was his stimulus to road construction. The country's transport system, as Gómez witnessed during the Libertadora revolution, was in an appalling state. A British engineer in 1911 described the country's roads as almost nonexistent except near large cities,[19] and the easiest and fastest form of travel was by sea, or where it existed, the small rail network.[20] The lack of an adequate road infrastructure meant that coffee exports from Táchira were first transported to Cúcuta in Colombia, and then sent by rail to Puerto Villamizar on the river Zulia, where the cargo was transferred on to small shallow craft to Encontrados and from there to Maracaibo. Such a cumbersome transport system meant that the cost of shipping coffee from Táchira to Maracaibo was $4 to $5 per bag, compared with $0.40 per bag from Maracaibo to New York.[21]

In order to draw the country together and bring greater unity, as well as create the infrastructure that increased the general prosperity of the country, on June 24, 1910, Gómez—advised by Dr. Román Cárdenas and Luis Velez—

initiated a massive program of repairing the existing roads as well as building new ones. Half the Public Works Ministry's annual budget was earmarked for this purpose. This was carried out to a remarkable extent: between 1910 and 1919 a total of $6.7 million, representing 55 percent of the ministry's annual budget, was spent on road construction.[22] Not surprisingly, given Gómez's background, the largest single project was the Carretera Central de Táchira, with a monthly budget of $3,106.[23] Nevertheless, despite the great efforts made by the government, the Second Pan American Economic Conference, held in Washington in January 1920, drew attention to Venezuela's "urgent need to improve the transport system,"[24] with Gómez immediately issuing orders to this effect to his state presidents. The result was that the construction of new roads increased significantly that year, and by 1924 many isolated communities were joined to each other, with Caracas linked directly with the Andes in 1934.[25]

Pressing International Problems

The first major international problem that Gómez faced was the reestablishment of diplomatic relations with the United States, the Netherlands, France, and Colombia, which had been suspended during Castro's administration. On January 2, 1909, Gómez rescinded the decrees of April 28 and May 14, 1908, which suspended trade between Venezuela and the British and Dutch Caribbean islands of Trinidad and Curacao, respectively. Holland in turn revoked the suspension of the 1894 Protocol with the result that the Dutch colonial government expelled all Venezuelan political exiles from the island and Nicolás Rolando's cache of arms on Curacao were expropriated by the Venezuelan government. Dr. José de Jesús Paúl, the former foreign minister, was sent as special envoy to France and Holland to reestablish diplomatic relations with those countries. During the next few months Gómez's foreign policy would come under increasing attack, but he defended himself by arguing that the terms for the renewal of diplomatic relations by both France and the Netherlands were unacceptable to the Venezuelan government. Diplomatic relations with Colombia were renewed on June 2, 1909, after Gómez reopened the Zulia River for Colombian vessels.

It was the United States, however, which, by taking advantage of the situation, caused the greatest amount of embarrassment to the government by pressing forcefully for its five outstanding claims. Dr. Paúl's December 14,

1908, request for a gunboat from the UK, France, Germany, Italy, and the United States to protect the property of their citizens in the country was seized by Theodore Roosevelt, the American president, to send a "first class man down there in order to be on the ground floor before the trouble takes place,"[26] and ultimately to press for a settlement of the outstanding American claims.[27] On December 19, the day that Gómez seized power, the cruiser USS *Des Moines* and the gunboat USS *Dolphin* were ordered to proceed from Port-au-Prince in Haiti to La Guaira, while the battleship USS *Maine* was dispatched from the United States to Venezuela. At the same time William Insco Buchanan, who had been instrumental in Panama's secession from Colombia in 1903, was sent by the American president as a special commissioner, sailing from Hampton Roads, Virginia, on December 22 on board the USS *North Carolina*. His mission was to reestablish diplomatic relations with the new government in Caracas and to get Gómez to accept arbitration of the US claims. It was not deemed necessary for Buchanan to "complete definitely the signing and submission to arbitration of the pending claims"[28] because the US government would be satisfied with the new Venezuelan government's acceptance to submit the claims to arbitration.

On December 25, the USS *Dolphin* arrived at La Guaira to the delight of the Venezuelan government. They thought that this would be the extent of the US presence because this was exactly what Paúl had in mind when he requested help from the United States and the other major European powers in mid-December. Commander Thomas Washington and four officers spent the night in Caracas and the following morning were received by the full cabinet at Miraflores Palace. Washington had a private fifteen-minute meeting with Gómez, from which the latter emerged highly satisfied with the outcome, and was then joined by the entire cabinet for an inspection of the closed US legation. The government felt that this was the first step toward the "rehabilitation of our diplomacy among the civilized countries of the world."[29] However, the arrival the following morning of Rear-Admiral Conway Hillyer Arnold[30] on the battleship USS *Maine* and Special Commissioner Buchanan on the cruiser USS *North Carolina* came as a complete surprise to Gómez and his government. The surprise was mutual because on his arrival Buchanan expected to find "the country in the throes of civil strife and to be called upon to exert his mediatory influence in favor of the new Administration."[31] Buchanan was therefore disappointed to find that Gómez was firmly in power and that his rule had been warmly accepted by most people and that "foreign support, moral or otherwise, had become superfluous."[32] To an impartial observer the small flotilla of American naval power anchored in La Guaira was a clear sign that the United States intended to force the new government to comply with its will, something that the American senate had refused to sanction following Roosevelt's request in 1908. It was difficult to escape the view that the United States wanted to follow a "big stick" policy similar to that pursued in Central America and the Caribbean during the first years of the twentieth century.

Buchanan's mission was to be a short one, but after formally presenting the US government's proposals for arbitration of the five US claims, he ran into a number of obstacles because the Venezuelan government increasingly resented his presence. Buchanan started to volunteer "advice in other matters in which the United States were not directly interested,"[33] notably the normalization of relations with Colombia and the constitutional position of Gómez. The new Gómez administration was proving to be more difficult to deal with than had been initially expected after the promises made by the coup leaders in the heady days before the December 19 putsch. Far from allowing all questions of injuries to foreigners allegedly inflicted by unconstitutional means or illegal actions by Castro to the judgment of some impartial arbitral tribunal, the new government started to show a distinct tendency to avail themselves of legal technicalities to maintain the position in which Castro placed them. Sir Vincent Corbett, the British minister, felt that if such a situation persisted the new government of Gómez would "prove as difficult to deal with as the late redoubtable President himself."[34]

Buchanan achieved his primary objective, however. Venezuela was forced to discuss the five US claims and by so doing admitting the claims as a legitimate object of diplomatic intervention, something that had been resolutely denied in the past. After protracted negotiations, during which the cabinet and the Council of State rejected several times the draft protocols, agreement was finally reached on February 13, much to the satisfaction of Robert Bacon, the US secretary of state, who telegraphed Buchanan: "Heartiest congratulations. Great Work."[35] For his efforts, Buchanan was decorated with the Second Class Order of El Libertador; he left Venezuela on the *Des Moines* on February 22.

Under the Buchanan–González Guinán Protocol, the claims pertaining to the Orinoco Steam Ship Company, the Orinoco Corporation, and Crichfield would be submitted to arbitration only if the parties were unable to reach an agreement with the Venezuelan government after a negotiating period of five months. In the Crichfield claim, the Venezuelan government offered at first to extend the concession to settle the claim, but was rejected owing to financial difficulties that prevented the company from working the concession. In order to regain the concession, on August 21, 1909, the company accepted the Venezuelan government's offer to pay $475,000 in eight equal installments. The same initial offer was made to the Orinoco Corporation, but it preferred to settle on the government's terms to regain possession of its concession by accepting $385,000 in eight equal installments. The International Court of Arbitration at the Hague on October 1, 1910, settled the Orinoco Steam Ship Company's claim, when Venezuela was ordered to pay $92,637 to the company.[36] The issue was of judicial importance, as the principle involved was whether a previous arbitral decision could be submitted for revision by another arbitral tribunal.

On February 13, 1909, two further agreements were reached concerning the Jaurett claim and the New York and Bermudez Company (NYB) claim. In the former claim, the French-born American citizen would receive $40,407[37] compensation for his treatment under Castro. In the case of NYB, the company accepted and recognized its involvement in the Libertadora revolution and agreed to pay the government compensation of $300,000. It also agreed to sell asphalt to the government for public works at 25 percent below the prevailing market price, and it would pay a tax of $0.75 per ton of asphalt exported per annum and a surface tax of $0.375 per hectare per annum. In return, the government allowed the company to retain its concession and equipment.

The settlement of these claims opened the way for the renewal of diplomatic relations between the two countries, and on March 20 William Russell was officially received in Caracas as the new US minister, while on May 2 Pedro Ezequiel Rojas took up his post as Venezuela's minister in Washington. The protocols caused great bitterness and resentment in Venezuela, as it was felt that Francisco González Guinán had surrendered the country to foreign interests and that "Venezuela was heading to join Panamá and become another American protectorate."[38] The result was that Gómez's position weakened during the months of February and March, with the public and the press clamoring "against any further concessions to the pretensions of foreign powers."[39] The influential *El Tiempo* newspaper wrote that public opinion increasingly felt that US policy was not to uphold the Monroe Doctrine but to intervene directly in the internal affairs of the country.[40]

In its first session in 1909, Congress, unable to criticize Gómez directly, vented its anger on Paúl, severely censuring him for his actions during the

December crisis and for his subsequent diplomatic efforts. Deputy R. Castillo Chapellín called on Congress to protest against the action that had brought American warships to Venezuela in December, making "the Venezuelan people appear to be taking the first step towards an embarrassing protectorate,"[41] and urged the legislative body not to ratify the American Protocol because by doing so "we can assume that our courts are closed to matters related to foreign affairs, and that we have abrogated our National Sovereignty to the Judicial Power."[42] In addition, Deputy Castillo Chapellín was not too happy with the NYB Company Protocol because "Venezuela only receives a small sum and not the fine imposed on the Company to indemnify the country for damages caused."[43] During the same session, Paúl was also criticized by deputy General Manuel Modesto Gallegos, who blamed him for the presence of US warships and accused him of being unfit to represent Venezuela. General Ignacio Pedroza, another deputy in Congress, stated that Paúl's acts do not "deserve a protest, but the curse of the Venezuelan people."[44] Alarmed at this intense popular feeling against the American Protocol, Gómez adopted a "pseudo-constitutional attitude leaving responsibility for all measures to Congress."[45]

Gómez's government was further criticized for its handling of the negotiations involving the renewal of diplomatic relations with the Netherlands and France. It was felt that Paúl, Venezuela's special envoy, had bungled the negotiations because he had been mistakenly advised that the French would only reestablish diplomatic relations once an agreement between the French Cable Company and the Venezuelan government was reached. Such an agreement was achieved on May 13, when the government annulled the $4.7 million fine imposed in 1906 and the company obtained a twenty-five-year lease to handle all external telegraphic communication, with the government retaining the coastal telegraphic line valued at $4.7 million. However, the French had also demanded as a sine qua non that the other outstanding French claims should be adjudicated by a mixed commission, something that the Venezuelan government did not approve, with negotiations breaking down in December 1909. The manner in which these claims were to be submitted kept both countries apart until 1913, when a compromise solution was reached and diplomatic relations were reestablished. Similarly, the Netherlands demanded as a condition for the renewal of diplomatic relations that Venezuela recognize the claims of its Dutch citizens, in particular that of Henrique Thielen, the son-in-law of Ramón Tello Mendoza, who had lost an estimated $77,670 because of the wanton destruction of his property in Caracas during the December disturbances. Venezuela failed to recognize the Dutch claims, and so negotiations continued until 1921, when finally both countries were able to renew diplomatic relations.

Power Struggles at the Local Level

Although there was a consensus at the national level about supporting Gómez, it was a different picture at state level, where there was a ferocious fight for power between four distinct groups: viz, the Liberals, the Nationalists, the Rolandistas, and, the Gomecistas. At this stage, it suited each non-Gomecista group to support Gómez, as they were all trying to rebuild their own power bases and it was felt that the president could be toppled later. Gómez for his part was aware of this, and he instructed the secretary general of each state to keep him informed of the level of support from each group.

Rolando was the last caudillo from the Matos revolution to be defeated by Gómez in 1903 in Ciudad Bolívar. In 1908 he was organizing an invasion of the country when Castro's government was overthrown. Since the Gómez coup, the Rolandistas had retained most of their support in eastern Venezuela, with Manuel María Guevara warning General Pedro Linares in January 1909 that the fight of the Liberals in Anzoátegui was against Rolandismo because the "dominance of General Rolando in the east means that the enemy will continue working to overthrow the Government of General Gómez."[46] In Rolando's hometown of Barcelona there was an intense political struggle, and although the governor was trying to comply with Gómez's orders, by March he had "put into practice the disastrous principle of personal ambition strengthening the party of General Rolando as the only political faction."[47] Consequently, the Liberals in Barcelona supported Gómez in order to defeat the Rolandistas. In Monagas State, the Rolandistas also had strong backing, but the Gomecistas were more powerful because support for the Mochistas was declining.

In Bolívar State, Arístides Tellería, the state president allied to Alcántara, the previous incumbent, was working against local Gómez supporters.[48] Domingo Antonio Coronil, the secretary general of the state, reported that there were five distinct political groups at the time: (1) the Nacionalistas Personalistas, followers of José Manuel Hernández (Mocho), who "with exquisite foot work intervenes in local government in order for them to hold public office in the various regions of this state";[49] (2) the Nacionalistas

No-incondicionales, who "in almost their totality are retailers, farmers, cattle ranchers"[50] and who Coronil considered would be "useful in the policy of assimilation that I have developed"[51] because of "the credit that they enjoy";[52] there was the Official Circle, who were all friends of Alcántara and therefore of the government; the Historic Liberals, "who behind the scenes are trying to impose their policies in the region, which at present remains in open opposition to what the Government wants to achieve";[53] and, finally, the Rolandistas, who were nothing to worry about. In May 1909, Coronil reported to Gómez that Rolando was trying to get a job for General Benigni, who had been his *jefe de guardia* during the Matos revolution but had not supported him "because it distances us further from the plan that is needed to achieve our goals here."[54]

In Zamora State, there was a certain amount of jealousy among the Liberals because of the deferential position given to the Nationalists. Carlos Jiménez Rebolledo, the secretary general of Zamora State, reported in April 1909 that the policy of the state government was not Mochista or Rolandista but Gomecista. The state of Mérida, according to Estebán Chalbaud Cardona, its secretary general, was anarchic "due to the insidious rumors propagated by people returning from the capital."[55] A mob in Tovar tried on April 22 to assassinate Pérez Soto, the military and civil chief of Tovar District of Mérida State. A further attempt on Pérez Soto's life was made a few days later in Mucuchíes.

Most of the various political factions claimed Gómez as their presidential candidate and supported his bid for the presidency even before he agreed to stand. At this stage, Gómez's close advisers were influential Liberals, such as his uncle José Rosario García Bustamante and Baptista, both key figures in the 1908 coup and both elected to the important Directorio Liberal of the Distrito Federal (Federal District), whose other members were Matos, José Antonio Velutini, and Rolando.[56] The Liberals enthusiastically embraced Gómez's foregone conclusion that he would launch his candidacy for the presidency. General Samuel Ortega Martínez, a Liberal, wrote in July 1909 that their "patriotic efforts"[57] had reached a climax because with Gómez elected president, all rights would be guaranteed.

The Liberals interpreted Gómez's plans for the country as "inspired in the purest liberalism,"[58] as "commerce and industry will be reborn to an active life because the black monster of monopoly had been killed."[59] In October 1909, a number of Gómez's Liberal friends realized that the "conspiracy between the Unionistas and Mocheros [*sic*] represents a real danger for your Government, because although each faction thinks it will win, your administration will be severely weakened."[60] Matos, who was involved in the reorganization of the Liberal Party, understood that there was a great deal of truth to these fears, noting that the Nacionalistas were gaining support and warning Gómez in November that "already all your best friends, closely allied to your Government, see the danger of a Cult developing because of what is happening in Caracas and La Guaira, where your orders have not been followed because of the influence of the Conservatives."[61] In the past, the "Conservatives had abandoned their leader, finding it more convenient to be with Castro, but today they have returned to Mocho,"[62] while the Liberals "preferred exile rather than serving Castro, and today are at your service, resolute and loyal, without any other leader than you."[63] Matos urged Gómez to take note "of the radical change undergone by the Liberals and Conservatives or Unionists, which for all intents and purposes are the same."[64]

Matos wanted all the Nationalist government officials transferred from Caracas and La Guaira and sent to states where the Conservative delegates were friendly to Gómez. The Conservatives at this juncture also embraced with enthusiasm Gómez's bid for the presidency because, as Mocho Hernández stated, this was "a sure guarantee that the acts of the new government are inspired by a spirit of serene fairness and a high degree of patriotism."[65] Mocho Hernández would later call on the whole nation to support Gómez "in the rehabilitation work in which you are committed, and if the case arises, defend it against possible aggressions from an irredeemable and obstinate despot."[66] Many of the other caudillos who returned to Caracas, including Rolando, Gregorio Segundo Riera, Ramón Guerra, Juan Pablo Peñaloza, Jacinto Lara, Carlos Rangel Garbiras, José Ignacio Pulido, Ramón Ayala, and Baptista endorsed the election of Gómez as president in a letter sent to General O. Pérez Bustamante, who had initiated the procedure to get him elected by the Conservatives. It was felt that only Gómez could complete the mission of ridding the country of the "nightmare of oppression and tyranny"[67] created by the previous administration.

Gómez Elected President and Council of State Established

With the enactment of the new constitution on August 4, 1909, Congress reacquired most of the powers lost under the 1904 constitution. The new constitution revived the establishment of a Council of State, did not allow the reelection of the president, and abolished the office of vice president. Congress would now elect the president and the Council of State, composed of ten members—one for each two states—as well as approving army promotions above the rank of lieutenant colonel. Congress also regained the power to declare war and decide on the annual intake for the army. The rationale behind the creation of the Council of State, which would be composed by the old caudillos, was to serve as a watchdog over the executive because presidential decisions would have to be approved by it. The council had two kinds of votes: a deliberative and a consultative one, with any presidential action coming under the aegis of the council's deliberative powers. It was felt that with this body in place Gómez would be "bound hand and foot to the political parties."[68]

According to Arellano Moreno, the Council of State was "a forum for those who refuse to recognize the new social order and who, underestimating the current situation, feel that a legal putsch can be set in motion to topple the new dictator."[69] The council was made up of eight Liberal generals (Riera, Peñaloza, Ramón Guerra, Pulido, Rolando, Ayala, Jacinto Lara, and Baptista) and two Nacionalista generals (Mocho Hernández and Carlos Rangel Garbiras). These caudillos, who represented the states where they held political power, would in turn nominate the state presidents. So, for instance, Rolando nominated his brother Armando Rolando to be president of Anzoátegui; Baptista nominated his brother Víctor in Trujillo; Alcántara nominated his brother-in-law Raimundo Andueza Palacios for Aragua; Riera nominated Arcaya for Falcón, but he declined; and Mocho Hernández nominated Zoilo Vidal for Guayana. Rolando, Riera, and Alcántara were the most distinguished political figures in the country, so it was natural for them to be represented by people they trusted. However, the appointment of close relatives as state presidents was not universally approved because it was felt that they should be independent appointees.

New Political Parties

In 1909, Gerónimo Maldonado advocated the need for political parties because they represent "the thinking side of the masses in its struggle and social ascent."[70] In early September 1909, Pedro Andara, Arcaya, Zumeta, Manuel Díaz Rodríguez, and Rufino Blanco Fombona explored the possibility of forming a political party that would be "radical, uphold civil rights, civilized, healthy, honest, and that fights against military barbarism."[71] The traditional parties such as the Liberal Amarillo (Liberals) and the Liberal Nacionalista (Conservatives) wanted to sanction Gómez, but, as we have seen, it was the

Liberal party that really took Gómez to its heart. General Francisco García, leader of the Liberals, gave a banquet for Gómez at General Raimundo Fonseca's Aragua estate of "La Providencia," to which both Liberals and Conservatives were invited. Fonseca during dinner toasted Gómez and stated that the Liberal party supported "the famous Decree of guarantees written with the blood of Zamora[72] and endorsed by the altruistic hand of Marshall Falcón,[73] so that the glory of fulfilling it fell on you, from the freedom of thought, without any restrictions, to the granting of rights and privileges to all the citizens, even the abolition of monopolies."[74]

Gómez reciprocated the gesture but did not give anything away when he raised his glass and toasted "the Fatherland and Union," adding, "I am here to prevent any fighting between Liberals and Conservatives,"[75] which summed up succinctly his political aspirations. Gómez felt that as long as he did not take sides he was powerful enough to struggle against these political factions; he did not see or care for any ideological differences manifested by the various political factions that were becoming increasingly active. Gómez's opinion, expressed by his close adviser Arcaya in his *Memorias,* was that only two political parties existed in the country, viz, "that of the government and that of the revolution."[76] Nevertheless, at this early juncture Gómez wanted to prevent the various factions from fighting each other, while he strengthened his own position. Moreover, just after his election to the presidency by Congress in September, Gómez issued a stern warning that he would not tolerate anarchy and chaos.[77]

A period of relatively free democratic participation appeared to be close at hand. Under the new constitution, a deputy would now be elected for each 35,000 inhabitants, with each state represented by two senators elected by the state legislative assembly. The election of deputies to Congress and state legislatures would take place during December 1909, and they in turn would form an electoral college that would elect the new president in April 1910. Both the Liberals and the Nacionalistas overwhelmingly supported Gómez's election as provisional president by Congress on August 11, 1909, until the end of the presidential period in 1910, when full elections were to take place for the new constitutional period.

Baptista's Influence Wanes

The influence of Baptista, who continually placed his friends in office, was affecting Gómez's popularity in the country. Gómez appeared almost subservient to Baptista, causing discontent among certain of his supporters. This view was further reinforced by General Antonio Pimentel, Gómez's confidant, who advised that if he "wished to retain the good will of all parties, it would be wise to broaden the base of his Cabinet and especially to include therein some of the so-called 'Guzman Blanco party.'"[78] It was felt that Baptista, while reviving the interests of Gómez, had also furthered his own end and that he was becoming a liability. By the end of the congressional session in 1909, Baptista's position in government had weakened by the action "of his opponents both inside and outside Congress."[79] Gómez, however, needed Baptista's advice and backing, as he did not want to end up with the support of just one group. He could not get rid of him just yet but was forced to find a new role for one of his closest advisers.[80]

With the promulgation of the new constitution and the election of Gómez to the provisional presidency, all sorts of intrigues were set "afoot by parties and interests anxious to be represented in the new government."[81] The most prominent among these groups were the Liberals and their closely connected associates, the Blohms, the Boultons, and other owners of large mercantile houses. Gómez did not want to alienate this Guzmán Blanco–Blohm-Boulton combination, as Sir Vincent Corbett referred to them, because he himself was engaged in many commercial schemes "and their support both politically and privately"[82] was very important to him.[83] At this stage, Gómez's initial intention was to remove Interior Minister Alcántara, Federal District Governor Iturbe, and two other cabinet members who were unfriendly to him, but in the end he was forced to sack Baptista, who was replaced by Abel Santos. As a result, in Gómez's new cabinet, Matos, who was married to Ana Teresa, Antonio Guzmán Blanco's daughter, returned to Caracas to take up his new post as finance minister, and General Juan Pietri, whose daughter Catalina was married to John Boulton Rojas, was appointed foreign affairs minister, with both representing the Guzmán Blanco–Boulton interests. General Antonio Pimentel, a close friend of Gómez and also closely connected with the Blohm family, was appointed secretary general. Baptista was offered the presidency of the Council of State, an important position because he would take over the functions of the president whenever Gómez was absent from Caracas, but he declined and left the capital. The political scene was thrown into confusion for a few days; the newspaper *El Día* published a series of articles by Federico Restrepo praising Baptista and warning that Gómez should not declare himself a dictator because "it would be equivalent to committing suicide in politics."[84]

Some of the new ministers such as Pietri refused to follow the policy of their predecessors and made their own decisions, while others sought orders from Gómez and his new secretary general but were unsuccessful. After a week of confusion with rumor and counter-rumor going around in Caracas, Gómez, according to Sir Vincent, "repented of his attempt to think for himself"[85] and summoned Baptista to return, who quickly regained his former influence. However, the "obnoxious Ministers are still there,"[86] hampering business with the British colonial islands. Sir Vincent was convinced that both Baptista and Gómez would be only too glad to settle the 30 percent surtax problem with Trinidad[87] and "escape from any importunities,"[88] but Pietri "comes to it with a fresh and strongly prejudicial mind and quite prepared to meet our demands with a point blank refusal and defy the consequences."[89] The dominant factor in the situation, according to Sir Vincent, was "the vacillating character of the President and his constant anxiety to be friends with all parties no doubt with an eye to the next Presidential elections."[90] Moreover, Gómez feared alienating the support of the Guzmán Blanco–Blohm-Boulton group.[91] In the past, the influence of Boulton and other mercantile houses had waned because of Castro's bias toward the Blohm trading house, with the Guzmán Blanco clique reduced to "impotence by General Castro, but since the return of the exiled generals, some of whom are closely allied to it, [it] has assumed a position of some importance and must be reckoned with."[92]

The xenophobic sentiment that was prevalent immediately after the signing of the American protocols made it impossible for the government to abolish the 30 percent surtax on goods imported from Trinidad and Curacao. The very success of the United States, however, directed the thoughts of the "Venezuelan Government towards seeking a counter point to the United States influence in the support of some other Power."[93] Gómez's natural tendency was to lean toward Britain, as Castro had been such a Germanophile, with British officials receiving hints from the Venezuelan government to oppose the influence of the United States. Sir Vincent reported that "the fear of eventual absorption by the United States is undoubtedly almost universal here, and it must be confessed that it is not entirely without cause."[94] The US government's action in Nicaragua at the time put an end to any consideration that the Venezuelan government had of removing the 30 percent surtax. As a result, the British found that there was no way of bringing pressure to bear on the Venezuelan government to modify its position without risking the loss of any advantages Trinidad derived from handling Venezuelan produce.

Congress, which according to Sir Vincent was "markedly Chauvinistic,"[95] did not at first approve the American Protocol; Baptista was compelled "to bring the whole weight of the Presidential authority to bear"[96] in order to secure safe passage of it. Such an experience convinced Baptista "that there were limits beyond which it would be unsafe to go."[97] A resolution authorizing the president to deal with the question of the 30 percent differential surtax was, however, passed by Congress "but owing to influences . . . was framed in terms less precise than those which Dr Baptista,"[98] at Sir Vincent's request, had suggested. Consequently, the protocol signed by Paúl with the Netherlands was dropped as well as "a hurriedly drafted Tariff Bill, which the Government endeavored to force through Congress in the last days of the session."[99] After much intense pressure from Gómez, Congress reluctantly ratified the American Protocol in September 1909, but it retaliated by not approving the protocol signed by Paúl with the Netherlands. Paúl, who was dismissed from his post as special envoy to France and Holland, served as a convenient scapegoat for Congress to blame, as there was little political reason for censuring Gómez, whose actions until then indicated that he was committed to the establishment of a genuinely democratic political system. Congress would be free for the first time to function without the "ambushes of power,"[100] as Senator Arístides Tellería stated in his speech opening the first session of Congress after the December 19 coup, with the country ready for the "dawn of a new era."[101]

1910 Elections

There was no doubt that Gómez would be elected president in 1910 because his popularity was fueled by a groundswell of support from both the Liberals and the Conservatives. The Liberals in particular embraced Gómez's candidature for the 1910 presidential elections with true political fervor. In the autumn of 1909, the Liberals from all corners of the country met to discuss and pledge their support to Gómez. On October 10, the Sociedad Liberal Eleccionaria of the Distrito Federal (Federal District), the most important of the Liberal branches, met at the Club Concordia to elect the Directorio del Partido Liberal of the federal district and also to pledge their support for Gómez at the forthcoming elections. José Ladislao Andara stated in his opening speech that the Liberals should unite to support Gómez the "virtuous Conductor of the republican and Liberal evolution of the 19 December."[102]

Matos, the previous regime's most ardent opponent who had plunged the country into a vicious eighteen-month long civil war that Gómez ended, followed Andara, declaring his wholehearted support for Gómez. Their Liberal manifesto stated that the 1908 coup had closed "forever the era of personal ambition, which favors individual interests against those of society in general, and determines that individuals are more important than political parties."[103] On October 22, the Directorio Liberal of Miranda State was formed, and two days later, a similar group was established in Táchira to endorse Gómez for the presidency.

Gómez for his part was grateful for the political support given by both parties, feeling that it was time to put an end to the political malaise that afflicted the country, which he pinpointed as being "the official tyranny and the intolerance of political parties."[104] Gómez's thinking was based on the premise that these two extremes had "always led to Liberals being killed, to civil war and the devastation of the Republic; terrible evils that can be radically cured during the current historical moment when by Providence, you all appear to be inspired by one common goal."[105] Gómez emphatically rejected the idea of a single political party because a country was composed of people with different views and aspirations. Consequently, all civilized countries "have formed and maintained various factions and groups with differing ideals, programs and intentions; and in keeping with the rate at which civilization advances in its luminous way, those parties have become compatible with greater tolerance for each other, respecting their opinions and principles, working for the good of the fatherland and taking turns in the peaceful exercise of power."[106] Gómez thus urged the political parties to cease their incessant bickering by working to create an atmosphere of mutual respect for each other in order for Venezuela to "equal itself with its continental sisters in civilized life and progress of all sorts."[107] There was little doubt that Gómez's political allegiance at this early stage was with the Liberals: they had supported him in the December coup d'état, and he also had close family ties to the party, such as his uncle García Bustamante, who was elected president of the Directorio del Partido Liberal of Caracas in December 1909. Nevertheless, his own position was that of a unifier of the two main political factions and a link between them during this transitional period.[108]

As part of this plan, Gómez saw the need to form a strong professional army to protect him and the policies he was pursuing. Although Castro had first decreed on July 5, 1903, the construction of the military academy building, which was completed on May 23, 1908, it was Gómez who requested

Congress in 1910 to create the military and naval academies.[109] The Chilean Colonel Samuel McGill, who would later turn against the dictator, headed the former institution.[110] Gómez further strengthened his own position by establishing during the same year the inspectorate general of the army "in order for the armed forces to be under constant and useful surveillance."[111]

The Nacionalistas also began to organize themselves, establishing new regional branches such as the Junta Central del Partido Liberal Nacionalista formed in September 1909 in Anzoátegui. They called on their supporters to assist Gómez politically and to collaborate with him for the "successful completion of his plans to rehabilitate the country."[112] Mocho Hernández felt that Gómez's election as president was "a safe guarantee that a spirit of serene fairness and judgment of pure patriotism will inspire the acts of the new Government."[113] The Liberals, who through Matos warned Gómez in October that any Mochistas in his government would hinder his political aims, mistrusted Mocho Hernández's intentions. This advice was not heeded, and Matos repeated it the following month, stating that the Nationalists were acquiring greater support "especially in Caracas and La Guaira where your orders have not been obeyed because of the prominent Conservative influence."[114] Matos wanted to see the Conservatives replaced by Gomecistas or better still by Liberals. Other Liberals, such as Pedro María Parra in Mérida, counseled that the Nationalists were threatening the peace established by Gómez.[115] Parra advised Gómez that a "loyal and genuine"[116] Liberal element was backing Cardona, the state president of Mérida, while "the doubters and speculators"[117] were with the Nationalists. Moreover, "I presume that only a small push is needed to destroy them, even as a political faction."[118] There was no love lost between the Liberals and Mochistas at this stage, and the fight between them carried on. This was important because the forthcoming elections for deputies to the national congress and to state legislatures would take place in December, and they in turn determined the presidential elections of 1910 by forming the electoral college that elected the president.

The elections that took place at state level were in effect a sham: Gómez and the state presidents selected the candidates in the main. Gómez essentially appointed the senators and congressmen, whose election was carried out in two phases. The first stage took place in the office of the interior minister, "who listens to the requests of those who aspire to form part of the Legislative Power and adds to the list the people who are trustworthy and of his liking."[119] The second phase was when the short list was taken to

Gómez, who decided who would be the lucky winners. Miguel Delgado Chalbaud, who was a member of the Directorio Liberal for Bolívar State, wanted Tellería, the state's provisional president, reappointed, but the latter could not accept because he was under strict orders from Gómez not to allow any discussion of elections until he had received the list of names to be included. The *directorio* then offered Zoilo Vidal the state's presidency, but he refused because he had already accepted the presidency of Sucre State.

The appointment of the legislative power of the states and the Concejos Municipales was slightly different. Here the state presidents had the right to appoint the *juntas electorales,* who elected the candidates, but it was Gómez who selected the candidates for election, and thus the councils appointed in the *jefaturas civiles* were the result of appointments made by the police officers who "drew up the affidavits and lists and deposited the votes specified by the law in the ballot boxes."[120] Gómez gave his state presidents firm instructions for selecting members of the state assembly. In December 1909, for instance, Gómez instructed General Gumersindo Méndez to hand over to General José María Colmenares Pacheco in Zulia "a list of the people who owing to their pledges I feel are best suited to be in the Legislative Assembly of that particular Federal entity"[121] and "drawn up with the agreement of our friends in Maracaibo."[122]

On December 20, the elections for deputies to Congress and state legislatures started, with General Pablo Giuseppi Monagas, the state president of Monagas, making sure that:

> his main responsibility before you is the result of those elections because the selection of the candidates must only be from your supporters who will contribute without hesitation nor dependency on any other political interest to the majority that you need in Congress for the successful outcome of the first constitutional period, and the alternates also have to be totally trustworthy for your own security and satisfaction of public opinion in this state.[123]

Giuseppi Monagas assured Gómez that Mochismo in the state "did not have any relevance"[124] and that the Rolandistas were on the decline, remaining only "proponents of bad law, and causing chaos."[125] It was not difficult to predict the outcome of the state elections. In the case of Monagas, he ensured that the men elected were supporters of Gómez, but in the case of Lara, where General Manuel L. Araujo, a supporter of Mocho Hernández, was president, the outcome of the state legislative elections was heavily in favor of the Mochistas. It was only in February 1910, when Mocho Hernández left the country to seek a cure for an illness, that Gómez started to move against the Nationalists by removing such prominent members as Oscar Blanco Fombona from the military command headquarters of La Guaira and by winning over General Rodríguez in Carayaca, a former Nationalist stronghold. Such moves were a hard blow to the Nationalists on the coast.[126]

Gómez Elected President

After presenting his annual message on April 19, 1910, Gómez resigned at six p.m. as provisional president together with the Council of State. Dr. Emilio Constantino Guerrero, head of the federal court, succeeded him as president, who immediately ratified the appointment of all the former ministers in their respective posts. Guerrero's acceptance speech continued the theme of progress to be made in basic industrial development together with a strong unified government. The country was rich in natural resources, and all that was needed was for people to work in unity to develop Venezuela. In order for this to occur there had to be forceful and progressive individuals as well as a strong government, whose role was to stimulate basic industries by creating the necessary infrastructure such as roads, "rivers of gold as the medieval hyperbole called them,"[127] which in turn would attract foreign capital. There was a need to expand credit facilities in order to avoid the establishment of the onerous monopolies that had been created in the past, with the result that the government started working on the tricky problem of fiscal reform. Finally, there was an urgent need to "guarantee the stability of government in order to enter into contracts with foreign associations for the exploitation of our innumerable mines."[128]

The following morning the senators elected González Guinán as president of the Senate, while the deputies elected General José Antonio Martínez Méndez, Gómez's brother-in-law, as the head of the chamber. New elections would take place for the president of the Council of State and the ex officio vice presidents. Three days later, on April 22, Gómez secured more power when Congress unanimously (103 votes) elected him commander in chief of the army, and on April 27, he was again unanimously elected president of the republic for the next four-year constitutional term.[129] At the same time, the Council of State, with two exceptions, was reelected, with Ayala as its new president. General Lara was not reelected, with his place taken by Pietri, and Ortega Martínez replaced Rangel Garbiras, who had died. Constantino Guerrero transferred power to Ayala, president of the Council of State, at four o'clock in the afternoon of April 29 at the Casa Amarilla. Five weeks later on June 3, at three thirty p.m., Gómez took the oath of allegiance to Congress and was confirmed president. On the same day, Gómez appointed his new cabinet composed of the following people: Alcántara, Interior Minister; Matos, Foreign Affairs Minister; Antonio Pimentel, Treasury Minister; Manuel Vicente Castro Zavala, Navy and War Minister; Bernabé Planas, Development Minister; Román Cárdenas, Public Works Minister; and Trino Baptista, Education Minister. According to William O'Reilly, the British minister, the new cabinet was not a "sensation, but they point to the predominance at present of the influence of General Alcántara; the new appointments are Amarillo Liberals as opposed to Godo conservatives, and the only two who can be reckoned as Andinos seem to be universally regarded as political cyphers."[130]

Financial Difficulties

When Gómez took over in December 1908, the new government found itself in a financial crisis. It inherited from Castro a budget deficit of $990,029, and it would remain in the red for the next couple of years. Consequently, it was no surprise when the Gómez government started acting in the same manner as its predecessor because of its financial difficulties, with the result that in 1909 some of the monopoly concessionaires who had their concessions rescinded during Castro's time were able to reacquire them. The Compañía Anónima Sales de Venezuela, for instance, acquired in July 1909 a fresh ten-year concession with a new British company, the National Salt Mines of Venezuela Ltd.[131] formed with half the equity held by the Venezuelan government and the rest by the company.[132] The contract, however, was rescinded in October 1909, and a new salt contract awarded to a company owned by Román Delgado Chalbaud, whose main shareholders were Gómez and General Manuel Corao. The Venezuelan Match Company was also able to secure a new concession that expired in December 1932.

The robbery and pilfering that went on at the various ministries at this time was on a "gigantic scale"[133] according to Sir Vincent, the British minister, who reported that Gómez's administration was "one of bunglers, who with perhaps much better intentions than Castro, are not conscious of the mess they are getting themselves into."[134] The administration was anxious to foster new sources of revenue because the government depended on customs receipts for 70 percent of its revenue. In 1910, customs receipts showed signs of declining, while government expenditure increased considerably during the same year. The only solution out of the impasse was to consider a foreign loan, rumored in 1909 to be $39 million, in return for various concessions.[135]

After a number of unsuccessful efforts to secure both American and French bank loans, it was decided that a possible way out would be the establishment of a foreign bank in Venezuela that could issue legal tender. There was a problem: the 1904 banking law only authorized the Banco de Venezuela to issue notes, acting in effect as the country's central bank. The other deposit banks and discount houses in the country were for legal purposes considered as ordinary businesses. The debate in 1910 was whether the banking system under the 1904 law, with its high interest rates, was a deterrent for progress in agriculture and industry because loans were difficult and expensive to obtain. There was a pressing need for long-term loans at reasonable interest rates; hence the attractiveness of allowing foreign banks to establish themselves in Venezuela. As a result, the 1910 bank law, drafted by Santos, the former finance minister, was enacted in order to allow this to happen. The new law had a further advantage, which was that the new banks would break the stranglehold that existing banks had on the financial system of the country, allowing Delgado Chalbaud, in particular, to prosper with his plans to set up foreign banks. Mr. Robert Wallis, the managing director of the Tram and Telephone Company, was approached on behalf of Gómez and invited to submit to a group of London investors, the most prominent being Lord St. David (the banker and financier behind the Tram and Telephone Company), a proposal for the formation of a bank backed by British capital. The new bank would have a capital of $5.8 million and would only deal with government business,[136] with a secured overdraft of $2.3 million at 6 percent interest. In addition, the bank would charge 1 percent commission on government business. Corao and Delgado Chalbaud, Gómez's aides, held secret preliminary talks with the British group that were concealed as long as possible from the cabinet in order not to arouse the suspicion of Foreign Minister Matos, who controlled the Banco de Caracas, and Finance Minister Pimentel, who owed his large fortune to the timely financial help given in the past by Blohm and Company and "who would strain every nerve to defeat them in defense of the vested interests of the Bank of Caracas and of the house of Blohm respectively."[137] As suspected by Gómez, as soon as the negotiations became known to a wider public they had to be suspended owing to the pressure brought to bear on the government—the terms for establishing the bank were too generous. Nevertheless, on November 18, 1910, a revised contract was signed between Pimentel and Román Delgado Chalbaud to establish a "Banco Comercial, Agrícola e Hipotecario."[138]

The need to secure a foreign loan was still a prime necessity. In an endeavor to raise a loan in New York, Gómez believed that if the Ethelburga Syndicate, which had previously financed the match company, was favorably disposed toward the country, then a loan would be easier to secure.[139] Hence, in early January 1911, the government restored the monopoly held by the Venezuelan Match Company under Castro's rule "in the hope of influencing the attitude of the London market in the matter of the Bank's scheme now being considered by the Phillips group."[140] The National Match Factory of Venezuela Ltd., as the new company was called, had its concession until December 1932, with the government compensating it for any losses incurred from its stamp duty revenue. This would not be the end of the Ethelburga Syndicate's involvement in Venezuela.

In August 1911, Delgado Chalbaud and Corao's company, the Compañía de Navegación Fluvial y Costanera, in which most members of the government had a stake and which was rumored to have Gómez as the largest shareholder, signed a contract with the Venezuelan government giving it the monopoly navigation rights over the lakes, rivers, and coastal waters of the country, as well as taking over the country's salt mines and the development and colonization of the Amazon territory. The contract was extremely unpopular among certain sectors of the population and a few firms in Ciudad Bolívar, such as Blohm and Company, had real grounds to fear the contract.[141] The main objections were that the contractors would make excessive profits because the contract resembled a monopoly, and if it was transferred to a foreign company then any dispute between the holders and the Venezuelan government would eventually be settled against the nation, forcing it to pay large sums in compensation.[142] Delgado Chalbaud also obtained a separate contract to supply Caracas with water and to build the city's sewage system. It was expected that both American and European capital would be attracted to this venture, and to this end Delgado Chalbaud and Corao traveled to England to secure funding, reaching an agreement with the London Ethelburga Syndicate, which was controlled by Otto Herbert Fuerth, Francis M. Voules, and Albert Pam. For its Venezuelan venture, the syndicate gained the support of the National City Bank of New York, and on November 15, 1911, Fuerth arrived in New York, meeting George Williams, the local manager of the National Match Factory of Venezuela Ltd. After talks with the National City Bank, the Ethelburga Syndicate signed a contract with the bank to guarantee a loan of $9.6 million. As a result, the navigation concession, together with the sanitary and water supply monopoly, was transferred to the Ethelburga Syndicate, who sent out a representative to the country.

In spite of these developments in the private sector, a loan to the government from the United States to cover its fiscal deficit during 1910–1911 was not raised. Corao and Delgado Chalbaud then traveled to Paris to get a number of French banks and finance houses interested in establishing in Caracas two banking institutions, viz, a National Bank of Venezuela and a Banco de Crédito Hipotecario.[143] While in Paris, Corao and Delgado Chalbaud met Paul Marie Boló (known as Boló Pasha),[144] who wanted to establish in Venezuela a financial institution to fund all kinds of businesses that would be floated subsequently on the Paris Stock Exchange.[145] Louis Dreyfus and Company and the Credit Français were the two French institutions closely associated with the enterprise. A total of $153,030 was deposited at the financial firm of Marcuard and Cie. as the initial capital for the National Bank of Venezuela and designated for use by the government of Venezuela. According to Luis Núñez, the former French Prime Minister Joseph Caillaux agreed to help Delgado Chalbaud and the Credit Français.[146] Caillaux assured Núñez that Dreyfus "requested from Marcuard and Demachy a credit of ONE MILLION to take with him to establish the Syndicate together with what we can subscribe."[147] Consequently, on September 13, 1911, Delgado Chalbaud entered an agreement with Boló Pasha to establish the National Bank of Venezuela, with a paid-up capital of $5.8 million, which would provide an unsecured loan to the Venezuelan government of $2.9 million. Under the terms of the contract, at least half the bank's capital would be raised in Venezuela.

Boló Pasha wanted to travel to Caracas, but Núñez advised that his trip should be kept "in reserve in order to avoid any intrigue and manipulation from Furst [*sic*], Marcuard and Demachy, the Bank of Venezuela and the Bank of Caracas,"[148] who were opposed to the scheme. Domingo B. Castillo convinced Vicente Lecuna, head of the Banco de Venezuela, that it would be unwise to establish a National Bank under Boló Pasha because Venezuela would be mortgaged to France, and this could provoke punitive action by the French government in the future. The result was that on Delgado Chalbaud's and Corao's return to Caracas, Gómez cancelled the agreement because its terms went against the interests of the country. Although Blohm and Company had something to do with the annulment, the main reason appeared to be that "members of the Government, and others, who had no 'pickings' in these transactions, astutely worked on his feelings by suggesting that he (Gómez) was selling the country in granting them."[149] According to Siso, Gómez rejected Delgado Chalbaud's financial maneuvers in 1912 because he felt that the naval admiral would gain a strong political and economic advantage from the deal and because the group of La Conjura,[150] formed by Alcántara, Iturbe (close to Manuel José Revenga), and Corao, backed the venture.[151] The outcome was that a new law on banks, the Ley de Bancos, was enacted by a Congreso Extraordinario later that year, making the establishment of foreign banks in the country almost impossible.[152] The failure of Delgado Chalbaud's banking scheme would also be the main reason for his plot against the government the following year.

Foreign Investments

Although Gómez during this early period continued to emphasize the need for unity and peace in order to exploit the wealth of the country, by 1911 it was becoming clear that his "economic-social"[153] plan to modernize and develop the country needed greater stimulus from financial institutions, with foreign capital the driving force in developing the country's natural resources. Part of Venezuela's problem was that it had a small population: labor was relatively difficult and costly to obtain. The effect of this was that the capacity "of production by cultivation or manufacture is consequently very limited, and it is found easier and more lucrative to collect natural produce than to employ labor in agricultural pursuits."[154] Since the heyday of the gold boom in the 1870s, Venezuela had attracted relatively little attention by British and American investors.[155] Venezuelan capitalists were not willing to take the necessary financial risks because in the view of some of the local mining entrepreneurs domestic capital was lacking "for the establishment of large companies.[156] Castillo felt this was due to the stranglehold that the foreign mercantile houses had on the country's economy, which did not foster the creation of a native commercial bourgeoisie.[157] Since his arrival in power, Gómez wanted Congress to legislate laws that attracted foreign capital and expertise. Following this theme, in 1909 Tellería, president of the Senate, during the opening sessions of Congress called on the chamber to enact laws that would "flatter the foreigner so that he will come to our shores to instruct us in their scientific advances and participate in our wealth; that they can offer credit facilities, and that they will exhibit us like Argentina, opening its arms to the immigrant."[158] In October 1911, Gómez addressing an extraordinary session of Congress referred to the need for

> capital, brawn, science and experience for our industrial develop-
> ment; and as we do not have such essential factors, it is necessary to
> receive them from the foreigner who offers it to us in good faith.
> We have natural wealth that remains unexploited; mostly unculti-
> vated fertile land, immense empty territories. Our industries lack
> the necessary resources for their development. Our mining treasures
> lie at the heart of the earth because there are insufficient funds to
> bring them to the surface. Our immense plains are scarcely filled
> with animal herds, because the cattle industry requires selection and
> crossbreeds that we have been unable to provide. Our agriculture
> demands the establishment of sugar mills and the intensive devel-
> opment of other crops. We have the possibility of supplying our own
> markets but owing to a lack of industrial development, we buy an
> infinite number of articles from foreign markets that we could pro-
> duce ourselves, with excellent purity and flavor.[159]

As part of the policy of attracting foreign capital, on 1 October 1912, Gómez paid off the remaining debt of the 1903 Washington protocols of $7.5 million, with the country's credit worthiness increasing immediately. Gómez hoped that this would allow the country to "concentrate entirely its resources and energies on the promotion of its multiple interests, increasing its well-being and laying the foundations of a solid base for its future enlargement."[160]

In the early years of the Gómez dictatorship, the country also experi-enced an expansion in trade. The 1909 constitution abolished all export duties, which together with the high prices for coffee in 1911, lead to an increase of trade with all of Venezuela's main trading partners, *viz*, the United States, United Kingdom, France, and Germany.

The expansion in trade would have been greater had the Venezuelan gov-ernment rescinded the 30 percent surtax on imports from the West Indies. While the government was ensured of a stable source of revenue from this source, it also favored German and other large foreign mercantile houses in

Table 4 Percentage Increase of Trade with Venezuela, 1909–11

	Imports	*Exports*
United States	66	17
United Kingdom	126	24
France	182	20
Germany	53	229

Source: Calculated from FO 368/755 Hartford to Grey, Mar 16, 1912.

Caracas. During the ensuing years the British and Dutch governments tried in vain to get the tax removed, but the influence of Blohm and Company and the other mercantile houses was too great to counter any advantage that the annulment of the tax would entail. Moreover, if Trinidad ceased trading with Venezuela as a protest, then the colony would lose "far more from the benefits it derived from handling Venezuelan produce than Venezuela."[161]

The greatest hope among government circles was that foreign capital would develop the country's mining resources. From the very beginning of Gómez's rule there was keen interest to develop the mineral wealth of the country because it would spearhead the general economic progress of the country as well as provide an independent source of income. General Rafael María Carabaño, Gómez's first development minister, in his 1909 annual report stated that the development of the mining industry "is designed to make the country's wealth productive by favoring its exploitation, and opening with such a patriotic attitude good prospects to the individual's effort in establishing new industries, as well as the improvement of those already working."[162]

Although the country was by no means "a concession hunters' paradise,"[163] Sir Vincent observed that the number of concessions awarded had increased considerably since Gómez's rise to power, mainly as a result of policies aimed at stimulating mining, since it was now much easier to obtain concessions. Gómez and his government, therefore, pinned their hopes increasingly on the additional revenue that the mining industry could bring. In spite of the incongruities of some of the offending clauses in the mining code, there were tangible results to Gómez's mining policies. Soon after it was announced in 1909 that the law was going to be reformed, Dr. Clodomiro Contreras, the owner of several gold mining titles, left for London to negotiate his titles with British capitalists, with the Venezuelan Syndicate Ltd. formed on February 26, 1910.[164] In June 1910, Charles Freeman obtained from Pedro María Mata a twenty-five-year contract to exploit and export the magnesium produced from deposits on Margarita Island, which he later transferred to the Magnesite Mining and Manufacturing Company in 1914.[165] A further success was achieved when an agreement between the government and the Pan American Iron Corporation was reached in August 1910 for the latter to exploit the extensive iron ore deposits at Imataca in the southern part of the country. The Canadian Venezuelan Ore Company Ltd., a subsidiary of the Dominion Steel Company of Halifax, Canada, acquired the concession on August 14, 1911.

Gómez's policy of attracting foreign capital to develop the agricultural potential of the country appeared also to be working at the time. In 1909, the United Fruit Company almost reached agreement with E. Garmendia to establish a banana plantation on his six-thousand-hectare estate between Tucacas and Puerto Cabello. United Fruit was more successful the following year, when it negotiated with Alejandro Rivas Vásquez a contract to exploit Feliciano Montenegro's twenty-five-year contract with the government to cultivate and export bananas from the country. The attraction of the latter contract, which had been obtained on June 25, 1910, was that no taxes were levied. The contract was held by the Venezuelan Improvement Company in which the United Fruit Company held 51 percent of the equity, with the remaining 49 percent held by Feliciano Montenegro. In addition, United Fruit would provide a $1 million loan to the company to start the new plantation. Rivas Vásquez felt that the contract allowed Gómez to "think with pride that we have opened the vast hinterland of the country where you will build together with all good Venezuelans the future of our beloved Venezuela."[166]

Early Oil Developments

The General Asphalt Company (hereinafter the Asphalt Company), which through its subsidiary NYB exploited the Guanoco asphalt deposits in eastern Venezuela, in 1910 diversified into oil production. On July 12, 1910, Rafael Max Valladares, a junior partner in the Bance law firm, acquired a concession in eastern Venezuela, which four days later was transferred to the Bermudez Company, a subsidiary of the Asphalt Company.[167] Just prior to the award of the Valladares concession another successful development that attracted foreign capital to the country's oil resources occurred when John Allen Tregelles, a former employee of S. Pearson and Sons Ltd. obtained on December 10, 1909, a concession covering over three thousand square miles of the country. Four days later, on December 14, Tregelles transferred his share of the concession to the Venezuelan Development Company Ltd., a British company that in March 1911 sold the concession to the Venezuelan Oilfields Exploration Company Ltd.[168] The British oil company at the end of its two-year exploration period ran into trouble when it applied for an extension of the exploration time allowed by the law. The government refused to renew it because, in the opinion of Iturbe, the company lacked the financial resources to develop its vast concession properly. The real reason for the refusal was that the Asphalt Company had taken steps to "prevent its extension for the additional year"[169] in order for it to acquire a similar concession covering the same area when the Tregelles concession lapsed in 1912. The British oil company did obtain five more mining titles in early 1912, but its lands were in the opinion of A. C. Veatch of S. Pearson and Sons Ltd. "inconsiderable and relatively unimportant."[170]

Valladares, "who is reported to be quite popular in certain circles in Caracas and to be capable of getting favors from the Government,"[171] was again to act as the intermediary between the government and the Asphalt Company, whose Caracas representative was Lewis J. Proctor. The Valladares contract, which was identical to the Tregelles one, was approved on January 2, 1912. Two days later, on January 4, the concession was transferred by government decree to the Caribbean Petroleum Company, a subsidiary of the Asphalt Company, incorporated in Camden, New Jersey, on November 17, 1911, with a capital of $145,800,000.[172] It had two years in which to complete its assessment of the property; thus a "rapid reconnaissance was made to determine the most attractive districts in which areas were selected to be re-examined geologically after 1914."[173]

Royal Dutch–Shell

In the ensuing years, Shell acquired the Aranguren, the Valladares, and the Vigas concessions, which were expected to yield "a large supply of liquid fuel"[174] quickly. Development plans were hampered during World War I because of the difficulty in getting equipment and machinery to the country from Britain and the United States. In spite of this setback, Shell in 1915 was confident that "a large field is opening for us here."[175] Shell became the largest

Table 5 Shell Crude Oil Production: Mexico and Venezuela (in millions of tons)

Year	Shell Total	Venezuela	%	Mexico	%
1923	14.7	0.5	3.7	4.6	31.5
1924	13.4	1.2	8.7	2.7	20.1
1925	12.3	1.6	13.4	1.4	11.1
1926	15.5	3.1	20.1	2.3	15.0
1927	17.0	4.5	26.5	1.6	9.3
1928	22.1	7.1	32.3	1.4	6.4
1929	25.2	8.8	35.0	2.1	8.2
1930	24.0	9.7	40.3	1.8	7.7
1931	20.5	8.7	42.4	1.7	8.4
1932	21.0	7.6	36.0	1.9	9.2
1933	22.0	7.6	34.6	2.0	9.2
1934	24.1	8.2	33.9	2.5	10.2
1935	26.6	8.5	31.8	3.1	11.8
1936	28.2	8.7	30.8	3.6	12.9

Source: Adapted from Royal Dutch Company annual reports, 1908–36.

oil producing company in the country, and Venezuela in turn became vitally important to the oil group, overtaking both the United States and Mexico as their major source of crude oil during the 1920s.

Gómez and Economic Development

The arrival of Gómez in power in December 1908 inaugurated an era of political liberalization that all political factions grabbed with an added sense of urgency because it could so easily end in failure. The brief political spring would not last for long, however, with Gómez increasingly giving the impression that he was not about to relinquish power as easily as some had thought when he first took over the presidency. At the same time, Gómez started to put the country's finances in order and to stimulate foreign investment to develop Venezuela's natural resources. As vice president during the Castro years, he was well aware of the problems that foreign capitalists and their governments could create, and was careful once he was in power to cultivate good relations with foreign capital as well as foreign governments. It was clear that when Gómez became president, he wanted to develop an independent source of government income away from the traditional customs receipts that depended so heavily on the state of the economy. The oil industry would eventually provide such an alternative source of income.

Gómez Takes Over

Gómez's coup appeared to open a new era of political freedom, with the promise of a real shift toward permanent democratic rule. One of Gómez's underlying assumptions, however, was that he would be the sole arbiter in deciding when this shift took place. While allowing political freedom to develop, Gómez would always remain in power to prevent the various factions from disturbing the peace and prosperity that he hoped to bring to the country. As soon as Venezuela appeared to be moving back into factional chaos, he put into action his plan to secure absolute power. Although there was some opposition to this, he received the wholehearted support of the country, especially from commercial circles, who were pleased with Gómez's efforts to regenerate the economy—between 1909 and 1911, for instance, exports grew by 41 percent and imports by 81 percent—and bring law and order, while maintaining a semblance of peace. Gómez would secure a kind of peace by establishing himself as the absolute ruler of the country.

Castro's Reaction

Gómez's coup came as a bombshell to Castro, who at the time was preparing to undergo an operation in Berlin. Castro was sent into deep shock and did not realize initially the magnitude of what had occurred to him. Paúl, Castro's former foreign affairs minister and one of the instigators of the coup, who soon afterwards was sent on a diplomatic mission to restore relations with France and the Netherlands, informed Gómez from Paris in February 1909 that Castro continues "bewildered without understanding the magnitude nor the causes of his exile."[1] Castro at the time was something of a celebrity in both Europe and the United States. His remarkable appetite for publicity continued to form the "subject for amused comment in the local press."[2] At this early stage, Castro felt that he could return to Caracas as a simple citizen, writing to Gómez on January 23, 1909, from Berlin, where he was recuperating from a kidney operation at Dr. Israel's clinic, that once he arrived in Venezuela he would retire from politics and resign from the presidency in May in front of Congress. Castro felt that this would end "the multitude of difficulties"[3] that the Gómez government faced in carrying out its political program. Furthermore, it would spare Castro the ignominy of spending the rest of his life in exile, "playing a ridiculous role outside the country that does not suit my character or name."[4] Castro preferred to "play a respectable role in a jail of my fatherland rather than being ridiculed and derided by the foreigner who has humiliated us so much."[5] Castro suggested that having served his sentence he would then retire to his farm in Mariara, but Gómez knew his old compadre too well to fall for this ruse and refused to countenance any of Castro's suggestions. From that moment until his death in 1924, Castro would devote his considerable energy toward regaining the presidency by trying every conceivable plan, even murder, to oust Gómez. Castro would also become the natural focal point for any revolutionary endeavors, using his own agents to rally support from Venezuelan exiles in both the Caribbean and Europe. At this early stage, Dr. Julio Torres Cárdenas and Ramón Tello Mendoza represented Castro in Europe, with Gumersindo Rivas acting as his agent in Cuba, while Luciano Mendible looked after his affairs in Trinidad when his brothers, Celestino and Carmelo,[6] were not on the island. Finally, Manuel Vicente Romerogarcía was a roving envoy for the deposed dictator.

Castro was still suffering from poor health, however. After leaving Israel's clinic in Berlin on February 6, 1909, he spent a further $9,740 on surgical expenses and $476 for hotel bills in Cologne before leaving for France. From Paris, Castro and his large retinue traveled to Bordeaux, from where he expected to travel to the West Indies. Castro was confident that once he reached the Caribbean, or, even better still, returned to Venezuela, he would recapture the magic of his former years and his followers would soon regroup around him and turn against Gómez. Castro's strategy was either to get back directly to Venezuela or as close to the country as possible so that he could organize a revolution against Gómez.

In Bordeaux, Castro was prevented from purchasing a ticket to La Guaira and had to travel instead on the French mail steamer *Guadeloupe,* the same one that brought him to Europe in November 1908, to Martinique. There he hoped to gain permission to continue his journey to Venezuela. Castro decided to stay away from Venezuela and settle in Trinidad after the Venezuelan government, in March at the Federal Court and of Cassation, started legal proceedings against him, bringing him up on criminal charges for ordering the murder of Antonio Paredes in 1907. (There were additional criminal and civil suits brought against Castro in Venezuela.) Castro felt that he could later slip into the country without much fuss.

Gómez, unaware that certain foreign powers would prevent Castro from landing in Trinidad or indeed from plotting the overthrow of his government, was convinced that the Cabito (Little Corporal), as he was referred to in disparaging terms, would eventually land at Port of Spain, Trinidad. Gómez was not unduly perturbed at this, confiding to General Ulises Anselmo that "it is almost certain that he will spend a long time there; this will naturally cause some alarm but nothing more."[7] There were strong rumors in Caracas, however, that Castro was planning an uprising, with reports that he was trying to gain support from the exiles in Colombia, and from the Colombians Felipe Angulo, a former treasury and war minister, and General Rafael Uribe Uribe, his old friend and military ally.[8] General Rafael Reyes, the president of Colombia, informed Gómez that "Castro is understood to have reached agreement with the revolutionaries of the country, Messrs. Felipe Angulo, Aborta and others to start a war simultaneously in Colombia and Venezuela."[9] Felipe Angulo was expected to establish a center of operations on Curacao Island.

Although Gómez appeared relaxed about Castro's trip to the Caribbean, neither the United States, France, the Netherlands, Colombia, or the United Kingdom were pleased. All these countries, with the exception of Colombia, reached an understanding that Castro should be barred from the Caribbean and were successful in keeping him out. According to US Secretary of War Huntingdon Wilson, Gómez's government was sufficiently weak that Castro could conceivably overthrow it and that such a move "would be disastrous not only to American but also to all foreign interests in that Republic."[10] The United States was so concerned about the possibility of Castro's return to his home country that toward the end of March 1909 it sent a warship to La

Guaira to keep a watchful eye on the ex-president's movements. The United States also requested Britain and other European powers "having special reasons, geographical or otherwise, for desiring a responsible government in Venezuela . . . to take all legitimate steps to prevent the use of their ships and territory to embarrass Venezuela in meeting the menace of Castro's return."[11] The United States regarded Castro as almost an outlaw, ordering three further American warships to shadow him on his return to the Caribbean. The Dutch also sent three men-of-war to Curacao to prevent Castro's arrival, and in early April, Sir Clement Courtney Knaggs, the acting governor of Trinidad, on instructions from the Earl of Crewe at the Colonial Office, issued an order preventing Castro from landing on the British colony. A further proclamation was issued by the British colony prohibiting the export of arms and ammunitions from the island. The action taken by the foreign powers against Castro was favorably received in Caracas, but the behavior of the United States was viewed as being too heavy handed and was "looked upon as a further offensive demonstration of their semi-parental pretensions."[12]

Castro was therefore forced to disembark from the *Guadeloupe* at Fort-de-France, Martinique, where he was informed that he would have to leave the French colony and return to Europe on the *Versailles,* but the former Venezuelan dictator feigned illness in order to remain on the island. Although Castro was examined by three different doctors who declared him fit to travel, he still continued to resist deportation and was eventually taken ignominiously on board on a stretcher wearing only his underwear for the return voyage to Europe, arriving in Seville, Spain, in May. At the same time his brother Carmelo Castro left the French colony heading instead for Trinidad, where he was immediately placed under surveillance. The Venezuelan consul wanted the colonial government to deport him, but the governor did not have the authority to do this. Once Castro left Caribbean waters, the proclamation prohibiting the exports of arms and ammunitions in Trinidad was revoked.

While this was happening, Celestino Castro left Curacao for Colombia, where rumors of plots continued unabated, to gain support for his brother in the neighboring republic. Caracas too was rife with rumors about Castro's impending return. In October, it was reported that the Castristas had seized the *Delta* ship, which supplied the asphalt workers at Guanoco, in order to invade through the Orinoco and make the Yuruary region their central base of operations. The following month, it was rumored that three important generals were plotting with Castro in Puerto Rico the downfall of Gómez.

In November, Celestino Castro traveled from Conejo to Gamarra, Colombia, where he spent five days in talks with pro-Castro supporters. As a result, many of Castro's "leaders and officers who were here in service with him"[13] left for Cúcuta. Moreover, at Romerogarcía's hacienda there were men working as peons waiting to invade Venezuela. It was thought that the revolutionaries had purchased a ship in the United States called the *Nanticoke,* captained by Chauncey B. Humphrey, who had received two telegrams from Caracas inviting him to join the plotters. The whereabouts of Castro at this time were unknown to the Venezuelan authorities, since he had last been spotted in Seville. For instance, Arreaza Calatrava, the Venezuelan consul in Seville, reported in October that Castro was in "bed in Salares,"[14] Colombia.

In spite of the colonial government's efforts, Trinidad at this juncture became the center of Venezuelan revolutionary activity. Carmelo Castro, Manuel Felipe Torres (Castro's illegitimate son), Mendible, and Carlos Lázaro were actively engaged on the island in planning a revolution against Gómez that would start in the Delta Amacuro region. Luis Paredes, the Venezuelan consul on the island, informed Gómez that Romerogarcía had left Trinidad for Europe and the "*Castristas* hope to put into play a vast military plan and they count on people of certain importance in Venezuela" (emphasis in original).[15] Paredes also warned Gómez that former President José Santos Zelaya of Nicaragua was helping Castro's revolution. Further details were given to Paredes at a dinner welcoming Romerogarcía back to Trinidad, when it was revealed that Castro was expected in Trinidad in May 1911 with "a boat, a cache of arms and artillery."[16] Paredes bribed Colonel José de Jesús Delgado with $80 for information on the plans, which included the names of the plotters in Venezuela, such as Anselmo Zapata in Yuruary, Luis Natera Carrera in Maturín, Marcial Azuaje in Calabozo, and Felipe Osorio in Tucupita. On his return to Europe, Castro persisted in his quest to settle in Trinidad, applying toward the end of October for permission to live on the island as an ordinary citizen.

The British government was unsure what to do. Governor Sir George Ruthven Le Hunte was aware that the British government had arrived at an understanding with France and the United States that Castro was to be barred from the Caribbean,[17] but it was felt that the new Gómez administration had not reciprocated the friendly action of the British in refusing to grant Castro asylum, with the result that it did not see why they should prevent the former Venezuelan president from landing in Trinidad until Gómez gave a strong indication of relaxing the 30 percent surtax on goods imported from Trinidad. The British government decided to defer any decision on Castro in order to give the Venezuelan government time to reconsider its position on the surtax question.[18] The Venezuelan government, however, was not willing to reconsider its position on the 30 percent surtax and warned that Castro should be treated "like an obdurate conspirator against the institutions of the Republic."[19] If Castro was allowed to take up residence in the British colony, Venezuela would take severe measures to ensure that he stayed out of the country, and would in turn impinge "very seriously on trade that we want to maintain in the most flourishing way possible with that West Indian island."[20] The Venezuelan government won a diplomatic point over the British, as the latter's reply confirmed that "it would be impolitic to let Castro land."[21]

Romerogarcía arrived in Trinidad in January 1910, meeting Castro's brothers and Mendible. It was rumored at the time that Castro was in Central America after reaching some sort of agreement with Rafael Reyes, the former president of Colombia,[22] and would soon be in a position to depose Gómez. Further reports reached Venezuela that Castro was spending considerable amounts of money to prevent Gómez being elected in the forthcoming elections.[23] This was pure fantasy, as Castro was in Málaga, leaving on February 5, 1910, for Santa Cruz de Tenerife, from where he would return to the Spanish mainland and then leave for the Canaries in December 1910. A contemporary account at the time described Castro as dressed in "a dark coat of heavy cloth, covering his head with a knot cap, without a cravat needle,"[24] and wearing a diamond "of extraordinary size"[25] on his finger. There were more rumors of plots against Gómez being allegedly planned by Castro in New Orleans. Jacinto López, the Venezuelan consul in New York, felt that this was possible because it was too far away from Venezuela, and that if the plot was being hatched in Trinidad the British government would never allow the island "to become an asylum and headquarters of the monster Cipriano. To the eyes of the Government of Washington, it would be an act of hostility against the United States. With it England would also offend its ally France."[26]

Castro at the time was a wealthy man with total cash balances of $765,000 distributed as follows: $175,000 at the Disconto Bank of Germany; $250,000 at Credit Lyonnais in Paris; between $200,000 and $225,000 at the Bank of England; and $140,000 at the Banco de España of Madrid. In Venezuela, Castro owned coffee estates, with an estimated value of $1,050,000,[27] and cattle ranches on the Orinoco plains extending over 150 square miles, with

60,000 head of cattle valued at $650,000.[28] In addition, it was alleged that Castro had interests in the Planta Eléctrica de la Guaira (valued at $200,000), the water works, Fuerza y Propiedad "Mornio" (valued at $200,000), a third of the capital of the Orinoco Steam Ship (valued at US $200,000),[29] giving a grand total of $2.35 million. All the properties were up for sale to an American concern for $1,250,000. Castro also had diamonds worth $500,000 and owned expensive automobiles but, according to a State Department note, lived modestly with his wife at the Villa Benítez in the Canaries, while maintaining two other properties for his mistresses.[30]

Castro continued his efforts to settle in Trinidad. On the advice of Alberto Alcazar, who had a certain amount of influence in the colony, Castro acquired Mendible's farm in Trinidad in 1910 in order to become a taxpayer and be entitled to take up residence. Romerogarcía also financed the acquisition of a small cocoa farm from Mrs. Dominga García, situated next to the sea front in Diego Martín (Grand Fond), close to Port of Spain and Venezuela, "in order to find employment for Castro's adherents."[31] It had the added advantage of having two landing sites at Macqueripe and Point Cumana from which the Castristas with some two hundred men intended to embark and invade Venezuela. Other pro-Castro supporters were employed working at the La Brea asphalt works. Communication between Castro's supporters in Venezuela and Trinidad was maintained through Nereo Muñoz, who owned a small boat that sailed between the two countries. The revolutionaries planned to take the arms hidden in Trinidad to Maturín on the *Constant,* but when Castro failed to appear, the ship was chartered by Tregelles and Leonard Dalton, "experts who are going to develop an oil mining business in Venezuela."[32] Preparations for the impending revolution continued, however. Pro-Castro supporters on the mainland were sounded out, and some, such as Colonel Ciriaco León, who had over 140 men working his balata[33] plantation at El Jabal on the Paría peninsula, pledged his support to Torres, Castro's illegitimate son.

For the uprising to have any chance of success, it was essential that Castro should lead it. Consequently, in February 1910 Castro, who was living in Tenerife, announced that he would travel to Trinidad, where he was expected to arrive with his wife, Zoila Martínez de Castro, at the end of the month or the beginning of March. However, the revolutionaries received a setback when the US consul at Barcelona prevented Castro from traveling to the Caribbean by canceling his passage to the British island colony. The British authorities were not informed of the impending plot because Paredes, the Venezuelan consul, wanted to catch Castro red-handed. With the non-appearance of Castro, Paredes took the opportunity to denounce the plotters to the colonial authorities, with the view of rounding up the pro-Castro fellow conspirators. G. D. Swain, Lieutenant Colonel Inspector General of Constabulary on Trinidad, offered to apprehend the conspirators whenever he got the order from Paredes and sent three noncommissioned officers dressed as laborers to an estate situated at Grand Fond, where they discovered that Romerogarcía had sold the property to Torres, with his brother Roberto managing it. In Venezuela, Mr. Wharton, manager of the Compañía de Navegación Fluvial y Costanera, together with Alberto Alcazar, hurriedly left the country once the plot was discovered.

A few days later Romerogarcía left Trinidad for Europe, traveling with General José del Rosario Marca, a Colombian, who had a letter for Castro from General Rafael Uribe Uribe, the leader of the Bloque Liberal in Colombia, stating that the party in the neighboring country was ready to take up arms on Castro's side against Gómez.[34] At the same time, Paredes instructed General José Pabón to detain Antonio Rodríguez, José Sánchez, and Federico Mosquera, Castroist supporters in Irapa. A Castrista revolutionary committee also existed in Colombia, composed of Pedro Vicente, Alberto Galbán, Simón Antonio Turé, Alejandro Mendible, Héctor Medina, and Juan Bautista Méndez, who were in constant communication with the Trinidad committee.[35]

After his disappointment in Barcelona, Castro traveled to Madrid, where he was consoled by, among others, Gumersindo Rivas, who toasted with champagne the success of the revolution. Castro soon recovered his spirits, and plans were made to acquire more arms and ammunition, with Rivas dispatched to Paris and London on such a mission. Romerogarcía returned to Trinidad from Europe to continue preparations for the forthcoming invasion. The plan was for Castro, together with 200 men, to enter Venezuela from Trinidad through the Quiniquirirá sandbar in the Orinoco Delta region of Pedernales. He would then proceed to Maturín to join his supporters in the city, such as Julio Ledesma, Francisco Flores Sánchez, and Federico Fernández Navarro, together with the Rondones of Urica. Castro was assured that if the rebels received arms from him they would take over the state. Cariaco León would transfer over 140 men who were working on his balata plantation on the Paria peninsula to Castro's farm in Trinidad, where the former president of Venezuela had 60 men working on his Diego Martín farm.

The first step toward entering Venezuela without arousing any suspicion would be to win over to their cause the head of the customs office at Pedernales. Francisco Belmote of Tucupita, a pro-Castro sympathizer, was entrusted with this delicate mission, but he refused for fear of being caught and accused of spying, with Romerogarcía at the end of May bribing the customs official. By then the *Constant* had returned to Trinidad and was refitted at Castro's expense. Paredes, the Venezuelan consul at Trinidad, who was himself bribing Morillo, one of the revolutionaries, thought that the revolution would move arms into Venezuela through British Guiana, requesting Gómez to reinforce Macuro, Güiria, and Irapa with one hundred men as well as some warships.

When the reports of an impending attack from Trinidad reached Gómez, a further rumor was heard in New York that Castro and the former Nicaraguan president José Santos Zelaya, working through President José Madriz Rodríguez, his political heir, were in discussions to overthrow Gómez. Zelaya's government, which was characterized by its anti-US policy, was helping Castro in order for the latter to reciprocate if the Madriz government was toppled. The whereabouts of Castro for most people were uncertain and were exaggerated to confuse Gómez's spy network. Castro, according to his brother Carmelo Castro, was in Nicaragua negotiating with Zelaya, from where he would leave for Trinidad "with officers and troops."[36] The revolutionary committee in Trinidad also believed that Castro was in Central America and would soon return to the island to begin military operations. On his return to Trinidad, Romerogarcía was sent to Santo Domingo to "receive orders from Zelaya who is there with a cache of arms,"[37] but owing to the plague his departure was delayed by several weeks; he was expected to return to Trinidad on July 20. It was almost certain that several barracks in Venezuela would rebel on May 23 against Gómez. Torres, Castro's illegitimate son, decided to move on that date regardless as to whether Castro was able to lead the rebels. Rondón of Urica was ready and willing to attack Maturín as soon as word reached him.[38] It was rumored that Castro would use two boats to invade Venezuela, with the British colony of Barbados acting as a transit port. Sea passages, ostensibly for Brazil, were arranged by Casa Grell. Paredes, the Venezuelan Consul, felt that as the "Gutieri" boat "had passed with 25 men believed to be heading for work in that country; the Barbadian consul would not be surprised if a meeting did not take place on the island using the same pretext."[39]

Gómez heeded Paredes's advice, placing General J. Sebastián Laclé, the commander in arms of Sucre State, on alert and sent the Venezuelan gunship

Zumbador. At the same time, Paredes requested the authorities at Trinidad to ascertain whether any arms had been stolen or purchased by the revolutionaries. The colonial authorities searched all businesses closely associated with the rebels, especially Stephens Ltd., where Castro had an open line of credit. The house of José Antonio Ortiz was also searched, and police officers were posted on the road that led to Diego Martín. With so much public interest, the revolutionaries were forced on the defensive, with Carmelo Castro leaving Barbados for Port of Spain and urging Torres to postpone his invasion. The propaganda against Gómez continued on the island. Carmelo Castro accused Gómez in a published letter of being an American puppet "which has brought on our fatherland the humiliation of foreign intervention, making us appear before the civilized world as a people incapable of self-government."[40] Carmelo Castro also stated that the American chancellery must have noted with delight the appeal made to its power by "the sadly illustrious Dr. Paúl at a time when all absorbing imperialism is extending its boa-like jaws over all Spanish America."[41]

Despite the rumor of Castro invading Venezuela, the man himself returned to Santa Cruz, Tenerife, in June 1910, staying initially at the Grand Hotel Battenberg, where he was closely watched by A. C. O. de Mongaillero, later moving to Villa Benítez, four miles outside the city. Castro's arrival on the island made quite an impact. He brought with him a motor car, and he scandalized the island's society with his five female assistants from Venezuela. Soon afterwards one left for Barcelona and another for Trinidad, but this still left Castro with three assistants, and his wife was none too pleased "with the conduct of his consort."[42] Eyewitness reports confirmed that Castro at the time was fit and well and his old self.[43] In an interview with A. Sacchetti, Castro insisted that he had retired from politics and wanted to return to Venezuela to pursue his business interests. Castro rejected the notion that he wanted to return to power through a revolution because the government was in the hands of his friends, although he was saddened that Venezuela had come under the influence of the United States "in the conditions of a semi-protectorate."[44] More importantly, Castro's private thoughts, expressed to his brother Celestino, were that Venezuela's foreign relations had sunk to such a level that even "the United States, which has done what it likes, is not satisfied!!! They are insatiable!!!"[45] The political situation had degenerated to such an extent that the "gangrene has already invaded all the social body! It would not be an exaggeration to say that Venezuela is a penitentiary let loose in a lunatic asylum."[46]

Although there was a lone uprising at Yaguaraparo against the police station, Castro did not intend to invade Venezuela during this period. The main reason for this was that Castro was sure his plot within the Gomecista circle in Venezuela would succeed. From Tenerife, on June 5, 1910, Castro informed his brother Celestino in Salazar, Colombia, that his secret plot would open the way for his triumphant return. Moreover, the "events are accelerating *and the moment of Gómez's expiation* is soon" (emphasis in original).[47] Mrs. Nieves Castro de Parra, Castro's sister, was in charge of organizing the plot against Gómez. The plan was for Castro de Parra to pay $30,000 to Carlos Gafaro, Pedro Nell Estrada, and Juan de Dios Jara to kidnap Gómez at his Vaquera de la Vega hacienda in Aragua State, forcing him to "call the Governor and General Galavís by telephone to hand over the barracks"[48] to pro-Castro men, and then to murder him. Many prominent people were involved in the plot, including Zoilo Vidal, Angel Bordas Robles, José Trinidad Pino, José Manuel Cabrera, Juan Valentín Borregales, Evaristo Angel Alvárez, Jesús Manuel Trejo, Eduardo Carrillo, José María Delgado, Ernesto Díaz, Eleazar Enaos, and Manuel Díaz. General José del Carmen Uribe of Táchira uncovered the plot when Gafaro of Pamplona, Colombia, tried to enlist his help. Castro de Parra was not arrested because Gómez "does not seek to take revenge on a lady"[49] but was later deported to Puerto Rico on August 18 together with forty-six other females. Zoilo Vidal, President of Sucre State, was arrested and sent to jail in the Puerto Cabello castle.

When this plot failed, it was rumored that Castro and the Mochistas would combine forces against Gómez, something the Venezuelan president gave little credence to because there was no "affinity between those two sects."[50] When Mocho Hernández heard of the Castro de Parra plot, he was appalled that such methods were even considered, repudiating "the vileness of murder and the disgrace that such an act bestows"[51] because it was against all tradition of political life. The real enemy for Gómez was Castro, "but as I have him in my sight, I can follow all his steps and I am in a position to hinder any plan that he tries to develop."[52] Gómez not only relied on the reports of his consuls dispersed around the world for his intelligence on Castro and other revolutionaries, but had at least one secret agent in Trinidad among the revolutionaries, Zapata, who was used to deliver letters between Castro and the plotters,[53] as well as A. C. O. de Mongaillero, who spied on the former president when he was in Tenerife.

Rumors of an impending Castro plot continued unabated however. In September, it was reported that Castro had organized a plot from the United

States, something that Gómez dismissed outright as preposterous. Gómez wrote to Rojas, the Venezuelan minister at Washington, that he thought it was "not only rash but almost impossible to purchase ships and armaments, as well as organizing any invasion in the United States against Venezuela,"[54] because the "American government and the industrialists who have business deals with our country, not only rejected him but hate him."[55] A more serious incident took place on October 6 at the San Carlos fort in Zulia that showed that Gómez's position was not impregnable. Led by Commander Cáceres and Artillery Captain Méndez, officers and soldiers mutinied because of low pay, releasing all prisoners, including the political ones. Gómez was both furious and shaken by this incident because it demonstrated publicly that factionalism, as he referred to it, was present in the ranks. Castro Zavala, the minister of war and navy, was ordered to punish severely the officers who had speculated with the troops' rations because "the soldier must feel happy with his treatment as he is nothing else than an armed citizen defending the nation."[56]

In August, Celestino Castro acquired a farm in Salazar, Colombia, while Torres later purchased a hotel in Cúcuta, "where he maintains many Venezuelan exiles, who are in permanent meetings,"[57] whose main leader was Juan Figueroa. Castro, who remained in Tenerife, also renewed his efforts to settle in Trinidad. Charles Wharton, who was Castro's secret agent in Venezuela when he was manager of the Compañía Fluvial y Costanera Venezolana, had a brother in Trinidad who was the colony's attorney general and who recommended that he should petition the British government to be allowed to live peacefully on the island developing and working his cacao plantation.[58] Wharton spent a month with Castro in Tenerife and then proceeded to London to request permission from the British government for Castro to be allowed to take up residence in Trinidad because the former Venezuelan president had acquired a large cacao estate, but the British authorities refused even to countenance such an idea.

The rumors of a forthcoming invasion by Castro persisted, and in September it was reported that he had smuggled arms into Venezuela through the Delta Amacuro region. Castro was expected to land in Trinidad on September 16, 1910. In December, Romerogarcía and Mendible reached agreement with the Venezuelan exiles in Colombia, waiting only for funds to be provided by Carmelo Castro and to receive final orders from Castro. It was also rumored that Castro offered the Colombian government "his group of supporters for the reintegration of Panama because that way the government will reciprocate by protecting him when he attacks us."[59] It was now felt that Castro would definitely attempt a revolution in Venezuela during the centenary independence celebrations of 1911. In Trinidad, Governor Le Hunte reported that Carmelo Torres during the coronation celebrations was organizing parties and taking arms across to Venezuela.[60]

Castro finally left Tenerife on May 10, 1911, with the intention of reaching either Trinidad or Curacao and entering Venezuela through the Guajira peninsula, where he had made arrangements with General Simón Bello, his brother-in-law, and two other officers, a sergeant and a private in the San Carlos fort at the entrance of Lake Maracaibo, to hand the fort over and thus open the "way for him to penetrate into the Táchira district."[61] At his departure from Spain, the Venezuelan espionage network was cranked into action, with González Guinán, Secretary General, informing Consul Hermán Leyba in Curacao to redouble his guard and to warn Theodorus Isaak Andreas Nuyens, the Dutch governor, of Castro's possible arrival. The Trinidad authorities immediately issued a proclamation banning Castro from landing on the island, a measure that Gómez felt was in the island's commercial interests. Castro was thus forced to change his travel itinerary to Cuba, hoping to reach Colombia from there.

Castro, however, failed to arrive in Cuba, and his whereabouts remained a mystery. His supporters felt that Castro would turn to the United States for help, but Gómez was sure that he would not go there. Another possibility put forward at the time was that Castro would charter a ship from Las Palmas to Haiti and from there take a small steamer with some loyal supporters to land on the Guajira peninsula. What is certain is that Castro left Cádiz for Las Palmas and then to Aruba, landing on July 4 near Santa Marta in Colombia. He then made his way to the Guajira peninsula. On his arrival, Castro learnt that Bello and his fellow conspirators in the San Carlos fort had been discovered and "that the Government was expecting him, hoping to take him prisoner."[62] Castro managed to escape Gómez's soldiers, arriving in Rio Hacha and then left for Puerto Gallina, proceeding along the coast to Paseo Caballeros Island, one of the Rosario chain of islands off Cartagena. The Colombian government sent three hundred men to arrest Castro on the island, but he escaped disguised as a river boatman, making his way up the river Magdalena on one of the many steamers, disembarking at either Lorma or Gamarra. From there Castro traveled to the Venezuelan border, intending to make his way to the Bello estate[63] to meet the Cárdenas brothers.

Castro's possible invasion was taken very seriously in Caracas. At that year's independence centenary dinner given by the special American envoy in honor of Gómez at the US legation on July 6, Sir Guy Gilliat-Smith, the British vice consul, reported that the only topic of conversation was Castro's landing at La Guajira. Gómez, who believed the news to be true, declared during the banquet that "he wished nothing better than to see Castro land, as he would then inevitably be taken prisoner, and a source of possible disturbance in the future would thus once and for all be removed."[64] The Venezuelan government believed that Castro was sheltering within the area enclosed by the towns of Cúcuta, Pamplona, Ocaña, and Concepción in Colombia. The Venezuelan government closed the customs houses on the Venezuelan side of the border to prevent Castro and his supporters from crossing into the country. Gómez ordered a contingent of six hundred men from Maracaibo and a further six hundred men from San Cristóbal to intercept Castro if he crossed the border into Venezuela.[65] It was unlikely, however, that Castro would make a move now, as it was the middle of the coffee harvest with a particularly abundant crop that year.

For their part, the Colombian authorities were very keen for Castro to be rendered harmless because they were determined not to give the Venezuelan government any grounds for complaints: they were in the process of negotiating a treaty with Venezuela that allowed Colombian goods the right of way using Venezuelan waterways. However, in October 1911 it was confirmed that Castro was in Cúcuta, with further troops dispatched to reinforce the defenses of Táchira. The Venezuelan government also retaliated against Colombia by increasing the levies imposed on goods imported by Colombian merchants through the customs houses on Lake Maracaibo. The Venezuelan government expected a revolution soon after the coffee harvest was over in February the following year.

Castro avoided being detained, slipping out of Colombia and returning in November to Cuba. Castro stayed at the Matanzas country house of Gumersindo Rivas, who was connected to Manuel Silveira, the owner of a Cuban bank where the former president had deposited a large sum of money. It was also rumored that Castro had a cache of arms and ammunition at Palmira, near Ciénfuegos, where two sailing ships were waiting to transfer them to Venezuela. According to R. Gil Garmendía, secretary of the Venezuelan legation in La Habana, Castro owned the *Olympia,* which was armed and camouflaged as a warship.[66] The area was a favorite place for fugitives because it was full of caves and underpopulated,[67] although nothing suspicious was revealed when the Cuban authorities searched the area.[68]

Other rebels at the time were also working to achieve the end of the Gómez regime. In May 1911, Alejandro Rivas Vásquez tried joining forces with Mocho Hernández but was initially rebuffed. Rivas Vásquez then set up in New York a Comité Patriótico Venezolano, which later established a *junta patriótica* headed by Luis R. Guzmán, with Charles F. Schmidt as treasurer and P. Fortoul Hurtado as secretary.[69] The intention of the junta was to bring together all exiles opposed to Gómez. In his pursuit of this objective, Rivas Vásquez arrived in Trinidad in November, openly boasting of his intention to invade Venezuela with an expeditionary force. As long as he was able to supply the necessary arms and ammunition, he could count on the cooperation of Mocho Hernández, but this came to nothing.[70] After talking to Romerogarcía and Mendible, Castro's agents on the island, Rivas Vásquez together with General Gabriel Valencia, left Trinidad on December 5 for Puerto Colombia "to join Castro and his adherents on the Colombian-Venezuelan frontier near Cúcuta."[71]

In early 1912, Rivas Vásquez founded a revolutionary cell in Barranquilla, which evolved into the Partido Progresista de Venezuela. Rivas Vásquez's aim, outlined in the party's manifesto, was not to change one person for another similar one but "to change a system of oppression and exploitation for another one with effective guarantees for both nationals and foreigners; of an honest administration of the interests of the people; and for the development of the country's resources."[72] When the Colombian authorities discovered the formation of the party[73] and its intention of starting an uprising in Venezuela, Rivas Vásquez was expelled on February 13, 1912, giving great "satisfaction to the Government of Venezuela."[74] The Colombian government also detained a number of Venezuelan suspects found near the frontier, and in December expelled Celestino Castro, who left on the Royal Mail steam packet *Atraco* for Trinidad. Despite the efforts made by the Colombian government, the Venezuelan government withdrew its 1909 permission for Colombians to export duty-free staple articles, mainly coffee, through Venezuela twice a year for a week at a time across the frontier near Cúcuta and San Antonio del Táchira.

Old Political Differences Surface

Within Venezuela, the old differences and intrigues between the Liberals and the Nacionalista Conservatives began to surface in a more concerted fashion during 1911. The Liberals appeared to gain the upper hand when the Conservatives lost their seats on the Council of State. Rufino Blanco Fombona in his usual acerbic way described the country's political situation as disastrous, with the "Andean barbarity" juxtaposed to the "exclusive oligarchy of the González Guzmán [*sic*] and other Guzmancistas. The cadavers have left their bones and are poisoning the air."[75] The most discredited men from the Septenio[76] and the Quinquenio[77] "manage the nation, together with the Alcántaras, Andueza Palacios, Yturbes and the other nonentities whose sole mention is a disgrace for Venezuela because generations of the same families have whipped and sacked the whole nation."[78] The country appeared to Blanco Fombona to be suffocating "under the foot of the triumphant beast."[79]

By the middle of 1911, it was apparent to many that the Guzmán Blanco clique, as Sir Vincent referred to them, were the most influential group supporting the government. As a result, Gómez lost in October the support of Mocho Hernández, who had left the country in December 1909 because of health reasons. At the time he left, Mocho Hernández assured Gómez that he had his full support,[80] requesting at his departure that his followers should rally around the new government. Mocho Hernández resigned his seat on the Council of State in October 1911 and issued a proclamation declaring himself officially an enemy of the government because the promises made by Gómez on December 20, 1908, to abolish, inter alia, monopolies had not been fulfilled. Moreover, new monopolies were being awarded in the mining sector that only served to attract foreign adventurers. It was clear to many that Gómez was just as corrupt as Castro. In 1911, a British frozen meat factory in Puerto Cabello handed over $243,000 to Gómez and his associates in "ordinary stock, the balance of the capital being only £100,000."[81] In another case, A. M. Louvet wanted to build a short railway line to the Orinoco river, but the president awarded the concession to a man of straw and then demanded $145,800 for the concession, with the money going into "the pockets of the President and Ministers."[82] Mocho Hernández was also disappointed with the way Gómez had managed state affairs because had he remained faithful to his December 20, 1908, plan, it would have "completely changed the destiny of the country and has indicated a very different course for the future of the fatherland."[83] Mocho Hernández disapproved strongly of a mining contract awarded in Guayana and the possible establishment of a bank by Delgado Chalbaud and Corao[84] that would issue its own paper notes. The only area of agreement that Mocho Hernández had with Gómez was that peace should be brought to the country, but only if it was "maintained with the public's well-being rather than with forces armed with bayonets."[85]

Gómez did not receive Mocho Hernández's criticism with equanimity, finding it puzzling, as he had never uttered a critical word against the president and had voluntarily retired from the Council of State for health reasons to seek a cure in Paris. Mocho Hernández had then received the maximum salary allowed of two months because an alternate was not called to replace him in order to keep his post open. Gómez had hoped that Mocho Hernández had been "enlightened in the school of experience, in the dictates of reason and the impositions of duty, in order to sow with a calm spirit the honorable footpath of patriotism and gratitude."[86] Gómez even lent Mocho Hernández money for his trip to Europe and now wanted it returned.

In spite of this setback, Gómez still entertained the notion that he could unite the Liberals and Nacionalistas in order to bring peace and democratic government to the country. In his address to an extraordinary session of Congress in 1911, Gómez stated clearly his future plans for the country, arguing that since 1903, when he established peace and order in the country, his behavior was "defined by duty and patriotism."[87] Moreover, when he took over as president in December 1908, his plans had been "ample, expansive and democratic,"[88] with the result that between the Liberals and the Nacionalistas "there should not be victors and vanquished because they are all children of the same fatherland."[89] Gómez was satisfied that he had accomplished both the political and the military tasks that he set himself since he ended civil strife and "opened to all my compatriots the luminous enclosure of the true Republic."[90] Gómez believed strongly that the "moral conquests are ephemeral when not based on material possessions,"[91] instituting a number of measures to increase prosperity. Any person threatening this outcome would be banished, with the result that on November 14, 1911, the Council of State reproached Mocho Hernández's "underhanded conduct"[92] because it was unpatriotic and "lacking all feeling of gratitude and honesty."[93] In spite of this, during the same month, Gómez informed the Nacionalista General David Gimón that he would be happy "if at the end of his administration he could hand over to his successor a country free of the monster of spiteful factionalism."[94]

End of Democracy

At the beginning of 1912, the Venezuelan government expected three revolutionary movements against it, led by Castro, Rivas Vásquez, and Mocho

Hernández. In anticipation, the government detailed five thousand troops scattered along the Táchira frontier. The rebels, however, received a severe setback both by the vigilance of the Colombian government and the troops amassed at the frontier; the revolutionaries were no match for them. Castro returned to Tenerife on April 13 and was later reported to be suffering from blood poisoning.

It was becoming clear to Gómez that the country was slowly drifting back to political chaos and that he could use this to his own advantage to end the quasi-democratic experiment that he and his advisers had instituted since 1908. At the time disagreements among the cabinet members arose because of personal animosities, with Samuel Dario Maldonado and Carlos León "embroiled in fisticuffs"[95] during a cabinet meeting, leading to Gómez requesting their mass resignation on April 29, 1912. This came as a complete surprise to most of the ministers, including Alcántara, Matos, Pimentel, Castro Zavala, Iturbe, Román Cárdenas, Gil Fortoul, and González Guinán.[96] The new cabinet,[97] which came to be known as the "Interim Cabinet" and was composed by the departmental heads at the various ministries, was appointed on the same day and did not contain a single Liberal or Nationalist. It was provisional by nature, as Gómez explained to José Ignacio Cárdenas, because he was "waiting for the right moment to make the real appointments."[98] Gómez would find the experiment of governing with director generals to be more "conducive to peace and good government, than governing or rather being governed by rapacious politicians whose jealousies and private animosities he was unable to curb,"[99] with no new ministers appointed until the end of the year.

The question of whether Gómez remained in power after his period of office ended was a source of intense debate. One rumor at the time was that Dr. Cárdenas would be elected president with Gómez as vice president, and that the former would soon afterwards leave or retire to Europe, leaving Gómez ipso facto president. Some of Gómez's enemies considered launching their own presidential candidate, but the Benemérito (Meritorious), as he was later called, would not agree to such an experiment. Gómez informed Murillo, the state president of Táchira, that "we are not in a period when a few easily deceived and amusing men can disturb the country with their electoral propaganda, undermining confidence in the regime's stability, and increasing the state of anarchy,"[100] and he was preparing "a remedy of *sixty pounds* that will make them come to their senses and force them to think about the happy destiny of the Republic" (emphasis in original).[101] By September that year, one contemporary observer reported that the former ministers had disappeared completely from the public eye, with Pimentel living in disgrace on his extensive coffee estates because he had abused his position, while Alcántara "rarely quits his fine house in Caracas."[102] The same was true of Matos, who lived on his estates, "and is also never seen now."[103] Some of the former ministers together with others were conspiring with Delgado Chalbaud, the young head of the small Venezuelan navy, to launch a coup d'état that was planned for the following year.

Gómez felt increasingly confident and powerful against his enemies. When there were renewed rumors of a possible Mocho Hernández–Castro alliance, he informed his friend José Ignacio Cárdenas that "the extravagant notions entertained by Castro and Hernández are of little concern to me. It is of little importance whether they join forces or not because together or individually they only inspire scorn. They know what to expect from me in the battlefield and will not dare move against me."[104] Moreover, Gómez had already decided that he would ban any form of electioneering during the 1913 congressional elections, which would eventually elect a new president for the following presidential term, as the country was not ready for democratic change.

On January 3, 1913, Gómez named his first cabinet composed of his own appointees with only the ministers for foreign affairs, interior, and development and secretary general remaining unchanged from the Interim Cabinet and composed of the following people: Zumeta, Interior Minister; Román Cárdenas, Finance Minister; Ladislao Andara, Foreign Minister; Pedro Emilio Coll, Development Minister; Victorino Márquez Bustillos, War and Navy Minister; Felipe Guevara Rojas, Education Minister; Domingo A. Coronil, Public Works Minister; and, Ezequiel A. Vivas, Secretary General. The cabinet was composed of young intellectuals, without a military man in sight, who were appointed to positions that they hardly dreamt would be theirs. This was the first time that ministers were appointed from outside the "panel of traditional oligarchs and they were chosen from among the leading figures of the intelligentsia."[105] Gómez was happy with his new cabinet, stating to José Ignacio Cárdenas in March that "it behaves well and I am satisfied with it."[106] Moreover, his program of "Peace, Union and Work" was a reality that "all Venezuelans could see, feel and smell and they are convinced that I have fulfilled to the letter everything that I have offered."[107]

This move did little to allay the fears that Gómez was seeking reelection. In addition, the increase in press coverage given to the achievements of the Gómez administration and the large sums of money spent on roads and public works in general only served to reinforce the impression that he was preparing "for the continuation of the present dictatorship."[108] Several people were actively disseminating the view that Gómez's rule had been beneficial to the country. For example, the Liberal general Samuel Ortega Martínez published a flysheet in January 1913 praising Gómez for being the "unifying link between all Venezuelans and whose conciliatory policies had eradicated factional anarchy."[109] Manuel M. Gallegos was of the opinion that the country needed a few more years of Gómez's rule for him to guide the country to stability and end the "regional and factional hatred neutralizing the sterile system of petty chieftains, in order to allow further transfer of power without fear or danger of violent reactions."[110] Much of the construction work on the roads was undertaken by Andinos, who could be trusted in case of a civil war to fight on Gómez's side. This slap in the face to the old caudillos and the old political parties that were fighting for power was taken as a signal for them to unite against Gómez in the Council of State, where they still had a stronghold. Their first big test of strength against the government was whether to ratify the French Protocol in 1913.

A Watershed

In early 1913, the political situation in the country pointed to a slow but sure gain of absolute power by Gómez, with rumors circulating that he would continue his presidential term of office after 1914. From New York, Fortoul-Hurtado and Nicanor Bolet Monagas informed Gómez that Venezuela faced two revolutions, "the one generated by you and the other in the heart of the popular masses that cannot tolerate a dictatorship or its imposition, and who are prepared at all costs to take vengeance on you and your family."[111] Consequently, the country "is not ready to support your dictatorship any more nor the circle of advisers that surrounds you." [112] Gómez dismissed such thoughts outright because such a move would lead to a period of instability. Moreover, he had a very convincing argument against the rumors, which was that in order for him to be reelected article 74 of the constitution, which prohibited reelection, needed to be amended. For such an amendment to be considered by Congress, the executive had to receive a request to this effect from three-quarters of the state legislatures. Moreover, Gómez would not gain from such a change because of a new clause inserted at his insistence in the 1909 constitution that prohibited the president from "benefiting from changes of this nature made during his tenure of office."[113] Consequently, even if Congress amended the constitution to allow reelection, Gómez could not be a candidate because this would be unconstitutional and would violate a safeguard he himself had inspired. The political consequences would surely lead to a new period of instability with added revolutionary activity—something that Gómez wanted to avoid at all costs.

Gómez faced his first real test of power in 1913. The revolutionaries continued with their plans to invade Venezuela, with Castro, the only person who could unite all exiled revolutionaries, at the forefront of the attack. The invasion would coincide with the political blow the former ministers were busy planning in Venezuela together with the Council of State, the bastion of the old political forces of the country, and Delgado Chalbaud's own military coup. The plan was for the Council of State to inflict such a political blow on Gómez that he would be unable to recover. At the same time, the exiles would invade the country, bringing with them sufficient arms to counter any defense made by Gómez's army, and then join forces with Delgado Chalbaud, who was masterminding a military coup.

The invasion plan was initially outlined to Castro in Tenerife in the summer months of 1912. The debate centered on what had gone wrong with previous attempts at invading the country, reaching the conclusion that there was a pressing need for the rebels to be better armed and with their own ship to transport them and their cache of arms to Venezuela. Castro was convinced that the success of the venture seemed assured now that Gómez appeared weaker and isolated from the strong regional political support he had hitherto commanded. Castro agreed to fund the purchase of a boat, while the additional cache of arms would be sourced from a number of places, including his friends in Cuba and Colombia.

In order to confuse Gómez's spies, Castro ostensibly traveled to Germany to seek a cure for gout/rheumatic fever, traveling from Tenerife under the assumed name of N. Quintero on December 6, and heading for Southampton, England. Max Erde, who was Castro's adjutant, joined him at Las Palmas. Castro did not intend to stay in England but used his arrival in the country as a decoy to try to escape Gómez's spies. Part of his luggage was sent with Erde to the Abban Court Hotel in London, where J. E. Pérez, the Venezuelan consul, had installed a spy to keep an eye on the former president's movements. Castro, however, continued his journey to Antwerp, where Antonio de Pietri Daudet met him, traveling second class to Brussels using the local train service in order to shake off Gómez's spies. Pérez was surprised by this move because he expected Castro to leave immediately for

Paris and in anticipation caught the fast train from Antwerp to the French capital. Far from suffering with ill-health Castro was perfectly fit, finding time in Brussels to be in a hotel room with a girl he picked up in the street, from where she left "very happy with the gift he gave her."[114]

Castro eventually made it to Paris for a series of meetings with Corao and Baltazar Vallenilla Lanz to iron out the final details of the invasion plan. In early December, Castro traveled from Le Havre using his mother's surname of Ruiz to New York to acquire a small boat. The American immigration authorities frustrated Castro's plans when he landed at Ellis Island on New Year's Eve, detaining him as an undesirable alien because it was thought that he was suffering from a contagious disease and would therefore have to undergo medical tests. The Taft administration felt that there were sufficient statutory grounds on which to deport the former Venezuelan president.[115] It also believed that Castro was under indictment for the murder of Paredes and for the attempted murder of Gómez,[116] and could therefore be held, according to Dr. O. J. Berg, "subject to my warrant sworn out as murder in first degree."[117] Castro challenged such a view and after a month of arguments and counterarguments was allowed into the United States. New York Governor William Sulzer immediately gave a banquet in Castro's honor at the Waldorf Astoria in order to embarrass the Taft administration and the Republicans. While in New York, Castro acquired the *Mina Swim,* a small boat moored in Gloucester, Massachusetts, for $4,000, paying with a check drawn on a Chicago bank account.[118] The boat would later sail for New Orleans, where it would load arms and ammunition. Castro remained in the United States for a few more weeks while he completed the purchase of the boat before departing for Cuba. Meanwhile, Carmelo Castro and Mendible arrived in Cúcuta in January 1913 to organize their end of the revolution. Castro's revolutionary committee in Cuba, where he had strong allies, also acquired a large cache of arms that would be transferred to Venezuela.

After the fracas of New York, Castro left for Havana to confer with President José Miguel Gómez of Cuba and former Colombian president Rafael Reyes. On February 26, Castro arrived to the enthusiastic welcome of the crowd that gathered in a small flotilla to escort his ship into Havana. Once the ship docked, Castro, "the little runt of an ex-tyrant"[119] as he was referred to disparagingly by the *Havana Telegraph* and who was "clad in a natty white flannel suit and jauntily carrying a silver cane,"[120] was met by Rivas and his partner, Manuel Silveira, who was reported to be backing Castro. The Havana municipal band played the national anthems of Cuba and Venezuela as Castro stepped ashore, with the former Venezuelan president having to push his way through the crowds at the dockside in order to leave, doffing his cap and exclaiming "Long Live Free Cuba," which was answered by an ebullient "Long Live Castro!"[121] Castro's arrival in Havana was "more like the return of a popular hero than that of an outcast from his own country."[122] Castro's warm reception at the hands of the Cuban people was due to his perceived nationalism and defiance of the United States.

The crowds followed Castro to his hotel, where Reyes was also staying, with the two men starting talks almost immediately. Former President Zelaya of Nicaragua, and an old friend of Castro's, was also expected in Havana soon. Later that afternoon, Castro saw President Gómez and attended a banquet in his honor that evening. The celebrations continued the following day with another banquet given to Castro by his friends on the island. In a defiant move, Castro intended to return to the United States, traveling to Washington via Key West on Saturday, March 1, to attend the inauguration of President-elect Woodrow Wilson.[123]

Gómez did not appear unduly perturbed at these plans, feeling that Castro had "definitively passed into history excreted by his crimes."[124] The United States did not share Gómez's complacent attitude; the government believed that Castro posed a real threat to the stability of the country. Undersecretary of State William Tecumseh Sherman Doyle advised President Wilson that their "previous action with regard to Castro was based much more on our feeling that he was an international nuisance than upon any desire of the Venezuelan Government that he may be excluded."[125] Doyle's advice was that Castro was "still an international nuisance and the mere fact that the Government of Venezuela at the present moment does not fear his activities would hardly seem a reason for treating him differently than he has been treated in the past."[126] Castro's behavior and the attitude adopted by the United States worried the British government, which enquired whether the State Department still wanted Castro kept out of the British West Indies. The Americans replied that "the antecedents and character of Castro are such that he will continue to be a menace to the public order in Venezuela and that if permitted to land in any neighboring territory he might abuse its hospitality thereby setting on foot a movement hostile to the Venezuelan Government."[127]

The Franco-Venezuelan treaty

The signs of an imminent split with the old caudillos who had hitherto supported Gómez showed itself in the imbroglio over the French Protocol. The

Council of State and the executive were now antagonistic forces, and each was out to inflict as much damage as possible on the other. The council was extremely powerful, as it united important regional chieftains who were not awarded ministries but who still commanded a significant following. The Venezuelan-French treaty would be a test of strength between the executive and the Council of State.

After a long illness General Juan Pietri, the vice president and member of the Council of State, died on May 28, 1911, with the result that the constitution was amended on July 11 to allow the alternates to meet if the council's full members could not do so. Such a change would be extremely important during the following months. Under Venezuelan law, all *ad referendum* treaties such as the Franco-Venezuelan Treaty needed the Council of State's consultative opinion before Congress could consider it for ratification. After several years of negotiations, on February 11, 1913, the Franco-Venezuelan Treaty was signed by the executive but without the Council of State being consulted. Congress, however, could not ratify it until it had the council's judgment. Consequently, the treaty was submitted to the council for its consultative opinion a month later, on March 10.

Gómez was aware that his enemies were arming themselves. In February, Gómez was informed that Blanco Fombona had acquired from Francois Lebon some 399 rifles, 50,000 rounds of ammunition, and two machine guns.[128] There was mounting internal unrest, especially in Trujillo State, which was controlled by Baptista. Gómez was convinced that Baptista's allies had enough arms and ammunition to start a rebellion on their own and thus ordered them to surrender. In March 1913, Gómez sent his first cousin García Velasco with added reinforcements to the state. García Velasco's mission was to convince General Víctor M. Baptista Galindo, the state president, and Ramón Colmenares, a member of the Council of State, that "their patriotic duty was to resign from the legislature that is currently in session."[129] Gómez also requested the resignation of Antonio Jacinto Villegas, an adviser to the state government. Once this was achieved García Velasco, General Timoleón Omaña, and General Vincencio Pérez Soto would head the presidency, the state assembly, and the new Council of State respectively. This was a hard blow against Baptista in his own backyard, but, as Gómez rather cynically explained to García, he was sure that his friends Víctor Baptista, Villegas, Colmenares, and Juan Bautista Araujo would understand that these new measures were designed to "achieve the harmony and well-being of the Trujillano people, and all of them, I repeat, will help in an effective and disciplined way to carry out my orders."[130] Reinforcements were later sent to Omaña to be deployed at the estates of people considered to be Gómez's enemies. According to Velásquez, Gómez ordered García Velasco "to take as prisoners the many local heads that are loyal to Baptista and to exchange them for a fixed number of arms. Timoleón Omaña, the State President, has powers of a Pro Consul. There is no punishment, such as imprisonment, land expropriation, banishment from the state, that should not be used against the followers of Doctor and General Baptista."[131] Gómez later confided somewhat optimistically to José Ignacio Cárdenas in Paris and to Murillo in Táchira that the country "continues its inexorable calm development through work and peace, and general contentment can be seen everywhere."[132] The political situation, however, was deteriorating.

It was at this stage that the old caudillos decided to make their move. This would be a coordinated attack against the government with the purpose of initially weakening and discrediting it and then toppling it. The conspirators included such members of the Council of State as Baptista and Alcántara, together with more than a hundred generals, colonels, lawyers, and priests. The caudillos, led by Baptista, would seize the opportunity to embarrass and weaken the government while at the same time planning a conspiracy to depose him, led by Delgado Chalbaud, head of the Venezuelan navy, and with the close involvement of González Guinán and Néstor Luis Pérez. Some of the exiles were also included in the conspiracy, which at one stage involved both Castro and Mocho Hernández.[133]

The subcommittee of the Council of State appointed to study the Franco-Venezuelan Treaty, composed of Trino Baptista, José E. Machado, and Colonel Ramón Ayala, did not accept the Foreign Ministry's report. They argued that there was nothing to consult, as the treaty had already been signed. At the council's full vote, six members, viz, Generals Pulido, Alejandro Ibarra, Peñaloza, Ayala, Baptista, and Ortega Martínez, opposed the agreement and were immediately placed under police surveillance, with only two, Generals Guerra and Mariano García, favoring the agreement. Congress was therefore unable to ratify the treaty, something the council felt would discredit the authority of the presidency and weaken Gómez's support. To further embarrass the government, the council spread the rumor that France was demanding compensation of $18.9 million in order to ratify the treaty. As it had not been discussed in Congress, any rumor could prove to be legitimate and provoke a crisis in favor of the conspirators. The treaty was resubmitted to the council on March 26 but was once again rejected. To compound matters, the council also met to decide on the forthcoming elections, declaring complete electoral freedom—something that would not serve Gómez's wishes.

Gómez's way out of this constitutional crisis, suggested by Arcaya, the attorney general, was to seek a ruling from the Supreme Court as to whether the government had made its "consultation" in ample time. There was another course that Gómez could have taken, which was to accuse the council of not fulfilling its constitutional role. This was a crime under the country's penal code, and would result in "the suspension of the council members who refused to emit judgment and, consequently, the substitution by the respective alternates,"[134] thus causing "irritation to the council members, re-opening again the debate, and creating disagreements and fights."[135] It was decided to follow the former course, with the Federal Court and of Cassation deciding on March 29 that the government had consulted the council with ample time because Congress had not debated the protocol, and hence the council's decision did not have any legal validity. Moreover, the discussion of the treaty showed that Venezuela did not have to pay $18.9 million to France, as it had been freely rumored at the time. The council was forced to meet again on April 1 when it voted against the treaty "because it forced the Venezuelan government to settle an unjust debt with France."[136] The council's decision meant that the treaty could now be debated by Congress, which found that the French demands had been exaggerated and approved it, paving the way for its approval and the renewal of diplomatic relations with France.

At this juncture Gómez had the greatest contempt for the council. He wrote to García Velasco that the council probably thought that "we find ourselves at the end of our Power. . . . This is what small-minded people, blinded by ambition, always do."[137] Gómez was most scathing about Baptista, "who owes so much to the current government,"[138] as he had been "one of the staunchest opponents in the Council of State, probably because of his irritation at the political changes in his home state where he so wants to be the leader."[139] Up to then, Baptista's popularity was due to his role in obtaining official backing for the government, and without seeming to acknowledge the irony, Gómez concluded that "a tribe governed by an authoritarian corporal was fine during the dark days of the Conquest but today in our enlightened age, the leaders and the people are fully aware of their ideas, rights and noble aspirations."[140] Equally, Gómez declared that any of the other caudillos who "followed the same route would find that within a brief period of time nobody would care for these *eminent* patriots" (emphasis in original).[141] Gómez's confidence in outwitting his opponents was helped by his knowledge of the plots being hatched. J. Abdón Vivas, his informer within the Council of State, who with the exception of Ayala joined Delgado

Chalbaud's conspiracy,[142] reported in April that Peñaloza had assured him that Castro and Mocho Hernández had reached agreement with each other, and that Régulo Olivares was the acknowledged leader of the forthcoming revolution. Peñaloza also referred to the forthcoming elections and the potential candidates, of whom the most "talked about was Román Cárdenas favored by the Zuluagas [*sic*] and Nationalists and confidentially today united with Abel Santos, Felix Galavís and the Dr. Márquez Bustillos."[143] There were other people in the country who also wanted to topple Gómez using any legal instruments at their disposal to weaken his government. The letters received by Gómez from Mocho Hernández and Rafael L. Dávila proved to him that the conspiracies organized abroad had ended "and that the clumsy and ungrateful attitude of the caudillos left in the country toward the government to whom they owed everything also put an end to the ridiculous aspirations of certain men who have the illusion of reaching the presidency."[144]

Delgado Chalbaud's coup was set for April 18, just before Congress opened its first session in 1913. Of crucial importance for the success of the conspirators' plan was their ability to take the San Carlos barracks, where the government stored most of its arsenal. Colonel Ramón Párraga was in charge of taking the barracks, offering a generous bribe to General Julio Olivar. On becoming aware of the plot, Gómez transferred General Carmelo Medina, the commander of the San Carlos barracks, to Margarita Island, and Olivar was moved to Maracaibo after being offered a counter bribe of a house and $3,788 to remain loyal to the regime. Caracas was filled with loyal troops from Maracay, and police officers were posted at the homes of council members.[145] Andara, the foreign affairs minister, reported in his annual message to Congress that the government had uncovered a plot to assassinate Gómez on April 29. The rebels needed a change of plan.

On May 6, Pulido, the head of the Council of State, informed Zumeta, the interior minister, that the council had not achieved its necessary quorum for the meeting that had to take place to renew its legal status because Gómez had instructed Guerra, Francisco Tosta García, and Mariano García not to attend because of ill health. Their substitutes could not be called because of their congressional duties. Furthermore, Rolando had left for Europe because of health reasons and was not expected to return until September. Prior to his departure, he had requested his supporters to help Gómez, especially at the forthcoming elections in Anzoátegui. Rolando gave strict orders that nothing could be done without Gómez's approval and was confident that his interests would be secure, as his brother General Armando Rolando was the constitutional president of the state and as such "the agent of the National Executive and my representative on all matters concerning our party."[146]

In May, Gómez felt sufficiently strong to move against the conspirators and the Council of State. On May 17, Delgado Chalbaud, president of the Orinoco and Coastal Navigation Company, was jailed together with his brothers Miguel and Salomón, friends, and relatives, amounting to between thirty and forty people, who were charged with conspiring together with the Council of State to induce a rebellion against the government.[147] In order to make the Delgado Chalbaud brothers talk, Gómez ordered General Luis de Pasquali, governor of the San Carlos barracks, to keep them manacled with *grillos* in separate cells.[148] Delgado Chalbaud was later transferred to the La Rotunda prison in Caracas, where he remained until 1927, when he was released after a general amnesty for political prisoners was declared.

Many of the conspirators, such as Baptista and Alcántara, managed to escape, with the former fleeing to Curacao first on hearing of Delgado Chalbaud's arrest, and then traveling to New York. Alcántara almost drowned when the small boat that carried him to Bonaire capsized. Although Gómez knew about the escape plans, he allowed his enemies to leave because they would pose less of a threat and a problem, explaining to García Velasco that "neither here nor abroad can Baptista be a threat to peace in Venezuela."[149] The same applied to the "other Members of the Council of Government who feel like leaving the country"[150] because Gómez was confident that they would be unable to unite in a common front against the government. Gómez concluded that the affair was "a great victory"[151] for his cause because "we have unmasked these ungrateful traitors who would have created a lot of trouble for us in the future."[152] At the same time, Gómez sent García Velasco in Trujillo a list of all Baptista's supporters in the state and ordered them to surrender their arms to the authorities because their leader's departure from the country had left them in a compromising situation with the government. If they did not do this voluntarily, then Gómez suggested that they should be bribed "as it is also necessary to flatter men's particular usefulness and money is always welcomed; it appears to me that at your own initiative you should offer in exchange for Baptista's cache of arms a financial inducement to the people who are hiding it, according to the number of arms surrendered, promising not to reveal to anybody how much has been paid."[153] With these changes, Gómez felt more secure, intimating to Juan Bautista Araujo that "the government feels stronger than ever to suppress instantaneously any subversive putsch."[154] Gómez would now face the forthcoming electoral process with even greater confidence. The procedure to elect a new president started in May 1913, with the registration of the new electoral roll and followed by the election of the state deputies and senators in October. They in turn elected the representatives, who would choose the new president in April 1914. However, the electoral procedure was derailed by Castro's abortive invasion in July 1913.

After his confrontation with the Council of State, Gómez wanted to do away with it completely. As we have seen, Congress on July 11, 1911, changed the constitution to enable the council to call alternates. The amendment to the constitution stated that if the council failed to meet because there was no quorum—that is, seven members—over a period of four consecutive meetings or fifteen days, the whole body would be dismissed, and the ten alternate members called to replace the councilors. If any of these were unavailable, due to illness or any other motive, then Congress, or the president of the Republic if Congress was not in session, would nominate the new members to fill any vacancies. The effect of this was that "if at any time the Executive is dissatisfied with the Council of Government and can secure the non-attendance of four councilors and the corresponding supplementary members, a new body can be constituted composed of ten supplementary members."[155] The three congressmen who were opposed to the change, viz, Trino Baptista and José E. Machado (both of whom had refused to accept the Foreign Ministry's report on the Franco-Venezuelan Treaty) and Pedro María Parra, were all forced to leave the country quickly. In May, General Antonio Fernández, one of the councilors, died, and Congress on May 21 voted for Gil Fortoul, who had only returned to Venezuela in 1912 after an absence of twenty-two years abroad serving as a diplomat, as his replacement.

On May 31, Zumeta, the interior minister, informed Congress that the council had not met since April 29 and that its *junta directiva* had not been elected. Consequently, the ten members of the Council of State, "some of the most influential political leaders and petty chieftains of Venezuela,"[156] were dismissed, including Baptista, Peñaloza, Riera, Rolando, and Pulido, with Congress electing their substitutes on June 3,[157] and naming Gil Fortoul as president. The new council was clearly expected to be much more submissive to Gómez than the former one. While these developments occurred it was hinted in Caracas, and reported by the British chargé d'affaires, that Gómez "would not be displeased if this arbitrary settlement of the Executive's dispute with the Council of Government would lead to an uprising headed by one or other of the above Generals, which in view of the improvement in the army of late years, he is apparently confident that he could crush."[158] In addition, the changes created by the invasion would allow Gómez to govern "until he saw fit to declare that peace had been re-established."[159] Such a situation was achieved with the pro-Castroist invasion of Falcón at the end of July.

In spite of the grave political events that took place during May, some people were convinced that free elections would take place that year. Inspired by Mocho Hernández and as a way of testing Gómez's real intentions at the forthcoming September elections, the presidential candidacy of Félix Montes, a young university law professor from Guayana, was launched on July 11 by Rafael Arévalo González, the editor of *El Pregonero* newspaper. The administration's intentions were soon felt: the newspaper editor was imprisoned, and the candidate fled the country to Curacao, where he published a flysheet, "Exposición Necesaria," explaining his reasons for launching his campaign.[160] At the imprisonment of Arévalo González, the university students demonstrated on the streets against the Gómez regime, but La Sagrada, Gómez's elite Praetorian guard, quickly put an end to this, with the university remaining closed for ten long years. Mocho Hernández would also launch his own presidential campaign but from the safe haven of Cuba.

A Trap for Castro

Soon after dealing with Delgado Chalbaud's abortive plot, Gómez started to set a trap to capture Castro, the only remaining person he perceived as a potential threat to his regime. Moreover, such a move also had the distinct advantage of securing his reelection. As long as constitutional guarantees were suspended under the constitution, Congress could not meet in April 1914 to elect a new president who would take office in June. Under the law, once elections were postponed, a Plenipotentiary Congress of the Municipalities would be convened to draft a new constitution.[161]

Such a situation developed in June 1913, when in the east Horacio Ducharne entered the country through Caño de Pedernales,[162] and Luis Mijares also took up arms in Maturín. F. Pulgar from New York warned Gómez that Castro had friends in Caracas with hand grenades willing to "throw them against the barracks and other buildings in combination with the sinister plans that they have organized."[163] Gil Fortoul counseled Gómez that, with rumors of Castro's invasion and a revolutionary uprising already in the Llanos (plains), this could be used as a legal pretext to declare martial law and thus prevent elections from taking place. While Castro, Olivares, and Blanco Fombona continued their preparations for an armed invasion, the other political exiles in New York called on Gómez to step down after 1914.

As we have seen, Castro and his supporters were organizing an invasion of Venezuela with three simultaneous uprisings: one in the East led by Castro's illegitimate son; one in the West through San Cristóbal; and, one through Falcón led by Castro and Bello in Coro. As part of the invasion plans, General Silverio González, prior to becoming the army commander at Coro, was offered a bribe of $18,939 by Bello to hand over the state capital to Castro. Gómez was aware of this and felt he could use it as a way of trapping his erstwhile friend. González informed Gómez of Castro's bribe; Gómez in turn ordered González to set the trap by accepting the money, but the general was later imprisoned as a precaution.[164] On hearing that the rebel's offer was accepted, Bello left for Coro to pay off González. At the same time, Gómez instructed León Jurado, the president of Falcón and a former Castro associate, to enter into negotiations with the rebels in Curacao and to place himself and his men at the disposal of the former president. It was felt that Castro would be enticed to invade through Falcón, where he would be captured by the government. Bello, believing that Jurado's offer was genuine, continued the preparations for an invasion. Gómez informed García Velasco that it was rumored that Castro would invade from Colombia in 1913, either through Los Castilletes bay or through the Ensenada de Cojoro in the Guajira peninsula. As a precaution, García Velasco was ordered to move two battalions closer to the zone in order to capture Castro. In the East, toward the end of June, José Betancourt, the special commissioner of Carmelo Castro and Torres, arrived in Cristóbal Colón from Trinidad with the news that all was ready for the invasion. All that was needed was the green light from Castro, when they would order Pecha Sayago, the government official at Cristóbal Colón (Macuro) in Paria Peninsula, to provide the revolutionaries with money and detain any government boats.[165] In early July, Carmelo Castro, Miguel Bethencourt, José Quintero, and Alejandro Ibarra left Barranquilla for Cúcuta in order to complete the revolutionary plans.[166] In Caracas, Castro's loyal supporters were ready to attack the city's army barracks.

Where Is Castro?

The whereabouts of Castro at this stage were unknown to most of the rebels and the government. As we have seen, Castro intended to go to the United

States in March, but it later transpired that he traveled instead to Germany to secure arms for the revolution. There he was almost imprisoned for using a false passport. The Cabito traveled first to Hamburg and then later stayed at the home of Herr Wolfrem in Dresden, where he met Olivares, who was rumored at the time to be looking for money to launch a revolution of his own later that year. While in Europe, Castro succeeded in securing and purchasing a cache of arms and ammunition for his revolution. The cache consisted of 17 cases of modern French rifles and 132 cases of ammunition. In May, the ordnance, described as "nuts and iron castings" in the bill of lading, was loaded in London onboard the Danish steamer *St. Croix* and shipped under the name of Castro's brother Carmelo, arriving on June 6 at Bridgetown, Barbados, where the colonial authorities impounded the consignment.

In Venezuela, the possibility of a Castro invasion increased considerably the tension felt in government circles. Abdón Rivas counseled Gómez on the need to purchase an armored boat because Castro "this time will try to snatch victory from your domination of the sea, allowing him to mobilize his supporters in the most effective way and preventing government troops from reaching and helping their own men."[167] Abdón Rivas also argued that Castro was aware that Táchira was well defended and that the Easterners were untrustworthy, and would thus only invade through "the coasts of the West; Tucacas for Barquisimeto; La Ceiba to hit Trujillo, or Coro to take advantage of the great antipathy that León Jurado with his monopolies and pilfering has brought against the government."[168] Castro would most probably choose Coro because of Jurado's unpopularity with the local population, who were "capable of going over to Castro or the devil to get rid of that adventurer hated by society, hated by the people and hated by the army."[169] The rumors of a forthcoming revolution intensified further in June, when it was stated that Mocho Hernández, who was living in New York,[170] together with Peñaloza would invade Venezuela through Coro.

Gómez was not unduly perturbed at the prospect of a Castro invasion, informing Manuel Sarmiento at Coro not to worry as he felt that "the revolutionary movement will no longer be important there, and that soon it will be extinguished forever owing to your efforts and that of General Laclé's."[171] Gómez was convinced that Castro was already in Venezuelan territorial waters, cruising on board a rebel ship and waiting for the right moment to strike. There is little doubt that Gómez respected Castro's military qualities. In an interview with the *New York Herald* Gómez felt that people such as Alcántara, Mocho Hernández, and Baptista, were "of little political or military importance,"[172] whereas Castro was the only man who was truly "dangerous, the only one that instills respect by his valor."[173] Gómez relished the thought of being close to capturing his former friend and was "calm and serene in the presence of this movement headed by that crazy person who in his madness imagines that the times of today are the same as yesterday and that the same men of 99 [*sic*] are present."[174]

There were persistent rumors that Castro was hiding on Curacao, making his headquarters at the St. Nicholas estate of General Ramón Guerra, situated some fifteen miles west of Willemstad. The estate had the great advantage of access to an open bay, where a landing by small boats at night could easily be made. Gómez believed that he was about to trap and capture Castro, ordering Jurado, the thirty-one-year old president of Falcón State, to persuade the insurgents to invade Venezuela. Jurado informed the rebels in Curacao that he was willing to help Castro disembark at La Vela to start the revolution. The rebels, according to Jurado, were "waiting for General Castro and they have been informed that they are short of arms and armaments."[175] It would appear that the rebels were also convinced that Castro was in a rebel ship cruising Venezuelan coastal waters in readiness for the appropriate moment to invade. Bello, believing that Jurado's offer was genuine, tried in vain to convince Castro's advisers to get the former president to reach La Vela. In spite of Castro's nonappearance, his proclamation was issued by his brother Carmelo in Curacao, though it was dated Coro, July 27, 1913. It called on all Venezuelans to "contribute to the salvation of our dear fatherland by taking up arms without hesitation,"[176] as the country had been "trampled by the dark savage who has destroyed the Venezuelan home and has even traded away the nation's honor."[177] This was done by "the idiotic and ferocious Gómez who for eternity will have his forehead marked with the inri [*sic*] of traitor."[178]

On the same day, Bello disembarked at La Vela de Coro, without Castro, to start the revolution together with the poet Alfredo Arévalo Larriva, Adolfo Rosales, Juan Liendo, Vicente Parra Castro, Félix Pérez, Porfirio Sierralta, and Julio Velasco Castro, a seventeen-year old nephew of Castro. They were quickly captured, and Bello, Rosales, and Liendo were sent to Puerto Cabello on August 3, putting an end to the possibility of enticing Castro to Venezuela. The following day, on July 28, the Castristas, headed by General Patrocinio Peñuela, invaded Táchira from Cúcuta but were soon defeated by government forces.[179] There were other minor uprisings in the country; the most important was José Asunción Rodríguez in eastern Venezuela, a Nationalist movement that had joined Castro's revolution.[180] Gómez was sure, however, that "not many days will pass before he is captured."[181] In Güiria, Torres left the town to raid Cristóbal Colón, while Luis Nieves invaded Venezuela by Apure "and his exploits have been to steal, murder and violate those defenseless homes."[182] Meanwhile, Carmelo Castro, Ibarra, and Quintero were arrested in Ocaña, Colombia, while forty-three other Venezuelan revolutionaries were captured at the estate of General José Rosario González on July 26.[183]

Gómez immediately placed his army chiefs and state presidents on full alert, sending Santos Matute Gómez with government reinforcements to Falcón.[184] On July 29, Gómez also ordered José Ignacio Cárdenas in Europe to purchase arms "because it was convenient from all aspects to have modern armaments supplied"[185] and owing to "revolutionary guerrilla movements that have appeared that undoubtedly follow orders from Castro, who is surely sailing in Venezuelan waters."[186] In Táchira, the rebels led by Olivares, managed to reach Rubio and Capacho before the local authorities dealt with them. The only place that offered some resistance to Gómez was the state of Trujillo, where the Baptistas had a strong following. Gómez dispatched Generals Eugenio Montana, Julio Moreno González, Marcial Padrón, and Rubén Espina to reinforce the garrison in Trujillo, manned by State President Omaña. The Baptistas and their supporters suffered severely, with Gómez ordering that "they should suffer the consequences of their subversive and disloyal behavior."[187]

In order to encourage other people involved in the plot to come out into the open, Gómez kept Coro incommunicado "because I still feel that such an expectation will feed the hope of those who are involved, and they will make a gesture in gratitude to their failed Leader."[188] Although Jurado, the Falcón state president, believed that the "enemy" appeared to suspect something, he made one last effort on August 7 to convince Castro to invade, sending a vessel carrying an intelligence agent to Curacao with a letter stating that "the situation for the revolutionaries was favorable."[189] This way the agent would enter "indirectly in communication with the revolutionaries, and will try discreetly to get them to trust him with some correspondence or some agent of theirs."[190] Jurado's premature move of taking Bello prisoner disturbed "the trap prepared for the *man* and he managed to escape" (emphasis in original).[191] Gómez informed José Ignacio Cárdenas in Paris that "the trap to which you refer to catch the mouse was prepared by me and you should not worry about appearances."[192]

It was at this time that Gómez put into action the plan that would secure his complete hold on the country. At an emergency cabinet meeting on Monday, July 29, the Venezuelan government requested both the British and Dutch governments to prohibit the export of arms and ammunition from their respective colonies, something agreed to by the colonial authorities. It was also agreed that the Council of State should suspend all constitutional guarantees. Gómez informed the state presidents that owing to a breakdown in law and order as a result of the various Castroist inspired rebellions, "people in the territory under your control should remain alert so that the government can act swiftly and strongly against the troublemakers."[193] Preparations for a major military campaign were under way, with troops placed on full alert. Gómez explained to his state presidents that the expeditionary force that he was mustering would be "an army as never before seen in Venezuela."[194]

As a mere formality, the Council of State met on July 30 to consider Gómez's requests for emergency powers to deal with the crisis provoked by Castro's putative invasion, agreeing to suspend all constitutional guarantees two days later, on August 1, with little opposition in the country. The feeling among commercial circles and the general public as a whole was that if Gómez retained the reins of government "without too flagrant a break of the Constitution, he [was] only too welcome to do so."[195] On Saturday, August 3, a week after Castro's alleged landing in Coro, Gómez left Caracas in the afternoon for Maracay at the head of his troops, estimated at around five thousand men. Gil Fortoul, head of the Council of State, was appointed acting president and Gómez's brother Juancho was named governor of the Federal District. Such a large army was needed in order to defeat anything that Castro could throw at Gómez but also to prevent any further uprisings getting out of hand. Gómez was accompanied by Félix Galavís,[196] *jefe del grande estado mayor general del ejército;* McGill, as *sub-jefe* to Galavís; and Pimentel as quartermaster. The army was divided into three brigades: Brigada No. 1, commanded by General Fernández; Brigada No. 2, commanded by General David Gimón; and Brigada No. 3, commanded by General Diógenes Torrellas Urquiola. In addition, several dozen "fighting cocks and five roulette tables were dispatched"[197] to Maracay on the same day. With such a large army in Maracay and with easy access to the rest of the country, Gómez was able to control the nation as well as give warning to others who might have wanted to join the rebellion. Gómez would remain in Maracay until early January the following year, raising doubts as to whether Castro had indeed invaded the country.

Elections Postponed

Soon after Gómez departed for Maracay a wave of skepticism about Castro's invasion spread over Caracas, with doubts "expressed as to whether Castro is anywhere in the neighborhood of Coro at all."[198] It was felt that Gómez had engineered Castro's invasion as a way of preventing the December congressional elections taking place. As elections could not be held while constitutional guarantees were suspended, the forthcoming April 1914 presidential elections were cancelled. The feeling that Castro's invasion was a figment of Gómez's imagination was also prevalent among certain foreign observers, in particular Guy Gilliat Smith, acting British chargé d'affaires. In order not to take any chances, Acting Governor Sir Clement Courtney Knaggs in Trinidad issued a proclamation prohibiting the export of arms and ammunition, gunpowder, and military and naval stores from the colony.

The United States, however, reacted in a panic because at the time it was badly represented in Caracas. Elliott Northcott, the American minister, had resigned, and Jefferson Caffery, the secretary of the legation, had been reassigned to the State Department. This left Richard Riggs, the legation's clerk, temporarily in charge, who requested a man-of-war to protect US citizens. The State Department believed that Castro's invasion was for real and not wanting to take any risks sent immediately a warship and a higher-ranking diplomat with instructions to protect American interests and report on the uprising. On August 2, the *Des Moines* left Brunswick, Georgia, carrying Harry F. Tennant, the newly appointed chargé d'affaires at the Caracas legation. After making a brief stop at the US Guantanamo naval base in Cuba and encountering bad weather, the *Des Moines* arrived at La Guaira on August 11. The American man-of-war would remain in La Guaira until August 18 because it did not have permission to travel to any other Venezuelan port and was used instead as a communications post with the outside world because the rebels had allegedly cut the telegraph line.

The newly arrived Tennant soon reached the same conclusion as the other diplomats in Caracas: that Gómez had manufactured the revolution in order to get himself reelected. The US consuls, Werner J. Leitner and Herbert Wright at Maracaibo and Puerto Cabello, respectively, also reported that events had been staged to trap Castro sympathizers in the country. On August 18, Andrew T. Long, commander of the *Des Moines*, left La Guaira for western Venezuela, remaining in Puerto Cabello until August 22, when he was allowed to proceed to Falcón after Gómez had declared an end to the uprising the previous day. The *Des Moines* arrived at La Vela on the morning of August 23 and returned to La Guaira the following day because it was clear that Castro had not been in Falcón. Tennant concluded that the "entire revolution has the appearance of having been manufactured for political reasons."[199] At the same time, on August 25, the Venezuelan warship *Mariscal*

Sucre was sent to La Vela to pick up sixteen prisoners, including Torres and three others from the east, who were later marched from Puerto Cabello to Maracay. It is a curious coincidence that with the *Des Moines* in Venezuelan waters the government decided to publish the correspondence between the military authorities and Gómez on uprisings that took place in various parts of the country. The official telegrams dated the capture of the insurgents to August 21, but it was on July 31 that the majority of them were apprehended and certainly no later than mid-August.[200]

The whereabouts of Castro during this time has never been established. Although I did not find any direct proof that Castro was in Curacao at the time, there is sufficient circumstantial evidence to indicate that he was on the island. If Castro was not in Curacao, it is difficult to explain why Bello and the others would sacrifice themselves in a senseless invasion and issue a proclamation that they knew would have little effect without the appearance of Castro. It is also highly unlikely that Castro would have allowed such a proclamation to be issued in his name if there was no serious intent of following it up. Any other explanation would be counterproductive for Castro's standing as the main opposition party to Gómez. It is thus possible that Castro was in Curacao waiting to see whether Jurado's offer was genuine and to gauge the country's reaction to his proclamation. If the country did rise up to support him, then he would land on Venezuelan soil and lead his advance on Caracas. The reason for believing this conjecture is that Gómez himself was convinced that Castro was near to Venezuela, as he confessed to his closest allies. In addition, Gómez was annoyed with Jurado's inept handling of the situation, which could have been out of loyalty based on his close collaboration with Castro when the latter was president. Moreover, Gómez did not need to mount the charade of a Castro invasion to usurp power because he had such a strong grip on the country, having got rid of the most dangerous members of the Council of State after the Delgado Chalbaud plot and replacing them with political ciphers. In addition, Zoila, Castro's wife, made a series of intriguing documented trips to Curacao at the time. At the end of August, Zoila Castro, accompanied by Dr. José Antonio Lares Ruiz and Gregorio Franco, left Santiago de Cuba for Puerto Rico, arriving a few weeks later in Curacao, where she stayed with relations, returning to Puerto Rico six days later on September 24.[201] There was no reason given for her visit, but it could have been to see Castro. Certainly it was assumed among "intelligent people"[202] of the island that Zoila Castro was in Curacao to meet Castro "and probably did so,"[203] as reported by Elias Cheney, the US consul on the island. Cheney also believed that during Zoila's stay, Jurado met Castro on board the yacht *Julia* for three days in September.

Cheney reported that Jurado saw Castro arriving at St. Nicholas with "his retinue of a dozen Venezuelans . . . in an auto party."[204] It was believed that Castro, while staying in the Otrabanda district of Willemstad, moved around the island disguised as a priest from a Catholic order that he had banished from Venezuela when president. Another intriguing piece of evidence comes from Antonio de Pietri Daudet, who was Castro's private secretary, when he wrote years later that while both were heading for Venezuela in 1913 on board the SS *Tagas,* the former president promised to have Gómez shot for treachery once he recovered the presidency.[205] According to Pietri Daudet, "the Revolution was lost both by Castro's organizational ineptitude and by the first skirmishes undertaken by his emissaries in San Antonio del Táchira."[206] Mocho Hernández was also convinced that the revolution was for real, declaring to the *Heraldo Español* that Castro's rebellion "was not a sham as people think it was but a revolution that did not go to plan," with Gómez taking "advantage of such a clumsy and scandalous farce."[207] Finally, the United States took the possibility of Castro's invasion seriously sending the *Des Moines* in order to prevent the Cabito from landing in Venezuela.

Castro's supporters were clearly not pleased with his nonappearance. General Asunción Rodríguez and Luis Felipe Nava, for example, complained bitterly to Zoila Castro when she was in Curacao in September that year, and withdrew their support.[208] Zoila Castro ignored their requests and had the "temerity to order these men to return to their respective homes until they received new orders. Naturally such action was rejected."[209] According to Hermán Leyba, the Venezuelan consul on the island, the attitude of Zoila Castro

> encapsulates Castro's thinking, that is, this man persists, despite his lamentable recent failure, in damaging the country without reparations. At Doña Zoila's demand, the ladies of the family that form Castrismo's general staff were present, but I know of one who is trying to return to Venezuela, arguing that she did not participate in the rebellion, which you should bear in mind to determine what to do with her.[210]

It was clear to Zoila Castro that Curacao was too closely watched by Gómez's spies and the United States to make it a sensible operational base for the revolution. While at Curacao, Zoila Castro managed to convince her husband to make Puerto Rico his permanent base. The island became the center of operations for revolutionary activity against Gómez until Castro's death in 1924. The revolutionary disturbances in Venezuela were real enough, but they had been aptly dealt with by the state presidents and did not warrant Gómez's direct intervention, as the rebels did not pose a real threat to his government or to the well-being of the country. It appeared then that Gómez seized on an invasion plan to suspend the constitutional guarantees and establish himself as the national savior and defender of his country against the former tyrant. Up to the end of July, a Castro invasion was expected, and although a number of small-scale uprisings took place in several parts of the country, Gómez wanted to lay a trap to catch his former compadre. Gómez also wanted people to believe that Castro had indeed invaded, allowing his proclamation issued in Curacao to be distributed in Venezuela. After it became obvious that Castro was not about to fall into his clutches, Gómez seized the opportunity for his own ends in order to remain in power after 1914.

Castro's abortive invasion allowed Gómez to demonstrate to the country the military might he had built up over the years and to discredit Castro as a leader. At the time, Gómez referred to Castro disparagingly as "that lunatic who has ended his career,"[211] and declared to his state presidents that his "reputation has ended, and I assure you that this man's career is over. The more cowardly and inept will now follow. The Mochistas will exploit Castro's defeat to attract his dispersed men to their side. Hernández, Baptista, Olivares, and others appear to be united and will launch their attack soon, but we shall make short shrift of them."[212] In my view Gómez did not invent the invasion ploy, as has been suggested by other writers, but seized the opportunity for his own advantage. Soon after the fracas of the Castro invasion of Venezuela, Mocho Hernández would take up the struggle against Gómez.

Gómez Returns to Caracas

The experience and support that Gómez received from the country during the crisis filled him with "great satisfaction and pride that I have not plowed in the sea,"[213] but more ominously for the country's political development, this episode inspired him to continue "working with greater will power for the enrichment of the fatherland and my fellow citizens."[214] On January 1,

1914, Gómez at the head of his five-thousand-man strong army returned to Caracas. The political crisis remained unresolved, however, with the state presidents pressing to know whether local elections should be organized to elect state deputies and senators, who in turn would choose the president. There was also the constitutional problem of article 74, which prohibited the reelection of the incumbent, whose successor had to assume office on April 19, 1914. The timetable for electing the new president, which began in May 1913, when registration of the electoral roll started, was disrupted by Castro's invasion and the imposition of martial law, with the result that the election of deputies and state legislatures planned for in October did not take place. Consequently, the state presidents at the beginning of 1914 were pressing to know whether the state legislatures should go ahead with the election of senators in January, as the law stipulated, so that they could convene a joint session of Congress in early April to elect a new president.[215] However, elections for senators could not be held in January 1914 because the composition of the state legislatures was unknown, since the October elections for deputies and state legislatures had not taken place. The result was that Congress was unable to elect Gómez's successor. Gómez, however, had already decided that elections would not take place and that the army would not be disbanded because of the conspiracies and rebellions that had taken place during the year. With a certain amount of political acumen F. D. Hartford, the British minister, reported that "this sudden move is more or less what has happened at the close of the first term of previous presidents who are in a way to become dictators."[216]

Gómez had decided that elections would only take place after he had appointed his own men as state presidents in order to ensure that he remained in power. For instance, his cousin Eustoquio Gómez was appointed president of Táchira, with Gómez emphasizing the need for probity in the "handling of the revenues of the State,"[217] applying with "honesty and without sterile wastefulness the largest share of the revenues for the progress of the people,"[218] something that was ignored by his relative. More importantly, Gómez counseled Eustoquio that the judicial power of government should be organized "with the most careful selection, always choosing civil employees who guarantee the inviolability of the Law and are faithful guardians of public interests."[219] Many saw Gómez's maneuver for what it was but were powerless to do anything about it apart from resigning or writing protest letters. Olivares, for instance, was one such person who resigned from the Council of Ministers as a protest against Eustoquio's appointment, and the exiled

Alcántara issued a flysheet on January 29, 1914, protesting against Gómez's reelection.[220] The university students also demonstrated against Gómez, with the result that a number of them were arrested, including the fifteen-year-olds Nicolás Zuloaga Ramírez and Gustavo Machado (son of Carlos Machado, who owned one of the biggest estates near Caracas). The Asociación General de Estudiantes was closed on February 18, with its headquarters demolished five days later.

Gómez's popularity declined during the second half of 1913 mainly because of his government's unconstitutional acts and his monopoly of the cattle trade. Gómez continued his policy of reaching a consensus with the various disparate factions remaining in the country, informing Eustoquio Gómez in Táchira that "I will not cease in trying to achieve harmony with all the good people."[221] Gómez appeared to be happy with the new political reorganization of the country, informing José Ignacio Cárdenas that the change had "caused great despair in the spirit of the revolutionaries"[222] because "the rebellion under these conditions is impossible and if there is war, failure is the sure outcome."[223] Mocho Hernández at the time was preparing a revolution in Trinidad that, with Castro's presence on the island, signaled the unity of these two forces. As we shall see, this or any other revolutionary plan never threatened the Gómez administration.

A Legal Way Is Found

The latest date allowed under the constitution for elections of the municipal councils, the deputies to the state legislative assemblies, and the deputies for the national Congress was February 20, 1914. Consequently, on January 14, the various state presidents, following an agreed formula, communicated to the interior minister that the states and municipalities would be without legislative, executive, and judicial officers after February 20 because elections were not held before November 30, 1913. Consequently, between January 17 and 21 each state proceeded to pass identical resolutions requesting the president of each state to call on the citizens to elect the municipal councilors on February 20, as well as two plenipotentiary deputies for each district of the state in order for the latter to meet at the state capital to appoint a provisional executive and the judicial functionaries and fix a provisional constitutional statute to be enforced until the definitive constitution of the state had been approved. This could only be done by the president of the plenipotentiary deputies of districts and would be a decision for each of the states, as the central government could not intervene. The plenipotentiary deputies of the districts was a new institution in Venezuela, formed to appoint temporary officers for the executive and judicial branches of state government and to enact a temporary constitutional statute under which the state could be ruled until a definite constitution had been approved by the people.

In early February 1914, popular assemblies or caucuses were selected to elect the suffrage boards, with the election for councilors or plenipotentiaries of districts taking place February 3–5. On February 6, the suffrage boards met to scrutinize the votes of each district, and on Friday, February 20, the plenipotentiaries gathered at the various state capitals to declare open an assembly and to receive the annual message from the state presidents. They would also appoint a provisional executive and the judicial officials to draft the provisional constitutional statutes to be in force during the framing and adoption by the people of a definite state constitution and under the deferral pact uniting them to deliberate upon the constitutional relations of one state with another. Finally, on February 26 a provisional state executive was appointed.

On April 19 the plenipotentiary Congress opened its sessions to elect a provisional president and draft a new constitution, which, according to Gómez, would be better adapted to the "aspirations of this historic moment and will facilitate the joint effort between the people and the government to accelerate the country's progress and prosperity."[224] Márquez Bustillos, the former defense minister, was elected acting president for the interim period between April 19, 1914, and April 19, 1915, to replace Gil Fortoul until elections took place in April 1915. The new Constitution, enacted on June 19, guaranteed "the freedom of industry,"[225] which according to Juvenal Anzola, the president of the Chamber of Deputies, had previously been "annulled by the privilege of servitude, constituted to please the parasitic classes whose coffers were filled by the tribute from all,"[226] and which under their influence "the expansion of monopoly power,"[227] threatened individual entrepreneurship, small private capital, and even property rights.

The new constitution embodied in law much of Gómez's December 1908 recovery plan for the country, such as stimulating industrial development by abolishing the concessionaire's privileges. In addition, it was felt that a strong government would be in a better position to attract foreign capital to develop the country's resources. Peñaloza, for example, speaking in Congress on May 7, drew attention to this when he stated that "peace is the only thing that glorifies our fatherland"[228] because strong governments attracted foreign capital. The constitution also established the "cardinal principle of equality of contributions, and extended the system of proportional distribution of revenues that correspond to the States."[229] The new constitution strengthened the executive's position considerably, with the presidential term increasing from four to seven years, and more importantly for Gómez, allowed his reelection. The reasoning behind the lengthening of the presidential period of office was in order to ensure that peace was maintained in the country.[230] According to Juvenal Anzola, the four-year term was seriously flawed because

> in its persistence to adapt to the social conditions of the country and to protect it from the historical political bosses, it formed a vicious maze of distrustful restrictions, accidental in the Constitution and in reality counterproductive because, on the one hand they forced the necessary amendments of the Pact, or caused reforms from interested parties with the object to deceive and on the other hand provided an excuse to those aspiring to reach Power to incite the people to rebellion.[231]

It was felt that with a seven-year presidency there would be a whole quinquennium of progress because the first year of the new term was devoted to discredit bureaucratic procedures, while the last year was earmarked for what was termed "political agitation." Under the new constitution, the president was vested with powers to appoint his successor in case of retirement or absence from the capital. The 1914 constitution also created the new post of commander in chief of the armed forces especially for Gómez, while the vice presidency and the Council of State were abolished. With the demise of the latter, the executive had a freer hand in all future negotiations of mining contracts. In order to forestall this happening article 58 was inserted into the new constitution that stated that Congress needed to approve all mining concessions and other contracts made by the government. The revision of the constitution required ratification by the legislative assemblies of the states and had to be approved by three-quarters of the assembly but it was a foregone conclusion that it would be enacted. For Gómez the new state of affairs marked the end of the old warmongering Venezuela he had known since childhood, stating at the end of April that "the process of civil wars in Venezuela had ended for ever,"[232] while continuing to tighten his grip on the country even further by creating a governing dynasty.

Gómez was even more active in trying to weed out the few remaining pockets of resistance to his rule, especially in Trujillo, where Baptista was organizing a plot against him in 1914. It was rumored that Omaña, Amador Uzcátegui, Gumersindo Méndez, and Jurado, the state presidents of Trujillo, Mérida, Zulia, and Falcón, respectively, would join in the uprising, which was set for April 19, 1914. Humberto Tejera and his brother Domingo were detailed to acquire arms for the rebels. Tejera traveled to Zulia and Falcón to coordinate the revolution with the exiles abroad but was unable to acquire the ordnance. In order to end the "old prevailing feudalism"[233] in Trujillo State associated with the Baptista family, Gómez wanted those who paid rent to Baptista to desist from doing so. General Polidoro Afriosmo as *jefe civil* of the Distrito Escuque, who commanded seventy soldiers, was appointed by Gómez to restore law and order in the district and stabilize the state. Further reinforcements were sent with Manuel Azuaje to Omaña in the state because "there is no need to give the enemy breathing space; it is imperative to leave him absolutely impotent from causing us harm."[234] Gómez strengthened his grip further on June 5, 1914, when León, who was Venezuela's permanent member at the International Court of Arbitration at the Hague and who had insisted on minimizing graft in public affairs while he was Federal District governor, was arrested because of his hostility toward the regime.

The country's new acting president was also from Trujillo State and a close friend of Baptista, who wanted Márquez Bustillos to assume all the powers conferred on him as provisional president. The latter, however, was fearful of the consequences[235] but did try to impose his will in June on what was formally his government when he unsuccessfully proposed to Gómez the appointment of Giuseppi Monagas as the new interior minister, Gustavo Sanabria as foreign affairs minister, and José Antonio Tagliaferro as public works minister. However, after the abortive Baptista plot, Márquez Bustillos began to fear for his political life, refusing to receive Baptista's messenger because he thought it was a ploy by Gómez to test his loyalty. As a result, the hope that some Caraqueños entertained that Márquez Bustillos would be able to exercise his functions of office independently from Gómez were dashed. Some of the newly exiled revolutionaries such as Olivares, who had also pinned their hopes on the provisional president, gave up at this juncture, accusing him of lacking political courage. On July 2, Baptista left Curacao for New York and then for Europe.

The situation for Gómez remained fluid with rumors in June that Olivares, who was in Santa Marta between June 3 and 4, was about to invade

Venezuela through Zulia. Alcántara in Barranquilla explained to the American consul there that the revolutionaries were looking for a final knockout blow with a revolutionary movement where all outside interests were to be combined or through a general uprising within the country in order to place Ortega Martínez in the presidential chair.[236] A number of state presidents were also not happy with Gómez continuing in power. Zoilo Vidal, president of Sucre State, was jailed in the Puerto Cabello fort because he was against Gómez remaining in power, and Tellería, president of Bolívar State, went into voluntary exile for the same reason. On May 26, 1914, General Pedro José Fernández Amparán launched an uprising in Upata to protest against Gómez continuing in power.[237] The political situation for Gómez was rapidly deteriorating according to Preston McGoodwin,[238] the US minister at Caracas, who reported that revolutionary cells were to be found all over Venezuela.[239] This was a gross exaggeration by the American minister; Gómez's political position was strengthening rather than weakening.

It is remarkable how Gómez, who was not known for his political acumen but rather the contrary (he was perceived by most contemporary commentators as being rather slow witted), managed to outwit in a spectacular manner the regional caudillos during this period. Baptista, his close collaborator and adviser in the 1908 coup, was certain that he would topple Gómez within six months, returning the country to the Liberals, after the painful experiment with the Tachirenses. However, they underestimated the quiet man from the Andes who outmaneuvered the old Liberal and Nationalist caudillos in the same way as he defeated them on the battlefield during Matos's 1901–1903 Libertadora revolution. The political freedom that Gómez appeared to bring to the country in 1908 was just a mirage, coming to an end in 1913, when he finally consolidated his power by defeating the opposition with ease during the abortive Castro invasion and at the same time seeing off his most feared foe. Moreover, the experience showed him the low level of support that Castro had in the country. Many of Venezuela's hitherto powerful caudillos were in exile plotting Gómez's downfall. Gómez would now have greater freedom to maneuver but was always aware and alert to the dangers associated with governing Venezuela.

CHAPTER THREE

An Opportunity for the Exiles

The political upheaval that took place in Venezuela during 1913 and 1914 encouraged the exiles to continue their efforts to unite under one banner to topple Gómez. After the failure of Curacao, Castro reached agreement with Mocho Hernández whereby the latter would invade Venezuela in April 1914 through British Guyana, while the former would follow from Trinidad either through Margarita Island or from Cumaná. Mocho Hernández had "assurances from many of General Gómez's officers"[1] that they would support him in an uprising. The presence of Venezuelan revolutionaries in Trinidad suited the British government because it acted as "a salutary check to the hostile attitude of the Venezuelan Government to British undertakings,"[2] especially the 30 percent surtax on goods transshipped from the island to Venezuela. The British policy toward the Venezuelan exiles just prior to World War I was one of tolerance, something which became highly relevant during the next few years, as a number of revolutions would be launched from the colony. The exiles also came close to getting formal support for their political aims from the United States. In most of the historiography written about this period of Venezuelan history, Gómez is portrayed as an American puppet, ready to do what was necessary to keep the American government happy. Venezuela's policy of strict neutrality during World War I was a source of great irritation to the United States, which unfairly branded Gómez as pro-German. The Woodrow Wilson administration was keen to see the Venezuelan dictator lose power, as it sought to increase its influence further afield than the Caribbean. The exiles took advantage of such a situation to persuade the US government to support their efforts to get rid of Gómez, with the Wilson administration coming close to sanctioning and helping a revolutionary movement against the Gómez dictatorship.

Mocho Hernández's Uprising

On October 27, 1913, Mocho Hernández arrived in Port of Spain from Puerto Rico to confer with Horacio Ducharne and other rebels on the island in order to reach agreement for a forthcoming revolution. He would return to Puerto Rico to consult with Castro.[3] Mocho Hernández's agents were negotiating in Hamburg an enormous cache of arms of ten thousand rifles, fifty machine guns, five cannons, two ships with a speed of twenty-five knots each, together with a large amount of ammunition. Mocho Hernández's political manifesto, outlined to the *Heraldo Español,* was to use government revenues to foster the development of the country's resources without creating monopolies, while increasing government spending on improving the country's educational standards. In addition, great efforts would be made to attract foreign capital and immigrants who would build railways and transport canals. Mocho Hernández would also abolish "the disastrous political intrigues and focus on establishing good government in order to attract to the country healthy and progressive people from other nations."[4] In addition to Castro, Baptista, Olivares, Ayala, and Tellería also supported the revolution.[5] However, in trying to reach an overall agreement the revolutionaries ran into difficulties and were unable to appoint "the managing council of the revolution."[6] Mocho Hernández ignored these difficulties and continued his preparations for the forthcoming invasion of Venezuela.

In mid-January 1914, Mocho Hernández returned to Trinidad and was allowed to enter as a way of setting the "Venezuelan Government's nerves on edge."[7] George Hereira and Dr. López, his two agents on the colony, secured a cache of arms from the *Bonanza* store of Mr. Smith who would "convey them to Carenage by motor lorry for shipment to Venezuela."[8] In order to finance the purchase, Mocho Hernández approached a Mr. Hunn "with a view of getting a loan of $5,000 for which he was prepared to pay back $15,000."[9] In preparation for the same revolution, Castro left from Southampton and entered Trinidad secretly in mid-January 1914, staying at 37 Dundonald Street, situated in the heart of Port of Spain near Savannah Park. The house, which was rented by Castro's brothers Trino and Carmelo, was sparsely furnished with a sitting room containing only a few chairs and a bedroom with only the bare necessities. Two female servants looked after Castro, who was drinking heavily and keeping several bottles of rum by his bedside. Unlike Mocho Hernández, Castro's supporters managed to smuggle into the island a cache of arms that was stored at the Hotel Orinoco, owned by Mrs. José Rafael Wendehake, a Venezuelan. Castro, however, was unable to reach agreement with Mocho Hernández and Alcántara about the forthcoming rebellion. Without an adequate supply of arms and ammunition, Mocho Hernández returned to the United States on February 10 to raise further funds for the coming revolution.

The Gómez regime aware of these preparations requested the British government to prevent the colony from being used as a base for a "conspiracy against the Venezuelan government."[10] Since Castro's proclamation of July 27, 1913, the export of arms and ammunition to Venezuela was prohibited and was strictly enforced to the extent of not allowing a consignment of hunting daggers and sporting guns invoiced by Messrs Th. W. Petersen and Company of Birmingham to a merchant in Ciudad Bolívar to be transshipped to Venezuela. In addition, the local police were slowly closing in on Castro. In mid-March the police raided the Hotel Orinoco, and found forty thousand to fifty thousand rounds of ammunition, a number of revolvers, a shotgun, and a Mauser carbine, all belonging to Pedro González Gutiérrez, a fictional name used by Castro.[11] Although the ammunition, which had been shipped from New York, belonged to Castro, the authorities could not prove it, concluding that there was "nothing to show that the ammunition was connected with Castro."[12] A few days after the raid and after almost a three-month search, the police discovered Castro's hiding place on the island.

On March 20 at about two in the afternoon, Sub-Inspector E. C. Willis together with Sub-Inspector M. Costelloe, armed with a search warrant, entered the house, where they found Castro locked in the lavatory and later appearing "very much excited and protested violently against the forcible entry into his house."[13] After his discovery, Castro sought to take up residency on the island, but approval depended on whether the Venezuelan government instructed the colonial authorities to keep a close watch on his movements to ensure against any breach of the Foreign Enlistment Act. Although Castro's presence on the island did not appear to pose any serious trouble in Venezuela, Hartford, the British minister at Caracas, felt that it would be inopportune for the colonial government to revoke the proclamation prohibiting the export of arms to Venezuela.[14] Castro was deported from the island and returned to Tenerife.

The deportation of Castro was a considerable setback for the revolutionaries in Trinidad, with very little revolutionary activity between February and April when Mocho Hernández returned to the island. In Caracas, the Alcantaristas and Hernandistas met clandestinely in the *botica* (pharmacy) of Manuel Romero, while the Venezuelan exiles in France continued to contribute meager funds for the purchase of arms for Mocho Hernández, Baptista, Olivares, and Alcántara. In March, Alcántara left Curacao for New York "in search of a cache of arms and money,"[15] hoping to return to the Dutch colony before April 19, when he would send firm instructions and details to Pulido, Ortega Martínez, Emilio Rivas, Peñaloza, and a group of army officials in Venezuela who were plotting Gómez's downfall.[16] Mocho Hernández, who insisted on being the leader of the group, also secured a cache of arms in the United States, but the main stumbling block remained finding sufficient funds to pay for them.

Mocho Hernández's raison d'être for his uprising was Gómez's reelection, something he considered was "a crime of usurpation that with unprecedented impudence has consumed the ill-fated Juan Vicente Gómez."[17] Mocho Hernández's rebellion would rid the country of the "usurpers," as he referred to the Gómez clique. Mocho Hernández writes:

> The usurpers are conspiring and planning their last attack, knitting
> a ridiculous farce of insurrection with the ghost of Castro at its head,
> inciting the people to insurrection and scaring the fainthearted with
> a large army, and conferring to the President of the Republic limited
> despotic powers that turn him into an irresponsible man, suspend-
> ing all constitutional guarantees and declaring martial law.[18]

Finally, with the opening of the Panama canal, the civilized world would focus more clearly on Venezuela and, according to Mocho Hernández, "claim imperiously, with more than enough justice, the definitive introduction of a political order that is based on the principles of law: we want to be respected as a free, independent and sovereign nation."[19]

Mocho Hernández made the trip south in April, stopping in Grenada to confer with the Nacionalistas Horacio Ducharne and Vicente Rodríguez. It was agreed that Ducharne would mortgage his cocoa estate on Trinidad to purchase the arms and ammunition needed for his expedition against Gómez, and that the revolution, which was initially planned for a day after the elections on April 20, 1914, would be postponed by a month, when it was confidently expected that three thousand rebels would be massed at the Colombian border to invade Venezuela. The plan was for Mocho Hernández, as head of the movement, to invade eastern Venezuela, followed by Ducharne who knew the terrain better than anyone else, while Baptista and Olivares invaded from Colombia. The three rebels left Grenada for Trinidad, arriving on April 22; there they met Baptista and Olivares, who had arrived from Puerto Rico, to finalize the details of the forthcoming rebellion. In spite of this progress, there was a great deal of pessimism in the Nacionalista ranks because it was felt that Mocho Hernández could not deliver what he had promised, with some even accusing him of deceit.[20] Nevertheless, the plans continued afoot, with Colonel Américo Spinetti sending Luis Irausquín to Ciudad Bolívar to ascertain whether Captain Fanerte, who commanded the First Company of Rivas Battalion in Bolívar State, "could be bought, and whether he would lead an insurrection in that city."[21] The Comité Hernández offered Fanerte $768 in cash and a check for $3,839 for him to join forces with Mocho Hernández. Fanerte took advice from Eleazar López Contreras, his commanding officer, who recommended that he should play along with the offer. By mid-May, all was ready with the revolutionaries traveling on the SS *Delta* to Venezuela. Irausquín saw Fanerte on May 17, informing him to be ready for the uprising on May 20, when Mocho Hernández issued his proclamation in Trinidad.

López Contreras, who wanted to catch the revolutionaries red-handed on the night of the uprising, failed because General Gimón "decided to take him [Spinetti] prisoner and all those implicated in the correspondence that came with the *Delta* steamboat, with the result that my plan failed."[22] A number of coordinated uprisings were planned for other parts of the country, especially Falcón, but Gómez was confident that Manuel Sarmiento in Coro and General Laclé would deal with it "because I know that the impertinent Mocho Hernández and his followers have no support among the people of Falcón, and Peñaloza, who you state should be treated carefully, is totally unknown here and completely useless at waging war."[23] Emilio Arévalo Cedeño, a telegraph operator at Cazorla, Guárico State, also took up arms for the first time on May 14, in what would become an almost annual event in support of Mocho Hernández's revolution. Arévalo Cedeño at the head of forty men successfully attacked Julio Robles, who commanded the government forces at the La Rubiera estate of Dr. Francisco Mier y Terán. Arévalo Cedeño returned to Cazorla, where he was acclaimed, and then left for western Guárico, attacking and taking by surprise Valle de la Pascua and some of the other nearby small towns. Arévalo Cedeño then attempted an attack on Calabozo, the state capital, but had to retreat and was defeated on June 16 by Francisco J. Sáez and Alfredo Acero at Caño del Medio, with the rebel fleeing to the Orinoco and eventually making his way to Trinidad.

After Mocho Hernández's abortive attempt to launch a revolution from Trinidad failed, Gómez was able to announce that all the Mochista leaders in the last nationalist stronghold of Carabobo had surrendered to the government. Gómez wrote to Eustoquio Gómez that

> the revolution has completely crumbled because the enemies of order, the enemies of peace, those who feel and think bad things of their country, were at the head of a movement that in part was there to justify their depredations and abuse of power. . . . They thought that my ambition was equal to theirs and they have made a great mistake; and now without reason, principle and flag, it appears to me they did not launch their rebellion; and if their anger gets the better of them and they do launch, then the ideal situation will be presented to us to judge them for what they are: that is to say we will call them a mob of criminals.[24]

Now that Gómez appeared to exercise complete dominance over the country, he channeled all his energy to weed out the few remaining pockets of resistance to his rule, especially in Trujillo State, because the "enemy should not be allowed a respite and it is necessary to leave him helpless in order not to cause any danger."[25] Baptista's supporters never had more than 2,000 arms,[26] and by September 1915 between 1,500 and 1,600 arms had been collected in the state with only 300 to 400 arms left hidden by Víctor Manuel Baptista and Maximiano Durán.

After the failure of Mocho Hernández's initial rebellion in May, a summit meeting was held in Trinidad between the latter, Castro, Mendible, and Arévalo Cedeño. There appeared to be a lack of direction to the revolution, with Arévalo Cedeño complaining bitterly that "everything was debated except the return to the fatherland to fight for its freedom and to end the ridiculous role played by winging exiles, who live a life of luxury, anarchy and tranquility."[27] Alcántara would later arrive in Trinidad from New York on July 12 "with the intention of finding out the true state of things and to see if it was possible to formalize something serious,"[28] and bringing the good news that he had secured through his friends at West Point[29] "some money and quite a lot or ordnance in Europe."[30] Within three months a large rebellion in which Peñaloza, Tellería, Ayala, Olivares, Arnoldo Morales, Ortega Martínez, and Alcántara were involved,[31] would take place in Venezuela before the state elections in October. However, after his discussions with the rebels on the island, Alcántara concluded that Mocho Hernández was "inept and petulant"[32] and referred to Olivares sarcastically as "the immaculate."[33] Nevertheless, an agreement with all the caudillos was achieved, with Alcántara leaving on July 14 for Curacao to confer with Peñaloza. It was agreed that most of the rebel leaders would meet in Paris later that year to elect a leader and secure finance. In early July, Baptista left Curacao for New York on his way to Paris. A month later, in August most revolutionaries, with the exception of Mocho Hernández and Castro, reached the French capital, electing Baptista as their overall leader. Their plans were adjourned when World War I started, as the promised financial help was no longer available. In mid-August, Alcántara and Tellería were back in Curacao discussing an alternative plan.[34]

In the meantime, Mocho Hernández, with very little support, decided to go ahead with his own invasion of Venezuela through British Guyana. Mocho Hernández could not have chosen a more inhospitable and difficult route, but it did have the advantage of taking him through the Yuruary region of Venezuela, which he knew well from his gold mining days of his youth. Mocho Hernández's invasion plans, however, were stillborn and woefully inadequate in terms of firepower, and not surprisingly, he did not get very far, avoiding by a whisker being apprehended by General Paulino Torres. Mocho Hernández was forced to return to Trinidad, from where he left for New York to try to secure more funding.

On August 31 in New York, Mocho Hernández entered into an agreement with Rudi de Graaf, John J. Sullivan, and William A. Rowan, known as the Graaf, Sullivan, and Rowan Syndicate, where he practically mortgaged the country to them in return for transporting him and his rebels from Trinidad to Ciudad Bolívar. The Venezuelan rebel would purchase the boat or boats needed for the operation for $25,000, payable a week after landing in Ciudad Bolívar. In addition, if Mocho Hernández became president with the right to award "contracts for any City, State or Governmental improvement, that the preference will be given to the said de Graaf, Sullivan and Rowan."[35]

While Mocho Hernández was in negotiations in New York, Horacio Ducharne, a nationalist supporter, toward the end of August 1914 invaded Venezuela with sixteen men and a small cache of arms obtained from France with funds raised by mortgaging his cacao estate. He first reached the small port of Yaguaraparo in Sucre State, where he hid a small cache of arms to be used by Mocho Hernández. Ducharne then sent for Sixto Gil, a trusted officer, who joined him from Guanoco, together with a number of his timber workers, and attacked and secured the customs post of Caño Colorado in the Orinoco delta. The rebel groups had by now swelled to around sixty men who moved on Guanoco and later engaged and defeated the government troops headed by General Arístides Fandeo at El Pilar in Sucre State. The rebels had the tacit help of the New York and Bermudez Company at Guanoco, allowing Ducharne the use of its motor launch as well as kerosene and grease for their arms. The rebel leader also used the *Viking*, the company's supply ship, to send messages to Trinidad.[36] In the meantime, General Elbano Mibelli, president of Monagas, ordered General Rafael Volcán, who had two hundred men stationed at Maturín, the state capital, to seek and destroy the rebels. Ducharne and his rebels, now numbering 130 men, reached an area known as Teresén, three kilometers away from Caripito, where he was informed that Volcán was about to attack him. Ducharne, in a coordinated pincer movement with Sixto Gil, defeated Volcán and his soldiers on the Maturín-Caripito road.

Mibelli was later surprised by Ducharne toward the end of October in a region known as Pararí, some six kilometers from Maturín, and forced to return to the state capital, where he started to organize the defense of the city. Ducharne did not attack Maturín straight away, as Sixto Gil counseled; he felt it was unnecessary because Mibelli would capitulate as soon as they attacked. Nevertheless, after failing to get Mibelli's conditional surrender, Ducharne attacked the city, accompanied by Sixto Gil, Juan Rescaniere, Ramón Aróstegui, and Simón Betancourt, among others. After thirty-six hours of hard fighting the government troops still controlled the city, and with José de Jesús Gabaldón fast approaching Maturín with over a thousand government soldiers, the rebels were forced to lift the partial siege and retreat. According to Mibelli, the failure of Ducharne to take Maturín was due to three factors: first, he did not exploit the Pararí success; second, a lack of ammunition prevented him from attacking the city; and finally, there was not enough time to make a siege count. Mibelli, hoping to meet up with Gabaldón, left Maturín to pursue Ducharne as he retreated, but the rebel leader anticipated the government's next move well and was able to attack and defeat the government troops at Guayabal on December 13, forcing the state president to return to Maturín.

In the meantime, Sixto Gil surprised Gabaldón at El Mango, some thirty kilometers to the east of Maturín, and defeated him, with the latter regrouping in Uracoa in Monagas State. At this stage, Ducharne left the relative safety of the jungle for the plains in order to secure as many horses as possible to increase the mobility of his troops but was attacked by a contingent of 150 government soldiers on January 25, 1915. Although wounded in the arm, Ducharne managed to defeat his attackers at Laguna Grande. During the following months, Ducharne maintained a low profile, waiting for events overseas to clarify the position of the rebel leaders. At this juncture, Ducharne decided that Sixto Gil should act independently from his own efforts. The government also made a few changes locally. In February 1915, General Manuel Rugeles replaced Elbano Mibelli as state president, and Francisco Antonio Colmenares Pacheco resigned his commission as inspector general of the army, to replace José de Jesús Gabaldón at the head of government troops fighting the rebels in eastern Venezuela, leaving on February 28 for Maturín on board the *Mariscal Sucre.*[37]

The Osceola *Affair*

Mocho Hernández's revolutionary plans were making progress in the United States after he secured funding from the Graaf, Sullivan, and Rowan Syndicate for the purchase of two ships, viz, the *Osceola*—140 feet long by 18 feet wide, with a displacement of 114 tons and a speed of twelve knots—and the *Velocity,* a smaller ship with a speed of ten knots. A number of Venezuelan exiles in New York, including Peñaloza, Olivares, Alcántara, Ortega Martínez, Julián Avelino Arroyo, and Mocho Hernández formed a revolutionary committee, headed by Baptista. The group divided Venezuela into three military zones, with Baptista acting as chief of staff, and the following division commanders: Olivares with responsibility for western Venezuela, with Mocho Hernández taking the eastern states, while Tellería concentrated his efforts on the central states.[38] In addition, Ducharne, who remained undefeated in eastern Venezuela, joined them. The revolution would be timed to coincide with the February 1915 presidential elections.[39]

The plan was for the *Osceola,* skippered by Rudi de Graaf, to sail first to Norfolk, Virginia, and then to Jacksonville, Florida, to take on arms and ammunition, and from there to Puerto Rico and Trinidad, entering Venezuela through Caño Colorado, where it would join up with Mocho Hernández's uprising through British Guyana.[40] The *Velocity* would proceed from New London, Connecticut, to Cuba to pick up Dávila and other rebels together with five hundred rifles and thirty thousand rounds of ammunition. The rebels' plans were scuttled when the US government in December 1914 prevented both the *Osceola* yacht and the *Velocity* from leaving for Venezuela.[41]

Gómez was well aware of these developments. In January 1915 he warned Eustoquio Gómez to prepare for war surreptitiously because he believed that Olivares, who had a farm near Cartagena, was about to invade together with other rebels. Gómez advised Eustoquio how to deploy his men in case of an attack because he wanted "this time to defeat those people on the day of the invasion and not allow them to reach Rubio and Capacho as happened with the war with Castro."[42] Gómez also wanted Eustoquio Gómez to set up a good spy network in Cúcuta, Colombia.

Elections Again

On December 19, 1914, popular assemblies gathered in all the state districts of the country to appoint the suffrage committees for the election of municipal councilors and deputies for the legislative assemblies of the states, which took place on January 6, 1915. On February 20, the legislative assemblies with their representatives gathered at the state capitals. Once the legislatures convened, the state presidents resigned, with executive power transferred to the chief justices of the state supreme courts until the election of constitutional governors. In many cases, the provisional presidents were retained, and on February 23, 1915, Arcaya, the interior minister, sent out the formal notification addressed to the various legislative assemblies.

There was little doubt who would be elected president in 1915. At the beginning of the year, a number of juntas were formed to encourage Gómez to launch his own candidature for the presidency. However, in a surprise move Commander in Chief Gómez informed the government on January 9 that he would not stand for office, writing to the state presidents that it would be inappropriate for him to do so and that they should "join our efforts in a firm and sound manner to maintain unharmed the majesty of the Law represented by the decisions made by the National Congress, which is charged to choose and elect the Constitutional President of the Republic."[43] Gómez, nevertheless, received assurances from his state presidents that they would support him if he did stand, and Congress on May 3, 1915, unanimously elected him to the presidency for the term running from 1915 to 1922. Although Gómez accepted the presidency during this period, he remained in Maracay, with Márquez Bustillos acting as provisional president in Caracas.[44] Gómez would now rule almost unchallenged until his death in December 17, 1935.

World War I

The start of World War I on August 4, 1914, and Venezuela's neutrality policy toward the conflict provided the exiles with a good reason for attracting the Wilson administration to their side. Arcaya, the interior minister, expressed the view prevalent in the government at the outbreak of war that there was no reason for Venezuela to "intrude in that quarrel,"[45] a sentiment shared by the other South American republics. Venezuela would stick to a strict policy of neutrality for the duration of the conflict, with Gómez issuing a number of "strict orders to maintain Venezuela's absolute neutrality in that bloody fight."[46] Although Venezuela's definition of neutrality conformed to the Hague Convention, it also included an amendment, which was first suggested by Chile, that "belligerent warships may only take, in Venezuelan ports, enough coal to enable them to reach the nearest neutral port."[47] In order to ensure that Venezuela was not the only Latin American country to remain neutral at the beginning of the war, Manuel Díaz Rodríguez, the Venezuelan foreign minister, who was felt to be "hostile to the cause of the Allies,"[48] called for a conference in Washington of all neutral governments to discuss their rights. This ambitious initiative was due, according to Hartford, the British minister at Caracas, to "national jealousy and conceit, for Venezuela has been in no way directly affected by the action of the belligerent nations."[49] In January 1915, a congress of South American nations opened in Washington, with Venezuela submitting a proposal "that all neutral powers should take into immediate consideration the question of common action for the support of neutral interests now threatened by the action of the belligerent powers."[50] Although the proposal was thought to emanate from the German legation in Caracas, with its chief support, apart from Venezuela, coming from Chile, most South American countries remained neutral until the United States entered the conflict in 1917. Venezuela, as we shall see, did not waver in its neutrality policy despite strong US pressure to change its position.

German Influence in Venezuela

The association between Germany and the German trading houses of Venezuela, which with the exception of H. L. Boulton and Sons were the largest in the country, was more historical than commercial because as good traders they looked for the cheapest and best available goods—invariably British or American. Nevertheless, during the first few years of Gómez's administration the Germans had made something of a commercial comeback in the country. The German trading houses such as Blohm and Company gained influence over Gómez initially through Pimentel, a close friend since the Castro days, who helped to finance the December 1908 coup. Pimentel, who had invested a large part of his wealth in Germany, persuaded Gómez just prior to the beginning of hostilities in 1914 to deposit more than $2 million with German banks.[51] This was almost 40 percent of the total wealth that Preston McGoodwin, the American minister, estimated Gómez had amassed since 1908. McGoodwin felt this was an underestimate, with Gómez's wealth easily doubling because César Vicentini, Gómez's agent and also head of the National Cigarette Company, had recently rejected an offer of $5.8 million for the dictator's landed estates.[52] The close ownership ties between the merchant houses and Germany gave rise to the label that Gómez, like his predecessor Castro, was pro-German.

For its part, the Wilson administration at the beginning of World War I was unwilling to enter into joint action with the Allies, as this was against his government's policy of embarking in "anything like a spirited foreign policy or to initiate any joint international action even on this continent."[53] Moreover, the United States, according to Sir Cecil Spring-Rice, the British ambassador at Washington, wanted to maintain absolute impartiality "in case it is asked to mediate."[54] For Castro and the Venezuelan opposition, the European conflict posed a financial strain, as most of the former president's money, including his wife's jewels, were deposited with German banks; they were unable to transfer any funds out of Germany.[55]

Ducharne Killed

The rebel invasions of Venezuela continued, with Arévalo Cedeño crossing into the country through Arauca for the second time in April 1915. At the same time, Ducharne, who was hiding in eastern Venezuela in order to gain greater momentum in the fight, started his second campaign without the help of Sixto Gil, who remained well dug in with his sixty men at Tres Cerros near Guanaguaná in Monagas State. Gómez ordered General Rugeles to put an end to Ducharne's rebellion, and in so doing severely depleted the state capital's defenses when he left Maturín with two battalions. Rugeles ordered Commander Alfredo Rugeles (no relation) and Juan Manuel Olivo to attack Tres Cerros, but they were repelled by Simón Betancourt with twenty men. In the meantime, Rugeles returned to Maturín, followed by his commanders, who were ordered to locate and capture Sixto Gil. Aware of Maturín's weak defenses, Sixto Gil attacked the city's jail on May 7 with eighty men, freeing twenty-eight political prisoners and also taking arms and ammunition. After a number of further skirmishes, Sixto Gil was forced to retreat to the hinterland with Rugeles in pursuit.

At the same time, Ducharne entered La Urbana in May 1915, and then proceeded to Caicara, leaving on June 6 for Barrancas, which he attacked two days later, securing fourteen rifles. The government reacted by sending a detachment of fifty soldiers from Ciudad Bolívar to Caicara on the SS *Arauca*. From Barrancas, Ducharne proceeded to Tucupita and then to Uracoa, arriving on June 16, with fifty men. Although he was tired, hungry, and sick and was advised by Rafael Núñez Sucre to return to Trinidad, Ducharne decided to carry on. After a period of recovery, Ducharne arrived at the farm of Joaquín Plaz on the banks of the river Guanipa on the afternoon of August 19, continuing shortly afterwards to a place called El Rabanal, where they decided to spend the night. A little later, Rugeles arrived at Plaz's farm and was informed that Ducharne's camp was only a few kilometers away. Rugeles decided to attack the rebels later that night while they slept secure in the mistaken belief that nobody knew their whereabouts. In the ensuing exchange of fire, Ducharne was wounded in the leg and was later killed by Juan Manuel Olivo carrying out Rugeles's orders. Ducharne's white beard was shaved off and exhibited as a war trophy in Maturín. Sixto Gil continued the fight for a few more weeks, keeping Tres Cerros as his center of operations, but eventually was forced back to Trinidad after being pursued by the relentless Rugeles. The news of Ducharne's death after a seven-month campaign was a blow to the revolutionaries, who concluded after much debate that he had been unsuccessful because of a lack of arms. It was imperative from now on to secure arms and to transport them to the battlefront in Venezuela.

Rebels Try to Secure US Assistance

The exiled rebels tried to exploit the antipathy the United States felt against Gómez for remaining neutral during World War I and curry favor for their cause. The revolutionaries also tried influencing American foreign policy by sending Robert Lansing, the secretary of state, details of Gómez's despotic rule. In a separate initiative, Mocho Hernández urged President Wilson in June 1915 not to recognize the Venezuelan administration following the US government's policy of not acknowledging any government that reached power by illegal means. This would be a recurring theme of the revolutionaries for the duration of the war and one that almost succeeded in deposing Gómez.[56]

At the beginning of July 1915, the relationship between the various exiled revolutionaries appeared to be one of conciliation. In early 1915, Baptista, Olivares, and Carabaño, together with Mocho Hernández, Roberto Vargas, Ortega Martínez, Ayala, and Tellería, met in New York to agree on a new revolutionary movement against Gómez.[57] The main argument revolved around securing funds to purchase arms and transport them to Venezuela. With Castro's small arsenal impounded in the West Indies, Mocho Hernández suggested that the only way forward was to reach a similar arrangement to the one concluded with the Graaf, Sullivan, and Rowan Syndicate the previous year.

The revolutionaries had no objection to Mocho Hernández securing this kind of arrangement because there was no alternative: he would proceed with or without their support. The problem lay in reaching an agreement with Mocho Hernández, because the rebel who controlled the supply of arms would invariably lead the revolution. Mocho Hernández, who by now was an old hand at this type of activity, soon reached an agreement with Joseph Montague Roberts,[58] who represented James J. O'Brien in New York. Under the agreement signed on November 17, 1915, Mocho Hernández would receive on credit ten thousand Springfield rifles caliber 303 Model 1903, which were sufficient to match those held by the government, estimated in July 1917 at eleven thousand Mauser carbines "oiled and clean," with a hundred thousand recycled bullets, although a further million rounds could be serviceable with some work.[59] In return, once he achieved power Mocho Hernández would grant Roberts the concession to build a railway between Caracas and Carenero and from the Orinoco to Yuruary "with the necessary Gold [*sic*] and land subsidies so as to make the proposition attractive to the concession holders and to the purchasers of the bonds that may be necessary to issue and authorize in order to finance the lines."[60] The concession would also "carry as much of the forest and mining rights as may be possible to grant in accordance with the laws, and will also include land concessions for terminals, warehouses and yards."[61] In addition, Mocho Hernández would give Messrs Roberts and O'Brien preference on all future contracts awarded for railway lines, public works, and public utilities necessary in any part of the country. The new Mochista government would grant rubber concessions on either side of the Orinoco or any other part of the country, with sufficient acreage to employ 2,500 men and in return they would pay the government a small percentage of the profits. The government would also grant them the iron ore concession at Imataca, receiving "all the moral support necessary to make their holding a paying investment, provided that in some way, the holders help in the expenses of the Administration from their profits, or develop new industries in connection with the same metal or mining holdings."[62]

The government would establish, under the management of O'Brien and Roberts, a development agency that would act as the fiscal agent of the government to stimulate agriculture and industrial development by issuing bonds either locally or abroad. Roberts and O'Brien also acquired the concession to exploit the oyster pearl beds off Margarita Island, with the government participating in the profits, and finally, for good measure, oil concessions were thrown in as well. O'Brien and Roberts would raise $10 million for the venture on the New York Stock Exchange by issuing a hundred thousand shares of $100 each in the Standard Venezuelan American Improvement Company. The funds raised would be used according to the prospectus for "the bettering of the conditions in Venezuela, from a social, business, agricultural and (political) [*sic*] standpoint,"[63] and in securing mining, railways, and navigation concessions once Mocho Hernández reached the presidency. The issue was a flop.

The revolution now was at a standstill without sufficient funds, with the strain between the rebels beginning to show. After the US government prevented the *Osceola* and *Velocity* leaving the country in April 1915, Baptista declared that he did not want to enter into any further revolutionary pacts. Ayala and Tellería were in Europe, and Ortega Martínez now fancied his chances of leading the revolutionary banner, but he would have to work hard to get recognition from such a disparate lot. Castro remained the key to any revolutionary plans as he had a cache of 1,200 Mauser carbines and 20,000 rounds of ammunition[64] that were impounded in 1913 by the colonial authorities of

Barbados, placing him in an unenviable position to lead an invasion of the country if he could secure the release of the arms and ammunition. However, Castro failed in his quest to get the arms released, returning to Trinidad. However, when Castro heard the news that the revolutionaries were meeting in Puerto Rico, he left for the island immediately on July 15. Castro traveled to the Danish island colony of St. Thomas, where he arrived four days later, but without any available passage to Puerto Rico he was forced to return to Trinidad on July 21. Deprived of his weapons, Castro decided to sell them to Gómez for $60,000, reasoning that this would demonstrate to the world that he was no longer interested or willing to fight Gómez. In addition, Castro wanted the sale of arms conditional on the release of all his jailed supporters in Venezuela. Castro also wanted the transaction kept a secret while negotiations were completed through the good offices of Barón Espejo. Castro knew that once the deal was agreed it would not remain a secret for long. The former Venezuelan president was also aware that he would be severely criticized by other revolutionaries for his action, but he wanted his supporters in Venezuela to regain their freedom because he was convinced that the revolution "will not prevail in Venezuela anymore; and the opposition will do nothing, much less while Europe is at war."[65]

Gómez agreed to purchase the ordnance, reasoning that this would deprive the rebels of a source of weapons to be used against him. He did not object either to releasing the Castristas, provided that those "agreements be made directly by the interested parties, without anybody interfering."[66] L. F. Calvani, the Venezuelan consul at Port of Spain, met Castro at eight p.m. on February 12 to agree on the final details, but at the last minute the deal fell through. As expected, Castro during the next few months was severely criticized by the other exiled revolutionaries for wanting to sell his arms to Gómez.[67]

In March 1916, Arévalo Cedeño, the eternal rebel, arrived in New York but soon became so disgusted at the amount of bickering and backstabbing among the revolutionaries, especially among Mocho Hernández, Ortega Martínez, Tellería, Vargas, Alcántara, Carabaño, Ayala, and Baptista, that he decided to leave, as he was getting nowhere with his efforts. He later wrote, "there was no hope for what I was looking for; I wanted us to fight Gómez but all we did was waste time with intrigues, accusations and selfishness."[68] Moreover, the opposition used the bickering as "a powerful weapon not to do anything, helping Gómez to thwart the plans being developed to overthrow the tyrant."[69]

United States Places Pressure on Gómez

As we shall see, there was little doubt that President Wilson wanted Gómez out of office. Carlos B. Figueredo, the Venezuelan consul in New York, advised Gómez that President Wilson was convinced of the need for a change in the Venezuelan regime but did not have "confidence in the success of a revolution brought on by men who appear to be the leaders."[70] Castro was an unlikely candidate for this role because of his past activities and also because he was perceived to be powerless, without any real prestige and money while suffering periodic malaria attacks. While Castro was out of the running and Mocho Hernández was "considered incapable and used up, a burnt match,"[71] the State Department felt that Ortega Martínez was the only rebel who had funds and a cache of arms and was supported by other rebels, such as Alcántara, Baptista, Peñaloza, Ayala, Asunción Rodríguez, Tellería, Carabaño, and Vargas. Only Olivares stood apart, branded most of the time by his fellow rebels as a "neurasthenic"[72] because of the scars that disfigured his face. Pulido, Rolando, and Riera were no longer referred to as real contenders, while Félix Montes felt he could become president once the revolution had successfully toppled Gómez. Despite the despondency of Arévalo Cedeño, the slow grind of organizing a revolution continued, but it was not easy to get agreement among so many petty chieftains who all wanted to be king.

In Caracas, Baptista's revolutionary committee representing the exiles functioned almost openly, meeting at the home of Iturbe, with Dr. Pedro Carrillo Márquez acting as a courier.[73] They were sure that funds had been acquired, and at a secret meeting in Caracas, Manuel Felipe Núñez read a letter from his brother Luis in Paris, who stated that the wherewithal had been secured and that they were ready for action. At the same meeting, Iturbe reported that the rebels in Cumaná and Barcelona were ready to take up arms.[74] Despite being aware of these arrangements, Gómez continued to allow Baptista to receive an income estimated at $1,550 per day from his properties in Venezuela,[75] a fact that was revealed in a legal dispute in New York between Baptista and José María Vargas Vila, the Colombian writer. Baptista and Gómez had been in business together, mainly in the cattle trade and other industries, with their combined interests estimated in 1912 to be worth in excess of $10 million. In March 1916, Gómez forwarded to Baptista $67,016 in "settlement of private business interests."[76]

Despite Castro's views that the revolution would not succeed during the European conflict, in June 1916 he departed from Trinidad to New York together with his wife, stopping first at Barbados for one last unsuccessful attempt to recover his cache of arms, and then on to New York. The Venezuelan government was also actively pursuing Castro's arms, and after a long protracted effort, J. M. Bethencourt, the Venezuelan consul at Barbados, finally got the Barbadian authorities to confiscate the cache of arms on November 28. The Venezuelan government later acquired the cache of arms for $7,000 and sent a gunboat to collect them in January 1917.[77]

On his arrival in New York, Castro held a number of meetings at the Hotel Savoy with his old Nicaraguan friend Zelaya, a number of Mexican revolutionaries, and many of the Venezuelan revolutionaries exiled in the city such as Ortega Martínez, Tellería, Peñaloza, Vargas, Ayala, and Carabaño. Castro still retained his political reputation and the promise of a large cache of arms. Soon afterwards, Castro was granted residence in Puerto Rico. It was decided that a summit meeting of the revolutionaries would take place in San Juan, Puerto Rico, shortly after Castro's arrival on the island on July 19 to form a united front to depose Gómez. At the meeting, Castro, Ortega Martínez, Alcántara, and Trino Baptista met together with representatives of Tellería and Olivares and elected Ortega Martínez their leader.[78] Their rationale for increasing their revolutionary efforts at this moment was that Gómez "by not taking up the Presidency . . . breaks the foundation of the constitutional period"[79] and that the "acts of President Márquez Bustillos are illegal because he completed his term of office over a year ago."[80] In Puerto Rico, Castro was under the surveillance of detective Bernstein working under the direct orders of W. R. Bennet, a US marshal in San Juan.

The Economic Situation

The economic situation in Venezuela improved in 1916 because of the large coffee and cocoa harvest of that year. The harvest of beans, peas, potatoes, vegetables, sugar cane, and tobacco was also very good. The following year conditions were less favorable because of lower coffee prices owing to the European conflict, with the result that large stocks were built up. Despite the increase in production, at the beginning of 1916 Zumeta from New York urged Gómez to stimulate agricultural production by forming Asociaciones de Crédito Agrícola to grant loans to the sector. Such a move was prompted by Senator William Joel Stone, chairman of the US Senate Foreign Relations

Commission, who declared in a speech that some of the weaker Latin American countries should become fiscal protectorates of their stronger brothers in order to attract foreign capital to develop their economies. Zumeta counseled that "we run a grave risk if we are unable to triple our harvests during the next six years with a big cooperative effort."[81]

There was progress on the political front for some. Laureano Vallenilla Lanz in his inaugural speech as a senator declared that the government did not represent one political faction but was an administration under which people could work and which did not divide the country. Laureano Vallenilla Lanz stated in 1916 that the current administration "is not a government of a political party"[82] and that the "intransigent ensign of a political faction no longer flies from the highest mast at the Capitol, but rather the sacred standard that in the early days of Independence was a symbol of redemption for the oppressed people."[83] Under such conditions, Venezuela in a short period had undergone "a social and economic transformation,"[84] with Gómez initiating the building of a large road network and developing the country's resources together with the "creation and organization of internal revenues, whose yield have surpassed the most optimistic estimates."[85] The result was that the states had been freed from their dependence on customs receipts, which up to then was their main source of income.

Although Venezuela wanted to remain isolated from World War I, it was dragged into the conflict indirectly after the United States declared war on the Central Powers on April 6, 1917. The entry of the United States in the European conflict produced in Venezuela something "like consternation among the mercantile and agricultural classes dependent upon New York."[86] The pressure on Venezuela to enter the conflict started in January 1916, when Trinidad placed the branches of the allegedly German trading houses of Blohm and Company and Wenzel and Company on the black list of enemy firms, as well as Dr. J. E. Sánchez Afanado and P. Liccioni, who were alleged to act as front men for Blohm and Company in their deals. In addition, "all transit trade with these firms or persons"[87] with Trinidad was prohibited. This suited the Trinidadian authorities who wanted Blohm and Company on the blacklist because they were the "chief opponents to the removal of the 30% surtax in Venezuela."[88] As Venezuela could not reverse its neutrality policy when the United States declared war on Germany, Márquez Bustillos held a meeting with McGoodwin at Miraflores Palace in which he reiterated the "firm and loyal friendship of Venezuela toward the government and people of the US."[89] The entry of the United States to World War I would have a cooling effect on relations between the United States and Venezuela, offering the opposition to Gómez an ideal chance for forging his demise.

US-Venezuelans Relations Cool

Although there was little doubt about Gómez's Germanophilic tendencies, there were other processes at work that were of far greater significance than the ostensible German bias. The Venezuelan opposition and the United States were to use this argument against him, so that when Gómez closed several pro-Ally newspapers for domestic political reasons, he was again labeled pro-German and incurred the wrath of the United States already irritated at Venezuela's refusal to follow America's lead in declaring war on the Central Powers. The possibility of a US intervention was strong and gaining momentum with every newspaper closure. As we shall see later, the United States openly contemplated intervening in the country, but its heavy commitments in other parts of the world prevented this happening. The threat of US intervention was a continuous one up to 1922, when the oil needs of the United States modified American policy toward the complete acceptance of the Gómez regime.

Since the beginning of the war, the *El Fonógrafo* newspaper had been an ardent supporter of the Allies, refusing to run advertisements for German-owned or pro-German commercial houses, arousing the hostility of the German community in Maracaibo, the capital of Zulia. The newspaper was warned about its anti-German stance, and in December 1916, the German minister at Caracas complained about an article against the Kaiser. The Spanish government was also suing the newspaper over an article against King Alfonso XIII of Spain. Carlos López Bustamante, the editor and proprietor, was annoyed at this interference and sought financial assistance from the Allies in his propaganda effort against the Germans. If he did not receive support, then he would be forced to stop printing or "end all propaganda in our newspaper in favor of the Cause"[90] before the authorities detained him.

Under the country's neutrality laws, the German minister acted in a correct manner, with H. D. Beaumont, the British minister, confessing that he would have reacted in a similar manner if the British sovereign had been the subject of such press abuse. Beaumont felt that as a result of "the correct attitude of the Venezuelan government in observing the strict impartiality in the present war"[91] any "protest made by one of the Allied representatives would result in not less effective action than that taken on a similar protest from the German Minister."[92] The newspaper ran into financial difficulties when its circulation declined, with López Bustamante deciding at this juncture to start a Caracas edition. López Bustamante raised $3,898 from Italian and French merchants in Maracaibo but still needed a further $5,848 to mount the presses in Caracas, which he sought to acquire from the British legation in the form of a loan.

Beaumont together with other Allied colleagues tried discouraging him because it was felt there was no room for another daily in the capital city and because *Nuevo Diario* and *El Universal* had shown complete impartiality. López Bustamante then turned to the Royal Bank of Canada for a loan, but the bank was unable to help because the law prevented it from doing so. In the end, López Bustamante raised the additional funds in the United States, where he bought the printing presses. The Caracas edition was managed by his half brother E. López Rivas, who informed the British minister in April 1917 that a printing shop and an office had been set up but they needed additional funds to get the modern equipment, paper, ink, and other items out of customs at La Guaira. According to López Rivas, the Venezuelan Oil Concessions Ltd. contributed $39, Don Pablo Prosperi a further $97.50, and others with smaller sums, with the proprietor appealing to the British legation for money to continue his work. Beaumont advanced $476 from the legation's Secret Services fund[93] and contributed a further $97.50 out of his own pocket, which together with $195 from four French citizens saved the situation. *El Fonógrafo* started publishing its Caracas edition.[94]

At the same time, certain pro-German newspapers in the country were having a field day. J. Robertson, British vice-consul at Maracaibo, reported to Beaumont that the *Panorama* and other smaller pro-German papers had become noticeably "voluble in the continued success of the German and Austrian forces, to such an extent that the local public would soon be convinced that the Central Powers are having things all their own way when it is otherwise."[95] The government toward the end of August warned both *El Fonógrafo* and *Ecos del Zulia* to adhere to the strict rule of neutrality imposed by the authorities, but its warnings went unheeded, and the newspapers were soon closed down.[96]

In May, the German-inspired newspaper *El Diario* of Caracas was closed and its editor imprisoned because it published an article condemning President Wilson and the entry of the United States into the war. The suppression was viewed in government circles as an "indication of the importance attached here to the scrupulous fulfillment of the duties of a neutral,"[97] as Beaumont reported. Moreover, the editor was viewed "with disfavor by the dictator,"[98] with the suppression causing no alarm among the diplomatic representatives of the Allied countries. Later during the year, after Márquez Bustillos read an article titled "Plegaria," which produced "just indignation because it attacked the prestige and glory"[99] of the government, Dr. E. Domínguez Acosta, the newspaper editor, was imprisoned on August 22. The following day the *Fonógrafo* newspapers of Caracas and Maracaibo were suppressed by the government because the paper published an article by Domínguez Acosta, titled "De Lejos y de Cerca," which had not been written specially for the newspaper but reprinted from *Dharma,* a local Theosophist review of small circulation that criticized the Hohenzollern dynasty in Germany and thereby breached Venezuela's neutrality stance. Such a move, according to Beaumont, was "popularly regarded as an open declaration"[100] of Gómez's pro-German sympathies, and a "direct affront to the Allied representatives all of whom have more or less favored and supported the enterprise of Sr López and his brothers, and because the up-to-date monotype press which the latter have put in Caracas was bought in the USA and still largely unpaid for."[101] Preston McGoodwin, the American minister, and a future Gómez ally, did not support the publication because from the outset he judged "inopportune the promotion of your country's interests in that newspaper."[102] This was in direct contrast with the British minister, who informed Ignacio Andrade Troconis, the Venezuelan foreign minister, that the arrest of the editor of *El Fonógrafo* "could be misunderstood as a hostile measure against the cause of the Allies."[103]

The banning of the pro-Allies newspapers such as *El Fonógrafo* led the Allied diplomatic representatives to believe that the political situation was getting out of hand, with an increase in the demands for "help or intervention of the United States to end an intolerable tyranny."[104] In addition, McGoodwin informed Beaumont that he had in his possession politically damaging material against the government, including the arbitrary arrest of numerous people, the misappropriation of government funds, the wholesale confiscation of private property, and numerous dossiers on political prisoners that would justify foreign intervention. In 1915, Preston McGoodwin estimated that Gómez's annual income between 1909 and 1914, mainly from the cattle and meat industry of the country and the River and Coastal Navigation Company,[105] could have been $5 million per annum, although he felt a more realistic figure would be nearer $10 million. McGoodwin also reported that Gómez had $2 million deposited in Germany and that in 1915 had paid $160,000 for the six-hundred-acre Santa Estella cocoa property with 170,000 bearing cocoa trees located in the Sangre Chiquito ward of Manzilla in Trinidad. Beaumont was of the opinion that Gómez's policy was to seize as many companies as possible for his own benefit.[106]

The reality of the situation, however, escaped the eyes of the foreign observers because Gómez, using the pretext of neutrality, closed the newspaper out of political expediency. Dr. Antonio María Delgado Briceño, secretary general to Juancho Gómez, explained to Beaumont that the imprisonment of Carlos López Bustamante was due to his suspected hostility to the government as well as his criticism of the country's foreign policy. Arcaya, speaking as a private citizen, also explained to the British minister that the closure of the newspaper was due to the internal policies of the government and had nothing to do with any hostilities against the Allies.[107] Nevertheless, Beaumont felt that strong action was called for against the Gómez regime but that this could only be undertaken by the United States. The Americans, however, were keeping their options open, sending Major C.C. Smith, the military attaché at the legation in Caracas, on a tour of inspection of the country's coastal defenses in order to ascertain whether there was any truth in the rumor that Gómez was thinking of selling Margarita Island to the Germans to provide an operational base for their submarines to strike at Allied shipping in the West Indies.

Major Smith started his tour in May, first visiting La Guaira and then traveling to Curacao and La Vela, giving the impression of "an inspection of the coasts of those Antilles and of the Republic."[108] The Venezuelan government was not contemplating the sale of Margarita Island and informed the Allies that it would not "consent to transfer the sovereignty of any part of its territory"[109] while taking the necessary steps to "prevent hostile action from Venezuelan territory directed against the United States."[110] McGoodwin also sought to place further pressure on the Venezuelan government to enter the European conflict through Gil Fortoul.[111] On a number of occasions McGoodwin had informed Caracciolo Parra Picón, the vice president of the country, that the United States "would one way or the other tear down the current political situation of Venezuela providing, if needed, arms and all sorts of help to the bad Venezuelans that are outside the country because of their criminal behavior."[112] Márquez Bustillos found such a declaration by a US diplomat "inconceivable,"[113] concluding that McGoodwin had acted on his own initiative "without receiving the slightest encouragement from his government."[114] It was felt that McGoodwin acted out of personal malice against Gómez rather than pursuing stated US policy, with his behavior influenced by "people opposed to the regime or revolutionaries."[115] McGoodwin's language was so brusque that the Casa Amarilla was compelled to send back a note received from him because of its offensive tone.

Santos Domínici in Washington had a long meeting with Secretary of State Lansing during which he reiterated Venezuela's strict neutrality and friendship toward the United States while lodging a strong protest at McGoodwin's behavior. Lansing was surprised at the American minister's behavior but could not give an immediate answer, as he had to consult President Wilson after his department had drafted a memorandum on the Venezuelan situation. Lansing did not lend much credence to the revolutionary press in New York that was trying to discredit Gómez.

New Hope for the Revolutionaries

The bad impression created by the Venezuelan government in Washington by its refusal to enter the world conflict and the attitude of McGoodwin in Caracas gave the exiled revolutionaries new hope of deposing Gómez. In March 1917, P. Fortoul-Hurtado wrote to Lansing requesting the United States to end diplomatic relations with the "barbarous government of the usurper Juan Vicente Gómez"[116] because the American government should sanction "the sacred doctrine praised"[117] by Wilson of not recognizing governments that had usurped power by force. The rebels claimed that the Gómez regime would soon fall by "the uprising organized and led by the exiles."[118]

While Ortega Martínez remained in New York, many of the other revolutionaries, such as Peñaloza, Alcántara, Vargas, Dávila, Nava, Montes, Carlos Rojas Castillo, and Baptista, sensing that the United States could change its mind over Gómez, gathered in Puerto Rico in May 1917 for discussions with Castro. It was agreed at the meeting that Castro should leave soon on a tour to Cuba, Mexico, and New York, giving the impression that he wanted to retire from politics and live peacefully in Trinidad, but in reality trying to gauge the level of support among the exiled revolutionaries for his leadership. The Gómez administration was well aware that the revolutionaries wanted to alienate Venezuela from the US government by spreading false rumors, and feared that if diplomatic relations were severed, "a revolutionary movement would take place in the country; and then the army commanded by General Gómez would find itself practically disarmed compared to the one formed by his enemies."[119]

The seriousness of the situation forced Venezuela to send Coronil to the United States in May 1917 to explain to the State Department its position on neutrality. Coronil's trip was ostensibly for health reasons, for which Gómez provided $4,000,[120] in order not to arouse suspicion within the country that the Gómez regime was not viewed favorably by the United States. It was important for Coronil to establish with the US government that Venezuela had declared its neutrality publicly at the beginning of the war, and he took with him a number of documents demonstrating such an action. Such a move was necessary, Márquez Bustillos explained to Santos Domínici, the Venezuelan minister at Washington, because the revolutionaries "have taken on themselves the unqualified task of propagating the view that Venezuela holds hostile feelings against the great neighboring country."[121]

The Regime Stumbles

The reports of an impending uprising during the middle of 1917 became more intense, with rumors that the Castristas and the Mochistas had joined forces and were once again planning an invasion of Venezuela. In the United States, a *gran junta*, grouping together a number of revolutionaries, was formed in August 1917 to denounce Zumeta, the new Venezuelan minister at Washington, as an enemy of the US government. It also sought the support of the American government's "benevolent neutrality"[122] in their struggle in order for them to "carry through the war, which we contemplate against the accursed Gómez in order to substitute the present odious despotism in our beloved country with a regime of order, constitutionalism and liberty."[123] Carabaño, a former public works minister during Castro's administration and for a brief period development minister during Gómez's first administration, wanted an old acquaintance, Albert Pam of the Ethelburga Syndicate Ltd. in London and a brother of Hugo Pam, the manager of the British Match Factory in Caracas, to persuade the British government to get the United States to support the revolutionaries. In return, the new government in Venezuela would abolish the 30 percent surtax "so that henceforth Germany would not be the only market for Venezuelan products, as it is at present, but the great English mercantile houses established in Trinidad would enter into competition with Blohm and such people."[124]

In August 1917, Rafael de la Cova, a former departmental director in the Education Ministry who, according to Pedro César Domínici, the Venezuelan minister at London, was "a protégé of Mr. Hartford, the former British Minister in Caracas, who has given him a third rate job in the Censor's office to write short articles in favor of the Allies for South American newspapers,"[125] issued in London a pamphlet condemning Venezuela's pro-German attitude. It was tacitly assumed by the exiles that the Gómez government was sympathetic toward the German cause, with the implication that the "only way to promptly terminate pro-German activities is to promptly terminate the Gómez Government."[126] A further way of placing pressure on Gómez was to limit American food imports, thereby reducing government revenue through lower customs receipts.

At the end of May, in an extensive memorandum written by Bolet Monagas, Fortoul Hurtado, and J. López Rivero to Secretary of State Lansing, the revolutionaries outlined their plans to reorganize the country after reaching power.[127] As a first step, the United States would have to stop recognizing Gómez's government. Ortega Martínez, the preferred candidate for the presidency, would establish a Liberal Democratic government. Once power was achieved, a national directorate composed of five members would reorganize the country politically, with no member of the directorate allowed to stand for the presidency during the remaining constitutional period. The directorate would declare in force the 1909 constitution and would have the same powers as the head of government under the former constitution, with matters decided only by a majority vote. The directorate would also assume the supreme command of the army and would elect a government from outside its own members, including the attorney general, a national delegate for each state, and the governor of the Federal District. In order to prevent any internal resistance, the directorate would follow Gómez's advisers in the December 1908 coup and invite the United States to place a war ship "in the waters of Venezuela, in order to prevent the establishment of any naval base by the enemy."[128] The directorate would also grant a General amnesty and release all political prisoners. Later, a national constituent assembly would be convoked, composed of deputies in equal number to that stipulated by the 1909 constitution and elected by each state. The aims of the constituent assembly would be to legalize the authority of the directorate, inspect the accounts of the directorate and ministers, and enact a new constitution to ensure the establishment of a democratic regime. Once the new constitution had been approved, the national delegate of each state would convoke elections for the constitution of the public powers of each sovereign entity and that of the state and municipal governments. Just as soon as they had been installed with all formalities, the directorate would hold elections for the nomination of all the national magistrates to be elected by popular vote according to the new constitution. Once this occurred, the directorate would then transfer power to the president.

Other revolutionaries kept up the pressure on the State Department, with Rivas Vásquez in New York writing to President Wilson with a detailed exposition of the Gómez regime, calling it "*the most sinister autocracy that this world has known*" (emphasis in original).[129] In another letter seeking help from the United States, Manuel Jové pointed out to President Wilson the awful political and social conditions created by the Gómez regime.[130] The revolutionaries were encouraged by the change in US foreign policy that the murder of Francisco Madero in Mexico had brought about, with the American government now opting for the nonrecognition of governments that came to power by the use of force. At this stage, it was reported that the United States would not support a Castro-led revolution but would instead encourage other revolutionaries, notably Ortega Martínez. In contrast, the British government would not offer any help to the revolutionaries. In a meeting with the State Department, Ortega Martínez explained that together with his colleagues he could rid Venezuela of Gómez but on account of World War I was unable to acquire the necessary arms and ammunition in Europe and the United States. A provisional government could be established on Margarita Island because Asunción Rodríguez, who was a local caudillo, had joined their conspiracy.

It was clear to the Americans from the interview with Ortega Martínez that the political situation in Venezuela was deteriorating, with an estimated 1,500 prominent Venezuelans in jail and 5,000 exiled, and what was probably worse, Gómez was under the influence of the German minister and the commercial trading house of Blohm and Company. The State Department concluded that the government of Venezuela was "manifestly at variance with the provisions of the Constitution and not entitled to be considered as a "constituted form of government."[131] Ortega Martínez sought both economic and military help from the United States and wanted it to "shut its eyes to the procuring of arms and ammunition."[132] The United States felt that it would be difficult to comply with such a request because of Wilson's policy of nonrecognition of governments reaching power by force against a legally constituted government.

The island of Santo Domingo was becoming an important center of operations for the revolutionaries against Gómez. Carabaño and Durán among others had settled on the island, and the plan at this stage was for Castro, disguised as a priest, to disembark at Santa Marta in Colombia, where he would be met by both the bishop of the city and Carlos Díaz Granados. Simultaneously, Peñuela would take San Cristóbal and capture an expected eight thousand rifles and $194,932, which Castro would then use to enter Venezuela, traveling from Santa Marta to Rio Hacha and then to Trujillo. The local rebel supporters had already been ordered to clear an old path from Santa Marta to Ocaña in Colombia's Norte de Santander Department. In Caracas, support was expected from certain army officers who would stage a coup to coincide with Castro's invasion of the country. The plan, however, suffered a major setback when Captain José Agustín Piñero gave the plotters away. In Colombia, the governor of the Norte de Santander Department detained Peñuela and Rosario González. The result was that in July 1917 the armed movement was postponed; none of the revolutionaries at the Colombian border with Táchira, with the exception of Durán and Guevara, were willing to join forces with Castro. The revolutionaries in New York and Puerto Rico did reach an agreement with Castro, but the ones in the West Indies remained undecided whether to join a future rebellion.

Castro at the time embarked on a trip to the United States, Mexico, and the West Indies to gather support for his revolution. On August 2, 1917, the former Venezuelan dictator arrived in Cuba on his way to Veracruz (Mexico), where he disembarked six days later. Soon afterwards, Castro returned to Cuba on September 10, leaving for New York and then returning to Trinidad. The US government was extremely worried about Castro's arrival on the British island on September 25, because of the possibility of his reentry to Venezuela. According to Colmenares Pacheco, Gómez's brother-in-law (married to his sister Emilia), President Wilson warned Gómez by telegram of Castro's arrival on the island and advised "him to take precautions."[133] At the same time on a more formal note, the State Department requested the British colonial authorities to prevent Castro from traveling to Venezuela.[134] Walter Long, the British secretary of state for the colonies, felt that Castro should be sent back to the United States at the first "opportunity unless you can make sure of preventing him proceeding to Venezuela."[135] On October 9, the former Venezuelan president was formally ordered to leave the island after a reasonable amount of time had elapsed for him to prepare his departure. Castro used this excuse to prolong his stay while he awaited the arrival of his baggage and remittances from Cuba. Castro's refusal to leave for the United States after a suitable time had elapsed compelled J. R. Chancellor to issue warrants for his arrest and expulsion of the island. On November 6, after his deportation order had been issued, Detective Sub-Inspector Costelloe escorted Castro to the *Vasair* of the Lamport and Holt shipping line, which left for New York the following day. On his arrival in the United States on November 18, Castro immediately set sail for Puerto Rico.

The plots outside Venezuela to depose Gómez continued unabated. The American government felt sure that a revolution was about to take place in the country in early March 1918. On November 26, 1917, Beaumont became aware of an impending plot when the Tennants Estates Company requested permission from the governor of Trinidad to ship 122,000 cartridges to Venezuela. Beaumont sought the opinion of the US minister, who "agreed that nothing was to be gained in any way compromising the Colonial authorities,"[136] with the US government appearing to be "disposed to place no interference in the way of conspirators"[137] while favoring Iturbe, the prospective presidential candidate. At the time of his departure from Trinidad, Castro informed Mr. Gress, the Associated Press correspondent, that certain American citizens offered to help the rebels as long as Francisco Javier Yanes, deputy director of the Pan American Union, was made president of Venezuela, but he had refused. Some of the rebels in New York thought that Yanes's refusal was due to the American government offering to help the exiles. At Yanes's refusal to stand as a candidate, the rebels offered the presidential candidature to Félix Montes in New York.[138] Oscar Blanco Fombona, who in December 1917 was in New York, abhorred the revolution being organized in the United States by Montes, with the alleged support of the American government, because "he had not stopped being a patriot."[139] Further proof of such a venture comes from M. Rodríguez Llamozas, a Venezuelan who sat at Castro's dining table during the voyage to New York. Castro at the time intimated to Rodríguez Llamozas that "the American government expelled him from Trinidad for being an obstacle to a revolution that said government was fostering and headed by Ortega, Tellería, Ayala and Olivares."[140]

It is untrue that the American government was directly involved in a Venezuelan revolution, but as certain rebels were trying to curry favor with the United States at the time, it is likely that the rumor was started in order to encourage others to join. Some revolutionaries, such as Pío Gil, had little confidence in Ortega Martínez and Baptista. Pío Gil writes that both revolutionaries had recently sold their properties in Venezuela for a considerable amount of money, showing the "respect that Gómez, who otherwise tramples over other people's property, has for these two revolutionaries, revealing that he does not consider them to be revolutionaries of action but instead of attitude and still expects and hopes to persuade them to join him."[141]

Sociedad Patriótica Joven Venezuela

Despite such malicious views, Ortega Martínez continued with his own invasion preparations. It was clear that in order to get any assistance from the United States the exiles would need to form a party or some form of political organization. Ortega Martínez returned to the State Department seeking help for his cause in early November, this time seeing William Russell, the former minister at Caracas when the American legation was closed in 1908. Ortega Martínez informed Russell that the situation in Venezuela was becoming desperate and that "it is openly asserted that an attempt will be made to assassinate Gomez."[142] Such action would plunge the country into anarchy because the state presidents would fight among themselves for the ultimate prize of the presidency. Ortega Martínez and some of the other exiles wanted to prevent this from happening but were unable to launch their own revolution because they could not get hold of the arms and ammunition owing to US export restrictions. At the end of the meeting, Russell concluded that if anarchy broke out in Venezuela, then the United States would "be obliged to intervene, and in our present harassed condition, this would to say the least, be very inconvenient."[143] Moreover, if the United States brought pressure to bear either unilaterally or in a joint effort with other countries against Gómez this would immediately arouse "the patriotism of Venezuelans against foreign interference and *would re-act seriously* against us" (emphasis in original).[144]

It was clear after the meeting that some form of political organization needed to be created. Consequently, on November 25, 1917, the Sociedad Patriótica Joven Venezuela, headed by Ortega Martínez together with Olivares, Baptista, Carabaño, and Tellería among others, was founded in New York with the purpose of deposing Gómez and replacing him with a democratically elected government because "we are completely opposed to the disastrous theories of personal rivalries that have caused so much damage to the country."[145] The group, which later issued a monthly newspaper, *La Joven Venezuela,* was against caudillos and "personal ambition or peculation"[146] but did not have a clear political program. Other émigrés such as Bernardo Suárez and Sergio Ruiz tried to unify the Venezuelan emigrants by forming the Unión Patriótica in New York.

The revolution led by Ortega Martínez—and it was thought with the tacit support of the American government—was expected to start on February 11, 1918. There was general agreement among all the various rebel factions, with Vargas, representing the Nacionalistas, joining Ortega Martínez. It was agreed that Peñaloza would command the forces in western Venezuela, while Asunción Rodríguez would head the eastern forces. In anticipation of the forthcoming invasion, Peñaloza left Curacao for New York on December 13, and Vargas, who was living at a modest hotel described as "very poor"[147] in Santo Domingo, left for Curacao at the end of 1917. In November 1917, Ovidio Córdova was sent from Trinidad to Anzoátegui State to secure the support of General José Mercedes Rodríguez and General Zacarias Lira in Guárico, but the rebel envoy was caught.[148]

As we have seen, certain members of the Venezuelan exiled community in the United States urged the American government to break off diplomatic relations or intervene openly to end the Gómez dictatorship. In Venezuela, some would-be revolutionaries also wanted the help of the United States. In Zulia, Pedro José Rojas, an engineer by trade and nephew of Pedro Ezequiel Rojas, the Venezuelan minister at Washington from 1910 until his death in 1914, founded in early 1918 what he called the "Constitutional Government Party," with the intention of organizing a coup by a "committee of correspondence" similar to one formed by the thirteen American colonies prior to the declaration of independence in the United States. The association was named Sociedad Pro-Patria Bolívar, with the aim of substituting the Gómez regime with a civilian government. Although the organizers claimed to have around 1,500 rifles and one million rounds of ammunition, they still felt they needed four thousand rifles, three million rounds of ammunition, six cannons, sixteen machine guns, four anti-aircraft guns, and three aircraft in order to ensure success. The difficulty with their plan was that the country's mail service was unreliable; they had to depend on delivery couriers.[149] Rojas was convinced that Maracaibo would fall into their hands without bloodshed, since the army and half the state legislature, together with many other influential people, were behind them. However, without the help of a foreign power, Rojas felt that his revolution was doomed and therefore wanted assurances from the United States that it would recognize the revolutionaries if they captured Zulia. The revolution was set for March 24, 1918, but without foreign assistance it was postponed indefinitely because they would be unable to resist the forces of the central government.

The State Department had previously ignored these pleas for help but toward the end of 1917 was beginning to lose patience with the "unconstitutional situation"[150] of the Gómez regime. It decided to apply some pressure on the Venezuelan government by placing an embargo on paper supplies to the country. Such a move was misguided and ultimately a foolish act because the anti-American press in Venezuela, as Britain argued, was "insignificant and harmless."[151] At this juncture, the intention of the American government was more to threaten Venezuela than to do anything more serious, but its displeasure against Gómez was fuelled further when McGoodwin failed to turn up to listen to the annual presidential message in 1917. During a long two-and-a-half-hour meeting, McGoodwin explained to Bernardino Mosquera, the foreign affairs minister, that his nonappearance was due to being ill on the day. McGoodwin was suffering with a sore throat, and was treated by Dr. Rafael González Rincones, who felt that such treatment "would not have any side effects, but the opposite occurred, provoking a choking and coughing fit that forced him to stay in bed at precisely the time that Congress met."[152] McGoodwin added further insult to injury when he stated to Mosquera that President Wilson, despite more important matters, would not "be more tolerant of injustices and criminal irregularities here than in Mexico . . . especially as he would have the vast majority of the Venezuelan people on his side."[153] McGoodwin was convinced that the political situation was deteriorating to such an extent that "nothing less than a peremptory demand for the immediate establishment of the Constitution, backed by force if necessary or a complete blockade, will have any effect,"[154] with only the "forcible removal of General Gómez"[155] having any real impact. The Italian ambassador at Washington had already received instructions from his government to discuss with the "State Department and his Allied colleagues means to be used against Venezuela"[156] in its pending claim.

Beaumont, the British minister, counseled that only a full-scale attack would succeed in getting rid of Gómez, and, in a lapse of diplomatic discretion, he almost urged the Foreign Office to back the revolutionaries in their bid for power. He argued that while unaided the rebels had no hope of succeeding, "with moral and material help from the United States the case would be different, and a rapid *coup de main* at Maracay, backed by American machine guns, would accomplish more than any protests, ultimatums or punitive economic measures that it might be possible to take."[157] The British government felt that "the responsibility of such a vigorous policy"[158] should be left to the United States to bear, as the Foreign Office could not sanction such a policy or associate themselves with the "removal of the President of a South American republic."[159]

Gómez Tries Appeasement

The Venezuelan government felt extremely vulnerable to the threat of any Allied power severing diplomatic relations, and more so in the case of the United States, as it believed this would signal its downfall, allowing a fierce revolutionary movement to sweep the country. There is little doubt that Gómez felt that he was in a tricky situation, since the United States was threatening to sever diplomatic relations. The United States was in a dilemma, too: it could not support the revolutionaries because this would go against its foreign policy. Consequently, President Wilson, before making up his mind on what to do with Gómez, commissioned Glenn Stewart to study the Venezuelan situation in detail and report his findings to him.

In Maracay, Gómez believed that something was needed to appease the Allies. He dismissed his most pro-German ministers, viz, Interior Minister Arcaya, Development Minister Díaz Rodríguez, and Education Minister Carlos Aristimuño Coll, and replaced them with Ignacio Andrade Troconis, Gumersindo Torres, and Rafael González Rincones in the respective ministerial posts. Although Gómez was convinced that he had done "everything that was required of him and satisfied [*sic*] the Allies,"[160] the United States would continue to encourage Venezuelan conspirators, with US-Venezuelan relations remaining strained until 1922, when US oil needs modified America's policy toward the country.

McGoodwin was well aware of the government's interpretation of his nonappearance at the year's annual presidential message, assuring the Venezuelan government that his actions were misinterpreted and that he was still well disposed toward it, so much so that at the request of local business leaders he was traveling to the United States to try to ameliorate the export restrictions imposed on Venezuelan produce into the country. Gómez felt that the imposition of such restrictions on the part of the US government was unjust and informed McGoodwin that "you have witnessed at close range my work and know that my only ambition is to do good things for my country, promoting industry, commerce, agriculture, animal husbandry and maintaining a cordial and honorable peace with all the people of my country."[161] However, Gómez's position in the United States was deteriorating further.

At the end of 1917 Stewart completed his report, which was a damning indictment of a friendly government. Stewart considered the Gómez administration to be "extra legal and unconstitutional"[162] and "founded on corruption, fear and force,"[163] where personal liberty and security did not exist, under conditions comparable only "to the worst days of the Inquisition."[164] Stewart concluded that the social and political conditions prevalent in Venezuela were "a disgrace to civilization and a living reproach to those who countenance it,"[165] with little possibility of improving them while Gómez was in power. The removal of the Venezuelan dictator, Stewart concluded, could "surely and speedily be done, should arms bound to Venezuela, slip out of the United States."[166] Stewart then considered the alternatives available to the US government to bring about the desired change in the country. He thought that the nonrecognition of the Gómez administration would achieve nothing, as Venezuela was financially and economically independent. A commercial embargo would hardly affect the country, as it did not levy export duties; moreover, the United States needed most of the country's exports, such as hides, skins, sugar, coffee, and cocoa. A US embargo would only affect the Venezuelan people and would have little real impact on the government. Moreover, a concerted effort to place strong diplomatic pressure on Venezuela would have no effect unless backed by arms, and "such an action would be doubly undesirable as it would unite Venezuela in arms and weaken the United States in her struggle against Germany."[167] Stewart concluded therefore that there was only one way of guaranteeing good government in the country under what he termed "Christian civilized conditions,"[168] and that was to "eliminate Gomez root and branch! Such an action would also promptly terminate German activities and any possible submarine activities."[169] This situation could be achieved by giving the exiled rebels tacit recognition through allowing them to purchase arms in the United States and being less strict "in the granting of one or two exports licenses."[170]

At the end of the first week of 1918, President Wilson had digested Stewart's report and had also read with interest McGoodwin's correspondence, concluding in mid-February that Gómez was a "scoundrel"[171] who "ought to be put out."[172] He sought Secretary of State Lansing's advice on the best way "in which we can do it that would not upset the peace of Latin America more than letting him alone will."[173] Secretary of State Lansing felt that Gómez was a pro-German sympathizer who constituted a "real danger to the United States and our war effort."[174] The elimination of Gómez, however, posed a problem for the United States as to who would best fill the political vacuum. It was clear to the Wilson administration that the exiled revolutionaries were not acceptable because they came from the same mould as Gómez. There were a number of other important reasons for President Wilson pulling back from actively deposing Gómez at this juncture. Wilson had adopted a nonintervention policy in the region, and "Dollar Diplomacy" was still fresh in Latin American–US relations, with the added complication that a Venezuelan incursion by US marines could threaten relations in the whole continent. Moreover, the United States was now deeply involved in World War 1 and could not afford the time, men, or equipment to get embroiled in what was viewed as a minor problem. The British government felt in February 1918 that Ortega Martínez could succeed Gómez as head of the Venezuelan government "especially if he could obtain the assistance of the United States or of the Allies,"[175] but would not go as far as financing the exiled rebel.

Although the United States was now engaged in the bitter European conflict, and ostensibly could not get actively involved in regime change in Venezuela, there was also a shift in US foreign policy that shied away from direct action. During the first two decades of the century, US foreign policy in the Caribbean and countries bordering the sea underwent a series of changes. President Theodore Roosevelt and Secretary of State Elihu Root only acted when they were forced to deal with emergencies in which action seemed necessary to prevent further bloodshed or European intervention. The Dominican Republic Customs Receivership was set up in 1905 because of the imminent seizure of one of its ports by European powers, and in Cuba an American government was established after the authorities refused to set up a government. Learning from their mistakes, US policy makers urged fiscal and political reforms that prevented such emergencies arising in the region.

The nonrecognition or the threat of nonrecognition was one of the chief means by which the United States attempted to discourage revolutionary changes of government in the Caribbean after 1909. The William Howard Taft government departed from this policy by bringing about the overthrow of the Madriz Rodríguez regime in Nicaragua in 1910 and by delaying recognition of the Jean Jacques Dessalines Haitian government until assurances were received that American interests would be protected. The Taft administration, with Secretary of State Philander C. Knox, went further in the meddling of the internal affairs of Caribbean countries under the theory that prevention was better than cure—it was more expedient to remedy conditions likely to cause foreign complications. The United States did not hesitate to use force when its advice went unheeded, such as in Nicaragua, and it especially sought to extend to other countries the same sort of financial control that until 1911 were so helpful in dealing with the Dominican Republic. The Taft administration went further than its predecessors in its emphasis on financial reform as a principal objective of its Caribbean policy. In Nicaragua, Honduras, Guatemala, and Haiti, the Americans attempted to have the old European-held bond debts refunded by loans floated in New York. It felt that the new role of the United States in the Caribbean required that American financial influence should be prominent there, and after its success in the Dominican Republic, the formulation of the "Dollar Diplomacy" with American control of the customs house was seen as a panacea for the ills of these countries.

President Wilson in dealing with General Felipe Adolfo de la Huerta in Mexico introduced a new concept in American policy when he made recognition of a government a matter of principle. Under Wilson's administration and subsequent governments, recognition of a new regime, especially in the Caribbean, came to signify that the government had the moral support of the United States, while nonrecognition was a means to discourage and compel revolutionary leaders to respect constitutional procedures. The recognition policy according to Munro "became one of the important instruments through which the United States influenced the course of internal politics"[176] in the region. In Central America, after the events of 1909–10, it was generally believed that a regime that failed to obtain American recognition had little chance of survival. With the Wilson presidency in 1913 an essentially similar policy was enforced but with the addition that the United States would only recognize constitutional governments. Wilson and his advisers attempted to attack the basic causes of Caribbean political instability by insisting on the establishment of efficient police forces, the reform of financial administrations, and the adoption of broad economic reforms. When these objectives were not achieved, there was little recourse left but force—thus Haiti and the Dominican Republic were occupied. At the end of the First World War, there was a gradual shift in US foreign policy; the European powers were in no position to challenge the Roosevelt Corollary to the Monroe Doctrine, and the behavior of the United States in the region was becoming repugnant to the American public. A course toward nonintervention was set in motion.

Throughout the period the United States was trying to put an end to conditions that threatened the independence of some of the Caribbean states and were consequently "a potential danger to the security of the United States."[177] It was felt that revolutions had to be discouraged as well as bad financial practices that weakened governments. Thus, the Platt Amendment in Cuba was an effort to achieve this end, and the Roosevelt Corollary to the Monroe Doctrine meant that the United States would achieve its objectives in the Caribbean. Throughout the 1901–21 period, then, the first objective of American policy in the Caribbean was to discourage revolutions because they were a source of friction with European powers, disrupting government finances as well as being an obstacle to "any sort of material or social progress."[178] Governments engaged with internal civil conflicts could do little to improve road construction and education or encourage investment. The development of the economy was a second objective after the improvement of the political situation of a country.

Nonintervention in Venezuela

After careful consideration of the evidence, President Wilson in the end decided that there were no grounds for intervening in Venezuela; he felt that the country did not constitute a security risk, and he opted instead to impose economic sanctions on the regime. The US government was deeply worried about Gómez's alleged pro-German sympathies and possible threat to the American war effort. However, Gómez, as we have seen, pursued a strong neutrality policy all along, had not entered the conflict on Germany's side, and thus could not be criticized on this point. Nevertheless, in February 1918 the United States began to consider blacklisting Gómez and placing him on the Enemy Trading List for the suppression of the pro-Ally newspapers in the country. The US administration also sought the opinion of the British minister at Caracas on the best way of dealing with the Gómez regime. Beaumont felt that Gómez had not been unduly harsh with Allied property, since the suppression of *El Fonógrafo* and other newspapers was due to the belief that the proprietors were "ill-disposed towards the government."[179] Moreover, the placing of Venezuela on the Enemy Trading List would amount practically to a rupture of relations and, according to the British minister, "would be justified if he had committed some act of positive hostility or if the effect were to promote a revolution which would drive him from power and cause him to be replaced by a successor more friendly disposed towards the Allies."[180]

Consequently, both Beaumont and McGoodwin did not think that it would be wise to blacklist Gómez because he would "retaliate with disastrous effect on Allies' enterprise in this country."[181] Although Gómez remained "obstinately determined to go his own way"[182] in refusing to favor rapprochement with the United States, Beaumont felt that a change of government could only be sanctioned on "moral principles and in the hopes of the establishment of a Government with more enlightened views ready to encourage foreign enterprise, rather than one definitely Alliophile [*sic*] but insufficiently strong to enforce law and order."[183] The British minister also felt that the best solution would be setting up a US-administered Venezuela for a few months "provided equal opportunities for all were thereby secured."[184] Such a view was strongly rejected by the Foreign Office, which in a stern message to Beaumont stated that it would not "view with favor the intervention of the United States in Venezuelan affairs."[185] The British position was made singularly clear to the US government when Lord Reading informed them that it did not matter who held office in Venezuela as long as "due protection is afforded to British interests and a settlement of a few small claims is affected."[186] The British government stressed the need to "propitiate rather than alienate"[187] Gómez in order to convince him that he had more to gain from being friendly to the Allies rather than to Germany because the regime had "no intention of allowing herself to become a mere satellite of the United States and shows an independent spirit,"[188] which was not at odds with British interests in the region despite its refusal to cease friendly relations with Germany. In addition, if a new Venezuelan government granted preferential treatment to the United States, similar to that given by Cuba, this would be fatal to future British commercial interests in the country after the war.

The United States, while not willing to intervene openly, nevertheless tried to make life difficult for Venezuela and, more specifically, for Gómez. In March 1918, the US government was wrongly reported to be almost sure that a revolution in Venezuela was about to take place with its blessing.[189] What happened was that customs officials at Puerto Rico seized a cargo of cigarette paper that the Spanish ship *Montserrat* was transporting from Montreal to Venezuela. When the ship docked in La Guaira, the Venezuelan government detained it for nondelivery of goods and imposed a fine of $115,830. The vessel was released after twenty-four hours because the US legation at

Caracas assured the government that the paper would be sent on the first ship leaving Puerto Rico for Venezuela. The settlement cleared the air, and the anxiety of the government was further allayed when it received information that other South American republics, including those that had broken off relations with Germany, had suffered no less than Venezuela from the restrictions imposed on exports from the United States because of the war. Beaumont informed Mosquera, the foreign affairs minister, that the main cause of US irritation was Gómez's failure to follow America's war policy. Many prominent Venezuelans, including Matos and Gil Fortoul, advised Gómez to follow the United States.[190] The Venezuelan government felt that it was unnecessary to break off relations with Germany but that a "frank official expression of sympathy with the course for which the US had entered the war"[191] would be sufficient. Gómez's annual message to Congress declaring Venezuela's intention to adhere to strict neutrality was enough to allay any fears the United States may harbor over the government's intentions.

In a further friendly gesture from Gómez to Beaumont, the government released López Bustamante from prison in April 1918. He left almost immediately for the United States, where he started to criticize the Gómez regime, beseeching President Wilson to stop recognizing the Venezuelan government.[192] López Bustamante's request did not fall on deaf ears, as he met R. C. Bannermann of the State Department. After discrediting Mc-Goodwin's misinterpretation of US policies because Gómez had bought him off by giving his wife $20,000,[193] López Bustamante outlined his plan for the United States to intervene in Venezuela to secure the release of the political prisoners. The United States, however, wanted to improve relations with Venezuela. The State Department sent Special Commissioner Ernesto Lara Gogorza in May 1918 on a mission to establish even better relations than "the existing ones between you and President Wilson, who appears to be a friend and trusted confidant,"[194] as he explained to Márquez Bustillos. Lara Gogorza wanted to reach a closer understanding with Gómez and disapproved of "the behavior of Minister McGoodwin and Mr. Phelps concerning our international relations with North America."[195] Such a view, Márquez Bustillos counseled, reflected President Wilson's "honest and correct attitude . . . and on Venezuela's neutrality, and is aware of the true nature of Minister Mc-Goodwin's behavior and the machinations of Phelps."[196] With the attitude of the US government mellowing, the Venezuelans tried to further appease them by allowing McGoodwin the use of the capitol building for a July 4 Independence Day celebration, to which more than four hundred people were invited. This was a rare privilege, "a unique distinction awarded in America to an American diplomat in the contemporary history of its relations."[197]

Despite the assurances of Lara Gogorza, the United States kept up its pressure on the Gómez government by seizing the SS *Guárico,* the former gunboat *Zamora,* and the flagship of the Compañía Venezolana de Navegación,[198] whose major shareholder was Gómez, on a technicality in Colón, Panama. It was alleged that the ship did not conform to US regulations on lifesaving equipment and wireless, but the reason behind the detention was to use the steamer "as a lever to induce the Company to cease accepting cargo for German or listed firms between Venezuelan ports."[199] There was no regular service to Panama because of the lack of trade between the two countries, with Foreign Affairs Minister Mosquera assuring Beaumont that the *Guárico* had not carried German goods. Secretary of State Lansing, however, felt that the owner of the ship was "not entirely free of his links with the enemy,"[200] and the ship was refused bunkering facilities in Panama. This would only be reinstated after the US War Trade Department had inspected the company's accounts and ascertained that it had not been trading with the enemy. The department was invited to examine the company's books, while a more permanent solution of subleasing the ship to the United States was contemplated. The same offer was extended to McGoodwin by Luis Pérez Bustamante so that he could "verify in a positive and absolute way the complete falsehood of the rumors that are going around abroad."[201] As the company only used Venezuelan coal, the only other pressure that could be exerted was to place the company on the Enemy Trading List if it continued to carry cargo for German firms. Such a penalty was hardly justified, as it had serious repercussions on the interests of Venezuelan and American traders in the country because the company's steamers acted as feeders and distributors of goods for American freight steamers trading with La Guaira, Puerto Cabello, and Maracaibo. However, it would be difficult to enforce: there were practically no German bondholders, and the company was a public utility, being the only carrier between certain ports in Venezuela. If the company was placed on the list, then "American citizens could not travel or dispatch any goods between La Guaira, Carúpano, Cumaná, Ciudad Bolivar and intermediate ports, except by sailing boats."[202] In addition, freight charges would increase further if sailboats were used to transport cargo.

The only financial penalty suffered by the owners while the ship was detained would be the loss of future earnings, since the *Guárico* had more than covered the charter for a year, estimated at $2,285,[203] with the voyage already made. As a concession to release the ship, the United States demanded that two US agents be posted on each of the company's boats to enforce and verify that the boycott of the German merchant houses was effective. Gómez refused resolutely to accept this for all his steamers, but he did not object to the *Guárico,* as this was the only international steamer in the fleet. The *Guárico* would remain in Panama a further three months, and the incident caused additional indignation in Venezuela "by the want of regard shown by the United States Authorities to Venezuelan susceptibilities."[204] The detention of the ship resulted in a decline in trade between Trinidad and Venezuela because of a fall in voyages.

A further source of irritation to the United States was the ill treatment by the Venezuelan government of the Bramon Estates Company (Bramon), an American agricultural company operating in Táchira that had invested $400,000 in the country and in 1917 entered into a legal dispute with Breuer Moller and Company, a German trading house in Maracaibo. Bramon had offered eight different solutions to settle the dispute, but none was acceptable to the Maracaibo trading company, which took the company to court in September 1918. As a result, McGoodwin demanded from Mosquera, the foreign affairs minister, "the immediate suspension of the proceedings against the company's property, to allow a clarification of this accusation."[205] After a long trial, the Juzgado de Primera Instancia of Táchira declared the Bramon company bankrupt, prompting McGoodwin to lodge a strong protest, stating that the company had suffered from the intervention by Ramón Vargas, who had coerced the free action of the tribunals. It was claimed that he handed the tribunal judge the written sentence to be imposed. The judge lost his job because he refused to comply, and was expelled from the state, with his replacement accepting the "impositions of Doctor Ramón Vargas."[206]

In a stern note, McGoodwin requested the Venezuelan government to "repeal the illegal acts committed against the company."[207] The US minister stated bluntly that a conflict with the United States would ensue if the Venezuelan government did not intervene but agreed to withdraw his note if the government ensured that the two companies reached a "proper agreement for which a period of two or three weeks was requested."[208] Gómez advised Eustoquio Gómez, the state president, that if the judge "proceeded wrongly when it declared an embargo, to wait for the Superior Courts to revoke the sentence because they will not be constituted by vagabonds and when it is firmly revoked and it is proved that the Judge violated the laws that he is obliged to follow, indict him or force him to resign and put another judge from our cause who will know how to perform his duty."[209] In the meantime, Eustoquio Gómez should not "intervene to avoid the justified complaints from the other side."[210]

Allied Victory Creates Problems for Gómez

The Venezuelan government took the threat of an invasion by the exiles seriously, requesting the Colombian government to either deport Peñaloza from the country or put an end to his revolutionary plans. In August 1918, Trino Baptista, who was on a mission for Mocho Hernández to get the United States to support the revolution by either declaring Gómez a persona non grata or allowing the shipment of five thousand rifles and five million rounds of ammunition to Venezuela for the revolutionaries,[211] was in Santo Domingo staying at Carabaño's farm. While on the island, Trino Baptista together with Francisco Rivero and Fernando Figueredo met with Colonel Alexander Bacon, a US military man, to gauge the level of support they would receive from the United States. In preparation for the forthcoming revolution both Carabaño and Durán in Santo Domingo sold their farms at the end of 1918. In Puerto Rico, Castro spent his time planning his next revolution while waiting for the European conflict to end.[212]

The Allied victory on November 11, 1918, caused open hostility to manifest itself in Caracas against Venezuela's neutrality during World War I, creating more headaches for Gómez. Now that the war was over, public resentment against the regime was more open, encouraged by the secret opposition and the exiles giving "such publicity to their views as is possible in a country where the Press is strictly muzzled and free expression of opinion prohibited."[213] The triumph of the Allies after the war stimulated the opposition to Gómez, both inside and outside the country, with Beaumont, the British minister, convinced that Gómez's days were numbered. In Caracas, a flysheet appeared extolling the virtues of Dr. Francisco Javier Yanes, deputy director of the Pan American Union, in Washington, as a good candidate for the country's presidency.

In Caracas the students seized the opportunity of King Albert of Belgium's birthday to demonstrate against the Gómez regime for not allowing any form of relief for the influenza epidemic known as "Spanish flu," which killed a great deal of people, including Alí Gómez, the dictator's favorite son on November 7.[214] Archbishop Felipe Rincón González tried to stop the march owing to the recent influenza pandemic but without success. Just prior to the protest march, McGoodwin on November 14 met with Mosquera, the foreign affairs minister, and Andrade Troconis, the interior minister, to discuss how the government would deal with any problems arising from the protest march. One of the student leaders was the son of Nicómedes Zuloaga and the fiancé of Mosquera's daughter. The following day, November 15, King Albert's birthday, the students first went to the Belgium legation, where Andrés Eloy Blanco, Jorge Luciani, Gonzalo Carnevali, and Rodolfo Moleiro addressed a crowd of approximately three hundred students.

The main reason for the protest was to draw attention to the political conditions in Venezuela, but the students were disappointed at not being allowed to organize any sort of relief for the influenza victims in Venezuela. The university students also protested the regime's neutrality policy and its refusal to allow people to congregate for the purpose of studying, to reopen the university, and to allow the Red Cross to set up a branch in Caracas. Jorge Luciani, in particular, accused Gómez of cowardice because he had abandoned Caracas during the influenza epidemic. The students then seized Belgian flags and other Allied flags from the floral tributes and while singing "La Marseillaise" went first to the British legation and then to the American one. Since the British and American ministers were not present, the students then marched to the French legation, where they toasted the Allied victory with champagne,[215] and declared that with the fall of the Kaiser there "remained only one despot in the world and appealed to the Allied Diplomatic agents to complete the task which President Wilson has characterized as a solemn duty."[216]

Pedro García, the chief of police, arrived and ordered the color bearers arrested but without success. The students headed to the Plaza Bolívar but were detained by Delgado Briceño, secretary general to Juan C. Gómez, the Federal District governor, who, with a detachment of sixty men with fixed bayonets, arrested twenty youths while the rest dispersed. Further arrests were made later. According to Cecil Dormer, the new British minister, the government required the use of even "more tyrannical"[217] methods to quash the demonstration. Although the press portrayed Gómez as being pro-Ally in order to allay the feelings that he was a secret pro-German supporter, the government was worried about the political unrest that appeared to be growing, ordering all churches, theatres, and public meeting places to close during the Christmas festivities for "fear of hostile demonstrations against the Dictator."[218]

In New York, there were two main revolutionary groups at the time: one led by Ortega Martínez, who deployed Peñaloza and Alcántara at the Colombian border, and the other headed by Baptista, Olivares, and Tellería. The efforts of the revolutionaries in the Ortega Martínez camp centered on getting US assistance for their revolution, encouraged by President Wilson's proclamation on November 28, 1918, regulating the import of certain Venezuelan products, including beans, sugar, hides, and skins, at an estimated loss in trade of over $2 million. The revolutionaries fanned anti-Gómez sentiment by insinuating to the US authorities that the pro-German merchant houses would seize this opportunity to start an anti-American campaign in Venezuela, which would also have the tacit support of the Gómez government, having already demonstrated its pro-German feelings. Thus by getting rid of the Gómez administration, such friendly feelings toward Germany would also end. They also argued that with a "liberal democratic government in control of Venezuela such as will be assured under Doctor Ortega Martínez, an end will be put to the narrow minded, anti-foreign and particularly anti-American legislation."[219] Hence, with the help of the Americans and Allies, Ortega Martínez would triumph over the despotism of Gómez, and so "Venezuela and her people look to the United States and President Wilson for their liberation."[220]

The United States, however, refused to help the revolutionaries on an individual basis, preferring to lend its support instead to organized political parties. Dormer, the British minister at Caracas, argued that it would be a mistake for Britain to intervene, as British interests in the country would be the easiest to attack if the Venezuelan government wanted to retaliate against foreign intervention. To the British government, Gómez was the "best guarantee that we have that British interests will not be interfered with."[221] This was not due to Gómez being openly pro-British but because "he wishes for British rather than American or other capital to develop the country."[222] Dormer added that the "ill-feeling between America and Britain is very bitter in these parts, and I fear is more than justified on the latter side."[223] McGoodwin's reputation in Caracas was bad, and "gossip says that he is not above bribes."[224] However, in early 1919 it was apparent to the revolutionaries in the United States that their efforts to gain the support of the American government were leading to a dead end. US foreign policy had shifted to one in which it preferred to prevent revolution, with an April 1919 State Department memorandum stating that "it was settled policy of the Department to discountenance all revolutionary activities in Central and South American countries."[225]

Despite rumors that Ortega Martínez, Rivas Vásquez, and Jacinto López wanted the United States to intervene in the country, the revolutionaries decided reluctantly to try to achieve agreement among themselves and go it alone. The leadership of the expedition was initially fought over by Ortega Martínez and Olivares, with the former winning. Ortega Martínez's plan for a military uprising in Venezuela to coincide with an assassination attempt against Gómez was set for February 1919 at the latest. The plotters felt that this would be an appropriate time to hit Gómez because he was still grieving the loss of his son Alí.[226] The new government would be headed by Ortega Martínez, with Baptista as first vice president and Mocho Hernández as second vice president. Castro also supported the rebels because he was promised "in addition to other privileges, the return of all his goods and compensation for his losses."[227]

The 1919 Military Uprising

In early 1919, the opposition to the Gómez regime would take the form of a military conspiracy that involved mainly officer cadets who had graduated two years previously from the military academy, as well as students, professionals, journalists, and employees of commercial houses—in effect the representatives of a nascent middle class. The purpose of the coup was to topple Gómez and set up a provisional civilian junta that would organize free and fair elections and proclaim the sovereignty of the people. The plan was to isolate Gómez in Maracay by gaining control of all the barracks in Caracas, where most of the army was stationed.

There were eight captains and eight lieutenants implicated in the conspiracy at the Caracas barracks in Mamey, La Trinidad (today San Carlos), El Cuño, El Hoyo, Palos Grandes, and La Planta. The civilian section was mostly composed of students who would wait "in small groups distributed in the most diverse places of the city; some of them either for pleasure or not were to meet at the two brothels next to the Mamey barracks, whose walls they would scale as soon as the signal was given."[228] The nerve center of the conspiracy was the office of the satirical magazine *Pitorreos*, directed by Leoncio Martínez (Leo) and Francisco Pimentel (Job Pim) and managed by Eduardo Coll and Antonio José Calcaño Herrera. The conspirators met at the university, which although closed still housed the "National Education Council and was generally used for examinations by the university schools that were located elsewhere and some other schools."[229] Old man Piña, "the porter of the building,"[230] would take the conspirators to some remote classrooms, where Captain Luis Rafael Pimentel and Commander Manuel María Aponte, José Rafael Pocaterra, Job Pim, Pedro Manuel Ruiz, Gustavo Machado, Pedro Zuloaga, Jesús Corao, and others met. The decision to form a government was made in January, with a junta composed of León, Rafael Arévalo González, Nestor Luis Pérez, Leopoldo Torres Abandero, Nicómedes Zuloaga, Pedro Manuel Anibar, and General Félix Anibar. According to Pimentel the rebels had "the support of the American Minister"[231] and also received funds from Pulido, who was very wealthy. A prisoner under torture later confessed that Giuseppi Monagas, who was chair of the Senate Committee on Foreign Relations, had received $100,000 from American citizens for revolutionary purposes.[232]

The army conspirators, Pimentel, Captain Francisco Angarita Arvelo, Second Lieutenant Luis Aranguren Moreno, Captains Miguel and Cristóbal Parra Entrena, Second Lieutenant Pedro Betancourt Grillet, Major Manuel María Aponte, José Agustín Badaracco, Captain Carlos Mendoza, Aníbal Molina, Félix Andrade Mora, Domingo Mujica, Lieutenant Julio C. Hernández, and Lieutenant Jorge Ramírez, were all officers between twenty and thirty years old. The civilian leaders were Pocaterra, Avelino Martínez, Job Pim, and Pedro Manuel Ruíz. It was estimated that half the Ministry of Foreign Affairs was involved, as well as other officials and employees in other ministries. Iturbe, one of the main conspirators, appointed Aristeguieta as chief of the revolution in the East.[233] Aristeguieta's brother Francisco de Paúla Aristeguieta was the only link between the revolutionaries in exile and those in eastern Venezuela.

The date chosen for the uprising was January 16 because the officers on duty at the San Carlos, Artillería, and La Planta barracks and at the military academy were fellow conspirators. The Miraflores barracks would be attacked first because it was not part of the conspiracy. The plan was for Colonel Roberto González to detain Márquez Bustillos at midnight on January 15 at Dos Caminos and force him to resign. Salvador de la Plaza and Martín Tovar Lange were to go by motorcycle to Los Teques "to give instructions and help organize the brigades that would bomb the rail tracks and bridges, and the advance parties that would harass government troops during their move forward."[234] Other regime supporters would be removed from office, and it was expected that by the time the counterattack was mounted, the rebels would have gained enough strength to defeat them. A cannon blast by Captain Andrés Mora at 4 o'clock in the morning from the San Carlos barracks was supposed to signal the start of the revolt, but this never occurred.

On the eve of the uprising, the civilians Job Pim and Tancredo Pimentel, De la Plaza, Pedro Zuloaga, Antonio José Calcaño, Luciani, and Ramón Feo Calcaño met at the offices of Pitorreos to distribute revolutionary propaganda. At around nine o'clock that evening, Pimentel together with Mendoza and Hernández saw Captain José Agustín Piñero at his office in the Mamey barracks, wanting to know whether they could count on his support and if not for him to keep quiet. Piñero did not join the rebels and informed Colonel Lollot Márquez what was happening, with the result that the movement failed. (Gómez later promoted Piñero to the rank of colonel and gave him $960 for denouncing the plot.) Pimentel, realizing that the Trinidad barracks had not been taken, decided to attack the Artillería barracks. Hernández went in first to see what was happening and was caught, followed later by Pimentel with a number of other rebel officers arrested. Around a hundred people were arrested, including Iturbe, who had been secretary general of the 1903 Ejército Pacificador, governor of Caracas, and development minister and was jailed together with Hector Briceño, brother-in-law of Mosquera, the foreign affairs minister.

On January 16, General Pedro Alcántara Leal, commander of No. 1 Brigade, interrogated Pimentel, Mendoza, and Hernández. They were then sent to Villa Zoila in the Paraiso district of Caracas, together with Captain Miguel Parra Entrena, Lieutenant José Ramírez R., Lieutenant Aníbal Ramírez, Sub-Lieutenant Ricardo Corredor, Arturo Lara, José Agustín Bodaraco, Mujica, Aranguren Moreno, Betancourt Grillet, and Cristóbal Pávora Entrena, for further interrogation by José Vicente Gómez (Vicentico), Alcántara Leal, Aparicio Gómez, Modesto Torres, and León Zapata. Later Betancourt Grillet related to Carlos Emilio Fernández how Vicentico tortured him, threatening to hang him by the testicles if he did not reveal the civilian conspirators and sign a full confession. Betancourt Grillet was later sent to La Rotunda for refusing to divulge the names of Corao and Carabaño, the most important civilians in the coup. Pimentel, leader of the coup, was tortured eleven times and would later play an important role in Delgado Chalbaud's *Falke* expedition. Six days later, on January 21, fourteen army officers were taken to Villa Zoila and "flogged to such an extent that they had to be carried back to the main entrance of the 'Rotunda' political prison."[235]

Oil Enters into the Political Equation

After the Armistice in November 1918 the prices for Venezuela's traditional exports rose sharply, producing a short-lived economic boom in the country. World War I showed that Venezuela could not depend on customs receipts as its main source of public finance. The government decided to tap a new source of revenue that would equal or surpass customs receipts and lessen its dependence on international trade for tax receipts. A number of laws were enacted, such as the Ley Orgánica de la Hacienda Nacional, the Ley de Aduanas, the Ley Orgánica de Renta de Salinas, and the Ley de Papel Sellado Nacional, that by 1922 generated annual revenues of Bs 44.47 million compared with customs receipts of Bs 43.22 million in the same year.[236]

The production of oil that started flowing in large quantities during the mid-1920s gave the government a new source of revenue free from the volatility of customs receipts. The Anglo-Dutch concern of Shell was first in the country, followed by the entry of the large American oil companies such as Gulf Oil and Standard Oil Company (Indiana), which later sold its interests to Standard Oil Company (New Jersey). Soon after World War I, crude oil production in Venezuela started to rise, becoming in 1928 the second largest oil producer in the world, accounting for 8 percent of the world's crude oil production. The country's rapid increase in oil production was accompanied by a huge rise in foreign capital invested in the country to develop the oil industry. US investments, for example, in 1914 stood at $8 million, rising to $247.2 million in 1930, concentrated almost exclusively in the oil industry, compared with $125 million for British investments.

The wealth generated by the oil companies had a relatively small effect on the general economic conditions of the country, but its effects on Zulia in general and Maracaibo in particular were startling, with property values increasing to astronomical levels. The companies also acted with little concern for local sensibilities; for example, part of the oil produced from wells in Lake Maracaibo spilled into the water, causing pollution and many fires, instilling terror in the local population, with the companies refusing initially to recognize any claims for damages arising from them. Labor relations in the oilfields were also extremely bad.[237] The increased mobility of people within Zulia and between the Dutch West Indies and the mainland was a constant source of worry to the local authorities because it was difficult to control political activities and the dissemination of political ideas and literature against the regime. Pérez Soto's political surveillance of the state when he was president of Zulia was effective because he had the active help of the oil companies. An agreement was in place between the companies and the state government to collaborate and to keep a close watch on any subversive propaganda that took place in the oilfields. In early 1928, rumors reached Maracaibo that a revolutionary committee headed by Esteban Gil Borges and Santos Domínici had been formed in New York and had introduced a small cache of arms into Venezuela that Rafael Simón Urbina and his men would later use when the call for arms was made. It was reported that Jesús María Irazabal had introduced arms into the oil villages of La Rosa and Cabimas to be used during a strike, which could develop into "a rebellion in that State and in Coro according to Baptista and Olivares who will disembark in Coro in order to invade Lara State."[238]

In spite of the increase in oil activity during the mid-1920s, the government still depended heavily on customs receipts. Although oil taxes at the end of Gómez's regime accounted for nearly a third of total government revenues, customs duties were still the most important source of revenue. The political fortune of Gómez, however, changed with the discovery of oil in the country. The general feeling at the time was that the world was about to run out of petroleum reserves when crude oil consumption was about to take off. Consequently, the strong antipathy of the US administration against Gómez would mellow to one of tolerance. After 1920, Venezuela would no longer feel the cold shoulder of the major international powers. In a number of oil-related legal cases, the British government defended the regime against the United States because of the need to preserve British oil concessions.[239]

The oil companies were a natural focus for the revolutionaries in need of funds, and they were approached several times for finance in exchange for better and larger oil concessions. There was nothing novel about this approach. Mocho Hernández in 1914 virtually pledged the country to the Graaf, Sullivan, and Rowan Syndicate in return for transporting his men safely to Venezuela.[240] The following year Mocho Hernández entered into a similar agreement with Joseph Montague Roberts and James O'Brien.[241] Arévalo Cedeño also refers to a similar proposal made to him by an American businessman in the early 1920s.[242] Although the oil companies, especially the American ones, were suspected of financing various abortive invasions, they had a very limited involvement with the exiled political leaders. As we shall see, in 1926 Captain Harald Lindblad, a former Royal Swedish navy officer and Norwegian consul at Trinidad, on behalf of Ortega Martínez approached unsuccessfully a number of British oil companies for finance. In his trawl of the US National Archives Duffy finds no evidence of American oil companies supporting revolutionary activity against Gómez. Similarly, I did not find any trace of support for Venezuelan rebels by British oil companies in the Foreign Office archives at the Public Record Office or in the US State Department Archives.

There was one important personal link between the oil industry and the exiled revolutionaries through General Antonio Aranguren, who held the concession operated by the Venezuelan Oil Concessions Ltd. (VOC), a Royal Dutch–Shell subsidiary. Aranguren was also involved in other oil deals and was the most successful Venezuelan broker of oil concessions. As well as being on the board of VOC, Aranguren was also a director of the Venezuelan Eastern Oilfields Ltd. and the Venezuelan Consolidated Oilfields Ltd. In the late 1920s, he successfully negotiated with Gil Fortoul the national reserves acquired by Gómez's own company, the Compañía Venezolana de Petróleo (CVP), which were transferred to the Creole Syndicate.[243] Nevertheless, Aranguren was a fierce opponent of Gómez, partly financing Ortega Martínez's *Odin* expedition in 1921,[244] Baptista's *Angelita* expedition of 1924,[245] Román Delgado Chalbaud's *Falke* expedition of 1929,[246] and probably Urbina's *Superior* expedition of 1931. Many of these expeditions also received backing from sources close to the Mexican government.

The exiles in 1917–18 almost succeeded in getting the US government to openly support an armed revolutionary expedition against Gómez. There is little doubt that the American administration found the Gómez dictatorship distasteful, especially as it was unwilling to follow the United States into World War I. It is clear that without the US entry into the war Wilson would have sanctioned a more robust help for the exiles than just imposing sanctions that hurt the United States more than Venezuela. The active support of the United States would have given the exiles more funds and time to prepare an armed revolution that had a greater chance of success. It should be noted that the involvement of the United States did not include the sending of marines, as in the case of Haiti in 1914 and the Dominican Republic in 1916, because the country was too large to secure safely. Captain Parker, the American military attaché in 1904, came to the same conclusion after touring the country and drawing up plans for a possible military intervention.[247]

PART II

Consolidation of Power, 1917 – 1928

CHAPTER FOUR

The *Odin/Harrier* Expedition

Gómez withstood the attempts by the United States during 1917–18 to bring him down and the abortive January 1919 coup. Having lost the support of the United States, the exiles during the 1920s gained the support of the Mexican governments of Alvaro Obregón (1920–24), Plutarco Elías Calles (1924–28), and what is termed the Maximato, when Calles was known as the *jefe máximo* and was the power behind presidents Emilio Portes Gil (1928–34), Pascual Ortiz Rubio (1930–32), and Abelardo L. Rodríguez (1932–34). The political pressure on Gómez would continue during the decade, with the exiles turning their attention to organizing an armed expedition from Europe, where there was a plentiful supply of arms after the end of World War I.

With the failure of the January 1919 coup attempt and without the help of the United States, the exiles began to consider the possibility of a direct armed attack against Gómez, especially now that arms were in plentiful supply in Europe after the war. Rivas Vásquez, who had previously formed a loose political association called the Partido Progresista de Venezuela, decided in early 1919 to revive the group after Bolet Monagas approached him with a proposal to study, together with a number of other exiles living in New York, the political problems of Venezuela and how to resolve them. This led to the founding of the Unión Patriótica Venezolana in New York on February 15, 1919,[1] with its first meeting at the Hotel Ansonia. It was not a political party but a loose association of "children of the same fatherland who are inspired by the same intentions and who aspire to establish in Venezuela governments based on the law and the exercise by its citizens of all their rights."[2] Rivas Vásquez at the founding meeting called for the end of *personalismo* (cult of the leader)[3] and dictatorship as a form of government. The association published a newspaper, the *Unión Patriótica,* edited by Domingo B. Castillo, Ramón Muñoz Tebar, José Heriberto López, and the brothers Horacio and Oscar Blanco Fombona.[4] Local branches in La Habana, Mexico, Costa Rica, Panama, Puerto Rico, and Colombia were soon established to discuss "the great interests of the fatherland,"[5] to end "for ever in Venezuela discretionary governments, . . . to put to an end feudalism and to establish an effective republic."[6]

In more concrete terms, Rivas Vasquez suggested establishing a central command to act as a mediator between the various revolutionary groupings. Under his proposal, Baptista would be appointed war minister, with the country divided into two military districts: the eastern states and certain central states would be headed by Ortega Martínez, while Mocho Hernández would lead the western states and the other central states.[7] Once the revolution succeeded, Ayala would be appointed the provisional president until presidential elections, under free and democratic rules, took place. The plan was opposed by the Peñalistas, Olivaristas, and Mochistas, and more particularly the Ciprianistas,[8] as they had their own plans. In September, Bolet Monagas, Oscar Blanco Fombona, Leónidas Brige, and A. Granado Rodríguez addressed a note to Venezuela's attorney general requesting him to restore the country to normality and to allow the formation of political parties.

Other Venezuelan exiles at the time with a different political ideology also established new political organizations. In Panama, the Venezuelan exiles Humberto Tejera, Horacio Blanco Fombona, L. Guevara Travieso, Luis Felipe Nava, and Juan Manuel Sanoja founded in 1919 the Partido Republicano de Venezuela, subscribing to the "fundamental propositions of universal socialism"[9] to establish a government "for the majorities, not for an oligarchic group, less for a sole leader; and for that reason we will destroy the large estates and distribute land among the farmers."[10] Although the party was more interested in agrarian issues, it would also sponsor labor unions despite the small proletariat in the country. It believed in federalism and would grant each state its economic independence.

The exiled regional caudillos continued organizing their filibustering expedition to topple Gómez, but the date was put back after the military plot in Venezuela failed. Ortega Martínez continued preparations for his Revolución Constitucionalista, with Baptista as *jefe de estado mayor.* Castro and his close family contributed funds toward the revolution, with the operational center based in Puerto Rico, where the Cabito lived. The revolutionaries planned their operations at the branch of the Unión Patriótica Venezolana, which operated in a club run by Rafael Martínez located next to Castro's own home in Santurce. Most of the revolutionaries stayed at the Hotel Palace, with L. González Pacheco, the Venezuelan consul at San Juan, Puerto Rico, moving into the hotel so that he could keep an even closer eye on developments.

After long and heated discussions the start of the revolution was set for April 22, 1919. The plan of attack conceived by the revolutionaries was modeled on the 1901–1903 Matos Libertadora revolution, and one that was repeated often over the next twelve years. This consisted of a simple pincer movement to isolate and concentrate Gómez's forces at Caracas. Peñaloza would attack from Colombia through Táchira, with one rebel group heading for Rubio and another to Colón. In a coordinated move, Ortega Martínez would land his troops in the East with the rebel forces converging on Caracas. Their initial plan was for Castro, together with Durán, Vargas, and General Rojas, to travel first to New York via Cuba and then, with arrangements finalized in Europe, to proceed to Colombia.

Once agreement was reached, the revolutionaries left Puerto Rico to organize their own theater of operations, with Peñaloza traveling to Cúcuta to prepare the western front. In March, Carabaño, who was Ortega Martínez's agent, together with Durán left Puerto Rico for Trinidad to brief the Castristas on the island, such as Mendible and Asunción Rodríguez, who would command the troops in eastern Venezuela with Carmelo Castro. Aristeguieta, who was in Trinidad at the time, immediately placed himself at the service of Asunción Rodríguez. Later, Mendible traveled with Horacio Maldonado to Rio Hacha in Colombia. Gómez's spy network kept abreast of what was happening, informing the dictator that an uprising would take place on April 27, 1919, in Rubio and Colón with good "officer material."[11] The Venezuelan government immediately requested Colombia to put an end to their plans by deporting Peñaloza,[12] who left for Puerto Rico on a schooner in August 1919, almost drowning during the voyage when he was swept overboard.

Although the funds for an expedition were secured through Dr. Luis Loreto Biamón,[13] who was married to Castro's niece, and Aranguren, their main problem was acquiring a cache of arms and ammunition and a vessel in Europe to transport it to Venezuela. In order to expedite matters, Ortega Martínez, Tellería, and Baptista traveled to Europe to acquire the ordnance and the ship. This was made easier through the good efforts of Castro, who managed to get the Nicaraguan government of Emiliano Chamorro Vargas to appoint the Venezuelan Carlos Villanueva as the new Nicaraguan chargé d'affaires at its legation in Paris.[14] Villanueva had been consul general of Venezuela in London in 1913, and later secretary of the Venezuelan legation at Paris, from where he was dismissed, turning against Gómez.

The revolutionaries received a further boost when Rivas Vásquez informed them that the Cuban government would support the revolution. Dr. Clemente Vásquez Bello, Rivas Vásquez's partner in Cuba who had been secretary to President Gerardo Machado y Morales, approached the Cuban government of Aurelio Mario Gabriel Francisco García Menocal y Deop and obtained the promise that the Cuban government would finance the revolution up to $325,000. The money came out of secret funds, and to disguise the expenditure, a share issue took place that was only subscribed by the government. Aristeguieta was sent to Cuba to supervise the establishment of a company and the transfer of funds to Europe. A few days after the shares were issued but before the money was paid in, Menocal and Colonel Charles Hernández, the interior minister, informed Rivas Vásquez that the Cuban government would not be involved in the revolution because everything would be provided by "a North American gentleman who is a good friend of yours and with a debt of gratitude, who in addition is a man of great wealth who had generously helped Cuba during its War of Independence."[15] Menocal promised, however, to cooperate if the offer of funds in New York did not materialize.

Aristeguieta left immediately for New York, where he met the US citizen, obtaining from him a verbal offer that he would provide a ship. Aristeguieta already had the promise of two thousand rifles from an undisclosed source believed to be the Mexican government. The progress made by the revolutionaries at this juncture was excellent, with Flores departing for Trinidad to help Asunción Rodríguez prepare for the invasion, while Tellería in Cuba and Baptista in New York were placed on alert. The enthusiasm soon vanished when the offer of a ship never materialized and Aristeguieta on his return to Cuba was greeted with the news that Menocal had definitely withdrawn his support, losing the $10,000 donated by Carlos Rojas[16] in a futile trip to the United States.

In Europe, Ortega Martínez continued his search for a ship with Henry Beaumont, the former British minister in Caracas, sending him the details of a stern wheeler ordered by the government of Mesopotamia that was suitable for navigating and transporting troops in the Upper Orinoco and could be purchased for $211,132. Further particulars followed on a thousand-ton steamer for transporting both passengers and cargo.[17] In the end, Ortega Martínez settled on purchasing a ship and arms in Germany, pending payment. His other lieutenants now joined him to acquire the arms and sail to Venezuela to start the revolution. Alcántara left Curacao for Puerto Rico on November 24, 1919, to continue his trip to Paris for treatment of an alleged ear infection but in reality to join Ortega Martínez and the other revolutionaries in Europe. While in Puerto Rico, Alcántara met Simón Barceló, his old friend and Gómez's agent, confiding in him his plans because he felt that his old compadre would be incapable of revealing his plans to the government. Once he arrived in France, Villanueva issued him a Nicaraguan passport on December 29, stating that he was the Nicaraguan legation's new secretary and authorizing him to acquire war material in Germany for the government of Nicaragua.[18]

The revolutionaries were in serious financial trouble, however. At a crisis meeting they estimated that $40,000 was needed to purchase the ship and arms, with Rivas Vásquez contributing $15,000 from his very profitable liquor factory, the Sociedad Anónima de la Creem du Vie (Ponche Crema), in Cuba. This still left a shortfall of $25,000. In November, Carabaño gave power of attorney to his nephew Manuel Morales Carabaño to sell his estates La Estancia and Quebrada de Apa in Venezuela to provide funds for the revolution. Toward the end of January 1920, Baptista and Víctor Barret de Nazaris left New York for Curacao, with many of the other revolutionaries departing from New York to go to Cuba. In Curacao, Baptista and his brother Víctor Manuel met Carabaño and Torcuato Ortega Martínez at their second-class Hotel Europa.[19] The other revolutionaries living in Curacao also met to prepare for the forthcoming revolution and to settle their financial affairs as well as keeping some of the other exiles living on the island and in Colombia informed of their plans. A brother of Olivares had six hundred rifles hidden in Curacao, which could be offered to the revolution. The Baptistas divided up their inheritance, valued at $26,871, not including a "property they left undivided, and empowered their brother Napoleón to either manage or sell it."[20] At the same time, J. C. Sotillo Picornell, together with members of the Venezuelan colony and students living in Curacao formed the Unión Libertadora Venezolana.[21] At the end of February, Baptista and Torcuato Ortega Martínez returned to New York, while Víctor Manuel Baptista and Carabaño and his wife departed for the Dominican Republic. Many of the revolutionaries such as Ayala, Vargas, and Carabaño traveled on false passports issued by other countries.[22]

Internal Politics

At the time, the Gómez regime was experiencing a number of labor disputes as well as incurring the displeasure of certain European countries. The Belgian chargé d'affaires Bourseaux, echoing the previous American and British sentiments, advised his government that foreign intervention was the only answer to the Gómez regime and that the Allied powers should topple the government on behalf of the political prisoners of the country and more specifically certain pro-Belgian students who had demonstrated against Gómez at the conclusion of the Armistice in November 1918. Dormer, the British minister, felt that this was impractical because it would be bitterly resented and "it would probably produce a revolution with all its attendant bloodshed, and the same oppression of opponents would continue under possibly another form but with some cloak of justification."[23] Britain had most to lose as the other countries that had been called in the joint intervention against Venezuela, viz, the United States, France, Brazil, Italy, and Cuba, only had small financial investments in the country and could contemplate such action "without any hesitation as to its effects."[24] The United States favored intervening not for humanitarian reasons but, as Dormer pointed out, because McGoodwin, the US minister at Caracas, was "aggrieved that he is not meeting with greater success in his various dealings with the Venezuelan Government,"[25] especially with a number of oil concessions. Without British support it was unlikely that any foreign government intervention would prosper.

Gómez also had to deal at the time with a potentially damaging industrial dispute in the port of La Guaira. On March 1, 1920, the workers of La Guaira port, operated by a British company, formed themselves into a union called the Asociación de Obreros de la Corporación del Puerto de la Guaira, with Miguel Bolívar as president and Francisco González Blanco as secretary, for the purpose of guaranteeing "our work for the Company, the defense of our interests, and the strict fulfillment of our duties.[26] J. H. Wall, the general manager, was surprised at the formation of such a society because he had never mistreated his employees. However, many workers refused to join the new grouping when it became plain that it was to be a union rather than a mutual aid society. Miguel Bolívar threatened the workers with the loss of their jobs if they left the association. Wall disagreed strongly with such a move because the association could not usurp the company's position of hiring or firing people, issuing a statement on March 8 banning the organization from operating within the company's property. The following day, both Bolívar and Blanco were fired, followed by the treasurer of the association, which led to a strike in protest at such an action. A total of 90 workers out of a workforce of 250 went on strike, preventing the *Manzanares* being loaded with cargo. Wall solved the problem by employing new workers to fill the 90 new vacancies. Wall also sought help from the local prefect, who "immediately detained the 3 agitators and then personally came to talk with the strikers."[27] The prefect tried to convince the strikers to return to work, but they ignored his advice because they wanted the three leaders reinstated at their old jobs, an impossibility because they had "meddled in the management of the Corporation."[28]

The Revolutionaries Continue Their Plans

The plan for an invasion of Venezuela continued apace. It was agreed that Castro would join Peñaloza at the appropriate time on the Colombian border in order to invade Venezuela. However, on the eve of his departure to Colombia Castro became very ill, with "a serious infection in the hand, and with acute and persistent pain over the whole arm,"[29] with the doctors noting "a gangrenous point"[30] on it. Castro was suffering with "very acute joint rheumatism that kept him in agony all day and night and screaming with pain";[31] the doctors considered amputating his arm but ultimately decided against it. His physical condition was further complicated by "an intestinal infection and congestion in the kidneys"[32] and his need of assistance for "his daily personal chores because his arm and leg are paralyzed."[33] Under such conditions, it was impossible for Castro to travel to Colombia; he went instead to Barranquitas in Puerto Rico to recuperate.

With Castro out of the picture for the time being and Ortega Martínez in Europe trying to secure a cache of arms, Peñaloza postponed his invasion plans and returned to New York in April, where he reached agreement with Olivares, Baptista, and Tellería to work jointly to support the coming revolution. The revolutionaries were further encouraged by the events happening in Guatemala; they still maintained a forlorn hope that the Americans would support their revolutionary activities. Manuel Jové and Flores arrived in Trinidad to brief the rebels on the island, especially Asunción Rodríguez, reassuring them that all was ready "with the exception of a good steam boat."[34] In early May, Castro returned from Barranquitas, having made a miraculous recovery, and was now working hard to secure funds for the revolution. Most of the money for the armed invasion of Venezuela would come from Biamón and Eduardo Georgetti, a Puerto Rican millionaire,[35] in exchange for "large concessions that will be awarded to them when they take power."[36] In addition, it is also likely that Aranguren contributed $113,435, while a number of other Venezuelans in New York, Puerto Rico, and Europe donated smaller sums.[37]

Georgetti was described by González Pacheco, the Venezuelan minister on the island, as a "rich financier and banker of this country, that has a stake in almost all the businesses of this island."[38] He was the main shareholder in the newspaper *La Democracia,* a leading politician of the Partido Unión, the largest on the island, and at the time was vice president of the island's Senate and a personal enemy of Governor Emmet Montgomery Reily.[39] Diego Agueros, the main partner in the merchant trading house of Diego Agueros and Company, was also a sworn enemy of Gómez on the island. Agueros was continually seen in secret meetings and was a "co-owner and agent of the *Meteor* schooner that frequently sails between Maracaibo, Puerto Cabello and Coro,"[40] with captain Vidal E. Prince, "an irreconcilable enemy of yours and the government."[41] In May 1920, Diego Agueros traveled to Maracaibo and Coro via Curacao, returning with "important business matters"[42] and boasting that "he met and dealt with many friends of the Venezuelan exiles in Puerto Rico, taking and bringing news, and by the means already indicated, he was able to fool the Consulate and the authorities in Venezuela."[43] Diego Agueros through his eponymous company allowed passengers and merchandise to leave for Venezuela without the consul's permission because most of it was sent to Curacao; he was in collusion with Waldemar E. Lee, vice-consul of the Netherlands in San Juan. The enemies of Gómez also used the Red "D" Line and obtained visas to Curacao through Lee.

One example of this was Plácido Martínez Areas, a twenty-seven-year-old Spaniard from Pontevedra, who first arrived in Puerto Rico in 1909 from Montreal. In Venezuela he called himself Daniel Plácido Martínez, but according to González Pacheco he was "a BANDIT, capable of doing everything that is bad, *because he is very clever*" (emphasis in original),[44] establishing a trading business called Martínez y Morales and obtaining "flour mills representations."[45] He placed large flour orders "that he sold here, pocketing the money, as the business failed due to fraud and not bankruptcy and this was repeated twice: the first time for around $70,000 and the second time for $35,000."[46] Later, Plácido Martínez was tried and deported from the island, settling in Venezuela. Since the consul refused to issue a visa, he obtained one in Curacao from Dutch Consul Lee and settled in La Guaira. Arthur Yager, the governor of Puerto Rico, assured González Pacheco that he would help to combat such subversive elements, but there was no law they could use to stop them. The use of this method allowed any correspondence or persons from Venezuela to come in and out of San Juan without González Pacheco knowing about it.[47]

Ortega Martínez Secures a Boat

In early February 1920, Ortega Martínez, who was now sixty-one years old and considered a wealthy person with a personal fortune estimated at $767,754,[48] was in London securing a boat and arms but without much success. Ortega Martínez was also trying to curry British government support by offering to "remove the 30 percent West Indian duty,"[49] but the British refused to help. After the disappointment of London, Ortega Martínez and Villanueva made a promising contact in Paris that offered the possibility of acquiring the necessary funds. Ysaac Ain Bendelac,[50] a French businessman living in Paris, allowed the plotters to use his Paris office as a central base for their operations. Bendelac was associated with the trading firm of Levy and Barros, which finally secured for the revolutionaries in Kiel the *Odin*[51] for the large sum of $109,800, making them "pay out double the budgeted amount."[52] The ship, which consumed large quantities of coal, was acquired by W. H. Melleman and Company and registered in Bendelac's name.

At the same time, the exiles continued their quest to obtain another ship and arms in Britain. While in Paris, Georgetti met William Henry Billal Quilliam, a former British solicitor who had been struck off the rolls in June 1909. Georgetti used Quilliam to ostensibly establish a company in London to finance a sugar plantation in the Dominican Republic, but he was to act as a decoy in acquiring arms for the revolutionaries through the Nicaraguan legation. Quilliam became the agent of the Venezuelan exiles in the purchase of a small gunboat in England, together with arms and ammunition, "because they had made a secret treaty with Colombia."[53] Quilliam believed that Carabaño was a general in the Nicaraguan army and that once the arms were acquired he would travel to Paris to inspect them. Later, on September 27, 1920, Villanueva authorized Alcántara to acquire war material for the Nicaraguan government, which would allegedly be sent to the port of Corinto[54] in Nicaragua. Toward the end of October 1920, while Alcántara was in Germany purchasing the *Odin,* Villanueva placed an order with Vickers Ltd. of the United Kingdom for a 250-foot-long sloop of the Flower class, together with two four-inch guns, ten thousand rifles, five million cartridges, two airplanes, fifty machine guns, and ammunition.[55] In order to fulfill the order, Vickers Ltd. needed the Foreign Office's approval, but Villanueva did not want the British government involved, as they would check with Managua and discover that there was no official Nicaraguan minister at Paris.

Toward the end of September there was great enthusiasm and expectation of events that were to unfold. The exiles scattered around the Caribbean and in Colombia were convinced that Ortega Martínez had acquired a boat with sufficient arms and was about to make the voyage south. Now that the revolution appeared to be getting off the ground, at the end of 1920 the revolutionaries in Europe, viz, Ortega Martínez, Baptista, Carabaño, Biamón, F.H. Rivero, Villanueva, and Aristeguieta signed the Pacto de Paris, which had as its main objective the toppling of Gómez. The pact would end on March 31, 1921,[56] and any opponent of Gómez was welcome to join. The members of the pact would elect a *jefe supremo de la revolución,* who would have under him a *jefe del estado mayor general,* a *sub-jefe del estado mayor general,* and a *secretario.* Ortega Martínez would head the revolution, and it was up to him to acquire the necessary arms. When the revolution reached Caracas, the "Supreme Leader will appoint a Junta composed of the heads of the Army Corps, and those who are absent will nominate their representatives, so that by a majority of votes they will elect three out of the seven members that will form the first Cabinet, with the Supreme Head designating the portfolios that these three Ministers will hold."[57] Once power was achieved, popular elections would take place to elect a president for a period of four years with no reelection allowed. The new government's main social agenda was to increase public health and education.

The plan was for Baptista to attack through the Andes, while Tellería invaded Coro from Curacao. Tellería, a fifty-year-old Coriano and related by marriage to Ortega Martínez, would lead the military offensive in the West. Alcántara, also fifty years old and a graduate of West Point, would be Ortega Martínez's chief of staff and war and navy minister in the new cabinet. Asunción Rodríguez, who was of humble origins and had taken up arms in 1913 supporting Castro's invasion with a large following in the East, especially on Margarita Island, would lead the eastern army. In the event of success, Asunción Rodríguez would be appointed either as a cabinet minister or Federal District governor. The other important members of the revolution were the Nacionalistas Mocho Hernandez, who was sixty-eight years old, and Vargas, a civil engineer by training who had a large following in Guárico and Apure states. Other members of the revolutionary council included González Guinán, one of the oldest and possibly a compromise candidate for the presidency; Alberto Smith, who was sixty years old, an engineer by profession, had worked in Cuba with the Cuban Sugar Cane Company, and was a possible education minister; Iturbe, forty-four years old and also an engineer, who according to a State Department note was "one of the leading political figures of Venezuela";[58] Augusto Pulido, forty-eight years old and married to Miss Bell, a wealthy American from Philadelphia; Pedro María Brito González, sixty-one years old and a lawyer; Carabaño, fifty years old, who started his political career with former president Joaquín Crespo; Baptista, fifty-five years old and a lawyer; and, finally Olivares, fifty years old.[59]

The *jefe de revolución* would be appointed interim president as soon as the rebels entered Caracas, with Ortega Martínez and his interim cabinet taking the necessary steps to pay back the "Revolution's contracted debt above all others."[60] Once the interim government was named, it would appoint provisional state presidents, and when two-thirds of the national territory was under control of the new government, elections would be held either directly or through the *concejos municipales,* which would "have arisen from direct popular suffrage,"[61] for a national constituent assembly and for state constituent assemblies, with each state represented by three deputies. The national assembly would be accountable to the interim president, approve a new constitution, and elect a provisional president.

In Paris, Aristeguieta agreed to join the pact and acknowledge Ortega Martínez's leadership. He nevertheless had strong reservations about how politically successful the revolution would be because "there is no remedy for Venezuela and it is likely to fall into an incurable abyss if from the beginning of this fight we do not break with the past and bury for ever the monster of absolutism,"[62] proposing instead that there should be no single overall leader. Aristeguieta returned to Trinidad to organize the rebels, while Ortega Martínez and Alcántara in August held a number of meetings with Tello Mendoza and Luis Núñez in Paris with negative results initially but in the end reaching agreement. All revolutionaries, with the exception of Olivares, who was against the pact because of its focus on the *personalismo* aspect referred to by Aristeguieta and therefore dependent on the whim of the leader,[63] were united in a front. The revolution was set for October.

The sale of the rebels' property continued to finance the revolution. Oscar Blanco Fombona sold his boarding house in Santo Domingo, while Carabaño sold his farm in Puerto Rico, and Durán was in the middle of selling the hotel he owned jointly with another Venezuelan exile.[64] Castro was so convinced of his return to Caracas that he requested his nephew, the son of his sister Dona Laurencia Castro de Lázaro (married to José Hilario Lázaro, a Colombian), to get the Venezuelan legation at Puerto Rico to grant power of attorney to George M. Curtis, the manager of the National City Bank of New York in Caracas, to inspect Villa Zoila, Castro's old residence in the El Paraiso district of the capital to see what repairs were needed.[65]

The plans were proceeding well for the revolutionaries. Peñaloza's son, who worked for the Globe Oil Company of Colombia, was so sure that the revolution would succeed that he openly broadcast the invasion plans, stating that the rebels "have a steam boat that will leave England shortly under the Dutch flag."[66] Peñaloza's son also promised the revolutionaries the use of the oil company's river barges to transport a cache of arms up the Magdalena River. The employment of Peñaloza's son by the American oil company also led to rumors among the exiled Venezuelan community in Colombia that an oil company was backing their cause in exchange for oil concessions in Venezuela. The rumors were so persistent that Peñaloza's son was dismissed by the company. In August, Peñaloza Sr. left Cartagena on board the *Crynssen* for Curacao to meet other revolutionaries to finalize plans before returning to Colombia, where in September he was joined by Carabaño from New York. It was clear that the Colombian authorities were aware of Peñaloza's invasion plan because the armed expedition was organized and planned in Cúcuta and the arms were purchased locally. Messages were sent to the rebels' supporters in Caracas using a longtime American resident, who also acted as the "intermediary between the rebels and the American Minister, who . . . has news that favors the interests of the revolution."[67]

In early October, Peñaloza launched his abortive revolution by crossing the Colombian/Venezuelan border at Michelena with eight hundred men in the mistaken belief that Ortega Martínez was about to disembark from Europe with a boat full of revolutionaries. In his *proclamación*, Peñaloza called for all Venezuelans to join the fight for "liberty and justice."[68] Peñaloza's rebellion was short-lived, as he was met by three thousand Venezuelan troops who quickly suppressed the rebellion, leaving seventy dead rebels, with the rest disbanding quickly. The Venezuelan government immediately launched a strong critical attack on the Colombian government. Dormer, the British minister, reported that the most sensational rumors emanated from the American legation, as the chargé d'affaires "had received a cable from his Government asking for news before most people here knew that anything had happened, and he took such a serious view of it that he seems to have contemplated asking for a warship."[69] The US government sent a warship, which in the absence of any internal disturbances demanded reparations for the wrongful imprisonment in October 1920 of the American manager of the National City Bank at Maracaibo, leading to strained diplomatic relations between the two countries for a while. The attitude of the US government toward the Venezuelan administration at the time was one of general disapproval that "they do not hesitate to make felt on the smallest provocation."[70] The Americans, according to Dormer, were "unpopular in the country, and their business methods have aroused widespread disgust."[71] The fear and suspicion that such an attitude created within the Gómez government was responsible for the Venezuelan dictator's failure to accept an American military mission and to set up an aviation school under American direction. Instead, a French offer to establish a flying school was accepted. The visit of the warship, however, made the Venezuelan government react and accept the US claim.

The news of Peñaloza's invasion initially encouraged the revolutionaries in New York to lower their guard, with reports circulating that the rebels had acquired in Germany a ship called the *Santiago* and were waiting for a captain (probably Guillermo Egea Mier) to sail it to Venezuela. The plan was for Alcántara, as *jefe de estado mayor de la revolución oriente,* to disembark with five hundred rifles in Caimancito in the Araya peninsula and then to distribute the arms among the rebels ready for a general uprising on December 20. In spite of these developments, despondency and recrimination among the revolutionaries in Puerto Rico started soon after receiving the news of Peñaloza's failure, who was accused of setting back the revolution by acting prematurely. Long meetings and debates took place to decide what to do next. Most of the Venezuelan revolutionaries on the island, including Carabaño, Durán, Vargas, Trino Baptista, and Luis López Méndez, met every morning at General Rojas's rooms to plan the rebellion. The exiles would also meet at a club they had at 10 Barcelona Street in Santurce, and then armed with a new plan they would confer with Castro. In order to confuse Gómez's spy network, Castro was portrayed as being very ill and not an active player, but González Pacheco, the Venezuelan consul, reported that this was a lie because he had fully recovered his health and was looking fit and strong.[72] The exiles on the Colombian border, who numbered between five thousand and seven thousand, wanted Castro to take up the leadership, but until the return of Biamón and Georgetti from Europe, it was not clear whether Ortega Martínez had acquired a ship. Hence the invasion plans were postponed until December 1920.

When Georgetti and Biamón returned from Europe, it was agreed that Carabaño, López Méndez, and others should travel to Europe to join Ortega Martínez to help him organize the expedition. Castro would later join them in Europe but would travel first to Cuba to convince Mocho Hernández to join the revolutionaries, and then proceed to the United States to cash in a letter of credit for $27,000 he had with the Guaranty Trust Company of New York. Consequently, in December 1920 Castro left Puerto Rico for Santiago de Cuba on the *Barcelona*, with his old equerry Enrique Acosta, Durán, and Rojas. Castro, who traveled under the assumed name of M. V. González in order to evade Gómez's spy network, arrived in Habana on December 28, where he was granted a three-day visa for the United States, since his alleged final destination was Spain.

Castro was suffering with a heavy cold and looked almost like a tramp when he arrived in Havana, with the Cuban secret police reporting that he was in a state of "filth that was shameful."[73] According to an eyewitness, Castro was "was badly dressed and ill with a cold; he looked like a beggar. Although appearances can be deceptive with this sly character, it is a fact that Castro is 'throwing his last shots' as they say, and if there is something that he is looking for at this stage is for you to apprehend him any day now."[74] Mocho Hernández was in no better shape, suffering from a bladder complaint "that every moment makes him scurry into the first establishment that he finds in the street to relieve the bladder."[75] It was clear that these enemies of Gómez were in no physical condition to undertake the rigors of an armed expedition, even if they managed to agree to the terms. Rafael Angel Ruiz, the Venezuelan consul general at Havana, described Castro and Mocho Hernández as two geriatrics "in total physical and moral ruin, dragging their old age . . . and it is no exaggeration to state that neither are in condition to resist three late nights or twenty-four hours on horse back."[76] While in Havana, Castro also met with Rivas Vásquez several times to discuss the Menocal episode.

Venezuelan Government Unaware of Events

The Venezuelan government up to November 1920 remained blissfully unaware of the preparations by the revolutionaries in Europe. It was only then, when Captain C. L. Hirschfeld, a German citizen previously employed at the Puerto Cabello shipyard, alerted Simón Barceló, the Venezuelan minister at

Paris, that the government became aware of these events.[77] Barceló immediately informed Gil Fortoul, the Venezuelan foreign affairs minister, and Herr Sturup, the Venezuelan consul in Hamburg, who with the cooperation of the German police located the *Odin* in Kiel loaded with arms and ammunition from Germany,[78] with Alcántara onboard and about to leave for Amsterdam.[79] The ship was registered in the Netherlands while it was refitted and loaded with more arms. In Amsterdam the subversive intentions of the rebels were confirmed when a crate allegedly containing a piano was found to be full of arms. According to the captain, the cargo brought to Amsterdam was in "long and heavy boxes, registered as machinery, that could not be transferred in the port here but would be offloaded either at sea or at an English port."[80] The Dutch authorities sequestered the boat, and Alcántara was arrested. José Ignacio Cárdenas used his influence with C. Beelaerts,[81] director of the *corps diplomatique* in the Hague, to sabotage the ship and prevent the rebels from slipping away unnoticed by the authorities. The Venezuelan diplomat reported that after "*that accident* [*sic*] we have given those blackguards a blow to the spinal cord that will keep them paralyzed,"[82] and "they were forced to leave it there, from where I hope it will never leave."[83]

The British Connection

In the meantime, Quilliam acquired in Britain the SS *Harrier* from a Mr. Sailes for $155,550 and registered the ship in his name. According to José Ignacio Cárdenas, Georgetti provided $95,160 for the purchase of a ship. The *Harrier* was completely refurbished and overhauled at a cost of $36,600 and was expected to sail in March. In January 1921, Villanueva placed another large ordnance order, this time through Quilliam, for a thousand rifles, a thousand cartridge belts, twenty-five machine guns, five million rounds of ammunition for rifles and machine guns, and one four-inch gun with a hundred rounds of ammunition.[84] Later, Villanueva would deny placing this order, but there is no doubt that he did because he freely admitted it when confronted in Paris by Ian I. Bannon and James McBrien of the Special Branch of Scotland Yard, confessing that it was a "private matter in which he alone was concerned and of which the Nicaraguan Government has no knowledge."[85] Quilliam however was convinced that he was acting on behalf of the Nicaraguan government and that the Foreign Office would have to approve the sale of arms from Vickers.[86]

The Venezuelan government was getting anxious at these events. On February 11, Gil Borges requested Beaumont to press for assistance to be rendered in London to prevent any transshipment of arms sent there. Beaumont felt that Gómez had been so helpful in the successful recent litigation by British oil companies[87] that the British government should give him all possible assistance, but warned that it had to act with caution because it did not want to offend the Nicaraguans. On February 16 R. Sperling at the Foreign Office requested the Board of Trade to keep him informed of any arms shipments to Nicaragua or to any countries bordering Venezuela. At the same time, Carabaño arrived in London to inspect the boat acquired by Quilliam and when questioned by Scotland Yard admitted to "collecting arms to overthrow President Gómez."[88] Soon afterwards he was deported, leaving for Paris, and warned not to return to the country. The same warning was given to Ortega Martínez, Alcántara, and Bendelac.

The admission of guilt already referred to by Villanueva when he was interviewed by the Special Branch in Paris was sufficient proof for the Foreign Office to request the Admiralty to render unworkable the engine of the SS *Harrier*, which was moored at Swansea. The departure of the *Harrier* was further delayed by the British authorities until proof of her final destination was confirmed, and Vickers was warned that it would be prosecuted under the Foreign Enlistment Act if it sold arms to the plotters. Later, the collector of customs executed a warrant for the seizure of the ship for contravening the Foreign Enlistment Act. At this moment most of the revolutionaries realized that the game was up. Castro, described by González Pacheco as "finished,"[89] returned to Puerto Rico from Cuba toward the end of February, spending most of his time recuperating at the Coamo baths.

The revolutionaries in March 1921 regrouped, with the pieces of the jigsaw falling into place. According to Juan Tinoco, a revolutionary who arrived in San Juan from New York, Olivares was near Táchira, while Vargas was in Apure, and others soon would be at their appointed posts. Castro had recovered his health, according to the testimony of Antonia Alvárez, his concubine. The plan now was for Baptista to invade through the Andes, while Tellería attacked Coro from Curacao. However, Tellería was not ready, after having traveled from New York to Santo Domingo in April 1921 and returning later to the United States.[90] Ortega Martínez remained in Paris, with Alcántara leaving for the United States in early April and Carabaño proceeding to Colombia after stopping at Puerto Rico on May 10. In June, Olivares, Baptista, Carabaño, and Peñaloza had returned from the Colombian border with Venezuela and were in Barranquilla ready to leave Colombia. It was clear, as the Venezuelan consul Luis F. Aranda reported at the time, that "anarchy reigns among the various personal factional enemy groups and they are very discouraged in their intentions."[91]

In early June, Olivares and Vargas, unaware that the *Odin* was detained, crossed into Venezuela at El Amparo, with about 500 badly armed men. The rebels marched toward Guasdualito to secure arms but were met by Pérez Soto, with 290 men killed on both sides.[92] In spite of this setback the revolutionaries continued with their preparations. The plan now was for Ortega Martínez and Alcántara to invade Venezuela from the Andes. The exiles also continued their efforts to persuade US President Warren G. Harding to support their cause.[93] They were further encouraged when Preston McGoodwin was replaced by Willis C. Cook as American minister, with Ortega Martínez informing Nicolás Hernández that "Gómez loses a good friend."[94] In the United States, Ortega Martínez together with the Peruvian minister in Washington saw Cook at the State Department "in the hope that some progress towards assisting the revolution might be made in this country."[95] In particular, Ortega Martínez wanted permission to purchase arms and ammunition in the United States and then to ship the cache of arms to Venezuela. He suspected that Shell had given him away, leading to the confiscation of the *Harrier* in the United Kingdom because Gómez had reached an understanding with the Anglo-Dutch oil company over certain disputed oil concessions.[96] In spite of this, at the meeting Ortega Martínez stressed that the rebels had reached an agreement with Shell to grant the company further oil concessions in the event of the revolution being successful, something that was untrue.

The revolution during this period lost one of its most enduring and unlucky caudillos when Mocho Hernández died in New York on August 25, 1921, at the age of sixty-eight. A few days later on August 30, Nicolás Hernández, Mocho's son, issued a flysheet in New York against Gómez titled "Política Venezolana al Nacionalismo," accusing the Venezuelan government of being dictated by "mercantilism" in that "a large number of politicians lack true patriotism: where the doctrinaire parties have disappeared to be replaced by personalist groups: where the dignity and love for the fatherland are exhausted: where foreign powers see us as savages and where the greatest horrors and outrages are carried out."[97]

The enquiries made by the Venezuelan foreign affairs minister with Managua showed that there was no Nicaraguan minister at Paris and that they were not aware of the purchase of "a ship by the Nicaraguan government"[98] as Beaumont informed the Foreign Office. This was confirmed by

M. W. Gaisford, British minister at Guatemala, who stated that the "Nicaraguan Government are totally unaware of what has happened."[99] This was clearly untrue, because Villanueva was known to the Nicaraguan government and was an accredited Nicaraguan diplomat who attended the Paris Peace Conference representing the country and had signed the accord that contained a clause forbidding the trade of German war surplus material. Indeed, the French government in mid-1921 conferred the Legion d'Honneur on Villanueva for his services at the Paris Peace Conference, hastily withdrawing it afterwards, claiming that the award was the result of a bureaucratic error. In mid-April 1921 the British government sought information from the US government on Villanueva, keeping the French abreast of what occurred. It also sought from the Nicaraguan government assurances that Villanueva's activities would cease in the future, but he had already left Paris for Italy.[100]

Cárdenas was so happy with the outcome in the Netherlands and the United Kingdom that he donated three hundred guilders to the Widows and Orphans Charity of the British police, while Paul Carlos Heyden Altuna, the Venezuelan consul in London, felt that the "Order of the Bust of the Liberator"[101] should be awarded to James McBrien, chief inspector of the Criminal Investigation Department of Scotland Yard. Gómez was also thrilled at the outcome because the intervention of the British government was of "the greatest assistance in helping to clear off a number of outstanding claims and disputes which have been spontaneously settled during the last few weeks by the direct intervention of General Gómez."[102] Cárdenas sent copies and photographs of the *Odin* that first appeared in the Spanish newspaper *El Financiero* to all senators and deputies in France as well as the Conseil de Legion d'Honneur and government ministers. Cárdenas also gave a dinner to Nicolas Johannes Laurentius Brantjes, the new governor of Curacao, "with whom I am in talks to persuade to come over to our cause to help us guard your peace."[103] The diplomatic wrangles with Nicaragua continued, with the Nicaraguan government sending Foreign Affairs Minister Máximo H. Zepeda to Paris to investigate the affair. In Paris, Zepeda met Cárdenas, who showed him the files, which "left him dumbfounded at the evidence of so much wrongdoing."[104]

Mexico Enters the Scene

While official support for the exiles from the United States diminished, the rebels in early 1920 started receiving financial and material backing from the

Mexican government. This was part of Mexico's foreign policy of trying to influence the internal affairs of other countries, especially in Central America, to adopt their own brand of nationalism and in so doing counterbalance the influence of the United States in the region. Although the involvement of the Mexican government in the internal affairs of Venezuela is not generally known, Mexico's embroilment in Central America, especially Nicaragua with Augusto César Sandino, is well documented.[105] Mexico considered Central America "as a natural sphere of influence,"[106] with the country playing "the role of a regional powerbroker . . . as a logical and consistent element in its foreign policy agenda."[107] Consequently, Mexico's support for the Liberals in the region during the 1920s was "anything but an isolated phenomenon insofar as its relations with the isthmian region are concerned."[108] According to Salisbury, the Nicaraguan Liberals often looked at Mexico "for assistance in their long-standing conflict with their Conservative opponents."[109]

Mexico's involvement in Nicaragua started in 1909, when the government of Porfirio Díaz (1884–1911) helped the Nicaraguan administration of Zelaya (1893–1909) to minimize the Guatemalan influence in the region.[110] Díaz also helped Madriz, Zelaya's successor, both politically and militarily.[111] The Venustiano Carranza administration (1915–20),[112] which came to power after the turbulent years following the fall of the Díaz dictatorship in 1911, increased Mexico's involvement in Central America. Carranza believed other nations in Latin America could use the Mexican revolution as the model to start their own reforms against the conservative elites. Carranza wanted Latin America to assume a united independent role in world affairs, believing that "nationalism would provide the foundation for such cooperation."[113] Central America presented the perfect arena to promote what became known as the Carranza Doctrine,[114] which was "the assertion in México of revolutionary nationalism and the creation internationally of a united Latin American anti-imperialist front to counter US economic and political hegemony."[115] The Carranza administration therefore "decided to challenge his northern neighbor by establishing throughout the isthmus Liberal regimes friendly to México."[116]

Carranza's successor, Alvaro Obregón, one of the ablest military men of the revolution, was elected president of Mexico on September 5, 1920. Obregón was closely allied to both the peasants and the workers as well as anti-clerical, and was backed in Congress by the Mexican Labor Party, which was established by Luis Napoleón Morones, head of the newly created Confederación Regional Obrera Mexicana (CROM), and the National Agrarian Party, representing the peasants. Within Latin America, Obregón tried to influence the development of the Pan American Union in order to counter the overwhelming influence of the United States in the region. Finally, in Central America, Obregón supported individuals and social movements that could bring about a second successful Latin American social revolution and in so doing end Mexico's political isolation among the conservative Latin American elite.[117] Obregón's involvement in Central America, particularly Nicaragua, was more subdued than his predecessor because he was involved in negotiating US recognition and did not want to upset the American government.[118] The Obregón government finally renewed diplomatic relations with the United States after the Bucareli Conference, which started on May 14, 1923.[119] Although Obregón's room for maneuver was restricted in Central America, his government would support certain Venezuelan exiles.

In 1924, Plutarco Elías Calles, who was reputedly "more radical and nationalist"[120] than his predecessor, succeeded Obregón. With Mexico joining the Pan American Union after reestablishing diplomatic relations with the United States in 1923, Calles would carry the country's "fight for legitimacy and revolutionary movements into the Latin American diplomatic setting."[121] It was clear, even before Calles was elected to the presidency, that he was against dictatorship. In a speech at Victoria, in Tamaulipas State, on April 29, 1924, Calles stated that "the time has come for tyrants to disappear from the face of the earth and for their names to exist only in the records of the past. The time has come, not only for the people of México, but also for the people of the world, to impose their powerful will and to conquer definitely their political liberties."[122] The Mexican government felt strong enough to challenge the Monroe Doctrine, with Genaro Estrada, the newly appointed foreign minister, in 1927 carrying the theme of diplomatic recognition to a new level and demanding that in the future any new government should receive diplomatic recognition regardless of the way it achieved power. Consequently, if such a policy was adopted, it followed that "Mexico could thus recognize any new revolutionary administration and end its ongoing political isolation in the Latin American setting."[123]

Calles started a fierce propaganda campaign against US gunboat diplomacy and the work of the US marines in the Caribbean and Central America, developing a special relationship with Cuba at a time when the island was struggling with its relationship with the United States. Calles went further in Central America than any of his predecessors in trying to change the Conservative regimes in the region, backing "diplomacy and propaganda with action, as in providing support and later asylum to the Nicaraguan revolutionary Sandino."[124] In Nicaragua, the CROM helped organize Nicaragua's labor movement, with Calles assisting the Conservative Carlos Solórzano as the presidential candidate and the Liberal Juan Bautista Sacasa running as vice president, to win the October 1924 elections. As Buchenau has pointed out, there were clear similarities between the goals of the Nicaraguan Liberals and the aims of the Mexican revolution, from the "spread of a well defined economic nationalism to the field of syndicalism."[125] Moreover, this was the first time in Central America that "a government was trying to form a political populist system with the participation of workers and peasants."[126]

On October 25, 1925, the Liberal faction of the Carlos Solórzano government was eliminated when the Conservative Emiliano Chamorro launched a successful coup d'état. Solórzano was initially reduced to a figurehead, and in December, Juan Bautista Sacasa was forced out of the vice presidency, with Solórzano following on January 14, 1926, to be replaced in the presidency by Emiliano Chamorro. The US government did not recognize the Chamorro Administration, and Sacasa, leading the Nicaraguan Constitutionalist rebels, tried to obtain military help from the United States. When this failed, Sacasa turned to the Mexicans, who provided "loans that were redeemable after victory by the insurgent faction, weapons and ammunition and the supply ships that were ostensibly part of the merchant navy but which supplied the ordnance to the scene of the battle."[127] Under the Calles-Sacasa Pact of 1926, Mexico provided "financial backing as well as military advisers, arms and ammunitions for the Liberal expeditionary force,"[128] and also agreed to transport the rebels from Mexico to Nicaragua. Luis Napoleón Morones, the Mexican industry minister and head of CROM, was in charge of supplying the arms, while General Joaquín Amaro was involved in the military planning of the operation. The Mexican government not only provided Sacasa with men and arms, but also equipped the Mexican commercial ships *Foam, Carmelita, Superior, Jalisco,* and *Tropical*[129] to support the Liberal revolution in Nicaragua. The *Tropical,* for example, set sail from Manzanillo port on the Pacific coast in mid-August 1926 with fifty Mexicans, most of whom were former army personnel, and allegedly carried 2,000 rifles with 1.2 million rounds of ammunition.[130] Furthermore, at the end of August 1926, Alfonso Cravioto, the Mexican minister in Guatemala, forwarded funds to Sacasa.[131] According to Buchenau, the economic and military help given to Sacasa by the Calles administration demonstrates that "revolutionary México was really interested in establishing neighboring regimes that supported vigorously the ideals of social transformation."[132] Further Mexican help was sent to the Nicaraguan Liberals when Adolfo Díaz replaced Chamorro as president on November 11, 1926.

However, matters deteriorated, and the US marines returned to Nicaragua in 1927. In April 1927, however, the Liberal rebellion ended with the signing of the Espino Negro pact, with the United States brokering a peace treaty in which Díaz remained in power until supervised elections by the American government took place in November 1928. Sandino, who had returned from Mexico to Nicaragua in early 1926 to join the fight against the Conservatives and had become the most powerful Liberal general in the North, continued the fight against the US troops, which remained in the country until 1933 in a vain attempt to capture the rebel. The Mexican government in 1928 consigned its Nicaraguan venture to history, proposing in 1929 that Sandino could move to Yucatán if the US marines left the country. This did not happen, and Sandino continued the struggle, but "the Mexican policy of anti-imperialism was already part of history."[133]

The Venezuelan Connection

The Mexican government had a strong antipathy toward the Gómez regime. The main instigator of such a policy was Licenciado José Vasconcelos, the education secretary. Prior to entering Obregón's government, Vasconcelos, as chancellor of the National University, delivered a speech on Columbus Day, October 12, 1920, in which he insulted the Gómez regime in front of the students and a number of invited South American diplomats. Vasconcelos referred to Gómez in particular as a "pig, a tyrant, an executioner"[134] and encouraged the "students to march against the government through the streets of the capital, taking with them the Venezuelan flag."[135] The reason for acting in such a manner, Vasconcelos later stated in his *Memoirs,* was that on the eve of his speech he recalled "the sad condition of our people, some in perpetual dictatorship in Central America and Venezuela."[136] The latter country "produced physical heart pain to me,"[137] because he had been an exile himself between 1915 and 1920 as a result of the "despotism of my country"[138] during the Carranza period, and had met many of the Venezuelan rebels in New York. A strong bond developed between him and the exiles, and on returning to Mexico, he decided to denounce the Gómez dictatorship. Although President Elect Obregón did not comment on the scandal that ensued, War Secretary

Calles was favorably disposed, stating that Vasconcelos, not "content with having contributed to the liberation of his own country, was fighting for freedom beyond the nation's frontiers."[139] According to Vasconcelos, Obregón's only response after a number of Venezuelan ladies requested the president to intervene "morally" was to organize "a group of Mexican ladies friendly towards Venezuela, headed by his wife."[140] As we shall see, Obregón's help went considerably further than Vasconcelos would have us believe in his *Memoirs.*

The Venezuelan exiles renewed their hope of obtaining new financial backing when Vasconcelos entered the Mexican government as the education secretary. Mexico from now on became a magnet for certain Venezuelan revolutionaries who descended from "the United States, Cuba, Panama, Colombia, Santo Domingo, Curacao, Trinidad and even Europe."[141] The less well-off were given employment by the Mexican government, while the financially secure demanded "greater support for their subversive aims."[142] Vasconcelos in his *Memoirs* states that soon after his Columbus Day speech many Venezuelan exiles appeared in Mexico, wanting "weapons and ammunition, something I could not give them, but when in Obregón's government, and Calles had gone to the Ministry, I took them to the president himself."[143] This was all part of a "continental Hispanic movement,"[144] which was Mexico's destiny to lead and which "started attracting the curiosity of the best of the Continent."[145] Such a situation would be a real threat to the Gómez dictatorship, as the Mexican government would give succor and financial support to the Venezuelan exiles, with many of the arms that President Obregón confiscated from his enemies, especially from Adolfo de la Huerta's failed rebellion in December 1923, ending up in Venezuelan hands.

Following the failure of the *Odin/Harrier* expedition, Castro sent Rivas Vásquez to Mexico in July 1921,[146] but President Obregón did not give him any encouragement, and he returned to Cuba. Later, Obregón changed his mind, and Vasconcelos invited Rivas Vásquez back to Mexico City because the Mexican government was now "interested"[147] in helping the Venezuelan exiles. At the same time, Obregón's Secretario de Concejo invited Ramón Ayala to Mexico "because General Obregón did not want to negotiate with Rivas Vásquez only."[148] This in turn attracted other rebels, who arrived in Mexico City because "the plans to supply large quantities of arms and ammunition confiscated by Obregón from the Mexican revolutionaries have been seriously discussed, if the revolutionaries can get hold of a boat."[149]

In 1922, while the Mexican government debated whether to back Ortega Martínez or Baptista, Arévalo Cedeño and León founded the Mexican branch of the Partido Republicano de Venezuela, with a directorate composed of a number of Venezuelans dispersed throughout Latin America. The president of the new party was L. Guevara Travieso, who was living in Guayaquil; the vice president was Horacio Blanco Fombona, who resided in Mexico, as did Humberto Tejera, the secretary; while Juan Manuel Sanoja, the second vice president, was living in Puerto Rico, and Luis Felipe Nava, the treasurer, was in New York.[150] The party was inspired by the ideals of the Mexican revolution. Its political objectives were the redistribution of land, the nationalization of the subsoil, the restriction of foreign investment, no reelection of the presidency, the formation of unions with a socialist focus, independence from the church for the education system, and universal suffrage. The Obregón government initially helped Arévalo Cedeño, the perennial Venezuelan revolutionary, with $8,000.[151]

The Venezuelan government was aware of Obregón's position and the help it was thinking of giving the Venezuelan exiles. Arcaya advised Gómez in November 1922 that "Mexico is today the biggest revolutionary center owing to the support that your enemies have found in Vasconcelos because, as his acts demonstrate, he is a buffoon who has the ear of Obregón."[152] Arcaya also felt that the criticism of the Gómez regime was exceedingly cynical on the part of a Mexican administration that had bloodied its hands with gruesome executions and murders. Arcaya counseled Gómez that it would be "very useful if a society was formed in Caracas that would work for the curtailment in Mexico of such horrors and the end of the bloody spectacle that has scandalized the world."[153]

The anti-Venezuelan campaign continued in Mexico, reaching its climax on October 29, 1923, when the country broke off diplomatic relations with Venezuela. The excuse used by the Mexican government was that the Venezuelan government had refused entry into the country of the Compañía de Teatro Mexicana because it was alleged that certain members of the theatrical troupe were communists who would spread malicious rumors about the government. In his criticism of the Venezuelan regime, Vasconcelos was influenced by Samuel Gompers, the head of the American Federation of Labor, who in December 1924 chaired the Pan American Federation of Labor Convention in Mexico City, which approved a resolution condemning the development of the Venezuelan oil industry and the exploitative measures adopted by the oil companies. The companies in Venezuela were quick to respond, sending a memorandum in which the resolution was seen as a "manifestation of a systematic and world-wide campaign of the Mexican

Government against the Venezuelan Government, actuated in part by the former's alarm at the transition of American oil operations from Mexico to Venezuela, and the feeling of the Mexican Government that it is its duty to institute throughout Latin America the program of destroying property rights it has so successfully carried out in Mexico."[154]

Obregón remained undecided whether to support Ortega Martínez or Baptista, opting in the end for the latter, to whom, as we shall see, he advanced $20,000 for the *Angelita* expedition in 1924. When Calles was elected president in 1924, José Ignacio Cárdenas insinuated to Gómez that he should try to reestablish diplomatic relations. The Venezuelan dictator felt, however, that it was not convenient for it to be "first suggested by our government,"[155] but if Calles broached the subject, Cárdenas should "indicate to him that Venezuela sees no reason why friendly relations with Mexico could not be re-established."[156] Calles pursued a similar policy toward Venezuela as his predecessor, with Mexico remaining a thorn in the side of the Gómez regime until the reestablishment of diplomatic relations in 1933.

Events in Venezuela

While the exiles were organizing their abortive expeditions and making new friends in Mexico, Gómez faced a number of small, irritating political problems as well as a stronger challenge from within his own ranks. On the institutional front, Gómez continued to modernize the armed forces by creating the Military Aviation School of Venezuela in August 1920. The law was framed in such a manner as to prohibit foreign companies from flying in the country out of fear that the revolutionaries would attack. Another law on foreign war vessels was enacted in order to take into account submarines because Gómez suspected that the revolutionaries in Europe would acquire one and use it against him.

There were signs of renewed labor unrest fanned by the university students. Toward the end of March 1921, the workers of the Caracas Tramway Company went on strike. The Centro de Estudiantes de Medicina wanted the Central Council of the students to support the strikers by declaring a boycott on the company. The students organized a protest meeting at the Plaza Bolívar, which Miguel Zúñiga Cisneros, the main organizer and second vice president of the Central Council, later admitted was overtly political in nature. The police allowed the meeting to take place initially, but once they learned of its subversive nature, it was violently suppressed by General Lorenzo Carvallo and Colonel Pedro García, with Zuñiga Cisneros and other students arrested. Many others were involved, including M. A. Pulido Méndez, Alfonso Bortone, Rodolfo Moleiro, Jacinto Fombona Pachano, Domingo Ramón Castillo, and Lt. Rafael Alvarado, who years later would lead the abortive military coup in 1928 and who at this early stage suggested the taking of the San Carlos barracks.[157] Many of the students sent to jail were the children of friends of Gómez. A number of these friends, including William H. Phelps, Carlos Zuloaga, H. Pérez Dupuy, Mosquera, and, surprisingly for a serving diplomat, McGoodwin, among others,[158] addressed a letter to Gómez on April 5, 1921, asking him to look into the matter to ascertain that the protest was not "intended to cause a public disruption."[159]

In November 1921, Ortega Martínez and Baptista arrived in Puerto Rico from New York to "reach an agreement with Carabaño and Castro."[160] However, the revolution was paralyzed without arms and transport. Ortega Martínez returned to the United States, possibly through Mexico, in order to acquire the *Odin* moored in the Netherlands, but for this to happen a front needed to be set up to confuse the authorities. The ruse involved Ortega Martínez's assumption of the name of Walter Scott Roberts in his pursuit of the *Odin*. Roberts became the major shareholder in the Pennsylvania Textile Company, with a capital of $2 million not fully paid up,[161] who was prepared to back the rebellion with $100,000. Cárdenas was sure that Roberts was an alias used by Ortega Martínez to confuse the authorities, citing as proof a letter by W. S. Roberts sent from New York and written on letterhead from the Pennsylvania Textile Company, to W. H. Melleman and Company, the agent in Amsterdam handling the sale of the *Odin*, informing the Dutch agent that he would pay the anchorage fees. For Cárdenas, "there is no doubt that the author of the correspondence is Ortega Martínez who hides behind the name of Roberts, and who could be the American who contributed one hundred thousand dollars to the revolution"[162] to create confusion. In order to reduce the "hefty monthly sum"[163] in anchorage fees, the boat was moved from Amsterdam to Rotterdam. The *Odin* was valued at around $20,000, and Bendelac was in the process of acquiring arms in Belgium.

The revolutionaries acquired five hundred perfectly working machine guns, together with another lot not in such good order, as well as "some 20 rapid-fire cannons for airplanes, that some were incomplete but easy to mend. There is more than 1 million rounds of ammunition in good order and others in not such good shape. There are 1000 very good pistols *para bellum*."[164] There were also some thousand mortars for the cannons and a telescope.[165] The plan was to sail the *Odin* under the Mexican flag to Hamburg, where it would be repaired cheaply and where armaments could be procured. The *Odin* would return to Amsterdam, from where the arms and ammunition would be transferred to another ship for the voyage to Mexico, and would then proceed to the United Kingdom to take a cargo of whisky for sale in the United States to defray the costs of the expedition. The *Odin,* however, was unable to depart because Cárdenas sabotaged the ship, informing Gómez that "the inspectorate of ships demanded (it conforms to the plan) that in order for the Odin to sail, it should be inspected at a special wharf where it was taken . . . once the inspection took place it was *established that the boilers were absolutely useless.* You understand" (emphasis in original).[166]

The rebels at the beginning of the 1920s managed to organize themselves, acquiring two ships and a respectable arsenal without the Gómez spy network detecting them, only to be frustrated at the last moment by the action of Cárdenas in alerting the relevant authorities on the case. The discovery of oil at this juncture helped Gómez on the economic front, but the rebels continued their fight to topple Gómez, with Mexico forming an increasingly important focal point for the revolutionaries.

CHAPTER FIVE

The *Angelita* Expedition

The effect of the collapse of the *Odin/Harrier* expedition on the morale of the exiles was contradictory. Some of the exiles felt that the Gómez regime would never be toppled, while others thought that the way forward was to unite all opponents of the regime under one political party. Some of the revolutionaries refused to join the new political organization, arguing that there was no difference between Gómez and the new political entity, leading directly in 1924 to what became known as the *Angelita* expedition.

The setback of the *Odin/Harrier*, according to Cárdenas, created a "strong mutual criticism among the revolutionaries in New York and Paris,"[1] with many exiles calling Alcántara a thief because they felt he had deceived them "by appearing to be more than he really is."[2] In some circles, it was felt that Alcántara had given away the rebels' secrets to the Venezuelan government. According to Arévalo Cedeño, Alcántara met with Barceló in Puerto Rico and informed him about his plans; he was sure that he would not reveal them to the authorities because he owed him a few favors. With the unfolding of events, Arévalo Cedeño felt vindicated in his view not to trust Barceló.[3] Among the rebel leaders, the most aggrieved was said to be Ortega Martínez.

The political energy of the exiles needed to be harnessed once again, with intense political activity taking place in the United States, the Caribbean, and Central America, where a new focus was given to the struggle. The erstwhile leaders of the *Odin/Harrier* would reunite again in a front in which all opponents to the Gómez regime could join to depose the dictator. At the time, it appeared as though a revolutionary party was being formed wherever Venezuelans were living in exile. Political activity against Gómez within Venezuela was also growing.

The Young Turks among the revolutionaries now started to assert themselves, producing a political program that bore closer resemblance to student politics rather than a viable and practical way of deposing Gómez. The sentiments were correct, but the execution was wrong because it did not take into account Venezuela's history or the large number of exiled ageing regional caudillos with the knowledge, wherewithal, and courage to launch a revolution against "the catfish of the Mulera," as Gómez was disparagingly referred to among the exiled community. The new grouping that formed the Unión Revolucionaria Venezuelana (URV) grew out of an idea by Aristeguieta to form a loose study group to ascertain whether there was enough support for deposing Gómez and, if so, the best way of achieving this end. The aim of the group was to "destroy tyranny and the personal ambition that has created and maintained it, in order to restore the republic with law abiding and responsible governments that guarantee the exercise of public liberties."[4] It sought initially approval for its aims from approximately forty exiled caudillos that formed a sanctum sanctorum of the Venezuelan opposition that would later establish a more permanent URV. Apart from Aristeguieta, the initial members of the group were Francisco H. Rivero, Eliseo Vivas Pérez, Manuel María Urbaneja, Ramón Muñoz Tebar, C. López Bustamante, L. Duarte, and A. Granado Rodríguez. Rodríguez was the editor of *El Venezolano,* the association's newspaper, who also wanted to establish a new circle of "people who did not have anything to do with the arrivistes."[5]

A party would later be established on a more formal basis with proper aims and statutes, with members voting for a committee structure. The *cuerpo directivo* would then call on the caudillos for its "installation, urging them to go to an Elected Assembly"[6] with a view of electing an *entidad revolucionaria* that was in charge of organizing the revolution and would form the national executive in the event of its being successful but be subordinated to the URV. Olivares felt that the association should grow by incorporating all groups opposed to Gómez under the banner of the now almost extinct Sociedad Patriótica Venezolana. Certain revolutionaries were quick to criticize the new group for being "caudillista" and an instrument of both Olivares and Baptista. In order to get further support for the revolution, it was revealed in New York that Baptista, who was in Europe trying to secure a ship for the rebels and unaware of these developments, had received $50,000 from Castro and Georgetti in Puerto Rico.[7] At the same time, Fernando Aristeguieta Badataco, Jorge Luciani, Rodolfo Rojas, Manuel Flores Cabrera, and Sergio Ruiz Urrutia formed another group, the Unión Cívica Venezolana, in New York.

The formation of the URV sparked a heated debate among the revolutionaries on the country's future political direction. Some of the exiles considered Gómez to be the sole enemy, with the country's political problem solved by simply deposing him. Others felt that such a move was simply a replacement of one tyrant by another and therefore wanted to link the struggle for power with the establishment of a genuine democracy, something that the Mexican government was deeply committed to in its support of certain rebels.[8] A number of exiles, such as Ortega Martínez, were clearly not in complete agreement with the URV because they did not like the cliquishness of the party selecting those who joined. Ortega Martínez's son, for example, felt that the URV was "an insignificant group of individuals, constituted per se in arbiters of the country's destiny,"[9] with the party generally accused of *personalismo,* a recurring theme over the next decade. The crux of the argument, according to Ortega Martínez, was that there was little difference between Gómez and the URV because it was "the policy of the clique in all its sterile meanness, formed by the blinding presumption of an unfounded moral and intellectual superiority on the part of a small group over the rest of its fellow citizens, with the eternal tendency to create privileges and to establish classes characteristic of the spirit of oligarchies."[10] José María Ortega Martínez Jr. felt that if "personal ambition represents a constant threat and a danger for the republic, the oligarchy is, however, the death to any democratic ideals."[11] While it was true that the people of Venezuela wanted to break "definitively the cycle of governments headed by personal cliques, it will never tolerate the ascendancy of a new oligarchy to power, as is abundantly demonstrated by the history of our popular revolutions."[12]

The URV was perceived as the party of the military and the caudillos. Moreover, the *junta directiva* would be in charge of political/military affairs and, once the revolution was successful, would form a government. Ortega Martínez Jr. felt that the URV did not have a mandate to do this, as the group had no government experience and therefore could not conceive of something that was more "antidemocratic and absurd."[13] Ortega Martínez Sr. intended to stand as a candidate in the presidential elections of 1922 because it was up to the electorate to decide who should form the government and not a small group of individuals. He argued that "however much the revolutionary group believes it has the prestige and merit, it cannot usurp that function whose exercise belongs exclusively to the great popular masses."[14] What the intellectual architects of the URV failed to see were the contradictions in their arguments, stating that they were anti-caudillista but later praising the important role played by the caudillos in bringing forth political change. Ortega Martínez junior reminded Aristeguieta that "despotism together with caudillismo is not the cause but just one of the innumerable effects of our lamentable social and political backwardness."[15] In addition, Olivares, Castillo, Muñoz Tébar, and José Heriberto López all shared the same fear that the caudillos would only launch a revolution in order to place themselves in power. Olivares also felt that there was a need to change the system because the government of a country was not up to one man's will.

Olivares was the only caudillo who embraced wholeheartedly the principles of democracy and who steadfastly refused to join any expedition that was not led by leaders committed to free elections soon after achieving power. This central tenet of his political ideology, which remained with him up to the *Falke* expedition in 1929, meant that he did not join Baptista and Ortega Martínez's *Angelita* expedition in 1924. Aristeguieta used the same argument in essence when he pointed out that the opposition to Gómez since 1913 represented the old Liberal Amarillo oligarchy that had produced tyrants over the past hundred years and had dismally failed to get rid of the Andean dictator. The armed struggle that so far had ended in failure was the result of inadequate planning and support within the country. Aristeguieta accused Ortega Martínez Jr. of striking a theatrical pose with his pamphlet, which he called "a comical political gesture,"[16] in order to sway public opinion to join forces with the rebels to topple Gómez and thus place an arbitrarily selected person in power. In October, Mocho Hernández's son, Nicolás Hernández, added his thoughts to the debate when in an open letter to Rivero, president of the *URV* New York chapter, he wrote that "our leading or representative classes are in part or totally responsible and supportive of the tyrannies and usurpation."[17] While these heated debates on the future of the revolution were conducted through pamphlets, others, such as Dr. José Guerrero,[18] issued flysheets defending the behavior of the exiles and calling on them to oust Gómez, while beseeching the US government to break off diplomatic relations with Venezuela. The feeling among many of the exiled community in New York at the end of 1922 was that Gómez would be murdered—either stabbed to death or blown up—and "to this end the New York Revolutionary

Committee offers ($25,000) twenty-five thousand pesos,"[19] to anyone who was able to assassinate the dictator.

Uprisings in Venezuela

While the exiles continued to debate their differences, in Venezuela in June 1922 there was a small uprising in Paraguas headed by Bolet Monagas, which failed because of insufficient funding and manpower. Bolet Monagas had fifteen men in Currucaisito and could muster a further twenty men to follow him, but he needed money for such a venture. He requested Alcántara to send the funds from Ciudad Bolívar, "and you will see the entire hinterland affected."[20] Alcántara, under the pseudonym of Alfredo, replied in July that "nothing can be done for the moment because the foreign Nations do not allow ordnance exports even though these have been obtained in sufficient quantities to allow us to triumph in all regions."[21]

Gómez's espionage network at the time started to yield reports of possible trouble in the future. In Panama, for example, Herbert de Lima was trying to acquire arms from the Panama government for the revolutionaries. In Zulia, a cache of arms was discovered in the home of General Adolfo Carroz, who through the París family of Maracaibo had connections with the exiles in Curacao and New York. It was clear, however, that these developments were not considered a threat because in July 1922 Pocaterra, who would play a critical role in the revolutionary field in the forthcoming years, was released from prison. He immediately left Caracas,[22] arriving in Curacao on July 16, leaving six days later for New York, and settling eventually in Montreal.

The failure of the *Harrier* and the *Odin* proved, albeit in a negative way, that the exiles could organize an armed expedition against Gómez. Despite the continuing ideological debates about the form the revolution should take, the serious business of organizing one continued. In the early part of 1922 Alcántara, Asunción Rodríguez, Asuaje, Flores, and others met in Trinidad to consider the possible success of a future armed expedition. It was felt that a properly organized invasion of the country could topple the Gómez administration. At the end of September 1922, Ortega Martínez, with the backing of Georgetti in Puerto Rico and Félix Córdova Dávila, the resident commissioner of Puerto Rico to the US House of Representatives in Washington, established a revolutionary junta in New York to fight against Gómez. Having lost $132,900 in the *Odin* debacle, Georgetti wanted to be the sole organizer of the expedition, forming an association under which all who contributed funds would be incorporated into the decision-making process. In addition, people who were promised a great variety of concessions once they were successful, including oil, sugar cane plantations, and cattle ranching among others, supported the exiles. The most enticing were oil concessions; the revolutionaries were also caught up in the oil fever that was sweeping the country that year. Promising oil contracts would be awarded in return for financial assistance. Pedro Rafael Rincones, the Venezuelan consul in New York, counseled that it was doubtful that any company would pay serious attention to these offers.[23] Rincones was right: the oil companies did not support the revolutionaries because oil concessions at this early stage of the industry's development were easily available in Venezuela. I have been unable to find in the archives examined proof of any active involvement in revolutionary activity by the established oil companies. Aranguren, Venezuela's richest oil intermediary, did support Ortega Martínez financially, and it is likely that the rumor of help from an oil company emanates from this source.

Georgetti started to organize the logistics and the fund-raising activities himself, with all exiles invited to join Ortega Martínez in the struggle against Gómez. Since 1915 Olivares had decided not to participate in an armed struggle in which the military leader of the campaign would also be head of government once power was achieved. He argued that the interim head of government who would appoint ministers, state presidents, and other government posts should be held in check so that he did not become a dictator and so as to allow genuine democratic elections to take place.[24] Olivares argued that the current political situation in Venezuela had generated "the unfortunate *system* of government by personal edict that is strangling us"[25] (emphasis in original). The same would happen with Ortega Martínez as the proclaimed leader of the revolution, because once power was achieved, he would distribute the various government posts among his friends. Olivares would only be willing to join Ortega Martínez if a central revolutionary entity was formed, consisting of five members and their alternates who constituted a Junta of Popular Defense entrusted to appoint the head of the armed expedition as well as organizing the invasion of Venezuela. Once one or more states were taken, the junta would install itself and organize a government in the area, and on reaching Caracas, it would appoint a provisional president and government, with elections taking place later.[26] Ortega Martínez rejected Olivares's suggestions, arguing that such a junta would have insufficient authority and legitimacy and therefore could not impose its will on the people of Venezuela.[27]

Ortega Martínez felt that the rebels could still use the *Odin* that was moored in Rotterdam. In Antwerp, Bendelac saw L. de Winter, of the firm of Amsterdansche Export en Import Maatschappij, who claimed he could get the *Odin* released as well as arming it with two cannons and two machine guns. To become seaworthy the *Odin* needed to undergo extensive repairs at a cost of $26,950, which was higher than the value of the boat. Nevertheless, Ortega Martínez, posing as Roberts, tried to get it released and delivered to the Venezuelan rebels. In September 1922 the Dutch police seized the ship. Roberts's visa was amended for immediate return to the United States, and he was informed that the "United States would not countenance any action by an American citizen tending to further any revolutionary movements against a Government with which the United States is at peace."[28] At the end of November, when it was rumored that Roberts was bankrupt, a legitimate buyer appeared for the *Odin,* and the ship was sold for $11,075 the following month. The affair cost the revolutionaries an initial $132,900 and a further $31,010 subsequently spent on repairing and maintaining the ship. Cárdenas's intention to ruin the rebels financially as well as destroying their plans worked to perfection.[29]

Ortega Martínez was not defeated yet, as there was the possibility of acquiring arms and a ship in Italy. In September 1922, it was reported that Baptista and Ayala were in Italy looking for arms for an expedition and that a boat had been acquired and equipped with "cannons, machine guns, airships, explosives and even suffocating gas."[30] Cárdenas reported: "New information has come to light that Baptista is negotiating with Bendelac and Villanueva, and that there is an employee in the Ministry in Belgium who was Chargé d'Affaires in Caracas and who could help the revolutionaries, because he does not hide his ill-will toward your nephew. I am trying to verify these facts, with the *help of the secret service here*"[31] (emphasis in original). Villanueva was also in Italy trying to secure arms from the Casa Ansaldo, which sold war surplus material from the Italian government. Díaz Rodríguez, the former Venezuelan consul in Italy, enquired about the purchase of a cache of arms that Eduardo Dagñino, the Venezuelan minister at the Holy See, had negotiated in January, allegedly for the Venezuelan government. The Marquis Della Torretta, the Italian foreign affairs minister, explained that the Italian government would not grant permission to sell arms and ships unless they were completely satisfied that they were for the Venezuelan government.

E. Urdaneta Braschi reported that Dagñino was in collusion with the revolutionaries to purchase arms in Italy, although the proof against the Venezuelan minister was a document that Guido Turin, who was married to a Venezuelan, had of a plan to invade Venezuela the previous September. Turin, however, did not want to deliver a copy of the document because many people were involved and he did not want to create a scandal. Turin informed E. Hurtado Machado, the Venezuelan consul, that the document referred to "a revolutionary plan that consisted in recruiting people here, that would have left in August or September of last year, under the pretext of emigrating to one of the Central American republics to later change course for Venezuela and disembark in Chichiriviche and from there attack Maracay with airplanes."[32]

When enquiries were made to purchase a boat, they found that it was too expensive, with the result that Díaz Rodríguez started a defamatory campaign against Dagñino, "which took as its starting point my negotiations with the Ansaldo House last year for the purchase of two war ships that the Venezuelan Legation in Paris and its Press Attaché were entrusted to acquire for the government of Venezuela."[33] Dagñino, however, tried to acquire two ships for the rebels in Paris through Buchetti, a rich Rome merchant, who was the intermediary between Dagñino and Casa Ansaldo. The Italian government gave clear assurances that it had no knowledge of any arms deal with Venezuela.

Gómez's Health Suffers

On October 25, 1921, Gómez suffered from a bad prostate that developed into uremia; later he contracted pneumonia and, at one stage, was believed close to death. Although the legal position was clear as to who would succeed Gómez in the event of his death, among political circles it was unclear what would happen. Article 83 of the 1914 constitution stated that the head of the Federal Court and of Cassation would assume the presidency until elections took place at Gómez's death. Gómez's close relatives were against this because the election for a new president for the 1922–29 constitutional period would in effect start that December, and "they were not prepared to relinquish power as it would doubtless be the case if the Acting President called for new elections to take place."[34] Gómez's faithful henchmen would not necessarily accept the outcome, leading to political uncertainty and "a relapse to the old conditions only too familiar in the history of the country."[35]

Gómez's son Vicentico, who was inspector general of the army, was ready to stage a military coup with part of the country's army if his father died. Vicentico was backed by Vicente Vizcaya, Julio Anselmo Santander, Amadeo Anselmi, and Isaías Vivas, as well as commanding the support of the Piar and Miranda barracks. Vicentico clearly wanted to become president but lacked "the natural shrewdness and intelligence of his father,"[36] according to Beaumont, the British minister. Cook, the American minister, considered Vicentico "a person of no competence and dominated by an ambitious wife."[37] It was felt that with the army behind him and the support of the states of Táchira and Mérida, Vicentico could seize the succession, but according to Beaumont "he would never be accepted willingly at Caracas or by Zulia or by the State of Bolivar."[38] Juan Crisóstomo Gómez, hereinafter referred to as Juancho, the dictator's brother, headed another group preparing their own coup against the military backing of Vicentico. Juancho commanded the support of the Girardot and the Bravos del Táchira battalions and had among his backers his cousin Eustoquio Gómez, Benicio Giménez, Isaías Nieto, José María Merchán, and David López Henríquez. Eleazar López Contreras, who became president after Gómez's death in 1935, acted as the go-between for the two groups, managing to diffuse the "split among those family members"[39] at the time. Gómez rewarded his loyalty by appointing him brigadier general on March 11, 1923.

The only opposition against the regime, according to Beaumont, the British minister, was among the political exiles, who tried bringing pressure to bear on the State Department to intervene in order to secure free elections in the country. Their efforts were doomed to failure because there was no channel through which pressure could be exercised in the face of an electoral Congress in which there was complete unanimity of purpose, even if the American government was persuaded to take action. Although there were faint murmurs supporting change, it was clear that most agreed that the "maintenance of internal peace and order is the first requirement, and that General Gómez is the only man capable of assuring this, the result of a perfectly free election might not be different from that which will shortly be achieved by a packed body of partisans of the present regime."[40] In effect, the beginning of the election for a new president started on June 22, 1921, when all legislative assemblies swore their loyalty to Gómez by asking him to continue at the presidency for the next constitutional period of 1922–1929. Congress interpreted "the exact desire of its representatives who have been given that award of gratitude and collective trust"[41] to Gómez. Itriago Chacín wrote that "this plebiscite has the merit of being a true expression of the national will that has been freely and spontaneously expressed, because the companies, the guilds and citizens have not received any official prompting to uphold what Congress agreed on the date mentioned."[42]

Nevertheless, two possible presidential candidates were mooted from outside the immediate entourage of the Gómez family: Márquez Bustillos, the Trujillano politician, and Esteban Gil Borges, the foreign minister. The latter would not remain in office for much longer, as he omitted to mention Gómez's name in his speech on April 19, 1921, at the unveiling of a statue of Bolívar in New York's Central Park during the centenary anniversary of Venezuela's independence. That same day two New York newspapers started a political campaign in favor of Gil Borges and against Gómez. J. M. Herrera Mendoza, together with Santos Domínici, the Venezuelan minister at Washington, and Santiago Rodríguez met to discuss tactics. They decided to warn the foreign minister by asking him to write an article disassociating himself from the suggestion that he wanted to stand for the elections, but Gil Borges refused. When another similar article appeared the following day, Gil Borges was urged again to disclaim the suggestion, but he was confident that Gómez understood that he had not inspired the articles. Accordingly, Gil Borges informed Pedro Itriago Chacín, the acting minister of foreign affairs, that he had been well received in New York by bankers and other businessmen.[43] Márquez Bustillos, who was the provisional president, clearly did not want Gil Borges to stand for the presidency, starting a whispering campaign calling into question the foreign minister's loyalty by stating that he wanted to topple Gómez and that he had spoken against the Venezuelan dictator while in the United States. It soon became an accepted fact in Caracas that Gil Borges had criticized the regime in New York, but Gómez was well aware of the contents of his speech, as he had approved it in January. More damaging possibly for Gil Borges was Cárdenas's accusation of his involvement in the abortive *Odin/Harrier* expeditions.

There were also signs that certain American oil interests were backing the plotters, with J. C. Clarke of the British Petroleum Department of the Board of Trade receiving a report from the British Controlled Oilfields Ltd. stating that while no direct support of the revolutionary movement by American oil interests could be proved, Gómez's "friendly attitude towards British company in recent legal proceedings had disappointed Standard Oil and other American concessions."[44] Furthermore, Cárdenas, the Venezuelan minister at the Hague, felt that the *Odin/Harrier* plot had been financed from the United States as part of a "campaign to secure the cancellation of concessions granted by the present administration in Venezuela"[45] to British oil companies. Cárdenas was more lucid when he saw Sir Edward Howard, the British ambassador at Madrid, stating that the two boats acquired by the revolutionaries had been chartered and fitted out at the "expense of the oil investment interests of the United States,"[46] from whom he believed they had received $400,000. This was arranged "by the American oil interests with the express object of removing President Gómez and bringing Señor Estebán Gil Borges back to power."[47] This was clearly untrue, but under such extreme pressure, Gil Borges resigned as foreign minister on July 7, 1921, and replaced by Itriago Chacín. A few days later, he left for voluntary exile in the United States, and soon afterwards was elected deputy director of the Pan American Union in Washington, DC.

With the departure of Gil Borges, two distinct groups were left fighting for power, viz, the Gómez clique and Márquez Bustillos. The Márquez Bustillos group had public opinion on its side as well as all the enemies of Gómez because, as a State Department report stated, he was "disposed to treat with the factions in exile and to release the political prisoners."[48] Márquez Bustillos also commanded some factions of the army, with many officers on his side. It was evident that Márquez Bustillos would have a hard time fighting the Gómez clan of Juancho, Vicentico, Eustoquio, and José Ignacio Cárdenas because with their military support they could force him to resign at any time and replace him with Dr. Jesús Rojas Hernández, the president of the Federal Court and of Cassation, as temporary head of the government. The regime was weakening somewhat, freeing in December 1921 some sixty men, including León, after more than two hundred women in Caracas implored US President Harding to use his influence to get the political prisoners released.

Under the constitution, Congress had to elect a president for the next presidential period of 1922–29. The initial plan was for Juancho to take over as president, but this was dropped owing to dissension within the inner Gómez family: Vicentico wanted the presidency and was opposed to his uncle.[49] Gómez opted to change the constitution in order to avoid a civil war among his supporters. Under the proposed new constitution, Gómez continued in power, but the office of vice president was introduced again. It was hoped that this would allow the election of at least one vice president. On May 3, 1922, at four p.m., Congress reelected Gómez as the president of the Republic. Gómez returned unannounced to Caracas from Maracay on June 22 and to everybody's surprise took up his post on June 24, immediately appointing a new cabinet. On the same day, the new constitution was also approved, with Congress electing two vice presidents, viz, Juancho, first vice president and Vicentico, second vice president. The new constitution also reduced the number of days Congress was in session. On June 26, Juancho Gómez was appointed governor of the Federal District, and on July 4 the Universidad Central de Venezuela was reopened.[50] The creation of a Gómez dynasty was greeted with moot silence except by Santos Domínici, the Venezuelan minister at Washington, who resigned on July 5 in protest at such a nepotistic move[51] and would now become a fierce opponent of the Gómez regime. In Venezuela, conspiracies to topple Gómez surfaced at the time, with Cook in August 1922 reporting the discovery of a military/naval plot led by half a dozen junior officers who planned to kidnap Gómez.[52] The plot leaders were later imprisoned in La Rotunda.[53]

Gómez Tightens his Grip

In Puerto Rico the collection of funds and organization of the revolution continued. Cayetano Coll y Cuchi, a lawyer and leader of the House of Representatives on the island, informed Galavís in Caracas that a revolution against Gómez was being organized both in the United States and on the island. Coll y Cuchi together with Santiago Iglesias Pantín, a naturalized US citizen, founded the Free Federation of Puerto Rican Workers, headed by the latter. In 1915, they formed the Socialist Party, which took Iglesias first into local government and then to the Insular Senate in 1920. González Pacheco, the Venezuelan consul, informed Gómez that Coll y Cuchi was "a man with a revolutionary nature and a great agitator of the masses . . . who is able to call a strike whenever he wants and needs money, because he is another one who likes an easy life, and who wants lots of money."[54]

Coll y Cuchi, who first met Galavís in 1920, when he arrived on the island to purchase machinery for a sugar mill, was also a good friend of both Biamón and Georgetti, who used him "for any undertaking that requires boldness, recklessness and Machiavellianism."[55] Although José María Ontiveros, the Venezuelan minister at Puerto Rico, was given a letter of introduction to Coll y Cuchi by Galavís, he felt that a spy should be sent to Puerto Rico who would operate independently of the legation. In addition, while Dr. Víctor Coll y Cuchi, brother of Cayetano, was in Caracas delivering a paper at a scientific conference, he saw Gómez together with Galavís. At the meeting, it was agreed that the plotters' plan had to be sabotaged and that the central character in this plot was Governor Reily, with a double agent introduced at the governor's office. Carlos Delfino, Gómez's son-in-law, on his way to negotiate a number of oil concessions in New York, stopped at San Juan to meet with Governor Reily about a possible revolution that was being organized on the island. Ontiveros thought that this was a "hoax" that appeared as though it was "a plot being hatched here, but which in our opinion is no more than a form of blackmail by the people involved to try to take out money, lots of money from Venezuela."[56] Nevertheless, Reily took the necessary precautions in case Ontiveros was wrong. On September 27, Coll y Cuchi returned to the legation to demand that the news about the plot be relayed to Gómez, stating that the governor had all in hand and that the conspiracy was being organized in Washington. Ontiveros, however, believed this to be political blackmail, while others, such as José Ignacio Cárdenas, Julio Velutini, and the Núñez clan, felt that they "work together, not only in revolutionary politics but also in their own private interests such as the Banco de Caracas, giving rise to the strong suspicion that the banking institution supports the revolutionary plans."[57]

In October, further revolutionary cells were formed, with the Liga Patriótica Venezolana established in San José de Costa Rica, headed by J. C. Sotillo Picornell, while in Colón, Panama, Rafael Nogales Méndez[58] and Arévalo Cedeño waited for orders at the Hotel Colombia. The latter wanted the New York committee to allow him to invade Venezuela, while the former was itching to attack the country through Táchira. Tejera, who was also in Panama and had been the presiding judge in the Bramon/Breuer case, joined the Partido Republicano Venezolano led by P. J. Jugo Delgado, who was Arévalo Cedeño's secretary and chief of staff. Tejera was offered the presidency, but he refused.[59] At this time, León, Horacio Blanco Fombona, Nava, and Guevara Travieso were also in Panama.

In December 1922, Arévalo Cedeño left Colón for New York in order to finalize plans with other revolutionaries in the city. Baptista was also in the city, back from Paris with news of the arms purchased in Europe, and in January 1923, Ortega Martínez was back in New York to purchase another ship. It was time to formalize their efforts under one banner. In early 1923, the statutes of the URV were modified to allow six of the most important revolutionaries to choose the interim president and cabinet ministers, who would then reorganize the country as soon as power was achieved. Once Venezuela was pacified, elections for deputies from each state would take place for a constituent assembly. As a result, in February 1923 Carabaño, Baptista, Olivares, and Biamón met in New York to join the URV, agreeing to pool their armed resources together as well as acquiring arms without offering "concessions or contracts that are onerous to the country, much less enter into agreements that compromise the integrity and dignity of the country."[60]

The new group soon received financial support. Rivero forwarded $5,000, and a further $15,000 came from a European source, most likely Aranguren. According to an anonymous note, Baptista was reported to have received $50,000 from Mibelli, Galavís, and surprisingly Márquez Bustillos.[61] In addition, Rivas Vásquez once again convinced President Menocal of Cuba to support the Venezuelan exiles. The previous Cuban government of Menocal had paid a monthly stipend of $300 to Juan Valentín Borregales, Rafael Rodríguez Santaella, and Flores, and $200 to P. López Bello, but the new government of Alfredo Zayas stopped the payments.[62] In the meantime, Baptista was busy trying to acquire arms and ammunition to invade the country through Falcón in order to meet up with other revolutionaries in Lara and Trujillo. Aristeguieta at the same time tried to get Arévalo Cedeño to return because he had an arms cache of five hundred rifles but no ammunition. It was decided to give Cedeño $5,000 to purchase ammunition and for him to invade Venezuela from the Colombian Arauca border. The URV would later send him a further $2,000.

Ortega Martínez and Tellería were not included in the group, with Baptista and Olivares sending an olive branch out to both men that did not work. Baptista and Olivares wanted their offer to Ortega Martínez and Tellería to remain open indefinitely, but Aristeguieta felt that this would further delay any action. On March 17, Alcántara arrived in Trinidad from New York to reach an agreement with Ortega Martínez. The executive directorate of the revolution, headed by Rivero, with the governing committee composed of Baptista, Carabaño, Olivares, and other military leaders, was called to a meeting to approve the URV's plans. A number of people did not follow these plans. Asunción Rodríguez, for instance, did not answer "the communications that were directed to you,"[63] whereas Félix Montes wanted to follow his own revolutionary plan, and, Gil Borges, who was working at the Pan American Union and did not want to abuse his stay in the United States, would "fulfill his duty when asked."[64]

Other revolutionaries in New York at the time centered their plans on Arévalo Cedeño and León, who formed a rival rebel group. In 1922, León,

Manuel Antonio Pulido Méndez, Miguel Zúñiga Cisneros, and Arévalo Cedeño founded the Partido Republicano in Mexico, with a branch soon afterwards established in Panama, headed by Jugo Delgado, Horacio Blanco Fombona, Nava, L. Guevara Travieso, and Humberto Tejera. In 1922, Arévalo Cedeño arrived in Panama by way of Colombia after his campaign, partly financed by $200 sent by Ortega Martínez, failed. In Panama, he met León and encountered the usual rivalries and difficulties to unify the various rebel factions. Arévalo Cedeño and León then traveled together to New York to attend a conference convened at Rivero's clinic in the city, and attended by, among others, Ortega Martínez, Baptista, Rivero, Olivares, and Tellería.

While in New York, Arévalo Cedeño and León initially joined the URV, requesting $20,000 to start their own revolution. This was rejected, and after an acrimonious meeting both men left the political party because it was "a caudillista instrument."[65] Biamón was willing to advance funds to Arévalo Cedeño if he secured sufficient outside support. Consequently, on November 3, 1922, Arévalo Cedeño, together with a Venezuelan youth organization headed by Sergio Ruiz Urrutía, sent a circular to all exiled Venezuelans inviting them to attend a meeting on November 11 at the Hotel Ansonia, 2109 Broadway, in New York. At the same time, León and Arévalo Cedeño met with a number of "innocent foreigners"[66] to establish themselves as part of the leadership of the Venezuelan opposition. The traditional caudillos, however, failed to show up at the New York hotel "because they knew that a Directorate of the Revolution would be proposed by all those present."[67]

At the meeting, it was agreed to form a supreme directorate of the reactionary revolution for the purpose of toppling Gómez. It was headed by León and composed of Rivero, Jugo Delgado, Fortoul Hurtado, Montes, and Jesús María Godoy Pinto,[68] with Arévalo Cedeño as military leader. Certain exiles, such as Nicolás Hernández, felt that the party's political program, which was written by León, was a "constant repetition of hollow verbiage that was completely wasted, by suggesting laws that are already on the statute books but are not applied."[69] Nevertheless, a number of different exiled groups such as the Unión Libertadora of Costa Rica, the Partido Republicano Venezolano of Panama, and the Unión Revolucionaria Venezolana and Sociedad Democrática Venezolana of New York joined the new organization.[70]

The most pressing problem was the need to acquire funds. Dr. Marco Aurelio Herradora, a Central American politician and head of a drug company in the United States "who had great influence on companies in the

United States and who was an expert in helping the Yankees to acquire contracts in the Central American republics, to the detriment of the country's sovereignty,"[71] offered to help the exiles. Herradora set up a meeting between León and Arévalo Cedeño and an American company represented by an American colonel, whose presence was interpreted "as the hand of American intervention and we prepared ourselves to resist the pretensions and the abuse of the Company."[72] At the end of the meeting, the rebels were offered a boat and guns, and "everything that we need for the Revolution and lots of money."[73] Arévalo Cedeño would command the ship from US waters and would repay the help offered with interest. According to Herradora, the company did not want to charge for the loan, but "once victorious, we will give the Company enough land for its business."[74] Such a deal, however, was unacceptable.

The revolution was thus stillborn, but some of the rebels continued with their quest to topple Gómez by whatever means possible. Other rebels by the early 1920s were not so keen to continue with the struggle. By 1923, Rolando buried his differences with Gómez and in April of that year left Caracas for Barcelona (Anzoátegui State), his hometown, to "busy myself with the aqueduct of said city."[75] The iron grip that ruled the country nevertheless appeared to be weakening, with a split among Gómez's own supporters, and although he was reelected in 1922, the future of his regime seemed in doubt.

Renewed Hope

In the early part of 1923, the rebel cause received a financial boost. In March, General Mario Terán arrived in New York with a $30,000 check from Mibelli to Baptista. At a meeting at Rivero's clinic, Baptista proposed to advance Arévalo Cedeño $5,000 for him to organize an invasion from Colombia, with further funds following later. President Obregón of Mexico had also sent $8,000 to Arévalo Cedeño, who never received it.[76] Although Arévalo Cedeño was unhappy with these arrangements because they were full of problems, he was willing to participate because revolutionary life in New York had become meaningless for him. Traveling under a false name, Arévalo Cedeño left the United States for Colombia, going first to Canada and then doubling back to the United States, from where he proceeded to Panama and finally reached Cúcuta, Colombia. Soon after his arrival, Arévalo Cedeño's plans collapsed because his invasion plan appeared in full in a Colombian newspaper soon after Carabaño and Alberto Smith met with Pedro Nel Ospina, the Colombian president, about the plot.

Despite Arévalo Cedeño's setback, in May 1923 Baptista, Castro, Alcántara, Peñaloza, Carabaño, Vargas, Olivares, León, Ortega Martínez, Rufino Blanco Fombona, Luis Núñez, Santos, Carmelo Castro, Arévalo Cedeño, Flores, Jacinto López, Tellería, Rivas Vásquez, and Francisco de Paúla Reyes signed a pact in New York to liberate Venezuela from its despotic regime and establish democracy there. Once the revolutionaries landed on Venezuelan soil, Baptista would be appointed provisional president and would appoint a provisional cabinet that included Castro as vice president. Soon after the country was secure, elections would take place for a constituent assembly that would meet in Caracas three months later.[77] The rebels approved the purchase by Baptista in the United States of the 1,100-ton yacht *Gloucester* of the Corsair type, with a top speed of sixteen knots. It was built in 1903 by William Armstrong and Company and used as a transport ship during the First World War. The yacht, which was registered in Panama and renamed *Angelita,* was moored at a pier on Twentieth Street in Brooklyn harbor, with Angel Dubuc, Baptista's German son-in-law,[78] the nominal owner. Virgilio Fuenmayor would captain the ship on its voyage to Venezuela.

Negotiations for a cache of arms in Europe still needed to be completed, with Carabaño leaving New York to finalize matters. Carabaño returned full of optimism, traveling to Washington "to meet with Dr. Gil Borges"[79] to convince him to join the exiles. It was now only a matter of refurbishing the *Angelita* "like a proper gunboat"[80] and deciding the date of the revolution. The refurbishment was a disaster; the engine room a complete mess with ill-fitting cabin doors. The repairs became a financial black hole into which the revolutionaries' meager funds disappeared. In the meantime, Baptista left for Colombia, with Arévalo Cedeño, now in Venezuela, requesting more funds to acquire further arms, as he claimed to have lost his arsenal. There was no money left; the cost of the *Angelita* itself together with the repairs to the boat depleted the rebels' financial resources.

With little progress made in Europe, Smith was entrusted to find out what was delaying matters. Certainly the acquisition of a cache of arms was not the problem, with Bendelac informing Smith that the ordnance had been secured. In June, Baptista left New York for Europe on board the *Aquitania,* with a special passport issued by Gil Borges. Aristeguieta was also on board traveling to Paris, with Baptista spending much of his time trying to convince him to join the expedition. To his consternation, Baptista discovered on his arrival in France that no arms had been acquired and that the funds were depleted. It was decided, however, to proceed with the venture after seeing Aranguren, who "promised to finance the enterprise."[81] Soon afterwards, Baptista left for the Colombian border, while Aristeguieta traveled to Trinidad to await further orders from Asunción Rodríguez. A number of agents from Venezuela also arrived in Trinidad at the time to receive orders. F. Veracoechea Briceño, the Venezuelan consul general in Trinidad, reported to E. Urdaneta Maya, Gómez's secretary general, that Alcántara had received funds from the New York exiles.[82] The American consul in Trinidad also indicated to Veracoechea Briceño that "the funds were made available by a North American oil company operating or about to start operations in Venezuela."[83] In June 1923, further reports reached Gómez that Galavís, who was also involved in the revolutionary plot, was in Trinidad seeing the exiles on the island.

Acción Radical Revolucionaria Venezolana

While this activity took place, other revolutionaries established political parties to fight Gómez. In 1923, Pío Tamayo, Francisco Laguado Jayme, Juan Montes, Alberto Ravell, and Luis Alfredo López Méndez founded in La Habana the Acción Radical Revolucionaria Venezolana, a left-wing organization that wanted to study the Venezuelan situation "from the point of view of the alienation of its economic classes in order to reach a coherent explanation and a revolutionary solution to the Gómez dictatorship."[84] The group rejected "all help by foreign governments and foreigners interested in our country, our petroleum and natural resources, but leaves open the way for the spontaneous co-operation of all good international revolutionaries."[85] The following year, in 1924 the Acción Radical Revolucionaria Venezolana invited all exiled Venezuelans to join the movement, issuing in Havana a flysheet, signed by Laguado Jaime, Pío Tamayo, Feliciano Montenegro, Gilberto Gil G., Juan Montes, and Ravell, calling for a revolution to take place in Venezuela.[86] In an open letter to Pérez, the group acknowledged the work done by individual exiles but felt that this was not focused in a coherent manner.[87]

For the nascent revolutionary group the problem with the current Venezuelan political opposition was that it was in the hands of three or four high-profile individuals. Although they did not want to create divisions among the exiles, "a fundamental error has been made in our view because they have tried and are preparing the revolution as if it was a conflict between nations in which there is a need to determine precisely the ordnance and resources."[88] The new group's main weapon would be public opinion and felt that it was a "waste of time to get those financial groups mentioned by you interested while the state of war in the country is not intensified as we are in agreement with you[89] that we are viewed with pity, indifference and at times with contempt."[90] While this debate continued, on October 23, 1923, young exiled Venezuelan workers in New York formed the Unión Obrera Venezolana, dedicated to "fighting the present tyranny in Venezuela," and once Gómez was toppled to work for the improvement of the "working class and people in general."[91] Its first secretary general was Bernardo Suárez.

Juancho's Murder

On June 30, 1923, the Gómez regime was rocked to its foundations when Juancho Gómez, who lived at the Miraflores presidential palace because Gómez was seldom in Caracas, was murdered in his sleep. The regime blamed the exiles as the intellectual authors of the crime, but to this date the murder has never been satisfactorily explained, especially as Miraflores was well guarded and Juancho did not appear to have any enemies, although it was alleged that he was bisexual.

On the night of June 29 Juancho went to the Olimpia theatre to watch an operetta called *El Ultimo Vals* presented by the Compañia de Marina Uguetti, returning to Miraflores at two o'clock in the morning. Juancho was given a sleeping potion by an attendant and was then murdered just before dawn in a horrific manner, with the killers stabbing and slashing his torso repeatedly and then cutting off his feet, hands, and head.[92] Juancho's dead body was found at six a.m., when security was alerted. At Juancho's bedside, a cup was found containing "a narcotic that was probably mixed with the hot drink he drank before going to sleep."[93] Later, Isidro Barrientos, Rafael Andara, Juan Araguainamo, Custodio Prieto, and Encarnación Mujica[94] were detained.

According to T. J. Morris, the British chargé d'affaires, the motive for the crime appeared to be either jealousy from a former mistress or a political enemy such as his nephew Vicentico, who as second vice president wanted to get closer to the presidency. The timing of the murder is significant because it took place five days before Congress ended its sessions, and there was a rumor at the time that Gómez would leave the country to be replaced by Juancho. The suspects for the murder have been reduced to three possibilities: (1) Gómez's common-law wife, Dionisia Bello, "who held an old grudge against Don Juancho for having seduced one of her daughters, and then abandoning her when she became pregnant";[95] (2) Eloy Tarazona, following orders from Gómez because Juancho was planning a coup; and (3) the official version, which was that certain exiles paid for the assassination.

Dionisia Bello's favorite child with Gómez was Vicentico. Prior to living with Gómez, Dionisia Bello was married to General Paulino Torres. From her first marriage, she had a daughter, Margarita Torres, who was engaged to Matute Gómez. However, just before his wedding Matute Gómez learnt from Juancho that his fiancé was not a virgin because he had slept with her. The marriage was cancelled, and Margarita was later found dead. She may have committed suicide, or she was murdered. Dionisia Bello was extremely angry at these events and decided to seek revenge using Isidro Barrientos, who was known to procure boys for Juancho and who had taken a particular fancy to "a strapping lad that was Barrientos's passion."[96] Dionisia Bello decided to make Barrientos so angry over the boy that he would kill Juancho in a fit of jealousy.

Dionisia convinced Vicentico to join the conspiracy because with his uncle's demise he would become first vice president. In this version, on Juancho's return to the Miraflores palace on the dawn of June 30, Encarnación Mujica gave him a sleeping potion, and Barrientos stabbed him twenty-seven times. Dionisia, dressed as a man, kept a look out in case others came to the vice president's rescue.[97] Barrientos, together with Mujica and Andara, were caught and sent to La Rotunda. At the infamous jail, General Julio Hidalgo, who replaced Juancho as the Federal District governor, tortured Barrientos, who refused resolutely to confess, wanting only to speak to Gómez, who could not accept Juancho's bisexuality. It was left to Ovidio Pérez Agreda of the *auditoría del ejército* (army auditors) to inform Gómez of his brother's bisexuality, with the dictator ordering the file to be destroyed and Barrientos killed.[98] Hidalgo reached his own conclusion over the assassination, which was that Gómez ordered the murder because Juancho wanted the presidential chair.[99]

Gerardo Gallegos also attributes Juancho's death to the intrigues of Dionisia, but in his version, she is jealous of losing Gómez to another woman, with Juancho supporting his brother's new love affair. Furthermore, Dionisia felt that Vicentico, her son and second vice president, should enjoy the benefits of being the first vice president. As a result, Dionisia started to plot against Juancho, devising a plan in which the vice president appeared to order the death of his brother by hiring Corporal Falero to do the deed but who prior to committing the crime would confess to Gómez, making Juancho look decidedly bad in his brother's eyes. Gómez wanted to ascertain who was behind the plot and paid Falero sufficient money for him to murder Juancho instead, thus revealing the real culprits behind the plot. Gómez ordered the duty guard to intervene and stop Falero just before he committed the crime in order to prevent his brother's death. However, there was a mix-up, and Ulises León, the guard on duty, arrived too late to prevent the crime. In this version, the murderers escaped to Ecuador, while León was killed in prison. Soon afterwards, Dionisia Bello departed for Europe.[100]

The official version was that the authors of the crime were, according to Gómez, "the same unhappy people who left Venezuela to develop their plans abroad."[101] Salazar Martínez quotes a letter sent to Gómez from a confidential agent in New York in which the detective agency employed to solve the murder concluded that Juancho's murder was "the work of the revolutionaries and was planned in Puerto Rico at a place called Sabana Seca between two Generals, probably Castro and Baptista."[102] It added that Wenceslao Borda, a rich Spaniard, provided the funds for the murder and "helped individuals to return to Venezuela."[103] It should also be noted that at the end of 1922 there was a belief among the rebels in New York that a reward of $25,000 was on offer to anyone who assassinated Gómez.[104]

Gómez explained to his cousin Eustoquio, in a letter delivered by Colonel Leal after the conclusion of the investigation of his brother's murder, that the assassination had been undertaken by "bad, ferocious and cowardly characters."[105] According to the official version, certain exiles bribed Andara, who worked in Miraflores as a dishwasher during the three months prior to the murder, to open a secret passage that connected the presidential palace to Caño Amarillo. The assassins then entered the palace between three and four in the morning, reaching Juancho's bedroom without alerting the palace guards and stabbing him first in the heart and then "two more by the stomach and the back, the last puncturing his lung and four further deep cuts were made in the forearm, severing the arteries of the arm that he instinctively used to shield himself."[106] The murderers then wrapped the body in the bed sheets, closed the mosquito net and "left without being seen nor felt, and from this we can deduce that they are probably professional criminals."[107] The reason for the assassination was that the regime's political enemies felt that by inflicting such a "hard moral blow"[108] on Gómez, he "would die or be disabled physically"[109] because of his poor health.

Whatever the motive, and it is unlikely that it will be known with any certainty in the future, by October 1923 most of the people alleged to be involved in the assassination were detained, with Gómez stating that what remained to be ascertained were the people who formed the Caracas Committee, "those who followed instructions from the enemy abroad, and who gave the order to execute him."[110] Gómez informed José Ignacio Cárdenas that he had sufficient proof in the form of intercepted letters, pamphlets, newspaper articles, and other documents to demonstrate that the exiled rebels had committed the crime. However, none of this was published, with the burden of proof falling on the regime to show that the exiles were the intellectual authors of the crime. In his annual message to Congress on April 26, 1924, Gómez declared Barrientos as the intellectual murderer who executed the assassination through "Rafael Andara, Juan Araguainamo, Custodio Prieto and Encarnación Mujica."[111]

Fund-Raising Continues

The caudillo revolutionaries continued their fund-raising activities. There was talk that the oil companies could provide funds, especially the German ones, a clear reference to the Stinnes Group, which was having problems in Venezuela.[112] At the time, contact was made with anti-Gomecista factions in Venezuela in order to raise funds. Baptista's son-in-law Dubuc, who worked for the Costa Rican firm of Montealegre and Bonilla, made two visits to Venezuela but was unable to secure funding because preparations were too early. He did get the promise of funds once the plot was closer to fruition. Additional assistance was secured from President Obregón of Mexico, who advanced $20,000[113] with the promise of a further $30,000. An American source also "offered $50,000 provided they received the 50 thousand from Mexico."[114] The funds would be used to purchase and arm two ships, with one acting as a decoy. Baptista at the time was busy buying arms and ammunitions, intending to attack through Falcón and then to meet up with other rebels in the states of Lara and Trujillo.[115]

Carlos Castillo in October 1923 informed Gómez from Curacao that a plot was being hatched in Haiti for an invasion force to disembark at Maracaibo and proclaim an independent state that would then be recognized by the United States. According to Castillo, the revolutionaries bribed American officers at Haiti to secure a place where they could deposit arms.[116] In the same month, the Venezuelan government requested the expulsion from Trinidad of Alcántara. Beaumont, the British minister, reported to London:

> From the point of view of British interests the important thing is not to do less than the Dutch at Curacao. If we fall short of any step they may be willing to take, there are many ways in which British Companies working in Venezuela could feel General Gómez's disappointment. The Dutch Minister at Caracas is on such friendly terms with the Venezuelan Government that he will certainly recommend all reasonable compliance with their wishes. Whatever may be thought of the Gómez rule we have nothing to gain by even indirectly assisting his enemies.[117]

As a result, Alcántara left the British island colony, with Pedro E. Betancourt Sucre, the Venezuelan minister, recommending that Colonel George Herbert May, the chief of police, be awarded the Orden del Libertador Third Class for his help in "shutting up the press and forcing Alcántara to leave."[118] It would appear that Alcántara managed to slip back into the island: at the end of December 1923 Betancourt Sucre advised from Port of Spain that a powerful revolution headed by Alcántara and Flores was under preparation because these revolutionaries have "received cash from certain financial people on the island and some other Venezuelans."[119]

There were plenty of arms to be had in Europe, especially in Belgium, where they had been left behind when the Germans retreated from the country at the end of World War I, as long as negotiations were kept away from the prying eyes of the British government. The Rousset House of Paris was either a partner or associated with the Yüngling House of Liege. The Venezuelan rebels commissioned a Mr. Darlow of Bedford in the United Kingdom, who was an agent of Yüngling and a "notorious dealer in arms,"[120] to purchase ordnance. This was confirmed by Belgium's director of public security, who informed Carlos Aristimuño Coll, the Venezuelan minister, that two thousand rifles belonging to Yüngling were going to an unknown destination that was suspected to be the Venezuelan revolutionaries.[121] In August 1923, Diógenes Escalante, the Venezuelan minister at London, reported on K. E(rik) Roeslin, a German citizen, who had been employed by the Gómez administration as head of the Puerto Cabello dock yard but was dismissed when he failed to complete the purchase of a steamship for the Venezuelan government. Since then he held a grudge against the government and had joined the rebels. Roeslin was extremely useful to the rebels, as he still carried official accreditation as an agent of the Venezuelan government. Roeslin left Germany for the United Kingdom to purchase a boat and arms for the Venezuelan revolutionaries, while Escalante, the Venezuelan minister, requested the British authorities to "impede the activities of Roeslin in Great Britain."[122] Roeslin, who was in Danzig between July 4 and 24 "making people believe he is a Swedish citizen involved in the oil industry,"[123] received $229 from the Hamburg-based arms dealer Benny Spiro to act as an intermediary. On July 29, Augusto Dupont, the Venezuelan consul in Antwerp, visited all the arms manufacturers in Liege "using the excuse of wanting to make cash purchases," and discovered "that a person called Yüngling . . . would send somebody called Spiro or his agent in Antwerp, a cache of 2000 rifles but that said arms were under surveillance by the Belgian police."[124]

At the same time, Dupont also met Castro's old arms dealer, who stated that for the past fifteen years no new shipments had been sent to the former Venezuelan president. Dupont then returned to Brussels and Antwerp to find Spiro but was unable to locate him, as he had left for Danzig to collect the arms. Dupont immediately informed Roberto Skutezki, Venezuela's consul in Danzig, about the possibility of the Venezuelan exiles smuggling arms between Danzig and Venezuela. Skutezki located Roeslin at the Danziger Hof hotel, but he refused to answer any questions. Smuggling at the free port of Danzig was easy, since merchandise was rarely inspected when it arrived by sea for transshipment.[125] Skutezki inspected the books of the Customs House and found in the register seventeen boxes of spare parts for cars that immediately aroused his suspicion because Danzig had no car assembly plants.

F. Díaz Paúl, the Venezuelan Consul at Genoa, also reported that he had received word in August that Roeslin was possibly in the city, alerting the authorities to increase their vigilance for any suspicious boat departing for Venezuela.[126] In September, it was reported that Roeslin was probably in Danzig or Hamburg and that a cache of two thousand rifles were destined for the *Gaspe,* which arrived in Antwerp from Boston on August 22. Alba Biagio, an Italian, was the new owner's agent who stated on his arrival in Antwerp that the ship would be sold. As the previous owner was Antonio Fauci, an Italian living in Boston, the Italian consulate in the American city informed his counterpart in Antwerp that it could not change its registry from Italian to French because the ship's papers were not in order. However, in October the *Gaspe* received the Italian government's consent to be sold, and it became a French ship called *Beatrice,* with a crew of four US citizens and eight Frenchmen who together with Biaggio sailed for Santiago de Cuba. The arms from Germany would be shipped to Mexico or Cuba to a secret destination and then transshipped to the *Angelita* but could not be found after four months of intensive cable communications.

The *Angelita* expedition was encountering other problems too. Biamón and Georgetti, who were in Paris at the time, confirmed that Castro was in poor health in Puerto Rico. According to Barceló, "Castro despises and fears Baptista, but he has to help any putsch against Gómez."[127] Zoila Castro was almost bankrupt because Elias Sayago, the administrator of her farms in Táchira, had not remitted any funds recently and "no lawyer wants to make a claim for fear of going to jail."[128] In addition, the government expropriated the land she owned near Caracas without compensation. The other revolutionaries in Puerto Rico at the time were Trino Baptista, Victor Manuel Baptista, Juan Manuel Sanoja, López Bello, and the Ramírez Monagas brothers. The Venezuelan consul reported that "Venezuelan inertia has joined the laggards here."[129] In October, Baptista was in Puerto Rico to determine whether Castro was able to do battle again and invade Venezuela. The former president declined, declaring that "his state of health would not allow him to go on a campaign nor return to his political activity,"[130] but that he would order all his officers to support Baptista. Once the revolution succeeded, Castro would travel to Caracas to start legal action against Gómez. In the meantime, Baptista was trying to negotiate with W. D. Henry the purchase of four thousand rifles and 1.5 million rounds of ammunition.[131]

Toward the end of the year, most of the revolutionaries gathered in Puerto Rico, where a Junta de Defensa Popular Venezolana was formed to discuss the invasion plan. In November, Tellería, Carabaño, and Trino Baptista were on the island, and were soon joined by Ortega Martínez, Baptista, and Núñez. Gómez's spy on the island reported that the exiles wanted to incorporate foreigners against Gómez, adding that "these people become more stupid by the day believing that they are already in La Guaira with a small boat and a small cache of arms ready to topple you."[132] A new deal on arms negotiated by Manuel Ayala brought together Baptista, Pérez, López, and Tellería. Aristeguieta urged Baptista to forget the *Angelita,* moored in Brooklyn for over eighteen months, because the arms would not be available for much longer. The dilemma was that if they acquired the ordnance, they would have to move quickly to make the *Angelita* seaworthy because they did not have sufficient money to purchase another boat. It should be noted that at the beginning of 1924, the Venezuelan government was unaware of the expedition. It was only through the intelligence service of a non-oil company with large interests in Venezuela that it found out that the "Venezuelan revolutionaries in New York were preparing said expedition in the steamboat *Gloucester.*"[133]

In January 1924, Carabaño was back in Santurce, Puerto Rico. He was almost bankrupt because Ortega Martínez's revolution and his trip to Europe two years ago together with other "losses on foreign exchange speculation and bad business deals that were also a result of that trip have set me back $10,000."[134] Carabaño, who only had assets of $5,000, distributed between a house and a representative agency he had in the Dominican Republic for an American machine tool manufacturer, was clearly despondent with the situation because there was very little they could do against Gómez. Carabaño explained to Durán that "we get hit wherever we show our faces: some day our luck will tire of punishing us and then our revenge will come: the thing is that it will find us very old, my hair is completely white, and I assume that you have lost the little hair that you had in the past."[135] At the same time, Víctor Baptista sold the farm at Aibonito he owned together with his brother Trino for $6,000.

Other revolutionaries were not so pessimistic about the possibility of change in Venezuela. In January 1924, Arévalo Cedeño and thirty-eight other rebels invaded Venezuela from Casanare, Colombia, and declared San Fernando de Atabapo the capital of Venezuela.[136] This was Arévalo Cedeño's fifth invasion of Venezuela, which he thought would place him at the head of the army that would march on Caracas. In New York there was confusion about whether Arévalo Cedeño should be supported by the other exiles. Aristeguieta expressed the general mood of the exiles when he stated that Arévalo Cedeño's action was a publicity stunt to assume the leadership of the revolution. Aristeguieta counseled Rivero that Arévalo Cedeño should not be backed.

León later joined Arévalo Cedeño, stating that the funds secured from Mexican President Obregón "were lost in useless operations of the Revolution and nothing could be expected from abroad."[137] After this failure, Arévalo Cedeño accompanied by León and Colonel Alejandro Agostiniet, arrived at Manaos to proceed to Belem. León, who had been secretary to Felipe Carrillo Puerto, the Socialist governor of Yucatán,[138] left for Mexico with a letter of introduction to President-elect Calles from his former Mexican employer. Arévalo Cedeño returned to New York, where "he extinguished himself on Columbus Avenue."[139] According to Aristeguieta "the so-called opposition was always inept and clumsy; nothing was achieved with the arrival in New York of León and Arévalo,"[140] with the revolution dying of paralysis while the caudillos "were always free spirits. León and Arévalo had the destiny of Venezuela in their hands."[141]

In the middle of June, Ortega Martínez, who according to Rivas Vásquez—who first met him in New York in 1917—was the "prototype of the vain man, without talent, nor aptitudes of any kind, holding on desperately to the illusion that he should be President of Venezuela,"[142] and Rolando joined the rebels. They rationalized their action by stating that the common enemy was Gómez: "it is Gómez who should be destroyed, and he is the one we must fight."[143] Olivares would lead the armed expedition that was rumored to have secured approximately 3,800 arms and rifles in Canada under Pocaterra's diplomatic immunity because he was the Dominican Republic's consul in Montreal. It was assumed that Pocaterra could acquire more ordnance using his diplomatic status. It was also reported at the time that Ortega Martínez and Baptista approached L. F. Hoover, an arms dealer in the United States, to acquire machine guns. Arcaya, the Venezuelan minister at Washington, dismissed the story as untrue because it was easier to purchase arms in Europe, especially in Belgium, the Netherlands, and Germany. In September 1924, Ortega Martínez and Baptista, through Major Frederic Shake of Berlin, who acted as an intermediary between the rebels and an unknown arms dealer, secured in the German capital an offer of 750 seven-millimeter rifles, with between 20,000 and 25,000 rounds of ammunition that were "hidden in a farm."[144] With the help of the Mexican legation, it would not be difficult to ship the cache of arms out of Germany. Although further supplies of the seven-millimeter rifles would be harder to secure, the 1888 model (eight-millimeter-caliber Mauser carbines) and the newer 1898 model could be obtained from "communist entities who have large deposits."[145] The 1898 model, with 1,000 rounds, would cost $28 each for orders of between 5,000 and 10,000 units, but for an order above 100,000 units a reduction of between $1 and $1.50 per rifle could be obtained. The cost of the older rifles, with 1,000 rounds of ammunition, was considerably lower, at $10 per unit. A boat to transport the cache of arms and the rebels could also be supplied for $44,160. Although we do not have conclusive proof that Mexico financed this expedition, according to Pulido Méndez, Baptista secured funding from Mexico on condition that he took the money before Calles came to power.[146] It is likely then that the funds placed at the disposal of the plotters by Mexico's President Obregón were used to purchase the arms, with the Mexican legation in Berlin used to ship the arms to the United States.

The revolution was now in full swing with contracts drawn and signed and a military plan masterminded by Eduardo Prince, a Venezuelan by birth but a naturalized Salvadorian. Prince recruited a number of mercenaries, including Victor M. Gordon, who was in charge of the military part of the plot, and a Mr. Friedman, who was responsible for securing the cache of arms and the revolution's finances. According to Delfino, Gómez's son-in-law who was in New York at the time, Friedman "represents certain important people, among them those who possess the arms, who are willing to place them at our disposal,"[147] with the cost of transport, the ship's charter, and general mobilization expenses borne "by these capitalists."[148] Delfino's informant was probably Sama de Atenero,[149] who as legal counselor at the US Justice Department, had "under my responsibility all matters related to the Hispanic-American revolutionaries, who made New York their operational headquarters,"[150] and who alerted Rincones as to what was happening. Ortega Martínez received $25,000 "for the dispatch of agents and the organization of our forces."[151] If the revolution succeeded, the value of the arms would be repaid, thirty days after the new government established itself, at three times the nominal purchase value of $44,160. In addition, the new government would pay Gordon and his mercenaries the astronomical sum of $1 million for services rendered, while Friedman would receive $800,000 for his financial backing and Prince would be paid $200,000 awarded in government bonds that could be sold "six months after its issue."[152]

In early November 1924, Baptista, Carabaño, Tellería, Olivares, and Pérez were in New York to discuss their revolutionary plans. Although they were against war because most revolutions only substituted one tyrant for another and so in essence maintained the dictatorial regime, they felt it was a necessary evil in the case of Venezuela. The result was that on November 19 they signed the "Pacto Revolucionario Antigomecista del 'Angelita.'" The pact was against *personalismo* and would fight to create a government that did not succumb to this tendency. Consequently, the rebels "agree to be *the guarantors of the agreement,* and that from now on not only the Supreme Director of the war but all the other leaders who carry arms will not for any reason or pretext be re-elected to the presidency of the country in the provisional government that is to be established"[153] (emphasis in original).

The *Angelita* underwent a last minute refurbishment, taking longer than the rebels anticipated, with its departure delayed by a few more days because the revolutionaries wanted to register the ship under the Panamanian flag but failed owing to the efforts of Rincones, the Venezuelan consul. In order to fool the Venezuelan authorities, Aristeguieta convinced the revolutionaries to sell the *Angelita* to Rivas Vásquez in Cuba on condition that in the event of failure and while she was still of service, he promised to "feed the officers and the ship's crew, to pay their wages and to repatriate them to their various destinations."[154]

The ship finally left the United States on November 18, with a passenger list of seven Americans and twenty-eight other members, none of whom appeared as Venezuelan nationals. However, most of the passengers, including Baptista, Olivares, Tellería, Manuel M. Urbaneja, and Pérez, were Venezuelans using assumed names and nationalities to avoid suspicion from Gómez's spies. Rincones reported that the other passengers were probably recruited by José Heriberto López from the Unión Obrera Venezolana.[155] Although the ship's stated destination was Cuba, it headed first for Mexico to pick up the cache of arms stored there. The ship did not get very far because twenty-four hours after leaving port it entered Newport News for repairs. It remained in port until November 26, when once again it headed south. A further complication arose when the rebels realized that the purchase of the arms had not been completed. Two telegrams were received requesting further payments of $3,000 and $6,000 respectively in order to finalize the purchase in Mexico. Although the request for further funds brought about the first disagreement among the revolutionaries, the money was wired to Manuel G. Betancourt at Plaza Orizaba, Mexico City, to complete the purchase. The ship suffered another technical breakdown on its way south and was forced to limp into Key West, Florida, for further repairs, as well as purchasing more coal, "since the fuel they had taken on in New York was of bad quality and was being consumed at double the rate calculated."[156]

A further $4,200 was forwarded on November 28 to Captain Alex Hager in order to complete the repairs.[157] W. Wainright, the ship's engineer, was paid what he was owed, and the ship left Key West only to come to a complete standstill after three hours of travel. Further repairs to the ship's turbines were made at four in the morning but all to no avail. To complicate matters further, the ship ran out of food and provisions owing to the rebels' miscalculation and "ignorance of this vital operation,"[158] almost causing a mutiny among the mercenaries that was averted at the last minute. After some hasty repairs, the ship limped back into Key West on November 30, where the crew took the ship's mate to court for nonpayment of wages, something the rebels were unable to prove and so were forced to "pay again the wages already paid by Dubuc and the fares to New York, a loss of several hundred dollars."[159] In Key West, Baptista requested from Aranguren a further $6,000 to pay for the additional repairs on the *Angelita.* Their position was hopeless, and the expedition was aborted when the arms in Mexico were no longer available because the contract time had elapsed. There is a certain amount of confusion about the ownership of the *Angelita,* but it seems likely that Rivas Vásquez in Cuba acquired the ship, placing her at "the disposal of the Revolutionary Committee there, for it to take on arms and ammunition, and that said boat then sailed under the Cuban flag for better protection."[160] Blas María España forwarded to Key West $2,000 from his own pocket and $1,000 from Rivas Vásquez to complete the necessary repairs to the ship, which sailed to Havana to load the arms.

A further blow to the revolutionaries came with the death of the sixty-six-year-old Castro on December 5, 1924. Apart from his nephews and nieces and two of Biamon's friends, there were only eight people outside Castro's immediate family present at his funeral.[161] Gómez was relieved to learn of the death of his erstwhile friend and mentor; he felt that the exiles were left without a leader. Gómez informed Francisco Jiménez Arraiz in Havana on January 15, 1925, that with Castro's death "the enemies are leaderless and will do nothing more than talk."[162] Gómez also wrote to Eustoquio Gómez that the government no longer had any enemies "because with Castro dead, everybody is aware that nobody is left abroad who could become a leader."[163] The American minister at Caracas reported that "great relief is felt in Government circles, not out of a fear of Castro instigating revolutionary activity, but of the possibility of provoking the assassination of Gomez."[164] After Castro's burial Gómez telegraphed Zoila Castro on January 15, 1925, informing her in a rather cryptic message that "your interests are guaranteed."[165]

The *Angelita* left Florida and headed for Cuba to pick up the revolutionaries. Rincones alerted Arcaya by telephone, who immediately informed Jiménez Arraiz, the Venezuelan minister at Havana, about the ship.[166] The *Angelita,* with a crew of fifteen Venezuelans and three Americans, reached Havana on December 19 and was impounded on its arrival, but it was later released thanks to the uproar made by the press and Rivas Vasquez.[167] It remained moored until April the following year, when it was towed by the *Donophan* to the Havana Marine Keys Company to "repair the boilers and to place double plates on the water line,"[168] at a cost of $6,000, which was paid by Victor M. Volcán and Nicolás Estensa. A year later, in June 1926, the *Angelita* was sold to Harry H. Root, manager of the Crenshaw Produce Company of Tampa, Florida, a fruit importer dealing mainly with Central America.

The *Angelita* plot was the last organized by the Unión Revolucionaria Venezolana. Gómez's spy network and bad planning by the plotters ensured that the movement failed. The revolutionary caudillos continued their dream of toppling the Gómez dictatorship by force, but from 1926 onwards they were joined by another form of opposition against the dictatorship. That year revolutionary action based on the Marxist tenet of class struggle began, drawing support from people such as León but, more importantly, from a younger generation of political activists such as Salvador de la Plaza, Gustavo Machado, Eduardo Machado, Alberto Ravell, and Francisco Laguado Jayme.

The Civil-Military Movements of 1928

The stability and development of the country together with the added commercial wealth accumulated during the first twenty years of the Gómez dictatorship created new social forces that wanted social reform and political freedom. The economic development of the country was accompanied by the softening of the regime, which decreed a number of general amnesties for political prisoners. This then was the situation in the country that led to the main political opposition publicly manifested during the Gómez regime: the students' revolt of March 1928 and the subsequent army uprising the following month. For their part, the exiles renewed their efforts with greater vigor, with Mexico continuing as an important center of their activities.

In May 1925, the Venezuelan constitution was amended to allow the vice president to perform the duties of the president whenever Gómez desired. Cook, the American minister, reported that such a change allowed Gómez to "turn over at will the powers of President to his son, thus accustoming the people to the idea that at any time José Vicente Gómez may exercise the Presidential office."[1] The new constitution extended the centralization of authority in the national executive even further because it empowered the president to delegate to the vice president the exercise of the executive functions, and it allowed the head of state to appoint provisional state governments until the states adopted the new constitution. Furthermore, the amendment of the constitution allowed the federal executive to locate its seat of government in any part of the country outside the Federal District. The executive could now dismiss all current state presidents to be replaced by presidential appointees until the respective state legislatures elected new incumbents. Such a change allowed Gómez to get rid of any state president he did not like or thought was a threat to Vicentico, in particular Eustoquio Gómez in Táchira and Matute Gómez in Zulia. The general feeling among the diplomatic community, as reported by Cook, the American minister, was that Gómez was trying not only to place Vicentico "in the most favorable position possible to one day succeed him, but to strengthen his own position and at the same time popularize himself with the people."[2]

With these constitutional changes in place there was an unmistakable trend toward favoring Vicentico, who up to now had "been regarded as weak and his father's supporters had opposed him for the reason that they felt a man of his caliber would not be kept in office for long."[3] Others felt that Vicentico showed "possibilities and that his influence will be for a betterment of conditions and preferable to that of other candidates."[4] Frederick C. Chabot, the US chargé d'affaires, reported:

> It is natural to believe that the Gomez family hopes for a Gomez to follow the present President. I am told that "Vicentico" is instrumental in removing the old Don Juancho set from Miraflores; and that he is doing everything in his power to strengthen his popularity in the Army of Venezuela. However, there exists that group of the Gomez family who scorn illegitimate issue taking predominance over themselves, and I understand that "Vicentico" could never take over the Government without bloodshed and the strong possibility of quick defeat.[5]

The diplomatic community felt at the time that Gómez would provoke a political crisis if he placed his son in the presidential office, with Cook, the American minister, reporting that the inevitable outcome would be a coup d'état.[6] As we have seen, the previous year there were rumors of a conspiracy taking place to separate the western section of Venezuela from the central government. At the time, it was alleged that the conspiracy was headed by Eustoquio Gómez and Matute Gómez together with influential Colombians who considered joining the revolt that would separate the states of Zulia, Táchira, and Trujillo and the Cúcuta district of Colombia from their respective parent republics. It was felt that to have any chance of success, the revolt needed the support of Pérez Soto, the president of Trujillo, who initially acquiesced. Pérez Soto later changed his mind, informing Gómez, who squashed the revolt and removed Eustoquio Gómez from Táchira and Matute Gómez from Zulia.[7] It is unlikely that such a plot existed because it is doubtful that any of the participants would have continued to form part of the regime's charmed circle of close advisers to Gómez and who would be found by his side at his deathbed in December 1935. The story no doubt surfaced as a way of discrediting the state presidents and gives a flavor to the type of rumors that Gómez coped with during his long dictatorship.

What is certain is that Eustoquio Gómez, Matute Gómez, and Jurado were against Vicentico replacing his father at the presidency, and it is for this reason that on July 1, 1925, they were replaced as state presidents. According to Cook, Eustoquio Gómez was paid "a large sum of money for quietly relinquishing control of the State of Táchira."[8] It is known that in March 1924 Eustoquio Gómez deposited $613,027 in the Banco de Venezuela,[9] and in May of the same year R. J. M. Donald, manager of the Royal Bank of Canada in Maracaibo, accepted from him a deposit of $574,712 and $766,284 in silver rather than in gold.[10] The following month Eustoquio Gómez deposited $220,091 at the same bank in Maracaibo, and in July transferred $400,000 to the bank's New York branch, leaving $1,204,045 in his account in Zulia.[11] On July 25, of the same year, Eustoquio Gómez transferred $126,017 from his account in the Banco de Venezuela to his account in the Royal Bank of Canada. According to Pedro Emilio Fernández, Matute Gómez in 1926 took refuge in Curacao, where he had $4,734,848 deposited in various banks.

The Regime Softens

In July 1924, Gómez informed General Martín Matos Arvelo that a general amnesty would be declared for political prisoners the following year when the road to Táchira was completed.[12] A small group of political prisoners was first released in May 1925, and a general amnesty was granted on July 5 that took effect on July 24, which was the birthday of both Simon Bolívar and Gómez. Dr. Rubén González Rincones was appointed to head the mission in Táchira to welcome back the large number of Venezuelans whom Eustoquio Gómez had driven into exile when state president. A delegation composed of Vicente Dávila, Samuel Niño, and Isaías Garbiras was sent to Táchira to welcome all returning exiles from Colombia. Many of Castro's former supporters, who were living in exile at the time of his death, now recognized Gómez as their leader, with many returning to Venezuela, including Carmelo Castro, "who seems on excellent terms with President Gomez."[13]

It was estimated that some fifteen thousand exiles, mainly Tachirenses and Trujillanos, returned together with Castro's brothers, Zoila Castro, the Peñuela brothers, Santos, and Pedro María Cárdenas, who was later appointed president of Táchira. In July, Zoila Castro was in Caracas to regain some of her late husband's property and was "well received by President Gomez and granted an interview."[14] Other political prisoners in Venezuela, estimated by the American minister to number five hundred, were released from various prisons, including Iturbe, who was freed from La Rotunda jail and appointed a senator. Pimentel, who would play an important role in the 1929 *Falke* expedition, was also released from La Rotunda prison and left immediately for Panama.[15] A number of important political prisoners, such as Delgado Chalbaud,[16] however, were not released, and many exiles remained abroad in opposition to the Gómez regime.

The softening of the regime was accompanied by a spate of labor disputes in 1925. The most dangerous and potentially damaging conflict was the oil workers' strikes at the Shell-operated Mene Grande and La Rosa oilfields.[17] The workers of the British-owned La Guaira and Caracas Railway also went on strike, followed by the Gran Ferrocarril de Venezuela, a German concern. In Caracas, the Workers Association of the Caracas Tramway Company threatened to strike if a particular obnoxious cashier was not sacked. The management refused, and all the drivers and conductors walked out, demanding at the same time an increase in wages in order to return to work. The demand was so sudden and peremptory that the company was unable to answer within the time required. The press and the general public were in favor of the strikers, with the government taking a neutral stand in the dispute. A few days later, however, one of the trams was smashed by a crowd near a central square of Caracas, forcing the police to disperse the mob with clubs and pistols. When the same scenes were repeated the following morning, Velasco Bustamante, the Federal District governor, intervened; the men's wages were increased, while the cashier, who was the motive for the initial labor unrest, was moved to another post. A few days later, a strike threatened by the workers of the Caracas-Valencia Railway Company was averted by the intervention of the government.

H. A. Hobson, the British minister, reported that the government's attitude was ambivalent toward the disputes because they cannot "wish to encourage trouble, yet their half hearted protection of the company and the innuendoes in the Government press, their sympathies were seen to have been wholly on the side of the workers."[18] Support for Gómez in Caracas came from the Confederación de Artesanos, Obreros e Industriales del Departamento Federal, which wanted to celebrate the Day of Peace on July 21,[19] with "a huge and magnificent manifestation."[20] Velasco Bustamante thought it was a good idea because it showed "full acceptance of your policies by the working classes."[21] Arcaya, the interior minister, addressed the demonstration, stating that "alienated men strive in foreign countries to use the power of the working class to destroy the current civilization."[22] At the same time, Gómez provided land for the Centro de Artesanos y Obreros to build its headquarters in Maracay.

Parting of the Ways

A distinct split among the exiled revolutionary community can be detected at that time. Up to then, all exiles essentially had as their major objective the toppling of the Andean tyrant. Political ideology was not at the forefront of the struggle, but from that point on it became more important. There was a distinct polarization between two groups of exiles, viz, a left-wing group based mainly in Mexico and the old caudillos, who remained mostly in New York and Europe. The efforts by left-wing exiles to form groups that appealed to a mass following continued unabated, albeit on a minuscule basis. On June 8, 1924, in Barranquilla, Pío Tamayo, Luis M. Arévalo, and a group of exiles founded the Unión Obrera Venezolana to fight for workers' rights and against Gómez; it was conceived as a "political party for the working classes."[23] According to Machado, the new organization was the "first Venezuelan organization to follow the teachings of Marx and Engels."[24] The following year, Salvador de la Plaza and Gustavo Machado, representing the Third International, arrived in Havana from Paris and published a Marxist interpretation of Venezuela's current political situation. In August of the same year, the newspaper *Venezuela Revolucionaria* started to circulate in Panama.[25]

Mexico became the central focus of the left-wing Venezuelan revolutionaries who received financial support from the CROM and the Mexican government. José Prevé, as a labor leader and a former member of the Regidores of Mexico City, had in the past recruited "enthusiastic Mexican laboristas [*sic*]"[26] to join the Venezuela revolutionaries. After the failure of the

Angelita, the Mexicans reconsidered their policy on political assistance and decided to support organized political parties instead of individual efforts. The change of heart occurred because the Mexicans felt that the Venezuelan exiles had taken advantage of their largesse. Prevé, one of the most important links between the Mexican government and the Venezuelan exiles, informed Smith in a direct and blunt manner that all Venezuelan exiles who had secured money from the Mexican government were crooks and "rogues that end up stealing the leader's money and that of several other members of the government."[27] There was a certain amount of sympathy for this view among a number of exiles, such as León and Arévalo Cedeño, who felt that the funds secured from Obregón had been "lost in useless operations of the Revolution."[28]

Nevertheless, the Mexican government still wanted to topple the Gómez regime. According to Gustavo Machado, León already had 1,500 rifles and 25 machine guns at his disposal from Carrillo Puerto,[29] and with a letter of introduction from the Yucatán governor he met with President-elect Calles.[30] The outcome of the meeting was that León, who was considered by the Mexicans as the only trustworthy person among the exiles, secured from the Mexican government "ten thousand rifles, and up to ten million rounds of ammunition,"[31] as long as he was the undisputed leader of the revolutionary movement, and the military campaign was headed by Arévalo Cedeño, who would step down after successfully establishing a rebel government and calling elections.

As a result, in 1926 León and Zúñiga Cisneros, at the insistence of Governor Adalberto Tejeda of Veracruz[32] and Morones, head of CROM, formally founded the Partido Revolucionario Venezolano (PRV) in Mexico City, through which the Mexican government would channel funds to certain Venezuelan exiles rather than provide financial support to individuals. The PRV, which also received financial backing from the Soviet Union, followed the same tenets as those of the Mexican revolution, that is, redistribution of land, nationalization of the subsoil wealth, restriction of foreign capital and investments, syndicalism, free education, and no presidential reelection.[33] The party was to be a pluralistic one, formed specifically to topple Gómez. It published the *Obrero Libre* newspaper together with the Unión Obrera Venezolana.

Once it had achieved power, the political program of the PRV, which in March 1928 was dubbed by Rómulo Betancourt as "Perros Rabiosos Venezolanos" (Venezuelan rabid dogs) would include the breakup of the large landed estates in Venezuela and the expropriation of Gómez's properties together with the emancipation of the peasants. The latter would be organized in peasant leagues, while industrial workers formed labor unions represented in Congress and other legislative assemblies. The separation of the church from the state and a revolutionary army would be established, with embezzlement made a criminal offense and punishable with prison sentences. Women were to be incorporated into political life, with state protection for both children and their mothers. The party also advocated the nationalization of utilities and all energy sources; the creation of a central bank, with land deeds to be negotiable like money; and strict control of foreign capital. State participation in all concessions granted would increase, with industrial and rural education to be established, together with the creation of universities for the masses. As we shall see later, the party organized the ill-fated invasion of Falcón through Curacao in 1929, while Prevé's plan was finally executed in 1931, when Rafael Simón Urbina set sail on the SS *Superior* to invade Venezuela. General Joaquín Amaro, the minister of war in the Mexican government, allowed the Venezuelan rebels to acquire arms and a ship in Mexico without difficulty. Prevé was appointed commander in chief just to make sure the funds were put to good use.

The Origins of the Falke *Expedition*

Despite the setback of the *Angelita*, the revolutionaries continued their quest for glory by trying to topple Gómez, but the same problems remained, namely a lack of finance and disputes among themselves as to who would lead the revolution. The problem of coordinating such disparate characters with varying aspirations, and living on different continents, was a difficult and thankless task. The expedition, which would later be known as the *Falke* and headed by Delgado Chalbaud, had its origins out of the failure of the *Angelita.* It would be the best planned and the one that had the greatest chance of succeeding, showing what a military mind could do in such circumstances. It was the only rebellion that really threatened Gómez and his government at a time when the repercussions of the Great Depression were about to be felt in the country.

At this stage, Román Delgado Chalbaud was not involved directly in the rebellion, as he remained imprisoned in La Rotunda in Caracas. Most of the revolutionaries involved with the *Angelita* fiasco met in March 1925 at

Aibonito, Puerto Rico. The Venezuelan consul reported that the rebels "have something in their hands"[34] because their "joy is palpable"[35] as a result of the involvement of Aranguren in funding their quest. The Venezuelan oilman, who was referred to as the mysterious "Mister" in the correspondence, together with Aristeguieta was planning a new revolution that would be headed by Arévalo Cedeño. Aranguren's sole condition for his financial help was that once the revolution succeeded he should be appointed president.

After their meeting at Aibonito, the revolutionaries renewed their peregrinations around the Caribbean, the United States, and Europe, alerting other exiles of their plans and seeking funds and support for the forthcoming revolution. Biamón also agreed to help, traveling to the United States, Spain, France, Switzerland, Italy, and the United Kingdom "in a trip for both recreational and study purposes"[36] to secure assistance for the revolution. Other revolutionaries such as Alcántara arrived in Curacao[37] on April 25, 1925, for consultation with the exiles on the island, leaving a few weeks later on June 10 for San Juan and then New York.[38] In September, Aristeguieta traveled to Europe to start negotiations with the "Mister," who according to Córdoba was "a very reserved foreigner, with more money than hair,"[39] who could finance the revolution but only if Domínici headed the revolutionary committee.

The Search Is On for New Funds

It was clear to the caudillo revolutionaries that Mexico was out of bounds for securing funds for their plans. Moreover, Aranguren, the millionaire oilman and eternal financier of failed rebel expeditions, was getting close to the end of his tether, with the result that the rebels would be unable to rely for funds from this source. It was felt that the obvious place to seek new funds for their plans, as in the past, would be with prospective or dissatisfied investors in the country, with some exiles beginning to focus their attention on the possibility of obtaining support from the oil companies, especially as the oil boom in the country was in full swing.

After the failure of the *Angelita,* Ortega Martínez continued to look for funds to finance another filibustering expedition. In 1924, Harold Lindblad, the Norwegian consul in Trinidad, who claimed that he was a former commander of the Swedish navy and that he could be useful in securing arms and sailing a ship for the rebels, met Alcántara in Port of Spain. Lindblad originally arrived on the British colonial island in June 1917 from Colón,

Panama, where he had worked for the Johnson Line Company, unsuccessfully seeking oil concessions in the British colony and in Venezuela. Lindblad then turned his attention to developing an agricultural estate acquired on the British colony. It is likely that Lindblad convinced Alcántara that certain oil companies would be interested in supporting his revolutionary activities. Consequently, Lindblad in September 1925 was appointed chief of naval staff and financial agent for the "Patriotic Movement for the Establishment of a Constitutional Government in Venezuela,"[40] traveling to New York to confer with a number of large American oil companies to ascertain whether they would support the rebels. The Standard Oil Company[41] agreed initially to participate through somebody identified as "L," but became alarmed once the plot was discovered by Gómez and withdrew their support. While in New York, the German Stinnes syndicate was approached, but all companies contacted in the United States turned down Lindblad's offer to participate in the revolution. Despite the refusal of Standard Oil, the revolutionaries still entertained the idea that once the affair quieted down, the oil company would be attracted to the venture again.

On his return to Trinidad, Lindblad met with Colonel Medlicott of the British Controlled Oilfields Ltd. (BCO), who was returning to England from Venezuela after trying to acquire further oil concessions for his company. Lindblad took this as his cue and suggested to Medlicott that if the BCO helped the revolutionaries with $48,600, Alcántara would grant "them as many concessions as they asked for"[42] on reaching power. Lindblad further explained to Medlicott that Alcántara preferred "to have British support,"[43] although the Standard Oil Company in New York and a German oil syndicate had been approached with a similar offer. Medlicott, however, did not commit himself because he wanted to find out more about the plot in order to inform the Venezuelan minister at London, and suggested that Lindblad should outline his plans to the company's board of directors in London. In order to avoid the erroneous impression that the company was involved in the plot, the Foreign Office ordered the British minister at Caracas to inform Gómez directly of Lindblad's efforts, since "rumours of subversive activities by oil companies are frequently heard in Venezuela."[44]

The recurring theme of a separatist Zulia state surfaced once again in April 1926, this time inspired by a Thomas Lee article[45] on the state's precocious oil fields. This was not taken seriously by the Caracas government because it was felt that the American oil companies would not favor such a movement as "they are well treated by the government, have large amounts invested in property, some of which is outside the Maracaibo district, and that the unsettled and troubled times would interfere with their operations."[46]

In Paris, Aristeguieta continued his efforts to persuade Aranguren to contribute funds to the revolution. At the beginning of 1926, E. Vivas Pérez briefed Aranguren on Venezuela's political situation, which was characterized as being in a complete state of anarchy. Aranguren was assured that a number of influential people close to the regime were maneuvering to place themselves in a favorable position in case of Gómez's demise, which was predicted to happen soon as a result of natural causes or by accident. The old Liberales Amarillos, headed by Matos, supported Vicentico "to reach power and later to betray the office,"[47] while others were making conspiratorial pacts with the military strongmen of the regime, with all convinced "that the rebellion will take place inside the country rather than outside."[48] The feeling conveyed to Aranguren was that the regime was tottering and on the brink of falling, with Gómez soon to be kicked out by his own close-knit circle of family, friends, and advisers. There was an urgent need to act soon because such a window of opportunity for the rebels would be lost once the new regime was installed in Caracas.

After several months of discussion Aranguren agreed in March 1926 to contribute up to $100,000 toward financing the rebellion, provided that Arévalo Cedeño's own revolutionary plans were not implemented by the time the rebels were ready. For his part, Arévalo Cedeño convinced Aranguren that he would succeed where others had failed because, among other things, he had the financial backing of the Mexican government. Arévalo Cedeño intended invading Venezuela either through Táchira, Arauca, or eastern Venezuela, with León as the proposed new president of the country. On March 14, the strange "Mister," according to Aristeguieta, finally gave his "formal promise that if we can organize ourselves according to Arévalo Cedeño and León's plan, we could automatically count with one hundred thousand dollars, a sum that is sufficient to guarantee our success."[49] At the time, Generals A. J. Sánchez and Barret de Nazaris, together with Y. Spinetti and Mr. Love, who was secretary and treasurer of the Tonopah Extension Mining Company,[50] wanted to acquire two thousand rifles, two million rounds of ammunition, and airplanes and to charter a steamer to carry them to one of the islands offshore from Venezuela, where they would meet other exiles to attack Ciudad Bolívar. Part of their funding activities included raising money on Wall Street, with the company issuing 400,000 new shares of preferred stock on March 4, 1926, to acquire new mining prospects.[51] The

Venezuelan rebels also contacted General Gray, a former British officer, and Major Ross, a former American officer, in New York for technical assistance, but both were unwilling to assume the risk.

The efforts to get British oil companies interested in funding the revolutionaries continued when on June 20 Lindblad, representing the rebels headed by Ortega Martínez, had an appointment to meet with Lord Buckmaster, chairman of BCO, at the company's London headquarters. Lindblad was shown to a waiting room, where instead of seeing the chairman he had a meeting with Colonel Medlicott and A.D. Butler, the company secretary. After presenting his credentials, Lindblad proceeded to state that the revolution would start in Trinidad with the full backing and control of the states of Guayana and Bolívar and Delta Amacuro Federal Territory as well as support in western Venezuela, with a Caracas garrison the only likely opposition to be encountered by the rebels. Lindblad further stated that he had failed to acquire arms in Belgium, Italy, and England but had secured in Germany a cache of arms and had chartered a two-hundred-ton trawler for ten weeks, which he would captain "to take arms to a rendezvous in Venezuela."[52] Lindblad wanted to purchase a further thousand rifles, a number of machine guns, and other arms and equipment in Germany at a total cost of approximately $48,600.[53] In return for financing the expedition, the BCO would "be given favourable terms and concessions"[54] in the country's expanding oil industry.

Lindblad was informed the following day that the BCO board had refused flatly to accept his proposal while giving their wholehearted support to Gómez.[55] Lindblad persisted and telephoned the BCO later that day, stating that Alcántara had received $24,300 from other sources, leaving only $24,300 for the company to finance, but he received no satisfaction. Lindblad also made a similar proposal to Andrew Agnew, a director of the Caribbean Petroleum Company, one of Shell's Venezuelan oil-producing subsidiaries, but the company "would naturally have nothing to do with the matter."[56] Lindblad then left for Germany to negotiate the purchase of arms. In the meantime, the Foreign Office was informed of Lindblad's activities, and they in turn briefed the Venezuelan government.

The Foreign Office debated whether Lindblad should be expelled from Britain. It would be easy to do this because it could be argued that Lindblad had overstayed and had given false information by calling himself commander of the Swedish Navy when he was only a Norwegian naval captain. The opinion of both Scotland Yard and the Foreign Office was that Lindblad should be allowed to remain in the United Kingdom "in order that if his intrigues against the Venezuelan government continue and seem likely to meet with success, we should then be in a position to act promptly."[57] Escalante, the Venezuelan minister, reported to Gómez on the Lindblad case that "the attitude of the oilmen here, as well as the Norwegian and British governments have been extremely friendly towards us."[58] The Foreign Office did apply pressure on Norway to recall its consul in Trinidad, with the result that Lindblad resigned from his consular post in the middle of July. Lindblad could, nevertheless, return to the British colony because he did not require an entry visa, and could only be prevented from entering by the colonial office instructing "the Governor of Trinidad to take steps to prevent his landing there."[59] The Venezuelan government placed pressure on the British government to stop Lindblad from returning to the island, alluding to the possibility that the good relations that existed between the two countries would be seriously interfered with by any "revolutionary movement, however harebrained and however easily suppressed which had been fomented on British territory."[60] There was no need to worry because N. Byatt, the governor of Trinidad, took immediate steps to prevent Lindblad from landing in Trinidad.

Prior to this, on April 22, Alcántara left Trinidad for Cuba, returning on July 13 via Santa Marta in Colombia onboard the SS *Canuto*. Two weeks later, on July 26, he was interviewed by M. Costelloe of the Trinidad constabulary, who concluded that Alcántara was "very keen to topple General Gómez but he does not feel he will do it from Trinidad as there are few Venezuelans at Trinidad as most have returned to Venezuela since Gómez proclaimed a political amnesty."[61] In spite of this, on August 26 Alcántara was served with an expulsion order from Trinidad, making his way to Martinique on the SS *Dominica* on September 3.[62]

Back to Square One

The rebels had failed in their efforts to secure finance for their revolutionary venture. In October 1926, Alcántara, Carabaño, López Bello, Francisco de Paúla Reyes, the Montes brothers, Juan Dolores, and Hilario Montenegro were back in Puerto Rico for what could be described as a summit meeting to decide the best way forward. On October 16, Georgetti joined them on his return from Europe. Juan Santaella, the Venezuelan consul in San Juan, with the help of E. B. Wilcox, hired a private detective to watch the revolutionaries on the island. Both the Venezuelan government and the island's authorities were very "interested in discovering if any of these men had subversive intentions, in order to apply the laws of the United States to those who are plotting against friendly governments."[63] The discussions proved difficult because the rebels' options were severely reduced without adequate financing. The meetings continued throughout October and into most of November with no agreement as to what needed to be done. As they approached the year's end, a sense of despondency gripped certain revolutionaries, with some having second thoughts about fighting Gómez. After many months of dithering, Alcántara left on February 14, 1927, for the Dominican Republic, convinced that "it is utter madness to think about overthrowing"[64] Gómez, because of the country's increasing prosperity and progress. Alcántara would eventually establish himself in Puerto Plata on the north side of the island, initially administering a sugar estate and later heading an urban project financed by the Compañía Anónima Cubana Industrial Antillana,[65] one of Rivas Vásquez's companies. The latter was now a declared friend of Gómez who no longer wanted to have anything to do with the exiles.

The rebels' spirits were lifted in early January 1927, when Aristeguieta secured from the "company" he had previously spoken to in Mexico City, and most probably the Mexican government, the offer to help the revolution by doubling the $100,000 credit available to it with no strings attached. Santos Domínici later assured Aristeguieta that up to $150,000 in credit could be secured, provided the "company" guaranteed delivery, and negotiations were to be concluded in Europe. Aristeguieta started immediately to negotiate "the arms with a subsidiary Company that was not exposed to the monitoring of the United States."[66] In February 1927, Arévalo Cedeño was back in San Juan to gauge the support he had among the other revolutionaries on the island, leaving soon afterwards for Mexico, where, together with León, he obtained the help of a Mr Salas by "promising the concession of the oil MONOPOLY IN VENEZUELA."[67] Salas soon found out that León and Arévalo Cedeño were in no position to offer concessions, remaining "once again disappointed."[68] Arévalo Cedeño and León then saw President Calles, who ordered Finance Minister Alberto J. Pani to pay León $5,000.[69] Separately, Eduardo Machado and Carlos Aponte saw former Mexican President Obregón at his Sonera hacienda; Obregón offered to supply the Venezuelan rebels with five hundred carbines, twenty-five machine guns, half a million rounds of ammunition, and various dynamite boxes.[70] Obregón wanted the Venezuelan rebels to include a number of "Villista" generals because they had become a nuisance for the Calles administration. The invasion would be led by Arévalo Cedeño, who was now in the Dominican Republic securing a boat. The rebels contacted Peñaloza in Cúcuta, Norberto Borges in Barlovento, and Zoilo Vidal in Valencia to invite them to join the rebellion.

In the Dominican Republic, Arévalo Cedeño acquired a schooner that transported large quantities of cargo and would be used to load the arms in Tampico.[71] Machado, Julio Antonio Mella, Carlos Aponte, De la Plaza, and Bartolomé Ferrer traveled to Tampico to await the ship's arrival. However, when the schooner arrived from the Dominican Republic, the Mexican authorities impounded it because it was carrying hundreds of cases of Dominican rum ("Ron Negrita") that Arévalo Cedeño was trying to smuggle into the country to make some money for himself.[72] As a result, Obregón withdrew his support for the venture, and the arms went back to the arsenal. Arévalo Cedeño was expelled from the PRV on September 9, 1927. Over the ensuing months the relationship between Arévalo Cedeño and León soured, and the two went their separate ways in October 1927.

Political Events in Venezuela

The regime in Venezuela appeared in 1927 to be changing, taking a softer political line under the influence of Francisco Baptista Galindo, Gómez's secretary general. The Federación de Estudiantes de Venezuela, banned since 1921, was reestablished on March 16, 1927, at a meeting held in the Teatro Ayacucho, with Jacinto Fombona Pachano elected as the students' leader.[73] Later that month, Gómez, who was convinced that he had extinguished for ever the "revolutionary spirit that is so anachronistic at this time of progress and welfare,"[74] was persuaded by Bishop Antonio Mejía of Guayana to declare a general political amnesty on March 24, releasing the remaining political prisoners from jail, including Delgado Chalbaud, who left La Rotunda after fourteen years of imprisonment.[75] Many of the revolutionaries in exile, such as Mibelli, Tellería, Vargas, and Rivas Vásquez took advantage of the amnesty and returned to Venezuela. Ortega Martínez, who on March 17 arrived in Puerto Rico from Europe to stay with Ramón Ayala, his son-in-law, also thought of returning to Venezuela, as he did not have a kind word to say about the revolutionaries on the island or in New York. According to him, all they did was "to ridicule him and talk about him very badly,"[76] especially after he had spent a great deal of his personal wealth on two abortive expeditions. Ramón Ayala left for Venezuela on March 28 to negotiate his father-in-law's return. In Barranquilla, Pablo César Peñaloza, son of Peñaloza, was also willing to return to Venezuela after the amnesty was decreed, with Gómez forwarding $189 for his trip. Peñaloza's father followed soon afterwards when he had sufficient money. General Emilio Barradas, Peñaloza's business manager, wanted to return but lacked the wherewithal to finance the trip.[77] By the middle of 1927 there were no political prisoners left in Venezuela, with Gómez boasting that no Venezuelan should remain in exile, because his government "does not close the door of the fatherland to anybody."[78] Gómez was also prudent in banning the possession of arms and started a campaign to collect firearms and ammunition from private individuals.

Many of the above plans changed once it was known that Delgado Chalbaud was organizing his own expedition against Gómez in Europe. Soon after his release from prison, Delgado Chalbaud left the country, having secured a medical certificate alleging ill health that required him to seek a cure in Europe. Despite his long sojourn in La Rotunda, Delgado Chalbaud had sufficient energy and stamina—but most important of all, a burning passion for revenge—to secure the financial backing and organize the logistics of the revolution while getting all the petty chieftains to work together. Delgado Chalbaud took up the banner of the opposition, working ceaselessly for the downfall of the Gómez regime.

The Delgado Chalbaud Revolution Takes Shape

Delgado Chalbaud was a curious character to unite the revolutionaries against the Gómez dictatorship. Egea Mier, his first naval commander, described Delgado Chalbaud, when he joined the SS *Vencedor* in 1899 from the naval school, as a tall and thin man who "only projected a thin shadow when the sun fell on him."[79] He always played his cards close to his chest, an "obstinate stutterer who delivered oratory lessons"[80] and had the natural caution and distrust of those born and bred in the Andes.

Delgado Chalbaud settled in Vichy, France, in order to recover his health from his long incarceration. At this stage, Delgado Chalbaud maintained a low profile to avoid drawing the attention of government spies; if he did not, Gómez would "mobilize his resources in order to watch and harass us and what is worse, I will lose my links with the friends in Venezuela, which are worth keeping."[81] Delgado Chalbaud played his role to perfection, with Barceló, the Venezuelan minister at Paris, reporting to Gómez after a lengthy conversation with him at the French spa town that "he is no longer the impulsive and conceited boy we knew, but a gentle and almost disillusioned man, who would be difficult to attract to any revolutionary activity."[82] Moreover, his "discreet and serious"[83] attitude impressed Barceló immensely. However, soon after Delgado Chalbaud arrived at Vichy, the meetings with revolutionary emissaries started. In the middle of April, María de León, León's wife, arrived from Mexico to explore the possibility of Delgado Chalbaud joining forces with León and Ortega Martínez. León's offer had tantalizing appeal: he had secured the backing of an American financial group, and the Mexican government had promised arms and ammunition.[84]

In a separate development in Mexico, Arévalo Cedeño, Pérez, and Rivero tried to persuade Aranguren to back their efforts. Arévalo Cedeño traveled to Paris, where he saw Santos Domínici and Smith, later crossing the Channel to London to meet with Aranguren, who was unable to help until he recovered the losses incurred by past revolutionary expeditions. Arévalo Cedeño then left for Havana to confer with Rivas Vásquez, returning to Paris a month later, when he tried again to persuade Aranguren to help. It was while Arévalo Cedeño was trying to secure funds that León sent the Mexican Colonel Prevé to Paris to confer with Aranguren. Prevé assured the oilman that Morones, the Mexican minister of industries and head of CROM, and other important Mexican politicians were willing "to help the Revolution."[85] Smith also helped Arévalo Cedeño to persuade Aranguren to part with his money, but all was to no avail: nothing was obtained from him except "the Mexican agent's return expenses"[86] and Arévalo Cedeño's return expenses to Martinique, where he was met by Mauricio Berrizbeitía, who agreed to provide $10,000 for his revolutionary cause.

When Arévalo Cedeño failed to obtain the necessary funds for his own rebellion, he decided to join Delgado Chalbaud, returning in August to Vichy to plan and coordinate the help of his Mexican backers.[87] Delgado Chalbaud had in mind an internal uprising that was linked with an external invasion on two fronts, viz, one in the East and the other in the West, from Colombia. The revolution would try to win over some of the young army officers in Venezuela for them to lead a putsch within the Gomecista rank and file army. Once he fully recovered his health, Delgado Chalbaud left Vichy and moved to 17 rue de Babylone in the seventh arrondissement in Paris, from where he started planning in earnest his invasion of Venezuela. In his endeavors, Delgado Chalbaud was helped by a number of people, including Gustave Coubert Gonfreville, a lawyer and secretary to Aristide Briand, who was prime minister of France on eleven occasions between 1909 and 1929, receiving the Nobel Peace Prize in 1926,[88] and who stood unsuccessfully for the presidency in 1931.

At the same time, Pocaterra in Montreal, fed up with the "many extravagances of the paper opposition,"[89] felt that it was the right time to form "a national, constitutional, civil rights party"[90] that brought together all exiles under one banner. Unity would be achieved by having a civilian such as Santos Domínici or Juan José Mendoza heading the organization. Pocaterra argued that most exiled groups followed one individual political line, with the result that little was achieved because each small group did not have the proper resources to achieve their goals. Pocaterra was convinced that the unity of the different revolutionary strands would bring the necessary financial backing for an armed expedition that would open the possibility of a putsch against the regime "in the bosom of Gómez's barracks and their surroundings."[91] Baptista, who discussed at length such an idea with Pocaterra, left for Europe in the middle of May for discussions with Delgado Chalbaud in Paris.[92] The chances of reaching such unity were not good, with Jacinto López and Olivares finding it impossible to reach agreement during this period. Many of the revolutionaries, however, felt that the two main opposition factions within the Gómez regime would probably support a revolutionary uprising if it took place.

The Political Situation in Venezuela Worsens

The political situation in Venezuela in 1927 did not materially improve and was to worsen as the economic situation deteriorated during the year. The sudden influx of wealth from the oil industry and the high price of coffee the previous year was treated by the population as though it was going to last forever, with many people burdened by large debts. The year's coffee crop was poor, and prices for the commodity dropped, with many firms incapable of meeting their export commitments and unable to collect their debts. The oil industry also encountered a minor recession because a large number of new oilfields in the United States started to produce that year, with companies in Venezuela reducing production. This was soon felt by Maracaibo's construction industry, which was forced to lay off thousands of workers when oil activities were halted in April.

The sudden blossoming of a Venezuelan political spring came to an abrupt end when Baptista Galindo died of malaria in May 1927. With his moderating influence gone, the political debate in Caracas centered on who would succeed Gómez. Vicentico, considered the front runner as recently as the previous year, was not even a contender now, unless the group supporting his father shifted their allegiance to him. Many people regarded Pérez Soto as the real challenger for the presidency: he was forceful, had a good knowledge of the country, and was ruthless. There was a determined effort within the regime to ensure that Gómez was not reelected in 1929. Some felt that the only way to achieve this objective was for the United States to make its displeasure known if Gómez continued in power. Gustavo Manrique Pacanins, a deputy in Congress, was the spokesman for this group, headed by Arcaya, the interior minister, who felt he had a good chance of succeeding Gómez if the latter decided not to run for office again. Manrique Pacanins informed Cook, the American minister, that Gómez had previously made it clear to a number of his close associates in April 1927 that he would not be a candidate "but that he and his friends would select a good man to succeed him."[93]

Soon afterwards, however, the Benemérito changed his mind and now wanted to stand for reelection. Manrique Pacanins informed the American minister that such a move would be a mistake because Gómez was "a greatly changed man, mentally exhausted, who had lost all interest in public work, avoiding, if possible, any discussion of public affairs even with members of his Cabinet."[94] Manrique Pacanins assured Cook that Gómez would not complete his term if reelected, but his forceful removal was ruled out because it would only lead to confrontation with the United States. The best solution, Manrique Pacanins insinuated, was for the State Department to intimate to Gómez "that it would be better if he were not re-elected."[95] Cook made it clear to Manrique Pacanins that the US government could not interfere directly or indirectly in the politics of the country, as it was up to the Venezuelans to decide who should rule them. Apart from the secret ambitions of Arcaya, the two other possible candidates for the presidency, viz, Gil Borges, the assistant director of the Pan American Union, and Santos Domínici, a practicing physician in Paris, were known opponents of the regime.

Financial Backing Remains a Problem

The major problem for the rebels remained financial backing. Aranguren was the one source where funds were plentiful, and he was a secret opponent of the Gómez regime. Aranguren had lost a small fortune backing the *Odin/ Harrier* and *Angelita* expeditions and would not be so forthcoming this time. Aranguren insisted on a number of conditions, the most important one being accepted as the sole leader, before backing the revolution. Over the next two years, to the increasing exasperation of the rebels, Aranguren would blow hot and cold on this issue, creating a great deal of frustration among the revolutionaries.

With the possibility of Aranguren's support, the rebels continued with their plans with greater energy, as Delgado Chalbaud was obsessed with organizing a revolution against Gómez. In New York, too, the "revolution business" aptly named by Figueredo, the Venezuelan consul, continued unabated, albeit at a slower pace. Delgado Chalbaud's ordnance requirements were ambitious and expensive, with a shopping list that comprised eight thousand rifles, two thousand carbines, four million rounds of ammunition, six machine guns, and a battery of four cannons. The total cost, including a ship to transport the equipment and men, was estimated at $1 million. Delgado Chalbaud between September and December 1927 traveled three times to London to reactivate his old associates in the United Kingdom who could support his new venture. The money was not forthcoming, and there was a wild rumor that the exiles in New York were planning a bond issue to raise $400,000 to add to the $600,000 already pledged in order to complete the $1 million needed to start the revolution.[96] In December 1927, Pocaterra managed to get hold of a supplier of arms and ammunition, with Delgado Chalbaud rather naively wanting to know whether the firm could deliver the arms to the West Indies or even Venezuela.[97]

At the end of 1927, there was great expectation in Barranquilla among the exiled community that Gómez's enemies in Europe had acquired two boats with sufficient arms to invade Venezuela in March of the following year.[98] Delgado Chalbaud was anxious about the revolutionaries in Mexico because their correspondence attacking him was published, thus alerting Gómez's espionage network that a revolution was being organized in Europe.[99] In March 1928, reports reached Gómez that the revolutionaries had acquired armaments in the United Kingdom that had been shipped to Cartagena, Colombia. It turned out that the arms were for insurgents in China, with the UK government assuring Escalante, the Venezuelan minister, that the shipment of arms to insurgents outside Venezuela from the British Isles would not be allowed.

Civil-Military Movements

At the beginning of 1928, a year that marked twenty years of Gómez rule, the Andean dictator was full of optimism and pride at bringing peace and prosperity to the country and, what was probably even more important to him, preventing the country from returning to the "very sad period of past civil wars."[100] There was no sign that Gómez was going to step down, but instead rumors that he would amend the constitution to extend the presidential term that expired in 1929. The next two years, however, were a period of intense political activity, beginning with the students' unrest in February and culminating with the *Falke* expedition of August 1929.

The 1928 civil-military movement is generally perceived as the beginning of a new period of Venezuelan politics. It is during this period that the future leaders of the political parties of the country started to take their first tentative political steps. The movement, which appeared to have no "organization of any type, and without any program,"[101] would be the first to mobilize a large part of public opinion, with its spontaneous "civil rights character"[102] appealing to its followers. The political situation within the regime, as we have seen, threw up a number of factions, some of which did not want Gómez reelected in 1929. López Contreras, who was the military commander of Caracas at the time and closely allied to the Gómez camp, stated later that the 1928 student movement "corresponded to a preconceived plan to prepare public opinion in the country to receive enthusiastically the Revolution that some compatriots were organizing with the support of individual committees inside Venezuela."[103] After all, Gómez was about to celebrate twenty years in power, which is a long time even by Latin American standards, and, as we have seen, there were rumblings among the Gomecistas that a change should take place within the political establishment, enhanced by the view that the dictator was becoming senile. Behind the group of friends of the regime there were one or two puppeteers who wanted to prevent Gómez's reelection in order to take over the presidency themselves. Gómez, unlike some of his ministers, took the events of the student rag week very seriously indeed, and when all counseled that he should take the soft option, he came down hard on the student agitators.

The Student Week

In early 1928 the Venezuelan Student Federation decided to sponsor a series of cultural events during the year. In order to raise funds for the event, a Semana del Estudiante (Student Week) was planned to coincide with the carnival season in February. The student-military movement would pose the main political threat for Gómez in 1928. In spite of a number of reports of possible trouble, Arcaya, the interior minister, and Velasco Bustamante, the Federal District governor, granted permission for the Student Week because they felt that it would not threaten the regime. The Student Week began on February 6, commemorating the Batalla de la Victoria, when the youth of Caracas under José Félix Ribas fought against the Spanish army of José Tomás Boves, and ended six days later on the twelfth. The aim of the students' celebrations was to collect funds to reopen the Casa de Estudiantes, which had been renamed "Casa Andrés Bello: Morada del Estudiante." Pío Tamayo,[104] who was one of the main leaders of the bloody "Huelga de Inquilinos"[105] in Panama and who would play a crucial role in the forthcoming events, arrived in Caracas in early 1928 and made contact with the university students through his friendship with Raúl Carrasquel y Valverde, the founder of *Elite* magazine.

The students elected Beatriz Peña Arreaza as their queen,[106] and started their celebrations on February 6 with a great procession from the university, which was situated facing today's National Assembly building, to the National Pantheon. There Beatriz, the, as yet, uncrowned queen of the students, deposited a floral arrangement, and Jóvito Villalba gave a speech in which he made certain disparaging remarks about the Gómez regime, and complained that the same level of political freedom existed in Venezuela as in Nicaragua under the dictatorship of Anastasio Somoza. Later, Guillermo Prince Lara, a medical student, "smashed a marble tablet with the name of the *Rehabilitador* in the School of Medicine."[107] From the National Pantheon the students walked to Andrés Bello's birthplace in La Pastora district of the city, where Rafael Angarita Arvelo gave an impromptu speech condemning the Gómez regime for having sold the country to foreign interests. The students then proceeded to the American legation, shouting "Down with the Yankees. Long live Sandino! Long Live Nicaragua!" The American chargé d'affaires did not feel threatened by this behavior, considering the student action part of a number of "childish pranks"[108] rather than a real political protest. Later in the afternoon, the students found themselves in Plaza Ribas, also in La Pastora district of the city, where Joaquín Gabaldón Márquez gave a speech in front of the Ribas monument, drawing attention to the "epic achievement of the Caracas students against Boves,"[109] and making an implicit comparison with the Gómez regime. That evening Beatriz was crowned in the Teatro Municipal, with Pío Tamayo reciting a poem calling for freedom,[110] followed by Juan Bautista Oropeza giving the coronation speech. Rosa Segnini later sang an aria, accompanied at the piano by A. J. Ramos, followed by a musical number by Israel Peña and Pardo Soublette. Jacinto Fombona Pacheco closed the act reciting his poem "Canto a la Reina de los Estudiantes" (Song for the Queen of the Students). The following day there was a car parade in the afternoon, with a gala dance in the evening held at the Club Venezolano. On February 8, there was a further poetry recital at the Teatro Rivolí, situated in front of the Capitolio, where Rómulo Betancourt delivered a speech.

During the course of the Student Week, Arcaya received reports warning him about the possibility of trouble, but he ignored them because he felt they were unimportant and "did not mention anything of this to General Gómez."[111] Velasco Bustamante also formed the same impression, but both men received an unwelcome surprise when Gómez sent them a stern telegram ordering them to keep the students in check to prevent events from getting out of hand.[112] There is little doubt in my view that Gómez felt that the activities of the Student Week were a concerted effort by the opposition to prepare public opinion for the revolution being organized abroad. Such a view has been categorically denied by Joaquín Gabaldón Márquez, one of the students, whose father later joined Delgado Chalbaud in a synchronized uprising with the *Falke*'s invasion of Venezuela. He states that the Student Week "was not a revolutionary movement planned beforehand, nor encouraged in any way by traditional political interests."[113] The two views are not contradictory because it is unlikely that the students were directly involved in any conspiracy. The regime was ready for some sort of coup, and it may well have suited certain members of the regime, such as Arcaya, to allow public opinion to vent its anger against Gómez and thus garner support for change within the Gomecista regime.

The first casualty of the students' "pranks" was Diego Carbonell, the university rector who was replaced by Juan Iturbe on February 9. At the same time, Raúl Leoni, leader of the Federation of Students, met with Velasco Bustamante, who personally made him responsible for any manifestations against the government. Although the Student Week was allowed to continue to the end, the main troublemakers would be detained afterwards. On February 13, the day after the celebrations ended, Velasco Bustamante detained Pío Tamayo, Jóvito Villalba, Rómulo Betancourt, and Guillermo Prince Lara at the El Cuño barracks. In a curious development, the detainees received gifts and fruit the following day from Josefina Revenga de Gómez, Vicentico's wife. Carlos Siso claims that García Velasco, who was the president of Carabobo State, was friendly with the students during the 1928 uprising and was aware of what was happening.[114]

Velasco Bustamante felt that it was unnecessary to imprison the students for a long period and wanted Arcaya to convince Gómez to allow him to free them.[115] Leoni, together with Juan Iturbe, saw Arcaya on Ash Wednesday and asked him to mediate with Gómez. The student leaders also saw Governor Velasco Bustamante but failed to reach a compromise. López Contreras, who was present at the same meeting, suggested that the students should be detained at the university. After this meeting, Velasco Bustamante, who up to then had sympathized with the students, now turned against them. For his part, Arcaya felt that the situation could only be defused if the three detained students were released.

While the government dithered, the political situation degenerated rapidly, with the possibility of slipping into a political crisis, with Arcaya traveling to Maracay to inform Gómez of the events. Prior to his meeting, Arcaya first saw Vicentico at Los Teques, who offered to support him and to change his father's "attitude toward the students,"[116] and to seek their release. Gómez, however, was very worried about the student action and was exceedingly irritated that Vicentico supported such a lenient line because he was convinced that the revolutionaries outside Venezuela were manipulating them. Gómez reasoned that if they were allowed to criticize the regime with impunity, then this would lead to further problems in Caracas. It was also clear that detaining the student leaders for a long period would only serve to aggravate the situation, with Gómez willing to release the students after a few days so long as no further protest marches took place. If, however, they did not agree to this, Gómez would draft them into the army because it was clear to him, at least, that they no longer had any wish to study.[117] Such an action would in itself create legal problems for the regime because it was illegal to send the students on military service because they were "legally exempt from the draft,"[118] as Arcaya pointed out to Gómez. The regime was in a quandary, given Gómez's own uncompromising orders from Maracay and the possible threat of further disturbances from such an innocuous source.

A further meeting took place in Caracas between Velasco Bustamante, Juan Iturbe, Colonel Pedro García (chief of police), and López Contreras to decide the best way of dealing with the situation. López Contreras maintained his view that the students should be confined within the compound of the university,[119] with a full battalion posted in front of the seat of learning. Arcaya then saw Leoni and urged the students to avoid "mass demonstrations against the Government because of the arrest by the police of our three colleagues."[120] Although the arrest warrants could not be revoked, it was proposed that if no further student demonstrations took place, they would be allowed to go free in a few days' time, but Leoni was unable to accept such terms. After this meeting, Gómez did not wait any longer to act, removing from their posts on February 17 the prefect, the chief of police of Caracas, and the secretary of the Federal District, who were replaced by General Guillermo Willet, General Tomás Cabrices, and General Rafael Cayama Martínez, respectively, with clear orders to act decisively. On the night of February 21, three hundred students were sent to Puerto Cabello on twenty buses, with each bus guarded by six soldiers with fixed bayonets. On their arrival at Puerto Cabello on February 24, the students were transferred to the dungeons of the Libertador castle. The twelve foot by nine foot cells were packed with forty students each, little sunlight, insufficient fresh air, and no food for two days. A few days later Hugo Fonseca Rivas, the *jefe civil* of Valencia, arrived at the Puerto Cabello castle and attempted to persuade the students to sign letters requesting Gómez's pardon and admitting that their actions were due to their youthful immaturity. The students refused to comply with the dictator's wishes. Some of the student inmates, according to Raúl Agudo Freytes, a fellow student prisoner, would pass the time away by forming a political science study group that met in the mornings. In the evenings, Pío Tamayo entertained the students with his travel stories.

The imprisonment of the students was followed by further repressive measures. Many of the old military leaders who had retired from active politics such as Zoilo Vidal, Mibelli, and Rafael Arvelo González, who launched the Montes presidential candidacy in 1913, were sent to prison after they tried to get the students released. Other students, together with some of the women who had tried to secure their freedom, were also imprisoned. The sermon at the San Francisco church on the following Sunday, for instance, was interrupted by Isbelia Jiménez Arraiz exhorting the congregation to demand the students' liberty. In addition, a group headed by Carlos Julio Ponte and René Borges Villegas visited the leaders of the banking, commercial, and industrial sectors to request "a stoppage to their activities as a gesture of solidarity with the demonstrators against the imprisonment of the students."[121] This was well received, with many of the young employees of the Banco de Venezuela, for instance, going on strike for several days in support of the students. Moreover, when news reached Caracas of the harsh treatment afforded to the students, many shops closed in protest on February 24, and the dock workers in La Guaira went on strike, with the telephone service in Caracas suspended as a sign of protest the following day. In addition, for three days there were no streetcars or taxis, with the government ordering the arrest of three hundred employees and clerks of the main companies of Caracas, whom it considered responsible for the "sympathetic strike" and sent to the Sombrero and Palenque labor camps. At the time, many handbills circulated in the capital, which became more revolutionary in their tone as the civil stoppage continued.

The students who initially had not been arrested thought of marching to Maracay to confront the dictator, but after much debate abandoned the idea, deciding instead to embarrass the regime by surrendering voluntarily to the police to share the same fate as the imprisoned students. The student group had become a mob when it arrived at the governor's palace, which was saved from being attacked by the measures adopted by Eustoquio Gómez in a brutal confrontation. The crowd dispersed through the streets of Caracas, shouting their demands that Gómez should step down as president, and by mid-afternoon two hundred students were behind bars.

López Contreras fought the stoppage by replacing the police officers guarding the city with troops who were "neither hated nor feared by the people."[122] At the same time, the workers at the San Agustín del Sur construction projects of Luis Roche, Diego Nucere Sardi, and César Salinas Monreal were placed at his disposal. The textile mills situated in the parish of San Agustín also went back to work.

The mothers of the imprisoned students approached Lila Richelet de d'Artillac Brill, the Argentinean wife of the Dutch minister who was the doyen of the diplomatic corps, to see whether she could secure the release of the students.[123] She sent a telegram to this effect to Gómez on March 1. The reply was that the students would be released after certain formalities were accomplished, such as getting the parents to sign a bond guaranteeing the good behavior of their children; this demand was rejected. A similar document requesting the students not take part in further political action was submitted to them in Puerto Cabello, but this was also refused. The government then suggested that the students draft their own release document, but they refused. When Gómez realized that the spirited resistance on the part of both students and parents was "receiving the wholehearted approval of public opinion, he was shrewd enough to see that he had gone too far,"[124] and on March 5, eleven days after the students were detained and after most people had given up hope, he ordered the release of the majority of the prisoners, with the exception of Arévalo González, Carmelo Castro, and General Márquez, who were suspected of more serious revolutionary designs. Pío

Tamayo remained in Puerto Cabello until his release in 1934, shortly before his death.[125] The prisoners taken during the rioting of February 24–25 also remained in jail.

The news of the release of the students was received with jubilation by the country, and their return to Caracas was "in the nature of a triumphal procession."[126] They received a particularly enthusiastic reception at Valencia, with the young men wearing their blue berets received with open arms, free drinks from the city's bars, innumerable parties, and "more than one romance flowering."[127] They were cheered at many other towns on the way to Caracas, where they were received as heroes coming back from a grisly war. By the time they arrived in Caracas, "their automobiles were filled with flowers thrown by women along the road."[128]

Rumors about the Uprising Increase

At the time, it was rumored that Vicentico had instigated the uprising as part of a general movement to topple his father from power. Gómez felt extremely threatened by what was superficially only a number of students letting off steam. This after all had happened before in 1913 and 1921, and the regime had coped without undue difficulty. The circumstantial evidence given for Vicentico's involvement was his subsequent expulsion from the *inspectoría general del ejército* (inspector general of the army) after the civil-military abortive coup and the elimination of the post. In addition, Vicentico's presence, together with a group of trustworthy high ranking officers, "at the door of his Los Teques mansion at dawn on the day of the transfer of the students to the Puerto Cabello castle"[129] is also cited as evidence of his complicity. Moreover, Vicentico's wife, Josefina Revenga, sent food parcels to the students. However, the munificence was not out of step with other high society ladies of Caracas. After all most of the students were very young and part of the Caraqueño elite, and there is no doubt that their plight touched the sympathy of friends, despite the political consequences. It was rumored that Vicentico had reached agreement with British vested interests, but there is no evidence of this in the archives. According to McGill, the Dutch minister P. J. d'Artillac Brill "was always on the side of the students and the revolution, even though there were some who believed the opposite."[130] Since 1928 García Velasco, with the support of his uncle García Bustamante, was maneuvering for power, and it was suggested in some circles that both had given informal support to the student protest in February. The American chargé d'affaires C. van H. Engert, in his report on the affair, concluded that the students had no intention of starting a revolution, nor did they have the backing of the organized opposition to a government that had been too repressive in its reaction, and they had alienated support for the regime because most of the students came from the wealthiest and most prominent families in Caracas. Nevertheless, the promptness and spontaneous support of the students by the general public was a source of worry for the supporters of Gómez.[131]

Many of the freed students left the country soon after their release in order to avoid the repression of the Gómez regime. Betancourt, Leoni, Miguel Otero Silva, Gustavo Reyes, Prince Lara, and Gustavo Tejera went initially to Curacao, where they lived in "a hovel that they called 'the nest' and . . . presented the disorderly appearance of an untidy house kept by boys who have just left their strict families."[132] The students had their meals at a "modest restaurant owned by a Venezuelan man of humble origins"[133] called Calderón. There were another three hundred Venezuelans on the island, mainly working at the oil refineries, who considered themselves enemies of Gómez. Among the refinery workers Domingo Lovera and Rafael Domingo Pegueso Pérez were the main organizers of the Gómez opposition movement on the island. Simón Betancourt, who accompanied Ducharne's assault on Maturín in 1914, was also living on the island at the time. Many of the students later moved to Barranquilla, Colombia, where they debated the ideas of Haya de la Torre and his party APRA, establishing the Asociación Revolucionaria de Izquierda (ARDI). The group, which "boasts about knowing Marxism,"[134] was revolutionary and anti-imperialist in focus, blaming, for example, a few companies such as Standard Oil Company (New Jersey), Royal Dutch–Shell, and the Royal Bank of Canada for controlling the Venezuelan economy.[135]

The political fight against Gómez continued after the students were freed, with clandestine meetings being held. According to somebody called Irazabal there were rumors of plots a few days before he left Caracas for Puerto Cabello toward the end of March, with Valentín García Tortosa informing him of a general uprising in Carabobo and Falcón states. It was alleged that García Tosta smuggled arms into the country in a small ship owned by a "Captain Gómez, who transports gasoline for the Lago company" and who also carries people "from Cabimas to La Rosa and other regions to link up with those in Falcón in order to attack the State of Lara."[136]

Revolutionary Committee Formed in Caracas

The Venezuelan revolutionaries in Europe received the news of the disturbances in Caracas with great enthusiasm, as it appeared that the regime was clearly weakening and that it was time to start preparing the way within the country for the forthcoming revolution. At the end of March, Delgado Chalbaud sent the poet Alfredo Arvelo Larriva[137] to establish contacts in Caracas to channel "the general unhappiness prevalent towards a simultaneous attack with the exiled opposition."[138] Arvelo Larriva's mission was to coordinate the simultaneous internal uprisings of José Rafael Gabaldón and Peñaloza, with Delgado Chalbaud's invasion. Mibelli, a wealthy landowner, who was detained for a short period after the student disturbances, was Delgado Chalbaud's permanent agent in Caracas and would help Arvelo Larriva coordinate meetings.

The secret revolutionary committee in Caracas, chaired by Enrique González Gorrondona, also included (apart from Mibelli) Antonio J. Silva, Ramón León, Luis Bigott,[139] General Hermán Febres Cordero, Alejandro Lara, Enrique Silva Pérez, Génaro Silva Pérez, José Antonio Gallegos, and Miguel Hernández Ron. At the time of Arvelo Larriva's arrival, the committee had collected a paltry $9,369.[140] Arvelo Larriva met with the committee at the house of Luis Horacio Ugarte in Guanare, Portuguesa State, and explained that a revolutionary movement was under way in Europe headed by Delgado Chalbaud together with Baptista and Olivares. Arvelo Larriva assured the secret committee that Delgado Chalbaud's revolution would be launched in either September or October of that year. Delgado Chalbaud received support in La Guaira, Valencia, Ocumare del Tuy, and El Tocuyo. Once everything was in place, Dr. Honorio Sigala from Carora in Lara State informed Delgado Chalbaud's agent in Caracas that the revolution would start soon. On the government's side, toward the end of March reports reached Gómez that a revolutionary committee was operating in New York, headed by Gil Borges and Santos Domínici, that supported Urbina's invasion through Coro.[141]

The preparations for Delgado Chalbaud's armed uprising were taking longer than expected, mainly because of insufficient financial backing. Delgado Chalbaud was not happy with Aranguren's terms to finance part of the revolution. Aranguren would back the project on condition that he was appointed president if they succeeded. Delgado Chalbaud had no option but to accept because funds were not readily available from other sources. In spite of securing some meager finance from New York, Delgado Chalbaud was still short of the bulk of the \$1 million that he needed to finance the expedition.[142] Some of the revolutionaries also felt that time was running out. Arévalo Cedeño, in particular, accused Delgado Chalbaud of dithering and scathingly lambasted him for only producing "deadlines and more deadlines, terms, deceits and throwing away money in a ridiculous and egotistical manner."[143] For his part, Delgado Chalbaud urged Arévalo Cedeño to refrain from invading Venezuela and to keep his promise of acting together because any action by him would alert Gómez, who would then strengthen the undermanned garrisons. Arévalo Cedeño did not pay attention to Delgado Chalbaud and continued his preparations, arriving in Trinidad on July 3 and leaving almost four weeks later on July 28 for the Colombian-Venezuelan border, where he was "chiefly interested in the hope of a revolutionary movement from the Colombian border."[144]

The April Army Revolt

The regime in Venezuela would be further shaken by the army revolt that took place during Easter that year. As Gómez suspected, the disturbances of the Semana del Estudiante only served to kindle the spirit of political freedom among some of the younger military officers. The country's arsenal was not in good shape, something which F. Conde García, the commander of the armed forces in Nueva Esparta, reported at the beginning of 1928. His stockpile of arms was "in an almost unusable state and the cache of arms stored here is completely useless as many do not have a firing pin and all are missing the extractors."[145] He had only 2,627 rounds of ammunition.

The April 7 military uprising was headed by Captain Rafael Alvarado Franco of the First Artillery Regiment, and Lieutenant Rafael Antonio Barrios Céliz, who were stationed at Miraflores, together with Lieutenant Agustín Fernández at the San Carlos barracks and Leonardo Leefmans at the military academy. General Félix Ambard was the most senior military man implicated in the abortive coup, joining the rebellion because Alvarado informed him that it was "a patriotic movement without personal interests of any kind that has as its only objective the election of a civilian candidate in completely free elections."[146] Two years earlier in 1926, Captain Alvarado Franco enlisted the help of Lieutenant Barrios Céliz in a plot he was organizing in the Girardot battalion. At the beginning of 1928, Lieutenant Fernández, who was also part of the conspiracy, was ordered by Vicentico to prepare the barracks for an insurrection. However, at this point "the two conspiratorial factions separated. Alvarado informed Barrios that the inspectorate belonged to Vicentico, and that he was not going to rebel to place another Gómez in power."[147] The majority of the leaders were between thirty and forty years old, with most of the cadets at the military academy involved, including cadet Eleazar López Wolmer, son of the military commander of Caracas, together with Benjamín Delgado Leefmans, José Antonio Ovalles Olavarría, and Armando Chávez, who would bear the brunt of the authorities' wrath when they were caught red-handed. Many of the cadets, including Delgado Leefmans, were inspired by the role played by the cadets at the Military School of Guatemala, who in 1920 deposed the dictator Manuel Estrada Cabrera. Others claimed later that many were also inspired by the 1917 Russian revolution.

The 1928 civil-military uprising contained five main groups made up of young officers, cadets recently graduated from the military academy, students at the military academy, students at the Central University, and a nucleus of youngsters and children of traders. Most of the university students, led by Juan José Palacios,[148] Víctor García Maldonado, and César Camejo Oberto, also joined the rebellion, prompted by a desire to get their colleagues in prison released. According to Palacios, most of the students soon after they were released from prison started placing pressure to free the other remaining prisoners, such as Pío Tamayo, Carmelo Castro, and Arévalo González. At the time, Palacios debated with Captain Alvarado whether the students should be asked to join the young army officers in an uprising scheduled for Easter, when Gómez would spend two days in Caracas on his way from Maracay to Macuto on the Caribbean coast. Alvarado Franco and Leefmans, who were instructors at the military academy, were detailed to persuade the cadets to join the rebellion. The assassination of Gómez at either Miraflores or Macuto was believed to be part of the plot.

As the above preparations took place, Mibelli asked Palacios to join Delgado Chalbaud's rebellion. Many of the students met to plot Gómez's downfall at Valderrama's apartment above the Farmacia de los Remedios, owned jointly by Palacios and Valderrama. Palacios was the intermediary between the students and the military, with the student leaders finally deciding to join Alvarado's revolt after a meeting at the house of Dr. Ramón Parpacén. It should be noted that the student movement was not large because most were away from Caracas for the Easter break. Moreover, once the rebellion started, they were only given a few hours' notice to group together.

A small group of civilians was also involved, including the writer Antonio Arraiz, Carlos Rovati, a public functionary, and Julio Naranjo and Francisco Betancourt, both retail workers.[149]

It appears that Vicentico was also implicated in the plot. Velasco Bustamante together with Colmenares Pacheco, José María García Velasco (a nephew of Velasco Bustamante), and Martínez Méndez saw Archbishop Monsignor Felipe Rincón González about Vicentico a few days before April 7, requesting the cleric to speak directly with Gómez for advice on how to proceed because they had proof that his son and heir was part of a military plot. Further proof came from Lieutenant Fernández, who during his interrogation after the abortive coup "stated that he joined the plot at the suggestion of officers in the Army Inspectorate . . . with General Vicentico never objecting to it."[150] Vicentico was later relieved of his duties and sent abroad after the meeting between Gómez and Archbishop Rincón González at Las Delicias in Maracay.

The main military objective of the uprising was to take the San Carlos barracks, with its large stockpile of arms and ammunition. The first step was to get Lieutenant Fernández transferred to the barracks. Lieutenant Barrios was certain that he could take Miraflores for the rebels, while Palacios was sure that he could deliver the support of the students affiliated to the FEV. Once the San Carlos barracks was secure, the plan was to invite López Contreras, the defense minister, to have a photograph taken with the rebel officers, at which point he would be asked to join the conspiracy. If they failed to convince López Contreras to join, a general alarm would be sounded for the students to stop other government officials from leaving their homes. If the rebel officers were unable to muster enough support from the troops, the students would dress up as soldiers to show the strength of support behind the rebellion in order to convince them to join the revolt.

The uprising was initially scheduled to start when Lieutenant Fernández was on guard duty at the San Carlos barracks during Easter Sunday, but the date was brought forward to Good Friday, April 6, because the government discovered the plot when the cadet son of General Rafael Garmendía Rodríguez tried to convince an officer to join the conspiracy. The details of the plot were passed to Prefect Guillermo Willet, who in turn told López Contreras. The cadet informed Alvarado and Leefmans of the possible new recruit, but they thought rightly that he was not trustworthy and so decided to bring forward their attack for that evening because with any further delay they ran the risk of being detained the following morning. An emergency meeting of the main conspirators was convened to coordinate their actions. Captain Alvarado, who would later die in Puerto Cabello's castle on October 12, 1933, asked Cecilia Núñez Sucre to inform Palacios to be ready, as the uprising would take place the following morning. It was imperative that the Casa del Estudiante should be opened that evening and that as many students as possible should be at their posts. They would leave from there to take up positions at the Plaza de el Panteón and Plazoleta de las Mercedes to wait for the signal that the San Carlos barracks had surrendered and so help to distribute arms.

Various people were to meet at Leefmans's house in La Pastora to receive arms and uniforms. Leefmans and Captain Pedro Dubornais, a Chilean colleague of Alvarado's at the academy, waited for them and at dawn one group went to Miraflores, where Barrios was waiting, while the other headed for San Carlos. Carlos Irazabal, Manuel José Arreaga, and Oropeza Bautista, who were in Macuto and not aware that the date of the uprising had been brought forward, left for Barquisimeto to meet Joaquín Gabaldón Márquez. Their presence there on April 7 aroused the suspicions of the authorities, who detained them at the Tres Torres prison.

Government army officers moved fast once they became aware of a possible military uprising. Colonel Elías Sayago, the director of the military academy, accompanied by two officers, saw López Contreras at his home at twelve thirty a.m. of the night of April 6, informing him that the "San Carlos barracks would revolt."[151] The San Carlos barracks posed the greatest threat to the regime because it held a large cache of six thousand rifles and five million rounds of ammunition. López Contreras realized the seriousness of the situation, and immediately contacted Colonels Eugenio Medina and Baltazar Díaz Peña, who were in charge of the arsenal at the barracks. He then contacted Miraflores Palace directly and ordered Captain Ramón González, the duty officer, to be outside the Palace barracks "with 30 soldiers and 2 officers"[152] so that López Contreras could proceed to the San Carlos barracks. López Contreras then telephoned Lieutenant Fernández at San Carlos, who cut the line when he realized who was speaking.

The civil-military rebellion started on Easter Saturday morning, when most people were away from Caracas. When Barrios entered the Miraflores barracks, he encountered Colonel Aníbal García, the duty officer, accompanied by Captain Ramón González. Barrios ordered their surrender, but the officers opened fire. In the exchange of fire, García was mortally wounded and died the following day. González also died from machete wounds inflicted on him in close body fighting. After this brief exchange of fire, Miraflores fell into rebel hands, with Barrios leaving immediately for the San Carlos barracks. Owing to a lack of transport, the rebels from Miraflores joined the main attacking force at San Carlos by foot, losing valuable time and allowing López Contreras to get there first. It was a tactical error to attack Miraflores first because most of the arms were at the San Carlos barracks. In addition, by not securing the central telephone exchange, the rebels allowed López Contreras to obtain up-to-the-minute information on what was happening at San Carlos. Finally, Regina Gómez, one of Gómez's daughters, who remained in the city for Easter and who lived near Miraflores, reported what was occurring directly to Velasco Bustamante.

López Contreras, accompanied by his orderly, Miguel Sanabria, left his home for the central police station, where he was informed that Miraflores was in rebel hands. He ordered Velasco Bustamante to deploy "a company of the Planta barracks and another from the Mamey barracks at the Bolívar square and the Banco de Venezuela respectively"[153] because he suspected that "the attackers would sack the Treasury reasoning that with sufficient money and arms the Revolution would prevail."[154] López Contreras then headed for the San Carlos barracks, observing on his way there that several groups and Captain Alvarado "were walking toward the Dos Pilitas."[155] López Contreras ordered Sanabria to follow Alvarado, "who started to run away on hearing my orders."[156] On his arrival at San Carlos, López Contreras ordered Sergeant Eleuterio Vásquez to open the barracks, while "Fernández remained surprised at the end of the guardhouse with his arms crossed."[157] López Contreras arrived at the barracks while it was preparing for the impending attack by the insurgents, so that when Barrios reached the San Carlos barracks he was surprised to find López Contreras and withdrew "toward the northwest part of the barracks,"[158] where he met with the cavalry but was not captured.[159] The students stationed at the corner of the Pantheon now went into action but soon surrendered after a twenty-five-minute exchange of fire. López Contreras ordered Captain Fermín Bracho to take twenty soldiers to the Dos Pilitas barracks and fire "on those posted in the rubble on its right side."[160]

López Contreras, later accompanied by thirty soldiers and two officers, left the north entrance of the San Carlos barracks when the firing stopped. López Contreras writes that his "presence there was another surprise for the students, civilians and others present."[161] According to the American chargé d'affaires, the attack on the San Carlos barracks left between thirty-five and forty dead or wounded, mostly on the rebel side.[162] In total, some 130 people were detained and taken to the Mamey and El Cubo barracks. Lt. Barrios and Leefmans managed to escape, however, with many of the students dispersing, but others, such as Ernesto Silva Tellería, Rolando Anzola, and Jóvito Villalba, were caught. Two months later Barrios was found hiding in the house of Hernán Nass, a future Acción Democrática leader, joining Alvarado in La Rotunda until 1933, when they were transferred to Puerto Cabello castle, with the latter dying soon afterwards. Others, such as Samuel McGill, owing to his friendship with Alvarado, were forced to flee the country, traveling to Paris, where he placed himself at Delgado Chalbaud's service.

Although the uprising was unsuccessful, it shook the regime to the core, with Gómez rushing a number of regiments to Caracas. Some thirty-three officers appeared in front of a military tribunal because of Alvarado's connection with the Chilean Captain Dubornais. Security at government buildings was increased, with police armed with rifles and revolvers, while all stores of arms and ammunition and military equipment not in use were transferred to Maracay. Gómez also implemented a recruitment drive of some five thousand men to work on public works at Maracay at $0.96 per day in order to have a reserve army if it was needed, as well as removing from Caracas a large number of the unemployed. More importantly, a number of state presidents were rotated, with Galavís moved to Yaracuy, Eustoquio Gómez to Lara, and Jurado to Falcón. In Caracas, on April 11 a new chief of police, General Clodomiro Sánchez, was appointed together with a new assistant chief of police, Colonel Pedro E. Gómez, and the new rector of the university, Dr. Plácido D. Rodríguez Rivero. The military academy was closed after the rebellion, and in its place the Escuela de Aspirantes a Oficiales was created in La Victoria, composed almost entirely of illiterate Tachirenses. Only students caught red-handed in the uprising were arrested, leaving free around a hundred students who were known by the authorities to be involved in the conspiracy but whom the authorities chose to ignore.

Gómez requested Congress to abolish the *inspectoría general del ejército* and the vice presidency, both posts occupied by his son Vicentico, who with his wife departed for Europe on May 20. He would never return to Venezuela, dying two years later in Paris from a medical complication stemming from his diabetes. Finally, López Contreras was banished to Táchira on July 2 as head of the army's Fourth Brigade. This was clearly a demotion and related to his alleged presidential aspirations. López Contreras was seen as a threat to the presidency for several reasons: He was instrumental in putting down the rebellion, and he was the only person capable of preventing the presidency from getting into the hands of such Gomecista stooges as Pérez Soto, José Ignacio Cárdenas, or Gil Fortoul. In addition, the day after the abortive army uprising, certain members of the business community wrote to López Contreras beseeching him that he should "never accept for one moment that the Gomezes should continue pursuing their daily vile attacks on Venezuelan society."[163]

Changes in the Regime

The regime between February and April 1928 suffered its worst political setback since possibly the threatened invasion of Castro in 1913. There was now open discussion and censure of the regime, which was perceived as wanting to turn the country into Gómez's family's inheritance, imposing his "son as . . . successor to the presidency."[164] Among certain social sectors there was exasperation with the regime. This was well formulated by Matos when he informed Gómez forthrightly that the country was in a nasty state, with the government spending too much on public works, and that the people "have threatened to smash the windows of photographers' shops if they do not remove your portraits."[165] Cook, the American minister, also reported that opposition to the administration was now "pretty general all over the country," with open criticism in Caracas, and that serious disturbances were likely to "occur during the months leading to the presidential election in April, unless the Liberal element is given satisfactory representation in the government."[166]

In order to allay these fears, Gómez requested Congress on April 23 to abolish the post of inspector general of the army, which was held by Vicentico, and informed the legislative body that he had advised his sons to stay away from politics. Gómez also wanted Congress to abolish the post of vice presidency, also held by Vicentico, because under the constitution any minister could replace the president for a short period. Moreover, Congress could elect a new replacement if it was felt that the president was going to be away for a long period. On May 20, two days before Congress enacted the new constitution, Vicentico left for France, stripped of his titles and military posts, to take a new job as a diplomat at the Paris legation. As a parting present, Gómez gave his son $382,409, and between December 1, 1928, and February 1930, the government credited Vicentico with $178,587, together with his monthly salary of $2,874. After Vicentico arrived in Paris, in October Delgado Chalbaud sued him for damages as a way of publicizing the rebels' plight and embarrassing the regime. However, under French law Vicentico could not be prosecuted because as a special counselor at the Venezuelan legation he was a member of the diplomatic corps.[167]

Congress duly followed Gómez's recommendations and on May 22 enacted a new constitution that allowed the head of state to be held temporarily by a minister appointed previously by the president. It is uncertain whether Gómez was convinced that Vicentico had conspired against him despite Archbishop Rincón González's advice on his son's intentions but it can be argued that he was the biggest loser in the rebellion as he was stripped of all his official roles and banished to Europe far away from the Gomecistas. It can also be speculated that as Vicentico was suffering from diabetes, and possibly did not have long to live, his father preferred to exile him in Europe rather than keep him in Venezuela under effective house arrest as this would only serve to weaken the Gomecista government apparatus. What is clear is that Vicentico was censored for his involvement in the rebellion when he was stripped of his place in the government.

Fossi and Urbina

The country would be rocked later that year by a further daring uprising in western Venezuela led by Colonel Roberto Fossi and Urbina. Fossi, an enemy of Gómez, returned to Venezuela when Gómez declared a general amnesty on July 24, 1925, and in March 1928 was offered the presidency of Monagas. He declined because he was secretly conspiring with the army uprising of April 7. Fossi did, however, accept the post of customs administrator at La Vela de Coro because "that location is of great strategic importance, giving us the right conditions to develop our revolutionary plans."[168] When he arrived at La Vela, Fossi appointed a number of Urbina's supporters living in the area, such as Abraham Navarro, Olegario Reyes, and Colonel Julio R. Hernández, to posts in the customs house. According to a contemporary account, Fossi "turned into a rat,"[169] taking bribes from both the traders and the schooners that plied between Curacao and La Vela.[170] Fossi's plan of attack was to take twenty men on July 24, Bolívar's birthday and a public holiday, and secure the barracks of La Vela, while Urbina with a further twenty men took control of the jail, and Abraham Navarro and ten men attacked the police station. Finally, another officer with three men would secure the telegraph and telephone offices. The plan called for the revolutionaries to be reinforced by three hundred Venezuelan and ninety Dominican supporters working in Curacao, but due to the speedy collapse of the rebellion they did not get off the Dutch island. The intention was to raise the revolutionary banner without State President General Argenis Asuaje at Coro knowing what was happening. As the telegraph was the only direct means of communication to Maracay, Fossi would feed Gómez false reports while the revolution gathered pace.

Urbina arrived at La Vela on July 24 to find Fossi totally unprepared for the uprising. Urbina gathered Hernandez, Reyes, Captain Eloy Hernández, Rámon Jiménez Mollejas, and Justiniano Arcila and "within ten minutes took the Governor's palace."[171] Asuaje was informed of events because Urbina allowed José María Fossi, Fossi's brother, to pass between La Vela de Coro and Cumarebo with José León Márquez, the mayor, as his prisoner. In order to stem any panic among the population Reyes was sent with four men by car to try to reach José María Fossi, but the driver panicked. Reyes and Enrique González Aranda released the chauffeur, who alerted the authorities in Coro. Asuaje later reported to Gómez that had the attack taken place as planned, the chances of success would have been greater because when the rebellion took place "I was with the government executive laying a floral tribute at the statue of the father of the nation."[172] However, when he received news of the rebellion he quickly organized his troops and posted them "in the plains that lead to La Vela in order to capture those rascals."[173] Meanwhile, Fossi and Urbina decided to attack Coro by car, but as they approached the city, they saw Asuaje's troops on maneuvers. After a heated discussion with Urbina, who still wanted to attack, Fossi retreated to the Sierra de Coro, having realized the futility of such a suicidal act and being chased by Asuaje, who after a few skirmishes declared that the state had been pacified.

Fossi and Urbina managed to commandeer a truck taking them to Décora, from where they managed to reach Aruba to be arrested and imprisoned for three days by the Dutch colonial authorities for illegal entry of the island. When the large number of revolutionaries on the island heard this, a protest march was organized that included the three hundred Venezuelan workers and ninety Dominican workers. On regaining their freedom, Fossi and Urbina made their separate ways to Colombia, arriving in Barranquilla, where Felipe Aristeguieta, who owned the Britania hat factory with Joaquín Briceño Maldonado, helped them for a time. Urbina published a pamphlet accusing Fossi of ineptitude, with the latter responding in kind. The Venezuelan government started extradition proceedings against the two rebels, but the delay in serving the summons gave Fossi ample time to leave the city, while the slack vigilance in the police jail allowed Urbina to escape. By September 1928 both had managed to leave the city.

A direct effect of the Urbina-Fossi attack was that Pérez Soto reorganized his small armory in Zulia State in readiness for an attack. Pérez Soto's arsenal was surprisingly small, with 202 rifles distributed among the army in the state and a further 113 in storage. The attack also had the effect of tightening up security on Curacao. Domingo S. Lovera, who headed the Oficina de Representación de Obreros Venezolanos at the Curacao refinery, financed by the refinery and Asuaje, was discovered to be an enemy of Gómez and one of the main instigators of the demonstration against the jailing of Fossi and Urbina. Leyba also secured in October 1928 the expulsion of Raúl Hernández, a Dominican leader of the two-hundred-strong Dominican contingency on the island, because his disruptive "presence was not conducive to good industrial relations."[174] Despite Leyba's and Asuaje's efforts some ninety Venezuelan workers arrived in October 1928 to work at the refinery. The Venezuelan consul felt that the curtailment of emigration to the islands should be legally enforced because the "larger the number of Venezuelan workers on the island the greater the threat to security."[175]

Repercussions of Student Affair Continues

In spite of the government's heavy-handed treatment of the students and military rebels, meetings against the government continued to be held in Caracas. A string of opposition leaflets attacking the government, such as León's "Nuestro Deber," which was published in Mexico in September 1928, were distributed in the capital city. In October, Joaquín Gabaldón Márquez wrote to Leoni, president of the Student Federation, stating that "the general situation of the country is worsening, especially in Caracas, the monopolies, the new businesses of the privileged, the daily ever increasing expansion of the pseudo-economic activities of that greedy family and their favorites are making life insufferable where the rules are the insecurity of business, the mistrust of the industrialists and the universal ruin of the working classes."[176] On October 2, Leoni sent a letter to Gómez requesting the release of the people arrested in February and April. This had the opposite effect, with 50 students detained three days later and sent to Petare to work on a construction site. The Student Federation responded with a further letter on October 11, signed by 150 students, protesting the arrest of the students after the October 2 letter, with more arrests following. Other students organized street demonstration during which a few shots were fired, with the loss of one or two lives. In total, 176 students were rounded up and sent to Colonia de Araira, near Guatire, to work in three groups of 58, 82, and 32 as forced labor on road construction. Velasco Bustamante's secretary wrote to Gómez that public order had been restored and that "life in the city has returned to normality after the Bolshevik students created a few hours of disorder, no doubt inspired by those abroad, and by the unbalanced women of Caracas."[177]

It remains a mystery as to who was the puppeteer pulling the strings of the events that shook Venezuela in 1928. It is clear from the foregoing that an intense power struggle within the Gomecista regime was taking place and that the Student Week was used by some to stimulate opposition, as well as giving Gómez a clear signal that his time was up. Some powerful figures within the regime, such as Pedro Manuel Arcaya, backed Vicentico, who was the regime's natural heir since the death of Juancho Gómez in 1923, while the García Bustamante group wanted García Velasco to become president. The Student Week, although not directly associated with elements of the regime, was used by them to send a strong signal of disapproval to Gómez. The military uprising of April 7 was an even stronger reminder to Gómez that parts of his beloved army were now against him, with the real possibility that Vicentico was behind it all.

Because of their middle class origins the students developed a liberal political view and were thus opposed to the rural oligarchy that governed the country. They also formed part of the intelligentsia that had as its goals "a political change in the country and the economic transformation of Venezuela."[178] Their role was to diffuse new values into society, to foster a new economic strategy, and, to develop the nation-state concept itself. It should be noted that the students belonging to the upper classes participated only in the Semana del Estudiante, dropping out once the movement became more serious. Fuenmayor rejects the myth that the "28th Generation" was made up of people of exceptional quality or even that it had a political job to do as if by divine right. What Fuenmayor shows is that the movement was the first in which the "masses actively participated and were at the forefront of the movement."[179] The 28th Movement was the start of democracy in Venezuelan politics, as it was the breeding ground for the future leaders of the political parties of Venezuela.

Gómez at the beginning of 1928 was clearly concerned about the political situation, reacting harshly to an event such as the Student Week, which did not need such strong handling. Other people within the government did not share his fear, but if we assume that his very existence was threatened, then we can see that his reaction was perfectly natural. Gómez had been in power for twenty years, and some elements within his regime wanted part of the booty for themselves, having served him faithfully for two decades. Gómez calculated that if he did relinquish power in favor of his son, Vicentico would be pushed aside in no time, as he was no match intellectually, politically, or militarily to some of the other possible contenders, such as García Velasco, Pérez Soto, Arcaya, or Eustoquio Gómez. Gómez understood perfectly well that his position was precarious, leading to a number of changes the following year in the constitution. Moreover, Gómez was now aware that his reelection in 1929 would not be politically acceptable and that other members of his regime would not tolerate his replacement by a close relation. It was thus necessary to punish and ban to Europe the most obvious and identifiable heir apparent.

We can speculate that Gómez exiled Vicentico in comfort for two reasons: (a) if he placed him in jail, it would weaken his own position and that of the regime at a time of political crisis, and (b) Vicentico's illness was known, and he needed treatment. It was also clear that in order to remain in power Gómez needed to retire temporarily from the presidency. His dilemma was how to achieve this goal without relinquishing real power, as otherwise he faced the possibility of either going into exile himself or having to fight back, and he was too old for both alternatives. The prospects for his old age, therefore, were not good.

PART III

Maintenance of Power, 1929 – 1935

Renewed Hope for the Rebels

The political events of March and April 1928 shook the Gómez regime and gave the political exiles renewed hope that the end of the Gómez dictatorship was fast approaching. The main problem for them was the usual one of securing enough financial backing to organize a filibustering expedition against the regime. The plan was to take advantage of the country's discontentment with Gómez and organize an invasion of Venezuela that coincided with a number of internal uprisings. The difficulty was keeping it a secret from Gómez's spies and coordinating events, especially as communication between the various exiles scattered around the Caribbean, Colombia, Europe, and the United States was difficult and slow.

In the summer of 1928, Baptista, who was living in New York, met Pocaterra at the New Hampshire–Quebec border town of Rousses Point to discuss whether an armed revolution could succeed against Gómez. They reached the same conclusion as the previous year, which was that any military action could only succeed if a recognized leader headed it. The mechanics of transferring power from the military rebel leaders to a democratically elected president were also discussed at the meeting. Baptista suggested that once the revolutionaries had secured one state, the head of the *directorio* would assume the presidency. On reaching Caracas, the president of the *directorio* would call for the election of a constituent assembly that would draft a new constitution, elect an interim president who would govern for four to six months, and guarantee general elections for a president. There was no agreement as to who would be the "the Provisional President, and even less so for the Constitutional Presidency."[1] It was decided, however, that once part of Venezuela had been occupied by the rebels, a *junta civil* would appoint a provisional president of the revolutionary government, who together with the field generals would be ineligible to stand at future presidential elections. The main problem for the rebels was to reach an agreement that gave Aranguren the possibility of becoming president without making it look too mercenary. A possible solution was for Aranguren to be recognized as the campaign president and then "elected publicly for such a role . . . when he is over there fighting,"[2] with new elections taking place when the rebels had secured Caracas. The rebels' directorate decided it was more appropriate to appoint as provisional president either Juan José Mendoza, the current president of the Bar Association of Caracas, or Santos Domínici, because this would then allow Aranguren to stand for the presidency when presidential elections took place.

Once Pocaterra reached agreement with Baptista, he traveled to New York to sign with Atilano Carnevali on June 8 a revolutionary pact for the establishment of a civilian presidential candidate, who would be Juan José Mendoza. At this juncture Gil Borges, who was "totally resolute to work for the country,"[3] also embraced the candidature of Mendoza. Atilano Carnevali met Senator Irving Lenroot, who was a keen follower of Venezuelan affairs because he had been legal counsel to the Caribbean Petroleum Company—a large oil-producing Shell subsidiary in Venezuela—to find out whether he was interested in toppling Gómez.[4] Other revolutionaries and supporters began to offer their assistance. Simón Betancourt would recruit between four hundred and eight hundred men from the Shell refinery on Curacao, together with a hundred Dominicans.[5]

The main problem remained finding someone to finance the expedition, as Aranguren had become more circumspect after his two previous failures. Gil Fortoul advised Aranguren not to inject any funds into the expedition because financing Delgado Chalbaud's revolution would be tantamount to "total madness, while reducing his funds without any hope of getting his money back."[6] Aranguren decided to back the revolution when he was persuaded by Pérez that Olivares was the best military leader for the expedition because he was the only rebel who could almost guarantee a successful outcome and therefore safeguard the oilman's pecuniary interests. Aranguren would back the rebellion on the condition that Olivares headed the expeditionary force.

It was now essential to convince Olivares to join Delgado Chalbaud's revolution, with a meeting arranged in London in mid-July between the two men at the Mayfair Hotel, Aranguren's favorite hostelry in the British capital. At the meeting, Olivares demanded a number of changes to some of the principal tenets that were driving the revolution. He was convinced that there should not be a single leader but rather power should be vested in a *directorio* that appointed the military command and a provisional cabinet that named a provisional president who would govern for three months. Olivares was also against the junta establishing a political party, because this was outside the remit of the liberating forces. Moreover, it was counterproductive, creating animosity among the revolutionary forces, which were formed by people with different political views.[7] Olivares was not against political parties per se but argued that such matters should be addressed after the overthrow of Gómez, and he felt that a simple declaration of intent to foster the creation of political parties would suffice because he wanted to "be totally free to join any political party . . . that holds the same aspirations as I."[8] Unless these conditions were met, Olivares would not join Delgado Chalbaud's expedition.[9] At the same time an agreement was reached in principle after several meetings in London between Delgado Chalbaud and Aranguren to form a Supreme Junta of the Venezuelan Revolution composed of five members, viz, Santos Domínici, Delgado Chalbaud, Smith, Pérez, and Baptista. The junta would study the political conditions of Venezuela, plan the revolution by securing funds and the necessary means to execute it, as well as form a political party. The junta would also appoint the war leader as well as the various military chiefs, who would resign once Caracas was taken and power transferred to a provisional cabinet and president.

Aranguren was not happy with Olivares's objections because this precluded his own participation and, worse still, would prevent him from becoming president. The revolution was now stuck in a catch-22 situation with the main financier not willing to support the struggle without the involvement of Olivares, who in turn would only accept if certain democratic principles were agreed beforehand. Without such assurances, Olivares returned to the United States, leaving Pérez to conduct all subsequent negotiations that would take place mainly in France. Pérez spent four days in Vichy with Aranguren discussing a new agreement that would be acceptable to both men. It was agreed that the *directorio* would be composed of civilians without Delgado Chalbaud, and that Pérez would draft the rebels' manifesto as well as the statutes of the new political party mentioned in the agreement. The sticking point remained Article 6 of the agreement, which named the military commander and stated that Delgado Chalbaud would be the president of the junta and also head the new revolutionary government.[10] Delgado Chalbaud, Smith, and Santos Domínici, the leaders of the expedition, assured Pérez that this would not be the case because "the election of the War Director will fall on another person who will not be President of the Junta, who will only preside over the revolutionary government as clause nine states."[11] In addition, different people would be appointed as head of the armed forces and the president of the Supreme Junta. Delgado Chalbaud accepted Pocaterra's suggestion that Santos Domínici should be the junta's figurehead, mainly because he was totally inoffensive and was perceived as a magnificent symbol "to preside over the Revolution."[12]

The revolution was faltering at this juncture, with the rebels in New York running out of funds. The group in Paris was in a worse position because Aranguren, described by Delgado Chalbaud as "a very slow and taciturn man who takes his time to make up his mind, and is today the center of a multitude of businesses that take up a great deal of his time and capital,"[13] would not forward any funds owing to the attitude adopted by both Olivares and Pérez, who "completely scared our banker, causing the venture to fail."[14] In Caracas it was asserted that Aranguren was helping the revolutionaries financially. José María García Velasco and Ovidio Márquez started the damaging rumor of his connection with the rebels in Europe. They circulated in Caracas a copy of a mortgage deed for Aranguren's properties in the city valued at $286,807, stating that the funds raised would be transferred to the revolutionaries. Aranguren had explained to Gómez in 1926 that the mortgage was in order to "take care of urgent business in the London Stock Exchange."[15]

The relationship among the left-wing opponents of Gómez in Mexico continued on a frosty note. In March 1928, Smith saw Gumersindo Torres, the Venezuelan minister at Madrid, and informed him that if León, De la Plaza, and others achieved power in Venezuela, he would place himself immediately at Gómez's orders.[16] In Paris, the PRV, with its committee composed of Gustavo Machado, Fortoul, and Pedro Brito, was also active.[17] Zumeta, the new Venezuelan minister at Paris, tried creating confusion among the various revolutionaries by starting a rumor that the rebels in the French capital were fraternizing with the "Venezuelan communists" and thereby provoking "a flysheet war that makes them look even more anarchic than they already are."[18] Zumeta also observed that Delgado Chalbaud and Aranguren were "exploiting their old acquaintances, offering them business deals, banks and oil."[19]

However, by the middle of 1928, especially after the events of Caracas in March and April, the government took the threat of a Delgado Chalbaud revolution more seriously. In October 1928, there was further talk in Caracas that Gómez was thinking of extending his presidency by two years by calling a special session of Congress in December, further aggravating the differences among the Gomecistas, who were divided into two groups. On the one hand, there was the powerful group led by García Bustamante, Gómez's uncle, and including García Velasco, Velasco Bustamante, Eustoquio Gómez, Colmenares Pacheco, and Jurado. The other group was headed by Pérez Soto with a number of the other state presidents. In order for the revolutionaries to succeed, they had to win over people in the army and "are said to have been making overtures to General López Contreras, the Commander of the Caracas garrison,"[20] because it was felt that he did not like Velasco Bustamante. Delgado Chalbaud confessed to Pocaterra in July that the disturbances in March and April resulted in Gómez "disabling a great deal of friends, including General Mibelli, whose help was of the utmost importance."[21] The imprisonment of Mibelli was a severe setback for the revolution because he had promised to donate $100,000 and had acted as Delgado Chalbaud's link between the Paris revolutionaries and their supporters in Venezuela, leaving the Paris committee "without any links with those people."[22] The Paris revolutionary committee in Caracas was now represented by a secret group headed by Dr. Alejandro Lara Núñez and composed of Enrique González Gorrondona, José Antonio Gallegos Rivero, Ramón León, Bernardo Guzmán Blanco, Luis Bigott, and Pedro Vallenilla. Some of the rebels, such as Pocaterra, urged Delgado Chalbaud to reach an understanding with the opponents of the regime within the country as well as those disaffected parts of the Gomecista regime.

It was felt that López Contreras would be easy to recruit because of his demotion to Táchira. At a social gathering at the home of Henrique Pérez Dupuy, Lara Núñez approached López Contreras before he left for his new army post, to see whether he would consider joining Delgado Chalbaud's revolution. López Contreras refused because he did not believe in treason, and although Gómez would be unable to "undertake a march by horse"[23] because of his age, he was "in good shape and can count on a group of important men that he can appoint as leaders of an expeditionary force."[24] López Contreras advised Delgado Chalbaud to wait for Gómez to die of natural causes, after which the army "would support a new state of affairs based on liberty, order and respect for human rights"[25] in order to "start a movement of democratic and patriotic union, and eliminating the disastrous chieftains."[26]

Other Sources of Funds

On October 29, Delgado Chalbaud made another effort to convince Aranguren to support his cause while he was staying at the Hotel Lutetia in Paris. Delgado Chalbaud pleaded with Aranguren for more than four hours to fund the revolution by pledging $382,409, offering to mortgage his Paris properties to the oilman, but all was to no avail.[27] Delgado Chalbaud then turned to other possible sources in the United Kingdom, where he was led up a cul-de-sac by John Thomson Jacobs, a British adventurer.[28] Jacobs, a political nephew of Emile Pusch,[29] the managing director of Barclays Bank and the Anglo-Egyptian Bank Ltd., as well as a partner in Lazard Brothers, a city merchant bank, made contact with Delgado Chalbaud in Paris through Madame Bremond. Jacobs was welcomed as an angel answering Delgado Chalbaud's prayers, as he offered to find financial backing for the rebellion through his political uncle. In November, Jacobs saw Pusch at the Hotel Hermitage in Monte Carlo, where the latter was on holiday. It was only after several further meetings that Jacobs plucked up enough courage to confess to his uncle that the motive for his various visits was that a rebel expedition was going to Venezuela to topple the government there, and he wanted an "introduction to Mr. Charles Sale, the Chairman of the Hudson Bay Company, with a view of chartering a ship,"[30] and a loan of $974,000 from Pusch's own bank. In return, the rebels offered Pusch various personal pecuniary inducements as well as granting oil and railway concessions to Lazard Brothers and allowing them to set up and manage a central bank.

Jacobs on his return to Paris reported initially to Madame Bremond that his uncle had examined his proposal thoroughly and that he "appeared to be willing to fall in with the request of those interested."[31] Jacobs also saw Delgado Chalbaud, informing him that Pusch had agreed to put up the remaining $974,000 needed to finance the revolution, provided certain guarantees were made. These were that Delgado Chalbaud guaranteed $487,000 in real estate, with the remaining $487,000 in promises of mining and railway concessions in Venezuela.[32] Delgado Chalbaud was clearly delighted with the news, as he felt it was only a matter time before he entered Caracas triumphantly. Jacobs was immediately commissioned to purchase war supplies in his own name because of his alleged commercial contacts in both London and Paris. Soon afterwards, Jacobs informed Delgado Chalbaud that he had placed an order with the Grahame White Aircraft Company to purchase two aircraft, with guns and ammunition and a ship from Vickers Ltd. However, Pusch changed his mind about the revolution, forwarding the correspondence between him and the rebels to the Foreign Office, including the letter from Madame Bremond. Pusch was then asked to play along with Bremond's letter, requesting more details and receiving an outline of the plot together with the benefits that would accrue to the United Kingdom. Bremond replied that "it might be a question, in effect, of the control of the oil of a country and commercial advantages, should England consent to give to the interested parties a moral support to their enterprise."[33] The aim of the plotters was to bring about "radical changes"[34] in the country and shift the balance of power away from the United States. However, the reluctance of Pusch to enter into the conspiracy put an end to "the machinations of the revolutionary Committee"[35] in the United Kingdom.

Arévalo Cedeño Strikes Again

While negotiations continued in Europe, Arévalo Cedeño arrived in Colombia to prepare his next invasion of Venezuela in October, which, to the despair of Delgado Chalbaud, would only serve to "discredit the revolution."[36] However, Arévalo Cedeño was unable to invade Venezuela because he was broke and could not get the rebels living in the border area and those abroad to finance him. Arévalo Cedeño wanted to reach Trinidad, where he felt his luck would change and would get the necessary financial support for his invasion but was forced instead to spend a month in hiding because the Colombian government wanted to expel him from the country. In Trinidad there was a large Venezuelan exile community, including General Bartolomé Ferrer, Dr. Alejandro Brito Salazar, who had a large medical practice and who since 1909 had been a member of the medical board of the colony, and General Valentín Figueredo, who lived from the income generated from his estate in Venezuela.[37] The Venezuelan government wanted the colonial authorities to act against the Venezuelan exiles, but the authorities were unable to do anything unless there was prima facie evidence of the rebels' revolutionary activities. Moreover, the authorities were confident that no attack would originate from the island, as Trinidad was only "a depot from which information is sent across the Gulf to malcontents in Venezuela and vice-versa."[38] Nevertheless, at the insistence of the Venezuelan government the colonial authorities banned Arévalo Cedeño from entering the island at the beginning of December. Delgado Chalbaud was considerably irritated at Arévalo Cedeño's "charlatanism" because "he has done us a great deal of harm in Venezuela."[39] This did not matter to Arévalo Cedeño, who had the utmost contempt for most of the exiles associated with Delgado Chalbaud because "they live the life of 'dolce far niente' in Paris, New York, and they are not able to help me because between them and me there is an enormous chasm: I am a patriot and they are cowardly speculators and a pack of rascals."[40]

José Rafael Gabaldón on the Attack

Gabaldón, who sensed that the country wanted to get rid of Gómez and who thought he had the support of a number of important Gomecistas, such as Fernández, López Contreras, Borges, and Dr. Hermán Febres Cordero, was persuaded by Arvelo Larriva that Delgado Chalbaud would invade the country in September. After the abortive April military uprising, Gabaldón urged Gómez to return the country to civilian rule, but the dictator ignored his pleas.[41] Gabaldón then joined Delgado Chalbaud's rebellion, seeking the support of generals Juan Bautista Araujo and Víctor Manuel Baptista in Trujillo State, Bartolo Yépez in Lara State, and Pedro Bereciarti in Portuguesa State, as well as important civilian elements such as Arturo Berti of Boconó, Trujillo State. On September 7, Gabaldón in an open letter to Gómez requested him to step down from the presidency before the country was engulfed in a civil war. As expected, Gabaldón did not receive a reply from Gómez and so occupied Guanare, with his son Joaquín Gabaldón Márquez and a number of his followers. José Antonio Baldó, president of Portuguesa, together with thirty officers and a hundred men, which was later reinforced by "a company from the army and another formed by Trujillano recruits,"[42] tried to apprehend Gabaldón but was instead wounded in the leg. According to Baldó, the battle against Gabaldón left two hundred men wounded or dead, with the rebel leader retreating on November 7 to his Santo Cristo estate.

Although the mountainous and heavily forested area made it difficult to capture Gabaldón, the surrounding government soldiers effectively imprisoned the rebel leader in his own estate. In the ensuing months, Gabaldón became increasingly anxious, as no word on Delgado Chalbaud's invasion of Venezuela reached him. In January 1929, Gabaldón decided to make a break and leave for either the United States or Europe through Colombia, requesting his friend Vargas to provide him with a number of men to get him out of the area clandestinely through Arauca. However, before leaving the country Gabaldón wanted to make doubly sure that there was still something he could do. He sent his agent Julio Alvarado Silva to "Barquisimeto, Maracaibo, Valencia and Caracas, to sound out the possibility of an insurrection using the existing forces in the interior of the country."[43] Alvarado Silva returned from his visit very optimistic because González Gorrondona, who was part of Delgado Chalbaud's secret committee in Caracas, informed him that although there were no further funds for a rebel uprising, the Gomecista regime was divided between Eustoquio Gómez, Velasco Bustamante, and others who favored the continuation of Gómez's rule and López Contreras, Fernández, and Borges, who wanted a change of government and therefore welcomed Gabaldón's rebellion.

This was not entirely correct, as we have seen that López Contreras at this stage was not willing to go against Gómez until after his constitutional period of office ended. Fernández, on the other hand, had no such scruples and tried to persuade López Contreras to join them sooner rather than later.[44] There was also the possibility that other opposition groups in Caracas that wanted a change of government, including the one led by García Velasco, and another, composed mainly by intellectuals, headed by Arcaya and Vallenilla Lanz,[45] would join the rebellion. With such encouraging news, Gabaldón postponed his trip out of Venezuela, and Alvarado Silva returned to Caracas to convince López Contreras to join the rebel cause because a number of his colleagues were allegedly ready to take up arms against Gómez. Alvarado Silva returned empty handed, with the warning that Gabaldón should not believe the rumors he had heard: "everything was a farce."[46]

Rumors of Delgado Chalbaud's Rebellion Reach Caracas

At the end of 1928, Gómez started to receive reports of a possible Delgado Chalbaud revolution, but as they came from third- or fourth-hand sources, the regime did not pay much attention. Luis Alcalá Sucre, the Venezuelan minister at Panama, reported in December that a Nicaraguan army officer and a Sandino supporter had stated that an expedition against Venezuela was planned and that "guns and ammunition have been sent"[47] to the rebels from Mexico. According to Alcalá Sucre's informer, the Delgado Chalbaud revolution involved leasing a ship to transport "arms and ammunition and a number of rebels that is still not determined."[48] The invasion would be a co-ordinated effort between the exiles and local sympathizers aimed initially at securing a number of states and then marching on Caracas. Baptista and Olivares would attack from the Andes, with Arévalo Cedeño invading the country from Casanare in the south and Aristeguieta opening an eastern front. The revolution had both military and civilian support in La Guaira, Maracay, Caracas, Barquisimeto, Maracaibo, Valencia, and other cities of the country. It was clear that many of the exiles believed that this invasion would soon take place. Arévalo Cedeño, for instance, when he reached New York toward the end of 1928, heard what later turned out to be a false rumor: that the old caudillos had wasted $95,000 provided by Aranguren in an abortive plot planned by Baptista, Tellería, and Olivares.

Clearly, the rumors of an imminent Delgado Chalbaud invasion were highly exaggerated, but it gave the superficial impression that the rebels had secured sufficient funds to mount the revolution. At the end of November, Delgado Chalbaud, confident that he had sufficient financial backing, appointed a revolutionary committee that later became the Paris directorate, headed by Santos Domínici, together with Delgado Chalbaud, Baptista, and Pérez representing Olivares. The political objective of most of the rebels associated with Delgado Chalbaud was not for a radical political change but rather to replace Gómez. Delgado Chalbaud did not agree with such an assessment, and after extensive debate with Santos Domínici at his 30 rue Miromesnil Paris flat, it was agreed that sufficient political guarantees should be given to ensure "a radical change to the system."[49] The small inner rebel group in turn appointed a Supreme Junta of the Venezuelan Revolution, whose primary aim was to acquire funds for the revolution. It was also charged with the creation of a political party that would guarantee the depersonalization of the revolution and the appointment of a war director, who would cease to hold office once the revolutionaries achieved power and entered Caracas. The elections for a national constituent assembly of deputies would soon follow. The entire junta would then travel to Venezuela as soon as one or two states had been secured, where it would form a revolutionary government headed by the president of the junta. Finally, the junta would also establish a multiparty political system as well as ensure free elections. Although Delgado Chalbaud already had from Pocaterra a general outline for a "party of national union,"[50] he instructed Blanco Fombona to start work on the manifesto of the revolution. It needed to "present something new,"[51] with "an eminently revolutionary program, but serious and political,"[52] which needed to be ready for April 19, 1929, because Gómez's reelection was almost certain. When the manifesto finally appeared, it was considered by some to be a "very feeble effort,"[53] especially as they had so many years to draft and polish it.

At the end of 1928, it was clear that many revolutionaries had decided to make their way to Paris to sign the revolutionary pact. On November 19, Aristeguieta in Mexico received the invitation from Delgado Chalbaud to join his revolution, and in December Francisco Angarita landed in Bristol just before Christmas, proceeding immediately to France. In New York, the Unión Cívica, which had strong links with the communists living in Mexico such as León—who had secured adequate financial backing from the Mexican government[54]—was reestablished in December 1928 under the presidency of Carnevali, with Luciani as secretary. The group published a newspaper called *Acción Cívica* from their headquarters at 24 Stone Street in New York.

Funds Not Forthcoming

Delgado Chalbaud, however, had still not solved his financial problems, returning to London on December 14 to pursue the Jacobs connection, but sadly discovering that the money would not be forthcoming. Delgado Chalbaud was not too despondent initially because during his week in London he reactivated his financial connections with the Ethelburga Syndicate made in 1912, as well as trying to "bring up the old matter of the 30 percent surtax and to flatter British interests by saying, among other lies, that the Government of Venezuela is granting everything to the Americans and that they will in the long run overtake the English."[55] In addition, Santos Domínici and Aranguren provided Delgado Chalbaud with the names of a number of people who could be interested in funding his expedition. All Delgado Chalbaud's efforts to obtain in the United Kingdom "financial support for their plans failed."[56]

On his return to France, a furious Delgado Chalbaud confronted Jacobs about his uncle's sudden lack of enthusiasm for the revolution and dismissed him from his team. Jacobs was short of funds and tried using his information on the forthcoming revolution to extract some money from the Venezuelan authorities. Jacobs, who was living in Monte Carlo, informed the Venezuelan vice-consul at Marseilles in February 1929 that he wanted to "communicate to a responsible agent of the Venezuelan Government the exact and complete facts in his opinion of a very important expedition organized in England that will leave for our coasts in the middle of this week."[57] On February 26, Picón Febres, the consul general in Paris, left for Marseilles, meeting Jacobs at the end of the month. Jacobs informed the Venezuelan consul that he had power of attorney from Delgado Chalbaud to supervise and coordinate all their revolutionary activities and supplies of arms and ammunition in Europe. Jacobs's grievance against the rebels was that he had been pushed to one side now that they had obtained their supplies of arms. Jacobs proceeded to give the Venezuelans the misleading information that two British registered ships would soon leave from Glasgow, with Delgado Chalbaud, McGill, and several other revolutionaries on board. Although the information was erroneous, it did alert the Venezuelan government of Delgado Chalbaud's activities in Europe, with the result that the organization of the revolution would have to be done in greater secrecy than had hitherto been the case.

Escalante, the Venezuelan minister at London, immediately informed the British government of the plot. R. L. Craigie at the Foreign Office assured Escalante that the British government would do their utmost to prevent the expedition, contacting Sir Haldane Porter and Mr. Scott of the Home Office to investigate the activities of all Venezuelans in the United Kingdom. Craigie also alerted the Scottish Office, which in turn ordered both A. D. Smith, the chief constable of Glasgow, and the collector of customs at Glasgow to keep a close watch on events.[58] After a careful check of hotels and boarding houses, Smith reported a few days later that no trace of Delgado Chalbaud or Aranguren could be found in the city. The only recent Venezuelan connection was a telephone message from a Mr. Rodonicich, the Venezuelan consul at Glasgow, concerning a party of tourists interested in traveling to Venezuela. A check was also made at Troon, Androssan, and Irvine to ascertain whether any ships were about to leave or had departed recently for Venezuela, but the search proved fruitless. The information that a consignment of arms from Glasgow to Venezuela was due to leave in boxes marked "machinery and agricultural implements"[59] was also misleading, as this could be sent to any port in Venezuela, Trinidad, or Curacao. Further enquiries revealed that L. Steinisten, a Norwegian shipbroker in Glasgow, had recently enquired about freight rates to Venezuela at the Venezuelan consulate in Glasgow, but no trace of the man was found in the city. Travel agents were also visited, but all reported that no enquiries had been made about trips to Venezuela. Finally, the steamship companies had not received any requests for passages to Venezuela.

In London, the Metropolitan Police discovered that in 1917 the Grahame White Aviation Company had ceased manufacturing the type of aircraft allegedly ordered by the rebels and were now dealers in motor cars and motor boats, having changed their name in 1928 to Grahame White Company. A careful search by A. Canning, an Inspector with the Special Branch of the Metropolitan Police, of the business records of Vickers Ltd. and Grahame White Company did not reveal anything that "would in any way confirm allegations that guns, machine rifles, ammunition and aircraft had been obtained from these firms."[60] Jacobs's allegations were a setback for the rebels because from March onwards Delgado Chalbaud and his fellow conspirators would not be allowed to return to the United Kingdom. In addition, the investigations carried out in the United Kingdom did not endear Aranguren to the revolutionaries because he had to consider his own business affairs; he was a director of a number of companies in Great Britain, and a great deal of his income was generated in the country. Aranguren at this stage was not optimistic about the revolution, and hence his financial backing would not be forthcoming. To compound Delgado Chalbaud's problems, Arévalo Cedeño was about to launch his next invasion of Venezuela.

At the end of 1928, Arévalo Cedeño arrived in the Dominican Republic from New York, leaving in January 1929 for the Arauca region of Colombia to plan his sixth invasion of Venezuela in fourteen years. Arévalo Cedeño crossed into the state of Apure on February 7, launching his proclamation "To the Venezuelans" from the Arauca border region, promising to "destroy the tyranny and establish order in the constitutional practices of all branches of public life."[61] In a separate document, Arévalo Cedeño placed his sword at the service of the country in this "redeeming struggle,"[62] with his cry "Republic or Death."[63] The rebellion did not last long, and Arévalo Cedeño was forced to return to Colombia.

The Paris Pact

All the political analysis received by Delgado Chalbaud at the time indicated that the reelection of Gómez would cause a large rift among the Gomecista clan. Consequently, this was the perfect moment to unite the disaffected erstwhile Gómez supporters, such as García Bustamante and García Velasco, with the exiles planning to invade Venezuela. Delgado Chalbaud concluded that the most appropriate time for his invasion would be just after Gómez's reelection in April 1929, with orders sent to Caracas, La Guaira, Valencia, and other cities for his supporters to be prepared to take up arms that month. Delgado Chalbaud would not be ready for this date because he was still trying to secure funds for his expedition to Venezuela.

Nevertheless, Delgado Chalbaud went ahead and convened a meeting of the revolutionaries in Paris on March 7 even though there was still no adequate funding. Delgado Chalbaud, Baptista (representing Carabaño and Olivares), Alcántara, Smith, McGill, Francisco Angarita Arvelo, Mendoza, Carnevali, Jugo Delgado, Aristeguieta, Blanco Fombona, Andrés Rodríguez Azpúrúa, Alejandro Ibarra, and Edmundo Urdaneta Auvert crammed into Santos Domínici's flat and signed the Pacto de Paris, which committed them to set up a junta to carry out a revolution on the same political lines previously agreed. Delgado Chalbaud explained to those present that his plan was to invade eastern Venezuela because the government patrolled that part of the country the least. Moreover, according to Aristeguieta, in eastern Venezuela "there is not a single arm that does not stretch across the ocean imploring for a rifle and some ammunition."[64]

As there was not enough money to purchase sufficient arms and ordnance to supply a general uprising of the country or even to arm all those in eastern Venezuela who wanted to join the revolution, it was decided to equip the first expedition with 1,500 rifles, half a dozen machine guns, and 1.5 million rounds of ammunition, and to transport it to Venezuela at a total cost of $100,000. Once eastern Venezuela was under rebel control, estimated to take between six and eight days after the initial landing, the rebels would forward to Aranguren between $100,000 and $150,000 for him to organize a second expedition with 3,000 to 4,000 rifles. If the second expedition could not leave, then Delgado Chalbaud would join forces with Arévalo Cedeño, who in April had mustered his supporters in Cúcuta but needed additional funds to acquire more arms in order to invade, and Gabaldón's rebellion in Portuguesa would be reactivated.

The financial situation of the revolution remained uncertain, as Aranguren continued to refuse to part with any of his money. Aristeguieta explained that "the oilman defends his money. He will not give a cent. He wants nothing with us."[65] It was clear that Aranguren was not comfortable being the sole backer of the rebels because he was not convinced that the revolution would succeed. Delgado Chalbaud tried again to secure his help by offering the military leadership to Baptista to see whether this would satisfy the Venezuelan millionaire. The question of his anonymity would be preserved if Aranguren desired, with only Domínici, Baptista, Delgado Chalbaud, and Aristeguieta aware of his financial contribution. On April 22, Aristeguieta tried again to convince Aranguren to place $150,000 in the revolution's coffers on condition that he could withdraw his financial support if Delgado Chalbaud and Domínici did not match his contribution. Aristeguieta explained to Aranguren that it was a foregone conclusion that the revolution would succeed because it now had the support of the García clan in Venezuela. Aristeguieta wrote:

> Gral. [*sic*] José María García in the Federal District Governor's Office is very close to getting to the Miraflores Palace. Uribe, the left arm of Don José Rosario at the Ministry of Defense, and Velasco, nephew of Don José Rosario and uncle of the other García in Finance, guarantees like a hammer blow this fast anticipated change, and the other García, the young one, is a novice in political matters, who will stop at nothing in his quest to hang Colmenares and Eustoquio if they cross him and will tie López Contreras to a telegraph post if he wavers.[66]

Although the Venezuelan authorities suspected Aranguren's alleged involvement in the plot, they ultimately dismissed the charge as malicious rumor. Escalante and Zumeta felt that Aranguren was not "engaged in any active conspiracy against the present regime"[67] and that he was free of "all complicity in the late attempt or alleged attempt to equip an armed expedition to sail from this country for Venezuela."[68] Moreover, Escalante informed Itriago Chacín at the end of April that Delgado Chalbaud's plot had failed to obtain any support or materials from the United Kingdom.[69]

The Delgado Chalbaud invasion would be coordinated with a number of internal rebellions planned in Venezuela during the period leading up to the reelection of Gómez. Henrique González Gorrondona, Hermán Febres Cordero, Pablo Vaamonde, and José Juan García in Caracas would start with their uprising on April 9, followed by Dr. J. S. Quintero's rebellion in La Guaira on April 15, and General Manuel Urbina's uprising in Valencia two days later on April 17. In addition, according to Fuenmayor, the following would take up arms: General Godofredo Massini and Dr. Hugo Parra Pérez in Mérida, Araujo in Trujillo, Yépez and Bereciarti in Barquisimeto, and Sigala in Carora.[70] All failed, however, because they were found out.

Gabaldón, who was also anxious to restart his own rebellion, was informed a few weeks later that López Contreras would lead an uprising on April 28 at six in the morning in Caracas. It was timed to coincide with Borges's own uprising in Ocumare del Tuy and Alvarado Silva's rebellion in El Tocuyo. The Borges plan consisted of a number of his supporters meeting in Los Teques to overpower the police station and barracks.[71] The plan was for Colonel Tadeo Sardi Carvallo in La Peña estate to rebel together with Pedro Borrego, who would then proceed to Los Teques, where he would receive 150 men with Mauser carbines and then proceed to join up with Borges to march to Ocumare del Tuy, while Carlos Acevedo attacked Los Teques with 50 men. In the event, on May 5 Sardi reached Los Teques with 20 men but was captured the following day, as there was no general uprising. Borges managed to reach Caracas but was captured by Elias Sayago on July 18.

Gabaldón relaunched his rebellion on April 28 but was informed a day later that May 5 was the new date for the general rebellion. At the time it was stated that Gabaldón had the tacit help of Severiano Giménez, the president of Yaracuy State,[72] because the prisoners taken by government troops were found to be using rifles with the Yaracuy state stamp on them, with many rebel prisoners stating that the state president was one of the main plotters. According to López Contreras, Gómez ordered the involvement of Severiano Giménez in order to justify a fourth term in the presidency. López Contreras writes:

> General Gómez was the one who placed him in that mess, as he wanted an uprising by anybody to justify his fourth usurpation of power. Until then nobody was thinking of Juan Bautista Pérez; Dr. Arcaya was more in the loop owing to his greater influence and favor of General Gómez. Matters worked out the way Gómez wanted when General Gabaldón launched his rebellion together with General Román Delgado, in order to help each other, who knows, and later on to fight for the presidency itself. Gómez got his way: ordering the Yaracuy President to deliver a few arms to the Civil Chief of Nirgua, Colonel Teodoro Méndez. The latter entered into an agreement with General Gabaldón and sent him the arms.[73]

On May 7, Baldó, president of Portuguesa, attacked Guanare, managing to penetrate the city, but was wounded, while the government troops retreated. The rebels captured General Gandica, who informed Gabaldón that López Contreras had not taken up arms. Gabaldón at this point understood that all was lost, as only Peñaloza and Borges took up arms simultaneously against the government. Gómez then ordered Eustoquio Gómez, Pedro María Cárdenas, Jurado, Galavís, and Juan Fernández to capture the rebels. Realizing that he was defeated, Gabaldón surrendered on June 23, together with his closest collaborators, José María Suárez, Carlos Sequera Cardot, and his son Joaquín Gabaldón Márquez. Gabaldón was treated as an ordinary prisoner and taken to the Tres Torres prison in Barquisimeto, where Eustoquio Gómez interrogated him. The rebel leader was later imprisoned in Puerto Cabello's castle, where he sought an explanation from his fellow inmates Enrique González Gorrondona and Alvarado Silva for the failure of the plan. González Gorrondona confessed that he had not spoken directly to López Contreras but to a close mutual friend of the defense minister, so there was no reason to distrust the "truthfulness of everything, even more so when the 'friend who died' had chosen Colonel Luis F. Fernández from Apure to act as a mediator between López Contreras and the Committee."[74] Finally, on May 5 Olivares in Colombia issued a *Proclama* threatening to invade Venezuela if Gómez was reelected president.

Gómez Stands Down

Gómez was well aware of the ill feeling against him among members of his own Gomecista clan and certain sectors of the population in general, but he was clearly not going to relinquish power because he felt that this would lead to anarchy and destroy all the good work done over the previous twenty years. Contrary to everybody's expectations, Gómez did not seek reelection but instead continued to hold power by controlling the army directly. It was García Bustamante who advised Gómez that he could remain in power without necessarily occupying the presidential chair by merely amending the constitution to create the new post of commander of the national army, which only he would occupy. Such a move had the added attraction that it would dispense with the need to be reelected and was accompanied by the promise that Gómez was not creating a Gomecista dynasty because he had abolished the post of inspector general of the army held by his son and had closed the military academy. The abolition of the vice presidency, which was also held by his son, still had to be approved by Congress. Gómez therefore informed Congress in April that as a result of the "the ingratitude received in politics,

I resolve that none of my children will be politicians and have closed the Inspectorate and the Military Academy. It is up to you to end the vice presidencies."[75]

As April 19 approached, it became clear that Gómez would remain in his El Trompillo estate near Maracay rather than travel to Caracas to deliver his annual presidential address to Congress. At four in the afternoon of April 19, Congress convened without Gómez, who sent General Julio Anselmo Santander, his aide-de-camp, to inform them that Arcaya, the interior minister, would deliver his presidential address. At the time Rubén González, the education minister, was the only cabinet member aware of Gómez's intention not to seek reelection, and he had only been informed twenty-four hours prior to Congress meeting. Under the constitution, if Congress failed to elect a president, a Supreme Court judge would then hold the post provisionally. All the Supreme Court judges were thus summoned to Maracay to see Gómez, with the dictator choosing Juan Bautista Pérez. Luciani described Pérez as a "shadowy lawyer, and a native of Caracas, whose innocuousness was perceived as meritorious, who led an exemplary and irreproachable private life, a virgin in political matters, a very distinguished man by his manners and very serious and graceful."[76] Pérez, whose appointment to the Supreme Court was his highest ambition because he only "ever wanted to be a judge,"[77] did not aspire to the presidency. The meeting between Pérez and Gómez was short and cordial, with the latter stating you are "my candidate and here is a list of the Ministers you must appoint."[78] Pérez felt that his appointment to the presidency by Gómez was due to his desire to "pay a debt of gratitude"[79] because his father had allowed him to stay in their house during "the days of the *Conjura,* when it was felt that Castro could detain him at any moment and even kill him. The man never forgot such a gesture."[80] Pérez thus became the provisional president, pending the full election by Congress of a president for the 1929–36 period.

Once Arcaya read the presidential message on April 19, General Santander handed a letter from Gómez to both Pérez, the provisional president, and González instructing them who should be appointed to the ministries. Pérez, who was expected to ratify the incumbent ministers, followed Gómez's advice and appointed the following, mainly Tachirenses, ministers: González (interior), Itriago Chacín (foreign affairs), Velasco Bustamante (finance), Tobias Uribe (war and navy), Gumersindo Torres (development), Samuel E. Niño (education), Luis María González Niño (public works), and García Velasco, Federal District governor.[81] The new cabinet accentuated the Andean regionalism of Gómez, which became more pronounced after 1928, when he started to surround himself with Tachirenses. González was instructed on April 22 to draft under the utmost secrecy "a letter to Congress in the manner indicated, but the minister managed to penetrate the inner conscience of General Gómez about what formula he wanted because it was clear that he had demonstrated his desire to remain in power."[82]

Congress was left in a quandary, repeatedly urging Gómez to seek reelection, with both houses reaching a unanimous decision on May 3 to reelect Gómez as president for the 1929–36 period. General Rafael Cayama Martínez, president of Congress, informed Gómez of their decision, but he refused to accept the appointment, confounding his critics by seeking to retire from public life because he felt the government no longer needed his services, with the country on a sound economic and prosperous base and in a state of peace. In a letter sent to Cayama Martínez on May 3 Gómez declared that "Venezuela knows me too well and I feel true satisfaction when saying it: I am a patriot always resolved to lift the country out of the quagmire that adverse circumstances in previous governments have led to; and that is why I want to serve her with the same enthusiasm and the same joy of a grateful son in what I feel is the greatest need of my fatherland: the development and encouragement of agriculture and stock raising."[83] Gómez wanted to return to his agricultural roots and hence "to give my fellow citizens, with my presence at the head of my interests and with my practical advice, strength, warmth and life, in order to reach a state when nothing is needed and when we are completely independent in our economic life."[84] Consequently, Gómez wanted to devote the rest of his life developing the country's agricultural riches:

> I want to complete the work of the Magistrate with the work of the laborer in the shade of the unalterable peace enjoyed and the prevailing order in all the branches of national activity. According to the present situation of Venezuela, as far as I am aware, all that is needed is for Congress to elect a citizen to the Presidency who will take care, conserve and improve the work done for the betterment of the fatherland: a man free of passion, who is honest and patriotic.[85]

All that was needed was for Congress to elect a caretaker president to conduct the country's affairs, as Gómez would always be there to ensure that the country remained on an even keel.

In spite of such assurances, Congress did not accept Gómez's wish to retire and on May 4 appointed a committee composed of five senators (Juan E. París, Luis Lizarraga, Pedro Miguel Queremel, Francisco E. Niño, and R. Gómez Pereza) and five deputies (Carlos A. Tamayo, Aurelio Beroes, S. Alvárez Michaud, Diego Arcay Smith, and Santiago Briceño Ayesterán) to persuade the Benemérito to change his mind. As they were unable to do so, two days later the entire Congress traveled to the hacienda of El Trompillo to persuade Gómez to relent, but all to no avail. Gómez would, however, consider becoming commander in chief of the armed forces, something that would be easy to do, as González had already drafted the modifications needed to the constitution by adding four new clauses, viz, numbers 128–131. It was decided that the election of a new president would not take place until the constitution had been amended, with Pérez continuing as provisional president. The creation of the new post would only be applicable to Gómez and was not intended to be a permanent change to the constitution. Gómez was clear about one thing: whoever was chosen as president had to "work in all senses according with my wishes, and in this way everything will work properly."[86] Gómez wrote:

> All the country is today aware that when I accepted the post of Commander in Chief of the Army from the National Congress that I would continue to maintain the peace, tranquility and well-being of Venezuela. I have this sacred obligation toward Congress and toward the Country and in this sense I do not have, nor should I omit any effort or sacrifice. All the work of the Government must focus on the highest and most humane patriotic aims in accordance to principles and action: to guarantee peace and the rights of the citizens, acting if necessary, with a vigorous and energetic strong hand.[87]

On May 9, Congress amended the constitution, separating the office of commander-in-chief of the army from that of the presidency. Pérez then handed his resignation to Gómez at his Trompillo estate before the constitutional changes became law. Pérez's resignation was not accepted, but "I understood that your desire was another and the following day I sent my letter of resignation to the Congress."[88] On May 24, the four amendments to the constitution were agreed upon, and once this was sanctioned by Congress, the election of a commander-in-chief and a president took place. O'Reilly, the British minister, reported that Gómez "will thus be left in complete control, but relieved of attending to anything which does not interest him."[89] It was a foregone conclusion that on May 31 Congress would elect Gómez as commander-in-chief and Pérez as president. In essence, two governments were created, with the constitutional president governing according to the orders of the commander-in-chief. Hence, it was not an abdication of his duties when Pérez consulted Gómez on certain matters, as has been suggested, but a constitutional prerequisite. The position created for Gómez was for his use only; in the event of his death the role of commander-in-chief would revert back to the constitutionally elected president of the republic.[90]

Gómez's position was helped by the general economic prosperity of the country with a bumper coffee crop that year; the economy was in good shape prior to the Great Depression. Moreover, Gómez's good health put an end to the "intrigues and speculations based on the possibility of his failure, and the loyalty of the army appears to be unshaken."[91] Soon afterwards García Bustamante, believing that Gómez had relinquished part of his power, started to conspire to get either Velasco Bustamante or García Velasco to replace Pérez. At the same time, owing to the news of an impeding invasion by Delgado Chalbaud, Gómez carried out a series of strategic changes at the state level to strengthen their defenses, with Pedro María Cárdenas sent to Táchira, Jurado to Falcón, Galavís to Yaracuy, Fernández to Sucre, and Eustoquio Gómez to Lara, to wipe out the "bad children of the fatherland."[92]

While these changes took place in Venezuela, the Delgado Chalbaud revolution appeared stillborn because it could not obtain the necessary funding, especially from a source that had hitherto been extremely generous. The invasion plan of the rebels, which had been coordinated with a series of internal uprisings to coincide with what was expected to be Gómez's fourth reelection, foundered when the exiles could not get their plans off the ground. There was now a desperate need to secure funds and invade Venezuela as soon as possible.

The *Falke* Expedition

The best equipped expeditionary force against the Gómez regime was organized by Delgado Chalbaud in 1929. The *Falke* expedition was the culmination of Delgado Chalbaud's opposition to Gómez, which started in 1913 with his abortive coup. Delgado Chalbaud started planning the expedition in 1927, soon after his release from La Rotunda jail after fourteen years in prison. The expedition would be the main attacking force in a coordinated assault against the government that joined together a number of internal uprisings in many cities, as well as an invasion force from Colombia in the west and Delgado Chalbaud's invasion in the east. Delgado Chalbaud's first need was to secure enough funds to mount his expedition.

At the end of May, the revolution had cash and mortgageable assets of $59,000, far short of the total needed to acquire and equip a ship with arms, ammunition, and a crew to take the revolutionaries to Venezuela. Delgado Chalbaud was back to square one without adequate backing and at the mercy of all the confidence tricksters and arms dealers that abounded in Europe at the time. Delgado Chalbaud could wait no longer for Aranguren's decision; he was getting more and more desperate to secure funds for his expedition, especially as all appeared to be ready in Venezuela. While Delgado Chalbaud wrestled with finding adequate financial backing for his revolution, his supporters and fellow rebels were also busy readying themselves for the forthcoming invasion of Venezuela. In eastern Venezuela, Francisco de Paúla

Aristeguieta, Flores, and Agustín Rodríguez were getting their supporters ready for the coming battle. It was clear that a new source of funds needed to be tapped, taking Delgado Chalbaud into the murky world of the European arms dealer.

Through Siegfried Kramarsky, a German banker and a director of the Lisser and Rosenkranz Bank in Amsterdam, McGill introduced Felix Prenzlau, one of the many arms dealers operating in Europe after World War I, to Delgado Chalbaud. Prenzlau had been the manager of the Nordische Seeschiffarts A.G. of Hamburg, which in 1925 together with the Lisser and Rosenkranz Bank supplied ten thousand rifles and a hundred million rounds of ammunition to Chang-tso-Ling[1] of Manchuria (China), which were shipped from Hamburg on the SS *George.* Prenzlau was also connected with Benny Spiro and Herr Ludwiggbing, both of whom were under suspicion for being connected with previous illicit shipments of arms from Hamburg and the purchase in the latter part of June 1927 of a ship to transport arms from the German port to Vladivostock, for which a $500,000 line of credit was opened at an American bank.[2]

Prenzlau informed Delgado Chalbaud that he only needed a modest down payment in order to supply his ordnance needs. Delgado Chalbaud, with properties in Paris worth approximately $50,000, decided to finance the enterprise himself by mortgaging his two houses on the rue Babylone and his wife's jewelry for $25,000 in favor of Kramarsky in part payment for the ship and arms needed for the revolution.[3] Consequently, on May 10 Delgado Chalbaud signed an agreement with Prenzlau of Hamburg for the latter to finance two expeditions at a cost of $1.5 million, distributed as follows: $500,000 to be paid after the first expedition reached its destination, with a further $250,000 paid after the second expedition reached Venezuela, and the remaining $750,000 paid one month after the new government was established in Caracas.[4] In addition, Prenzlau under article 16 of the contract would receive a bonus of $500,000 once Delgado Chalbaud formed a government in Caracas.[5] In return, Prenzlau would supply Delgado Chalbaud with the following Polish war-surplus ordnance at a cost of $37,000: two thousand Mauser carbines, twenty-five cavalry carbines, twenty-five pistols Parabellum, twenty-five sabers, one thousand cartridge belts, twenty thousand rounds of ammunition for pistols, two million rounds of ammunition for Mauser carbines, and four machine guns. The munitions, originally manufactured for the Afghanistan government, would be delivered by the Polish army to the port of Gdynia.[6]

Delgado Chalbaud needed little persuasion in accepting Prenzlau's tantalizing offer of a ship, crew, and ordnance that could be secured for a relatively modest deposit, with the bulk of the payment settled once the revolutionaries entered Caracas and formed a government. It was initially agreed that the ship would take the rebels to Venezuela and then proceed to Trinidad, with an option for the revolutionaries to acquire it outright if sufficient funds were transferred. A second expedition, more heavily armed with artillery and airplanes, and commanded by McGill, would leave three weeks later with the president of the junta and other members of the government. In order for this scenario to be triggered, the necessary funds would first have to be transferred to Prenzlau's account.

Prenzlau was unable to find a suitable ship to hire, purchasing instead the *Falke* from Lues and Wilhems on June 22, 1929. The ship was acquired in the names of A. G. Kauferlei and Kramarsky, registered in Altona, Hamburg, and described in its certificate of registration as a salvage steamer. The steel hull of the *Falke,* built in Hull in 1902 for Earle's Ship Company Ltd., was 73.37 meters long, 10.16 meters wide, and 4.95 meters tall; it was steam driven, with a gross tonnage of 1,140 tons and a relatively fast top speed of sixteen nautical miles per hour. It had three cabins and was fitted with radio communication. The *Falke* had previously been used as a cargo ship transporting herrings, butter, and fresh meat; as a salvage steamer; and for towing targets for naval practice. In 1921, the *Falke* had supplied the Rif of Morocco with arms to support the insurrection of Abd-al-Krim,[7] and in 1927 it sailed for South Africa with a cargo of arms and ammunition worth $243,000. At the time of purchase, the ship had been laid up in dry dock in Hamburg for nine months and needed to be refurbished before the long voyage to Venezuela was undertaken.

The Prenzlau agreement provided the revolutionaries with plenty of arms and ammunition as well as a ship. Prenzlau wanted as an act of good faith to be paid "two hundred thousand dollars"[8] as part payment for the first expedition before he would release the ship and arms. Aristeguieta explained that the "foreigners need that, only that, as proof of our confidence in our success."[9] However, the Venezuelan revolutionaries who had the wherewithal were not willing to contribute any money, except for Aranguren, and he did not want to be seen as the only one. Delgado Chalbaud continued to meet with Aranguren almost daily to garner his support, but other revolutionaries were becoming more disillusioned with the oilman. Aristeguieta wrote, "I have not been in touch with the oilman, the man of the hour. I have made three or four wounding remarks to him but he remains unmoved."[10] In reality, Aranguren was the only person who could guarantee the financial viability of the revolution because Delgado Chalbaud had already appealed to everybody he knew in Europe for funds with negative results. In a desperate last move, Delgado Chalbaud urged Blanco Fombona to see whether his Spanish banking friends would lend $250,000, which would be repaid four months later in full together with a further payment of $250,000 a month after the new government was established in Venezuela. As a guarantee he would issue a promissory note redeemable in a year's time for $250,000, which in turn was guaranteed by Aranguren.[11] Delgado Chalbaud's last hope lay in Madrid, but Blanco Fombona's negative results dashed any forlorn hopes he may have harbored.

Delgado Chalbaud did obtain the promise from a company for half the sum of money on condition that another company or individual came up with the remaining $100,000.[12] The company sent a telegram to Aranguren inviting him to "contribute equal amounts in the enterprise,"[13] with the result that the oilman on May 28 at last promised to contribute $100,000 but under the condition that the foreign company accepted a limit on "the amount of arms to half the original estimate."[14] The revolutionaries did not agree with this request, with the result that on June 2 Aranguren withdrew from the project.[15] In June, Blanco Fombona at the last minute brought with him $10,000 from Spain[16] secured from Dr. Carlos Machado Hernández, Andrés Rodríguez Azpurúa, Urdaneta Aubert, Enrique Castro, and Alejandro Ibarra.[17]

Without any further funds forthcoming, Prenzlau was willing to continue under the original agreement. The *Falke* was never acquired by Delgado Chalbaud, as clause 7 of the contract made it perfectly clear that the ship would be chartered for the first expedition and then purchased (clause 9), if so desired, for the second one, which never took place. The cost of chartering the ship for the first expedition was $23,000, with the arms costing a further $37,000. Prenzlau accepted as payment Delgado Chalbaud's two mortgaged properties in Paris and $2,000 in cash. The Polish army surplus material was sold by the firm of Hartwig and Company to the Dutch arms dealers of Agrumaria of Amsterdam in exchange for general merchandise sold by the latter to Poland. It was reported that the arms were manufactured at the Skoda factory in Czechoslovakia. The refurbishment of the ship and the wages of the crew were estimated to cost between $8,000 and $10,000, which was borne by Prenzlau. Under the contract between Felix Prenzlau and Company and Delgado Chalbaud, the *Falke* would be under the command of the

Venezuelan admiral, euphemistically referred to in the contract as the purser (*sobrecarga*), and the cargo in the ship's hold was owned by the same "purser." The *Falke* would only stay at the destination port for a maximum of four weeks, so that if no new orders were received from Prenzlau, the ship would return to Hamburg.

The contract allowed Delgado Chalbaud to make a number of small voyages within fifteen days of reaching their final destination, and furthermore, "if in the meantime the second expedition was planned and they left port, the captain will receive instructions from the fitters that the boat belonged to the purser."[18] If this happened, then the cost of returning the crew and captain would be borne by Delgado Chalbaud. In order to safeguard his investment, Prenzlau appointed Ernest Ziplitt as captain, Heinrich Kolling as first officer, Wilhelm Schneider as second officer, and Martin Esser as third officer, who would all be paid $1,000 per month,[19] and a bonus of $25,000 each by Delgado Chalbaud. In addition, Prenzlau also appointed three German engineers and his own crew of twenty-six men.

This was a high-risk policy for Delgado Chalbaud because in the event of the revolution failing he would face financial ruin, having exchanged his prison life for that of a destitute person in a cold and foreign land. But it is likely that Delgado Chalbaud left a possible escape route: Prenzlau agreed in clause 18 of the contract to submit an affidavit with the maritime authorities stating that the ship and the arms were the property of the former head of the Venezuelan navy, but "the handing over of the document as instructed by him was not verified, nor was the declaration before the naval authorities."[20] As such an affidavit was not deposited with the port authorities, the contract was rendered null and void. It is possible then that in the event of the revolution not succeeding, Delgado Chalbaud would not be left destitute, as he could argue that the mortgage issued to Prenzlau was worthless (there had been a clear breach of contract). This may explain why Pocaterra together with Carlos Delgado[21] felt inclined, as we shall see, to dump the ordnance overboard after the failure of the Cumaná invasion.

At the end of May, all appeared ready, and on June 4 the momentous occasion arrived for all the revolutionaries when Delgado Chalbaud together with Prenzlau signed the contract in Paris that provided transport, arms, and ammunition for the revolution. It was difficult to believe that just over two years after his release from La Rotunda prison, the moment Delgado Chalbaud had dreamt of for the past fourteen years was about to happen. All that was left to do was to advise the rebels of the impending revolution and for the revolutionary pact to be signed in Paris. Telegrams were sent to all of Delgado Chalbaud's closest supporters to gather in Paris for a summit meeting. For instance, Guillermo Egea Mier was summoned from Panama, while Pimentel in San José, Costa Rica, received a similar notice on June 18. The next day Pimentel boarded the *Ariguani,* which stopped at Colón, where Egea Mier and López Méndez joined him, arriving in Paris on July 8, three days late for the summit meeting of July 5. Pocaterra also missed the meeting because he arrived on July 7. On July 9, Pimentel left for Fontainebleau, where most of the rebels were staying because they feared that Gómez's spies in Paris would recognize them.

Revolutionary Pact Signed

On July 3, Baptista, who allegedly represented Olivares and Pérez, together with Carabaño, Blanco Fombona, Alcántara, Jugo Delgado, Aristeguieta, Carnevali (representing Manuel Flores Cabrera, who in turn represented the F.E.V. and the Asociación Obrera), McGill, Augusto Pulido, Flores, Mendoza, Delgado Chalbaud, and Edmundo Urdaneta (representing Peñaloza) crammed into the small dining room of Santos Domínici's apartment. Smith was absent because he was away on holiday. The powerful erstwhile caudillos, with a sprinkling of intellectuals, resembled more a geriatric convention than a revolutionary force. Some of the fellow conspirators had not set eyes on each other for more than twenty years, so it came as a shock to see how they had all aged during those long years in exile, with Blanco Fombona later describing the group as "caricatures of people whom I had not seen for over a quarter of a century."[22] Baptista had grey hair, Alcántara was deaf and whispered when he spoke, while Jugo Delgado "whom I left with blond hair is a geriatric with sad eyes and grey hair."[23] Delgado Chalbaud took the chair, and Atilano Carnevali acted as secretary, with the assembled revolutionaries heaving a collective sigh of relief when they were informed that a ship and arms had been procured. At last, the revolution was on.

A preparatory committee was formed to elect a junta to direct the liberation movement according to the Union Pact agreement drafted previously by the main participants at the assembly. The pact was to be "debated by all those present as this will govern the acts of the Supreme Junta that we are trying to elect."[24] The elected Supreme Junta for the Liberation of Venezuela would study the current political situation in the country and advise on the most practical way of making "despotism and barbarism disappear and . . . to substitute the current odious system with a regime of liberty and justice."[25] A committee composed of Santos Domínici, Smith, and Blanco Fombona was elected to study and approve the contract signed between Delgado Chalbaud and Felix Prenzlau and Company.

Two days later a general assembly took place at the rue Miromesnil flat, with further rebels arriving from the United States, Canada, Colombia, Central America, the West Indies, and Spain to sign the Union Pact, which was dated July 5 in Geneva in order to confuse Gómez's spies. Delgado Chalbaud wanted Aranguren to sign the *Proclama,* but he declined because he allegedly did not aspire to the presidency and only wanted business deals when Delgado Chalbaud reached the presidency.[26] The pact was very similar to the one approved in 1928, except that the junta was now composed of ten people instead of five, the formation of a political party was dropped, and the war director could not be the president of the Supreme Junta or the "designated *interim* President of the Republic" (emphasis in original).[27] The Supreme Junta for Liberation would substitute the Gomecista form of "despotism for a regime of freedom and justice in perfect harmony with the constitution."[28] The military members accepted that they had to "resign all personal ambition"[29] so that free elections could take place once power was achieved.

Delgado Chalbaud declared to the assembled rebels that with these changes the revolution would be unique in Venezuela's history in that it "yields to the civilians over the military."[30] The assembly then proceeded to elect the following people to the junta: Santos Domínici, a medical doctor with a practice in Paris, as head of the committee; Smith, a former public works minister and former professor of mathematics and rector of the Universidad Central as vice president; Jugo Delgado, a medical doctor with a practice in New York, as treasurer; and the writer Blanco Fombona as secretary. Pocaterra, Pérez, Flores Cabrera, Aristeguieta Rojas, and Carnevali were elected substitutes. The war junta was also elected, with Delgado Chalbaud as war director and treasurer, Baptista as commander in chief, and Pocaterra as secretary general.

The revolutionary manifesto, which was approved and issued by the rebels at the meeting, stressed that there was no need for an ideological struggle among the various rebel factions because it was time to fight for the very existence of Venezuela, declaring that all ideologies "even the more audacious are collaborating in the patriotic work. We are all united, we all want to be united in the brotherhood of preventing the total ruin of our fatherland at the hands of a senile despot."[31] The essence of their fight was to enlighten a country that had been in the political wilderness for over twenty years, portraying themselves as essentially bringing civilization to a country taken over by the barbarians of the Gomecista regime. The junta, however, drew the line at communism by declaring its total opposition to this form of government.

Once power was achieved, a constituent assembly would be formed to give the judicial power its independence, while the university would regain its autonomy. Measures would later be enacted to increase primary and scientific education and to raise the civic pride of the country's population as a whole, as well as increasing expenditure on health. Immigration would also be encouraged in order to help with the development of agriculture and the country's nascent industries. Other measures contained in the manifesto included the fostering of closer relations with other countries, especially in the Western Hemisphere; the abolition of monopolies; the punishment of corruption; the enactment of laws favoring the well-being and social conditions of the working class and peasants; the holding of effective elections; the stimulation of free speech and thought through political parties with well-defined policies; the encouragement of foreign investment; and, finally, the improvement of the living conditions of the armed forces to make the army a national institution.

The declaration of principles contained in the manifesto was fine, but the rebels needed to conquer the country before this could be enforced. The military plan was to open two fronts at each end of the country and then to march on Caracas. The western front would be organized and led by Olivares, Baptista, and Peñaloza; and, the eastern front would be coordinated by Delgado Chalbaud on board the *Falke*. The plan was for Olivares as head of the western army, after conferring with Peñaloza, to invade from Cúcuta sometime between August 9 and 10. On the other side of the country, Aristeguieta, in an undated memorandum written sometime in 1928, argued that he could attack Cumaná with two thousand men and then proceed to secure other areas of eastern Venezuela. Aristeguieta felt that, while the rebel troops were still fresh, it would be wise to attack first Fernández, the president of Sucre based at Cumaná, the state capital, and perceived to be one of Gómez's ablest soldiers, because then the rest of the Gómez military would collapse like a pack of cards. In addition, Aristeguieta was aware that the government's arsenal at Cumaná contained only two hundred rifles, "a good many in bad shape, and some eighty to one hundred distributed,"[32] with fifteen thousand to twenty thousand rounds of ammunition, so that "victory is on our side, possibly without fighting."[33] Finally, Simón Betancourt would supply around a hundred men from the Dominican Republic to rendezvous with the *Falke* offshore Venezuela.

The plan then was to secure Cumaná, Barcelona, or Carúpano, while Carabaño occupied Güiría at the extreme end of the Araya peninsula. Guanta would also be taken; with its very good natural harbor, it had the added advantage of being the shipping outlet for the coal mined at Naricual and thus would supply the *Falke* with fuel. The port would also form a secure base for the second expedition to launch its offensive on the Tuy valleys. While this was happening, Baptista and Peñaloza in the West would tie down Gómez's army; with the northern part of eastern Venezuela occupied by the rebels, a second expedition led by McGill would leave Europe with a larger cache of arms and ammunition. The revolutionary junta would also travel on this expedition together with Blanco Fombona, Ibarra, and Carnevali. The final decision on which city to attack first would be taken later, but Cumaná had a special meaning for Delgado Chalbaud, as it was the first city founded by the Spaniards on the mainland of the continent in 1521. Hence it had a strong symbolic gesture as the first city liberated by the new enlightened era that the former admiral was about to bring forth.

There were signs of dissent with the plan even at this late stage, with some rebels expressing serious doubts about Delgado Chalbaud's military plan because of the "the lack of preparation in which we find ourselves."[34] Arévalo Cedeño, who had invaded Venezuela earlier that year, voiced a feeling held by some of the more experienced military men that Delgado Chalbaud "was very brave but was not a military man."[35] The plan, as Baptista understood it, was for Delgado Chalbaud to make a surprise attack on Barcelona in order to establish a secure base and then capture a number of government naval vessels that would be detained out of harm's way in nearby Guanta. From Barcelona, Delgado could easily dominate Cumaná, Maturín, and Ciudad Bolívar and would then threaten government forces stationed at the center of the country. Olivares together with Peñaloza would invade Venezuela from Colombia on the night of August 9, while at the other end of the country Carabaño, with the help of Francisco Gutiérrez in Güiría, would take up arms against the government. Baptista's military plan was to create as much trouble as possible for Gómez at the two extreme flanks of the country in order for the government to deploy its forces along three fronts and hence relieve the pressure on Delgado Chalbaud and the rebel cache of arms.

The plan, however, suffered from a serious flaw, which was a lack of funds to mount a full attack from Colombia. With sufficient funding Baptista would be able to send commissioners to Caracas, Trujillo, and Lara and appoint a non-Venezuelan agent in Curacao to prepare the ground for his attack. It was estimated that the lack of financial resources would mean delaying the arrival of the second expedition to Venezuela by two months, giving Gómez enough time to "assemble almost all the means available to him to attack you [Delgado Chalbaud]."[36] If Delgado Chalbaud was unable to achieve his two objectives, or in the worst case only one, then according to Baptista "we are in a very serious situation, because without any preparation or rifles and ammunition in the whole country we can not expect much support, and we can only count with what you can achieve in your area of action."[37] Baptista argued that the Olivares uprising in the West was of the utmost importance for Delgado Chalbaud on two counts: first, to avoid government forces from "strangling you," and second, to raise the spirits "to frighten Gómez and encourage our friends, while forcing those abroad to help us with money to complete the sum needed to pay your arms' suppliers."[38]

The situation then for Baptista could not have been blacker when he stated bluntly to Delgado Chalbaud in July that "our situation at the beginning is very dark"[39] because they did not have a clear idea of the strength or numbers of Gómez's forces. Moreover, the revolutionaries would only have at their disposal the arms and ammunition that the expeditionary force delivered and "the small amount they are trying to obtain from the opposite side of the country; without any hope of obtaining more until two months after the fighting begins."[40] Baptista was expected in Barranquilla on July 27 and if necessary would make a quick trip to Bogotá or Cúcuta but would be back in the city on August 20.

In France, Carnevali and Delgado, the representatives of the revolution in the United States, left from Cherbourg on July 13 for New York, with the former continuing to the Caribbean to organize Simón Betancourt's expedition in the Dominican Republic. Aristeguieta also departed from France two days later to prepare his supporters in eastern Venezuela. In the United States, Jugo Delgado's first assignment was to get Gil Borges to join the rebel junta and, failing this, to get him to persuade the US government of the rebels' just cause. However, Gil Borges declined to join the revolution on July 6 because his position at the Pan American Union "did not allow any interference in the internal politics of the countries of America without breaking my duty and commitments of honor."[41] He did suggest that as the recently elected Herbert

Hoover administration was about to initiate a new Latin American policy unfavorable to dictatorships, Dr. Ed C. McGuire, who was working on a report on Venezuela for the president, could "be extremely helpful"[42] and might work with the junta because he was a person "who enjoys exceptional influence with the government and the press, and who is also notably interested in the fate of Venezuela."[43]

Jugo Delgado, together with Carnevali, were also directed to get US support for the revolution, and failing that, to neutralize America against their plans. Atilano Carnevali briefed Senator Lenroot, who was Hoover's intimate friend and one of his biggest campaign supporters, on the adverse political conditions in Venezuela. The result, according to Lenroot, was that President Hoover was perfectly aware of the situation in the country and had cancelled a trip to Venezuela during his recent Latin American visit not for the official reason of lack of time, but because he did not want to legitimize "an unjustifiable regime."[44] Jugo Delgado also sought to influence the new US administration through Major General Frank McCoy, a friend of his and Alcántara's. It was hoped that McCoy, who was on friendly terms with Henry Lewis Stimson, the new secretary of state, would explain to Hoover the revolutionaries' plans. The United States would only consider supporting the rebels if the new regime guaranteed the establishment of democracy in the country. The intense lobbying paid off because in July McCoy informed Jugo Delgado that the United States would assume a neutral role in the conflict after receiving assurances from Delgado Chalbaud that the new government would foster political freedom and would not enter into shady deals with oil companies or foreign governments.

On July 6, Baptista left Paris for New York on his way to Colombia, with orders for Olivares to invade Venezuela from the West. However, Olivares, who was not consulted about the plan, did not approve the revolution's manifesto. As we have seen, Olivares was approached to join the pact on July 17, 1928, but had refused because the president of the *directorio,* who had power over all matters, would be both the military leader and the interim president. The basis for the liberation movement was the Union Pact, which had been intensely debated by the Paris and New York revolutionaries and entered into in Paris when Olivares, together with Delgado Chalbaud, Baptista, and Pérez signed the agreement of November 28, 1928. However, Olivares argued that he had signed it under the clear impression, acknowledged by the Supreme Junta, that a number of modifications would be made. It was assumed that Baptista on his arrival in Europe in early 1929 to finalize arrangements brought with him a power of attorney from Olivares that "authorized him to act on his behalf and to sign the Pact as long as those modifications had been adhered to."[45]

The junta felt that Baptista, Olivares's representative, must have been satisfied with the changes, since he subsequently signed the agreement as well as attended the assembly that elected the ten members of the Supreme Junta. Although those present, who also represented absent supporters, signed the pact, Baptista did not have Olivares's authorization to commit to the venture on his behalf. Delgado Chalbaud and Domínici assumed that Baptista had power of attorney to act on behalf of Olivares. According to Olivares himself, however, he was only represented "on the understanding that the representation did not force me to accept what had been agreed, because as you know he did not have power of attorney from me."[46] Olivares immediately informed Baptista to convey his position to the Paris committee, which Baptista did on three occasions, viz, July 12, 13, and 14 but his name was included in the pact on purpose despite his statement.

Olivares was not willing to join Delgado Chalbaud's revolution initially because he disagreed with the way it was organized and felt that its aims were fundamentally flawed. He wanted to depersonalize the revolution and was convinced that Venezuela's main political problem was "the system of personal government where the will of a man replaces the law."[47] This had led to the establishment of the military as a fourth power in government, who, "in the person of the Commander in Chief of the Army, completely strips the Constitutional President of its inherent distinctive authority, thus preventing the reestablishment of individual guarantees and public liberty to the people."[48] Olivares was always willing to fight such an "unfortunate system under which civic life is impossible,"[49] but there was an urgent need for a guarantee that political parties would be established immediately after reaching power. Olivares was against the notion that the main financial backer should be the de facto leader of the revolution and not somebody with proven military skills. This had been the sad experience since the Matos Libertadora revolution in 1901–1903, and had been in his view the reason for the failure of all subsequent revolutions.

Moreover, Olivares felt that certain members of the junta were not acceptable to the people of Venezuela and argued that the struggle against Gómez could take two forms: (a) either under the "Leader of the Revolution" syndrome, or (2) under a *directorio*. There was a fundamental difference between the two options, because the first one meant that the victorious leader of the revolution would automatically become president, while the second alternative gave the *directorio* the power to appoint the president. It was clear to Olivares that although most leaders of the revolution or war directors had chosen Baptista as chief of staff in 1921, 1928, and 1929, his military experience was neutralized by having to receive orders from a "maximum leader" who was not a military man.

Ortega Martínez did not accept Olivares's reasoning for the junta to appoint the military commander because "the unity of leadership is indispensable for its success,"[50] but felt instead that a group of men should appoint the leader to head the military rebellion and also establish a provisional government. Ortega Martínez argued that whatever agreement was adopted, it had to state that the main aim of the revolution was the establishment of a civilian government, as well as agreeing to the military leader transferring power to the junta once Caracas was occupied and the country pacified. The junta would appoint the interim president, vice president, ministers, governors, and others by majority vote. A national constituent assembly would then be elected, composed of three deputies for each state and for the Federal District, which in turn would appoint the provisional president (who could not be the interim president) and vice president and draft a new electoral law for senators and deputies. Delgado Chalbaud and his collaborators in the junta also felt that Olivares had changed his mind about the success of the rebellion and was using a rather imaginative interpretation of events in order to justify his position. However, in a final frantic request the junta urged Olivares to maintain a high profile in Cúcuta in order to give the impression that he was about to invade Venezuela. Olivares agreed to attack Táchira together with Baptista but using his own men and arms and without the support of Delgado Chalbaud.[51] At the time of Delgado Chalbaud's invasion in August, the town of Capacho would be taken by the rebels by attacking the barracks and kidnapping López Contreras to allow the exiles easier access to Venezuela from Colombia.

The PRV and Its Curacao Adventure

While Delgado Chalbaud was organizing his expedition, the PRV in Mexico was also planning a daring attack from Curacao through what it perceived was the Achilles' heel of the Gómez fortress of Venezuela. The PRV was scornful of Delgado Chalbaud and his cohorts and severely criticized him for his efforts. The party's newspaper, *Libertad,* referred to the "revolutionaries' political ideology of that of simply 'Unión,'"[52] as there was no social agenda, with the rebels wanting to replace Gómez in order to reap the benefits of government for themselves.[53] Santos Domínici was perceived by the PRV as "Román Delgado's stooge,"[54] while the acknowledgment of the admiral's leadership by Ortega Martínez and Baptista only showed what sort of "traitors" they were.

The oil boom of Venezuela during the 1920s had the effect of increasing the prosperity of the Dutch West Indies, with the majority of the Venezuelan workers on the islands employed at the large oil refineries. The development of the oil industry in Venezuela produced a trading surplus in Curacao, and the island's standard of living increased by 540 percent between 1914 and 1929, with the shipping tonnage handled by Curacao surpassing that of Amsterdam in 1930.[55] The excellent cover afforded by the large number of Venezuelans, as well as the proximity and easy access to the mainland, attracted exiled political groups to the islands, which they viewed as a natural starting point of revolutionary activity in Venezuela. A similar consideration also prevailed in the British island colony of Trinidad. The Venezuelan government was acutely aware of this situation and kept a close watch on the activities of the Venezuelan workers on the island in order to preempt any revolutionary attack emanating from the colony. In 1922, for example, Urbina arrived in Curacao and was detained by the colonial government at the request of the Venezuelan government. Although released later, Urbina was kept under close surveillance and had to report to the police daily. The Venezuelan workers also posed a threat of sorts to the colonial government because of labor disputes between local workers and Venezuelan immigrants. With the increase in the activities of the oil industry in the early 1920s, the shipping companies of Curacao, for instance, started to hire Venezuelan stevedores because the local ones demanded higher wages and better working conditions. The dispute came to a head on July 17, 1922, when the local stevedores rioted against the shipping companies using Venezuelan labor.

In 1927, there were some 1,500 Venezuelan workers in Curacao and Aruba, mostly employed by the Curacaosche Petroleum Industrie Maatschappij, the Shell refinery company on the island. The Curacaosche Petroleum Industrie Maatschappij employed its Venezuelan labor through a subcontractor who brought men over from Coro. The treatment of the Venezuelan workforce at the refineries left much to be desired, so much so that in 1926 many of the workers complained to Leyba, the Venezuelan consul on the island, that their wages had not been paid in full. Leyba found that the workers were underpaid and was later successful in forcing the company to make up the difference. The company faced a more serious problem a few months later, when four hundred of its Venezuelan labor force went on strike for higher wages and a nine-hour day. Angry scenes broke out outside the refinery when management conceded the nine-hour day but refused to increase wages; only Leyba could calm the workers.

In Curacao, most of the Venezuelan workers lived next to the refinery, where liquor was sold from mobile cantinas and workers were encouraged by unscrupulous racketeers to gamble their earnings, estimated at approximately $3,831, on a Saturday night. The Dutch colonial authorities were helpless in preventing these practices because the land belonged to fifty different people; they were forced to post ten to twelve policemen permanently on duty outside the refinery to keep the peace. The concentration of Venezuelan workers in such a small area made political activity easier for the exiled Venezuelan opposition groups, who were able to inculcate the workers with "communist, subversive or revolutionary ideas in general against our government,"[56] as Asuaje, the president of Falcón State, the closest Venezuelan state to Curacao, informed Gómez. Simón Betancourt, who arrived from Trinidad and worked as a photographer and was in constant correspondence with Flores, was one of the main "enemy propagandists among the workers, making them believe many things, which only that type of person can think."[57]

In late 1927, Consul Leyba and Asuaje recommended to Gómez the curtailment of emigration of Venezuelans to the islands because opposition to the Gómez regime among the workers was growing all the time, with two opposition newspapers, the *Obrero Libre* and *Venezuela Libre*,[58] distributed among Venezuelan workers. It was too easy, as Pérez Soto, the president of Zulia, explained to Gómez, for undesirables to enter the country, first traveling from Curacao to Amuay in Falcón, and then by local oil tankers to the oilfields of Cabimas, Lagunillas, or other Zulian cities. Gómez heeded this advice and on June 12, 1928, recommended to Asuaje that emigration from Falcón be stopped immediately. The Venezuelan government was not slow either in infiltrating these labor groups, planting its own confidential agents, such as Carlos Malpica, among the workers. Criticism against Gómez and the colonial authorities intensified during the ensuing months, and an alarmed Leyba visited the island's governor and military commander to draw their attention for the need to take stronger measures to be taken to "counteract the insidious campaign," while at the same time bringing to their attention the "contents of a pamphlet and other inflammatory publications, from which it could be clearly deduced that a plot against our government is being organized in Curacao."[59]

At the time, there were also renewed efforts to associate Pérez Soto with a fictitious Zulian secessionist movement. P. M. Reyes, a Colombian in Paris, notified Gómez that Gustavo Manrique Pacanins, a Venezuelan lawyer, told him that "important people of the United States, that is, oilmen or people he says have contacts in the State Department, have briefed them on General Pérez Soto's aptitude or talent towards governing."[60] Further reports on the creation of a Republic of Zulia by US oil interests appeared in exiled opposition newspapers such as *El Republicano* of Panama and in the Colombian press such as *La Vanguardia Liberal* of Bucaramanga. Acisclo Boscán from the United States accused Pérez Soto of secretly plotting with Rivas Vásquez, an enemy of Gómez living in Cuba, to create such a republic. Pérez Soto, according to Boscán, had recently made two special trips to the United States, and once the Zulian Republic had seceded, then both the US government and Machado's Cuban government would recognize it.[61] Pérez Soto dismissed these rumors as "treason against my fatherland and an immense dishonor."[62]

The catalyst for setting up a branch of the PRV in Curacao was the general strike among refinery workers held at the end of August 1928 to stop the repatriation of eleven Venezuelan rebels who took part in the Fossi-Urbina abortive invasion of Venezuela that year. Hilario Montenegro[63] was closely involved with the Venezuelan refinery workers, distributing the PRV newspaper *Libertad,* which was edited in Mexico. The PRV also helped in defending workers' rights, with Montenegro establishing a workers' union, the Unión General de Trabajadores, with Andrés Avila as secretary general. The PRV felt that the large expatriate community of Venezuelan workers on the island would be fertile ground to establish a branch of their opposition party. The Salvadorian Carlos Flores, a member of the Anti-Imperialist League of the Americas, was sent by party headquarters to set up the PRV in Curacao. Dutch colonial law did not allow political parties to be established, so the PRV on September 17 founded its branch under the name "Sociedad 28 de Octubre." Montenegro was elected secretary general, and at the end of 1928 the society had over thirty members. Carlos Flores then moved to the neighboring island of Aruba to set up another branch of the party.

When Montenegro heard at the end of 1928 that Delgado Chalbaud was planning to invade Venezuela, he proposed to party headquarters to join the rebels by attacking the Amsterdam fortress in Curacao, arming the workers in the refineries, and invading Venezuela. Montenegro was convinced that there were sufficient arms for eight hundred to a thousand people. The plan was approved by the PRV but on condition that an eastern rebellion in Venezuela was started simultaneously. The plans received a setback on January 24, 1929, when Delfín Pérez murdered Montenegro, with the oil workers protesting the death of the union leader.[64] Gustavo Machado, who received funds from the Soviet Union,[65] was then sent to Curacao, arriving on March 4, 1929, with $100 to organize the operation. Carlos Aponte, who was fighting with Sandino in Nicaragua, was sent to Trinidad to help the military preparations there. On his way to the British colony, he arrived in Curacao on May 10, continuing a few days later to Trinidad to join Bartolomé Ferrer and Eduardo Machado to start preparations for an eastern Venezuela invasion. During his stay in Curacao, Aponte discussed with Machado the attack on the Amsterdam fort and showed a small group of rebels how to manufacture homemade bombs.

The attack on Venezuela was initially headed by Gustavo Machado and Carlos Aponte, but the latter decided to remain in Trinidad. This meant that Machado needed to reinforce his military operation, with somebody who knew the Falcón terrain well. Alonso Ramírez Astier, secretary general of the PRV in Panama, suggested Urbina to Machado because he was "anti-caudillista and anti-imperialist."[66] Urbina, a native of the state, accepted the challenge,[67] arriving in Curacao on May 31 on board the *Buenos Aires*. Machado would regret his choice, as he later labeled Urbina "clumsy" because of his preference for surprise attacks without proper preparation.[68]

When Urbina arrived in Curacao from Panama at the end of May, Leyba immediately requested his extradition from the island to Venezuela but was unsuccessful.[69] In order not to arouse any suspicion, the plotters on Saturday night, June 8, met at Mi Deseo, an isolated house rented by Machado situated two kilometers from the refinery, for a bogus christening, during which a small cache of arms consisting of twenty-five machetes and two colt pistols were distributed. Gustavo Machado and Urbina headed the attack, with Gustavo Reyes, Ramón Torres, and the students Pablo González Méndez, José Tomás Jiménez Arraiz, Gustavo Ponte, Miguel Otero Silva, and Guillermo Prince León. At about half past nine that evening two buses, with a total of approximately forty men, headed for the waterfront; the men were split into two groups. While a leaflet proclaiming the revolution was issued,[70] one group attacked and overpowered in less than fifteen minutes the twenty-four men guarding the island's Amsterdam fort and arsenal. The rest of the garrison and active police force were on duty patrolling the streets of Willemstad and other parts of the island. In the ensuing skirmish, around five people died, and several others were wounded,[71] with the rebels removing 150 rifles, a large number of automatic pistols, 3 Lewis guns, and 3,000 rounds of ammunition. Colonel A. F. Borren, the commander in chief of the Dutch garrison and known as the Tiger of Amsterdam because he was reputedly responsible for thirty thousand deaths in Indonesia, was captured when he arrived at the fort.

Meanwhile, another band of insurgents overpowered the residence of Dr. Leonard Albert Fruytier, the island's governor, and took him prisoner. Urbina ordered an immediate search for Consul Leyba and issued an order for his execution for his many "crimes committed against Venezuelans."[72] Leyba was not located, but according to Urbina's testimony, his mother-in-law died of shock, and his pregnant wife aborted when the rebels rampaged through the consulate. In the meantime, the exiled Venezuelan students resident on the island and some 30 Dominican workers joined the insurgents at the waterfront, with the number of revolutionaries swelling from 40 to 250 men. A ship to transport the rebels to the Venezuelan mainland was requested by Urbina from the manager of the Curacaosche Petroleum Industrie Maatschappij,[73] threatening to blow up the refinery and pillage the town and then set it on fire if he did not obtain a ship. The SS *Maracaibo* of the Red "D" Line was placed at the disposal of the rebels, but Captain A. G. Morris refused to sail at first, relenting only when Urbina threatened to hang the governor and his family if he refused to comply with his orders. Around 140 rebels landed at La Vela de Coro, where they first encountered government troops. The rebels overpowered the town, but then disorder and a lack of experience took over, forcing them to withdraw to the surrounding hills. After several skirmishes at Mucuquita, Socopero, and San Francisco, the group disintegrated, with each rebel making his own way out of the country.

The attack caused a certain amount of consternation in the Dutch parliament. On June 19 Mr. Colijn, leader of the Anti-Revolutionary Party, expressed surprise at the lack of intelligence and activity on the part of the island's police, to which the Dutch minister of the colonies replied that the attack had been well executed and planned and that "no information concerning the plot had reached the secret police, so that no special measures had been taken,"[74] even though Leyba had warned of such an event taking place. In Caracas, there was an inclination to believe that some Dutch officials had been privy to the venture, but the British minister there doubted that the Venezuelan government would bring any claims against the Dutch. On the other hand, it was felt that the United States welcomed another incident of this nature, as it would allow them to take over the defenses of the island. Odo Russell of the British legation at Caracas reported at the time that "the activities of the Dutch government in Curacao are very closely scrutinized by the United States Legation here."[75] However, such a move, as the British consul at Curacao reported, would probably be unacceptable to "the thinking section of the community" because "the Petroleum interests are bringing most of them great prosperity."[76]

The Venezuelan government complained to the Dutch authorities about their negligence. Itriago Chacín, the Venezuelan foreign affairs minister, could not understand how eighty men "armed with machetes and some revolvers"[77] could overpower the Dutch garrison. In addition, the commander-in-chief had not mounted a counterattack. At first the colonial authorities stated that the revolutionaries had landed on the island on June 7 from a sailboat, but this was denied categorically by Itriago Chacín because it was confirmed that the "assault and subsequent landing in Venezuela was organized exclusively on that island and that such a view is manifestly tendentious."[78] Moreover, the Dutch authorities stated that circumstances had forced the governor of Curacao to order the departure of the SS *Maracaibo*. Such a view, Itriago Chacín felt, was the most serious charge against the colonial authorities because the governor knew that the rebels were about to attack a friendly country. After expelling many known agitators from the islands, the Dutch government court-martialed Lieutenant Bergen, in charge of the garrison on the night of the attack, as well as the governor's personal adjutant, with the former dismissed from the service with dishonor and the latter severely reprimanded and losing a rank.[79]

Problems at the Colombian Border

In the meantime, the Delgado Chalbaud revolution had stalled at the Colombian frontier. The rebels up to early July had not purchased any arms, and Olivares was placing so many conditions for his participation that there was no certainty that they could rely on his support.[80] Baptista also felt that it would be difficult to act together with Peñaloza in Táchira because of the "deep political jealousy that exists in that region."[81] The situation in Cúcuta was not as depressing as Baptista painted, since revolutionaries, such as Durán, Guillermo Power, and Héctor Blanco Fombona, had arrived from Barranquilla in mid-July bringing with them $5,000. The rebels formed a revolutionary committee under the aegis of Olivares and purchased around four hundred Mauser carbines and fifteen thousand rounds of ammunition. Peñaloza had a further two hundred arms of different caliber with twenty thousand rounds of ammunition hidden near Cúcuta.

Baptista arrived in Barranquilla on July 30 and received orders to invade Táchira on August 5, an impossible task because it took nine days to reach Cúcuta from the coast. Baptista left Cartagena on August 6 for the Venezuelan frontier, with Olivares following him the next day.[82] When Baptista arrived in Cúcuta in early August, he canceled the purchase of arms because "he was able to buy the cache of arms that allegedly belonged to General Ramón González Valencia and that remained in the custody of his former officers."[83] The Colombian border town was full of rumors of Peñaloza's rebellion and its coordination with a large revolution taking place in Venezuela.[84]

The Falke *Leaves*

The *Falke* was completely refurbished between June 21 and July 9, with its engines repaired, its pumps cleaned and overhauled, and a new coat of paint applied. Ernest Ziplitt, the ship's captain prepared the ship for a voyage lasting two months, taking on 205 tons of coal at Hamburg. On July 8 two cases of light machine guns, which originally came from Antwerp, Belgium, were delivered from the arms depot (Kriegswaffendepots) of Hamburg port and loaded on the ship under the supervision of the Hamburg Free Port Authorities for the account of Ludwig Bing and Company. The following day, the *Falke,* with Jorge Parisot on board, left the German port bound for Gdingen (Gdynia), thirty miles from Danzig in Poland, arriving on July 11, two days after Prenzlau reached the Polish port. The *Falke* was scheduled to spend a week in Gdingen while it loaded more coal and arms and the Venezuelan rebels boarded the ship.

In Paris, early on the afternoon of July 13, the bulk of the Venezuelan revolutionaries, after bidding farewell to their friends and relatives, traveled to Fontainebleau to join Delgado Chalbaud on the evening before embarking on the first leg of what they expected to be the liberation of Venezuela. During the evening, War Director Delgado Chalbaud assigned the various ranks and posts. Alcántara was appointed chief of staff, assisted by Flores and Commodore Egea Mier; Lieutenant Colonel López Méndez, quartermaster; the Frenchman Parisot, who was an intimate friend of Delgado Chalbaud and who acted as a kind of secretary and aide-de-camp, was appointed *comisario de guerra, jefe interno del parque;* Captain Carlos Julio Rojas, adjutant of orders; Lieutenant Colonel Pimentel, head of artillery; Lieutenant Colonel Mendoza, head of cavalry; Lieutenant Colonel Rafael Angarita Arvelo, first assistant; Lieutenant Colonel Carlos Delgado Chalbaud Gómez, aide-de-camp; Lieutenant Armando Zuloaga Blanco, aide-de-camp; Lieutenant Juan Colmenares Pacheco, staff adjutant; Lieutenant Julio McGill Sarria, staff adjutant; Captain Edmundo Urdaneta Auvert, adjutant to general staff. The other rebels were Alfredo Russián; Raúl Castro Gómez; Pocaterra; Julien Graftieux, Delgado Chalbaud's French servant; Rafael Vegas; Captain Ernest Ziplitt (a German), captain of the *Falke;* Martin Essner (a German), third officer on the *Falke;* and Captain Franz Zucal (a German), chief of machine guns.

Early the next day, on July 14, Delgado Chalbaud, Alcántara, Flores, Pocaterra, Pimentel, McGill, Mendoza, Carlos Julio Rojas, McGill Sarria, Rafael Vegas, Zuloaga Blanco, Juan Colmenares Chacón, Angarita Arvelo, López Méndez, Urdaneta Aubert, Raúl Castro, Delgado Chalbaud Gómez, Egea Mier, and Graftieux left at eight o'clock in the morning by bus from Fontainbleu for the Gare du Nord, giving the impression that they were a party of tourists led by Colonel Alejandro Ibarra on their way to the Exhibition of Poland at Warsaw. The rebels caught the midday Paris-Berlin express, with Danzig as their final destination. Delgado Chalbaud, Pocaterra, and McGill, after bidding the motley crew farewell until they rejoined them in Danzig on July 17,[85] left the train station to meet up with Marcos Bunomovich[86] and Zucal to make the final arrangements before they themselves left Paris the following day for Danzig. Kramarsky would join them in Berlin to continue the trip together to Danzig.

The following day, on July 15, at three o'clock in the afternoon, McGill, who would remain behind to lead the second expedition to Venezuela, which would bring with it the Supreme Junta, saw Delgado Chalbaud, Pocaterra, and Bunomovich off on the Paris-Berlin express. During the trip Delgado Chalbaud drafted a telegram for Baptista to be ready to invade Venezuela together with Peñaloza by August 10 at the latest. He also urged them to convince Olivares, who no longer was in agreement with the junta, to at least let Gómez's spies in Cúcuta think that he was about to invade. In Berlin,

Prenzlau, Kramarsky, and Zucal met up with the group traveling to Danzig via Malbork in Poland, arriving at the Hotel Danziger Hoff at seven p.m. on July 16, where the majority of the rebels were staying. A further hundred revolutionaries had previously arrived from Spain, staying at the same hotel, where they sipped cognac and went out very little while they waited to be transported to the ship. It is difficult to imagine what sort of impression such a large group of Venezuelans must have made on the town, which by all accounts was not used to such an influx of Latin blood "smelling of rum and perfumed hair tonic,"[87] as a contemporary account reported.

The arms and ammunition soon arrived by railway from Warsaw, which according to the ship's manifest were destined for Durazzo (Durres), Albania.[88] At seven thirty a.m. on July 17 the ship's crew started to load the first consignment of some 2,400 reconditioned carbines of the 1888 Mauser type, which were handed over by Germany to Poland under the Treaty of Versailles, together with 950 cases of ammunition and 4 machine guns, finishing at three o'clock the following morning, some 1,248 cases in all.[89] The rifles were in a bad state, as "they were all patched guns,"[90] according to Franz Zucal, who was on board the *Falke* and was a locksmith by training. The crew, who were unaware of the nature of the cargo or their destination, became worried when they accidentally discovered that the cases contained arms and ammunition. The crew demanded an explanation from Ziplitt, but none was given until Prenzlau and his partner "personally declared that the freight had been declared in the proper manner and was being sent from one Government to the other,"[91] and that the ship was not transporting contraband, as the customs authorities had authorized the shipment, "which is proved by the Customs seals."[92]

At the same time, according to Heinrich Kolling, first officer on the *Falke*, the ship took on board 650 tons of bunker coal, 100 tons less than they had paid for, something which became critical when they reached the Caribbean.[93] In spite of the assurances, the crew demanded more money, which Prenzlau at first refused to countenance but which Delgado Chalbaud accepted, with the added incentive that every member of the crew had their wages doubled and were promised a bonus of $119 at the end of the voyage. With the arms and coal stored safely in the ship's hold, it was time to celebrate, with Prenzlau, Kramarsky, Bunomovich, and a Polish government representative taking Delgado Chalbaud, Alcántara, and Pocaterra to dinner at the Hotel Casino de Zopott (Sopot), "one of most famous in Europe and a seaside resort of incomparable beauty."[94] When they arrived for dinner at the hotel, they found a dance in full swing, with the Bürgermeister present celebrating a national holiday. During the meal Delgado Chalbaud remarked that the restaurant was full of beautiful women, but knowing that they had to get up early the next morning, they resisted temptation because "we were not here for that and at twelve each little owl returned to his olive tree."[95]

The following morning, July 19, at six o'clock the expeditionary force took a small boat from the Free City of Danzig[96] to Gdynia[97] in Poland, where more passengers joined the ship, including Delgado Chalbaud, Alcántara, Flores, López Mendez, Mendoza, Castro Gómez, McGill, Delgado Chalbaud Gómez, and Pocaterra,[98] all of whom "made a passable impression and aroused no suspicion of any kind."[99] Once on board, Bunomovich took many photographs, mainly to show Aranguren how he had spent his money. Soon afterwards, twenty other passengers came on board, with Delgado Chalbaud taking the captain's cabin and finding a floral arrangement wishing him good luck in Spanish. At nine-thirty in the morning, the *Falke* left Gdynia to rendezvous with a sailing ship from Hel on the Mierzeja Helska peninsula to pick up the remaining seventy revolutionaries and then set a course for the North Sea. The German crew was unaware of their destination or what use the arms were for, with Delgado Chalbaud promising to tell them their destination at sea. Apart from Ziplitt and Zucal, employed by Prenzlau to instruct the revolutionaries in gunnery and weapon handling allegedly in a new army that was under formation in South America, none of the crew knew the military nature of the expedition. After crossing the English Channel, the ship set a course for Blanquilla Island, off the eastern coast of Venezuela to rendezvous some time on August 7 with Pedro Elias Aristeguieta and Francisco Gutiérrez.

Venezuelan Government Discovers Plot Too Late

In early July, the Venezuelan legation at Paris learned of the activities of Delgado Chalbaud when a German citizen revealed the plot to Zumeta, the Venezuelan minister, in revenge for the alleged bad treatment received from Delgado Chalbaud. At the time, Zumeta believed that Delgado Chalbaud was staying at the Dinard Hotel in Paris, but in fact he had left on July 10.[100] Although Zumeta believed that his informers had confused Delgado Chalbaud Gómez with his father, Román, from August 9 onwards the Venezuelan diplomat tried to get the French authorities to act against the plotters. French law, however, did not consider conspiratorial meetings as sufficiently serious to warrant expulsion from the country. Under French law, Zumeta needed to find a cache of arms on French territory that belonged to the rebels or catch the plotters red-handed for an expulsion order to be issued. Zumeta suspected that the French government's lack of interest was because it sympathized with Delgado Chalbaud, who had contacts with "French political men interested in the old Delgado-Boló negotiation."[101] Zumeta feared that any sanction "applied to Delgado would be exploited to promote a great press and parliamentary debate with the help of socialist and communist groups."[102] The French government did not take a great deal of interest in the affair, assuring Zumeta soon after Delgado Chalbaud had died in Cumaná that he was still at the Dinard Hotel in Paris.

The reports of an impending revolution were now beginning to reach Caracas from other sources. Figueredo, the Venezuelan consul in New York, informed Gómez on July 28 about the *Falke* expedition. Later, Carlos J. Grisanti, the Venezuelan minister at Washington, and Pedro R. Rincones, the consul general at New York, sent a confusing telegram on August 9 stating that Olivares would land in Venezuela on a "ship coming from Mexico or Colombia, with a cache of arms obtained in those Republics."[103] On this occasion there is little doubt that Gómez's espionage network did not work well, and had it not been for the German sneak, Delgado Chalbaud's arrival in Venezuela would have taken the government by complete surprise. However, once alerted, the Venezuelan authorities immediately notified other Venezuelan consuls around the world. Dr. Noguera Moreno, the Venezuelan consul in Trinidad, informed the colonial authorities in July 1929 of a revolutionary plot against Venezuela, something which the Trinidad police, after a full investigation, concluded was totally unfounded and even suggested that it had been fabricated by the consul for personal reasons.[104] Alejandro Fuenmayor, the Venezuelan minister in the Dominican Republic, complained to the government that a revolutionary plot was being organized almost publicly on the island and wanted to know what measures the government was taking to stop it.[105] The Dominican government made a number of enquiries and in early August informed Fuenmayor that Simón Betancourt and Rómulo Betancourt were organizing some form of revolutionary action but that their destination was unknown.[106]

Crossing the Atlantic

The mood on board the *Falke* at first was that of a cruise ship, with the crew in general high spirits, snapping pictures and reading books on the deck. The ship had three individual cabins on board, with Delgado Chalbaud occupying one and another taken by Alcántara, who was not feeling well and receiving medical treatment from Vegas; a third cabin was reserved for Pocaterra but was occupied by Egea Mier, who was also ill. The rest of the crew and expeditionary force slept in hammocks in an open space below the small dining room, which had a large chart showing the ship's daily progress. Although the ship was capable of a maximum speed of sixteen knots, the voyage to the Caribbean was at a leisurely eleven to twelve knots in order to conserve their coal stocks.

Two days after leaving Gdynia, the Venezuelan rebels were armed with revolvers and daggers and started receiving weapons training on how to use and maintain their old carbines. Once the ship had passed the Azores, Ziplitt before the assembled crew took his oath of allegiance to the Venezuelan flag on condition that in the event of the raids being successful he would be promoted to the rank of Venezuelan admiral, with a salary of $958 a month. After the ceremony, machine guns were posted and erected on the deck of the bow, and when the German crew, now thoroughly alarmed, "enquired into the meaning of these precautions, Ziplitt declared with brutal simplicity that 'I am master here and answerable for whatever is done on board.'"[107] The crew was only calmed by promises of further remuneration. On July 24, Bolivar's birthday, the *Falke* was renamed *Crucero General Anzoátegui,* and the rebels' flag, with the same colors as the Venezuelan one except that the bands were vertical and without a shield or stars, was raised for the first time.

A Change in the Plans

Although a plan of sorts was agreed prior to embarkation, Delgado Chalbaud's military campaign was unclear to many on board. Four days out of Poland, Delgado Chalbaud informed Alcántara that the military plan he had agreed to in Paris had changed and that he was now going to attack either Barcelona or Cumaná. Alcántara was so taken aback, and his disagreement was so strongly felt, that had he known of these plans he would not have joined the rebellion. In his account of the ill-fated expedition, Pimentel criticized Delgado Chalbaud for not explaining more fully his plan of attack, stating that during the voyage to Blanquilla he tried repeatedly to get some sort of indication of what the admiral intended doing but was unable to ascertain "even the name of the place where we would first engage the enemy."[108]

Egea Mier found Delgado Chalbaud's attitude on board the ship "something exotic, not to say implausible."[109] In order to calm the nerves of all those on board, Delgado Chalbaud agreed to hold a war council at Blanquilla Island, but this never took place.

There were more practical problems facing the expedition at this stage, with Egea Mier worried that the ship would run out of fuel. Both Ziplitt and Delgado Chalbaud were sure that they had taken on board approximately 800 tons of coal, but just before arriving at Blanquilla Island, it was discovered that they only had 70 tons of coal left, enough for a further three days of sailing. We have estimated that the *Falke* had 830 tons of coal onboard when it left Poland, and with the ship consuming 40 tons per day, a total of 760 tons on its nineteen-day voyage to Blanquilla Island, leaving 70 tons of fuel, which was insufficient to escape if they encountered and were chased by government gunboats. Such a critical situation would now have a direct bearing on any plans made before the rebellion started. Egea Mier later wrote that "our luck is desperate, our situation would make us change all the plans so carefully drawn up by D.[elgado]."[110] A crisis meeting was summoned by Delgado Chalbaud, with Alcántara, Carlos Julio Rojas, and Pocaterra deciding to attack Guanta first to secure additional supplies of coal.

The Guariare Ranch

Meanwhile in Venezuela, Francisco de Paúla Aristeguieta met his brother Pedro Elias on July 31 at the family ranch at Guariare, close to the fishing beach of Peñas Negras, situated near the Laguna Grande stream on the Gulf of Cariaco, and an hour and a half away from Caiguire, which was at the center of Francisco de Paúla Aristeguieta's fish processing business. Aristeguieta ordered Alfredo Russián on July 30 to meet him at their ranch three days later on August 2, and to ready himself to take delivery of arms between August 6 and 10 on the *Esmeralda* vessel.[111] The weapons would then be transported in *piraguas* (canoes) from Peñas Negras to Cumaná ready for when the *Falke* attacked.

On August 6, the *Falke* arrived off Blanquilla Island expecting to find Simón Betancourt and Carnevali with 150 volunteers from Santo Domingo, but there was no sign of these men. The *Falke* slow-steamed around the island, which is approximately twenty kilometers wide and almost square in shape, to establish whether there was anybody there because it was known that two or three people lived on the island. Although the place looked deserted, a search party, composed of Flores, Carlos Julio Rojas, Mendoza, López Méndez, and Colmenares, was sent to ascertain whether this was the case, because they did not want anybody giving their position away to the authorities. The search party found Fernando Rodríguez, the *oficial del resguardo de sal* and owner of the small goat herd on the island, an old man called Marcano, together with two peons who looked after the goats, who hid while the *Falke* circled the island. Rodríguez informed Delgado Chalbaud and Alcántara that the coast guard boat usually arrived with provisions every fortnight but that it was now more than two weeks overdue. The watchman had seen a schooner some three days before, but it had not stopped at the island. The rebels reasoned that the spotted vessel had transported Aristeguieta's messengers to the island and that they remained in hiding. A further search of Blanquilla carried out during the afternoon revealed Aristeguieta's three commissioners hiding in an upturned boat waiting to make a positive identification of the *Falke* in case the ship belonged to the government.

Aristeguieta's agents assured Delgado Chalbaud that the state of morale of the Cumaná barracks was poor; that the rebels had many supporters in Cumaná, and that having secured the state capital they could launch an attack on Carúpano and Barcelona. Aristeguieta also felt that Cumaná offered an easier target to attack than Barcelona because the rebels could perform a pincer movement from land and sea. Aristeguieta would attack Cumaná with a landward assault, while the *Falke* attacked the city from the sea. Later that day, at yet another meeting, it was decided that if the second expedition had not arrived from Santo Domingo as planned, then the *Falke* would proceed to Guanta to replenish its coal stocks. Aristeguieta wanted the *Falke* to rendezvous at Peñas Negras on August 11, when a final decision would be made on whether to attack Guanta or Cumaná. At Blanquilla, fresh provisions were taken on board, including a number of goats, while any seaworthy boat was rendered useless so that anybody who remained undiscovered would not alert the government of the whereabouts of the *Falke*. Later that day, Angarita Arvelo and Pocaterra proceeded to the mainland to find a place called Tres Puños. The German crew, further alarmed at what they were witnessing, saw Ziplitt on August 6 stating that they did not want to continue with the voyage, demanding to be taken to the nearest port with a German consul. The crew's fears were assuaged with a further payment of $100 each to continue on course.

A day after arriving off Blanquilla, Delgado Chalbaud on August 7 issued his revolutionary proclamation, stating that "the tyranny that has enslaved us for thirty years is still standing. We are going to overthrow it. Our flag is: FREEDOM, JUSTICE, SANCTION. Your duty is to join us to show the world that we want to be, that we should be, and that we can be free."[112] At about five in the afternoon the motor launch *Ponemah,* owned by Francisco Gutiérrez and captained by Nicanor Piñerua R., approached the *Falke.* It was confidently expected that the launch was bringing some fifty rebels from Santo Domingo, but instead it came from Trinidad with Carabaño, Colonels Leopoldo Pellicer and David López, Major Andrés Gutiérrez, surgeon Roseliano Pérez Frontado (a young medical doctor and the son of General Francisco Roseliano Pérez), Armando Morales Carabaño, nephew of Carabaño, and Juan Ramón Frontado. General Gutiérrez had lent the *Ponemah* to Roseliano Pérez to sail between the coast of the Gulf of Paria and Trinidad and then to Puerto Cabello. The following day, on August 8, the schooner *Ave María* arrived, and about five cases of rifles and twenty-five cases of ammunition were transshipped to the boat, which left the following morning. There was hope that the rebels from Santo Domingo would soon join them because Carabaño brought the encouraging news that the Dominican expedition left on July 30, so that by August 9 at the latest they would rendezvous with Delgado Chalbaud. It was decided that it was worth waiting for them, and consequently, at midnight on August 8 Aristeguieta's agents were dispatched with instructions that they should rendezvous with him at Peñas Negras on August 10. The wait for the Santo Domingo rebels would be in vain because they never showed up.

The Santo Domingo Expedition

The organization of the Santo Domingo expedition started in March 1929, when Simón Betancourt arrived in Barranquilla and met with Felipe Aristeguieta, the owner of the Britania hat factory, and a brother of Aristeguieta and Francisco de Paúla Aristeguieta, who promised to fund Víctor Power with $5,000 and Durán with $10,000 to acquire arms in Santo Domingo.[113] Later in Curacao, Simón Betancourt secured the services of Leandro Frontado, whose vessel was in Puerto Rico, to transport the rebels and arms from Santo Domingo to eastern Venezuela. Simón Betancourt traveled to the island to ensure that the boat was seaworthy. Other revolutionaries in Barranquilla also contributed with money towards the rebels' cause, but certain left-wing rebels in Mexico, such as De la Plaza of the PRV, advised certain of their possible supporters, such as Rómulo Betancourt, that Pocaterra was a fraud and that they should not associate with him or any of his endeavors.[114] In spite of this, Simón Betancourt together with Rómulo Betancourt (not related) left for Santo Domingo, with their supporters in Barranquilla following once everything was in order. In the Dominican Republic Simón Betancourt met his old friend Rodolfo Paradas, a Venezuelan of Dominican parents, who was part of Urbina's 1928 attack on Curacao.

After Urbina's attack on Curacao in June 1929, the Barranquilla group, composed of Raúl Leoni, Pedro Rodríguez Berroeta, Hernando de Castro, Bernardo Suárez, Carlos Cabrera, and Rafael Angel Castillo, received on June 17–18 orders from Rómulo Betancourt to leave immediately for Santo Domingo. Carlos Julio Ponte in Santa Marta also traveled with them, arriving in Santo Domingo on June 28, when they started a fruitless wait for Frontado to arrive with his refurbished boat from Puerto Rico. The group had grown to around twenty-five men, including a few Dominicans.

There was a great deal of optimism because Felipe Aristeguieta appeared to have secured some two hundred rifles with twenty-five thousand rounds of ammunition during the first few days of July in Puerto Limón, Costa Rica, which he requested Simón Betancourt to pick up. At the same time, Frontado was ordered to leave for Santo Domingo immediately, but this was impossible, as his schooner was undergoing repairs, with the rebels losing their cache of arms. Betancourt was, nevertheless, convinced that he could muster in the Dominican Republic two hundred men and forty officers with a total cache of twenty rifles and thirty revolvers to leave for Venezuela. In spite of his previous experience, he was convinced that Frontado would not disappoint him, requesting from Delgado Chalbaud only $1,000 for expenses. No financial assistance was forthcoming from Europe, but he did secure $1,000 from the university students and a further $1,000 from Aristeguieta, $3,000 short of the promised $5,000 to fund the rebellion. The money should have been spent primarily on purchasing military equipment but was used on more pressing items such as food and lodgings for the revolutionaries. In the mistaken belief that the Dominican revolutionaries were ready with sufficient ordnance, Delgado Chalbaud ordered Simón Betancourt to leave on July 31, immediately after Carnevali, the rebel leader's envoy, arrived with the exact rendezvous location in Venezuela.

The telegrams sent between the beginning of July and the nineteenth of the month, when the *Falke* left Europe, crossed each other,[115] with Carnevali arriving in New York on July 18 from Paris. On his arrival in Puerto Rico eight days later, Carnevali sent a note to Simón Betancourt to leave the

Dominican Republic on July 31, with sufficient provisions for a fifteen- to twenty-day voyage. Betancourt was penniless, however, and without a boat. In spite of Frontado's assurances that he would be in Santo Domingo by July 25 at the latest, he had sailed instead for another island in the West Indies with the intention of returning to Puerto Rico during the middle of August. Betancourt could only ask for more funds from Carnevali to hire another ship. While in Puerto Rico, Carnevali briefed Ortega Martínez and Carabaño, but the latter did not want to join the expedition from Santo Domingo because of the difficulty of reaching eastern Venezuela from the Dominican Republic by sea during that time of year, preferring to leave instead with five others for St. Thomas and from there to Trinidad. Owing to the prevailing winds at that time of the year, it took approximately four days to travel directly from Santo Domingo to La Guaira instead of the usual two days.

On July 29, Carnevali boarded a ship for the relatively short trip across the Mona channel to Santo Domingo, with Delgado Chalbaud's instructions that Simón Betancourt and his people should be waiting for the main expeditionary force at La Blanquilla during the first week of August. On his arrival, Carnevali found only despair and almost panic at being let down by Frontado.[116] Carnevali had with him $1,400 but soon realized that more money was needed, cabling New York for more funds but only receiving $300. From this moment the expedition was doomed, as they only had $1,700 to charter a ship and a crew and purchase provisions. With Rómulo Betancourt trying desperately to get more money from Felipe Aristeguieta and others in Barranquilla, the rebels started looking for a ship to charter with the certainty of arousing the suspicions of Gómez's spies and the local authorities. Nevertheless, a frantic search was started, with Carnevali in San Pedro de Macoris, Simón Betancourt in La Romana, and Rómulo Betancourt in Santo Domingo looking to secure a boat. Simón Betancourt, who had previously found a motorboat and two schooners in San Pedro de Macoris, in desperation paid the owner to start making them seaworthy, but on July 29 the captain changed his mind. It seemed impossible to secure a ship at such short notice at either San Pedro de Macoris or La Romana, but in Santo Domingo they at last located a Dominican captain who was willing to travel a hundred miles due south for $700. The captain warned the rebels that his ship, the *Gisela,* would not cross the Mona channel. In desperation, the rebels accepted, reasoning that they would force the captain to proceed to Blanquilla once they were at sea.

The *Gisela* intended initially to sail from the port of Barahona in order not to arouse suspicion but in so doing would delay its departure further because the Dominican supporters in La Romana and San Pedro de Macoris[117] to the east of the island would have to travel to the port. A decision was made to leave on the night of July 31 from Santo Domingo with only the arms that Rafael Vidal had obtained. The Venezuelan rebels proceeded to Santo Domingo, where they expected approximately one hundred Dominicans to join them. The ship was due to leave at two in the morning, but the police became suspicious, and the captain of the *Gisela* feared for his license. The rebels started to panic, and in the rush that followed only forty people armed with two or three revolvers boarded the ship that departed at eleven p.m. Soon after the ship set sail, Vidal arrived with more men and arms.[118] The voyage was extremely rough, with Carnevali falling and knocking himself out for six or seven hours. When he woke up, he opened Delgado Chalbaud's orders that they were to sail to Blanquilla Island and wait for the *Falke*'s arrival. The captain, however, refused to sail to the Venezuelan island because it would be impossible to navigate a course, as he had no sextant or compass and was certain that the boat would capsize. It was already taking on water, and the pumps could not cope. Moreover, it was impossible to reach Blanquilla for the August 10 rendezvous, since the voyage would take ten to twelve days. Betancourt reluctantly concluded that they had to return to the Dominican Republic.

The nearest Dominican port was Barahona, and once they disembarked, Simón Betancourt and Rómulo Betancourt returned to Santo Domingo, where they continued their now pointless quest of getting another ship together with more men and arms for an expedition against Gómez.[119] Desperately needed funds now arrived with Guillermo Power, who left Barranquilla on August 8 for Santo Domingo with $15,000 in cash—$5,000 from Felipe Aristeguieta and $10,000 from Durán.[120]

Alejandro Fuenmayor, the Venezuelan consul in Santo Domingo who was recovering from an operation in a clinic, was frantic that the Dominican authorities were not doing enough to prevent the revolutionaries from pursuing their activities. On August 4, Telésforo Calderón, an official from the foreign affairs ministry, General Wenceslao Figuereo, head of police, and Colonel Andrés Santana, head of the secret police, informed Fuenmayor that although they believed Simón Betancourt and Rómulo Betancourt were organizing an expedition, they were unable to do anything unless they were caught red-handed. That same day Fuenmayor sent a formal note to the Dominican government requesting that it put an end to the rebels' plan.[121]

The Attack on Cumaná

The poor state of the Cumaná barracks according to Aristeguieta's envoys meant that he could attack the city with three hundred men and protect the rebels landing from the *Falke* by diverting the attention of government troops. The plan of attack on Cumaná was a pincer movement, "firing on the castle from the surrounding hills that tower over it, and to be at the Manzanares river by five in the morning,"[122] with Aristeguieta's troops attacking the city from the side of Santa Inés. Once government troops engaged Aristeguieta, Delgado Chalbaud would disembark and attack the Altagracia district of the city, "since the troops of General Fernandez would be engaged in fighting at another place,"[123] with rebel troops soon occupying the city. On the night of August 7, the war council agreed to this plan, with Delgado Chalbaud arguing that Aristeguieta knew the terrain well and had better intelligence on the state of the government troops in Cumaná than any of the other rebels. It was suggested that the *Falke* could transport the troops to Cumaná, but Aristeguieta disagreed with this because everything was ready and "the plan would suffer if there was any modification."[124] The *Falke* would meet Aristeguieta at Peñas Negras at dawn on August 10 to disembark men and arms and then proceed to Cumaná, with one of Aristeguieta's envoys, a Margariteño, remaining onboard to act as a pilot. Delgado Chalbaud's plan also envisaged distributing arms and ammunition to his supporters along the coast, but with critically low coal stocks it was decided to send the *Ponemah* with a cache of arms to General Gutiérrez "for him to wait in the port of Güiría from the 13 to 14."[125] The problem was persuading Piñerua, the captain of the schooner, to undertake the dangerous mission because the vessel belonged to a known political opponent of Gómez and was carefully watched.

Delgado Chalbaud spent the night of August 8 trying to persuade a reluctant Piñerua to undertake the voyage; Piñerua finally relented as dawn approached. The *Ponemah* left at four o'clock with two hundred Mauser carbines in five cases and fifty thousand rounds of ammunition in twenty-eight cases for Gutiérrez in Güiría, who would open another front there. Colonel David López, Commander Leopoldo Vicente Pellicer, and Egea Mier, who was seriously ill and was returning to New York for an operation, accompanied the cache of arms. When the *Ponemah* arrived at the Boca de Monos channel, with its direct access to Trinidad, they did not find Gutierrez's agents to inform them that the arms had arrived. By this time, the rebel attack on Cumaná had failed, and the country was on a general military alert, so they set sail for Güiría but found a government patrol boat in the harbor. They managed later to hand over the arms and ammunition to Gutiérrez and finally made their way to Trinidad on August 16.[126]

Events in Venezuela

In January 1929, Cumaná suffered a ferocious earthquake that left many dead and wounded and devastated a large section of the city. Gómez immediately dispatched the SS *Guárico* with food and medicine together with the large sum of $95,785 to distribute among the victims.[127] The SS *Colón* followed the next day with more tents and provisions, while additional medical supplies were provided by the US Red Lions organization.[128]

As we have seen, later in the year a number of state presidents were changed when Gómez vacated the presidency in a political maneuver (see chapter 7). At the time, Gómez offered Fernández the choice of four state presidencies, viz, Sucre, Bolívar, Monagas, or Guárico. Fernández chose Sucre because he felt he could do a good job at reconstructing the devastated city after the earthquake. Consequently, on May 23 Fernández arrived in Cumaná as the new state president with specific orders from Gómez to jail Francisco de Paúla Aristeguieta at the slightest suspicion that he was acting against the government. Fernández was loath to carry out such orders, as Francisco de Paúla Aristeguieta was a descendant of the Gran Mariscal Sucre, a Wars of Independence hero, and felt that he would not do anything against the government. Fernández believed that the best way of solving this conflict was to explain his predicament to de Paúla Aristeguieta and ask for his word of honor that nothing would happen. De Paúla Aristeguieta agreed to such a modus vivendi, and Fernández left him in peace.

The small cache of arms and ammunition at the disposal of government troops at Cumaná was puny compared with the arsenal the rebels had on board the *Falke,* with only sixty relatively well maintained rifles purchased in 1902 and ten thousand rounds of ammunition, most of which were in "bad shape because of age, humidity and saltpeter."[129] The earthquake had also killed a number of soldiers who were not replaced and damaged part of the arsenal. Fernández only had seventy men including officers at his disposal at the state capital, with the nearest reinforcements located some sixty kilometers away under the command of Arturo Galavís, the *jefe civil* of the Montes District.

The Rebels Attack

The *Falke* remained off Blanquilla Island until August 9, when at seven in the evening, having lost hope of the Santo Domingo contingency arriving, Delgado Chalbaud gave the order to head southwards to Peñas Negras on the northern side of the Araya peninsula to meet Pedro Elías Aristeguieta, who had been waiting since August 5 with his brother Francisco and Russián and almost two hundred men. At five in the morning, the ship dropped anchor at Taguapire, and soon afterwards Aristeguieta and his brother boarded the ship to discuss tactics with Delgado Chalbaud and the other officers in the ship's small dining room. It was agreed that Aristeguieta would attack Cumaná to capture "Fernández between two fires."[130] This way Aristeguieta could isolate the government's rearguard troops and be in Caiguire, just outside Cumaná, by four in the morning, securing the Guzmán Blanco Bridge an hour later in order to safeguard the landing of the *Falke* rebels and meet Delgado Chalbaud there. Aristeguieta was aware that the success of the revolution in the initial stages depended crucially on his action succeeding, confessing to his brother Francisco that "Delgado Chalbaud placed on my shoulders a load that was greater than my talent and my means of action."[131] Aristeguieta was, nevertheless, extremely grateful because of the trust placed on him.[132] Delgado Chalbaud suggested that Carabaño and then Flores should be Aristeguieta's chief of staff, but Pimentel was chosen instead.

Soon afterwards, some 225 rifles and 30,000 rounds of ammunition were off-loaded, with Pimentel barely having two hours to prepare the raw recruits on weapons handling. It was clearly an impossible task, especially as most had not seen, let alone handled, a rifle before and would now have to carry three Mauser carbines and three ammunition belts during the night because Aristeguieta expected a further 100 men to join him on his way to Cumaná. Pimentel, with Aristeguieta as second in command, divided the men into three groups headed by Colonels Pedro María Yegres, Antonio J. Gómez Rubio, and Luis Mago, with a security escort to guard the arms and ammunition. In all 110 men left with Aristeguieta, with some 75 Guaiqueríes[133] proceeding in the *Falke* to Cumaná. Russián would also stay on board because of a leg infection.

There was a certain amount of confusion among the leaders aboard the *Falke* and the contingency from Araya about the initial objective of the expedition. According to Aristeguieta, Pimentel did not inform him of the attack on Cumaná the following day. Pimentel later claimed that neither Delgado

Chalbaud nor Aristeguieta properly briefed him on what was happening. The situation became so tense that Delgado Chalbaud challenged Pimentel on whether he had any confidence in him because Pimentel persistently questioned the military objectives of the expedition. Nevertheless, Pimentel remained in the dark about the objectives, stating later that "I knew absolutely nothing about what we were going to do when we landed."[134]

The Aristeguieta group's orders were to march from Peñas Negras to Taguapire and from there to Angoleta, where they would use *piraguas* to cross the Cariaco Gulf, then disembark in Caiguire, and attack Cumaná at dawn. This entailed a night march of twenty kilometers, something that seemed almost impossible to achieve within the time constraints. According to Pocaterra, the march from Peñas Negras to Cumaná was at most five to six hours because "the leaders, especially the troops (native fishermen familiar with that coast) knew that terrain like the back of their hands."[135] Pocaterra also asserted that in a worst case scenario "those troops had more than enough time and could even rest before opening fire on the backs of the enemy at *four o'clock in the morning* as agreed on board the *Falke* and to be on Cumaná's 'Guzmán Blanco' bridge at five in the morning"[136] (emphasis in original). In the event, it took them almost ten hours to reach Cumaná because the route from Peñas Negras to Angoleta was a difficult one especially at night, made even more onerous when loaded with weaponry. This meant that in order for Aristeguieta to have reached Cumaná at five a.m., the rebels should have left Peñas Negras at seven p.m. the previous evening—not at midnight.

Government Preparations for the Invasion

On August 7, a general alert from Gómez was issued to all state presidents, including Fernández in Sucre, of a possible sea invasion by Delgado Chalbaud. Fernández immediately declared a state of emergency, advising his officers to be ready for an invasion. Fernández and General Tovar Díaz, his military commander, had between 100 and 125 men under their command and enough ammunition for one hour of fierce combat. On August 10, at eight in the evening, Luis Rodríguez, the owner of a fish processing factory who was working at a place called El Guanacho on the Araya peninsula, raised the alarm. He informed Fernández that both his fishermen and those who worked for Francisco de Paúla Aristeguieta had disappeared and that a ship with arms had dropped anchor at Peñas Negras and was likely to be in Cumaná in a few hours time.[137]

Fernández together with Lieutenant Arturo Briceño and another guard left in a car to go to Caiguire and the surrounding villages to see for themselves what was happening. On their arrival, they found the villages deserted when they should have been full of activity on a Saturday night. Fernández was now convinced that something was about to unfold, hurrying back to Cumaná to prepare the city's defenses. On his way back, he stopped at the Puerto Sucre customs house to warn the guards of a possible attack. The few remaining watchmen requested reinforcements, which Fernández did not have; he ordered them instead to give token resistance to the rebels and then to retreat back to the city. Fernández, who probably reasoned that the rebels would have a fair idea of his weak position in terms of men and arms, felt that Cumaná could be attacked on two fronts: from the Guzmán Blanco Bridge facing toward the customs house and Caiguire and from the southeast, where the San Antonio fortress was located. Fernández placed barrels of cement at the approach of the Guzmán Blanco Bridge and posted a number of civilian volunteers at the San Antonio fortress to give the false notion that he had recently received reinforcements. In order to scare the rebels, Fernández also ordered the old cannon to be fired using black powder, to give the impression that live shells were being fired. Finally, Fernández left his home open on purpose with government telegrams scattered on his desk to distract the attention of the attackers and gain more time, as they would inevitably stop to read them.

The Falke *Heads for Cumaná*

Once Pimentel and Aristeguieta disembarked at Peñás Negras, the duty officer spotted a motor launch "sailing toward Barlovento"[138] that could alert the authorities of the presence of an unknown vessel in Venezuelan coastal waters. Delgado Chalbaud reasoned that it was pointless following the vessel, as they would be in Cumaná at five the following morning. The motor launch belonged to Customs and was sent by Fernández to "inspect the coasts, and following orders the crew continued to Margarita instead of returning to Cumaná"[139] to warn the state president. Meanwhile at seven in the evening the *Falke* proceeded to Punta Moreno, where it was met by some five canoes with around 120 men in all. After they armed themselves, the *Falke* continued its journey with the rest of the rebels on board. Soon after leaving, Delgado Chalbaud set a course for Cumaná.

The moment that Delgado Chalbaud had spent sixteen long years dreaming of, that he hoped would culminate with the end of the Gomecista regime and place him as head of government, was about to take place. On the way to Cumaná, two of the *piraguas* towed by the *Falke* broke loose and drifted away. At 4:45 that morning, later than intended and with its lights off, the *Falke* slipped into Cumaná. It was clear that Aristeguieta had not arrived, as there was no sign of fighting from the south of the city, near the cemetery, where he was expected to attack first. Alcántara immediately counseled that the best plan was to go to Guanta, where they could take on coal and then return to Cumaná a few hours later, when it was hoped that by then Aristeguieta would have arrived in the city. With first light fast approaching, a decision had to be made whether to stay or retreat until Aristeguieta's arrival. Delgado Chalbaud opted to attack Cumaná, reasoning that if Aristeguieta had not arrived, then the expedition could suffer a major setback, as the ship could not remain exposed to an air or sea attack for long. Delgado Chalbaud was correct in this assessment; later that day a Dutch schooner, which was in Cumaná to pick up a cargo of manure, was bombed by mistake by government aircraft but did not suffer any damage.

Aristeguieta and his troops would not arrive for another seven hours because they got lost during the night. According to Aristeguieta, in order to be in Cumaná by four the following morning, they should have left at eleven the previous evening, but Pimentel wanted to depart two hours earlier, at nine, in order for the men to rest and eat before the main attack. In spite of Pimentel posting guides at the front and rear of the columns, the rebels got hopelessly lost in the innumerable ravines trying to reach Angoleta. In addition, Pimentel, who suffered with varicose veins, had to stop four times during the night for a short rest of only two to three minutes because of the intense pain in his leg.[140] The result was that they lost contact with the main column of men. Medardo Martínez, the best guide in the area and the man who carried the water supplies and Aristeguieta's luggage, did not realize that the group had stopped and continued his trek through the night. Pimentel started following a stream, which at one point divided into two, and took the wrong course.[141] After an hour trying to find the trail again, they realized that they were lost and started to "send agents in all probable directions and to navigate by the stars to find a route."[142] The rebels spent more than three hours looking for a way out, breaking cover by using electric torches, but despite all their efforts at climbing steep ridges and descending into deep gorges, they were unable to find a way out and could not continue until daylight. Although Francisco de Paúla Aristeguieta blamed Pimentel's varicose veins for the loss of contact with the main body of men, Carlos

Emilio Fernández placed the fault squarely on Aristeguieta, as he had no excuse for getting lost because he knew the terrain well. Ortega Martínez was also scathing in his criticism of Aristeguieta, stating that it was a scandal for a general to lose his troops, especially as this was his own plan that he had been unwilling to change.

At seven in the morning, Aristeguieta and his men finally made it to Langoleta, where some of the troops who had not gotten lost, together with a further fifty men, were waiting for him with canoes to cross the bay. The 140 men got into four *piraguas* taking three and a half hours of continuous paddling to reach the other side of the bay at El Peñón, located some six kilometers from Cumaná. Although Aristeguieta had calculated a two-hour crossing, it took the rebels five hours to travel from Langoleta to the outskirts of Cumaná, so that even if they had reached Langoleta at three in the morning, they still would have arrived at Cumaná three hours later than had been agreed and too late to attack Cumaná by five in the morning. Whatever the reason for not getting to Cumaná on time, the trek route seems strange: Aristeguieta and his men could have disembarked at El Peñón, which is much closer to Cumaná, or at Caiguire, which is almost next to the Sucre capital. The reason given for Delgado Chalbaud sticking to the original plan was to pick up more men on the way to Cumaná, but these rebels could have gathered at Langoleta and thus avoided a treacherous march across the peninsula and a bay crossing that was very close to the enemy. Although Pimentel was aware that it was too late to do anything when he disembarked at Peñas Negras, he did not want to further mortify Aristeguieta and so continued toward Cumaná. Cipriano Heredía defended what happened when he wrote that the journey was a difficult and complicated one and hence "all or some of these considerations makes it likely that some of the participants would have doubts about the undertaking. The inexplicable fatigue that affected Pimentel . . . was another negative factor."[143]

The Attack on Cumaná

As the *Falke* approached Cumaná, a total of ninety-nine men were divided into three columns, with a guard of honor acting as a reserve column. At four thirty a.m., just before entering the harbor, the three columns boarded the two *chulapas* and the one remaining *piragua,* to be towed approximately one hundred meters from the harbor, from where the rebels paddled to the shore.

Flores, Angarita Arvelo, and Raúl Castro commanded the first column, with twenty soldiers. Alcántara headed the second column, with López Méndez, Vegas, Juan Colmenares Pacheco, and twenty soldiers. Carabaño commanded the third column, with Antonio Morales Carabaño, Frontado, McGill Sarría, and twenty soldiers. Zucal, Esser, Schneider, and four others were in charge of the machine guns. The guard of honor was headed by Delgado Chalbaud, together with Mendoza, Urdaneta Auvert, Roseliano Pérez, Carlos Julio Rojas, Zuloaga Blanco, and fifteen soldiers. Delgado Chalbaud, before getting into the *chulapa*, busied himself giving last minute orders to Pocaterra, including one that he should not trust the German crew.[144] The Flores column descended first, followed by the Alcántara and Carabaño columns, and then by the fifteen men who made up the guard of honor, together with Captain Zucal and Esser with the two machine guns and second officer Schneider. There were also four German volunteers, two members of the crew, Knoche and Baumgaertel, as well as steward Walenczak. Pocaterra, Parisot, Andrés Gutiérrez (medic), Delgado Chalbaud Gómez, Russián, two deserters, and one prisoner taken on. Blanquilla remained on board to guard the stores and ammunition. The pealing of the city's church bells would signal a rebel victory, but if disaster struck, Pocaterra's orders were to save the leased boat and the cache of arms.[145]

Government Troops

As dawn broke, government troops sipped strong coffee to wade off the slumber of a night waiting for the revolutionaries to make their first move on Venezuelan soil. At five in the morning they heard "numerous detonations in the direction of Puerto Sucre,"[146] with government troops returning fire and forcing the rebels to abandon their craft and wade ashore. Flores was first to reach land, followed by Angarita and Raúl Castro. When Flores reached the beach, the government troops stationed at the customs house continued firing at the rebels, and in the first volley Frontado was killed. The rebels returned fire, and the customs house was taken quickly, with the government troops retreating back to the city as planned. The rebel officers had problems getting the men under their command to fight; some threw their rifles away and fled in a panic at the first volley of fire from government troops.[147]

Fernández, his son Carlos Emilio, and Lieutenant Arturo Briceño, followed by a platoon, took a car and crossed the Manzanares River by the

Guzmán Blanco Bridge, taking the Calle Larga toward the sea. On the way there, they found the officers of the "defense force, who faithful to their motto, fell back after firing on their attackers from the old rambling Customs house."[148] Fernández ordered J. M. López Centeno to inform General Tovar Diaz to retreat back to the city with all the remaining troops, leaving only a small contingent in the fort together with the refuse workers, "in order for it to appear as though it was really equipped and thus to deceive the enemy."[149] A telegram was sent to Gómez in Maracay informing him that a ship with Venezuelan revolutionaries had disembarked and that government troops were resisting their attack.

Rebels Advance

Flores, Alcántara, Carabaño, and Delgado Chalbaud reached the ruins situated between the customs house and the city, where a number of men were already posted by Flores and where the leaders took time to review their situation. A heated exchange took place between Flores and Delgado Chalbaud, the former counseling that the attack on the city should not proceed until Aristeguieta's arrival. Delgado Chalbaud, who was convinced that Aristeguieta was already in the city, rejected the advice, ordering the men to proceed to the bridge and telling Alcántara to take their colors. The latter refused, as he felt it was madness. It was left to Flores to carry the flag, repeating again his view that there was no reason to engage the enemy at this point. Nevertheless, with the rallying cry of "To the Bridge!" the advance to the Guzmán Blanco Bridge took place with Delgado Chalbaud at the center, flanked on his left by Mendoza, who was accompanied by Urdaneta, Carlos Julio Rojas, and Zuloaga, and on his right by Flores and Castro. Delgado Chalbaud was convinced that the government troops posted at the bridge were part of Aristeguieta's contingency.[150]

On the government side, Fernández, with eight sharpshooters and one officer, was trying to draw the rebels to follow them to the Guzmán Blanco Bridge, where the main body of troops, some fifty men, were deployed waiting to engage the revolutionaries. They were stationed in the following manner: a platoon was deployed in the center of the bridge protected by cement barrels brought in from a nearby cement works, with Tovar Díaz situated to the left flank behind the wall by the river; on the right flank Briceño, Captain Pablo Emilio Fernández, Carlos Fernández, and another platoon;

and behind them, protected by another wall, a number of policemen and government employees with only knives and revolvers. Another platoon was stationed in the square situated near the river to execute a surprise rear attack. Minutes later officers with sharpshooters who remained at El Salado returned to incorporate themselves into the main body of soldiers. Fernández then informed his officers that "we must fight them one by one, as I cannot think that they are so clumsy as to attack us by a single front."[151]

Delgado Chalbaud continued toward the Guzmán Blanco Bridge, where Fernández was waiting for him. The rebels managed to cross El Salado without any problems, although Angarita Arvelo was wounded. In order to reach the bridge, the rebels had to go up Calle Larga, where many fell wounded, including Carlos Julio Rojas, Carabaño, López Méndez, Pérez Frontado, and McGill Sarría. As they approached the bridge, the rebels gave the impression that they did not expect resistance: when Delgado Chalbaud arrived at it, he thought it was Aristeguieta who was waiting for him, though Flores thought otherwise. Fernández gave strict orders not to fire against the rebels[152] until they were no more than three hundred meters away. When the rebels ascertained that government troops were at the bridge, they started to shoot first, but many of their rifles malfunctioned, with the pins jamming. The result was that "our soldiers left their guns in the ground and they fell back to take refuge in the lateral sidewalk."[153] The rebels, however, gained ground with the help of Zucal and the machine guns under his command; with "some bursts of machine guns [they] swept the bridge; officers and soldiers followed the revolutionary leader not without certain distrust by the silence that reigned on the other side of the river, from where not a single shot could be heard."[154] Delgado Chalbaud advanced slowly, noticing when Flores was wounded by their own machine gun fire[155] and yelling at Urdaneta Auvert to bring forward the machine guns. Both Urdaneta Aubert and Zuloaga decided to fetch the guns, but when the latter crossed the street, he was mortally wounded. While Urdaneta informed Alcántara of Flores's orders, Zucal was wounded in the shoulder. Soon afterwards, the wounded Flores reached Alcántara and Carabaño, requesting them to send the machine guns to help Delgado Chalbaud. At the same time, Delgado Chalbaud picked up the rebels' flag from the wounded Angarita but was himself shot, falling on his bottom on top of the flag. A second shot in the chest soon afterwards killed him, as he uttered, "Damn, what a pain," as witnessed by Alcántara, who was very close to him.[156]

With Delgado Chalbaud dead, the rebel officers started to retreat, since their rifles were jamming (they had not been properly maintained). Flores ordered Urdaneta Auvert to take eleven men to secure the cemetery and to wait for Aristeguieta's arrival. Alcántara and Flores later arrived at the cemetery, together with Vegas and Colmenares; Urdaneta suggested that they should return to the *Falke*. It was decided instead to wait for Aristeguieta, with the small group moving to a location where they expected him to enter the city.

There were casualties on the government side too, with Fernández first wounded in the arm and his son shot through the chest, with the bullet piercing his lung and exiting by the back. Moments later Fernández received another shot, this time through the chest, and was taken by car to the home of Casimiro Valderama, where he died soon afterwards.[157] Captain Emiro Hernández took command of government troops. Hernández retreated from the Guzmán Blanco Bridge, taking his troops across the Manzanares River into the Altagracia sector of the city, where they dispersed.

Rebels Regroup

After the initial skirmish, the wounded Zucal, Mendoza, and Raúl Castro returned to the boat with the news that Delgado Chalbaud was dead. At around eight in the morning, government troops were back in the harbor shooting at the *Falke*. It was decided not to return fire because "the dispersed colleagues who tried reaching the boat thought that the vessel had been taken by the enemy because of the shots coming from there, losing any hope of rescue."[158] It was clear that there was a good chance that the *Falke* would be captured "without the glory of putting up a fight and to the ridicule of the revolution with a 1,200-ton boat and a cache of arms."[159] Pocaterra, facing the possibility of losing the ship,[160] gave the order at eight-thirty in the morning to leave port immediately, reasoning that without the expedition from Santo Domingo and the forces of Aristeguieta and Pimentel, the revolution was doomed, and he was not going to hand over to Gómez the boat and arms. Delgado Chalbaud had instructed Pocaterra that he should save the ship and cache of arms at all costs, stating to "sink the boat if it can not be saved rather than letting it fall into the hands of Gómez because apart from looking silly, it would mean my family's total ruin because as you know all that we possess is guaranteed by the mortgage held on my wife's and children's assets."[161] This way the Delgado Chalbaud family would not go bankrupt, as the ship was leased. In addition, the five Venezuelans on board were no match for the twenty-eight-man crew, who it was felt were willing to betray the rebels to the government. It has also been suggested that both Pocaterra and Delgado Chalbaud Gómez were extremely tired after "three nights of guard duty and nervous tension"[162] and that this accounts for what appears superficially to be an extremely strange act. Pocaterra felt that it would be irresponsible to remain in Cumaná any longer without any coal and a demoralized crew, with the *Falke* becoming in essence a sitting duck at the mercy of government artillery and war planes.

Pocaterra was severely criticized for what appeared to be a rash action. A number of the rebels, such as Russián, believed that Pocaterra gave the order to leave Cumaná when the "city had been taken by our colleagues,"[163] a view that was wrong and not shared by Pocaterra who, in a letter dated September 18, reiterated his view that Cumaná was never held by the revolutionaries.[164] Russián further accused Pocaterra of cowardice and of aborting the expedition because had he not "fled in the 'Falke' in such a miserable and shameful way . . . our fate and that of our beloved fatherland would be another."[165] Alcántara also accused Pocaterra of abandoning the rebels in Cumaná on the *Falke* owing to what he described as "our eternal misfortune: personal ambition,"[166] a view shared by Luciani when he wrote:

> That is the truth. Personal ambition presided over the composition of the Supreme Liberation Junta established in Paris; the doubts expressed by Régulo Olivares and Dr. Néstor Luis Pérez were not addressed because of personal ambition; and for the same reason José Rafael Pocaterra was both first alternate of the Junta and Secretary of the War Directorate; for personal ambition it was decided not to use the help of prestigious people in Eastern Venezuela; while insignificant people were used, it would appear from all sources that personal ambition drove Pocaterra to throw overboard the cache of arms and for personal ambitions after the death of Delgado Chalbaud the Supreme Liberation Junta of Paris was dissolved.[167]

Rafael Bruzual López believed that the expedition failed because it was sheer adventurism, feeling that in the end it is ideas that triumph because "it is not about a new fighting campaign in the old political feudalist style to substitute one dictator for another one, nor a commercial enterprise in which the moral and patriotic representation of the people is less important than whoever contributes the largest sum of money because by default he can award commands and reward his followers with sinecures."[168] Smith could not fathom how Pocaterra was left in charge of the ship, describing him as the one who "utterly terrified leaves all in port and can only think to flee in a boat that is not even under attack."[169]

In Cumaná, Alcántara, Flores, Vegas, and Colmenares waited initially for Aristeguieta at the cemetery but then left for Taguapire to see if they could signal to the *Falke*. They crossed the Manzanares river and at eleven in the morning heard shots and so continued toward Caiguire, but they only reached El Peñón, where they remained until ten that night, leaving by boat to La Angoleta. There they rested and slept, intending to leave the next day for Peñas Negras but instead headed for Taguapire. In the evening they took a rowing boat and arrived at Puerto Nuevo, where they remained hidden during the following four days. They then decided to return to Taguapire but, on hearing that government troops had retaken it, proceeded to Cariaco, staying in the home of General Ricardo Fuentes, where they were later joined by Francisco de Paúla Aristeguieta, who was extremely helpful. The rebels would remain hidden in this place for four months.

Aristeguieta Attacks Cumaná

Aristeguieta and Pimentel together with the other rebels started to cross the bay at 6:35 a.m., disembarking at a point six kilometers away from Cumaná. Soon after 11 o'clock, Aristeguieta was greeted by news of the *Falke*'s attack and the announcement that State President Fernández was dead. As they neared the city, Pimentel realized that it was still in government hands because two airplanes had flown by and nobody had tried to shoot them down. This caused great anxiety to Aristeguieta, as he felt that the rebels had lost the fight owing to his inability to reach the city earlier. The officers debated whether to continue with their plan and attack the city, or retreat. Their intelligence was patchy: they had been told that the soldiers were billeted in the open because the recent earthquake had destroyed the fort, which was built on the only high point in Cumaná. Although this was untrue, Aristeguieta "was going crazy, and said that the only thing that could vindicate our delay was to attack with our 150 men."[170] Pimentel was opposed to this, since he was sure that half the men would be lost before reaching the city, and decided instead to deploy his men "in four columns, maneuvering them in an encircling movement to attack the square and for the best of them to engage the shooters from the castle."[171]

At 11:55 a.m. they reached the outskirts of Cumaná, with Pimentel setting up his four columns headed by F. Z. Serrano, L. Mago, A. Valei, and I. A. Arismendi and commanded by Colonels Pedro María Yegres and Gómez Rubio. Yegres would try to take the fort, while another column was deployed "at the foot of the hills,"[172] with the remaining two attacking Cumaná by the beach after taking Caiguire. Just before 12:30 p.m. Aristeguieta and Pimentel positioned themselves by the cemetery and started their attack, which lasted four hours. The second attack took the government troops by surprise, especially the use of their "modern rifles, machine guns and unlimited ammunition,"[173] with the soldiers retreating to the old fort. The battle at the fort continued for the rest of the day, with Tovar Díaz and others escaping at night to Barcelona. Aristeguieta's forces were pushed toward the seashore, but Yegres and his troops came to his rescue, with the city falling into rebel hands the following morning, on Tuesday, August 13. After two days of almost continuous fighting the government garrison surrendered, "leaving the revolutionaries in possession of the town."[174] Prisoners such as Carabaño were set free, and the National Treasury that held the funds sent to reconstruct the city after the earthquake[175] was ransacked in order to pay the rebel troops. A total of \$61,409[176] was taken, after the state treasurer demanded a receipt from Aristeguieta. An airplane trainer, piloted by Robert Guerin, a French instructor, dropped several hand grenades over the city during a number of flights over Cumaná. According to Uldaric Hasall, captain of the Dutch-registered schooner *Vivian Smith*, which was in Cumaná during the attack, at around midday two airplanes flew over them with one dropping "bombs at the stern of the vessel in the water,"[177] and a fragment of one falling on the deck, with the bombing stopping soon after the Dutch flag was hoisted. The rebel attack left 70 dead and 115 wounded among rebel and army troops.

Soon after entering Cumaná, which was occupied for less than forty-eight hours, disagreement on who should command the troops was apparent, with Flores and Alcántara going their separate ways. It was clear that without any further help, it would be difficult for the rebels to hold on to Cumaná. In the afternoon of August 11, government reinforcements from Cumanacoa, commanded by General Agustín Rodríguez Córdoba and Panfilo Castro, arrived and managed to restore order on August 13. At the same time, the Venezuelan man-of-war *Mariscal Sucre* was dispatched from Guanta to assist government troops, but it could not deploy its guns because the harbor authorities at Cumaná flew the US flag (the port was leased to an American company). At eleven o'clock on the night of August 13, the rebels left Cumaná and headed in the direction of Mariguita, where they would regroup. Some rebels retreated southwards to Maturín to try to join Arévalo Cedeño, who had also invaded Venezuela by the Llanos to meet up with Delgado Chalbaud but was defeated at La Panchita by Lino Diaz, abandoning the city before government reinforcements arrived. When Aristeguieta left Cumaná, he headed for the Gulf of Cariaco, while others left for San Antonio del Golfo by *piraguas* to Puerto Nuevo. Once there, the rebels regrouped and formed three flanks: the front was commanded by Colonel Faustino Abreu; the center by Generals Agustín Rodríguez and Pánfilo Castro; and the rear by Aristeguieta and Colonel Guzmán, marching on August 21 toward Santa Ana, some thirty-five kilometers from Carúpano.

On August 14, further government reinforcements arrived in Cumaná, with General Faría bringing part of the troops stationed at Barcelona. He was later joined by General José Rosario González, the head of the Eastern Expeditionary Army, who arrived with 250 well-armed men from Maracay. González soon left Cumaná for Carúpano to try and stop Aristeguieta's retreat. Flores and the others continued from Angoleta to Peñas Negras, where they thought the *Falke* would be waiting for them. Once it became clear that the ship would not show up, the rebels took a boat and reached Puerto Nuevo, where they stayed for four days and were later joined by Francisco de Paúla Aristeguieta, who knew the terrain well. The rebels reached El Pilar, with government forces, now numbering four hundred men, chasing them to the Santa Ana settlement, where they stopped momentarily for lunch. Government troops then engaged the rebels in a fierce battle that lasted until four in the afternoon, with Aristeguieta wounded in the groin. When all hope of winning was dashed, Colonel Guzmán and Metheus got the upper hand, and the government troops were defeated on August 22. In spite of this victory, the rebels soon afterwards surrendered because they realized the futility of their sacrifice, as nobody else in the country had taken up arms against the government.

Alcántara, Flores, and Francisco de Paúla Aristeguieta traveled to Grenada on board the *Venus,* owned by José María Velásquez[178] and captained by Delfín Rivas. When they reached their destination, they heard that the *Falke* was in Trinidad and that General P. Alcántara Leal had blockaded the coast preventing any escape, with Carabaño and his officers capitulating. Urdaneta Auvert and Juan de Dios Gómez Rubio accompanied by the Spanish priest Venencio Fenosa were sent to negotiate their surrender with González, who was close to Carúpano. Finally, after much pleading, Colonel Conde, a commissioner, was sent to receive Carabaño's capitulation, which was drafted by Carlos Julio Rojas. Two days later, Conde García, accompanied by Urdaneta Auvert, returned to Carúpano, and on August 25 Carabaño, López Méndez, Aristeguieta, McGill Sarría, Juan de Dios Gómez Rubio, Urdaneta Aubert, and Anselmo Valerio surrendered. Government troops later entered El Pilar, where the rebels handed over guns and only $28,736 out of the $61,409 taken from the National Treasury at Cumaná and deposited by the rebels at the agency of the Banco de Venezuela at Carúpano. The prisoners were transferred to Cumaná for medical treatment, in particular Aristeguieta, who was seriously ill with gangrene from a bullet lodged in his bladder. He died later, on the morning of August 27. Pimentel was imprisoned in the Puerto Cabello castle, where he spend the next six years. The second rebel attack on Cumaná ultimately failed because of a lack of support, the panic by the Guaiqueríes and officers, and Pimentel leading the attack with a wounded left leg.

The Falke *Heads for Grenada*

On the *Falke*'s departure from Cumaná, Ziplitt set a course for Trinidad, but a few hours later Pocaterra changed the destination to Grenada in order to minimize any contact with the Venezuelan navy[179] and to conserve their coal supplies, which were insufficient to reach Trinidad. Dr. Gutiérrez, who joined the ship at Blanquilla and was a medical officer, felt that the reason for heading for Grenada instead of Trinidad was because the German crew would take the Venezuelans prisoner in order to be paid the money owed to them. Captain Ziplitt during the voyage formed the opinion that there was only enough coal to get to Grenada, but I have estimated that the *Falke* had approximately fifty tons of coal on board, just about enough to reach Trinidad, if we assume that the *Falke*'s fuel consumption was 7.4 kilometers per ton and the distance between Cumaná and Port of Spain (Trinidad) is approximately 360 kilometers. The reason for opting to go to Grenada according to Pocaterra is that it is 64 kilometers closer to Cumaná than Trinidad, but in reality the island is 50 kilometers closer to Cumaná than Grenada, and the ship would have used most of its coal supplies reaching the latter British colony. The main reason for heading for Grenada was that there was less chance of encountering a Venezuelan man-of-war than if the *Falke* headed for Trinidad.

The most controversial incident of this ill-fated expedition would now happen when, according to Ziplitt at the enquiry that was later held in

Trinidad, the arms on board the ship were dumped overboard between Cumaná and Grenada "by my orders and those of Pocaterra."[180] According to Russián, who was on board the *Falke,* at around ten in the morning, one and a half hours after leaving Cumaná, Parisot arrived on the bridge, stating that the captain was going to dispose of the ship's ordnance in order to reach a British Caribbean colony[181] and so lessen the boat's value as "'good bounty' and to save the Revolution from future embarrassment."[182] Russián's protestations were useless because the ordnance belonged to Delgado Chalbaud Gómez, who preferred it dumped "into the sea before it fell into government hands."[183] The cache of arms together with every other military and non-military item such as suitcases were thrown overboard.[184] When the *Falke* reached British colonial waters, the remaining "guns together with boxes of ammunition that were still on board were thrown into the water."[185]

The decision to off-load the arms and ammunition was not taken lightly, as the gravity of the situation was immense. The Venezuelan rebels debated among themselves whether they could hide the arms on the coast, with Mateo Salazar suggesting that they dump the arms at a safe haven on the Cariaco shore or possibly leave them on the Hermanos Island before reaching Trinidad.[186] They also considered burying the arms at a secret location, but with approximately 1,200 to 1,300 rifles, 2 machine guns, and 1.5 million rounds of ammunition,[187] the tonnage was too great for it to be buried quickly without running the risk of getting caught by the Venezuelan authorities. There was also the question of finding a place to bury them and later to retrieve the cache of arms safely. Moreover, there was not enough manpower to undertake the sheer physical work of ferrying the ordnance ashore. The German crew could not be trusted to help because they were terrified of ending up in a Venezuelan jail if caught in Venezuelan territorial waters with the arms on board. In addition, the German crew became very agitated when Zucal returned wounded to the ship. Finally, the rebels reasoned that the ordnance would not fall into Gómez's hands if it was thrown overboard and would thus avoid any complications with the British authorities when they arrived in Grenada, as otherwise they could be arrested for possessing arms and ammunition. Arévalo Cedeño later exonerated Pocaterra and the other Venezuelans on board the *Falke* by blaming the German crew because they were "at the mercy of the thirty-two German sailors, who once aware of the defeat and the death of General Delgado Chalbaud, revolted and threatened Pocaterra and his colleagues, forcing him to leave rather quickly for Grenada and to dump the cache of arms into the sea."[188]

The decision to off-load the arms was made unanimously by all six Venezuelan rebels on board. As the arms were owned by Delgado Chalbaud, his son Carlos Delgado Chalbaud authorized Pocaterra "to proceed to do it that way without any kind of scruples."[189] Delgado Chalbaud Gómez felt that Pocaterra "behaved according to circumstances"[190] and was willing to "carry the same responsibility with which he is tarred with."[191] So when Ziplitt gave the order to dump the arms, the crew did it with relish all the way to Grenada, working until eleven that night and "starting again at six the following morning."[192] After a voyage of just under twenty-seven hours, on August 11 the *Falke* dropped anchor at Glovers Island, off Grenada, where it took sixteen tons of coal and a small amount of provisions. Two days later, on August 13 at six p.m., the *Falke* left the British colony for Trinidad, reaching the island at about eight p.m. the following day. Eleven passengers, including Delgado Chalbaud Gómez, Parisot, Mendoza, Castro, and Dr. Gutiérrez landed at Grenada. Five left on August 15 for Saint Lucia, with another four intending to catch another ship to Martinique and thence to France, while one proceeded to St. John's, Antigua. Of the remaining six, five left for Trinidad by sloop on August 18, while Dr. Gutiérrez, the remaining rebel member, left Grenada on August 21 for Trinidad.

Preparations at the Colombian Border

After the Cumaná disaster, Baptista urged Peñaloza to telegraph the Paris committee to recommend his appointment as the new leader of the revolution, something that the latter agreed to do, uniting the two further. On August 12, Baptista held a meeting with General Guillermo Coti, the head of the North and South Santander Military Zone of Colombia, and Olivares at the Mercedes Abrega tavern at one in the morning. It was decided that Peñaloza should sell his arms hidden near Cúcuta to Olivares. Peñaloza later changed his mind, arguing that he owed everything to the people of those regions, with Baptista requesting the former to accompany him in his planned invasion of Coro. Olivares also refused to join the rebellion, with Baptista handing over to "Peñaloza the $2,000 sent as a gift to General Delgado Chalbaud, and promised to send a further $4,000 when he reached Barranquilla to complete all the preparations."[193] Baptista left Cúcuta for the Colombian Atlantic coast, while Olivares stayed hidden in an estate waiting for further developments. With the additional funds Peñaloza purchased a further 200 arms, 20,000 rounds of ammunition, and 1,500 kilos of explosives to manufacture marine mines with 50 pounds of explosives each, and some 200 land mines of 8 to 10 pounds. The rivers Encontrados and Zulia would be mined to prevent government forces from entering the region, while a small group of men kept the government forces occupied.[194] A number of land mines would be detonated to make the government army believe that a battle was taking place in order to draw them to an area already mined and "to explode them using two magnetos he had."[195] Fences would also be electrified to "slow down government forces."[196]

The rebel force totaled three hundred men, a third armed with Mauser carbines and the rest with machetes, with the invasion to take place through Encontrados to surprise the government troops stationed at El Guayabo and then pass to Santa Bárbara. There they would mine the river and acquire more arms to return to Las Frias, "where they were to meet with the revolutionaries from La Grita, Guaraque, Seboruco, Pregonero, and all that region north of Táchira."[197] In South Táchira, the Bramon estates would be attacked, and then Rubio, Capacho, and the San Cristóbal barracks bombed. Rubén Faría writes, "They would place a bomb in an uneven part at the back of the barracks to cause a disturbance in the barracks and when López Contreras, who does not live in the barracks but in an adjoining house, left there would be eight or more men with bombs ready to capture him, and at that same time other revolutionaries would take Capacho."[198] These plans did not take place because of the failure of the Cumaná attack.

The Falke *Declared a Pirate Ship*

As the scale of Delgado Chalbaud's invasion became known, the Venezuelan foreign service went into action. A day after the Cumaná attack on August 12, Pérez, the nominal president of Venezuela, declared the *Falke* an international pirate ship, a dubious legal ploy in this context but one the Venezuelan government felt would give it sufficient flexibility to pursue its case against Delgado Chalbaud through the courts in Trinidad and Germany. In Europe, Escalante, the Venezuelan minister at London, cut short his holiday at Chateau Guyon in France and returned to London on August 19, requesting the British government to detain the *Falke* in Trinidad, arguing that if the ship was allowed to take on coal, the rebellion against Venezuela could continue and the ship would then fall under the Foreign Enlistment Act. The *Falke* was denied coal and supplies by the colonial authorities at Trinidad pending an inquiry by the governor of the British colony.

The British government did not consider the *Falke* a pirate ship since there was nothing in international law that gave rise to legal action against it: it had not committed "acts of piracy on the high seas and [the government considers] it as solely at the service of the failed opponents of the Venezuelan Government in the Cumaná putsch."[199] Moreover, the expedition was not organized on British territory, with the main legal action against the rebels taking place in Germany, where the ship was registered. The revolutionaries in the United States lobbied hard to prevent the American government from recognizing the *Falke* as a pirate ship, alluding to the fact that the revolutionary council wanted closer relations with the United States and would favor American capital investment.[200]

On August 30, the colonial government of Trinidad instituted a Commission of Enquiry Ordinance under C. W. W. Greenidge, acting Puisne judge, to look into the activities of the *Falke*. After twelve days, on September 11, Greenidge reported that the ship was not a pirate because such an entity pursued gains for private ends, whereas the ship was clearly intended to topple a government, an act that could not be considered for private gain. It was argued that a pirate was primarily a person who satisfied his personal greed or vengeance by robbery or murder in places beyond the jurisdiction of the state. The act of piracy was an international crime, which by definition could only be committed on the open seas. It was also held that the ship moored in Trinidad had not committed an infringement of the 1870 Foreign Enlistment Act because sections 8 to 11 of the Act, which specifically dealt with illegal expeditions, stated that a ship needed to have been equipped and dispatched from a British dominion in order to break the law. It did not fall within these sections because the *Falke* had docked at a British port after the debacle of Cumaná, and there was no evidence that it was fitted at the British colony to proceed on a military or naval expedition against a friendly state. It thus followed that the provisions of sections 23 and 24 of the 1870 Act giving authority to detain the ship did not apply.

Greenidge believed that Ziplitt knew the nature of the expedition from the very beginning for the following reasons: he accepted the post of nautical adviser to the revolutionaries, he took an active part with Prenzlau at Gdynia in pacifying the crew when they voiced their concerns when so much war matériel was loaded on the ship, and he encouraged the crew to accept Delgado Chalbaud's offer of a reward bonus to take part in the attack on Cumaná. Greenidge believed that Ziplitt would not cause any further trouble, as only he had acted for personal gain and there was no point in carrying on now that the revolution was defeated. S.M. Crier, the acting governor, also believed that the *Falke* should not be allowed to leave under the command of Ziplitt or any other officer related to Felix Prenzlau and his fellow rebels and that "she must be detained until a Captain approved by the German government is placed in charge of her,"[201] who ensured that the ship returned to Germany. Crier argued that Ziplitt "could give no assurances that the 'Falke' would not be used for the purpose of assisting further the Venezuelan revolutionary movement,"[202] and therefore should not be commanded by him. There was little that Greenidge could do but recommend that the ship be released to Paul Ulrich, the German consul "to equip her for a voyage back to Germany" on his assurance that she would not be commanded by Ziplitt or any other member of the former crew.[203]

The British government could not keep the ship in Trinidad indefinitely; moreover, the authorities went as far as it was legally possible in detaining the ship while they ascertained its true ownership and under which flag it was registered. Although the German government wanted to cooperate as much as possible with Venezuela and punish the culprits "severely and to indicate to the Government of Venezuela the route to take to reach this end," it was not "responsible for some delinquents taking on such a risky criminal enterprise."[204] It was up to the Venezuelan government to start immediate legal action "in Germany, through our Legation in Berlin, against the owners of the Falke for damages and financial losses as well as requesting measures to embargo the ship,"[205] as Germany was willing to punish the culprits.

Legal Action in Germany

The Venezuelan government argued that the culprits should be punished not only for the damage done in Venezuela but also as a warning to future revolutionaries. The Venezuelan government failed to get the *Falke* declared a pirate under international law, so it argued that the international community should recognize a new form of piracy that it labeled "domestic piracy."[206] This did not prosper, and on September 19 the Venezuelan government tried again informing the German minister at Caracas of its new definition of piracy. This was based on article 153 of the Venezuelan penal code, which introduced a new concept in international law, namely "piracy according to Venezuelan law."[207] The difference between this type of piracy and that recognized by international law was that under domestic piracy "the target is a certain State and in exceptional circumstances against one or more States."[208] This would be a new precedent in international relations, and, just as slavery and heresy had been abolished after they had been in existence for some time, the Venezuelans argued that it was now time for the world to recognize this new form of political instability. The "domestic pirate" was not an enemy of other countries as such but did damage "their relations and international trade, and regularly tries to win your sympathy disguising his actions with an apparent motive for justice or acting as a victim of tyranny of the State against which it exerts his violence."[209]

The Venezuelans argued that the *Falke* came under such a category as well as the normal definition of piracy because it had sailed under an unknown flag, outside the jurisdiction of any country, and had attacked and expropriated Cumaná's earthquake relief funds. Itriago Chacín, the Venezuelan foreign affairs minister, did not want to go to court until all diplomatic channels had been pursued, but in the end the Venezuelan government viewed the problem of the *Falke* in the following manner: "The Falke is not German, and in that case, far from obstructing the negotiations of the Government of Venezuela, Germany should also prosecute the owner and the supplier of the boat, as well as the other nationals that took part in the punishable acts committed by them, or if it is German then it should try to punish those who carried out the attack and abused the German flag."[210]

The Falke *Released*

The Venezuelan government was working toward a tripartite agreement between London, Berlin, and Caracas in order to prevent the *Falke* from leaving Trinidad. The intention of Eduardo Dagñino, the Venezuelan minister at Berlin, was for the August 12 decree declaring the *Falke* a pirate to be given "moral force and granted legal effect" and for the German government to hand over the ship as "moral reparation."[211] The Venezuelan government also insisted that Germany punish its citizens who took part in the *Falke* expedition. In Germany, the criminal proceedings against the owners and master of the *Falke* started in Hamburg in December. The matter remained bogged down in legal arguments until May 27, 1930, when the Venezuelan government sent a formal memorandum to the German Foreign Office concluding that the German government was partly to blame for the *Falke* debacle and that its nationals should be punished for their deeds. The German government for its part reiterated its deepest regrets for the events and its desire to "get an account of the events by the guilty ones so that the appropriate punishment can be determined" because it felt that the principal actors could be accused of participating in a "revolutionary attempt against Venezuela"[212] and could thus be charged for treason under the penal code. Although the German government wanted to try the people concerned for treason, it was unable to do so until the Venezuelan government brought a case against them because it did not consider the *Falke* a pirate ship. The German government felt that Venezuela had unfairly criticized its handling of the affair, and, as much as it regretted the incident, it did not admit any guilt and rejected "in the strongest way possible any censure in the matter that it or any other German authority had not acted in an appropriate manner or had omitted something."[213]

The Venezuelan government would not consent to the *Falke* leaving Trinidad before the Venezuelan-German affair had been concluded.[214] The ship could not remain there indefinitely, especially as the new owners had given the colonial authorities guarantees that the *Isle Vormauer,* as the *Falke* was renamed, was not "associated with any revolutionary group, nor in political matters of any sort that would endanger the peace and harmony of any friendly nation."[215] The new owner, Ernst Vormauer, a businessman from Bargteheide near Hamburg, also gave assurances that he wanted to take the ship back to Germany with a crew brought to Trinidad on the SS *Cárdenas,* one of Vormauer's ships. The *Falke* would now be used for pleasure cruises only in the Baltic sea and other European waters.

At this juncture, the British government had no reason for detaining the ship further, especially as Vormauer had acquired the *Falke.* The German consul also felt that with the new owner and the guarantees given, the ship could be released from Trinidad. However, the Venezuelan government still demanded the ship back as reparations. As a way of breaking the impasse, the German government in August proposed to submit the outstanding points of difference in the *Falke* affair to a "commission composed of two members, one named by the Government of Germany, another one by the government of Venezuela and a third in case of disagreement named by these two."[216] Dagñino counseled that if the Venezuelan government accepted this offer, they could lose the matter, something that was unacceptable, as "reason and justice is completely on our side."[217] In early October, both Julius Curtius and August Zaleski, the German and Polish foreign affairs ministers respectively, guaranteed that future Venezuelan revolutions would not depart from their respective countries.

On November 7, 1930, the *Ilse Vormauer* finally sailed from Port of Spain to Jamaica.[218] In December, the German government proposed to compensate Gómez with a piece of jewelry "as testimony of the high personal esteem"[219] that Field Marshall Paul von Hindenburg had for the dictator if the Venezuelan government renounced its claims against the *Falke*. At the end of 1930 a solution had still not been reached, with Venezuela still seeking moral reparation and feeling that only the delivery of the ship would suffice.[220] It was also clear that the Venezuelan government was unable to shift the German position, and so on December 17, 1930, the centennial anniversary of Bolivar's death, the Venezuelan government decided to call an end to the *Falke* affair.

Prenzlau was now without the *Falke,* and the mortgage on the Delgado Chalbaud properties would take time for the courts to recognize. Prenzlau sold the mortgage to the Amsterdam banker Florsheim, who brought a court action against Delgado Chalbaud's heirs in Paris on June 10, 1932. Gustave Gonfreville, who had helped Delgado Chalbaud in his expedition, represented his heirs. The Seine Civil Tribunal decided on July 2, 1932, that Prenzlau's action was unfounded because "the nature of the main contract was unlawful as it was destined to alter international public order, and consequently the subsidiary contracts were cancelled as the main reason for the contract was null and void."[221]

The failure of the *Falke* expedition shows the difficult conditions under which the exiles operated. They were constrained by funding problems, but possibly more importantly, it was difficult to coordinate activities given the problems of communication and Gómez's spy network. It is likely that had the *Falke* expedition been a success, with the coordinated attack from the west, east, and south of the country, together with the many internal uprisings that took place and the general implosion within the Gomecista ranks, the regime would have been terminally weakened. The difficulty of coordinating all the various strands of the rebellion played into Gómez's hand, as none of the uprisings were sufficiently strong to pose any threat to the regime. In essence, the *Falke* expedition showed the many insurmountable problems associated with planning, equipping, and executing an armed rebellion in a foreign land. It was also, as Velásquez argues, "the final act in the long performance of the Liberal and Nationalist politicians and military men, who since 1913 were the main opposition to the Gómez dictatorship."[222] From that point on, Gómez would rule without any real threat from the exiles, with the exception of the *Superior* expedition of 1931, which was quickly dealt with by local forces in Falcón State.

CHAPTER NINE

One Last Try

The Gómez regime was shaken by the events of 1928 and 1929, and would now endure the impact of the Great Depression, which would bring with it the threat of further possible disturbances. The Venezuelan dictator was one of the few in Latin America to survive intact the savagery of the world's greatest economic depression. There are three main reasons for such an outcome: there was a lack of a concerted opposition, as most were in exile and without sufficient energy after the fiasco of the *Falke;* Gómez pursued a prudent political policy; and the good fortune of sufficient oil revenues allowed the government to cancel its entire foreign debt at a time when the world economy was about to contract severely. The development of the nascent oil industry in the early 1920s had a positive effect on government revenues, contributing largely to cushion the country from the effects of the Great Depression and in so doing underpinning Venezuela's financial and political stability. Moreover, as the American chargé d'affaires commented at the end of 1929, Gómez held the deep belief that "he was chosen by Providence to save his country from chaos and anarchy," so that "risen by his own will power and sheer physical courage from very humble origins, he developed a bold and sagacious leadership which has earned him the respect even of those who do not approve of his methods."[1]

The Economy and the Great Depression

The country's main export commodity was coffee until oil took off in the late 1920s. During the early part of that decade, coffee prices remained low, having an adverse effect on the country's balance of payments. The deficit was reflected in the bolívar's exchange rate, which was devalued in relation to the dollar by 6.5 percent in 1920, 16 percent in 1921, 5 percent in 1922 and 1 percent in 1923, only reaching parity again in 1924. The country was able to face the economic crisis because the nascent oil industry injected a large amount of money into the economy. Government revenues, primarily from customs receipts, expanded considerably as long as oil production increased, giving the government a greater margin of error in balancing its accounts. For example, the government's budget in 1917–18 was exceeded by 25 percent and in 1924 by 100 percent, but when oil companies curtailed production in 1927, there was an immediate impact on government revenues and on effective demand directly in Zulia, and to a lesser extent on the whole country, giving rise to a budget deficit in 1928, which increased to Bs 51 million in 1930–31. Many of the lines of credit that Venezuela were promised did not materialize, and in order to balance the books it was necessary to dip into the country's gold reserves, which declined by 50 percent.

The reduction in government expenditure had an immediate deflationary impact on the economy, with the situation further aggravated by Venezuela's lack of a central bank that could manage the supply of money and the exchange rate of the bolívar. At the time, six leading private banks were authorized to issue bank notes that had to be backed 100 percent with gold, with the Banco de Venezuela acting as the government's fiscal agent. Although the bolívar was probably the strongest gold-backed currency in the world at the time, it did not ensure an adequate money supply because unsupervised commercial and financial transactions drained the economy of its liquidity, exerting a deflationary effect on the economy. The lack of a central bank also meant that the bolívar's international exchange rate was determined by the commercial transactions of the private banks. With an increasing current account deficit in the balance of payments, the bolívar depreciated in relation to the US dollar, and the government was unable to maintain parity because it could not intervene in the markets. As the economic depression worsened during the early 1930s, the bolívar depreciated further, reaching an exchange rate of Bs 7 to the US dollar in 1931. This favored the oil companies but also alleviated slightly the plight of the agricultural exporters, who found that their products were now relatively cheaper to sell in foreign markets. The oil companies had a vested interest in maintaining a high dollar rate of exchange because it meant that their costs in the local currency were lower in relation to their dollar earnings.

The Agricultural Sector

The downturn in oil activity in 1927 and the subsequent release of men from the oilfields once again focused attention on the need to stimulate agriculture, with the influential Caracas Chamber of Commerce renewing its call for the creation of an agricultural bank. This time around, the government, encouraged by Santos, the former finance minister, heeded its advice and prepared a bill for the creation of the Banco Agrícola y Pecuario, which was approved by Congress during its 1928 sessions. With a capital of $6 million, financed wholly out of current revenue, the bank replaced the German trading houses as the main source of finance for the agricultural sector. The newly created bank distributed a fair amount of money among the farmers of the country, lending $1.12 million between July and December 1930 to 177 applicants, of which 44 percent was used to pay off mortgages, 38 percent to help agricultural farmers, and 18 percent to assist cattle farmers. The bank had a limited impact, though, because the landowners, having mortgaged their land to the bank, preferred to use the funds to finance other commercial ventures or go into the construction business instead of investing in the agricultural sector. When it was time to repay the loan, the landowners preferred to keep their new businesses, as the value of the land had declined due to the Great Depression, so the bank was left holding the mortgaged land. The bank then did not alleviate the major problem facing the agricultural and coffee growers, which was a chronic lack of investment that became ever more acute as the Depression started to bite in the early 1930s.

The drop in coffee prices from $26.82 per hundredweight[2] in 1929 to $9.36 per hundredweight in 1933 produced a further decline in the country's agricultural export sector, aggravated by the refusal of the traditional commercial houses and banks to extend credit to the coffee producers. The plight of the coffee growers, therefore, worsened as the economic depression deepened, and the value of coffee exports fell from $25.5 million in 1929 to $10 million in 1931. Although the bolívar strengthened considerably in 1934, coffee producers still faced a fall in coffee prices, with a hundredweight declining to

$7.34 in 1934, forcing many people with loans from the Banco Agrícola y Pecuario and other banking institutions to default on their payments. It was not only coffee that suffered, as other agricultural sectors such as cattle breeding also felt the impact of the worsening economic situation. Cattle exports, which in 1929 stood at 450 head of cattle per month to the Dutch Antilles, fell considerably by 1933. According to Edward A. Keeling, the special British envoy, not a single cow could be moved without Gómez's consent, as he owned the slaughterhouse and fixed prices, with the result that the "President is rich and the stock-breeders are ruined."[3] The same was true for other industries according to Keeling, who felt that "the ruling party either sucks the life blood of the concern as 'partners' or else takes it over."[4] This had a deleterious effect on the country's development as "no one dare be original and successful or he will be noticed," with the result that Venezuela, "which could grow wheat, potatoes, rice and other crops enough to feed herself and export and become a great cattle breeding country, is largely dependent on the foreigners for her food and one or two established industries for her support."[5] The effect of the Great Depression was to reduce activity in commerce and public construction as well as a tightening of credit, with merchants in large towns either going bankrupt or reducing their activities considerably because they were unable to collect their debts. H. L. Boulton, the long established trading house, for instance, sought a "moratorium on his debts"[6] from the government. In addition, low prices for other agricultural crops meant that many were not harvested, with a large number of people abandoning the land.

The coffee growers of Táchira in particular were severely affected by the Great Depression, and the lack of investment in the past hampered any recovery hopes, as the coffee bushes were at least twenty years old. During a period of high prices this did not matter, but when prices fell to rock bottom, the productivity of the coffee bushes was very important. In 1914, for example, coffee plantations produced on average 400 kilograms of coffee beans per hectare, one of the highest yields in the world, but by the end of the Gómez period production was down to 250 kilograms per hectare. During this period, no effort was made to improve yields or to mechanize coffee production, as was the case in Brazil and Colombia. Wages for farm laborers also declined significantly, reaching $0.12 per day in the early 1930s. In desperation, many farmers took out large loans at high interest rates, which proved impossible to pay back, especially for the small holder. As a result, during the 1930s, the banks ended owning many farms by default, which were later abandoned. To further aggravate matters, Colombia devalued its currency from Bs1=C$0.20 in 1929 to Bs1=C$0.50 in 1933, which meant that the terms of trade favored Venezuela's neighbor, with an increase of trade from Colombia to Táchira. There was, therefore, little liquid cash to finance the coffee crisis, and much of the textiles, cars, and other large consumer items were imported from Colombia.[7]

The establishment of the Banco Agrícola y Pecuario in 1928 was seen as an answer to the plight of the farmers because they could set aside part of their land for cultivation, receiving generous loans from the bank, and of those in Zulia particularly because they could sell their land to the oil companies. In 1934, the Coffee Growers Commission in a desperate move approached Gómez to request the government to waive the interest on loans extended by the Banco Agrícola y Pecuario. The government agreed to grant an interest-free loan of $2.8 million on July 24, 1934, to growers who could prove their need without any quid pro quo. The intention was to give the industry a boost by providing wages for the workers and enabling growers who continued to cultivate their land to receive a reasonable return. However, once the growers secured a loan, they looked on it as a net profit because there was no need to provide collateral or repayment, and so they did not bother developing their plantations. One immediate effect was that the sugar growers requested a subsidy of $706,215 million for their industry, and later the Cocoa Producers Association was founded for the sole purpose initially of requesting a similar type of loan.

Debt Cancelled

It was during this period of economic uncertainty that Gómez achieved his greatest financial achievement by paying off the country's large foreign debt while at the same time reducing substantially the domestic public debt. When Gómez came to power in December 1908, the foreign debt stood at $43.3 million, declining by 36 percent to $29.5 million in 1918 and by May 1930, when the government had a budget surplus of $20.6 million, shrinking to a mere $3.9 million, which was paid off in full on December 17, 1930, to celebrate the centenary anniversary of Bolívar's death. Similarly, the domestic public debt in 1908 stood at $13.9 million, declining to $5.9 million in 1929, and was almost completely paid off by the time of Gómez's death in December 1935.

Gómez viewed this achievement as economic liberation and on equal terms to Bolívar's independence movement, so that "I thought to myself that if they achieved political independence then I must complete the work by gaining economic independence, establishing peace and organizing public finances to ensure that the country's credit worthiness is stronger than its previous parlous state when I started."[8] In the United States there was enormous surprise at the cancellation of the country's foreign debt, with Arcaya, the Venezuelan minister at Washington, reporting that even taxi drivers commented favorably on the achievement and among "diplomatic and official circles the surprise is also large and has destroyed the enemy's propaganda."[9] It should be noted that the policy to repay the country's debt was initiated long before oil revenues assumed any importance in the late 1920s, as by then the debt had declined considerably. There is little doubt, however, that oil revenues contributed considerably to the acceleration in the rate of repayment.

Regional Impact of the Great Depression on Zulia

The impact of the Great Depression on Maracaibo was swift and severe, with the region experiencing a decline in economic activity with the fall in oil and coffee exports. Lower coffee prices restricted the trading community from extending credit to their customers in the interior of the country, with many small businesses going bankrupt. In addition, the drop in wages and salaries also led to the closure of many establishments catering to the needs of the workers who flocked to Maracaibo and other oil centers. In order to alleviate unemployment in Zulia, Pérez Soto, the state president, ordered that all unemployed non-Zulians should return to their respective home states, providing them with assisted passages and a small cash sum. The policy of repatriating non-Zulians only shifted the problem to other states that were less able to cope. Falcón, for example, not only had to deal with workers returning from Zulia but also with unemployed Venezuelans returning from Curacao and Aruba. At the same time Zulians sought to return to the land, but jobs were hard to get owing to the decline of agriculture and because sufficient people were already working the land.

The economic situation did not improve in the ensuing years, but once the 1931 harvest was collected, Gómez took the initiative and advised his state presidents that food prices should be reduced owing to the bumper crop, reasoning that it was not "equitable nor lawful that prices should continue high to the detriment of the proletariat."[10] Pérez Soto took up this initiative with renewed vigor, decreeing the establishment of an *inspector de abasto* (retail inspector),[11] headed by Colonel José Manuel Ruiz, and freezing prices on essential products such as meat, milk, sugar, flour, beans, coal, plantains, charcoal, rice, and other essential products. A maximum profit was allowed for each item, varying from 10 percent on plantains to 40 percent on beans. Each week a committee composed of the retail inspector, the central market manager, a wholesaler, and a retailer met to set prices for the coming week. As the economic situation worsened, Gómez was forced to issue on June 13, 1932, a general decree ordering food prices to fall.[12]

Party Politics

From 1930 onwards, there were two opposing fronts that can be broadly categorized as the Liberals, along with a small nascent left-wing movement. This was divided into the Machado/De la Plaza group, with its communist orientation closely tied to the Union of Soviet Socialist Republics and advocating working class revolution, and the Asociación Revolucionaria de Izquierda (ARDI) inspired by the APRA of Peru and formed by a group calling themselves "scholars of Marxism,"[13] composed of Betancourt, Leoni, Valmore Rodríguez, and Ricardo Montilla. According to Fuenmayor, from 1929 onwards other class regroupings appear, "but such political regroupings, derived from the defeats of 1928 and 1929, ended in economic stratifications with political projects that later culminated in the adoption of bourgeois ways by the masses and in the national betrayal by those who once in power accelerated the surrender of the country's resources to the voracity of foreign contractors."[14]

The students that remained in the country continued to be a thorn in the side of the government. In September 1929, they requested the release of the country's political prisoners, but soon after they were arrested and sent to the concentration camps at Palenque, Chinita, and Las Colonias. They were transferred in January 1930 to the Libertador castle in Puerto Cabello, where they remained for another seven months. This brought a virtual end to the Federation of Students, as many of the social differences between the members were highlighted at this time, with the majority of the students receiving money from home to buy food while others were dying of hunger because of a lack of funds. The experience was useful for some because they met people such as Pío Tamayo, Alberto Ravell, and Juan Montes, who gave them a clear vision of what was happening in Venezuela. Fuenmayor, a detained student, would later write that this was the start of the "regrouping of classes that later would play an outstanding role in the political activity of the country."[15]

On November 19, 1929, most of the 180 students detained previously without criminal charges against them were released from the Libertador castle in Puerto Cabello. Soon afterwards, the beginning of the communist movement of Venezuela can be traced when a small group of students headed by Francisco José (Kotepa) Delgado, Juan B. Fuenmayor, and Rodolfo Quintero formed a left-wing organization aimed at championing the political interests of the fledgling group of industrial workers in the country. There had been previous attempts to form a left-wing workers' party in Venezuela. In September 1923, the Venezuelan communist Maximiliano Schenburn Monroy was expelled from France. At the time, Monroy informed L. Parra Márquez, the Venezuelan consul general in Antwerp, that a number of communists, including Joseph Jeminski, Gregorio Lanski, Abrasca Rachtenber, Maxim Abranowith, Ignacio Rodríguez, Nicolás Agromonte, José Montenegro, and Octavio Uriarte, were traveling to Venezuela to start a communist party. When Eduardo Machado, his brother Gustavo Machado, and De la Plaza were in Cuba between 1924 and 1925, they were directly involved with Julio Antonio Mella, Carlos Baliño, and José Miguel Pérez[16] in the founding of the Communist Party of Cuba on August 16–17, 1925. In 1928, a number of left-wing Venezuelans in Paris, such as Aurelio Fortoul, Carmen Fortoul, De la Plaza, Eduardo Machado, Pedro Brito, and Anita Toledo, met to discuss the possibility of setting up a Communist Party in Venezuela. Aurelio Fortoul was a member of the French Communist Party, and his sister Carmen Fortoul was married to Guillermo Hernández Rodríguez, who was the secretary general of the Socialist Party of Colombia, which later became the Communist Party of Colombia. Carmen Fortoul met her husband when they both studied at the Lenin School of Political Warfare in Moscow.

Partido Comunista de Venezuela

Some historians consider that the PRV was part of what has been termed the prehistory of the Communist Party of Venezuela (PCV), but, as Fuenmayor argues, it cannot be considered as such because the party's focus was not "directed to the diffusion of Marxism in Venezuela, nor to the organization of the working class, but exclusively to the overthrow of the dictatorship of Juan Vicente Gómez by means of armed invasions."[17] The Gomecista regime was aware of the political threat that communism posed, with Arcaya in 1926 requesting permission from Gómez to allow him to bring into the country left-wing material to study this new form of political organization. The origins of the PCV can be traced to a meeting that took place in Angel J. Márquez's house in Caracas toward the end of 1930. Raúl Osorio Lazo, a student from Valencia, wanted to establish a Communist Party; he and a number of communist sympathizers, including Víctor García Maldonado, Fuenmayor, Quintero, Kotepa Delgado, Eloy Lares Martínez, and José Antonio Mayobre, who were influenced by Ravell, Pío Tamayo, and Montes, gathered at the home of Márquez to discuss the formation of a Communist Party. In July 1930, the group established a Communist Study Circle, which was expanded to include Josefina Juliac, Carmen Clemente Travieso, Elba Arraiz, and other sympathizers. In November they adopted what Aurelio Fortoul calls the "pompous"[18] name of the Communist Party of Venezuela and subscribed to the "Erfurt Program" and the statutes of the Social Democratic Party of Germany. The party agreed to work toward the physical elimination of Gómez by bombing his Maracay residence, although nothing ever came of this idea.

At the time, Moscow sent Joachim Michel, under the direction of Eusie Goldstein in Berlin, to Venezuela with $15,000 to support the fledgling party. The Group soon started publishing *Lo que debe saber todo obrero,* an information pamphlet that highlighted the injustices of the capitalist system. However, there were soon splits in the organization with the formation of a new group headed by Quintero, Fuenmayor, and Kotepa Delgado. The new group started publishing a series of weekly pamphlets entitled *25 Lecciones para obreros,* which although similar to *Lo que debe saber todo obrero* was more anarchic in its political orientation. Quintero wrote the first editions of *25 Lecciones para obreros,* while Kotepa Delgado and Fuenmayor penned later numbers. In all, seventeen *Lecciones* were edited by Fuenmayor and printed at the FEV until the police put a stop to the organization. The first *Lecciones* were printed twice a week, with a print run of between four hundred and six hundred copies, but most remained in storage and were not distributed.

The movement expanded further in 1931, when the Fortoul brothers returned to Venezuela. On March 3 of that year the first cell of the PCV was formed; it organized on April 7 a demonstration in the Plaza Bolívar by three hundred unemployed workers seeking work. Eduardo Machado in New York requested the US Communist Party to provide an experienced militant, with the American Joseph Kornfeder,[19] a delegate of the Communist International, arriving in Caracas from Bogotá the following month. Kornfeder brought with him the first communist manifesto by the fledgling Venezuelan party, *La Lucha por el Pan y la Tierra / Manifesto del Partido Comunista al Pueblo Trabajador de Venezuela,*[20] which was printed in Colombia on May 1 and published by the Comité Central Provisional del Partido Comunista Venezolano, Sección Venezolana de la Internacional Comunista.[21] Caballero postulates that the authors of the manifesto were Kornfeder, Carmen Fortoul, Hernández Rodríguez, and Ignacio Torres Giraldo, a Colombian member of the recently formed Communist Party of Colombia. On his arrival in Caracas, Kornfeder started giving lessons on communism together with Víctor García Maldonado at the offices of Aurelio Fortoul. The nascent Communist Party decided to concentrate their efforts in organizing unions, focusing on the Sociedad Benéfica de Panaderos, the most militant of the mutual aid societies in Caracas. However, their activities soon ended.

In a lapse of security, on May 29, 1931, the authorities raided the offices of the nascent communist group at Aurelio Fortoul's architectural practice. Kornfeder was arrested by the police but was later released after the US minister intervened.[22] In 1932, three communist cells were formed at the homes of Márquez, Fernando Key, and Mayobre. In the same year, a Venezuelan communist cell in Philadelphia started publishing *El Martillo,* a newspaper that was introduced clandestinely into Venezuela.[23] A further communist cell was formed on March 5, 1934, with a second edition of *El Martillo* published. It should be borne in mind that the number of militants was minuscule, with Caballero estimating that up to 1934 there were at most between forty and fifty communist sympathizers in the country.[24]

Plan de Barranquilla

After the failed *Falke* expedition, Betancourt in 1931 joined Ricardo Montilla, Valmore Rodríguez, Pedro Juliac, Raúl Leoni, and others in Barranquilla, where they published a biweekly specialized newsletter called *Extracto Notarial y de Juzgados,* selling it to local businesses and banks and generating revenues of around $1,500 per month.[25] The group in general, and Betancourt in particular, was alleged to be attracted by Raúl Haya de la Torre's APRA party in Peru. However, Betancourt's major influences were the Mexican revolution and the experience of the Chinese Kuomintang that led directly to the declaration known as the Plan de Barranquilla, issued on March 22, 1931.[26] The plan was signed by Betancourt, Leoni, Valmore Rodríguez, Pedro Juliac, Ricardo Montilla, Carlos Peña Uslar, Mario Plaza Ponte, P. Rodríguez Berroeta, and Simón Betancourt and later evolved into the Asociación Revolucionaria de Izquierda (ARDI). The Plan de Barranquilla was a political program that used Marxist methodology to analyze the political situation in Venezuela and identified military caudillismo, the latifundio, and the penetration of the Venezuelan economy by economic imperialism—mainly oil companies—as the main reasons for the backwardness of the country. The manifesto called for the confiscation of the assets of the Gómez family and their closest advisers, the renegotiation of oil contracts, and a social revolution that just fell short of a radical Marxist political change. The group argued that a revolution in Venezuela could not rely on the small working class recently created by the country's nascent oil industry but instead needed to be based on a multi-class, revolutionary, anti-oligarchic, and anti-imperialist party.

Later that year, Betancourt left for Costa Rica, while Gustavo Machado moved to Bogotá and De la Plaza to Trinidad, with Leoni, Montilla, and others staying in Barranquilla. In Costa Rica, Betancourt joined the Communist Party and helped organize a strike by the banana workers in Panama. Betancourt was later expelled from the Communist Party for his action during the strike and deported from Costa Rica but was allowed to stay after an appeal, remaining in the country until Gómez's death. In 1932, he published *Con quien estamos y contra quien estamos*, which started a political debate among the exiled community. In his pamphlet Betancourt rejected the stance taken by the New York group Venezuela Futura of Carlos López Bustamante, Rafael Bruzual López, and Jacinto López, who argued that only by getting rid of all the Andeans from government would Venezuela prosper. Betancourt also rejected the position of the PCV because of its need for support from a nonexistent working class in Venezuela. Betancourt was against what he considered to be an international imperialist bourgeoisie and their native allies, with their large commercial interests and "the military chieftains," proposing instead to create a multi-class party that would oppose the powerful traditional interests that Gómez represented.

With Gómez becoming more elderly and frail, the traditional Catholic interests started worrying about the political succession. Stimulated by the trip of Rafael Caldera to the 1934 Congreso de la Juventud de Acción Católica in Rome, which resolved that political parties with a Christian backing needed to be formed in all Latin America to counter the rising number of communist parties, the first tentative steps were taken toward the creation of COPEI, Venezuela's Christian Social party.

Students Demonstrate

A political demonstration was planned by the students for December 17, 1930, the centenary anniversary of Bolívar's death. The official program to commemorate the anniversary started with a church Mass held at the capital's cathedral, followed by a solemn celebration at the National Pantheon, where Pérez and his retinue of ministers were present. The plan was for the students at this stage to approach the president to request the release of the political prisoners from the country's jails. However, on that day a small group of demonstrators got hold of a number of national flags that were flying outside most houses in Caracas to mark the anniversary, and headed for La Rotunda jail seeking the freedom of the political prisoners and shouting "Long live liberty! Down with the government. Die Gómez. Down with the Andeans." General Volcán, the same officer who was defeated by Ducharne in 1914 and who was now in charge of the jail, ordered his troops to fire at the crowd, killing five people and wounding three. Eight businesses also suffered damage, losing merchandise to looters, with the shoe shop El Sol and the Pedigón and Bustillos offices suffering broken windows. Elias Sayago, together with sixteen police officers, managed to take away the flags and disperse the crowd. The demonstrators then proceeded to Plaza Bolívar; around a hundred people were later detained.

Gómez explained to Arcaya that this type of demonstration "happens daily in all capitals and main cities of the world, including the United States, when the authorities are forced to repel the threats of the communists and other rebels."[27] However, later in the year, in July 1931, Arcaya advised Gómez that keeping harmless people in prison gave the country a bad name and that he should release Carlos Borregales, Silva Tellería, and Rafael Arévalo González; moreover

> it would have a salutary effect if the Consulates issued a notice stating that all those with peaceful intentions can return to Venezuela with all their safeguards guaranteed and that the indigent will get assisted passages. The cost to the government would be small, it

would not even reach ten thousand dollars—and that notice to-gether with the news of the release of the detainees would put an end to any adverse propaganda.[28]

Gómez Reinforces His State Presidents

The disaster of the *Falke* sapped the energy of many of the exiles, with most of them venting their anger and frustration at Pocaterra for having dumped the large cache of arms in the sea. In October 1929, it was reported that the Unión Cívica Venezolana in New York "remained under the exclusive domain of the closest relatives of the deceased Pedro Elias Aristeguieta."[29] Aranguren still appeared eager to determine the state of morale among the army commanders, as he was willing to "use money or whatever is needed to buy some of them."[30]

Once the impact of Delgado Chalbaud's invasion subsided, Gómez immediately instituted a check on all the states to reinforce their defenses. General Lino Díaz, the president of Monagas, for example, felt that Maturín, especially Caripito and Quiriquire, which were growing oil towns with two thousand oil workers, needed to be strengthened. Maturín, the state capital, only had a squad of fifty men, the same as Barrancas, but without a proper barracks, so that there was a pressing need to build one. In addition, a squad of soldiers, even if it were only half a company in Caripito, would "protect those places to their advantage."[31] The case of Zulia was more critical because of its important oil industry and, as we have seen, because it was particularly vulnerable to attacks from the Dutch West Indies or Colombia. Pérez Soto advised Gómez to increase the army in the state because in the event of an attack from the Guajira peninsula, he would need to leave Maracaibo to engage the rebels, with the rest of the state, especially the oil fields, left defenseless and opening the door "to disorder when the government was occupied with a major emergency."[32] The situation could become even more critical if a simultaneous enemy attack started at Encontrados and the Guajira, because then he had to "divide the men at my disposal, with the result that each reduced group is not sufficient to guarantee the immediate success we are looking for."[33] Pérez Soto also wanted to increase his meager arsenal of 345 Mauser carbines, of which 100 belonged to the police force of Maracaibo, but Gómez refused, knowing that those very weapons could be used against him if captured by his enemies or in the event of a former friend turning against him. As we have seen, there was an outside chance of a Zulia Republic being formed, and Gómez remembered what happened in 1913, when the possibility existed of combining the forces of the Andean states together with Zulia to depose him.

Pérez Soto's fears of a revolutionary attack were continuously fanned by the numerous rumors and reports that were always present in Maracaibo. In June 1930, the manager of the Creole Petroleum Corp. handed Pérez Soto a long list of alleged communist infiltrators and agitators in the country, which the state president refused to give any credence.[34] Later, the *New York Times* reported that Pérez Soto had prolonged his stay in Caracas because he was soon to be appointed vice president by the Pérez government.[35] Pérez Soto was also the subject of personal attacks that questioned his integrity. In 1931, for instance, a rumor rapidly spread in Maracaibo that Pérez Soto had acquired steel pipes from the Richmond Petroleum Company for use on his farm without paying the import tax. He was forced to explain to Gómez that he had paid the proper import taxes and had not acted wrongfully, with Pérez Soto dismissing these rumors as "*mischief* by the enemies who persist in creating displeasure and discord among the men who are loyal to you"[36] (emphasis in original).

Rebels Try to Regroup

Flores, Pimentel, and Ferrer in September 1929 were back in Paris eager to start a rebellion against Gómez but unable to find financial assistance. The main hope remained Aranguren, who, as we have seen, wanted to know who the new army commanders in Venezuela were in order to "buy some of them."[37] In 1929, Bunomovich was in Paris, and in the autumn of that year it was reported that his agents are "looking for an exit in the Baltic or the Adriatic."[38] The Gómez regime was confident that an armed revolution against it was highly unlikely because as Figueredo, the Venezuelan consul in New York, reported, "there is a lack of military men with even some prestige and a lack of funds because they can only raise at most $20,000, and it is utter nonsense to think that they can defeat militarily a situation that you defend so well with such a small amount."[39] Nevertheless, rumors of possible revolutions continued to be reported, with Ortega Martínez and Alcántara keeping alive the hopes of the exiles.[40] In September 1929, Matos Arvelo, Teodoro Ramírez, Alberto Ordoñez, and Antonio Santana met at General Peñaloza's home ready to take up arms against Gómez but decided that they were in no condition to invade Venezuela, as they lacked sufficient arms.[41] At this stage, the revolutionary movement abroad appeared to Figueredo not to be a "revolution in all its form, but a plot to topple you, coinciding with a number of small uprisings in the country."[42] At the end of 1929, Ortega Martínez secured some meager funds from Aranguren for his forthcoming revolution, establishing in Paris a Supreme Command, with himself in control and Alcántara, who was in Puerto Rico, responsible for western Venezuela. Baptista was also thought to be keen to join the revolution. In February 1930, Ortega Martínez headed for New York to secure further financial help.[43]

The exiled students in Barranquilla were becoming more vociferous, with their experience giving them enough optimism to think that they could defeat Gómez. In February 1930, it was rumored that Rómulo Betancourt had secured a ship in Santo Domingo but lacked arms and ammunition. The truth was that Betancourt had secured an option to purchase a ship in Puerto Rico for $10,000 but was unable to find financial backers who were willing to purchase it outright.[44]

In early 1930, it was also rumored that Olivares in Cúcuta was pressing Baptista to launch a general revolution because they had between them 2,800 Mauser carbines. However, both Baptista and Olivares lacked funds for a revolution and traveled together to Bogotá, Colombia's capital, to raise a loan among the "rich retailers of the plains who live in Bogotá and Girardot."[45] Olivares remained in the Colombian department of Girardot, while Baptista returned to Cúcuta. The more than 400 arms that Olivares acquired from González Valencia ended up in the hands of "Antonio Reyes, a rich Venezuelan exile in Cúcuta, and his brother Pedro."[46] On August 9, Carlos J. Grisanti, the Venezuelan minister at Washington, informed Gómez that he believed that Olivares would invade Venezuela "with a boat coming from México and Colombia, with arms acquired in those republics."[47]

According to reports by the Venezuelan consul in Cúcuta, the rebels in August were openly talking about Peñaloza's next revolution, but because he was stingy and had no resources of his own it was unlikely to take place. The consul reported that the exiles expected a rebellion to "erupt in Venezuela, with Olivares and Baptista in the center and Flores and others in the eastern part of the country."[48] Toward the end of 1930, reports reached Gómez that the rebels in Colombia, headed by Alcántara and Flores, would soon invade the country.[49] A separate invasion by Peñaloza was also expected soon, but Ortega Martínez did not forward the funds needed for the rebellion.[50] It was reported that Olivares and Baptista had united and had the "cooperation of Arévalo Cedeño and Urbina, but there is not sufficient money to help these individuals, and they are urgently looking for $40,000 because Urbina has a mediocre cache of arms supplied by the Mexican government, but has no transport and only two hundred and fifty rifles that are not very good."[51] If they could not get funding, the Olivares/Baptista group would force Urbina to take "whatever boat is available, as they are interested in two or three theatrical blows in order to get more money from Aranguren in Europe."[52] In September 1930, Baptista was in Trinidad "to see if he could hold on to the situation, and get what remained of the revolution, as well as the leaders and officers to acknowledge him as the supreme leader."[53] Figueredo felt that this would not happen unless Baptista provided the necessary funds.

The Venezuelan government remained confident that the revolutionaries had run out of steam, receiving a shock in February 1930 that the rebel boat *Victoria* was allegedly about to leave the United States for Venezuela. The regime, which did not want to be caught off guard as in the *Falke* case, started a frantic search to ascertain whether this was true. Grisanti, who felt that both the State Department and George Summerlin, the US minister at Caracas who had been at West Point with Alcántara,[54] were "very knowledgeable about the revolution in Hispanic-American countries,"[55] requested help from the US government. President Hoover, Figueredo reported, was also "totally opposed to any type of armed movement in our countries."[56] The Venezuelan government employed a private detective to watch the rebels. On February 27, Inspector Edward P. Hughes, the head of a detective agency, advised Rincones to report his fears either to the police commissioner or to an inspector of the secret police. As the former was absent, Rincones saw Inspector John O'Brien and then Lieutenant Charles Newman, second in command of the secret police, who assured him that a secret agent would be assigned to the case. It later transpired that the only ship that left at around that time and had a remotely similar name to "Victoria" was the *Victolite*, an oil tanker belonging to the Tropical Oil Company, which departed from Bayonne, New Jersey, bound for Cartagena, Colombia. Rincones, wanting to be absolutely sure, checked the Lloyd's Register at the Globe Insurance Company the following day, February 28, and found that there were twenty-two ships with the same name. The only suspicious *Victoria* ship was one of 2,747 tons that left Galveston on February 22 bound for British Columbia in Canada and from there to Trinidad and Barbados, but owing to propeller problems was forced to remain in Canada. There was no further news about the revolution until April, when it was rumored that the Doheny Oil Company had offered financial help to the revolutionaries, something the State Department was unable to verify. The situation on the Colombian border seemed more alarming for the Venezuelan government because Alcántara, Baptista, and Olivares had gathered there, each wanting to head the rebel movement. It was reported that Cúcuta was filled to the brim with rebels, with "an estimated 2,800 arms in the hands of Peñaloza and the Olivaristas."[57]

Ortega Martínez continued his preparations for his own revolution, trying to convince people in Curacao and Aruba to attack Coro,[58] while Pocaterra was dispatched to Mexico in March to revive old friendships in the Aztec capital to ascertain whether the rebels could count on their support. Mexico promised Raúl Castro, Egea Mier, and Urbina a cache of arms as long as they could find a suitable means of transport. With such a promise, Jugo Delgado tried acquiring the *Falke* for $12,000, which would then be registered in the name of a foreigner and used as a merchant ship until the revolutionaries needed it. By the end of March 1930, Raúl and Henrique Castro had assembled some two hundred men, mainly Mexicans, with a group of officers and pilots who were willing to topple the Gómez regime. The question remained whether they could acquire a ship in Canada for $20,000.[59] These preparations would eventually lead to Urbina's *Superior* expedition in 1931.

In the meantime, Ortega Martínez in New York failed to raise any funds for his own rebellion, deciding to return to France to try again to convince Aranguren and other Venezuelans in Paris to contribute "with a sum larger than that promised."[60] He also felt he could strike a similar deal to the one made between Delgado Chalbaud and Prenzlau to obtain a ship and arms.[61] In early May, Ortega Martínez boarded the SS *Paris* for the voyage to Europe with his two sisters, Teresa and Trina, and his daughter, Altagracia de Ayala, who was very ill and traveling to France for medical treatment. In July, Ortega Martínez met Aranguren in Vichy for more talks and was expected back in New York on August 12. In the end, his revolution would not get off the ground.

In October 1930, Colonel Juan Bautista Carrillo and Valmore Rodríguez arrived in Rio Hacha, Colombia. It was rumored that the revolutionaries in Barranquilla were planning an attack on Zulia using two schooners acquired by Urbina from Sandino in Nicaragua. It was also rumored that some of the revolutionaries in Barranquilla, including Rómulo Betancourt, Carnevali, Guevara Travieso, and Horacio Blanco Fombona, left for Peru to "request new resources from the new Peruvian Government."[62] They changed their plans, however, once news reached them that Urbina would mount his attack on Falcón and that Colonel Carrillo and Valmore Rodríguez had landed on the Colombian Guajira peninsula. From Rio Hacha, they would invade Venezuela through Zulia in a coordinated attack with Urbina's Falcón landing. Olivares and Baptista, who were hiding in the Colombian banana zone ready to attack, would invade Venezuela through Catatumbo and Táchira, respectively. Peñaloza at the same time secretly tried to win over the oil workers at the El Cubo oil field, which bordered on Colombia. Olivares in the end did not accept the *jefatura* because he had no faith in the men behind it and because the $60,000 offered by both the New York and the Venezuelan revolutionaries in Colombia was insufficient; he had been promised initially $100,000.

It was further reported that Colombian President Enrique Alfredo Olaya Herrera "was committed to helping the revolutionary Committee, in exchange for granting Colombia a free trade port for the import and export of merchandise without having to make a transfer"[63] in Maracaibo. Spencer S. Dickson, the British minister at Bogotá, reported that certain oil companies were suspected of encouraging disaffection in both Cúcuta and Maracaibo, which would lead to the formation of a Zulia republic that would encompass the oil fields of the Venezuelan state and those of Norte de Santander in Colombia. Dickson reported that although the "imputation of such sinister designs to the oil companies is possibly fantastic, it is nevertheless true that sentiment both in Cúcuta and Maracaibo is rather provincial than national and that the creation of such an entity as the Republic of Zulia is within the bounds of possibility."[64] Víctor Sambrano, the Venezuelan consul at Cúcuta, reported that the Colombian authorities had been helpful to the revolutionaries and "all you hear people talking about in this city is the imminent fall of the government of Venezuela and the help that all of them would contribute because the trading houses and the people want free navigation and a fall in rates etc.; in addition, the large number of unemployed people are only waiting for the invasion order."[65]

Peñaloza's home was used as a central meeting place by the revolutionaries, who were waiting for the order to take up arms. The plan was to attack Tovar and Mérida first because both cities were lightly armed. Although the invasion did not take place, the government intensified its already extensive secret service in the oil camps to cover white-collar workers, bars, and restaurants. The cost of such a network, both across the state and in Maracaibo, was expensive, "since the situation is very delicate."[66] The oil companies contributed funds toward the maintenance of the network, as it was in their own interest to maintain law and order: a single match could set on fire "the large petroleum deposits and ruin the fields with such a disaster."[67] The spy network, as we have seen, also extended to Curacao and Aruba, with the government infiltrating most workers' organizations.

The efforts to get the revolution under way continued. Arévalo Cedeño left for Manaos in Brazil, where he was assured there was a cache of arms belonging to the Peruvian government. In October 1930, Gonzalo Carnevali remitted to Arévalo Cedeño $11,418 through the Banco Anglo Sud Americano in Manaos. In the middle of November, Baptista's agents were in Caracas trying to ascertain the level of support for the revolution,[68] and during the same month, Alcántara tried to enlist Summerlin, his former classmate at West Point and the American minister at Caracas, in their cause but without success. Alcántara returned to New York in December, spending his time "strolling down the streets, womanizing and with little money."[69] There was, however, a ray of hope when in early 1931 it was rumored that Urbina and Alcántara would lead an expedition from Martinique in the *Ponemah* schooner of *Falke* fame. Other revolutionaries would also leave at the same time from Trinidad.

In Venezuela, there were minor incidents that continually kept the regime in a state of alert. In February 1931, General Manuel Urbina proposed to Leoncio Hilmond, a Frenchman by birth but a naturalized Venezuelan and a mechanic by profession, to join a conspiracy against Gómez in Maracay. The plan was to assassinate Gómez in Maracay by either shooting him or bombing his car. Dr. Nouel and Diego Morales manufactured ten bombs in all, with Dimas Villegas transporting them to Maracay on April 22 to detonate them four days later. The idea was to throw a party at Leoncio Hilmond's house during the centenary anniversary of Bolívar's death and from there "to intercept the traffic at the moment when General Gómez passes, exploding nine demijohns of gasoline and to attack him with revolvers."[70] At the last moment they got scared, and the attack was not carried out, with Urbina calling them "a bunch of arseholes [*sic*] and that he was going to bring a number of Coriano troops, so that they would know how matters are handled, because he is an expert in that matter."[71] General Manuel Urbina was arrested along with all the other conspirators. In the early part of 1931, Nogales Méndez, Horacio Blanco Fombona, Rafael de la Cova, Isidro Ramírez, and others formed a revolutionary committee, but by June it had dissolved, with Nogales Méndez leaving for Germany.[72]

At the same time, the grey-haired Peñaloza, who was reputed to have received money and arms from the *directorio liberal* of Colombia,[73] accompanied by Roberto Fossi,[74] invaded Venezuela with a small force near Cúcuta and took possession of a railway station on the track running from Táchira to Encontrados in Zulia. Peñaloza was later captured in Pregonero in Lara and taken to Barquisimeto, where Eustoquio Gómez was state president. According to Rafael Antonio Alamo, an eyewitness, Peñaloza was brutally beaten, given "a gaping wound to the upper lip, and a marked limp on the right side, was weighed down with chains and manacles and his appearance was not good."[75] The next day he lost an eye during his interrogation by Eustoquio Gómez because he resolutely refused to give details of his fellow conspirators. He was sent to the Libertador castle in Puerto Cabello, where Gómez ordered him to be "caressed by the tortol in order to loosen his tongue."[76] Corporal Matallana then suspended Peñaloza by the testicles, and he "stayed in that position from six in the afternoon to close to midnight, when General Peñaloza stopped screaming because he lost conscience, leading them to think that he had passed away."[77] Peñaloza had only fainted and was later subjected to more torture, when "they pulled out his finger and toe nails, and the head tortol was applied."[78] According to Telmo A. Arellano, the leaflet published by Rafael Antonio Alamo on Peñaloza was utter nonsense, as the old general in 1931 "enjoys relative good health in the Puerto Cabello castle."[79]

The reports of an imminent invasion of Venezuela reached Caracas in early 1931.[80] It was mistakenly concluded that Alcántara and Urbina[81] would lead a revolution from Martinique and enter Venezuela through Yaguaraparo using the *Ponemah* schooner.[82] Other reports stated that Alcántara had organized his own revolution without the help of Urbina and that Peñaloza would soon invade from Colombia. Olivares was unable to do anything, "as he does not have friends or money."[83] The rebels claimed, as Carnevali stated in a interview in the *Washington Herald,* that Gómez was "protected in his power by Dutch and British warships that patrol the coast of the country,"[84] together with "Dutch and American oil interests that support him and have been able to secure for him the support of their governments"[85] In April 1931, Arévalo Cedeño crossed into Venezuela once again and captured the Llanos town of Amparo on the river Arauca on the Colombian border and gained a minor success against government troops sent after him.

It was becoming clear to some of the regime's supporters that opposition to Gómez was weakening. In March 1931, Figueredo, the former Venezuelan consul general in New York, wrote to Gómez from Madrid:

My presence in New York was not needed because our enemies there, without any money and divided, cannot achieve their criminal intentions of interrupting that fecund and glorious Peace founded and imposed by you, that is the basis for the rehabilitation of the fatherland, all made possible by your efforts. The enemies can only think of waging a paper and talk war, trying to achieve their treason or unexpected rebellions. I do not believe them because you also need money for such a venture and a leader who is willing to take risks, and I do not see such a person willing to do that.[86]

Urbina's Expedition

The last major filibustering expedition to hit Venezuela during Gómez's time was organized in 1931 by Urbina, with help from the Mexican government, which provided a hundred officers, soldiers, and transport to reach Venezuela.[87] Arévalo Cedeño and the rebels were billeted at the estate of a "high ranking official, close to Yucatán, where they will remain hidden until they are given the orders to embark."[88] It was certain, Arcaya counseled Gómez in September 1930, that if Urbina acquired even a small cache of arms, "he would reappear again in Venezuelan coastal waters."[89] Moreover, it was likely that the Colombian government would help Urbina now that Eduardo Santos, a "declared enemy of ours,"[90] was the foreign affairs minister in the new Colombian government of President Olaya Herrera, because "the Colombian Liberals have always opposed you,"[91] and the Conservatives who had hitherto supported him "will also be against us because of the events in Venezuela with the Catholic Church[92] after Dr. Pérez became president."[93]

In October 1930, Urbina and Pocaterra were in the Chiapas city of Tapachula, Mexico, planning with the Nicaraguan rebel Sandino "the acquisition of men and arms for a new rebellion."[94] The plan was to land arms at the Guajira peninsula and then take Falcón State. However, before going ahead they wanted to know whether there was an appetite for a revolution. An agent was sent to Puerto Cumarebo in Falcón State, where the rebels would invade, to gauge the extent of local support for a revolution. The envoy on his return reported that there was ample backing for the rebellion as long as the rebels received "arms, ammunition, money and everything that was needed, but if this was not the case they would not join the revolutionary movement because they were happy working for their livelihood."[95]

An invasion of the country was imminent, as the old rebel leaders appeared to be organizing themselves close to the Venezuelan border. Toward the end of January 1931, Francisco de Paúla Aristeguieta left for the Colombian banana region of the Departamento Magdalena, where his friends Negrón, Ildefenzo del Moral, and others were located. It was also rumored that Baptista and Olivares had reached an agreement, and were to enter Venezuela incognito. In addition, Durán in Colombia "was getting ready to march as soon as Baptista arrives,"[96] and the students in Barranquilla were also ready.

On February 7, 1931, on his way to Havana to seek funds for his revolution, Urbina arrived in Colón, Panama, where he gained the support of Joaquín Maldonado Briceño, who together with Felipe Aristeguieta and other revolutionaries in Barranquilla were waiting for the arrival of Baptista. In April 1931, Urbina returned to Mexico and met with León and Isidro Núñez to organize his new expedition together with the Mexicans Amador Ogendis Guillén and Major Guzmán. According to Arcaya, they had the financial wherewithal and support of "important people"[97] of Mexico for their "socialist revolution," as Urbina called it. Arcaya reached this conclusion because otherwise it would have been impossible for the rebels to acquire arms and ammunition without necessarily informing "President Ortiz Rubio or General Calles."[98] Eudoro Urdaneta, another source of information for the Venezuelan government, suggested that Urbina's revolution was also financed by "Mexican oil interests, and that Mr. Antenor Sala had spent in this some $60,000, encouraged by the promise that he would manage all the private land that was to be confiscated and distributed among the poor."[99]

Some of the arms were obtained from Bartolomé García Correa, the governor of Yucatán, who was an intimate friend of Diego Córdoba, "from whom he seems ready to obtain arms for the revolutionaries against you; as there is nobody in Mexico who will finance them."[100] Isidro Núñez contributed the largest sum—$5,000—but Aranguren also donated an unknown amount to the war chest. Urbina's group was later joined by Zúñiga Cisneros, Manuel Antonio Hernández and Julio Hernández, Pedro Campos, and Arturo Mujica as well as the Mexicans, General Prevé, and Colonels Julio Linares Tejera and Carlos Torres Guerra.[101] In Táchira, León's supporters organized themselves in a committee in Colón, with a secretary, treasurer and local president, together with a propaganda chief and people in charge of general recruitment to the cause.[102]

On their way to Veracruz on July 5, Urbina, Núñez, Guzmán, and Ogendis were detained at the jail of Belén but were released two days later on $476 bail. Arcaya was alerted by a Mexican secret agent while at the Conferencia Comercial Panamericana in Washington in October 1931 that Urbina, according to León, "was acquiring arms for a movement in Venezuela, that he was remanded in custody for those purchases but later the detention decree was revoked and he was freed on bail, where he continues with his plans."[103] The merchant ship *Superior,* the same ship that was part of the flotilla sent by Calles in 1926 to help Sacasa's rebellion in Nicaragua, sailed from Veracruz to Puerto Morelos,[104] a small fishing village in the Mexican territory of Quintana Roo, where the rebels and Urbina boarded the ship under false names. According to Urbina the rifles were packed "in long boxes . . . labeled as if they were machetes sent to a company producing chicle in Payobispo [*sic*], in Yucatán; the ammunition was labeled as axes; the machine guns were in our suitcases together with the dynamite."[105]

A few days before Urbina's expedition left from Mexico, it was freely rumored in Caracas that an insurrection from that country was about to take place, which was curious in view of the preparations made in connection with his previous raid at Curacao in 1929 in far more difficult circumstances. Furthermore, the feeling in some quarters in Caracas was that the usual sources of revolutionary funds must have been exhausted by previous attempts, as it was not clear who could have paid for the ship and for the services of the presumably mercenary Mexicans, with some believing that the "affair was provoked and secretly subsidized by General Gómez."[106] Moreover, other revolutionaries in Mexico such as Egea Mier, Ortega Martínez, Córdoba, and Tejera disassociated themselves from Urbina and León.

Owing to a small collision, the departure of the ship was delayed from Veracruz, but on September 30, 1931, the *Superior* finally departed for Quintana Roo with 130 men on board. It was later rumored that many on board were minors and inexperienced people who were not aware of the aims of the rebellion. This was untrue,[107] as the rebels' plan was to seize the ship on its voyage to the Yucatán peninsula during the telegraph operator's lunch break just before one o'clock. Prevé and Leopoldo Caroti, an Italian adventurer, captured the ship's captain, while Captain Campos and Colonel Julio Ramón Hernández seized the engine room. At the same time, José Angel Cano would be waiting in the bows with a number of men, and Colonel Ogendis would be posted at the stern, while the remaining rebels were having lunch in readiness to seize the telegraph operator.[108] On the day of the mutiny, Arturo Mujica informed Urbina at twelve thirty p.m. that the telegraph operator was having lunch, with the uprising beginning soon afterwards, and with many of the passengers and crew joining Urbina's adventure.[109]

Once the ship was in rebel hands, a war council was convened, and the various appointments were ratified: Urbina was the commander-in-chief of the Revolutionary Expeditionary Army; Caroti was appointed the captain of the *Superior;* General Prevé was the chief of staff; Colonel Torres Guerra was chief of operations; Colonel José Angel Cano was in charge of the machine guns; Colonel F. Linares Tejera was in charge of the combat engineers and dynamite blasters; and, Dr. Maxtio was chief of the grenadiers. The various companies were headed by Captains Ogendis, José Guillén Puente, Campos, and Major Guzmán; Julio Hernández and Manuel Hernández were officers in the general staff; Isidro Núñez was in charge of ordnance; Mujica was an instructor; and, finally, Zúñiga Cisneros was general secretary and medical officer. The ship's name was changed to *Elvira,* and it was repainted.

The initial plan was for the rebels to land at Mitara, near Sabaneta, and then attack Coro. Urbina and Caroti, however, decided instead to land at Puerto Gutiérrez, an oil company port on the Paraguaná peninsula, because the ship suffered mechanical problems in the boiler rooms, only managing a top speed of eight knots an hour. Worse was to happen: they ran out of fuel, with the ship drifting toward the coast of Falcón, arriving on October 11. They were forced to launch two boats carrying twenty men each, with a third ferrying the arms as they approached the coast. León Jurado, president of Falcón State, alerted by Gómez, who "was well briefed by his spies in Mexico,"[110] was waiting for them at La Vela. He informed the dictator that "tomorrow the vultures of Coro will feast on Mexican meat."[111] In a heated exchange of fire, the rebels were routed, with Urbina managing to escape to Colombia. Gómez pardoned the Mexican invaders on December 19, 1931, and returned the ship to Mexico, with General Rafael Falcón giving each Mexican $163, which was later reimbursed by Gómez.[112]

Further Expeditions

After the *Superior* incident, there were a number of wild rumors about further expeditions organized in Mexico against Venezuela. Arcaya reported a possible plot organized under the aegis of Mrs. Delgado Chalbaud, "and the people who they are trying to impress are those who took part in the Falke adventure with Alcántara, Flores and others from Eastern Venezuela."[113] A further report came from Dr. Ernst Demer, a German vet who worked for Gómez and was later expelled from the country. He reported in October that two more expeditions would leave for Venezuela, one from Yucatán and another from Puerto de México. Arévalo Cedeño left Barranquilla in November 1931 for Mexico to find "the rest of Urbina's failed filibustering expedition" and later entered Zulia State "in a sailboat, through the Castilletes region,"[114] with Pérez Soto leaving Maracaibo to capture him. In early November, Antonio Bremont, a Venezuelan living in New York, reported that a second expedition to support Urbina was being organized in Mexico, with Manuel C. Téllez, the interior minister, and many other Mexicans involved, such as Generals Prevé, Guillén, and Pedro Solorzano.[115] Arcaya did not give much credence to such reports because he felt that after Urbina's failure no further expeditions would sail from Mexico. In addition, the departure from the Mexican government of General Amaro, who had been the rebels' supporter, had "upset all the projects that could be maturing."[116] Arcaya advised that a new "adventure is unlikely at this moment when Mexico is going through a tremendous period of agitation where a split between Calles and several army chiefs and prominent men from his party has taken place, which is thought will end, as is the usual fashion, in the outbreak of a new and formidable revolution."[117]

The Peruvian Connection

Soon after the failure of the *Superior*, the Peruvian presidential candidate Luis H. Sánchez Cerro promised to supply Arévalo Cedeño with arms and ammunition if he was elected to the presidency.[118] When this occurred in 1931 an ad hoc committee composed of Jugo Delgado, David López, Miguel Delgado, and others, known as the Junta Civil de la Liberación de Venezuela, was quickly organized in New York to appoint Arévalo Cedeño their representative in the southern cone republics, and more specifically to Peru.[119] Arévalo Cedeño, through his friend Colonel Manuel Esteban Rodríguez, who was *jefe de la casa militar,* saw Sánchez Cerro, the new Peruvian president, in Lima, who kept his word to "obtain the liberation of my fatherland,"[120] promising to supply six hundred to eight hundred rifles, while at the same time agreeing to recognize the new rebel government. According to Andrés E. Rota, the Venezuelan consul, the help offered by Sánchez Cerro amounted to "the delivery of rifles, some machine guns and above all ammunition cartridges,"[121] as well as campaign tents. The arms would be shipped to the Amazon region of Peru on the SS *Marañón* of the Compañía Nacional, and "no suspicion will fall on the vessel because it had already made a voyage to Iquitos for the Peruvian government via the Panama Canal."[122] Moreover, the vessel would carry "sufficient Peruvian products to conceal from the authorities the real cargo transported"[123] when it crossed the canal.

Arévalo Cedeño already had 270 rifles hidden at the Brazilian/ Venezuelan border, which together with Sánchez Cerro's arms would be transported from Iquitos to the border. While Arévalo Cedeño was in Lima, he received news from Alcántara in Puerto Rico that he had obtained a ship on the island[124] ready to transport armaments. The plans were frustrated when in early 1932 Sánchez Cerro was assassinated and Arévalo Cedeño lost his Peruvian cache of arms. Arévalo Cedeño eventually left Lima for Panama and from there to Manaos in order to enter Venezuela from the south.

During this period, there were a number of small mutinies in the army, especially in the more remote areas of the countries. In Puerto Ayacucho, Rafael Yaguaracuto, Rubén Dario Morett, Antonio Cegarra, Virgilio Suárez, Pedro Afanador, Numas Contreras, Francisco Salazar, Manuel Toledo, Marcos González, Víctor Guippe, Nicolás Farreras, Nicolás Rosales, Domingo Arévalo, Miguel Bethencourt, and Cruz Malpico planned to take over the garrison in anticipation of joining Arévalo Cedeño's rebellion, which he estimated would cost him $6,000. On November 1, 1931, at 11:45 p.m., part of the garrison at the Cuartel de la Sagrada in Puerto Ayacucho mutinied, killing Colonel Eduardo Carrillo, the governor of the federal territory of Amazonas, and officers Custodio Sanz and Ricardo Mota. Their bodies were horribly mutilated by the rebels, who later went on the rampage, sacking the homes of the murdered officers as well as others and stealing $1,633.[125] The rebel leader Yaguaracuto was shot dead by Atilio Zapata when he was boarding a boat.[126]

Among certain Venezuelan revolutionaries there was a mood to shift the political battle away from filibustering expeditions and toward political parties and organizations. In February 1931, an organization calling themselves the Organo de Combate Contra la Tiranía de Venezuela published in Mexico City the first issue of its newspaper *Pativilca,* edited by Tejera and Egea Mier. In the newspaper, Córdoba called for the end of the "ruling regime in Venezuela" in order to "undertake the urgent social revolution, renew the state with new people ideologically prepared to steer the country through to democratic life" and to begin soon afterwards its "political organization with the parties . . . that represent the ideas and wishes of the different sectors of public opinion."[127] Córdoba also argued that it was naive and arrogant to think that a small group of exiled rebels should "abrogate the right to form political organizations or parties that cannot have any popular appeal nor any practical aim within the social needs of Venezuela; since these parties are meaningless when they are far removed from the reality of the country, its anxieties, and public opinion."[128] Moreover, "any new party has to emerge from its own revolutionary milieu, to form its ideas on the civic fight and to baptize themselves with the people's unction."[129]

The Welch Case

Gómez at this time faced possible censure from the United States when the regime's authoritarian methods were amply publicized by a number of American senators and congressmen supporting the Welch case against the Venezuelan government. James E. Welch, an American artesian well drilling engineer, became sexually involved with Ana Isabel Salazar, a thirteen-year-old girl who later gave birth to Irma Francisca Salazar, who was born outside of wedlock. In 1920, Isabel López de Salazar, the mother of the minor Ana Isabel, secured a judicial order over and above that which by law she was obliged to obtain from Pedro C. Salazar, her husband, to perform certain legal acts. Although Ana Isabel no longer resided at her mother's house, her daughter Irma Francisca remained with her grandmother. On February 19, 1929, Welch forcibly took his daughter away from her grandmother, with the result that he was accused of a criminal offence by Isabel López de Salazar and was detained in Ciudad Bolívar. Welch was freed forty-three days later[130] when the court ruled that the 1920 judicial authority granted to Isabel López de Salazar "was insufficient to enable her to lodge a criminal accusation without express consent of her husband."[131]

Welch finally secured custody of his daughter in Zulia, where the Salazar family had moved. Pedro C. Salazar was summoned to appear before the court to release the parental jurisdiction he had over Welch's daughter, something he did on July 6, 1929. Welch's common-law wife was bribed with $1,149 to contradict her first statement,[132] something which Pérez Soto, the state president, confirmed when he looked at the file and concluded that "Welch's crime is completely proven; but with money and influence, and with legal artifices pertaining to the legal profession, he managed to get the file misplaced."[133] Welch was prevented from taking his daughter out of the country with him, traveling instead on his own to the United States to press for parental jurisdiction from the Venezuelan government and to start in July 1930 a court action for damages of $500,000 against Venezuela for his ill-treatment. Welch also accused the State Department of bolstering American oil interests in Venezuela instead of assisting its citizens because of its refusal to help him in such a weak case.

At the time, Welch was approached by Miguel Delgado Chalbaud, Delgado Chalbaud's brother, and Jugo Delgado who wanted to use the Welch case as a cause célèbre to embarrass the Gómez regime while gaining the support of the State Department. For this purpose, they enlisted the help of Welch's congressman, Allard H. Gasque of South Carolina, as well as Congressman John Sandlin and Senator Joseph Eugene Ransdell, both of Louisiana. Some of the damaging press coverage on Venezuela that appeared in certain American newspapers at the time was inspired by Arthur Locke King, a lawyer who took up the rebels' cause and was a good friend of both Gasque and Welch. In Congress, Gasque called for a Congressional investigation into the political conditions in Venezuela brought to light by Welch, arguing that if one one-thousandth of the charges made by Pocaterra in his book against Gómez[134] were true, then "his countenance in power by the aid, directly or indirectly, of the United States is one of the foulest blots upon the record of this country."[135] The Venezuelan government countered by paying $400 to the *Washington Post* alone to publish an article favorable to the country. The government spent a total of $3,000 placing articles in other newspapers.

The importance of the Welch case lies in the use that certain anti-Gomecistas made of it by publicizing the political conditions that existed in the country, resulting in "considerable unfavorable press coverage for Gómez and the entire matter became extremely exasperating to the State Department."[136] However, not all rebels were willing to support the cause, with King trying to enlist the help of Pérez, Santos Domínici, and Smith, who all refused. Other exiles such as Olivares and Baptista did not support Welch, "demonstrating that above all, when it is about foreigners they are good patriots."[137]

In September 1930, Welch paraded in front of the White House with seventy-five-pound shackles on his ankles to focus attention on his case and to embarrass the Venezuelan government. The following year the International Committee for Political Prisoners issued a pamphlet detailing the unruly treatment given to US citizens in Venezuela and stating that there were 5,000 political prisoners and 100,000 people exiled from the country.[138] This prompted Senator Ransdell and Congressman Gasque to produce further evidence indicating that Gómez had the support of the State Department, and requesting an investigation to ascertain whether the United States was giving moral support to the Venezuelan dictator. Welch finally secured custody of his daughter in 1933 in Venezuela, returning to the United States in October that year with the intention of continuing his court action against the Venezuelan government for damages that had now grown to $1.5 million.

A Political Crisis Averted

The political crisis brewing in Venezuela with Pérez came to a head during the Congressional sessions in May–June 1931. At the time, it was felt that Gómez's health was declining, and although this was far from the truth, the Gomecistas reasoned that if the Benemérito died, then the command of the army would revert to President Pérez, placing him in a powerful position. They believed that he would no doubt change the cabinet and leave all the Tachirenses out in the cold. The status quo, led by García Bustamante, Gómez's Colombian uncle, wanted to prevent this by placing their own man in Miraflores Palace, because they feared that Gómez was about to abandon his old friends. Their real problem was Rubén González, the interior minister. Pérez was perceived as weak, filling Congress at the instigation of González with new young faces. García Bustamante wanted to substitute his nephew García Velasco for Pérez. The rationale behind such a maneuver was that the current head of government was weak and inept and that a stronger hand than Pérez was needed at the helm to manage the economic crisis created by the Great Depression. Deputies Carlos S. Tamayo and Aurelio Beroes in mid-May formally introduced a petition in Congress signed by many deputies requesting the substitution of Pérez by Gómez. More signatures were added the next day "because it was understood that whoever abstained from signing it did not consider the presence of General Gómez at the head of the country as necessary."[139]

González, the interior minister, immediately met with Pérez and counseled that the legal position was clear that he had to complete his constitutional period, but that he should see Gómez to advise him that "such a procedure, was simply a 'congressional' coup d'etat."[140] The invisible hand behind the Tamayo and Beroes petition was Gómez himself. The dictator explained to the unfortunate Pérez when they met in Maracay that he was the "brains behind the maneuver"[141] because he wanted to find out who wanted to get rid of him within his inner circle. Gómez also considered that "this movement could overshadow the natural rhythm of political events, and therefore gave Dr. Pérez complete freedom to resign or stay because General Gómez could not force him to continue performing his duty when he felt he was unjustly attacked."[142]

At the end of the meeting, Pérez remained undecided which way to move. González sustained his judicial thesis because "he had a public mandate, which as it was conferred for a determined period could only be revoked by specific causes expressly established by the Constitution or by the law."[143] Moreover, Pérez had given no cause for his impeachment, as only two weeks before "all his acts were formally approved in definitive form."[144] Gómez sided with González's view that Pérez should not be pressured to resign, but he did not understand "how the President could have vacillated in assuming a determined attitude that in the future could undermine the constitutional authority vested in him."[145] In the meantime, Gómez took precautions by reinforcing the various barracks in case there was trouble. Pérez was asked to resign privately, but the president refused to do so,[146] forcing Congress, instigated by García Bustamante, on June 12 to request that if he did not resign within twenty-four hours they would take the necessary measures to impeach him. This threat was enough for Pérez to submit his resignation the following day on June 13, which was accepted by a joint session of Congress, and Itriago Chacín, the foreign affairs minister, was appointed caretaker president.[147]

Six days later, Congress elected Gómez as president, but to their consternation he refused. Gómez suggested instead that the legislative body should freely elect a president from their own ranks, throwing the proceedings into chaos. Congress was left in a quandary, as it could not elect anybody else but Gómez. García Bustamante traveled to Maracay to consult with Gómez, who expressed his desire to remain commander in chief of the armed forces but not head of government. Gómez was interested in knowing García Bustamante's choice for head of government, and when García Velasco's name was mentioned, he knew he had uncovered a conspiracy. Gómez banned García Bustamante from Maracay and sacked García Velasco, who was Federal District governor, from the cabinet.

Itriago Chacín on June 16, 1931, informed Congress of the problems that Gómez "is suffering as a result of the latest political events between Congress and the former President of the Republic"[148] and requested the Benemérito to "be at the head of the nation's destiny."[149] Gómez would only accept if Congress amended the constitution again, reverting back to the situation where the president was also chief of the armed forces. The modification only meant canceling the temporary changes made to articles 128–131 of the constitution. On July 11, Gómez accepted the presidency, stating that the "National Representation has demanded in the name of the fatherland my services to the Presidency. I am willing to take up the challenge with the same dedication as always."[150] Gómez accepted the appointment "as in other occasions, as Congress knows, I welcome it as a duty,"[151] and on July 13, 1931, at eleven a.m. he took the oath of allegiance.

González was left in a difficult position because if he had sided with Pérez he would be attacked for preventing Gómez's return, and if he had gone against Pérez, he could be accused of being part of the conspiracy. What González did in the end was to assume an attitude of indifference because if Pérez fought a legal battle to retain the presidency, then Congress and government would be split, and Pérez did not have the political acumen to deal with this. González admitted that the conspiracy was also against him, and thus when Gómez assumed power he was replaced by Pedro Rafael Tinoco.[152]

Rebels Gather Their Breath

After the ill-fated *Superior* expedition Urbina returned to Nice to brief Aranguren, who had partly financed the expedition.[153] In early January 1932, a directorate was formed presided over by Ortega Martínez, with Baptista, the war director, and Carabaño as chief of staff.[154] The revolutionaries also sought finance from the Mexican government, especially from Calles, who was now secretary for war. A number of plans were discussed with Aranguren, who was approached by several other revolutionaries for financial help up to the time of Gómez's death in December 1935. Urbina returned to Panama, where his situation "was relatively comfortable thanks to the aid that General Aranguren religiously sends from Europe."[155] Secure in his European homes, he continued his secret fight against Gómez. José Ignacio Cárdenas felt that Heyden Altuna, Aranguren's son-in-law, was plotting with his father-in-law to murder Gómez in Venezuela. Heyden Altuna, who enriched himself under Gómez's government "in close contact with his family,"[156] owned the trading firm of J. Roessner and Company, of which

Aranguren's son was a partner and which had special permission from the German government to export arms to Central and South America.

In June 1931, McGill took up residence in Barcelona (Spain) at a place called Nonanova, and a few months later, Ortega Martínez in September moved to Badalona, near Barcelona. M. Bustillos, the Venezuelan consul general at Barcelona, employed Antonio de Nait, a private detective, to keep an eye on McGill, "who nobody takes into account."[157] Ortega Martínez had not been idle with his time, and using McGill as chief negotiator, secured in Italy a ship of 1,500 tons with a maximum speed of fifteen knots, together with four thousand to five thousand Malinger rifles, one battery of field guns, three million rounds of ammunition, twenty-four machine guns, two thousand hand grenades, a hundred pistols, two navy cannons, six cannons, eight hundred shells for the above, four airplanes, four hundred bombs for airplanes together with minor items such as pistols and swords and half a ton of dynamite. The cost of this large arsenal was put at $350,000 but the seller was willing to take half with delivery of the ordnance and the rest "would be paid after victory."[158] The main problem, as usual, was the lack of funds, with the rebels turning to Aranguren for help; he was sufficiently intrigued to take a closer look. Aranguren was willing to fund the venture if others such as the Mexican government supported the rebels, sending for his trusted friend Urbina in Panama for a summit meeting in Nice with his aides.

In March 1932, Urbina set off for Europe, arriving in Hamburg in April, where he was met by Heyden Altuna.[159] Both men traveled to Paris, where Urbina acquired a new wardrobe and saw Roberto Machado Morales. Later, Urbina arrived in Nice for the summit meeting between Aranguren, Pedro Térega Fombona, and Heyden Altuna. The outcome was that Aranguren would back Ortega Martínez with Urbina as his chief of staff.[160] Héctor Aranda, the Venezuelan consul in Nice, kept a close watch of the rebels, but as a precaution another spy was sent in case they suspected him.[161] Urbina left Nice for Paris on May 16, with Aranguren following him to the French capital two days later. Heyden Altuna was sent on a secret mission to Mexico to meet Ortega Martínez Jr. and Alberto Mascareñas, the head of the Mexican central bank, and if possible Calles, to discuss Venezuela's liberation. Mascareñas would be briefed about Ortega Martínez, the group backing him, and the formation of a new political party, for him to persuade Calles "our great friend, with respect to the situation of Venezuela and the aid we expected from you."[162] For his part, Ortega Martínez from his base in Barcelona also alerted Calles that Mascareñas would discuss with him "a matter that when favorably resolved means liberation, and the eternal gratitude of a people from a neighboring country."[163] By early July, Heyden Altuna was back in Nice with encouraging news for Aranguren.

Political Debate among Rebels

While Ortega Martínez pursued his revolutionary dream, a political debate opened up in 1932 among the left-wing revolutionaries on the political strategy needed to topple Gómez. The PRV, led by Pulido Méndez and Zúñiga Cisneros, decided in early 1932 to make "a peaceful penetration into Venezuela by means of agents and propaganda."[164] Pocaterra was no longer interested in working with people who only made promises and was fed up with improvised plans because "they do not have a program nor a road to follow, nor an ideal but everything is resolved by reaching agreement with the *compadres* and sometimes with 'monkey business'"[165] (emphasis in original), and therefore "they imagine that we are all the same."[166] A good example of this occurred in Aruba after the 1929 Urbina/Fossi raid, when Fruytier, the Dutch governor, was recalled and replaced by Herman Schonberg, a military officer, and a warship was stationed permanently offshore from the island. In 1932, the Dutch authorities of Aruba uncovered a Venezuelan plot to "commit incendiarism [*sic*] and seize arms," which was very similar to the 1929 Urbina/Machado rebellion launched from neighboring Curacao.[167] According to Russell the "details had been carefully elaborated and if the plan had been carried out Aruba would have fallen prey to a great disaster."[168]

Pocaterra felt that the revolutionaries should no longer accept "*conditionally* money or men" because "the temptation not to comply and to lead one up the creek without a paddle"[169] was too great. Consequently, in July 1932 Pocaterra tried to get people "of certain caliber among the men *of action*"[170] (emphasis in original) to start a Unión Nacional Venezolana (UNV) in Montreal, with Arévalo Cedeño as commander in chief of the army. The supreme leader was Pocaterra, with Santos Domínici as the president of the revolutionary junta and Rufino Blanco Fombona as secretary.[171] The UNV was a loose group of individuals under the guidance of Pocaterra trying to achieve a unified front without a formal structure such as an organizing committee, with no "agendas, or things like that,"[172] in order to strike when the time was ripe. Pocaterra asked Rómulo Betancourt and his ARDI organization to join them until Gómez had been defeated, when all parties would be free to carry out whatever policies they pursued. The UNV wanted to attack both eastern and western Venezuela simultaneously, to take Maracaibo and the Tuy valley, with Pocaterra invading via Borburata.

In pursuit of his goal, Pocaterra at the beginning of September 1932 located in Mexico a cache of arms together with "two Corsair airplanes, sufficient bombs, five hundred rifles with half a million rounds and forty five Tompson [*sic*] that are decisive in the fast attack that I am going to carry out."[173] All that was needed was $4,000 to pay for a ship to take the men and arms to Venezuela. In New York the talk among the revolutionaries was about "Pocaterra's revolution," and it was even rumored that he had acquired "some military material in Canada and $150,000 in cash." Pocaterra felt that the time was ripe and was willing to go to Europe to organize the expedition.[174] Pocaterra tried again in November to persuade Aranguren to part with the $25,000 needed to secure the arms, writing to both Aranguren and Smith:

> Until yesterday a small group of two or three "caudillos" would pledge their reduced wherewithal to achieve what they wanted, but not now, because it is no longer a *military* problem that at times is reduced to two or three encounters, with the *strongest encounter at a predetermined point*—but to have the flexibility and political energy to know when to *sweep inside* until we can determine—now in the field of battle—the natural course the revolution should take and to present the manifesto of "Venezuelan National Union" as a reality, in a strong doctrinaire fashion and *armed*, well armed, Don Antonio.[175] (emphasis in original)

While Pocaterra organized his rebellion, negotiations for a ship and arms for the Ortega Martínez revolution proceeded relatively well. McGill kept the identity of the main arms supplier hidden in order to maintain secrecy, but the vendor would travel on board the ship with the crew and officers.[176] As usual, the trouble was securing sufficient funds for the revolution. In August 1932, Ortega Martínez appealed to Aranguren for at least $100,000, which would be the initial down payment; by the end of the month it was reduced to $70,000, "but in that case, the steamboat on the list should not appear as sold but leased, with the option to purchase at an agreed price after our success."[177] Aranguren was not too impressed with the plan because with $100,000 it would be possible to obtain "sufficient material including a ship and airplanes, because there are adventurers that would join the rebellion in order to profit from its success."[178] The rebels received a boost when Arturo Alessandri Palma in Chile was elected president because the Chilean-born McGill felt that he could be "very helpful in certain ways."[179]

In the meantime, Aranguren negotiated with M. K. de Trairup, the head of the British European Consolidating Trust, an advance for $150,000 to the revolution by promising to treble the money invested once the revolutionaries achieved power together with the award of oil concessions.[180] Aranguren was convinced that the British company would put up the money, but no firm commitment was reached, and negotiations were discontinued. Unable to find any backers,[181] Aranguren refused to commit his money to an underfinanced venture. The money needed for the revolution was around $350,000,[182] but Aranguren was only willing to finance a part of it. Consequently, the expedition that united Ortega Martínez, Urbina, Pocaterra, and McGill was cancelled because of insufficient funds.[183]

Mexico Withdraws

The Venezuelan rebels received a further blow when in 1933 they lost the support of the Mexican government because it wanted to renew diplomatic relations with Venezuela. The Mexican government was finding that its rupture of diplomatic relations with Venezuela and also Peru was isolating it from the rest of Latin America. In May 1933, José Manuel Puig Casauranc, the Mexican foreign affairs minister, informed Calles, the *jefe máximo,* that its broken diplomatic relations with both Venezuela and Peru were causing "problems with other countries that are of greater interest to us."[184] Moreover, the Mexicans wanted to get the United States to accept the policy of nonintervention that was to be discussed at the forthcoming Seventh Pan American Conference at Montevideo in December 1933. It was felt that Mexico's position would have greater resonance if the country did not have any outstanding diplomatic problems in the region. Arcaya counseled Gómez that "General Calles, who is the one governing there, has never been your enemy. General Obregón, directed by Vasconcelos, was your enemy but when Calles succeeded him in 1925 he suspended the expedition organized by Obregón."[185] Although Urbina was helped later by Generals Amaro and Juan Almazán, Arcaya felt that Calles and the nominal president Ortiz Rubio were sincere and advised that "in my judgment the renewal of diplomatic relations would be convenient in order to take away from the enemies that conspiratorial nest and if Mexico appointed D [*sic*] Nemesio García Naranjo as Minister in Venezuela, this would be a tremendous feather in your cap."[186] Diplomatic relations between Mexico and Venezuela were renewed on July 24, 1933.

Rebels Continue their Quest

At the beginning of 1933 Aranguren was convinced that Gómez was very ill and near death and that Eustoquio Gómez would replace him. Aranguren's own revolutionary plans, headed by Ortega Martínez, with McGill second in command, were stalled because of a lack of financial support. Aranguren now sought to secure the backing of those who had hitherto favored Gómez, such as his friend Julio Méndez, Gómez's son-in-law, who in turn would attract others to his cause.[187] Ortega Martínez urged Aranguren to continue his pressure "until he convinces his friends" about the money because "you need to be blind not to see that the opportunity is *unique*"[188] (emphasis in original).

Gómez's spies in Europe reported that Aranguren's revolutionary activity was on the increase. Heyden Altuna was negotiating weapons with a "Belgian rogue, condemned to jail in Belgium prior to this."[189] Soon afterwards, Aranguren called off the deal with the Belgians, with Ortega Martínez complaining bitterly that "tomorrow these gentlemen will regret not listening to the deal proposed by you with a 90 percent chance of success, or to be more exact a deal without risk."[190] The rebels still felt that they could count on the $70,000 offered by Aranguren, but this too was not forthcoming. McGill started getting impatient about the lack of progress, pressing Aranguren for a firm answer by March 1933, while Ortega Martínez wanted to know whether he could count on the $70,000 offered to him.[191] Aranguren, however, concluded in April that it was "pointless to continue trying to solve the problem in the erroneous way that we have pursued so far. New routes are available now and it is not possible or patriotic to abandon hope of reconquering our beloved fatherland."[192] Soon after this disappointment, disillusionment set in, as the revolutionaries realized that they would have to wait until Gómez's death to see their country liberated from his rule. Ortega Martínez wrote to Aranguren in April 1933, stating that "what is certain is that after so many lost efforts we will have to resign ourselves to wait for the 'Unico' to die."[193]

Pocaterra, however, did not give up hope, stating in May 1933 that support for the rebels in Venezuela was on the increase especially in Caracas, with "people who have control of forces etc."[194] and that "onepower [*sic*]" had been "dismissed by his supporters with the 'malaise' of the people he had close to government."[195] The demands of the rebels were reduced in May, with Pocaterra wanting to know whether it would be possible to get $50,000 from Aranguren. The Venezuelan oil man finally relented, promising to contribute toward the expedition,[196] but this proved an empty gesture as no funds were forthcoming. At the end of 1933, McGill lost all hope of getting support from "the man in the air who looks for new directions that will lead him to the same result."[197] In May 1934, it was reported that Nogales Méndez, alias Rafael Inchauste, was trying to secure funds for a revolution he was planning, but the revolutionaries in Spain, such as the McGill family and Ortega Martínez, who had a prostate operation in August 1934, were in a poor economic state. Ortega Martínez was very fat, and his family lived in "an economic situation that is rather poor not to say outright misery, cheap hotel of 8 to 10 pesetas, in the so-called Piedra Paseo de Gracia,"[198] with his son running a poultry business in Badalona. In contrast, Aranguren had an apartment in Madrid and did not lack money, increasing his wealth in 1934, when he sold his shares in the Creole Syndicate, a company registered in Delaware, in which the Venezuelan oil millionaire held a production royalty and which had acquired the National Reserves held by the Compañia Venezolana de Petróleo.[199]

Arévalo Cedeño Tries Peru Again

Arévalo Cedeño was one rebel who did not give up his revolutionary dream. The new Peruvian government of General Oscar Benavides in 1933 offered Arévalo Cedeño a cache of arms, giving Pocaterra's revolutionary plans a boost. Arévalo Cedeño received word that the generous offer made by Sánchez Cerro prior to his assassination would be reactivated by Benavides. On May 4, 1933, Arévalo Cedeño and a Venezuelan colleague named Chifoni arrived in El Callao and quickly made their way to Lima, where Pedro Ugarteche of the Peruvian Foreign Affairs Ministry met them. Andrés E. Rota, the Venezuelan consul, had his own detective follow Arévalo Cedeño. The following day, Arévalo Cedeño saw Dr. Luis A. Flores, the minister of the navy and air force, who also headed the Sanchezcerrista Party, informing him that all or part of the cache of arms promised by Sánchez Cerro "would be available for his revolutionary plans."[200] Arévalo Cedeño met with Luis Velazco Aragón, who represented the province of Cuzco, as well as Colonel Manuel Esteban Rodríguez, the military chief of the presidential palace, who occupied the same position during Sánchez Cerro's short presidency.[201] At the meeting, Colonel Rodríguez gave Arévalo Cedeño the impression that he was speaking on behalf of Benavides, who promised delivery of the arms and ammunition.[202] However, when Arévalo Cedeño saw Benavides, the meeting lasted only ten minutes, leading Rota to suspect that the Venezuelan revolutionary's quest for help had been fruitless.

Arévalo Cedeño continued his talks with Ugarteche and Manuel Fernández, his representative in Peru, and Major Morán of the Peruvian general staff of the army in the vain hope of obtaining some of the arms, with Rota reporting that "negotiations have become more difficult."[203] Nevertheless, Arévalo Cedeño continued with his plans, acquiring a ship in Kingston, Jamaica, in May 1933. The boat would be used to attack eastern Venezuela and then proceed to Puerto Cabello. Arévalo Cedeño would use the same plan as in 1931: he would fly to Iquitos to pick up the ordnance and then proceed to Manaos and enter Venezuela by San Fernando de Atabapo, where he had a further cache of rifles hidden. Benavides at the last minute changed his mind and did not release the arms to Arévalo Cedeño, informing Rota that he only wanted cordial relations with Venezuela.

The Doroteo Flores Rebellion

At the end of 1933, Flores mounted an expedition from Trinidad to invade Venezuela. A number of arms and ammunition were secretly sent to Venezuela hidden in barrels of cement and sent to the Lower Orinoco, while other arms were buried in the Gulf of Paria. One of the main organizers was Enrique Silva Pérez. Later, Arévalo Cedeño, Sixto Gil, and Urbina met at Ducharne's farm at Filet in Trinidad to see whether they could secure the cache of arms that Flores had lost or buried in the Gulf of Paria. The plan was "to distract attention with their movement in the East to encourage the mobilization of Government troops toward that part of the country, while the rebels attacked Puerto Cabello."[204] On November 16, 1933, the *Margarita*, a Venezuelan ship of 196 tons, arrived in Trinidad from Martinique carrying on board Captain Camps de Fense. He brought Arévalo Cedeño's news to the Venezuelan revolutionaries resident in Trinidad that Captain Hansen of the *Margarita* had promised to "help the subversive movement."[205]

On Saturday, December 16, the *Delta* left Trinidad for Ciudad Bolívar at nine o'clock in the evening. When it reached Boca de Pedernales at two thirty a.m., it found the Standard Oil Company light tower at Capure out of order. The captain was surprised at this but was informed that the lighthouse had been switched off because it was Saturday, with the rebels having to wait until the morning before they could cross the sandbar. Flores, De Fense, and Arévalo Cedeño planned to take the *Delta*, but the ship had sailed two days earlier than planned in order to pick up former Minister and Bolívar State President Alamo and his family in Ciudad Bolívar before December 19. Although the expedition was not ready and had insufficient arms, the two leaders, Flores and Bartolomé Ferrer, received last minute orders to attack.[206] The revolutionaries would use two ships, the *Margarita* and *Samson* to attack the *Delta* before it reached the Orinoco, with a Shell tug boat, captained by De Fense, following with armed men to attack Tucupita. The *Delta* would then be used to attack other settlements on the coast while supporting a general uprising in Monagas. There were thirty-five men in total, mostly made up of "delinquents and fugitives from Venezuelan prisons imprisoned for common crimes."[207] The Flores revolution had a red and black flag with the insignia "By Reason or By Force. Long Live the Revolution." A few days before the attack, however, the *Margarita* became separated from the convoy, and the captain of the *Samson*, believing that the authorities had uncovered the plot, "escaped to San Vicente from where he has not returned."[208] Flores was in his own boat, the *Blanca*, but this sunk after hitting a rock in dense fog off Pedernales, with both Flores and Benjamín drowning.[209] After rescuing the survivors, the other launch returned to Trinidad, where Arévalo Cedeño and Urbina were waiting. The small cache of arms of forty rifles, eighteen Mauser carbines, ten hand grenades, and eighteen dozen machetes, together with ammunition that was saved after the failure of the revolution in Trinidad, was first hidden on Gasparillo Island and then moved to Barataria, close to Port of Spain.[210] P. López Tejera, the Venezuelan consul on the island, convinced the authorities to expel Hansen, the engineer Jack Dunn, and two other sailors, "calling the rest of the crew to the Office of the General Consulate to advise them of the danger they faced."[211] A new captain, Valentín Chávez, was appointed who was "worthy of confidence."[212]

The *Unión Nacional*

In Cuba, Eduardo Héctor Machado headed the Unión Nacional (Agrupación Cívico Militar Venezolana). He arrived in the country in 1929 and immediately started to organize local opposition groups, making contact with the university students to "organize them in a secret association," which according to Machado was the "precursor of ABC and its main founders."[213] Machado was also involved "with all the other revolutionary sectors, making and teaching how to manufacture bombs, grenades and mines; I smuggled arms and exiled men, and got others out whose lives were in danger,"[214] while conspiring with navy officers. Moreover, "Colonel Mendieta, the current President, appointed me an officer on his military staff prior to the failed 1931 coup."[215] In the 1933 revolution, Machado was involved in street skirmishes and was given command of a platoon. As a reward, he was promised a gift of a thousand rifles, half a million rounds, four machine guns with tripod and four hand machine guns, two cannons, and a boat "that is in bad shape but repairable."[216] The Cuban government was also selling four thousand rifles, with Eduardo Machado urging Aranguren to acquire them. In June 1934, Eduardo Machado, who was now an instructor with the Cuban navy at the Ariel Naval Academy, spoke with Colonel Fulgencio Batista at his home in Camp Columbia, who reinforced his offer "to help our enterprise giving us guns and ammunition, . . . machine guns, a few boxes of hand grenades and mortars and possibly . . . two Corsair airplanes."[217] Batista would be repaid after the revolution had been a success.

In October 1934, after the Cuban government acquired the *Falke* from its owners in Hull, Eduardo Machado tried convincing Aranguren to purchase the ship; no suspicion would be raised because "the boat is owned by the Navy and through them I will act in a very discreet manner."[218] When Aranguren declined, Eduardo Machado turned to Rivas Vásquez, whose business partner in Havana was Clemente Vázquez Bello, secretary to President Machado, seeking $10,000 to purchase the *Falke*, but Machado was unsuccessful.[219] José Heriberto López then suggested to Aranguren that the ship *Yuque* should be acquired in Cuba. The revolutionaries would gather in Havana and plan the expedition, especially as there was so much goodwill on the part of the Cuban authorities toward the Venezuelan rebels.

The idea was later taken up in April 1935, when President Carlos Mendieta of Cuba offered to help "in various ways the Venezuelan subversives."[220] Machado started selling bonds "at the rate of between five and ten dollars, with a guarantee of one hectare of Venezuelan land for every five dollars."[221] The bonds were marketed by López Méndez, Simón Betancourt, Rafael Martínez Duarte, E. Piñango Lara, and others. The aim was to raise $20,000 from people in New York to acquire the ship and arms from the Cuban government. An expedition against Venezuela, captained by Urbina, who was forced to leave Cuba for Panama after Carlos Aponte shot and wounded him in the leg,[222] would then be organized. The harbor costs would be paid later. According to Rincones, Machado was taking special care of the *Falke,* "preparing it and taking it out to sea once in a while."[223] Machado counted on the "the greed of Fulgencio Batista, who would do anything when offered the $20,000."[224] These plans would soon be confined to the waste paper bin when Gómez died in his sleep on December 19, 1935.

The Pérez presidency showed that with Gómez in the wings it was better to have him at the helm rather than as a puppet master. The maneuver for his succession revealed the internal divisions within the Gomecista regime that Gómez stamped out in a masterly political stroke. After the failure of the *Superior* expedition, it was clear that the exiles would have to wait until Gómez's death to continue their struggle for political change in the country. Although attempts to topple Gómez continued up until his death of natural causes in 1935, the dictator was never in danger of being ousted. Ultimately his longevity sapped the energy of the exiles, with most admitting defeat. The revolutionaries toward the end of the Gómez regime were a spent force, with many having lost much of their funds and living in poverty. Ortega Martínez, a rich man in 1908, was living in poverty in Spain. Arévalo Cedeño in November 1934 was in St. Thomas managing a small trading business of "fighting cockerels and firewater,"[225] which allowed him to travel around the West Indies. In Cuba, Urbina, after his encounter with Aponte, left for Panama, where he was in an "almost miserable state."[226]

CHAPTER TEN

The Succession Is Resolved

After Gómez took over the presidency in 1931, his health began to deteriorate; he became physically frail and visibly elderly, although he remained mentally alert. Gómez was convinced that his army continued to back him, stating in 1932 that the armed forces had "deserved, as always, special attention"[1] because although "I have not maintained it perfectly organized from the material point of view . . . I have given it the highest recompense needed to maintain an efficient environment of morality, order and discipline."[2] At the time, Gómez's travel movements were shrouded in mystery, only allowing people to know his final destination at the last minute. When he moved from Maracay to Caracas, the move was extremely competently organized by a former Uhlan officer, previously connected with the German espionage service. According to Keeling "as soon as the word is given lorry after lorry pours out, carrying beds, furniture, linen, crockery, German waiters, jazz bands, not to mention food and all supplies."[3] Once all this was ready, at a given moment "the President himself appears always beaming at the head of the cortege of Lincoln cars, followed by his suite."[4]

The regime appeared to be mellowing, with Gómez accepting Arcaya's suggestion in July 1934 that a goodwill gesture by the government would be to "empty the jails of political prisoners and to allow the return of all Venezuelans who want to come back as peaceful and orderly people."[5] He freed 150 political prisoners on December 19 of that year. Many of the newly released prisoners, who had been held in La Rotunda, were expelled from the country because of their communist ideas. Most headed for Cúcuta, but those with sufficient wherewithal traveled to the United States, France, Spain, or Trinidad. At the beginning of 1935, more political prisoners were released, including Gabaldón, Mibelli, and those captured during the *Falke* imbroglio. Delgado Chalbaud Gómez wrote, "It is clear that Gómez does not govern in an absolute manner, because that general amnesty is against all his principles."[6] Within the Gomecista regime it was decided that the best way forward politically would be to allow Gómez to rule until 1936, when a new president would be elected. In the event of Gómez's death preceding the end of his term of office, Gil Fortoul in 1933 designed a compromise solution known as the Peace Pact, which was agreed to by a number of influential people. The pact allowed López Contreras to take over the presidency until Congress elected a provisional president, who would govern for the remainder of the constitutional period; during that time "free political debate by the candidates would be allowed and one of these will be *elected by the people*"[7] (emphasis in original).

Although Gómez was now physically frail, his mental capacity had not left him, and at the end of 1933 he summoned to Caracas seven of his state presidents. They eventually remained for a year in Caracas while the respective secretary generals governed the states in their absence. Gómez's health continued to deteriorate, however. Although it was apparent to some influential ministers that Gómez would be unable to govern during the following presidential period of 1936–43, there were people who still wanted him to continue in power. On July 17, 1935, E. Ramón París organized a workers' manifestation "in support and exaltation of you for the Presidency of the Republic for the next presidential period."[8] The Workers Association and Civic Groups of the Federal District met to organize a march in support of Gómez. However, Velasco Bustamante, the Federal District governor, and Tinoco, the interior minister did not allow it. The main problem for the regime remained the succession to the Benemérito. There were two main political factions within the Gomecista regime, namely, López Contreras and Eustoquio Gómez, with Delgado Chalbaud Gómez commenting in January 1935 that "one will have to eliminate the other."[9] Gómez and his political opponents were well aware that if he died without a clear and acceptable successor, the country could degenerate into anarchy.

Gómez's candidate for the succession was López Contreras, who according to Nemesio Parada had the support of a "great number of heads of barracks,"[10] most of the state presidents, many of the secretary generals of the regional governments, as well as "priests, retailers and intellectuals in all parts of the country."[11] López Contreras, who appeared to be incorruptible and the best bet for a smooth transition in 1936, had, according to John Simon, the British minister, the "extraordinary record of being the only Venezuelan politician who ever remained poor."[12] López Contreras started in 1933 to prepare his way to the presidency using José Murillo as his intermediary between the Gomecistas and the non-Gomecistas. Murillo's job was to secure as much support as possible for the defense minister, with Pérez Soto the first to join the López Contreras camp. Isaías Medina Angarita, who was López Contreras's secretary, was one of his most enthusiastic collaborators, getting the support of Jurado, García Velasco, Velasco Bustamante, Sayago, and Ernesto Velasco Ibarra, who headed the troops stationed in Maracay. In Táchira, Father Moncada acted as the intermediary between López Contreras and the revolutionaries in Colombia such as Olivares, who was living in Bucaramanga.[13] López Contreras between 1933 and 1934 extended his network of supporters in the Andes, which included the "Araujos, Doctor Alfonzo Mejía and other distinguished Trujillano politicians,"[14] General Gofredo Massini and Hugo Parra Pérez in Mérida, and General José Antonio González and Amenodoro Rangel Lemus in Táchira. Gómez's death in December 1935 put an end to these plans.

Eustoquio Gómez and Tinoco, the interior minister, were two other possible candidates for the presidency, with the latter allegedly at the time receiving oil company backing. Eustoquio Gómez had the support of his son Josué, president of Portuguesa, and Colonel Pedro José Gómez, head of the Batallón de la Guarnición of Maracay and Tarazona. The rest of the Gómez clan did not want Eustoquio to assume power. The clan Núñez, which dominated Maracay just prior to Gómez's death, was instrumental in removing Rafael Requena, the president's secretary. Keeling, the special British envoy, commented that the dictator's sons "are unlikely to play any great political role, though one of them takes an interest in petroleum and other commercial questions and concession hunters consider it useful to have him on their side."[15]

Ortega Martínez explained to Aranguren in 1934 that when Gómez finally died, the country could degenerate into "bloody chaos that would be translated in the rural districts into agrarian banditry, Aztec style, and in the cities in the union of gangsters, with the consequent ruin of the country and lowering the value of property and other industrial assets."[16] The problem was that if it was not managed properly, then "the men of moral responsibility have defrauded the masses in their wishes for vindication and freedom, throwing themselves unquestionably into the hands of Communism, and not precisely Soviet communism, but libertarian or anarchic communism without any constructive aspiration but only to destroy and rob."[17] There was thus a new, far greater threat to the stability of the country, one that was much more dangerous than the previous regime. Keeling reported in the early part of 1934 that until recently "the view held by even his most violent opponents has been that bad as the Gómez regime is, any other would be infinitely worse."[18] With the political situation deteriorating, the opinion now among what he called the "more responsible commercial elements" was that "almost any change of government would be an advantage."[19] Moreover, it was felt that if these feelings of restlessness were not properly managed by those at the center who saw themselves as the legitimate successors, then the situation could develop "into serious trouble in the event of the death of the President."[20]

There was further trouble on the horizon in the Dutch colonial islands. In Aruba, the Liga Obrera, headed by J. H. Eman, was formed on November 1, 1934, to fight for workers' protection and compensation as a result of the Lago Oil and Transport Company reducing wages by between 20 and 30 percent at its Aruba refinery. As with other workers' associations in Curacao, Venezuelan government agents infiltrated the league, with Gómez kept well informed on possible future disturbances or strikes. Despite these measures, some of the oil companies were sure that once Gómez was out of the picture there would be trouble in the oil fields similar to that experienced by Mexico. Mr. Watson, manager of the Caribbean Petroleum Company confided to Keeling, the special British envoy, that he anticipated trouble at Gómez's death. Doyle, the former undersecretary of state, who subsequently became the doyen of oilmen in Venezuela and knew the country well, was more sanguine about the future and did not share these fears.[21]

At the beginning of 1934, there were three distinct groups among the exiled groups opposed to the Gómez regime. One group was headed by Flores Cabrera and Juan A. Padilla, another by Jorge Luciani and Manuel Jové, who spent most of the time arguing among themselves; and, finally there were the communists, including Carlos López Bustamante, Carlos Fleury, López Octavio, and José Antonio Gil, who were financially supported by the Soviet Union. Other exiles such as Cesareo Suárez, who was a cousin of Smith, were involved in establishing a labor movement, working on the first edition of *Obrero Libre* as well as being involved with two other groups in New York, the Pro-Presos Políticos Venezolanos and the Centro Venezolano de Trabajores. At the end of 1934, a number of factions within the country started to gravitate toward one of the two Gomecista groups that were maneuvering for power to prepare for the 1936 elections. Florencio Gómez Núñez, Gómez's youngest son, founded the *El Venezolano* newspaper, which was edited by Arturo Uslar Pietri.[22] It was clear at the beginning of 1935 that there were two strong factions with a real chance of succeeding Gómez, viz, López Contreras and Eustoquio Gómez, the president of Lara State, since he could also count on the support of Josué Gómez, Galavís, Jurado, Silverio González, and Salvador Uzcátegui, presidents of Portuguesa, Yaracuy, Falcón, Trujillo, and Barinas respectively, as well as the Fourth Army Brigade stationed in Táchira, headed by Tarazona, together with numerous other officers stationed in Maracay, Valencia, and Ocumare.

The End Is Near

In the early days of December 1935, with Gomez's health deteriorating rapidly, Eustoquio Gómez informed Colonel Eloy Montenegro, the civil chief of Barquisimeto, that "the General leaves nothing organized, so that the situation for us is quite alarming."[23] Gómez at his Maracay residence early in the morning of December 13 sent for his personal physicians, Drs. Leopoldo López Rodríguez and Ramón Ignacio Méndez Llamozas, informing them that "last night I felt something so great that I felt I would die,"[24] but "I struggled strongly with death and . . . I won."[25] After this heart attack it was becoming clear that Gómez was dying, although there was an outside chance that he might recover.

Meanwhile, at the Defense Ministry in Caracas, López Contreras received a delegation, headed by General Ernesto Velasco Ibarra, who informed him that they would support his candidacy for the presidency in the event of Gómez's death. Pérez Soto, Eustoquio Gómez, and Galavís saw López Contreras after Velasco Ibarra left, wanting him to smooth the succession after Gómez's death. López Contreras did not reveal his hand, informing them that he could only work within the framework set by the constitution. Later, Eustoquio Gómez and López Contreras met again at the house of Regina Gómez (Gómez's daughter) in Maracay together with Colmenares Pacheco and his wife, Emilia Gómez. López Contreras told Eustoquio Gómez the unpalatable truth that the country would degenerate into anarchy if the Gomecistas did not cooperate with a transitional government. Eustoquio Gómez agreed to back López Contreras for the time being but was already scheming to take power, with his trusted Tarazona mobilizing his supporters on Gómez's farms in Aragua and Carabobo in order to arm them when they reached Maracay. Tarazona had already commandeered the national police for his own service. On December 15, Eustoquio Gómez suggested to Montenegro that he should remain loyal, obeying his orders and not those of López Contreras, and start organizing his own supporters while awaiting instructions. The same orders were repeated to other chiefs. Tarazona meanwhile kept mobilizing peasants and officers, such as Colonel Pedro Gómez and Captain Leal to support Eustoquio Gómez, and the *jefe de guarnición* of Barquisimeto was bribed with $510,204 to join their ranks. Colonel Leopoldo Briceño Torres informed López Contreras that Commander Guillermo Abreu from the Limón barracks had sent him five large boxes of arms, two from the Girardot battalion and three from the Sucre battalion. Moreover, Briceño Torres stated that the "revolution would be at close range using revolvers; that the brothers Gómez and Don Eustoquio are giving General Lopez a sweet hand in order to seize him and force him to hand over command."[26]

López Contreras, before leaving Caracas for Maracay, reinforced the capital's barracks with loyal troops as well as distributing arms to close supporters in Maracay and La Victoria. López Contreras arrived in the capital of Aragua State "with sufficient troops and war matériel to dominate or to beat anyone in the indicated cities or any strong groups that opposed my authority."[27] On December 16, the Gomecista conspiracy was uncovered when a telegram from Eustoquio Gómez to Montenegro was intercepted. Tarazona and the officers under his command in the battalions of Maracay and Ocumare were detained. On hearing the news, Eustoquio Gómez, accompanied by his brothers, rushed to see López Contreras to inquire whether such a measure was appropriate. The defense minister's reply was very clear, informing the conspirators that he was "against all opposition, resolving to maintain my authority and order in Maracay and in the rest of the country, being responsible to General Gómez while he is alive, and later to the Cabinet."[28] The following morning, there was intense agitation in Maracay over Tarazona's conspiracy, after Tarazona was arrested at ten a.m. together with other officers. Eustoquio Gómez was now alone, having lost his main co-conspirator.

While this activity was happening, Gómez, in the privacy of his Spartan bedroom, was given some corn porridge at ten in the morning by Ulises

Sánchez, his son-in-law. This turned out to be his last meal. Moments later, he had another attack of delirium and at one in the afternoon entered into a diabetic coma that proved fatal. A blood transfusion from his grandson Carlos Eduardo Cárdenas Gómez extended Gómez's life until just before midnight, when "the tyrant par excellence that America produced,"[29] as Federico García Lorca would later write, finally passed away in his sleep at 11:45 p.m. Soon afterwards his close family entered the room one by one to pay their last respects, followed by several officers, with Colonel José María Márquez "vividly moved, his eyes awash with tears."[30] On hearing the news of Gómez's death, Eustoquio Gómez expressed his grief and admiration when he stated that Gómez had been a "hell of a man. Even death had to struggle to knock him down."[31]

Politics Continues

It was imperative to appoint a successor immediately in order to avoid any possible disruption. Forty-five minutes after Gómez had taken his last breath, the cabinet gathered in Maracay at twelve thirty a.m. to appoint an interim president. There were two candidates, López Contreras, the defense minister, and Tinoco, the interior minister. Although it was a foregone conclusion who would be appointed, a debate took place on the merit of both candidates. Efraín González, the finance minister, favored López Contreras, arguing that he was the man needed for the occasion because he would preserve law and order. Tinoco argued that a civilian was needed to guarantee oil investments in the country. In the end, it was a one-horse race, with López Contreras winning by seven votes to one and appointed interim president. Later that morning, in a conciliatory gesture to the country, López Contreras freed a number of political prisoners. This was badly received by the Gómez clan, especially Eustoquio Gómez, who considered the presidential chair as his rightful inheritance. The move was interpreted as an ominous sign that the power of the Gómez clan was diminishing. López Contreras also refused to appoint Medina Angarita, who was related to Gómez and was *comandante interino* of Maracay and *jefe del batallón* of the Cuartel Nacional. It was clear that Eustoquio and López Contreras were on a collusion course. When López Contreras paid his last respects to Gómez, he bumped into Eustoquio Gómez, who "at the very moment that I entered, left violently accompanied by his brothers."[32]

While Gómez was buried in Maracay on December 19 in a large solemn funeral, a mob in Caracas gathered at the Pabellón del Hipódromo and then proceeded to the governor's residence in Plaza Bolívar. Velasco Bustamante, looking very pale and agitated, appeared on the balcony to appease the mob, which was growing angrier by the minute. The governor had more than $255,102 in the palace safe and wanted permission from the secretary of the presidency to use force to keep the mob under control. The cistern lorries of the refuse collection service used their water hoses to disperse the mob, but they were hijacked by the crowd, who started throwing stones and breaking windows. After a few minutes, the governor withdrew, and the soldiers drawn in front of the building in a protective cordon were ordered to fire over the heads of the mob. However, a number of civil servants "acting evidently under Velasco Bustamante's orders, opened fire from the balcony with revolvers and, it is alleged, with a machine gun."[33] In the ensuing panic a massacre took place, with about twenty people killed and approximately forty wounded.[34] The municipal police chased the mob, firing repeatedly with their revolvers, "while from the ceiling and windows of the government building other shots were fired."[35] Soon the palace was cleared, but owing to the large number of deaths, Velasco Bustamante was replaced that evening by Galavís. The mob then sacked the *Nuevo Diario* newspaper and Velasco Bustamante's house.

In the afternoon of December 20, López Contreras entered Caracas triumphantly and in charge of the government. Eustoquio Gómez, who was determined to be the eventual president of Venezuela and maintain the Gomecista grip on the country, arrived in Caracas the following day with his brother Fernando and son-in-law Leopoldo Briceño Torres. Eustoquio Gómez saw López Contreras at Miraflores, "making a strong representation over what had been agreed in Las Delicias prior to the death of the Dictator."[36] Clearly, López Contreras disagreed and advised him to leave for Maracay, where he would be safer than in Barquisimeto, where he was still state president, because "many acts against him personally had already taken place."[37] As an alternative, López Contreras offered to fly him to Curacao, but Eustoquio Gómez opted for Maracay, leaving the Miraflores palace at nine in the morning and heading for Governor Galavís's office, where a mob once again gathered outside. When the mob saw him, they started shouting, "Death to the Gómezes! Down with the Gómezes," with Eustoquio Gómez replying, "Damn it, there are still some Gómezes alive!" and daring them to "kill me."[38]

Following Eustoquio Gómez's departure, López Contreras immediately telephoned Galavís, who was accompanied by Jesús Corao, to warn him of the forthcoming visit and to make sure that the governor saw him straight away. At the meeting, Corao rather tactlessly advised Galavís in the presence of Eustoquio that law and order in Caracas would be difficult to maintain while "that man"[39] (Eustoquio Gómez) was in the city. Eustoquio Gómez, offended by Corao's tone, admonished him: "More respect, young man. I am General Eustoquio Gómez."[40] At this point Corao was ordered to leave the room, and Eustoquio tried to get Galavís on his side by confiding to him that López Contreras had betrayed him. Galavís repeated the advice given to him by the acting president that his life was in danger and that he should leave for Maracay, where he would be given armed protection. Eustoquio Gómez continued to argue his case for staying in the capital. Aware that nothing was accomplished, Galavís telephoned López Contreras at ten that morning and told him that Eustoquio Gómez was not being helpful. At this point López Contreras ordered Eustoquio Gómez arrested and sent to Maracay, where he would be placed on an airplane to Curacao if he did not cooperate.

Galavís tried one last time to get Eustoquio Gómez to leave peacefully, threatening him with arrest if he did not leave, but he refused and made a gesture as though he was going to pull his gun out. Before this happened, Galavís grabbed his two hands, disarming and arresting him. Eustoquio Gómez was immediately taken "by force toward the private salon of the Governor," where moments later "two shots were heard and Don Eustoquio fell headlong on a leather armchair," with one bullet destroying his liver.[41] Briceño Torres was also disarmed without trouble, but he accused them of murdering a sick man suffering from hemiplegia.[42] Eustoquio Gómez's body was later placed on a campaign bed at the entrance of the urinal at the police headquarters that had direct access from the governor's palace. Eustoquio Gómez's assassin is unknown, but the prime suspect was Jesús Corao. López Contreras in his memoirs is adamant that if Eustoquio Gómez had not died, he would have murdered Galavís during his arrest.

Reaction to Gómez's Death

As soon as news reached Maracaibo of Gómez's death, a group of youths took over the radio station Ecos del Zulia and started to "harangue the people to assume a revolutionary attitude appropriate for the moment."[43] The adverse reaction to Gómez's death was greater in Maracaibo than in Caracas, with Pérez Soto, who was in Maracay at the time, appealing to the population to remain calm. He was warned, however, that his life was in danger if he returned to Zulia. In the meantime, the rebels held talks with Colonel Chacón, the army commander of Zulia, to gain his support, but he remained loyal to the government. Nevertheless, the relationship between the national guard and the police became appreciably tense, "and there were sporadic clashes in the streets, culminating in an exchange of shots between the Veterans barracks and the Government Palace, which had posted guards on the roof,"[44] with Severiano Rodríguez Hernández, a young law student, killed during this encounter. At his funeral, a skirmish took place among the large crowd that attended, and a further ten people were killed, with twenty-eight shops sacked at an estimated loss of $1,020,408.

In the oil towns of Lagunillas and Cabimas, Gómez's death was openly celebrated, with the oil workers going on strike while others sought revenge on every police officer they could find. The number of people killed in the two towns was estimated at two hundred. An eyewitness account related how a bloodthirsty crowd armed with machetes and about twelve rifles soaked an obnoxious watchman in gasoline and set him on fire. On December 22, a fire was deliberately started in the center of Maracaibo, destroying many businesses situated between the lakeshore and La Industria Avenue. Further rioting and pillaging followed, with the loss of millions of bolívares in merchandise. Jurado was appointed the new president of Zulia by the newly formed government of López Contreras. On his arrival in Maracaibo on Christmas Eve, Jurado immediately sent 150 troops to the oil fields, managing to restore law and order and ending the oil workers' strike on December 27.

A day after Gómez's funeral, on December 20, Congress was ordered to reconvene on December 26 to elect a new president, who would be López Contreras.[45] In February 1936, López Contreras instructed Dr. Carmelo París, consul general in Curacao, to persuade the Gómez family, who had recently arrived in Curacao, not to return to Venezuela, and to tell them that they should instruct their attorneys in Venezuela how to manage their property. Part of their farms and real estate would be handed over to a number of small farmers so that they could look after them. Moreover, París should "keep close control on the activities of the communists in his jurisdiction and you will refrain from issuing passports and visas to people professing said doctrines, watching very closely the clandestine exits."[46] The nightmare that the Venezuelan exiles had been living for almost a quarter of a century was about to end.

At the end of Gómez's life, the various exiles were scattered around the Caribbean and in New York. Olivares was in Ocaña in Colombia, Mendible in Barranquilla, Alcántara in Costa Rica, Ortega Martínez in the Canary Islands, and Arévalo Cedeño in New York after he had been kicked out of the French and British colonies in the West Indies. On December 27, Aranguren pledged his support for the new government,[47] and over the next few months exiles such as Olivares, Alcántara, León, Smith, and Félix Montes returned to Venezuela to rebuild the country, with some appointed to the López Contreras cabinet.

Conclusion

Gómez's December 1908 coup d'état was a popular move because the country was tired of the excesses of the previous Castro government, which followed a ruinous economic and foreign policy isolating the country from the rest of the world. Gómez, with his "rural and affable aspect,"[1] surrounded himself with enlightened and prestigious men who helped modernize the country. Gómez's administration at first appeared to open a new era of political freedom for the country with the promise of a real shift toward permanent democratic rule. However, one of his underlying assumptions was that he would be the sole arbiter of when this shift occurred. Consequently, while allowing some political freedom to develop initially, he would always remain in power to prevent the various factions from disturbing the peace and prosperity that he hoped to bring to the country. According to Octavio Baptista, the simplicity of Gómez's life, "his punctuality in fulfilling his obligations and his probity in business gave him access to credit for his commercial and financial pursuits, and he was accepted wherever he went, and held in high esteem."[2] Moreover "the life that he led and the understanding of the men whom he had always dealt with, inspired his belief that by enriching subordinates, favoring the capitalists, the large landowners and all those who could harm him and disabling his opponents, he could govern as the omnipotent owner and grow vain in power."[3]

Although Gómez started his regime with a modernization effect, submitting the country to his own good common sense, which had made him a successful and wealthy cattle trader in his youth in Táchira, it should not be forgotten that the Benemérito was in a relatively weak position when he first arrived in power. He was surrounded by a Castroist government machinery; Baptista, his bête noire, predicted that the new president would only be a short-term problem. The Gómez coup in 1908 initially signaled a change at only the head of the former Castroist structure of government. However, the political freedom that he brought to the country was immediately seized upon by various political factions to consolidate and renew their political activity. A period of free democratic participation appeared close at hand, reinforced by the promulgation on August 4, 1909, of the new constitution, which increased the power of Congress and revived the establishment of a Council of State. The creation of such a body, composed of the old caudillos, would serve as a watchdog over the executive because any presidential decision had to be approved by the council.

For Gómez, however, there were no ideological differences between the two leading political factions present in the country and known as Liberalismo Amarillo and Liberalismo Nacionalista, roughly equivalent to Liberals and Conservatives. Arcaya, one of the country's leading intellectuals and arch-bastion of the regime, later explained that the ideology of both parties "seemed false and its manifestoes mere words,"[4] as they "contemplated only the conditions of men."[5] Gómez saw his political role as the need to "unite Venezuelans without distinction of parties, in Government and under the glorious shade of the tricolor standard to work together for the progress of the fatherland."[6] Hence "Gómez Unico," one of the regime's mottos, had an intellectual basis; up to then the political development of the country was seen as the attainment of power that had to be maintained at all costs. There were only two political factors at play, that of the government and that of the revolution, a notion that was perfectly clear to Gómez and one that he often repeated in speeches and in his private correspondence. Arcaya gave an intellectual backing to this view by arguing that the country's history up to then demonstrated that not even the Federal Wars could be perceived as a clash of ideology between Liberals and Conservatives or even democracy against dictatorship.

Gil Fortoul, another pillar of Gomecismo and a leading intellectual, argued that there was no need for political parties, as real opposition could be achieved by "newspapers and conferences and in meetings without the need to enlist any doctrinaire party."[7] The feeling, especially by the leading intellectuals of the time, was that the country needed a period of rest from the long and debilitating wars that afflicted political life during the nineteenth century in order to reflect and take stock of the direction the country was taking. In essence, it needed "a strong power that proved the futility of all revolutionary endeavors until the people forget about revolutions."[8] Such a positivist interpretation of the country's needs served to justify the Gómez dictatorship in some quarters. Gómez, however, needed no intellectual justification for his regime except the preservation of his hold over the country.

As soon as the country appeared to be moving back into factional chaos, Gómez put into action a plan whereby he maintained absolute power. Although at the time there was some opposition to this, mainly from the old caudillos, the country on the whole, especially the business community, was pleased with Gómez's efforts to regenerate the economy and bring law and order. Gómez would provide such a period of relative stability, and certainly at his death at the end of 1935 the country's political and economic life had been transformed. By establishing peace and order, Gómez created a more appropriate environment in which economic progress could take place, with improved agricultural yields, as there was no fear of crops being destroyed because of political strife. The effect of this was the rise of investment in agriculture and industry, especially after the oil industry was established in the 1920s. With an increase in foreign investments, the first foreign bank, the Commercial Bank of Spanish America, a subsidiary of the Anglo South American Bank Ltd., was established in the country in 1913. This was followed in 1916 by branches of the Royal Bank of Canada and the National City Bank of New York, joined in 1920 by the Banco Holandés de las Indias Occidentales. After the excesses of so many former presidents, Gómez established the economic and political stability that the country needed and on which future generations built by forming political parties. The long Gómez dictatorship meant that two generations of Venezuelans were brought up "in the shade of peace, without chieftains, nor arms," becoming a strong base from which to establish "a flexible organic policy, evolutive and tolerant."[9]

The Gómez government by 1917 had its finances and administration in order and was on such a sound footing that the government could have cancelled the country's foreign debt even if oil revenues had not started flowing that year. Moreover, the large investments in road construction initiated in 1909 had the effect of binding the country together. The progress made on the economic side can be partly traced to the luck of finding huge reserves of oil within the country's borders, but Gómez should be credited with stimulating the development of this gift of nature. The Gómez regime, as Roldán Oliarte wrote, was a "moderate centralized dictatorship under a federal constitution,"[10] with the dictator's authority "regulated and dependent on the aims of social integration and political evolution."[11] Gómez's twenty-seven years in power, therefore, allowed the country to unite more closely in both a commercial and a political sense. The long period of relative political stability during the Gómez era made possible the next stage of political development in the country.

Gómez ruled almost unchallenged from 1913 until his death in December 1935, but he did not feel totally secure until after Castro's death in 1924. Once his former mentor disappeared, he was confident that his enemies would "do nothing but talk,"[12] as he so succinctly expressed it in 1925. Consequently, he allowed the many Tachirenses exiled in Colombia to return to the country and in 1927 released all political prisoners from La Rotunda jail. Although Gómez was able to bring to an end the "caudillo era" of Venezuelan history, a number of incidents that showed that there were always dissenting elements willing to fight against his regime both within the Gomecista clique and outside it. The abortive civil-military uprising of 1928 and the events of 1929, which included Gabaldón's uprising in Lara, Urbina's invasion of Falcón from Curacao, and Delgado Chalbaud's *Falke* invasion of Cumaná, undermined Gómez's confidence. Gómez was well aware that he had enemies who were constantly plotting against him.

The political opposition encountered during Gómez's years in power came mainly from the following groups: former members of his government exiled in Europe, the United States, the Caribbean, and Colombia; a small dissenting group of young officers; various left-wing groups; and an incipient middle class. These various groups organized approximately twenty-five conspiratorial movements, including twelve invasions, with Gómez relying mainly on his loyal state presidents to deal with them. Gómez also used peasants to fight local guerrillas because they knew the terrain better than the regular soldiers, receiving a small supplement from the government during peacetime. The state presidents ceased to have any regional importance, as was the case previously since they were appointed to fulfill Gómez's wishes. Gómez's views were well expressed in a letter to Eustoquio Gómez in 1915, when he advised his cousin about the art of government: "I am not in favor of prisons but the need to preserve law places us under the inescapable duty to punish unruly persons and to lock up the vagabonds and rogues that are harmful to society."[13] Gómez added that the army was the "security on which good government and its organization are based,"[14] with the need to "maintain keen vigilance on the officers who form it and to be very confident of their discipline, loyalty, their value and competence in order to be on top of any situation that may occur at any time."[15] Gómez also had to deal with the *jefes civiles* who would exploit local conditions for their own personal gain.

Although Gómez's government was based on a strong loyal army, Gómez ensured that he controlled the vast majority of the country's armory by only allowing his state presidents a small cache of arms. For example, in 1917 the national armory at Caracas held 11,000 Mausers, while the important state of Zulia in 1928 could count on only 315 rifles for the protection of the state and its oil fields. It should not be forgotten that the path of Gómez's longevity had been partly cleared for him during the Castro regime when the power of the regional caudillos was lost forever at the battle of La Victoria in October 1902, with the government defeating the Libertadora revolution. After this battle, Gómez himself swept away all remaining opposition when he defeated Rolando in Ciudad Bolívar on July 21, 1903. Although the caudillos and their followers remained powerful figureheads, as the century wore on and the country started to modernize, their power began to wane. They became stunted political figures with only a few faithful followers at the end of the Gómez era. Their isolation and solitary individualism meant that they were unable to breach the Gómez defenses, lacking adequate manpower and financial resources.

As we have seen, the "caudillo-type" uprisings against Gómez such as the *Odin/Harrier, Angelita, Falke,* and *Superior* were difficult to organize. They needed to attract a large following, have deep pockets, good military and organizational skills, and luck. This combination of factors was a precarious base on which to build any nascent type of struggle. It should be noted, however, that many of the rebel expeditions were linked to simultaneous uprisings in the country and support from countries such as Mexico that did not favor Gómez, and that they demonstrate greater political acumen by the rebels than current historiography portrays. In certain cases the rebels showed a great deal of stoicism, as many did not waver in their fight against the dictator even after countless failures, with many losing fortunes during the long years of exile. The core caudillos, such as Ortega Martínez, Baptista, and Alcántara lost a great deal of money in their various expeditions, with Ortega Martínez at the end of the Gómez dictatorship living almost in poverty in Spain. The personal sacrifice of the exiles, together with the long years away from their home country, should not be underestimated.

Gómez was also careful to cultivate good foreign relations "while avoiding any intimacies"[16] with all the major foreign powers. Gómez was able to use the problem of the 30 percent surtax on imported goods from Curacao and Trinidad as an important negotiating lever to get Britain and the Netherlands to keep a close check on the exiles living on the colonial islands. The result was that the British and Dutch governments during the 1920s assisted José Ignacio Cárdenas, Gómez's able diplomat in Europe, to uncover and thwart a number of revolutionary plots. For example, in 1921 the Dutch government sequestered Ortega Martínez's ship the SS *Odin,* while the British government prevented the SS *Harrier,* a ship also acquired by Ortega Martínez in the same year, from sailing. Later, the British government prevented Captain Lindblad, the Norwegian consul in Trinidad, who in 1926 was acting as Ortega Martínez's naval adviser, from returning to Trinidad. Delgado Chalbaud's activities in Britain during the late 1920s were also closely monitored when he was in London organizing what would become the *Falke* expedition, as were those British subjects who were involved with his activities during 1928 and 1929.

In the United States, the Venezuelan political exiles tried without success to get the government to break off relations with Gómez. The rebels almost succeeded during 1917–18, when US-Venezuelan relations were at a low ebb and would seize the Welch case thirteen years later to publicize their grievances against Gómez. At the time, Congressmen Lenroot and McGuire in 1929 and later Senator Ransdell and Congressmen Gasque and Sandlin were prominent opponents of the Gómez regime, lending their support and influence to the Venezuelan exiles, especially during the Welch case in 1931. Many of the Venezuelan exiles, viz, Smith, Santos Domínici, Pérez, Baptista, and Olivares did not approve of Welch's case, but others, such as Miguel Delgado Chalbaud and Jugo Delgado, seized the opportunity to publicize the political conditions in Venezuela. The United States, however, remained on friendly terms with Gómez until his death in 1935.

Mexico was the only country that showed any open hostility toward Gómez, breaking off diplomatic relations in 1923 and renewing them almost ten years later, on July 24, 1933. During this period, the Venezuelan exiled groups received the support of President Obregón, Education Secretary Vasconcelos, and other members of the Mexican government in their endeavor to topple Gómez. Obregón invited Rivas Vásquez and Ramón Ayala to Mexico to explore the possibilities of his government helping the exiles. The outcome was that in 1923 Obregón sent Arévalo Cedeño, the perennial Venezuelan revolutionary, a check for $8,000. The following year, Obregón was un-decided whether to support Ortega Martínez or Baptista, in the end opting for the latter, to whom he advanced $20,000 for his *Angelita* expedition of the same year. After the failure of the expedition, the Mexican government shifted their assistance away from individuals to political parties. In 1925 Prevé, one of the most important links between the Mexican government and the Venezuelan exiles, informed Smith, an exiled opponent of Gómez, that all the Venezuelans over there were crooks.[17] Only León remained trustworthy, with the Mexican government supporting him with ten thousand rifles and one million rounds of ammunition as long as he was recognized as the leader of the revolutionary movement. Consequently, in 1926 the PRV was estab-lished in Mexico through which the Mexican government channeled funds to the Venezuelan exiles. Although the PRV organized the ill-fated 1929 in-vasion of Falcón through Curacao, Prevé's plan was finally executed in 1931, when Urbina captured the *Superior* and invaded Venezuela. General Amaro of the Mexican government allowed them to acquire arms in Mexico without difficulty, and Prevé was appointed head of general staff in the unsuccessful attempt. Although Mexico was the only country openly opposed to the Gómez regime, other republics in the hemisphere such as Colombia, Cuba, Nicaragua, and Peru at different times also supported various exile groups in their quest to oust Gómez.

The oil companies, especially the American ones, at various times were suspected of financing various abortive revolutions, but they had a limited involvement with the exiled political leaders. Certain oil companies did, however, help the government by providing information on political activity at the various camps, and as Blendon points out, the captains of tankers would keep a lookout for revolutionary filibustering expeditions.[18] There was also one important personal and local link between the oil industry and the exiled revolutionaries through Aranguren, who held the oil concession oper-ated by the Venezuelan Oil Concessions Ltd., a Shell subsidiary. Aranguren became a fierce opponent of Gómez from the early 1920s, partly financing Ortega Martínez's *Odin/Harrier* expedition in 1921,[19] Baptista's *Angelita* ex-pedition of 1924,[20] Román Delgado Chalbaud's *Falke* expedition of 1929,[21] and probably Urbina's *Superior* expedition of 1931.

We have seen that Gómez's instinct from the beginning was to remain in power for as long as possible, something he achieved, as he died in his sleep while still president on December 17, 1935. The history of the period has been written to show a remarkably easy and linear political progression for the regime, almost as though it were preordained to be this way. Such a view has only served to mask the political acumen that Gómez had, for not only did he survive during the Castro years as the second most important figure in the country, but he managed to remain in power for a further twenty-seven years as the undisputed leader of the country, a period that was extremely difficult at times. What has also been overlooked by the history of the period is the internal strife that took place within the Gomecista ranks. With the prosperity of the country increasing, especially after Venezuela became a major oil-producing country, it was not unnatural for some of the faithful Gomecistas to want to share the benefits more fully. With this in mind the events of 1928 take on a more crucial role, as it appears that Vicentico stimulated the student quasi-revolt of March and the April abortive military uprising in a bid to oust his father. Hence, Gómez's harsh reaction to the Student Week was due to his perception that the event was a prelude to a much more important and harmful event, which was the abortive military uprising in April. The stripping of all Vicentico's titles and position in the government and his appointment as a minor diplomat in Paris demonstrate that Gómez was convinced of his son's intentions against his regime. Gómez showed his political astuteness here, as he was able to react to these events in a flexible manner, retiring from politics at the end of his constitutional period in 1929, only to return two years later by popular acclaim. It was a clever political move: it showed the country that Gómez did not want to build a Gomecista dynasty.

Although Gómez has been portrayed as the "shame of America" for his callous, savage, and uncouth methods of dealing with his opponents, it is debatable whether his modus operandi was more extreme than those of his contemporaries. Gómez did show an independence of mind that at times very nearly plunged the country into a major international conflict, but he was able to compromise with his opponents when the situation warranted such an action. Gómez's keen political awareness and shrewd political mind ensured the defeat of all his opponents and his survival for twenty-seven years as Venezuela's strong man.

Background Information on Important Political Actors of the Gómez Era

Note: Most of the information provided here has been adapted from Fundacíon Polar, *Diccionario de Historia de Venezuela.*

Alamo, Antonio (1878-1953). Historian, lawyer, and politician. Participated in Manuel Antonio Matos's Revolución Libertadora (1901-1903). Substitute senator for Lara State (1905-1909). Senator for Lara State (1919-21). Development minister (1922-28). President of Sucre State (1929-31) and Bolívar State (1933-35).

Alcántara, Francisco Linares (1876-1958). Military man and politician. Son of General Francisco Linares Alcántara, president of Venezuela (1877-78). Graduate of West Point Military Academy (1897). Chief of staff for the Caracas Army Division (1900). President of Aragua State (1900-1907) and Bolívar State (1907). Interior minister (1908-12). He becomes a political exile in 1913.

Andrade Troconis, Ignacio (1836-1925). Military man and politician. President of Venezuela (1898-99). Foreign affairs minister (1914-16), interior minister (1917-21).

Aranguren, Antonio (1868-1954). Oil concessionaire and oil broker. Although born in Caracas, he is a member of a distinguished Maracaibo family. In 1913 he transfers his 1907 oil concession over the districts of Bolívar and Maracaibo in Zulia State to the Venezuelan Oil Concessions Ltd., where he is a member of the board of directors. The company is later acquired by the Royal Dutch–Shell Group and becomes the largest oil-producing company in the country. Aranguen is reputed to be the richest man in Venezuela during Gómez's regime. Since the early 1920s he becomes a secret opponent to the Gómez regime.

Arcaya, Pedro Manuel (1874–1958). Lawyer, jurist, sociologist, historian, and politician. Attorney general of the republic (1912). Interior minister (1914–17, 1926–29). Senator for Falcón State and president of Congress (1918–22). Venezuelan plenipotentiary minister at Washington (1922–24, 1930–35).

Arévalo Cedeño, Emilio (1882–1965). Political opponent. He is born in Valle de la Pascua, Guárico State, and trains and works as a telegraph operator between 1900 and 1913. On May 19, 1914, he initiates the first of his many uprisings against the Gómez regime. Congressional deputy for Guárico State (1936).

Arévalo González, Rafael (1866–1935). Journalist, telegraph operator, writer, and politician. In 1892, he establishes with Odoardo León Ponte the newspaper *El Pregonero*. He publishes the novel *Escombros!* (1892) and *Maldita Juventud!* (1904). He is a contributor to the magazine *Atenas* (1913). He is jailed in La Rotunda (1913–22).

Aristeguieta, Pedro Elías (1885–1929). Military man and political activist. He is educated at the Colegio Nacional de Cumaná. He lives in the United States between 1909 and 1911, when he accompanies his uncle, Pedro Ezequiel Rojas, the Venezuelan plenipotentiary minister in Washington. In 1911 he returns to Venezuela to manage his family's fishing business. In 1919, he joins Luis Rafael Pimentel's conspiracy and is forced to leave the country.

Ayala, Ramón (1850–1920). Military man and politician. He fights the government of General José Ruperto Monagas (1868–70). He joins Antonio Guzmán Blanco's Revolución Liberal (1870). Vice president of Bolívar State (1878). He is exiled between 1884 and 1890. President of Zulia State (1890). Deputy for the Gran Estado Miranda (1890, 1892). He supports President Raimundo Andueza Palacios against Joaquín Crespo's Revolución Legalista (1892). He is exiled between 1892 and 1898. Senator for the Gran Estado Miranda (1898). He joins Cipriano Castro's Revolución Restauradora (1899). Provisional vice president (1901). President of the Council of State (1909). He becomes a political exile in 1913.

Baptista Galindo, Francisco (1880–1927). Lawyer and politician. Deputy for Mérida State (1917–18). Secretary general of Nueva Esparta State (1919–20). Private secretary to Gómez (1920–22). Interior minister (1922–25). Secretary general of the presidency (1925–27).

Baptista, Leopoldo (1869–1931). Military man and politician. Founding member of the Unión Democrática party (1889). Deputy for the Gran Estado Los Andes (1890). Minister of post and telegraph (1892, 1893). Development minister (1893). Secretary general of Trujillo State (1900). Deputy for Trujillo State (1900, 1905). President of Trujillo State (1901, 1903). Puerto Cabello customs administrator (1904). Interior minister (1906). Private secretary to Juan Vicente Gómez (1908). Secretary general of the presidency (1908–1909). Member of the Council of State (1909–13). He becomes a political exile in 1913.

Baptista, Trino (1870–1944). Lawyer and politician. Brother of Leopoldo Baptista. Secretary general of Trujillo State (1905–1909). President of Trujillo State (1909). Education minister (1909–11). Deputy for Trujillo State (1913). He becomes a political exile in 1913.

Barceló, Simón (1873–1938). Writer and journalist. He is exiled in 1889. Venezuelan consul in Puerto Rico and Haiti (1900–1906). Venezuelan minister in France (1923).

Bigott, Luis (1878–1945). Entrepreneur and philanthropist. He sets up a small cigarette factory in Caracas, the Cigarrera Bigott, which in 1920 becomes the largest cigarette manufacturer in the country. In 1922, he sells the company to the British American Tobacco Company and starts a new company, Cigarrillos San Luis. In 1932, he establishes a school for the children of his employees and starts an urbanization project to provide housing for his employees.

Blanco Fombona, Horacio (1889–1948). Poet, journalist, and politician. Representative of the Students Association of Gran Colombia meeting in Caracas in 1911. He becomes a permanent exile in 1912.

Blanco Fombona, Rufino (1874-1944). Writer and politician. He participates in Joaquín Crespo's Revolución Legalista (1892). Venezuelan consul in Philadelphia (1892-95). In 1895 he publishes his first poem, "Patria." Cultural attaché at the Venezuelan legation in the Netherlands (1896). Secretary general of Zulia State (1900). Venezuelan consul at the Hague (1901-1904). Governor of Amazonas (1905). Congressional deputy (1909). He is jailed for opposing Gómez (1909-10) and exiled thereafter. In 1915 he establishes the publishing house of Editorial América in Madrid, and in 1925 he is nominated for the Nobel Prize for Literature.

Bolet Monagas, Nicanor (1868-?). Son of Nicanor Bolet Peraza. He lives most of his life in the United States, where he achieves great economic success.

Bolet Peraza, Nicanor (1838-1906). Costumbrista writer, journalist, politician. He edits the magazine *El Oasis* (1856), founds the Museo Venezolano (1865-66), edits in New York the *Revista Ilustrada de Nueva York* (1885), and helps establish *Las Tres Américas* magazine (1893-97), which promotes modernist Latin American literature in the United States. In Venezuela he works on *El Cojo Ilustrado* and *Cosmópolis*.

Bruzual López, Rafael (1886-1932). Writer and jurist. Contributes to the *El Cojo Ilustrado* (1906-1907). Editor of the provincial newspapers *El Genio y El Alba.* From 1919 he becomes a permanent political exile.

Bueno, Adolfo (1881-1967). Medical doctor and entrepreneur. Partner with José Rafael Revenga in a medical clinic (1907). He works in the Vargas Hospital and the military hospital in Caracas. President of the chamber of deputies (1921). Deputy for Carabobo State (1921). Private secretary to Gómez (1921-27). He lives in Paris (1927-37).

Carabaño, Rafael María (1867-1933). Journalist and politician. He collaborates with Carlos León in editing the political weekly *El Carácter* (1889). He supports Joaquín Crespo in his Revolución Legalista (1892). He lives in Paris (1892-93), when his father is appointed attaché at the Venezuelan legation at Paris. He is appointed public surveyor of Miranda State (1896). Commander of arms of San Fernando de Apure (1898). Military chief of the states of Guárico (1899) and Aragua (1900). President of Apure State (1901). Senator for Apure State (1902, 1904). Public works minister (1902–1903). Deputy for Aragua State (1905). Development minister (1908–10).

Cárdenas, José Ignacio (1874–1949). Medical doctor and diplomat. Venezuelan diplomat in France and the Netherlands between 1910 and 1925. Public works minister (1927). Development minister (1929).

Cárdenas, Pedro María (1870–1938). Military man and politician. He defends government of Raimundo Andueza Palacios against Joaquín Crespo's Revolución Legalista. He is exiled in Colombia between 1892 and 1899. He joins Cipriano Castro's Revolución Restauradora (1899). President of Táchira State (1901), second vice president of Táchira State (1902). Commander in chief of the Federal District (1904), governor of western part of the Federal District (1905), commander in chief of Falcón State (1907). First vice president of Falcón State (1907). He is exiled between 1909 and 1924. He returns to Venezuela in 1925. Senator for Táchira (1928). President of Lara State (1928), Táchira State (1929–31), and Sucre State (1931–35). He is exiled after 1936.

Cárdenas, Román (1862–1950). Engineer and Civil Servant. Constructs Capacho's market and the bridge over the Uribante river in Táchira. Public works minister (1910–12), finance minister (1912–22).

Castillo, Domingo B. (1865–1941). Lawyer, writer, and diplomat. He forms part of a group that opposes President Raimundo Andueza Palacios and his intention of continuing in power in 1892. He supports Cipriano Castro's government in 1899. Political exile from 1911.

Castro, Carmelo (1875–1957). Half brother of Cipriano Castro. He joins the Revolución Restauradora (1899). He is Quartermaster of the Venezuelan army that invades Colombia in 1901 and is defeated at the battle of Carazúa. He fails to get into West Point and attends instead the Manlius Military Academy of New York (1904–1905). Superintendent of tobacco and liquor revenues of Bermúdez State (1906). He becomes a political exile in 1909. He returns to Venezuela after his brother's death in 1924 but is jailed after the 1928 army rebellion.

Castro, Celestino (1856–1924). Eldest brother of Cipriano Castro. President of Táchira State (1900, 1904). Commander in chief of the army when Carlos

Rangel Garbiras invades the country in 1901. Becomes a political exile when Gómez assumes the presidency in December 1908.

Castro, Cipriano (1858–1924). Military man and politician. President of Venezuela, 1899–1908. He lives in exile from 1908 until his death in 1924.

Cayama Martínez, Rafael (1874–1944). Military man and politician. He takes part in Matos's Revolución Libertadora (1901–1903) against President Cipriano Castro. He is imprisoned for three years (1901–1904) in the San Carlos fortress prison in Zulia State. Deputy for Falcón (1914) and Anzoátegui (1922). Secretary to the governor of the Federal District (1926). Senator for Falcón State (1929). President of National Congress (1929). Development minister (1931–35).

Centeno Graü, Melchor (1867–1949). Engineer and politician. Manager of the Naricual coal mines (1896–1899). Deputy for Monagas State (1914). Manager of the Gran Ferrocarril del Táchira (1915) and the Compañía de Navegación Fluvial y Costanera de Venezuela (1917). Finance minister (1922–29). Senator for Carabobo State (1932). Public works minister (1931–32). Director of the Banco Obrero (1933).

Coll, Pedro Emilio (1872–1947). Writer and journalist. He establishes, together with Luis M. Urbaneja Achelpohl and Pedro César Domínici, the literary magazine *Cosmópolis* (1894–95), considered the birthplace of the modernist movement in Venezuelan literature. Contributes to *El Cojo Ilustrado* (1895–1907). Venezuelan consul in Southampton (UK) (1897–99). Director general of the Development Ministry (1900). Development minister (1912–13). Venezuelan consul general in France (1915), secretary to the Venezuelan legation in Madrid (1916–24). Supervisor of banks and Senator for Anzoátegui State (1924–26). President of National Congress (1926). Inspector of consulates in Europe (1927–33).

Colmenares Pacheco, Francisco Antonio (1875–1937). Military man and politician. Married to Emilia Gómez (1897), Gómez's sister. Assistant to the general chief of staff of the Revolución Restauradora (1899). He fights on the side of the government during Matos's Revolución Libertadora (1901–1903). He intercedes on behalf of Antonio Aranguren for the government to award him an oil concession in Zulia State (1907). Governor of the

Federal District (1909–11). Inspector general of the armed forces (1912–14). Director general of telegraphs and telephones (1923, 1928). He establishes AYRE (1926), the first radio station in the country.

Chalbaud Cardona, Estebán (1859–1927). Military man and politician. He supports Joaquín Crespo's bid for the presidency in 1892. In 1899 he joins the new government of Castro, who appoints him civil and military chief of Mérida State (1900) and provisional president of Mérida State (1900–1901). senator (1905–1908), president of Mérida State (1909–13).

Dagñino, Eduardo J. (dates unknown). Lawyer, politician, and diplomat. Secretary general of Lara State (1909), Federal District (1909), and Bolívar State (1911). Venezuelan consul in Hamburg (1914–18). Venezuelan minister at the Holy See (1924–27) and at Berlin (1927–35).

Delfino, Carlos (1884–1944). Entrepreneur. Manager of the Fábrica de Cementos La Vega (1910). In 1912, he marries Josefa, Gómez's daughter. Deputy for Aragua State (1915). Important broker of oil concessions.

Delgado Chalbaud, Román (1882–1929). Navy and politics. He serves as a rating on board the navy's school yacht *Ana Jacinta* (1895–98). In 1901, he captains the Venezuelan gunboat *Restaurador* that chases the *Ban Righ,* a rebel ship that distributes arms and transports men along the Venezuelan coast during Matos's Revolución Libertadora. In 1909, he establishes the Compañía Anónima de Navegación Fluvial y Costanera. He is imprisoned in La Rotunda (1913–27). He is exiled in 1927 and dies in Cumaná in 1929.

Domínici, Pedro César (1872–1954). Writer and diplomat. Brother of Santos Aníbal Domínici. In 1894, he establishes *Cosmópolis,* with Pedro Emilio Coll and Luis M. Urbaneja Achelpohl. He publishes the magazine *Venezuela* in Paris (1905–1909). Chargé d'affaires at Venezuelan legation in Madrid, Venezuelan consul general in Rome (1909–15). Venezuelan plenipotentiary minister in London (1915). Venezuelan minister to Argentina, Chile, and Uruguay (1922–36).

Domínici, Santos Aníbal (1869–1954). Medical doctor, writer, diplomat, and politician. Brother of Pedro César Domínici. He graduates as a medical doctor in 1890 at the Universidad Central de Venezuela. He does postgraduate medical studies in Paris and in 1895 establishes the Instituto Pasteur de Caracas. Chancellor of the Universidad Central de Venezuela (1899–1901). He joins Matos's Revolución Libertadora in 1901 and after a short prison sentence is exiled from the country. Venezuelan plenipotentiary minister to Germany (1910), United Kingdom (1911–15), and the United States (1915–22). In 1922 he becomes an enemy of Gómez.

Ducharne, Horacio (1865–1915). Caudillo. He is educated in Trinidad. He joins Matos's Revolución Libertadora in 1901 and invades Venezuela from Trinidad. He is captured and imprisoned in the Libertador Castle in Puerto Cabello (1903–1906). After he is freed, he leads another uprising in 1907 and is captured and sent to prison until he regains his freedom after the fall of Cipriano Castro in December 1908.

Egea Mier, Guillermo (1870–1935). Naval man and journalist. Graduate of the Naval School of Puerto Cabello (1890). He establishes and edits *Oiga,* a newspaper in the Dominican Republic against the government of Castro (1899–1908). He returns to Venezuela in 1908 for a short period but then leaves as a political exile. In Mexico he edits the newspaper *Pativilca.*

Escalante, Diógenes (1879 –1964). Politician, diplomat, and journalist. Secretary to the governor of the Federal District (1901–1902). Venezuelan consul at Liverpool (1904–1906), consul general at Berlin (1906–1908), consul in the Netherlands and France (1909–10). Secretary general of Táchira State (1910–11). Director of the Imprenta Nacional (1911–12). Establishes the *El Nuevo Diario* newspaper in 1913. Deputy for Sucre State at the plenipotentiary Congress of 1914. Substitute Senator for Táchira (1915). Venezuelan delegate to the League of Nations (1920–33). Venezuelan minister at London (1922–35).

Fernández, Emilio (1870–1929). Military man and politician. He supports Castro's Revolución Restauradora of 1899. President of Monagas State (1910–13, 1921–23), Carabobo State (1915–20), Sucre (1929).

Flores, Doroteo (1880–1933). Caudillo. He joins Matos's Revolución Libertadora in 1901. Vice president of Monagas State (1909). He leaves Venezuela as a political exile in 1913.

Fossi Becerra, Roberto (1895–1952). Military man and politician. He is forced into exile by the government of Eustoquio Gómez in Táchira State (1914–25).

Federal District policeman (1927–28). Administrator of La Vela de Coro Customs House (1928). In July 1928 he launches a failed uprising with Urbina.

Gabaldón, José Rafael (1882–1975). Caudillo. Governor of Boconó District of Trujillo State (1904) and *jefe civil* of Puerto Cabello (1905). President of Portuguesa State (1909–10).

Galavís, Félix (1877–1941). Military man and politician. Fighting under Juan Pablo Pañaloza, he defends Táchira against Castro's invasion of 1899. Later he forms part of Gómez's army against Matos's Revolución Libertadora. Inspector general of the army (1909). Head of the armed forces general staff (1910–14). President of Aragua State (1911–14) and Yaracuy State (1929–35). Vice president of the States of Táchira (1918–21) and Lara (1921–24).

García Bustamante, José Rosario (1860–1934). Lawyer and politician. Gómez's uncle. Secretary to Gómez during Matos's Revolución Libertadora (1901–1903). Political adviser to Gómez.

García Velasco, José María (1874–1954). Military man and politician. Nephew of José Rosario García Bustamante and first cousin of Gómez. Part of Cipriano Castro's Revolución Restauradora of 1899, reaching the rank of general. Civil and military head of Northern Táchira (1900). He fights the invading army of Carlos Rangel Garbiras (1902). Administrator of the municipal revenues of the Federal District (1903). Senator for the State of Aragua (1905, 1909) and Falcón (1910). President of the Council of Government for the legislative assembly of Zulia State. Commander in chief of Zulia State (1910). President of Trujillo State (1912–14) and Zulia State (1914–18). Vice president of Trujillo State (1918–21). Inspector of consulates in Europe and the United States (1921–22). Plenipotentiary minister in Peru (1922). President of Carabobo State (1928). Governor of the Federal District (1929–30). Finance minister (1930–31).

Gil Borges, Esteban (1879–1942). Politician, diplomat and writer. President of the Supreme Court of Justice of the Federal District. Secretary to the Venezuelan legation in Washington, counselor at the Venezuelan legation at Paris, and chargé d'affaires at the Venezuelan legation in Madrid (1910–18). Foreign affairs minister (1919–21). Assistant director of the Pan American Union in Washington (1922–36).

Gil Fortoul, José (1861–1943). Writer, historian, sociologist, and politician. Commercial attaché at Bern (1894). Consul at Bordeaux (1886), Liverpool (1890–92, 1902–1905). Consul at Trinidad (1900). Venezuelan representative to the Second International Pan American Conference in Mexico (1901). Secretary to the Venezuelan legation in Paris (1892, 1902–1905). During this time he publishes numerous books on philosophy, poetry, and fiction. Commercial attaché at Berlin (1906). In 1906, the first volume of his *Historia Constitucional de Venezuela* is published. He attends the Second Peace Conference at the Hague (1907). Plenipotentiary minister at Berlin (1909). In 1909, the second volume of his *Historia Constitucional de Venezuela* is published. He returns to Venezuela in 1910 and is appointed Senator (1910–11, 1914–16), education minister (1911–12). Acting president (1913).

Gil, Pío. See Morantes, Pedro María.

Giménez, Juan Victoriano (1874–1923). Military man and politician. He joins Cipriano Castro's Revolución Restauradora in Cabudarse. He fights against Matos's Revolución Libertadora (1901–1903) and distinguishes himself at the battle of La Victoria (1902). Secretary of Lara State government (1905), Governor of Yaracuy Section of the Gran Estado Lara (1907–1908), senator for Yaracuy State (1910), president of Yaracuy State (1913–23).

Gimón Pérez, David (1869–1957). Military man. He receives his primary and secondary education in Trinidad. He participates in the Queipa uprising (1898). Joins Matos's Revolución Libertadora (1901–1903). President of Guárico State (1911–12) and Lara State (1916–20).

Giuseppi Monagas, Pablo (1850–1919). Politician and military man. President of Miranda State (1891), Maturín State (1891), and Monagas State (1909). President of the Senate (1911).

Gómez, Eustoquio (1868–1935). Military man and politician. First cousin of Gómez. He starts his military career during the presidency of Castro (1899–1908). He fights in Táchira the invasions of Carlos Rangel Garbiras (1901) and accompanies Gómez in his military campaign in eastern Venezuela during Matos's Revolución Libertadora (1901–1903). Military commander of Maracay (1904). Commander of arms of Miranda State (1904) and of Falcón State (1905). He kills the Federal District governor in a drunken brawl in 1907 and is sentenced to fifteen years in prison. He is freed in 1909, when Gómez assumes the presidency in December 1908. He is appointed military commander of San Carlos fort in Zulia State. President of Táchira State (1915–25) and Lara State (1929–35).

Gómez, José Vicente (1888–1930). Military man and politician. Gómez's son. Deputy for Aragua State (1914). Inspector general of the armed forces (1914–29). Second vice president (1922–29).

Gómez, Josefina Revenga de (dates unknown). Married to José Vicente Gómez.

Gómez, Juan Crisóstomo (Juancho) (1860–1923). Politician and farmer. Brother of Gómez. President of Miranda State (1911–1914). Governor of the Federal District (1913–23).

Gómez, Santos Matute (dates unknown). Military man and politician. Gómez's half brother. Commander of the San Carlos fort in Zulia State (1912). President of Zulia State (1918–24, 1925–26), Carabobo State (1929–35).

González, Silverio (1859–1938). Educator. He studies law at the Univeridad Central de Venezuela but does not graduate. Head of Colegio Nacional de Cumaná (1886–1921). Deputy for Sucre (1905) and president of Anzoátegui State (1915–17, 1923–24), Sucre State (1918–21), and Trujillo State (1935).

González Gorrondona, Enrique (1886–1975). Landowner, entrepreneur, and politician. In his youth he works in his family cattle business. In 1907, he establishes one of the first industrial lumber companies in the country at Tucacas, Falcón State, to manufacture wooden boxes and rail sleepers. In 1920, he starts Almacén Internacional, a business importing agricultural machinery and pumping jacks. He also starts a funeral service company called La Venezolana and is one of the first people to install a milk pasteurizing plant in Caracas in 1926. He joins the uprising of José Rafael Gabaldón of 1929 and is imprisoned during 1929–35, first at the Rotunda prison and later at the Libertador castle in Puerto Cabello.

González Guinán, Francisco (1841–1932). Lawyer, journalist, historian, and politician. Secretary general of the Revolución Reivindicadora (1879).

Development minister (1879) during Antonio Guzmán Blanco's administration. President of Carabobo State (1879). Interior minister (1884, 1887). Education minister (1886). He starts to write his monumental *Historia Contemporánea de Venezuela* in 1889. Senator for Carabobo State (1895). Deputy for Zamora State (1901). President of the Deputy Chamber of Congress (1901). Foreign affairs minister (1908–1909). Secretary general (1910–12). Senator for Carabobo State (1913).

González Rincones, Rafael (1885–1958). Medical doctor, entrepreneur, and politician. Director of the Sanitary Office (1913–15). Deputy for Táchira State (1914). Senator for Táchira State (1915, 1931). Education minister (1917–18, 1931–35).

González, Rubén (1875–1939). Lawyer and politician. Secretary general to the President of Táchira State (1900–1908). He is jailed in the San Carlos fort in Zulia State. Political exile in Colombia (1910–17). Deputy for Táchira State (1919–22). President of the Chamber of Deputies (1920, 1922). Legal adviser to the Finance Ministry (1920–22). Education minister (1922–29). Interior minister (1929–31).

Hernández, José Manuel "El Mocho" (1853–1921). Caudillo. Mocho Hernández earns his nickname when at the tender age of seventeen he is wounded in the battle of Los Lirios in August 1870. Prior to entering politics, Hernández has a colorful career working as a gold miner in Yuruary. With Alejandro Urbaneja he founds the Partido Democrático during the presidency of Juan Pablo Rojas Paúl. Inspector of public works for Yuruary (1890). He joins Joaquín Crespo's Revolución Legalista (1892). Deputy for Bermúdez State (1893). He is jailed in La Rotunda (Caracas) (1898–99) and in San Carlos fort (Zulia State) (1900–1902).Venezuelan plenipotentiary minister at Washington (1903). He is exiled in the United States (1904–1908). Member of the Council of State (1909–11). In 1911, he declares himself an enemy of Gómez and remains in exile until his death in 1921.

Iturbe, Aquiles (1875–1941). Engineer, military man, and politician. Secretary to the Venezuelan legation at Washington (1895). Chief engineer in the construction of the Guanare aqueduct (1896–97). Secretary general of Portuguesa State (1898–1899). President of Portuguesa State (1901–1902). Secretary and chief of staff of expeditionary force commanded by Gómez (1903). President of Zamora State (1904). Military commander (1904) and president of Bermúdez State (1904–1907). President of Táchira State (1908, 1909–10). Governor of the Federal District (1908–1909). Development minister (1911–12). He is imprisoned in La Rotunda jail (1919–26).

Hernández Ron, José Angel (1855–1932). Military man. Deputy for Gran Estado Miranda (1890–92). He supports the presidential candidacy of José Manuel Hernández (El Mocho) (1897) and participates in the Queipa uprising (1898). A strong supporter of El Mocho, he leads an uprising in 1899 against Castro's government. Joins Matos's Revolución Libertadora (1901–1903). President of Guárico State (1910–11).

Jiménez Rebolledo, Carlos (1869–1951). Lawyer and politician. In 1886 he joins Cipriano Castro in an uprising against General Juan Bautista Araujo, president of the Gran Estado de los Andes. He studies law and politics at the University of Merida and Universidad Central de Venezuela. Secretary general of the state of Cojedes (1909–11), president of Zamora State (1911–15), war director of War and Navy Ministry (1915–17), war and navy minister (1917–29). He drafts a new military code in 1923. Senator for Zamora State (1930–33).

Jurado, León (1874–1958). Military man and politician. He only completes primary education and leaves home at sixteen years old. Head of security, Maracaibo harbor (1892). He joins Castro's Revolución Restauradora (1899). He accompanies Juan Vicente Gómez during his campaign against Matos's Revolución Libertadora (1901–1903). Commander in chief, Coro (1903, 1906–1908). President of Falcón State (1910–23, 1929–35).

Key Ayala, Santiago (1874–1959). Essayist and historian. Contributor to *El Cojo Ilustrado* and *Cosmópolis*. He works at the Ministry of Foreign Relations. He represents Venezuela at the Plenipotentiary Conference on the border between Venezuela and Colombia (1920–21). He is a delegate at the League of Nations, the Pan American Conference at Havana, and the Hague's International Tribunal.

Laguado Jayme, Francisco (1901–29). Debater and political fighter. Student activist. He becomes a political exile in 1920.

Lara Núñez, Alejandro (1874–1972). Lawyer, entrepreneur, and politician. President of Supreme Court of Sucre State (1897). President of the Banco de Venezuela (1924). Member of the board of directors of the following companies: Cervecería de Caracas, Cervecería Nacional, Telares de Caracas, and Telares de Valencia. Director and Legal Counsel of the Banco Venezolano de Crédito (1925). He lives in Paris between 1927 and 1931. He returns to Venezuela in 1931.

León Carrillo, Carlos (1868–1942). Lawyer, jurist, academic, and politician. He collaborates with Rafael María Carabaño in editing the political weekly *El Carácter* (1889). He supports Joaquín Crespo in his Revolución Legalista (1892). Attaché at the Venezuelan legation in Paris (1893–94). Secretary to the Chamber of Deputies (1894) and treasurer to the Public Works Ministry (1894). Member of the Federal Court of Cassation (1904–1905). He lectures in political economy and sociology at the Universidad Central de Venezuela (1901–1904). Education minister (1906). He becomes a political exile in 1906, returning to Venezuela in 1909. Governor of the Federal District (1909). He is jailed in La Rotunda for eight years, between 1914 and 1922. He becomes a political exile in 1922.

León, Ramón David (1890–1980). Journalist, writer, and diplomat. Features editor of the *El Universal* newspaper (1922–24). He founds the newspaper *La Esfera* in 1926 and remains as editor until 1957.

López Contreras, Eleazar (1883–1973). Military man, politician, and president of Venezuela. He forms part of Cipriano Castro's uprising in Táchira in May 1899. Equerry to the President of Venezuela (1900). Chief of Tucacas Garrison (1901). Second Assistant of the Chief of Staff of the Barcelona Fortress (1902). Chief of Security of Cristóbal Colón (1907) and of the La Vela Customs House (1908). Manager of the Araya salt mines (1913). In 1914 he begins active military duty, becoming first commander of the Rivas Battalion. War director (1919). War and navy minister (1931–35).

López, Jacinto (1864–1942). Writer and political journalist. In 1890 he founds, with Ramón Mijares, the weekly magazine *El Avisador*. In Valencia he edits the conservative newspaper *El Constitucional* (1894) and writes for *El Cojo Ilustrado*. He supports the presidential candidacy of José Manuel Hernández in 1897. He leaves the country as a political exile in 1903 to live in Puerto

Rico and returns at the end of 1908. He leaves as a political exile again in 1911, residing in New York until his death.

Luciani, Jorge (1894–1956). Essayist, historian, and politician. Student activist. He becomes a political exile in 1920.

Maldonado, Samuel Dario (1870–1925). Surgeon, anthropologist, writer, journalist, and politician. He graduates from Mérida University as medical doctor (1893). He contributes to *El Cojo Ilustrado*. Political exile from 1901 until 1908. Education minister (1908–10). He starts the Office of National Health (1911) and directs many national campaigns to eradicate yellow fever, smallpox, bubonic plague, malaria, and dysentery. Governor of Territorio Delta Amacuro (1919), president of Aragua (1921) and senator for Tachira (1925). His most important novels are *Tropicales: Marina o la hija de las olas* (1906) and *Tierra nuestra (Por el río Caura)* (1920).

Márquez Bustillos, Victorino (1858–1941). Writer and politician. Director of newspaper *El Trujillano* (1877–87). Deputy for the Gran Estado Los Andes (1890). President of the Gran Estado Los Andes (1892). Brigadier general (1893). Secretary of the government for Trujillo State (1902–1904). Deputy of Trujillo District to the state assembly (1904–1906). Secretary of government for Zulia State (1909). Senator for Trujillo State (1910–14). Governor of the Federal District (1911–13). Defense marine minister (1913–14). Provisional president (1915–22).

McGill, Samuel (1877–1955). Military man. He is born in Chile. From 1900 he is a military instructor in Nicaragua, Honduras, El Salvador, and Ecuador. McGill arrives in Venezuela in 1904 and is appointed Venezuelan consul general in Panama (1904–1908). General instructor of the army at the military school in Caracas (1910). Chilean consul general in Venezuela (1921–27). On May 2, 1928, he is expelled from the country.

Méndez, Gumersindo (1848–1914). Military man and politician. He joins Castro's Revolución Restauradora (1899). Commander of arms for Lara State (1904), provisional president of Bermúdez State (1904), Commander of arms for Guayana (1904). President of Guayana (1904). Commander of arms for Táchira State (1905) and Zulia State (1907). President of Zulia State (1909–14).

Mendible, Luciano (1880–1940). Lawyer, military man, and politician. Deputy for Guárico State (1904–1909). President of Guárico State (1906–1908). He becomes a political exile in 1909.

Mendoza, Juan José (1875–1959). Lawyer and historian. Venezuelan plenipotentiary minister at Washington (1912–15). Legal counselor at the Foreign Affairs Ministry (1916). Lecturer at the Universidad Central de Venezuela in administrative law and roman law (1924–44).

Mibelli, Elbano (1869–1946). Military man and politician. He forms part of Cipriano Castro's 1899 Revolución Restauradora. He fights on the government's side during Matos's Revolución Libertadora (1901–1903). Civil chief of Carúpano, prefect of Vargas Department of Monagas State (1908–12). President of Monagas State (1914).

Montes, Félix (1878–1942). Lawyer, academic, writer, and politician. He contributes to the magazine *El Cojo Ilustrado* in the 1890s. He becomes a political exile in 1913.

Morantes, Pedro María (Pío Gil) (1863–1918). Writer and political commentator. He graduates as a lawyer and in 1903, after publishing a number of books on poetry and articles in *El Tribuno de Mérida* and *El Eco de Occidente*, goes to work at the Foreign Affairs Ministry and is later appointed as a judge in a lower court. In 1908, he leaves Venezuela.

Mosquera, Bernardino (1855–1923). Medical doctor and politician. He graduates in medicine from the University of Pennsylvania. He pioneers the study of bacteriology in Venezuela. Founding member of the Academy of Medicine (1904). Education minister (1899). Foreign affairs minister (1917–18).

Niño, Samuel Eugenio (1869–1941). Medical doctor, composer, writer, and politician. He graduates as a medical doctor from the Univeridad Central de Venezuela. He is head of the Partido Liberal Amarillo together with Juan Pablo Pañaloza. In 1897 he joins Castro's rebellion. Secretary general of Tachira State (1905). Deputy for Tachira State in National Congress (1905), president of Carabobo State (1907–1909), deputy for Trujillo State (1919–24), education minister (1929–31), senator for Zamora State (1927–30), president of Zamora State (1931–35).

Olivares, Régulo (1873–1952). Military man and politician. He joins the army of General Espiritú Santo Morales in Táchira, which rebels against the government and is part of Joaquín Crespo's Revolución Legalista (1892). Later, he joins Castro's Revolución Restauradora (1899). Chief of border security in Táchira State (1900), Commander of arms in Trujillo State (1900) and Maracaibo (1900). President and senator of Zulia (1901). Head of army division for Sucre, Bolívar, and Falcón states during the Revolución Libertadora (1901–1903). President of Zulia (1904–1907). Defense minister (1908–10). President of Táchira State (1910–11). He becomes a political exile in 1913.

Ortega Martínez, José María (1859–1933). Military man and politician. Public works minister (1896). Deputy for Carabobo State (1896). Military and civil chief of Maracaibo (1899). Deputy for Apure State (1901). He joins Matos's Revolución Libertadora (1901–1903), where he commands the revolutionary army in the center of the country and is private secretary to Matos. He is captured and imprisoned (1903–1906). He is exiled (1906–1909). Public works minister (1909–10). Member of the Council of State (1913). He becomes a political exile in 1913.

Peñaloza, Juan Pablo (1855–1933). Caudillo and military man. He joins the army of General Espiritú Santo Morales in Táchira, which rebels against the government and is part of Joaquín Crespo's Revolución Legalista (1892). Deputy to the legislative assembly of the Gran Estado Los Andes, Táchira section (1898–99). He defends the government of Ignacio Andrade Troconis against the invasion of Cipriano Castro in 1899. With the triumph of Castro, Peñaloza leaves the country. He returns during Matos's Revolución Libertadora (1901–1903) and is appointed chief of staff. With the defeat of Matos, Peñaloza becomes a political exile again and tries unsuccessfully to invade the country in 1907. Member of the Council of State (1908–13). He becomes a political exile in 1913.

Pérez Soto, Vincencio (1883–1955). Military man and politician. He starts his military career under General Rafael González Pacheco and fights in a number of combats during Matos's Revolución Libertadora (1901–1903). After the death of González Pacheco, Pérez Soto serves under Gómez as head of battalion, chief of regiment, and chief of staff for arms of Lara State. Under Gómez, Pérez Soto is appointed military and civil chief of the Tovar District of Mérida State. Military and civil chief in Lara, Falcón, and districts of Mérida State (1909). President of Apure, Portuguesa (1913, 1918–21), Bolívar State (1921–24), Trujillo State (1924–25), and Zulia State (1926–35).

Pérez, Juan Bautista (1869–1952). Lawyer and president of Venezuela (1929–31). In 1900, he joins the magistracy and becomes in 1929 head of the Federal Court of Cassation.

Pérez, Néstor Luis (1883–1949). Lawyer, jurist, and politician. President of Municipal Council of Maracaibo (1910). He is jailed in the San Carlos fort (1911) and in La Rotunda (1912–22). He becomes a political exile in 1924.

Pimentel, Antonio (1865–1938). Landowner and politician. At the end of the nineteenth century he is one of the richest coffee and cattle landowners in the states of Carabobo and Guárico. Gómez names him as the godfather of his son Florencio (1908). Secretary general (1909). Finance minister (1910–12). Inspector general of the army (1913).

Pimentel, Luis Rafael (1891–1959). Military man and politician. Instructor of artillery at the military school (1910). He is sent to the Chorrillos Military School in Peru (1910–12). He is appointed army captain (1914). Instructor of the artillery regiment of Montaña No. 1, based at the Mamey Barracks in Caracas (1916). He is a leader of the conspiracy against the government in 1919 and is imprisoned in La Rotunda until 1927.

Pocaterra, José Rafael (1889–1955). Writer and politician. He writes for the opposition *Caín* newspaper in 1907 and is jailed for one year. Secretary to public works minister (1909). Private secretary to José Angel Hernández Ron. He writes his first novel, *El doctor Bebé,* in 1912. Supervisor of uncultivated lands, Zulia State (1914). He writes for *El Fonógrafo* newspaper of Maracaibo (1914). Recorder of state property, Zulia State (1916). Director of finance and development of the Zulia State government. President of the deputy chamber of the legislative assembly of Zulia State (1918). He is jailed from 1919 to 1922 for being part of the Luis Rafael Pimentel conspiracy of 1919. He becomes a political exile in 1922.

Pulido Méndez, Manuel Antonio (1898–1965). Medical doctor, academic, and diplomat. In 1921 he is jailed for being involved with the strike by the tram workers. He becomes a political exile in 1921.

Ramírez, Juan Alberto (1865–1936). Politician. He is a shoe repairer and musician in his youth. He joins Castro's Restauradora revolution in 1899. He distinguishes himself in the campaigns against Matos's Revolución Libertadora (1901–1903). President of the states of Apure (1915–16), Nueva Esparta (1917–21), Sucre (1921–25), Táchira (1925–29), and Guárico (1929–35).

Ravell, Alberto (1905–1960). Writer and politician. He joins Pimentel's uprising in 1919 and is jailed in Puerto Cabello. He becomes a political exile in 1921.

Requena, Rafael (1879–1946). Medical doctor, diplomat, and politician. He graduates in medicine from Universidad Central de Venezuela (1904). He does medical postgraduate studies at the University of Paris (1904–1906). Consul general in Trinidad (1911–13). Head of customs, Puerto Cabello (1913–15) and Maracaibo (1915–16). Head of the National Library (1917–18). Senator for the Federal District (1918–21) and for Nueva Esparta State (1922–23). President of the National Congress (1921, 1923). President of Aragua State (1929–31).

Rivas Vásquez, Alejandro (1880–?). Lawyer, academic, and entrepreneur. Public works minister (1907). He becomes a political exile in 1910.

Rivero, Francisco Hermógenes (1875–1962). Civil engineer and medical doctor. He graduates from the Universidad Central de Venezuela with degrees in natural sciences (1890), civil engineering (1893), and medicine (1895). He practices medicine in Venezuela, Puerto Rico, the Dominican Republic, and from 1921 the United States. He is a political opponent of Gómez as soon as Gómez comes to power in December 1908.

Santos, Abel (1863–1933). Lawyer, jurist, and politician. Finance minister (1909). Venezuelan plenipotentiary minister in Colombia (1911). He becomes an exile between 1913 and 1925. Legal adviser to the Interior Ministry (1929). Attorney general (1931).

Sayago, Elías (1885–1976). Military man and public servant. He is part of Cipriano Castro's Revolución Restauradora of 1899. He fights under Gómez against Matos's Revolución Libertadora (1901–1903). Director of military school in Caracas (1919–20).

Smith, Alberto (1861–1942). Engineer and politician. Founding shareholder of Eléctricidad de Caracas (1895), Fábrica Nacional de Cemento, and the Jockey Club of Caracas. Development minister (1895). Rector of Universidad Central de Venezuela (1897, 1911). Venezuelan plenipotentiary minister in Peru (1908). He becomes a political exile in 1913.

Sotillo Picornell, José C. (1882–1957). Journalist, writer, and politician. He becomes a political exile almost as soon as Gómez comes to power in December 1908.

Tamayo, José Pío (1898–1935). Poet and politician. In 1917 he establishes the literary magazine *Renacimiento.* He becomes a political exile in 1922.

Tarazona, Eloy (1880–1952). Military man. He joins Gómez as an exile in Colombia (1892–99). He participates in Castro's Revolución Restauradora (1899). He is in charge of the personal security of Gómez.

Tejera, Humberto (1892–1971). Poet, jurist, and journalist. He contributes to the literary magazine *Génesis* (1905–1908) and to the newspaper *Ecos de la Sierra.* He works as a judge until 1918, when he becomes a political exile.

Tellería, Arístides (1861–1952). Military man and politician. Customs administrator for San Antonio del Táchira (1893, 1894). Deputy for Falcón State (1894, 1901). He supports Cipriano Castro's Revolución Restauradora of 1899. Customs administrator for Coro (1900, 1904). President of Falcón State (1903). Customs administrator of Puerto Cabello (1904). Senator for Falcón (1905). Development minister (1906). President of Bolívar State (1909–11, 1912–13). He becomes a political exile in 1914.

Toledo Trujillo, Henrique (1885–1986). Medical surgeon, university professor, and health expert. He graduates in medicine from the Universidad Central de Venezuela (1910). He specializes in orthopedic surgery and works as a medical doctor and surgeon until 1925. Head of Public Health (1925). Health minister (1929–31, 1932–35). He modernizes urban refuse collection in Caracas and other cities and founds the School of Agriculture.

Torrellas Urquiola, Diógenes (1860–1916). Military man, journalist, and politician. Head of the Yaracuy armed forces that fight against Matos's Revolución Libertadora (1901-1903) under generals Rafael González Pacheco and Santiago Briceño Ayesterán. President of Yaracuy State (1910-13) and Lara State (1913-16).

Torres, Gumersindo (1875-1947). Medical doctor and politician. He graduates in medicine in 1897. Development minister (1917-22, 1929-31). Under his advice, Congress enacts the country's first oil law (1920).

Urbina, Rafael Simón (1897-1950). Caudillo and politician. He spends a year at the military school (1910) and then leaves for Ciudad Bolívar and joins José Manuel Hernández's uprising in 1914; he is imprisoned between 1914 and 1915. He then becomes a small shopkeeper in Curimagua in Falcón State, where he takes up arms in 1919, together with his uncle Manuel Urbina, and spends the next four years fighting in the hinterland of Falcón State. He becomes a political exile and returns to the country in 1925. In July 1928 he launches a failed uprising with Fossi.

Urdaneta Maya, Enrique (1870-1928). Lawyer, politician, judge, journalist, and writer. He starts his political career at the side of Leopoldo Baptista in Trujillo State. President of Congress (1910). Member of the Federal Court of Cassation (1910-18). Secretary to Gómez (1918-25). Secretary general (1918-24).

Vallenilla Lanz, Laureano (1870-1936). Sociologist, historian, journalist. Inspector of the Guanta Customs (1892). Secretary to the president of Anzoátegui State (1892). Venezuelan consul at Amsterdam (1904-10). Inspector of education (1910). Editor of the newspaper *El Nuevo Diario* (1915-1931). Senator for Apure State (1916). President of the Senate (1920, 1923, 1930-31). Plenipotentiary minister in Paris (1931). His most famous book on the subject of positivism is *Cesarismo Democrático*, first published in 1919.

Vargas, Roberto (Tuerto) (1860-1948). Engineer, caudillo, and politician. Leading member of the Partido Liberal Nacionalista (1897), which supports the presidential candidacy of José Manuel Hernández. He is part of the uprising by Luciano Mendoza in 1901 against Cipriano Castro's government. He supports Matos's Revolución Libertadora (1901-1903). Public works minister (1908-1909). President of Guárico State (1909). He takes part in Emilio Arévalo Cedeño's 1914 uprising. He becomes a political exile in 1914, returning to Venezuela in 1925. Senator for Apure State (1935).

Velasco Bustamante, Rafael María (1874–1948). Military man, journalist, teacher, and politician. He marries Cipriano Castro's sister, José del Carmen Castro. His sister, Mercedes, is married to José María García Velasco. He starts his working life as a school teacher in San Cristóbal, Táchira, where he establishes a school and contributes articles to the newspaper *Ecos de Occidente*. He joins Castro's Revolución Restauradora as an officer in the chief of staff and is an equerry to Castro. Governor of the Federal District (1899–1900, 1902). Customs administrator at Puerto Cabello (1900). Provisional president of Mérida State (1901). Superintendent of tobacco and liquor rents (1904). Deputy for the states of Mérida (1904) and Lara (1905). Deputy for Táchira State (1909). President of Aragua State (1918–21) and Lara State (1921–27). Governor of the Federal District (1925–29, 1931–35). Finance minister (1929–1931).

Vélez, Luis (1860–1935). Land surveyor and engineer. Chief engineer for the construction of the road to Táchira (1911). Public Works Minister (1915–22, 1933–34).

Vidal, Zoilo (1866–1930). Military man and politician. He joins Jose Manuel Hernández (El "Mocho") in April 1892 in Guayana to support Joaquín Crespo's Revolución Legalista. He supports Mocho's uprising in 1898 against President Ignacio Andrade Troconis, and in 1899 against Cipriano Castro. Joins Matos's Revolución Libertadora against President Castro. He is exiled in Curacao until 1909, when he returns to Venezuela and is appointed president of Sucre State (1909–10). In 1913 he joins the conspiracy to oust Gómez and is jailed in La Rotunda until 1921, when he transferred to the Caracas lunatic asylum until his death in 1930.

Zuloaga Blanco, Armando (1905–1929). Politician. Member of the executive board of the Venezuelan Federation of Students (1928). He is one of the organizers of Student Week in 1928. He is later jailed at the Libertador castle in Puerto Cabello.

Zumeta, César (1863–1955). Writer, journalist, diplomat, and politician. He is expelled from the country in 1883 for his opposition to the administration of Antonio Guzmán Blanco. He returns the following year during the government of Joaquín Crespo but is imprisoned and exiled. In New York he manages the Casa Editorial Hispanoamericana (1894). Venezuelan consul general in London (1904). He returns to Venezuela after Gómez's coup of December 1908. Political director of Interior Ministry (1913). Interior minister (1912–1914). From 1915 to 1932 he has various diplomatic posts, principally as representative of Venezuela at the League of Nations. He returns to Venezuela in 1932 and is appointed president of Congress.

Zúñiga Cisneros, Miguel (1897–1984). Medical doctor, academic, and politician. President of the Nacional Council of Students (1921). He supports the strike by the tram workers of Caracas (1921). He is jailed and then expelled from the country.

Year	Interior	Foreign Affairs	Defense	Finance	Development
1908	Francisco Linares Alcántara	Francisco González Guinán	Régulo Olivares	Jesús Muñoz Tebar	Rafael María Carabaño
1909	Francisco Linares Alcántara	Francisco González Guinán / Juan Pietri	Régulo Olivares	Jesús Muñoz Tebar / Abel Santos	Rafael María Carabaño
1910	Francisco Linares Alcántara	Ángel César Rivas / Manuel Antonio Matos	Régulo Olivares / Manuel Vicente Castro Zavala	Manuel Porras / Antonio Pimentel	Rafael María Carabaño / Bernabé Planas
1911	Francisco Linares Alcántara	Manuel Antonio Matos	Manuel Vicente Castro Zavala	Antonio Pimentel	Aquiles Iturbe
1912	Francisco Linares Alcántara / César Zumeta	Manuel Antonio Matos / José Ladislao Andara	Manuel Vicente Castro Zavala / Ismael Pereira Alvárez / Victorino Márquez Bustillos	Antonio Pimentel / Manuel Porras Echenagucia / Román Cárdenas	Aquiles Iturbe / Pedro Emilio Coll
1913	César Zumeta	José Ladislao Andara	Victorino Márquez Bustillos	Román Cárdenas	Pedro Emilio Coll
1914	César Zumeta / Pedro Manuel Arcaya	Manuel Díaz Rodríguez / Ignacio Andrade Troconis	Manuel Vicente Castro Zavala	Román Cárdenas	Pedro Emilio Coll / Santiago Fontiveros
1915	Pedro Manuel Arcaya	Ignacio Andrade Troconis	Manuel Vicente Castro Zavala	Román Cárdenas	Santiago Fontiveros
1916	Pedro Manuel Arcaya	Ignacio Andrade Troconis	Manuel Vicente Castro Zavala	Román Cárdenas	Manuel Díaz Rodríguez
1917	Pedro Manuel Arcaya / Ignacio Andrade Troconis	Bernardino Mosquera	Carlos Jiménez Rebolledo	Román Cárdenas	Manuel Díaz Rodríguez / Gumersindo Torres

Ministry

Public Works	Education	Health	Secretary General	Federal District Governor
Roberto Vargas	Samuel Darío Maldonado	Ministry created in 1929	Leopoldo Baptista	Aquiles Iturbe
Roberto Vargas / José María Ortega Martínez	Samuel Darío Maldonado / Trino Baptista		Leopoldo Baptista / Antonio Pimentel	Aquiles Iturbe / Carlos León / Francisco Antonio Colmenares Pacheco
Rafael R. Alvárez / Román Cárdenas	Trino Baptista		Francisco González Guinán	Francisco Antonio Colmenares Pacheco
Román Cárdenas	Trino Baptista / José Gil Fortoul		Francisco González Guinán	Francisco Antonio Colmenares Pacheco / Victorino Márquez Bustillos
Román Cárdenas / Rafael R. Alvárez	José Gil Fortoul / Domingo Arreaza Monagas / Felipe Guevara Rojas		Francisco González Guinán / Ezequiel A. Vivas	Victorino Márquez Bustillos / Juan Crisóstomo Gómez
Domingo Antonio Coronil	Felipe Guevara Rojas		Ezequiel A. Vivas	Juan Crisóstomo Gómez
Luis Vélez	Felipe Guevara Rojas		Ezequiel A. Vivas	Juan Crisóstomo Gómez
Luis Vélez	Felipe Guevara Rojas		Ezequiel A. Vivas	Juan Crisóstomo Gómez
Luis Vélez	Carlos Aristimuño Coll		Ezequiel A. Vivas	Juan Crisóstomo Gómez
Luis Vélez	Carlos Aristimuño Coll / Rafael González Rincones		Ezequiel A. Vivas	Juan Crisóstomo Gómez

Year	Interior	Foreign Affairs	Defense	Finance	Development
1918	Ignacio Andrade Troconis	Bernardino Mosquera	Carlos Jiménez Rebolledo	Román Cárdenas	Gumersindo Torres
1919 1920	Ignacio Andrade Troconis	Estebán Gil Borges	Carlos Jiménez Rebolledo	Román Cárdenas	Gumersindo Torres
1921	Ignacio Andrade Troconis	Estebán Gil Borges / Pedro Itriago Chacín	Carlos Jiménez Rebolledo	Román Cárdenas	Gumersindo Torres
1922	Francisco Baptista Galindo	Pedro Itriago Chacín	Carlos Jiménez Rebolledo	Román Cárdenas / Melchor Centeno Graü	Gumersindo Torres / Antonio Alamo
1923	Francisco Baptista Galindo	Pedro Itriago Chacín	Carlos Jiménez Rebolledo	Melchor Centeno Graü	Antonio Alamo
1924	Francisco Baptista Galindo	Pedro Itriago Chacín	Carlos Jiménez Rebolledo	Melchor Centeno Graü	Antonio Alamo
1925	Francisco Baptista Galindo / Pedro Manuel Arcaya	Pedro Itriago Chacín	Carlos Jiménez Rebolledo	Melchor Centeno Graü	Antonio Alamo
1926	Pedro Manuel Arcaya	Pedro Itriago Chacín	Carlos Jiménez Rebolledo	Melchor Centeno Graü	Antonio Alamo
1927	Pedro Manuel Arcaya	Pedro Itriago Chacín	Carlos Jiménez Rebolledo	Melchor Centeno Graü	Antonio Alamo
1928	Pedro Manuel Arcaya	Pedro Itriago Chacín	Carlos Jiménez Rebolledo	Melchor Centeno Graü	Antonio Alamo
1929	Pedro Manuel Arcaya / Rubén González	Pedro Itriago Chacín	Tobías Uribe	Melchor Centeno Graü / Rafael María Velasco Bustamante	José Ignacio Cárdenas / Gumersindo Torres

	Ministry			
Public Works	*Education*	*Health*	*Secretary General*	*Federal District Governor*
Luis Vélez	Rafael González Rincones		Elías Rodríguez / Enrique Urdaneta Maya	Juan Crisóstomo Gómez
Luis Vélez	José Antonio Linares		Enrique Urdaneta Maya	Juan Crisóstomo Gómez
Luis Vélez	José Antonio Linares		Enrique Urdaneta Maya	Juan Crisóstomo Gómez
Tomás Bueno	José Ladislao Andara / Rubén González		Enrique Urdaneta Maya	Juan Crisóstomo Gómez
Tomás Bueno	Rubén González		Enrique Urdaneta Maya	Juan Crisóstomo Gómez / Julio Hidalgo
Tomás Bueno	Rubén González		Enrique Urdaneta Maya	Julio Hidalgo
Tomás Bueno	Rubén González		Francisco Baptista Galindo	Rafael María Velasco Bustamante
Tomás Bueno	Rubén González		Francisco Baptista Galindo	Rafael María Velasco Bustamante
José Ignacio Cárdenas	Rubén González		Francisco Baptista Galindo	Rafael María Velasco Bustamante
José Ignacio Cárdenas	Rubén González		Francisco Baptista Galindo	Rafael María Velasco Bustamante
Luis María González Niño	Rubén González / Samuel E. Niño	Henrique Toledo Trujillo	Sixto Tovar	Rafael María Velasco Bustamante / José María García Velasco

Cabinet Ministers, 1908–1935 (continued)

Year	Interior	Foreign Affairs	Defense	Finance	Development
1930	Rubén González	Pedro Itriago Chacín	Tobías Uribe	Rafael María Velasco Bustamante	Gumersindo Torres
1931	Rubén González / Pedro Rafael Tinoco	Santiago Key Ayala / Pedro Itriago Chacín	Eleazar López Contreras	Efraín González	Gumersindo Torres / Rafael Cayama Martínez
1932	Pedro Rafael Tinoco	Pedro Itriago Chacín	Eleazar López Contreras	Efraín González	Rafael Cayama Martínez
1933	Pedro Rafael Tinoco	Pedro Itriago Chacín	Eleazar López Contreras	Efraín González	Rafael Cayama Martínez
1934	Pedro Rafael Tinoco	Pedro Itriago Chacín	Eleazar López Contreras	Efraín González	Rafael Cayama Martínez
1935	Pedro Rafael Tinoco	Pedro Itriago Chacín	Eleazar López Contreras	Efraín González	Rafael Cayama Martínez

Source: Adapted from MinRelInt, *Memoria*, 1908–1935; Fernández, *Gómez, El Rehabilitador*, pp. 328–32; Fundación Pola *Diccionario de Historia de Venezuela*; and Velásquez, *Confidencias Imaginarias de Juan Vicente Gómez*, pp. 429–505.

Ministry

Public Works	Education	Health	Secretary General	Federal District Governor
Luis María González Niño / Federico Alvárez Feo	Samuel E. Niño	Henrique Toledo Trujillo	Sixto Tovar	José María García Velasco
Melchor Centeno Graü	Rafael González Rincones	Henrique Toledo Trujillo / Juan E. París	Rafael Requena	José María García Velasco / Rafael María Velasco Bustamante
Melchor Centeno Graü	Rafael González Rincones	Henrique Toledo Trujillo	Rafael Requena	Rafael María Velasco Bustamante
Luis Vélez	Rafael González Rincones	Henrique Toledo Trujillo	Rafael Requena / Enrique Urdaneta Carrillo	Rafael María Velasco Bustamante
Luis Vélez	Rafael González Rincones	Henrique Toledo Trujillo	Enrique Urdaneta Carrillo	Rafael María Velasco Bustamante
Antonio Díaz González	Rafael González Rincones	Henrique Toledo Trujillo	Enrique Urdaneta Carrillo	Rafael María Velasco Bustamante

Cabinet Ministers: Distribution between Single, Double, and Multiple Ministry Occupation

Single Ministry

Minister	Ministry	Period	Years
Alamo, Antonio	Development	1922–29	6.50
Alcántara, Francisco Linares	Interior	1908–12	3.50
Alvárez Feo, Federico	Public Works	1930	0.50
Aristimuño Coll, Carlos	Education	1916–17	1.5
Arreaza Monagas, Domingo	Education	1912	0.25
Baptista, Leopoldo	Secretary General	1908–1909	1.25
Baptista, Trino	Education	1909–11	2
Bueno, Tomás	Public Works	1922–26	5
Carabaño, Rafael María	Development	1908–10	1.5
Cayama Martínez, Rafael	Development	1931–35	4.50
Coll, Pedro Emilio	Development	1912–14	2.00
Colmenares Pacheco, Francisco Antonio	Fed. District Governor	1909–11	2.00
Coronil, Domingo Antonio	Public Works	1913	1.00
Díaz González, Antonio	Public Works	1935	1.00
Fontiveros, Santiago	Development	1914–15	1.50
García Velasco, José María	Fed. District Governor	1929–31	2.00
Gil Borges, Esteban	Foreign Affairs	1919–21	2.50
Gil Fortoul, José	Education	1911–12	1.00
Gómez, Juan Crisóstomo	Fed. District Governor	1912–23	11.00
González Niño, Luis María	Public Works	1929–30	1.50
González, Efraín	Finance	1931–35	5.00
Guevara Rojas, Felipe	Education	1912–15	3.25
Hidalgo, Julio	Federal District Governor	1923–24	1.50
Jiménez Rebolledo, Carlos	Defense	1917–28	12.00
Key Ayala, Santiago	Foreign Affairs	1931	0.50
León, Carlos	Federal District Governor	1909	0.25
Linares, José Antonio	Education	1919–21	3.00
López Contreras, Eleazar	Defense	1931–35	5.00
Maldonado, Samuel Darío	Education	1908–1909	0.50
Matos, Manuel Antonio	Foreign Affairs	1910–12	2.00
Mosquera, Bernardino	Foreign Affairs	1917–18	2.00
Muñoz Tebar, Jesús	Finance	1908–1909	0.50
Niño, Samuel E.	Education	1929–30	1.50
Olivares, Régulo L.	Defense	1908–10	1.50
Ortega Martínez, José María	Public Works	1909	0.50
París, Juan E	Health	1931	0.50
Pereira Alvárez, Ismael	Defense	1912	0.25
Pietri, Juan	Foreign Affairs	1909–10	0.50
Planas., Bernabé	Development	1910	0.50
Porras Echenagucia, Manuel	Finance	1912	0.25
Porras, Manuel	Finance	1910	0.50
Requena, Rafael	Secretary General	1931–33	2.50
Rivas, Angel César	Foreign Affairs	1910	0.50
Rodríguez, Elias	Secretary General	1918	0.50
Santos, Abel	Finance	1909	0.50
Tinoco, Pedro Rafael	Interior	1931–35	4.50
Tovar, Sixto	Secretary General	1928–30	3.00
Urdaneta Carrillo, Enrique	Secretary General	1933–35	2.50
Urdaneta Maya, Enrique	Secretary General	1918–24	6.50
Uribe, Tobías	Defense	1929–30	2.00
Vargas, Roberto	Public Works	1908–1909	0.50
Vivas, Ezequiel A.	Secretary General	1912–17	5.50
Zumeta, César	Interior	1912–14	2.00

No. of Ministers: 53   *Years in Office:* 124   *% of Total:* 49.6

Minister	Ministry	Period	Years
Alvárez, Rafael R.	Public Works	1910	0.50
	Public Works	1912	0.50
Andrade Troconis, Ignacio	Foreign Affairs	1914–16	2.50
	Interior	1917–21	4.50
Arcaya, Pedro Manuel	Interior	1914–17	3.00
	Interior	1925–29	4.00
Baptista Galindo, Francisco	Interior	1922–25	3.5
	Secretary General	1925–27	2
Cárdenas, José Ignacio	Public Works	1927–29	2.00
	Development	1929	0.50
Cárdenas, Román	Public Works	1910–12	2.00
	Finance	1912–22	10.00
Castro Zavala, Manuel Vicente	Defense	1910–12	2.00
	Defense	1914–16	3.00
Centeno Graü, Melchor	Finance	1922–29	7.00
	Public Works	1931–32	2.00
Díaz Rodríguez, Manuel	Foreign Affairs	1914	0.50
	Development	1916–17	1.50
González Guinán, Francisco	Foreign Affairs	1908–1909	0.50
	Secretary General	1910–12	2.50
González Rincones, Rafael	Education	1917–18	1.50
	Education	1931–35	5.00
González, Rubén	Education	1922–29	7.00
	Interior	1929–31	2.00
Itriago Chacín, Pedro	Foreign Affairs	1921–30	9.50
	Foreign Affairs	1931–35	4.50
Iturbe, Aquiles	Federal District Governor	1908–1909	0.25
	Development	1911–12	1.50
Ladislao Andara, José	Foreign Affairs	1912–14	1.50
	Education	1922	0.50
Márquez Bustillos, Victorino	Defense	1912–13	1.25
	Federal District Governor	1911–12	1.00
Pimentel, Antonio	Secretary General	1909–10	0.75
	Finance	1910–12	1.75
Toledo Trujillo, Henrique	Health	1929–31	2.50
	Health	1932–5	4.00
Torres, Gumersindo	Development	1917–22	5.00
	Development	1929–31	2.00
Vélez, Luis	Public Works	1914–21	8.00
	Public Works	1933–34	2.00

No. of Ministers: 20   *Years in Office: 115.5*   *% of Total: 46.2*

Multiple Ministry (Three +)

Minister	Ministry	Period	Years
Rafael María Velasco Bustamante	Federal District Governor	1925–28	4.50
	Finance	1929–30	1.50
	Federal District Governor	1931–35	4.50

No. of Ministers: 1   *Years in Office: 10.5*   *% of Total: 4.2*

Source: Adapted from table given above.

State Presidents, 1909–1935

State Presidents, 1909–1921

State	1909	1910	1911	1912	1913	1914
Anzoátegui	Baltazar Vallenilla Lanz	Armando Rolando	Armando Rolando	Armando Rolando	Armando Rolando / Manuel Antonio Guevara	Manuel Antonio Guevara
Apure	Julio Rodríguez Silva / José de Jesús Gabaldón	José de Jesús Gabaldón	I. Quintana / José de Jesús Gabaldón	José de Jesús Gabaldón	José de Jesús Gabaldón	José de Jesús Gabaldón
Aragua	A. Carnevali M. / Raimundo Andueza Palacios	Raimundo Andueza Palacios	Raimundo Andueza Palacios / Santiago González Guinán / Félix Galavís	Félix Galavís	Félix Galavís	Félix Galavís / Julio Hidalgo
Barinas (Zamora)	Carlos Jiménez Rebolledo	Carlos Jiménez Rebolledo	Carlos Jiménez Rebolledo	Carlos Jiménez Rebolledo	Carlos Jiménez Rebolledo	Carlos Jiménez Rebolledo
Bolívar	Antonio Delgado / L. Godoy / Arístides Tellería	Arístides Tellería	Arístides Tellería / L. Godoy	L. Godoy / Arístides Tellería	Arístides Tellería	Arístides Tellería / Marcelino Torres García
Carabobo	Samuel E. Niño / J. A. Martínez Méndez	J. A. Martínez Méndez	J. A. Martínez Méndez / Gregorio Cedeño	Gregorio Cedeño	Gregorio Cedeño	Emilio Fernández
Cojedes	Francisco Parra Pacheco / José Rafael Luque	José Rafael Luque	José Rafael Luque	José Rafael Luque	José Rafael Luque	José Rafael Luque
Falcón	Mariano García / Amábile Solagnie	Amábile Solagnie / León Jurado	León Jurado	León Jurado	León Jurado	León Jurado

1915	1916	1917	1918	1919	1920	1921
Silverio González	Silverio González	Silverio González	Manuel Antonio Guevara	Manuel Antonio Guevara	Manuel Antonio Guevara	Luis Godoy
Juan Alberto Ramírez	Juan Alberto Ramírez	Juan Alberto Ramírez	Vincencio Pérez Soto	Vincencio Pérez Soto	Vincencio Pérez Soto	Vincencio Pérez Soto / Hermán Febres Cordero
Julio Hidalgo	Julio Hidalgo	Julio Hidalgo	Julio Hidalgo / Rafael María Velasco Bustamante	Rafael María Velasco Bustamante	Rafael María Velasco Bustamante	Samuel Darío Maldonado
Carlos Jiménez Rebolledo	Isilio Febres Cordero	Isilio Febres Cordero	Isilio Febres Cordero	Isilio Febres Cordero	Isilio Febres Cordero	Isilio Febres Cordero
Marcelino Torres García	Marcelino Torres García	Marcelino Torres García	Marcelino Torres García	Marcelino Torres García	Marcelino Torres García	Vincencio Pérez Soto
Emilio Fernández	Emilio Fernández	Emilio Fernández	Emilio Fernández	Emilio Fernández	Emilio Fernández	José A. Baldó
José Felipe Arcay	José Felipe Arcay	José Felipe Arcay	José Felipe Arcay	José Felipe Arcay	José Felipe Arcay	José Felipe Arcay
León Jurado	León Jurado	León Jurado	León Jurado	León Jurado	León Jurado	León Jurado

State	*1909*	*1910*	*1911*	*1912*	*1913*	*1914*
Guárico	Manuel Sarmiento / Roberto Vargas	J. A. Hernández Ron	J. A. Hernández Ron / David Gimón	David Gimón	Manuel Sarmiento	Manuel Sarmiento
Lara	Carlos Liscano / Diego Bautista Ferrer	Manuel S. Araujo	Manuel S. Araujo / Rafael Garmendía Rodríguez	Rafael Garmendía Rodríguez	Rafael Garmendía Rodríguez / Diógenes Torrellas Urquiola	Diógenes Torrellas Urquiola
Mérida	Amador Uzcátegui G. / Estebán Chalbaud Cardona	Estebán Chalbaud Cardona	Estebán Chalbaud Cardona	Estebán Chalbaud Cardona	Estebán Chalbaud Cardona	Amador Uzcátegui
Miranda	Benjamín Arriens U.	Benjamín Arriens U.	Benjamín Arriens U. / Juan Crisóstomo Gómez	Juan Crisóstomo Gómez	Juan Crisóstomo Gómez	Juan Crisóstom Gómez
Monagas	Carlos Herrera / P. Giuseppi Monagas	P. Giuseppi Monagas / Emilio Fernández	Emilio Fernández	Emilio Fernández	Emilio Fernández	Elbano Mibelli
Nueva Esparta	Pedro Ducharne	Pedro Ducharne	Pedro Ducharne	Pedro Ducharne	Pedro Ducharne	Pedro Ducharne
Portuguesa	Ovidio María Abreu	Ovidio María Abreu	Ovidio María Abreu / José Rafael Gabaldón	José Rafael Gabaldón	Vincencio Pérez Soto	José Antonio Baldó
Sucre	Froilán Prato / Zoilo Vidal	Zoilo Vidal / Eliseo Sarmiento	Eliseo Sarmiento	Eliseo Sarmiento	Eliseo Sarmiento	Eliseo Sarmiento
Táchira	Jesús Velasco Bustamante / Aquiles Iturbe	Aquiles Iturbe / Régulo L. Olivares	Régulo L. Olivares / Pedro Murillo	Pedro Murillo	Pedro Murillo	José Manu Centeno Pacheco / Eustoquio Gómez

1915	1916	1917	1918	1919	1920	1921
Manuel Sarmiento	Manuel Sarmiento	Manuel Sarmiento	Manuel Sarmiento	Manuel Sarmiento	Manuel Sarmiento	Manuel Sarmiento
Diógenes Torrellas Urquiola	Diógenes Torrellas Urquiola	David Gimón	David Gimón	David Gimón	David Gimón	Rafael María Velasco Bustamante
Amador Uzcátegui	Amador Uzcátegui	Amador Uzcátegui	Amador Uzcátegui	Amador Uzcátegui	Amador Uzcátegui	Amador Uzcátegui
José Luna	José Luna	José Luna	Antonio B. Medina	Antonio B. Medina	Antonio B. Medina	Antonio B. Medina
Manuel Rugeles	Manuel Rugeles	Manuel Rugeles	Manuel Ledezma	Manuel Ledezma	Manuel Ledezma	Emilio Fernández
Pedro Ducharne	Pedro Ducharne	Juan Alberto Ramírez	Juan Alberto Ramírez	Juan Alberto Ramírez	Juan Alberto Ramírez	Juan Alberto Ramírez / Antonio José Cárdenas
José Antonio Baldó	José Antonio Baldó	José Antonio Baldó	José Antonio Baldó	José Antonio Baldó	José Antonio Baldó	Gregorio Cedeño
Eliseo Sarmiento	Eliseo Sarmiento	Eliseo Sarmiento	Silverio González	Silverio González	Silverio González	Silverio González / Juan Alberto Ramírez
Eustoquio Gómez	Eustoquio Gómez	Eustoquio Gómez	Eustoquio Gómez	Eustoquio Gómez	Eustoquio Gómez	Eustoquio Gómez

State Presidents, 1909–1921 *(continued)*

State	1909	1910	1911	1912	1913	1914
Trujillo	Trino Baptista / Víctor M. Baptista	Víctor M. Baptista	Víctor M. Baptista	Víctor M. Baptista / Rafael Román Colmenares / Timoleón Omaña / José María García Velasco	José María García Velasco	José María García Velasco / Santiago Fontiveros
Yaracuy	Rafael Garmendia Rodríguez	Diógenes Torrellas Urquiola	Diógenes Torrellas Urquiola	Diógenes Torrellas Urquiola	Diógenes Torrellas Urquiola / Juan Victoriano Giménez	Juan Victoriano Giménez
Zulia	José I. Lares / Gumersindo Méndez	Gumersindo Méndez	Gumersindo Méndez	Gumersindo Méndez	Gumersindo Méndez	Gumersindo Méndez / José María García Velasco

State Presidents, 1922–1935

State	1922	1923	1924	1925	1926	1927
Anzoátegui	Luis Godoy	Luis Godoy / Silverio González	Silverio González / Lino Díaz	Lino Díaz	Lino Díaz	Lino Díaz
Apure	Hermán Febres Cordero	Hermán Febres Cordero	José Domínguez	José Domínguez	José Domínguez	José Domíngue
Aragua	Samuel Darío Maldonado	Samuel Darío Maldonado / Ignacio Andrade Sosa	Ignacio Andrade Sosa	Ignacio Andrade Sosa	Ignacio Andrade Sosa	Ignacio Andrade S

1915	1916	1917	1918	1919	1920	1921
Santiago Fontiveros	Santiago Fontiveros	Santiago Fontiveros	Timoleón Omaña	Timoleón Omaña	Timoleón Omaña	Santiago Fontiveros
Juan Victoriano Giménez	Juan Victoriano Giménez	Juan Victoriano Giménez	Juan Victoriano Giménez	Juan Victoriano Giménez	Juan Victoriano Giménez	Juan Victoriano Giménez
José María García Velasco	José María García Velasco	José María García Velasco	José María García Velasco / Santos Matute Gómez	Santos Matute Gómez	Santos Matute Gómez	Santos Matute Gómez

1928	1929	1930	1931	1932	1933	1934	1935
Lino Díaz	Lino Díaz / José de Jesús Gabaldón	José de Jesús Gabaldón	José de Jesús Gabaldón / Juan Francisco Castillo	Juan Francisco Castillo	Juan Francisco Castillo	Juan Francisco Castillo	Juan Francisco Castillo
José Domínguez	José Domínguez	José Domínguez	José Domínguez	José Domínguez	José Domínguez	José Domínguez	José Domínguez
Ignacio Andrade Sosa	Rafael Requena	Rafael Requena	Rafael Requena / Samuel E. Niño	Samuel E. Niño	Samuel E. Niño	Samuel E. Niño	Samuel E. Niño

State	1922	1923	1924	1925	1926	1927
Barinas (Zamora)	Isilio Febres Cordero	Isilio Febres Cordero	Ismael Arellano	Ismael Arellano	Ismael Arellano	Ismael Arellano
Bolívar	Vincencio Pérez Soto	Vincencio Pérez Soto / Silverio González	Silverio González	Silverio González	Silverio González	Silverio González
Carabobo	José A. Baldó	José A. Baldó	José A. Baldó / José Felipe Arcay	José Felipe Arcay	José Felipe Arcay	José Felipe Arcay
Cojedes	José Felipe Arcay	José Felipe Arcay	José Felipe Arcay / Guillermo Barreto Méndez	Guillermo Barreto Méndez	Guillermo Barreto Méndez	Guillermo Barreto Méndez
Falcón	León Jurado	León Jurado / Argenis Asuaje	Argenis Asuaje	Argenis Asuaje	Argenis Asuaje	Argenis Asuaje
Guárico	Manuel Sarmiento	Manuel Sarmiento / León Jurado	León Jurado	León Jurado	León Jurado	León Jurado
Lara	Rafael María Velasco Bustamante	Rafael María Velasco Bustamante	Rafael María Velasco Bustamante	Rafael María Velasco Bustamante / Pedro Lizárraga	Pedro Lizárraga	Pedro Lizárraga
Mérida	Amador Uzcátegui	Amador Uzcátegui	Amador Uzcátegui	Amador Uzcátegui	Amador Uzcátegui	Amador Uzcátegui
Miranda	Antonio B. Medina	Antonio B. Medina	José Rafael Luque	José Rafael Luque	José Rafael Luque	José Rafael Luque
Monagas	Emilio Fernández	Emilio Fernández / Pedro Ducharne	Manuel Ledesma	Manuel Ledesma	Manuel Ledesma	Manuel Ledesma
Nueva Esparta	Antonio José Cárdenas	J. M. Bermúdez / Antonio José Cárdenas	Antonio José Cárdenas	Antonio José Cárdenas / Manuel Díaz Rodríguez	Antonio José Cárdenas	Antonio José Cárdenas

1928	1929	1930	1931	1932	1933	1934	1935
Ismael Arellano	Ismael Arellano	Salvador Uzcátegui	Salvador Uzcátegui	Salvador Uzcátegui	Salvador Uzcátegui	Salvador Uzcátegui	Salvador Uzcátegui
Silverio González	Silverio González	Silverio González	José de Jesús Gabaldón	José de Jesús Gabaldón	Antonio Alamo	Antonio Alamo	Antonio Alamo
José María García Velasco	Santos Matute Gómez	Santos Matute Gómez	Santos Matute Gómez	Santos Matute Gómez	Santos Matute Gómez	Santos Matute Gómez	Santos Matute Gómez
Guillermo Barreto Méndez	Guillermo Barreto Méndez	Guillermo Barreto Méndez	Guillermo Barreto Méndez	Guillermo Barreto Méndez	Guillermo Barreto Méndez	Guillermo Barreto Méndez	Guillermo Barreto Méndez
Argenis Asuaje	Argenis Asuaje / León Jurado	León Jurado	León Jurado	León Jurado	León Jurado	León Jurado	León Jurado
León Jurado	León Jurado / Juan Alberto Ramírez	Juan Alberto Ramírez	Juan Alberto Ramírez	Juan Alberto Ramírez	Juan Alberto Ramírez	Juan Alberto Ramírez	Juan Alberto Ramírez
Pedro María Cárdenas	Eustoquio Gómez	Eustoquio Gómez	Eustoquio Gómez	Eustoquio Gómez	Eustoquio Gómez	Eustoquio Gómez	Eustoquio Gómez
José R. Dávila	José R. Dávila	José R. Dávila	José R. Dávila	José R. Dávila	Rafael Paredes Urdaneta	Rafael Paredes Urdaneta	Rafael Paredes Urdaneta
José Rafael Luque	José Rafael Luque	José Rafael Luque	José Rafael Luque	José Rafael Luque	José Rafael Luque	José Rafael Luque	José Rafael Luque
José de Jesús Gabaldón	José de Jesús Gabaldón	Lino Díaz	Lino Díaz	Lino Díaz	Lino Díaz	Lino Díaz	Lino Díaz
Antonio José Cárdenas	Antonio José Cárdenas / José Garbi	José Garbi / J. M. Bermúdez	J. M. Bermúdez	Manuel Díaz Rodríguez	Manuel Díaz Rodríguez	Manuel Díaz Rodríguez	Rafael Falcón

State	1922	1923	1924	1925	1926	1927
Portuguesa	Gregorio Cedeño	Gregorio Cedeño	Paulino Camero	Paulino Camero / José Garbi	Paulino Camero	Paulino Camero
Sucre	Juan Alberto Ramírez	Juan Alberto Ramírez	Juan Alberto Ramírez	Juan Alberto Ramírez / Carlos Sardi	Carlos Sardi	Carlos Sardi
Táchira	Eustoquio Gómez	Eustoquio Gómez	Eustoquio Gómez	Eustoquio Gómez / Juan Alberto Ramírez	Juan Alberto Ramírez	Juan Alberto Ramírez
Trujillo	Santiago Fontiveros	Santiago Fontiveros	Santiago Fontiveros	Santiago Fontiveros / Vincencio Pérez Soto	Vincencio Pérez Soto / José Antonio Baldó	Emilio Rivas
Yaracuy	Juan Victoriano Giménez	Juan Victoriano Giménez	José Antonio Baldó	José Antonio Baldó	José Antonio Baldó	Severiano Giménez
Zulia	Santos Matute Gómez	Santos Matute Gómez	Santos Matute Gómez	Isilio Febres Cordero	Santos Matute Gómez / Vincencio Pérez Soto	Vincencio Pérez Soto

Source: Adapted from MinRelInt, *Memoria,* 1908–35; Fernández, *Gómez, El Rehabilitador,* pp. 333–39; Fundación Polar, *Diccionario de Historia de Venezuela;* and Velásquez, *Confidencias Imaginarias de Juan Vicente Gómez,* pp. 429–505.

1928	1929	1930	1931	1932	1933	1934	1935
José A. Baldó	José A. Baldó	José A. Baldó	José A. Baldó	Josué Gómez	Josué Gómez	Josué Gómez	Josué Gómez
Carlos Sardi / José Garbi	José Garbi / Emilio Fernández / Antonio Alamo	Antonio Alamo	Antonio Alamo / Pedro María Cárdenas	Pedro María Cárdenas	Pedro María Cárdenas	Pedro María Cárdenas	Pedro María Cárdenas
Juan Alberto Ramírez	Juan Alberto Ramírez / Pedro María Cárdenas	Pedro María Cárdenas	Pedro María Cárdenas / José Antonio González	José Antonio González	José Antonio González	José Antonio González	José Antonio González
Emilio Rivas	Emilio Rivas	Emilio Rivas	Emilio Rivas / Juan Fernández Amparán	Juan Fernández Amparán	Juan Fernández Amparán	Juan Fernández Amparán	Silverio González
Severiano Giménez	Severiano Giménez / Félix Galavís	Félix Galavís	Félix Galavís	Félix Galavís	Félix Galavís	Félix Galavís	Félix Galavís
Vincencio Pérez Soto	Vincencio Pérez Soto	Vincencio Pérez Soto	Vincencio Pérez Soto	Vincencio Pérez Soto	Vincencio Pérez Soto	Vincencio Pérez Soto	Vincencio Pérez Soto

State Presidents: Distribution between Single, Double, and Multiple State Presidencies

Single State Presidency

State President	State	Period	Years
Abreu, O. M.	Portuguesa	1909–11	2.50
Andrade Sosa, Ignacio	Aragua	1923–28	6.00
Andueza Palacios, Raimundo	Aragua	1909–11	2.00
Araujo, Manuel S.	Lara	1910–11	1.50
Arellano, Ismael	Barinas	1924–29	6.00
Arriens U., Benjamín	Miranda	1909–11	2.50
Asuaje, Argenis	Falcón	1923–29	6.00
Baptista, Trino	Trujillo	1909	0.50
Baptista, Víctor M.	Trujillo	1909–12	2.75
Barreto Méndez, Guillermo	Cojedes	1924–35	11.50
Carnevali M., A.	Aragua	1909	0.50
Castillo, Juan Francisco	Anzoátegui	1931–35	4.50
Chalbaud Cardona, Esteban	Mérida	1909–13	4.50
Colmenares Pacheco, José Manuel	Táchira	1914	0.50
Dávila, José R.	Mérida	1928–32	5.00
Delgado, Antonio	Bolivar	1909	0.50
Domínguez, José	Apure	1924–35	12.00
Falcón, Rafael	Nueva Esparta	1935	1.00
Febres Cordero, Hermán	Apure	1921–1923	2.50
Fernández Amparán, Juan	Trujillo	1931–34	3.50
Ferrer, Diego Bautista	Lara	1909	0.50
Gabaldón, Jose Rafael	Portuguesa	1911–12	1.50
García, Mariano	Falcón	1909	0.50
Giménez, Juan Victoriano	Yaracuy	1913–23	10.50
Giménez, Severiano	Yaracuy	1927–29	2.50
Giuseppi Monagas, Pablo	Monagas	1909–10	1.00
Gómez, Josué	Portuguesa	1932–35	4.00
Gómez, Juan Crisóstomo	Miranda	1911–14	3.50
González Guinán, Santiago	Aragua	1911	0.50
González, José Antonio	Táchira	1931–35	4.50
Hernández Ron, J.A.	Guárico	1910–11	1.50
Herrera, Carlos	Monagas	1909	0.50
Hidalgo, Julio	Aragua	1914–18	4.00
Iturbe, Aquiles	Táchira	1909–10	1.00
Jiménez Rebolledo, Carlos	Barinas	1909–15	7.00
Lares, José I.	Zulia	1909	0.50
Liscano, Carlos	Lara	1909	0.50
Lizárraga, Pedro	Lara	1925–27	2.50
Luna, José	Miranda	1915–17	3.00
Maldonado, Samuel Darío	Aragua	1921–23	2.50
Martínez Méndez, J.A.	Carabobo	1909–11	2.00
Medina, Antonio B.	Miranda	1918–23	6.00
Méndez, Gumersindo	Zulia	1909–14	5.00
Mibelli, Elbano	Monagas	1914	1.00
Murillo, Pedro	Táchira	1911–13	2.50
Olivares, Régulo L.	Táchira	1910–11	1.00
Paredes Urdaneta, Rafael	Mérida	1933–35	3.00
Parra Pacheco, Francisco	Cojedes	1909	0.50
Prato, Froilán	Sucre	1909	0.50
Quintana, I.	Apure	1911	0.50
Requena, Rafael	Aragua	1929–31	2.50
Rivas, Emilio	Trujillo	1926–31	4.50

Rodríguez Silva, Julio	Apure	1909	0.50
Rolando, Armando	Anzoátegui	1910–13	3.50
Román Colmenares, Rafael	Trujillo	1912	0.25
Rugeles, Manuel	Monagas	1915–17	3.00
Sardi, Carlos	Sucre	1925–28	3.00
Sarmiento, Eliseo	Sucre	1910–17	7.50
Solagnie, Amabile	Falcón	1909–10	1.00
Torres García, Marcelino	Bolívar	1914–20	6.50
Uzcátegui, Salvador	Barinas	1930–35	6.00
Vallenilla Lanz, Baltazar	Anzoátegui	1909	1.00
Vargas, Roberto	Guárico	1909	0.50
Velasco Bustamante, Jesús	Táchira	1909	0.50

No. of Presidents: 65 *Years in Offices: 191.0* *% of Total: 35.3*

Double State Presidency

State President	State	Period	Years
Alamo, Antonio	Sucre	1929–31	2.00
	Bolívar	1933–5	3.00
Arcay, José Felipe	Cojedes	1915–24	9.50
	Carabobo	1924–27	3.50
Bermúdez, J. M.	Nueva Esparta	1923	0.50
	Nueva Esparta	1930–31	1.50
Camero, Paulino	Portuguesa	1924–25	1.50
	Portuguesa	1926–27	2.00
Cárdenas, Antonio José	Nueva Esparta	1921–22	1.50
	Nueva Esparta	1923–25	2.00
	Nueva Esparta	1926–29	3.50
Cedeño, Gregorio	Carabobo	1911–13	2.50
	Portuguesa	1921–23	3.00
Díaz Rodríguez, Manuel	Nueva Esparta	1925	0.50
	Nueva Esparta	1932–34	3.00
Díaz, Lino	Anzoátegui	1924–29	4.50
	Monagas	1930–35	6.00
Ducharne, Pedro	Nueva Esparta	1909–16	8.00
	Monagas	1923	0.50
Febres Cordero, Isilio	Barinas	1916–23	8.00
	Zulia	1925	1.00
Fontiveros, Santiago	Trujillo	1914–17	3.50
	Trujillo	1921–25	4.50
Galavís, Félix	Aragua	1911–14	3.00
	Yaracuy	1929–35	6.50
Garmendia Rodríguez, Rafael	Yaracuy	1909	1.00
	Lara	1911–13	2.00
Gimón, David	Guárico	1911–12	1.50
	Lara	1917–20	4.00
Gómez, Eustoquio	Táchira	1914–25	11.00
	Lara	1929–35	7.00
Gómez, Santos Matute	Zulia	1918–24	6.50
	Zulia	1925	0.50
	Carabobo	1929–35	7.00

Guevara, Manuel Antonio	Anzoátegui	1913–14	1.50
	Anzoátegui	1918–20	3.00
Jurado, León	Falcón	1910–23	13.00
	Guárico	1923–29	6.00
	Falcón	1929–35	6.50
Ledesma, Manuel	Monagas	1918–20	3.00
	Monagas	1924–27	4.00
Luque, José Rafael	Cojedes	1909–14	5.50
	Miranda	1924–35	12.00
Niño, Samuel E.	Carabobo	1909	0.50
	Aragua	1931–35	4.50
Omaña, Timoleón	Trujillo	1912	0.25
	Trujillo	1918–20	3.00
Sarmiento, Manuel	Guárico	1909	0.50
	Guárico	1913–23	10.50
Tellería, Arístides	Bolívar	1909–10	1.75
	Bolívar	1912–14	2.00
Torrellas Urquiola, Diógenes	Yaracuy	1910–13	3.50
	Guárico	1913–16	3.50
Uzcátegui G., Amador	Mérida	1909	0.50
	Mérida	1914–27	14.00
Velasco Bustamante, Rafael María	Aragua	1918–20	2.50
	Lara	1921–25	4.50

No. of Presidents: 27 | *Years in Offices: 231.5* | *% of Total: 42.8*

Multiple State Presidency

State President	*State*	*Period*	*Years*
Baldó, José Antonio	Portuguesa	1914–20	7.00
	Carabobo	1921–24	3.50
	Yaracuy	1924–26	3.00
	Trujillo	1926	0.50
	Portuguesa	1928–31	4.00
Cárdenas, Pedro María	Lara	1928	1.00
	Sucre	1931–5	4.50
	Táchira	1929–31	2.00
Fernández, Emilio	Monagas	1910–13	3.50
	Carabobo	1914–20	7.00
	Monagas	1921–23	2.50
	Sucre	1929	0.25
Gabaldón, José de Jesús	Apure	1909–10	1.50
	Apure	1911–14	3.50
	Monagas	1928–29	2.00
	Anzoátegui	1929–31	2.00
	Bolívar	1931–32	2.00
Garbi, José	Portuguesa	1925	0.50
	Sucre	1928–29	0.75
	Nueva Esparta	1929–30	1.00
García Velasco, José María	Trujillo	1912–14	1.75
	Zulia	1914–18	4.00
	Carabobo	1928	1.00

Godoy, Luis	Bolívar	1909	0.25
	Bolívar	1911–12	1.00
	Anzoátegui	1921–23	3.00
González, Silverio	Anzoátegui	1915–17	3.00
	Sucre	1918–21	3.50
	Anzoátegui	1922–23	1.00
	Bolívar	1924–30	6.50
	Trujillo	1935	1.00
Pérez Soto, Vincencio	Portuguesa	1913	1.00
	Apure	1918–21	3.50
	Bolívar	1921–24	3.50
	Trujillo	1924–25	1.00
	Zulia	1926–35	9.50
Ramirez, Juan Alberto	Apure	19–15–17	3.00
	Nueva Esparta	1917–21	4.50
	Sucre	1921–25	4.00
	Táchira	1925–29	4.00
	Guárico	1929–35	6.50
No. of Presidents: 10	*Years in Offices: 118.5*	*% of Total: 21.9*	

Source: Adapted from table given above.

Currency and Exchange Rate Information

Annual Exchange Rates for Bolívar, 1913–35

Year	US $	British £	Dutch Fls	French FFr
1913	5.28	26.02	2.15	1.01
1914	5.21	26.13	2.18	1.03
1915	5.31	25.55	2.17	0.96
1916	5.16	24.66	2.18	0.88
1917	5.13	24.44	2.18	0.88
1918	5.18	22.26	2.2	0.82
1919	5.21	21.64	2.05	0.7
1920	n/a	n/a	n/a	n/a
1921	5.97	23.75	n/a	0.45
1922	5.45	24.23	2.16	0.41
1923	5.32	23.95	2.07	0.31
1924	5.22	23.39	2.01	0.28
1925	5.19	24.23	2.08	0.24
1926	5.28	25.61	2.12	0.17
1927	5.3	25.8	2.14	0.21
1928	5.23	25.93	2.05	0.2
1929	5.22	25.4	2.09	0.21

Annual Exchange Rates for Bolívar, 1913–35 (continued)

Year	US $	British £	Dutch Fls	French FFr
1930	5.43	26.38	2.19	0.21
1931	6.12	26.7	2.47	0.24
1932	6.85	23.68	2.79	0.272
1933	5.34	21.82	2.71	0.27
1934	3.54	17.85	2.43	0.24
1935	3.92	19.28	2.67	0.26

Source: Fundación Polar, *Diccionario de Historia de Venezuela*, pp. 1241–44.

Annual Exchange Rate between Sterling and Dollar, 1909–35

Year	US $	Year	US $
1909	4.87	1923	4.58
1910	4.86	1924	4.42
1911	4.86	1925	4.83
1912	4.87	1926	4.86
1913	4.87	1927	4.86
1914	4.93	1928	4.87
1915	4.76	1929	4.86
1916	4.77	1930	4.86
1917	4.76	1931	4.54
1918	4.76	1932	3.51
1919	4.43	1933	4.24
1920	3.66	1934	5.04
1921	3.85	1935	4.90
1922	4.43		

Source: http://eh.net/hmit/exchangerates.

Present Day (2003) Multiplier of US Dollar, 1909–35

Year	US $	Multiplier (x)
1909	1	19.5
1910	1	19.5
1911	1	18.84
1912	1	18.84
1913	1	18.19
1914	1	17.76
1915	1	17.53
1916	1	17.36
1917	1	16.14
1918	1	13.74
1919	1	11.71
1920	1	10.19
1921	1	8.8
1922	1	9.85
1923	1	10.52
1924	1	10.33
1925	1	10.31
1926	1	10.06
1927	1	9.96
1928	1	10.15
1929	1	10.28
1930	1	10.28
1931	1	10.55
1932	1	11.57
1933	1	12.89
1934	1	13.59
1935	1	13.14

Source: http://www.westegg.com/inflation.

Introduction

1. For a detailed account of Gómez's coup see McBeth, *Gunboats, Corruption, and Claims.*

2. Cf. McBeth, *British Oil Policy, 1919–1939.*

3. Cf. McBeth, *Gunboats, Corruption, and Claims.*

4. Cf. Harwich, "Arma y Coraza"; idem, *Arma y Coraza;* idem, "Venezuelan Positivism and Modernity"; Siso Martínez et al., *El Concepto de la Historia de José Gil Fortoul;* and Siso Martínez et al., *El Concepto de la Historia en Laureano Vallenilla Lanz).* It should be noted that the term "positivism" in Venezuela is used in a very general way. With the exception of Rafael Villavicencio none of the people associated with positivism, such as Vallenilla Lanz and Gil Fortoul, were trained as philosophers (cf. Cappelletti, *Positivismo y evolucionismo en Venezuela).*

5. The roots of the philosophy lie with Hippolite Adolphe Taine, Georges Sores, Maurice Barres, Gustav Le Bon, and Sapiro Sighele.

6. In a study published by the Office of the Comptroller General in 1938, Crisalida Dupuy estimates that Gómez's wealth in 1932 amounted to $32 million, which increased to $48 million at the time of his death (cf. Polanco Alcántara, *Juan Vicente Gómez),* pp. 454–55.

7. Velásquez, *La Caída del Liberalismo Amarillo,* p. 364.

8. "Mensaje que el General Juan Vicente Gómez, Presidente de la República, presenta al Congreso," Caracas, May 29, 1909, in Gómez, *Documentos para la historia,* p. 21.

9. Ibid.

10. Juan Vicente Gómez, "A Los Venezolanos," Dec 20, 1908, in Gómez, *Documentos para la historia,* p. 4.

11. Cf. Griffin, "Regionalism's Role in Venezuelan Politics."

12. Pocaterra, *Gómez: The Shame of America.*

13. Cf. McBeth, *Gunboats,* pp. 81–104.

14. AAA File 2, A Térega Fombona to Aranguren, Aug 14, 1934, and Térega Fombona to Santos Domínici, Sept 2, 1934; McBeth, *Gómez and the Oil Companies,* p. 104.

15. Cf. Brito Figueroa, *Venezuela Siglo XX;* Carlos Brandt, *La época del terror en el país;* Rangel, *Los Andinos en el poder;* idem, *Capital y Desarrollo,* vol. 2; idem, *Gómez el amo del poder;* Polanco Alcántara, *Juan Vicente Gómez;* Caballero, *Gómez*

el tirano liberal; Siso, *La formación del pueblo venezolano;* Fuenmayor, *1928–1948;* idem, *Historia de la Venezuela Política Contemporánea, 1899–1969;* Baptista, *Venezuela, su historia y sus métodos de Gobierno;* Pocaterra, *Gómez: The Shame of America;* Betancourt, *Venezuela.*

CHAPTER ONE   *A New Era*

1. Fuenmayor, *Historia de la Venezuela Contemporánea,* vol. 1, p. 198.

2. Venezuela, Distrito Federal, Juzgado de Primera Instancia en lo Penal, *Alegatos ante la Corte Superior del Distrito Federal en la Causa seguida contra el General Eustoquio Gómez por homicidio,* p. 14. Isaías Nieto and Rafael de la Cova were also absolved, but the court requested that Eloy Tarazona be tried for the murder of the governor.

3. Velásquez, *La Caída del Liberalismo Amarillo,* p. xviii.

4. AHMSGPRCP Apr 16-30, 1909, P. Giuseppi Monagas to Gómez, Apr 16, 1909.

5. AHMCOP 100, Gómez to Pedro Murillo, Jan 1, 1909.

6. Ibid.

7. Velásquez, *La Caída del Liberalismo,* p. xviii.

8. Ibid.

9. Ibid., p. xvii.

10. Gómez to Alcántara, Sep 26, 1909, in Gómez, *Documentos para la historia,* p. 196; Arcaya, *Memorias del Doctor Pedro Manuel Arcaya,* p. 88.

11. Altuve Carrillo, *Prólogo,* in Siso, *Castro y Gómez,* pp. 21–22.

12. "Mensaje que el General Juan Vicente Gómez, Presidente de la República, presenta al Congreso," Caracas, May 29, 1909, in Gómez, *Documentos para la Historia,* p. 21. The Council of State had been previously created on four other occasions: 1857, 1881, 1891, and 1893. The 1881 and 1891 constitutions made it the highest power in the land, which was used by Guzmán Blanco to nominate presidential candidates.

13. *Gaceta Oficial* vol. 38, no. 6, No. 11034, Jun 22, 1910.

14. Venezuela, Congreso Nacional, *Discurso pronunciado por el General Arístides Tellería,* p. 5.

15. This ended its functions on January 6, 1910, when the Consejo Superior de Higiene y Salubridad Pública was formed. On the same day the Dirección de Higiene y Salubridad Pública was created within the Interior Ministry. Later this was centralized in the Oficina de Sanidad Nacional, administered directly by the presidency. On August 11, 1930, the Ministerio de Salubridad y Agricultura y Cría was created (Venezuela, Ministerio de Salubridad y de Agricultura y Cría, *La Sanidad en Venezuela, 1909–1930,* p. 495).

16. Some observers were not convinced of the genuine intent of these reforms. E. Keeling, the British minister, many years later reported that the improvement of the water supply and the repairs to certain hospitals "are more than

anything else for the improvement of the capital as a show place and a personal monument for the glorification of General Gómez" (FO 371/4623 E. Keeling to Lord Curzon, Apr 29, 1934).

17. Venezuela, Ministerio de Hacienda (MinHa), *Historical Sketch of the Fiscal Life of Venezuela,* p. xii.

18. Ibid., p. xiii.

19. Booth, "Venezuela," pp. 226–43, 226–27.

20. In 1909, according to Hiram Bingham, there was between Valencia and Barinas "a passable cart road" (Bingham, *The Journal of an Expedition across Venezuela and Colombia, 1906–1907,* p. 37) open only during the dry season from December to March and impossible to use during the rainy season.

21. Cf. Rayburn, "Some Aspects of the Impact of Anglo-Saxon Capital and Technology in Venezuela"; Muñoz, "The Táchira Frontier, 1881–1899"; and Bingham, *The Journal of an Expedition across Venezuela and Colombia, 1906–1907.*

22. Ministerio de Obras Públicas (MOP), *Memoria 1917,* Exposición, Cuadro, p. 4, and MOP *Memoria 1920,* Cuadro, p. 10.

23. In 1915, the First Pan American Road Congress held in Buenos Aires acknowledged Gómez's efforts by electing him honorary president.

24. AHMSGPRCP Feb 1–28, 1920, N. Veloz Goiticoa, "Reseña sinóptica confidencial sobre la segunda conferencia Financiera Panamericana," undated.

25. Cf. Jahn, *El desarrollo de las vías de comunicación en Venezuela;* and, Vallenilla Marcano, *Carreteras de Venezuela.* The first automobile to reach the country was imported by Doña Zoila, Castro's wife, when she returned from a trip to Paris in 1904 (cf. Schael, *Apuntes para la historia*). Some 2,562 cars were imported into the country between 1911 and 1916, the majority destined for Caracas and Maracaibo, but by the end of the 1910 there were fifteen cars in Táchira and sixteen in Monagas (MOP, *Memoria 1917,* vol. 1, "Exposición," p. viii.).

26. T. Roosevelt to E. Root, Dec 17, 1908, in Hendrickson, "The New Venezuelan Controversy," p. 184.

27. Cf. McBeth, *Gunboats, Corruption, and Claims.*

28. US Department of State, Papers Relating to the Foreign Relations of the United States of America, *House Document no. 101,* vol. 1, 1909, 61 Cong 2 Sess. 1909–10, pp. 609–35, E. Root to W. I. Buchanan, Dec 21, 1908, p. 610.

29. Ministerio de Relaciones Interiores (MinRelInt), *Memoria 1908,* Alcántara to Presidentes de Estado, Dec 26, 1908, p. 323.

30. The author is indebted to Bob Brandt for providing Arnold's full name.

31. FO 199/240, Sir Vincent Corbett to Grey, Feb 24, 1909.

32. Ibid.

33. Ibid.

34. FO 199/275, Corbett to Grey, Feb 12, 1909.

35. Robert Bacon to Buchanan, Feb 13, 1909; US Department of State, *House Document no. 101,* p. 629.

36. The three arbitrators were M. A. Beernaert, the Belgian minister of state, representing the United States; M. Gonzalo de Quesada, the Cuban minister at

Berlin, representing Venezuela; and Professor Henry Lammarch, who held the chair of international law at Vienna University and was the deciding magistrate.

37. The original figure was 3,000 pesos gold, which equates to 100 ounces of gold (30 pesos = 1 ounce) at a gold price of $20.67 in 1909.

38. FO 199/250 Corbett to Grey, Feb 24, 1909.

39. FO 199/215 Corbett to Grey, Jul 29, 1909.

40. *El Tiempo,* "La Actitud de los Estados Unidos," Apr 12, 1909.

41. *DDCS* Month 1(9) Jun 9, 1909, p. 54.

42. Ibid., p. 55.

43. Ibid., p. 54.

44. *DDCS* Vol. 1(9) No. 10, Jun 15, 1909, p. 58.

45. FO 420/251 Corbett to Grey, Apr 25, 1909.

46. AHMSGPRCP Jan 20–31, 1909, Manuel María Guevara to General Pedro Linares, Jan 28, 1909.

47. AHMSGPRCP Mar 20–31, 1909, José L. Baiz to Gómez, Mar 31, 1909.

48. AHMSGPRCP Feb 1–14, 1909, El Comandante de Armas de Estado Bolívar to Gómez, Feb 4, 1909.

49. AHMSGPRCP Apr 1–15, 1909, D. A. Coronil to Gómez, Apr 2, 1909.

50. AHMSGPRCP Feb 1–14, 1909, Bolívar to Gómez, Feb 4, 1909.

51. Ibid.

52. Ibid.

53. AHMSGPRCP Apr 1–15, 1909, Coronil to Gómez, Apr 2, 1909.

54. AHMSGPRCP May 1–14, 1909, Coronil to Gómez, May 6, 1909.

55. AHMSGPRCP Apr 16–30, 1909, Estebán Chalbaud Cardona to Gómez, Apr 23, 1909.

56. *El Nuevo Evangelio Liberal.*

57. AHMSGPRCP Apr 1–30, 1919, General Samuel Ortega Martínez (*Boletín de la Sociedad "El Voto Liberal"*) to Ciudadanos, Jul 18, 1909 (misfiled).

58. AHMSGPRCP Jan 9–19, 1909, Carlos A. Martínez, "Renacimiento," Loose sheet, San Juan, Puerto Rico, Jan 16, 1909.

59. Ibid.

60. AHMSGPRCP Oct 22–31, 1909, Manuel Antonio Matos to Gómez, Oct 31, 1909.

61. AHMSGPRCP Nov 1–15, 1909, Matos to Gómez, Nov 3, 1909.

62. Ibid.

63. Ibid.

64. Ibid.

65. AHMSGPRCP Aug 11–19, 1909, José Manuel Hernández "Carta Abierta," Aug 11, 1909.

66. AHMSGPRCP Oct 1–7, 1909, Hernández, "Carta Abierta," Oct 6, 1909.

67. Roldán Oliarte, *El General Juan Vicente Gómez,* p. 77; letter in *El Tiempo,* Oct 4, 1909.

68. Fuenmayor, *Historia de la Venezuela Contemporánea,* p. 200.

69. Arellano Moreno, *Mirador de Historia Política de Venezuela,* p. 13.

70. Maldonado, *Cuestión Social,* p. 36.

71. Blanco Fombona, *Camino de Imperfección,* p. 176.

72. Ezequiel Zamora was a nineteenth-century military caudillo who supported social movements in the country.

73. Juan Crisóstomo Falcón, president of Venezuela from 1863 to 1868 and Zamora's brother-in-law.

74. Roldán Oliarte, *Gómez,* pp. 79–80.

75. AHM Alemania 1926 César Zumeta to Gómez, Jun 13, 1926.

76. Arcaya, *Memorias,* p. 88.

77. Gómez to Alcántara, Sep 26, 1909, in Gómez, *Documentos para la historia,* pp. 195–96, 196; Moros, *Por la Justicia,* p. 6.

78. CO 295/454 Corbett to Grey, Sep 3, 1909.

79. Ibid.

80. Ibid. Such action, according to Sir Vincent, showed that Gómez lacked "both strength of character and decision of purpose, and his sense of loyalty . . . is to say the least, Quixotic" (ibid.).

81. Ibid.

82. Ibid.

83. Cf. McBeth, *Gunboats, Corruption, and Claims.*

84. Núñez and Restrepo, *Constitucionalidad o Dictadura,* p. 11.

85. CO 295/454 Corbett to Grey, Sep 3, 1909.

86. Ibid.

87. This tax was imposed in 1881 to force importers to use Venezuelan ports rather than tranship goods at either Trinidad or Curacao.

88. CO 295/454 Corbett to Grey, Sep 3, 1909.

89. Ibid.

90. Ibid.

91. Ibid.

92. Ibid.

93. FO 371/1026 Corbett to Grey, Apr 23, 1909.

94. Ibid.

95. CO 295/454 Corbett to Grey, Sep 3, 1909.

96. Ibid.

97. Ibid.

98. Ibid.

99. Ibid.

100. Venezuela, Congreso Nacional, *Discurso pronunciado por el General Arístides Tellería,* p. 4.

101. Ibid., p. 5.

102. *El Nuevo Evangelio Liberal.* The Directorio was made up of the following people: José Ignacio Pulido, Ramón Ayala, Ramón Guerra, Nicolás Rolando, Baptista, Jacinto Lara, Manuel Antonio Matos, José Antonio Velutini, R. Fonseca, F. Tosta García, José María García Gómez, Julio Sarria Hurtado, V. Rodríguez, L. Villanueva, M.M. Iturbe, E. Urdaneta, B. Mila de la Roca, A. Lutowsky, and

Julio Calcaño. The alternates were: G. T. Villegas Pulido, Alejandro Ibarra, J. L. Andara, J. L. Arismendi, F. Arroyo Parejo, Lino Duarte, Torcuato Ortega Martínez, Andrés Vigas, Alberto Smith, Bernabé Planas, Eloy González, C. Benito Figueredo, Domingo Monagas, Antonio Guzmán Blanco, Alberto Térega Fombona, Julio C. Velutini, Luis Razetti, E. Medina Torres, Eduardo J. Dagñino, P. M. Brito González, and Rafael Matos.

103. *El Nuevo Evangelio Liberal;* "Manifiesto del Directorio," Caracas Oct 10, 1909, pp. 12–14.

104. *El Nuevo Evangelio Liberal;* Gómez to José I. Pulido et al y demás miembros del Directorio Liberal de Caracas y Generales J. M. Hernández y Nicolás Rolando, Oct 13, 1909, pp. 15–17, 15.

105. Ibid.; Gómez, *Documentos para la historia,* p. 198.

106. Gómez to Pulido et al., p. 16; Gómez, *Documentos para la historia,* pp. 197–98, 198.

107. Gómez to Pulido et al., p. 16; Gómez, *Documentos para la historia,* pp. 197–98, 198.

108. Gómez to Pulido et al., p. 16; Gómez, *Documentos para la historia,* pp. 197–98, 198.

109. Cf. García Villasmil, *Escuelas para la formación de oficiales del Ejército;* Giacopini-Zárraga, "Juan Vicente Gómez Militar."

110. McGill trained in Chile and in 1900 went to Nicaragua as *instructor general del ejército,* and when his contract expired and the Escuela Militar de Managua was established, he traveled to San Salvador as *instructor general del ejército* and organized the Escuela Politécnica Militar. From there he went to Quito as military attaché at the Chilean Military Mission, which was organizing the Ecuadorian army. McGill was also involved in setting up the Ecuadorian Military School and acted as its sub-director (assistant) for one year. He then returned to Chile for a short while, soon afterwards leaving for Honduras to be an army instructor; he was later commissioned to organize the military school at Tegucigalpa (AHMSGPRCP Jun 1–10, 1910, S. McGill to M. V. Castro Zavala, May 20, 1910). In 1908 he was the Venezuelan consul in Panama (AHMSGPRCP Oct 14–31, 1908, S. McGill to Castro, Oct 31, 1908).

111. "Mensaje que el General Juan Vicente Gómez (Presidente Provisional de la Republica) presenta al Congreso Nacional en 1910," Apr 19, 1910, in Gómez, *Documentos para la historia,* p. 55.

112. AHMSGPRCP Oct 1–7, 1909, Hernández, "Carta Abierta," Oct 6, 1909.

113. AHMSGPRCP Aug 11–19, 1909, Hernández, "Carta Abierta," Caracas, Aug 11, 1909.

114. AHMSGPRCP Nov 1–15, 1909, Matos to Gómez, Nov 3, 1909.

115. AHMSGPRCP Jan 1–15, 1910, Pedro María Parra to Gómez, Jan 13, 1910.

116. Ibid.

117. Ibid.

118. Ibid.

119. Velásquez, *La caída del Liberalismo Amarillo*, p. xviii.

120. Ibid., p. xix.

121. AHMCOP 100 Gómez to Méndez, Dec 8, 1909.

122. Ibid.

123. AHMSGPRCP Nov 16–30, 1909, Giuseppi Monagas to Gómez, undated.

124. Ibid.

125. Ibid.

126. AHMSGPRCP Mar 1–14, 1910, Julio Hidalgo to Gómez, Mar 5, 1910.

127. Emilio Constantino Guerrero, "Alocución," Apr 19, 1910, in Venezuela, MinRelInt, *Memoria 1910*, pp. 6–17, 10–11.

128. Ibid., p. 14.

129. Gómez informed his "great and good friend" William Howard Taft, the US President, of his election victory (DS 831.001/6 Gómez to President of the United States, Jun 4, 1910).

130. FO 199/232 Draft W. E. O'Reilly to Grey, Jun 11, 1910.

131. MinHa, *Memoria 1909*, Doc. 122, Jul 1, 1909, pp. 507–8.

132. The rental income was guaranteed at $718,686 per annum, but if sales were less than 16 million kilograms of salt per annum, then the government would credit the company with $0.04 cents per kilogram. However, the company would pay an additional tax of $0.04 cents per kilogram to the government if production rose above 16 million kilograms. Finally, if profits were above $200,000, then 50 percent of the incremental earnings would go to the Venezuelan treasury (ibid.).

133. FO 199/208 Corbett to Mr. Cooper, Mar 6, 1910.

134. Ibid.

135. FO 199/208 Corbett to Grey, Dec 12, 1909.

136. FO 199/208 O'Reilly to Grey, Nov 27, 1910.

137. Ibid.

138. Capriles Méndez, *Los Negocios de Román Delgado Chalbaud*, Doc 3.3.3, pp. 343–49.

139. It owned the Corton oil shale mine in Dorset, England. In 1906 Manuel Tejera was granted the monopoly to manufacture matches. The National Match Factory of Venezuela was registered in London and funded by the Ethelburga Syndicate, which owned 60 percent of the company with the remaining 40 percent held by Tejera.

140. FO 368/620 O'Reilly to Grey, Jan 1, 1911.

141. CO 295/470 Guy Gilliat-Smith to Grey, Aug 10, 1911.

142. It should be noted that the memory of American foreign claims was still very much alive.

143. Delgado Chalbaud, *Por mi Jefe, por mi Causa y por mi Nombre*, pp. 20–21.

144. Paul Marie Boló, alias Boló-Pasha, was born in Marseilles in 1871. Boló-Pasha, together with Joseph Marie Auguste Caillaux, the former French prime

minister, and Louis Malvy, a senior politician and interior minister, were arrested for treason in November 1917, when Georges Clemenceau became prime minister. Boló Pasha was found guilty of spying for the German government and was executed by the French authorities in April 1918. In 1920, Caillaux was tried and acquitted of treason but was found guilty of damaging the external security of the state.

145. Delgado Chalbaud writes:

> The contract for the National Bank was signed and the outline for the "Project for the Mortgage Bank" approved—eight hundred thousand francs (FFr 800,000) were deposited at Marcuard & Co. to establish the former institution and for the use of the Venezuelan government, with enough guarantees for the establishment of either one, as both banks would be formed backed by the respectable banking houses of Louis Dreyfus & Co. and Credit Français. (*Por mi Jefe,* pp. 20–21)

146. AHM Documents 1899–1914, Luis Núñez to Ezequiel Vivas, Dec 4, 1912.

147. Ibid.

148. Ibid.

149. FO 199/275, F. D. Hartford to Grey, Mar 8, 1912.

150. A period in 1907 during Castro's government when the president was thought to be dying and all his supporters conspired to prevent Gómez, the vice president, from taking over (cf. McBeth, *Gunboats, Corruption, and Claims,* pp. 156–60).

151. Cf. Siso, *Castro y Gómez.*

152. Cf. Castillo, *Memorias de Mano Lobo.*

153. "Mensaje del General Juan Vicente Gómez para el Congreso en Sesiones Extra," October 15, 1911, in Gómez, *Documentos para la historia,* pp. 92–93.

154. Consul de Lemos, "Venezuela, Report for the Year 1905 on the Trade and Commerce of Ciudad Bolivar."

155. In 1911, the *South American Journal* estimated that British capital, which had the largest share of foreign investment in the country, amounted to $48.6 million, concentrated mainly in gold and copper mines, railways, the match and salt factories of Caracas, and dock development projects. The country's largest port at La Guaira was owned by the British firm the La Guaira Harbour Corporation.

156. AHMSGPRCP Jan 9–19, 1909, A. Wittmerg, J. Pastori, J. Torres Carrero to Gómez, Jan 13, 1909.

157. Castillo, *La cuestión monetaria en Venezuela,* 1912, p. iv.

158. Venezuela, Congreso, Cámara del Senado, *Discurso pronunciado por el General Arístides Tellería,* pp. 12–13.

159. Ibid., pp. 92–93.

160. Venezuela, MinRelInt, *Memoria 1912,* Gómez, "A los Venezolanos," Oct 1, 1912, p. 35.

161. CO 295/455, "Venezuelan 30 % differential Surtax: Notes on Conversation between deputation from the Glasgow West India Association and Mr T McKinnon Wood, MP at an interview at Glasgow on February 12 1909 with comments added by Mr Thomas Prentice," undated.

162. Venezuela, MinFo, *Memoria 1907–08,* Exposición, p. v.

163. Vice Consul Gilliat-Smith, "Venezuela: Report for the Year 1909–10 on the Trade of Venezuela and the Consular District of Caracas," p. 773.

164. FO 368/620, O'Reilly to Grey, Jul 10, 1910.

165. Cf. Venezuela, Corte Federal y de Casación, *Juicios seguidos por la señora Ella Robinson y por el Señor Harry O. Robinson contra la "Magnesite Mining and Manufacturing Company."*

166. Cf. AHMSGPRCP Nov 1–14, 1910, Alejandro Rivas Vásquez to Gómez, Nov 12, 1910.

167. Venezuela, Consejo de Gobierno, *Exposición documentada,* pp. 294–301.

168. On March 30, 1911, the company was registered in London with an authorized capital of £157,500 in 150,000 participating preference shares of £1 each and 150,000 deferred shares of one shilling each, of which 38,334 participating preference shares and 10,000 deferred shares were fully paid. The company was promoted by the Oilfields Finance Corporation Ltd. registered in London on April 20, 1910, with an authorized capital of £256,250, to finance petroleum development projects, and was engaged in Romanian developments (cf. *Skinner's Oil Manual,* 1912, pp. 99, 143; and, *The Stock Exchange Yearbook,* 1913).

169. Pearson Archive, Mr. Ribon, "Memorandum," Oct 2, 1912.

170. Pearson Archive A. C. Veatch, "Memorandum," Jul 17, 1912. On April 19, 1919, the company's concession expired.

171. Pearson Archive, Mr. Ribon, "Memorandum," Oct 2, 1912.

172. Cf. *Skinner's Oil Manual,* 1921.

173. Arnold, Macready, and Barrington, *The First Big Oil Hunt,* p. 46.

174. Royal Dutch Company, *Annual Report, 1914,* p. 12.

175. Royal Dutch Company, *Annual Report, 1915,* pp. 20–21.

CHAPTER TWO   *Gómez Takes Over*

1. AHMSGPRCP Feb 1–14, 1909, Paúl to Gómez, Feb 10, 1909.

2. CO 295/454 R. McDonald to Grey, Mar 26, 1909.

3. Salazar Martínez, *Tiempo de Compadres,* p. 67.

4. Ibid.

5. Ibid.

6. Carmelo Castro was educated at Manlius Military Academy, New York.

7. AHMCOP 105 Gómez to Anselmo Mar 30, 1909.

8. Uribe Uribe was one of the leading Liberals in the Guerra de Mil Días in Colombia in 1899. At the turn of the century, Castro sought to unite

Venezuela, Colombia, Ecuador, Nicaragua, and several other Central American republics to form a supranational Liberal entente. Uribe Uribe was part of Castro's project to re-create a new Gran Colombia state. The Liberal presidents of Ecuador, Eloy Alfaro, and Nicaragua, José Santos Zelaya, an old friend of Castro's, were also involved (cf. McBeth, *Gunboats, Corruption, and Claims,* pp. 33–35). William M. Sullivan writes:

> The plan for unification was simple: General Castro would invade Colombia from the east, Ecuadorian president Eloy Alfaro would attack from the south, and the Nicaraguan leader Jose Santos Zelaya would advance against Panama in the north; all the while, dissident Colombian Liberals would undermine the Conservative regime from within. A 5,000-man expedition would sail from Managua after Bogotá fell to assist General Zelaya in conquering Central America. ("The Rise of Despotism in Venezuela," p. 218)

Castro saw this as a way of establishing Liberalism as the predominant force in politics in the region.

9. AHMSGPRCP Mar 20–31, 1909, Reyes to Gómez, Mar 20, 1909.

10. Wilson to Secretary of Navy, Mar 29, 1910; Hendrickson, "The New Venezuelan Controversy," p. 234.

11. CO 295/454 "Memorandum: American Embassy," Mar 31, 1909.

12. CO 295/450 Corbett to Knaggs, Apr 14, 1909.

13. AHMSGPRCP Nov 1–15, 1909, Antonio Darío Noguera to Juan Pablo Peñaloza, Nov 6, 1909.

14. AHMSGPRCP Oct 22–31, 1909, J. F. Calatrava to Gómez, Oct 27, 1909.

15. AHMSGPRCP Nov 1–15, 1909, Héctor Paredes to Gómez, Dec 5, 1909 (misfiled).

16. AHMSGPRCP Jan 1–15, 1910 Paredes to Juan Pietri, Jan 13, 1910.

17. CO 295/452 G. Le Hunte to Earl of Crewe, Oct 29, 1909.

18. CO 295/452 G. V. Fiddes to Foreign Office, Nov 24, 1909.

19. AHMSGPRCP Dec 11–20, 1909, Pietri to Corbett, undated (copy).

20. Ibid.

21. CO 295/457 Minute, Initialed G. V. H., Mar 24, 1910.

22. AHMSGPRCP Jan 1–15, 1910, N. A. Ricos to Gómez, Jan 15, 1910. This seems unlikely because Reyes was a Conservative and Castro was a Liberal.

23. AHMSGPRCP Mar 1–14, 1910, Juan Valbuena to Gómez, Mar 1, 1910.

24. DS 831.00 "El ex-Presidente de Venezuela," *Diario de Cádiz,* Dec 5, 1910.

25. Ibid.

26. AHMSGPRCP Apr 1–14, 1910, Jacinto López to Gómez, Apr 8, 1910.

27. These were:

Mariara	$400,000
La Trinidad	$300,000
El Banco	$150,000

El Funita $150,000
Cagua $150,000

(cf. DS 831.00/304 Department of State, "Note," Jul 27, 1910)

28. These were:

Hato de la Candelaria $500,000
Hato de la Santa Isabel $100,000

(cf. ibid.)

29. The Orinoco Steam Ship Company was sold off for a nominal sum, so his shares were worthless.

30. DS 831.00/304 Department of State, "Note," Jul 27, 1910.

31. CO 295/457 G. D. Swain to Governor, Mar 2, 1910.

32. AHMSGPRCP Apr 1–14, 1910, Paredes to Gómez, Mar 5, 1910. See pages 42–43.

33. A hardwood tropical tree yielding balata gum and heavy red timber.

34. AHMSGPRCP Mar 1–14, 1910, Paredes to Gómez, Mar 7, 1910.

35. AHMSGPRCP Oct 1–15, 1910, Francisco A. Prada to Tellería, Sep 17, 1910 (misfiled).

36. AHMSGPRCP Apr 15–30, 1910, Paredes to Gómez, Apr 24, 1910.

37. AHMSGPRCP Apr 1–14, 1910, Paredes to Gómez, Apr 26, 1910.

38. AHMSGPRCP Jun 21–20, 1910, Paredes to Gómez, Jun 27, 1910.

39. AHMSGPRCP Jul 15–31, 1910, Paredes to Gómez, Jul 19, 1910.

40. FO 371/1024 Carmelo Castro " Leaflet," Jul 20, 1910.

41. Ibid.

42. AHMSGPRCP Aug 1–10, 1910, Pedro César Domínici to Gómez, Aug 7, 1910.

43. AHMSGPRCP Oct 1–15, 1910, A. Sacchetti, "Una visita al General Cipriano Castro," undated.

44. Ibid.

45. Salazar Martínez, *Tiempo de Compadres*, p. 79.

46. Ibid., p. 78.

47. "El Jefe de la Conjuración," p. 10, in *Conjuración contra la vida del General Juan Vicente Gómez, Presidente Constitucional de la República.*

48. Ibid., p. 10.

49. Alcántara to Governor of Federal District, Aug 9, 1910, p. 37, in *Conjuración contra la vida del General Juan Vicente Gómez, Presidente Constitucional de la República.*

50. AHMCOP 100 Gómez to Pedro Murillo, Aug 12, 1910.

51. AHMSGPRCP Oct 1–15, 1910, Hernández to Gómez, Oct 25, 1910.

52. AHMCOP 100 Gómez to Murillo, Aug 12, 1910.

53. AHMSGPRCP Jul 15–31, 1910, Juan Valbuena to Gómez, Jul 17, 1910.

54. AHMCOP 120 Gómez to Pedro Ezequiel Rojas, Sep 20, 1910.

55. Ibid.

56. Gómez to Castro Zavala, Oct 9, 1910, in Gómez, *Documentos para la historia,* pp. 214–15, 215.

57. AHMSGPRCP Oct 1–15, 1910, A. Sacchetti, "Una visita al General Cipriano Castro," undated.

58. AHMSGPRCP Aug 21–31, 1910, Giuseppi-Monagas to Gómez, Aug 23, 1910.

59. AHMSGPRCP Dec 16–31, 1910, Manuel E. Cabrices to Gómez, Dec 17, 1910.

60. CO 295/466 G. Le Hunte to Colonial Office, Jun 9, 1911.

61. CO 295/470 Guy Gilliat-Smith to Grey, Dec 19, 1911.

62. Ibid.

63. CO 295/479 Douglas Young to Grey, Dec 30, 1911.

64. CO 295/470 Gilliat-Smith to Grey, Jul 27, 1911.

65. DS 831.00/443 Lt. Commander J.L. Sticht to Commanding Officer, USS *North Carolina*, Jul 8, 1911.

66. DS 831.00/453 US Minister to Secretary of State, Aug 7, 1911.

67. DS 831.00/457 Gibson to Secretary of State, Aug 28, 1911.

68. DS 831.00/456 Wilson to Caracas Legation, Aug 26, 1911.

69. In July 1911, Rojas informed Philander C. Knox, US Secretary of State, that a junta of exiled Venezuelans was organizing a revolutionary plot against Gómez in New York (DS 831.00/437 Rojas to Philander C. Knox, Jul 10, 1911).

70. Alejandro Rivas Vásquez, "A mis Amigos de Venezuela," San José, Costa Rica, Jan 26, 1919; Congreso de la República, *La Oposición a la Dictadura Gomecista*, vol. 2 (3), Doc 47, pp. 403–6.

71. CO 295/479 F D Hartford to Grey, Dec 19, 1911.

72. Labor Patriótica, *El Partido Progresista de Venezuela*, p. 5.

73. Ibid.

74. FO 199/231 Draft Hartford to George Le Hunt, Feb 23, 1912.

75. Rufino Blanco Fombona to Hernández, Nov 1, 1911, in Blanco Fombona, *Camino de Imperfección*, p. 208.

76. A period of government during the Guzmán Blanco era in the nineteenth century.

77. Ibid.

78. Blanco Fombona to Hernández, Nov 1, 1911, in Blanco Fombona, *Camino de Imperfección*, p. 208.

79. Ibid.

80. AHMSGPRCP Feb 16–28, 1910, Hernández to Gómez, Feb 24, 1910.

81. CO 295/470 Hartford to Grey, Nov 13, 1911.

82. Ibid.

83. Hernández to Gómez, Oct 28, 1911, in Varios, *Verdades para el pueblo*, p. 25.

84. See pages 36–37.

85. Hernández to Gómez, Oct 28, 1911, in Varios, *Verdades para el pueblo* pp. 23–29, 24.

86. AHMCOP 115 Gómez to Hernández, Nov 9, 1911; Gómez, *Documentos para la historia*, pp. 242–48; and Varios, *Verdad es para el pueblo*, p. 25.

87. "Mensaje del General Juan Vicente Gómez al Congreso Nacional en sus Sesiones Extraordinarias de 1911," Oct 15, 1911, in Gómez, *Documentos para la historia,* pp. 91–94, 91–92.

88. Ibid.

89. Ibid.

90. Ibid., p. 92.

91. Ibid.

92. Consejo de Gobierno, *Memoria, 1912,* p. 318.

93. Ibid.

94. Gómez to Gimón, Nov 5, 1911, in Varios, *Verdades para el pueblo,* pp. 77–78.

95. Venezuela, MinRelInt, *Memoria 1912,* pp. 5–6.

96. Ibid.

97. The new cabinet was composed of the following people (listed with their former posts in parentheses): Interior Minister César Zumeta (*director de la sección administrativa*); Foreign Affairs Minister José Ladislao Andara (*jefe de protocolo*); Finance Minister Manuel Porras Echenagucia (*director de crédito público*); War and Navy Minister General Ismael Pereira Alvárez (*director de marina*); Development Minister Pedro Emilio Coll (*director de correos y telégrafos*); Public Works Minister Rafael R. Alvárez (*director de vias de comunicación y acueductos*); Education Minister General Domingo Arreaza Monagas (*director de estadística y contabilidad*); and Secretary General Ezequiel A. Vivas.

98. AHMCOP 132 Gómez to José Ignacio Cárdenas, May 9, 1912.

99. FO 199/232 Hartford to Grey, Jul 20, 1912.

100. AHMCOP 100 Gómez to Murillo, Aug 20, 1912.

101. Ibid.

102. FO 199/232 Hartford to Grey, Sep 17, 1912.

103. Ibid.

104. AHMCOP 132 Gómez to Cárdenas, May 9, 1912.

105. Roldán Oliarte, *El General Juan Vicente Gómez,* p. 84.

106. AHMCOP 136 Gómez to José Ignacio Cárdenas, Mar 8, 1913.

107. Ibid.

108. FO 371/1861 Hartford to Grey, Jan 4, 1913.

109. AHMSGPRCP Apr 1–30, 1919, José María Ortega Martínez, *Por mi patria y por mi Jefe,* Caracas, Jan 1, 1913 (misfiled).

110. AHM Documents 1913 Gallegos to Gómez, Mar 11, 1913.

111. AHM Documents 1913 P Fortoul-Hurtado and Nicanor Bolet Monagas to Gómez, Mar 4, 1913.

112. Ibid.

113. FO 199/232 Hartford to Grey, Sep 17, 1912.

114. AHM Documents 1899–1914 J E Pérez to Gómez, Dec 8, 1912.

115. DS 831.00 Wilson to Charles Nagel, Dec 24, 1912.

116. DS 831.00/532 Knox to Nagel, Dec 31, 1912.

117. DS 831.001C27/1 Dr. O.J. Berg to Knox, Jan 5, 1913.

118. AHM Documents 1913, "Barco de Guerra del General Castro," *New York Herald,* Feb 25, 1913.

119. DS 831.001C27/19 "Castro Playing for Popularity," *Havana Telegraph,* Feb 28, 1913.

120. DS 831.001C27/19 "Castro Acclaimed on Arrival Here," *The Havana Post,* Mar 27, 1913.

121. AHM Documents 1913, "El Señor Castro en Cuba," *Financial News,* Feb 28, 1913.

122. DS 831.001C27/19 "Castro Acclaimed on Arrival Here," *The Havana Post,* Mar 27, 1913.

123. DS 831.001C27/16 Beaupré to Knox, Feb 27, 1913.

124. AHMCOP 136 Gómez to Cárdenas, Mar 8, 1913

125. DS 831.001C27/23 Doyle to Wilson, Mar 15, 1913.

126. Ibid.

127. DS 831.001C27/21 Alvey A. Adee to James Bryce, Mar 25, 1913.

128. AHM Documents, A. Gentini to Gómez, Feb 14, 1913.

129. Ibid.

130. Ibid.

131. Velásquez, *La caída del Liberalismo Amarillo,* p. xvi.

132. AHMCOP 136, Gómez to José Ignacio Cárdenas, Apr 18, 1913.

133. Penzini Hernández, *Vida y Obra de José Gil Fortoul,* p. 209.

134. Roldán Oliarte, *El General Juan Vicente Gómez,* p. 87.

135. Ibid.

136. Arellano Moreno, *Mirador de Historia Política,* p. 13.

137. AHMCOP 136, Gómez to José María García Velasco, Apr 9, 1913.

138. Ibid.

139. Ibid.

140. Ibid.

141. Ibid.

142. According to Miguel Delgado Chalbaud the conspiracy within the Council of State was betrayed by Nicolás Rolando a few days prior to his departure on April 13 to Europe to seek a health cure.

143. AHM Documents 1913, J. Abdón Vivas to Gómez, Apr 28, 1913.

144. AHMCOP 136, Gómez to Murillo, Apr 23, 1913.

145. Cf. Párraga, "Memorias," pp. 84–94.

146. AHMSGPRCP May 1–10, 1913, Rolando to Señor, May 10, 1913.

147. AHMCOP 136, Gómez to García Velasco, May 22, 1913.

148. AHMCOP 136, Gómez to Luis de Pasquali, May 22, 1913. According to Miguel Delgado Chalbaud, his brother Román was forced to sell his properties, which were valued at $1 million, to Gómez for $100,000.

149. AHMCOP 136, Gómez to García Velasco, May 22, 1913.

150. Ibid.

151. Ibid.

152. Ibid.

153. Ibid.

154. AHMCOP 136, Gómez to Juan Bautista Araujo, Jun 11, 1913.

155. FO 199/232 Draft, Gilliat Smith to Grey, Jun 9, 1913.

156. Ibid.

157. All were generals with the exception of Gil Fortoul. The substitutes were generals Víctor Rodríguez, Emilio Vivas, Julio Sarría, José María García Gómez, Augusto Lutowsky, Pedro Linares, Leoncio Quintana, Francisco Vásquez, F. Tosta García, and Dr. José Gil Fortoul.

158. FO 199/232, Gilliat Smith to Grey, Jun 9, 1913.

159. Ibid.

160. Félix Montes, "Exposición Necesaria," Curacao, Oct 25, 1913. He later issued a flysheet against Gómez on December 19, titled "Carta de Actualidad."

161. Penzini Hernández, *Vida y Obra de José Gil Fortoul*, p. 209.

162. AHMSGPRCP Jun 20–30, 1913, Pecha Sayago to Gómez, Jun 27, 1913.

163. AHMSGPRCP Jul 11–21, 1913, F. Pulgar to Gómez, Jul 23, 1913.

164. DS 831.00/589 Herbert R. Wright (Consul, Puerto Cabello) Aug 18, 1913.

165. AHMSGPRCP Jun 20–30, 1913, Pecha Sayago to Gómez, Jun 27, 1913.

166. DS 831.00/550 Harrison to William Jennings Bryan, Bogotá, Jul 12, 1913.

167. AHM Documents 1913, Abdón Rivas to Gómez, Jun 27, 1913.

168. Ibid.

169. Ibid.

170. The *New York Evening Post* described Mocho Hernández as "a lean, brown old man with a shovel-shaped head, scarred and battered from much cavalry fighting"; his "brows beetle, his eyes are keen and black, his form is little and sinewy, and is no token of his sixty years, and his manner is energetic, even Rooseveltian" (DS 831.00/532 *Evening Post*, "El Mocho Awaits Call," May 31, 1913).

171. AHMSGPRCP Jun 20–30, 1913, Pecha Sayago to Gómez, Jun 27, 1913.

172. Salazar Martínez, *Tiempo de Compadres*, p. 130.

173. Ibid.

174. AHMCOP 136, Gómez to José Ignacio Cárdenas, Jun 29, 1913.

175. Jurado to Gómez, Aug 1, 1913, in "León Jurado y la Segunda invasión de Castro," p. 229.

176. FO 199/232 "La Proclama Revolucionaria de Cipriano Castro," Coro, *El Nuevo Diario*, Jul 27, 1913.

177. Ibid.

178. Ibid.

179. Pedro Murillo to Gómez, Jul 28, 1913, and Eustoquio Gómez to Gómez, Jul 28, 1913, in "La Revolución de Castro: El desembarco en La Vela: La invasión del Táchira," *El Universal*, Jul 29, 1913.

180. AHMSGPRCP Aug 16–31, 1913, F. A. Vásquez to Gómez, Aug 23, 1913.

181. AHMCOP 238A Gómez to Murillo and Eustoquio Gómez, Aug 13, 1913.

182. AHMSGPRCP Aug 16–31, 1913, F. A. Vásquez to Gómez, Aug 23, 1913.

183. DS 831.00/552 Harrison to Bryan, Jul 29, 1913.

184. Pedro Murillo to Gómez, Jul 28, 1913, and Eustoquio Gómez to Gómez, Jul 28, 1913, in "La Revolución de Castro."

185. AHMCOP 136 Gómez to José Ignacio Cárdenas, Jul 29, 1913.

186. Ibid.

187. Ibid.

188. AHMCOP 238A Gómez to Murillo and Gómez, Aug 13, 1913.

189. Jurado to Gómez, Aug 8, 1913, in "León Jurado y la Segunda invasión de Castro," p. 254.

190. Ibid.

191. AHMCOP 238A Gómez to Murillo and Eustoquio Gómez, Aug 13, 1913.

192. AHMCOP 136 Gómez to José Ignacio Cárdenas, Jul 29, 1913.

193. Gómez to Presidentes de Estados, Jul 29, 1913, in Gómez, *Documentos para la historia*, p. 172.

194. AHMCOP 238A Gómez to Murillo and Gómez, Aug 13, 1913.

195. CO 295/487 Gilliat Smith to Grey, Sep 1, 1913.

196. In 1911, Galavís sold the Miraflores Palace to the government for $94,607 (MinRelInt, *Memoria,* 1911, Doc. 94, Jun 15, 1911, p. 351).

197. CO 295/487 Gilliat Smith to Grey, Aug 9, 1913.

198. Ibid.

199. DS 831.00/582 Teleg Tennant to Bryan, Aug 21, 1913.

200. CO 295/487 Gilliat Smith to Grey, Sep 1, 1913.

201. DS 831.001C27/31 Elias H. Cheney to Bryan, undated, received Oct 9, 1913.

202. DS 831.001C27/32 Cheney to Bryan, Oct 1, 1913.

203. Ibid.

204. Ibid.

205. AHMSGPRCS Oct 1922 Antonio de Pietri-Daudet to Enrique Urdaneta Maya, Oct 15, 1922.

206. Ibid.

207. "El General Don José Manuel Hernández: Importantes Declaraciones, *Heraldo Español,* San Juan, in Venezuela, Congreso de la República, *La Oposición a la Dictadura Gomecista,* Doc 27, vol. 2 (3), pp. 265–71, 265.

208. AHMSGPRCP Sep 15–30, 1913, H. Leyba to Gómez, Sep 29, 1913.

209. Ibid.

210. Ibid.

211. AHMCOP 136 Gómez to Jurado, Jul 30, 1913.

212. AHMCOP 238A Gómez to Murillo and Eustoquio Gómez, Aug 13, 1913.

213. Ibid.

214. Ibid.

215. DS 831.00B96/1 R. Bingham, "Memorandum: President Gomez and the Constitution of Venezuela," Jul 15, 1914.

216. FO 199/232 Draft, Hartford to Grey, Jan 17, 1914.

217. AHMCOP 238a Gómez to Eustoquio Gómez, Jan 29, 1914.

218. Ibid.

219. Ibid.

220. DS 831.00 Alcántara, "Protesta," Jan 29, 1914.

221. AHMCOP 238A Gómez to Eustoquio Gómez, Mar 23, 1914.

222. AHMCOP 238A Gómez to José Ignacio Cárdenas, Mar 9, 1914.

223. Ibid.

224. AHMCOP 238A Gómez to Eustoquio Gómez, Mar 23, 1914.

225. Venezuela, Congreso de Diputados Plenipotenciarios, *Exposición*, p. 6.

226. Ibid.

227. Ibid.

228. *Diario de Debates del Congreso de Diputados Plenipotenciarios de los Estados Unidos de Venezuela*, 1914, Month 2 (2), May 22, 1914, Sesión Vespertina, May 7, 1914.

229. Venezuela, Congreso de Diputados Plenipotenciarios, *Exposición*, p. 7.

230. It was reasoned that

> it was necessary to consider the urgent need to protect with all sorts of security measures the public's wish of exclusive dedication to peace and work, a desire frustrated over successive generations by those who use false theories to invoke at the end of each constitutional period the specter of corruption to immolate thousands of farm laborers and workers and to paralyze industry and commerce with disorder to disgrace property. (Ibid., p. 8)

Thus

> The presidential term of two to four years without re-election tested during a century, represents 100 years of failure and explains the sterility of the efforts of some of our better governors; the discontinuity of the tendency to mend and build something constructive hindered or trampled on by the impetuosity of the revolution, the instability of the institutions, the distressing lack of progress and the expansion of production, consumption and national wealth and the regressive characters that had already in 1908 assumed those evolutionary agencies of the nation. It was necessary to return to a period that took into account the unheeded lessons of our history, adapted to the needs the laboring and producing guilds have against political agitation, ensuring that the president has sufficient time to put into practice such an administrative program. (Ibid., p. 8)

231. Ibid., p. 9.

232. Gómez to E. Gómez, Apr 26, 1914, in Gómez, *Documentos para la historia*, p. 267.

233. AHMCOP 238A Gómez to Timoleón Omaña, Jul 11, 1914.

234. AHMCOP 238A Gómez to Omaña, Jun 23, 1914.

235. DS 831.00/671 Preston McGoodwin to Bryan, Jun 20, 1914.

236. DS 831.00/683 American Consul, Barranquilla, Jul 25, 1914.

237. "Proclama del General Pedro José Fernández Amparán al alzarse en armas en el estado Bolívar contra el gobierno del General Juan Vicente Gómez," May 26, 1914, in Congreso de la República, *La Oposición a la Dictadura Gomecista.* Doc 34, vol. 1 (3), pp. 299–301.

238. The American minister was born on August 12, 1880, in Princeton, Kentucky, and was educated at a military academy and at the Central University. Before entering the diplomatic service he earned his living as a journalist and publisher.

239. DS 831.00/668 McGoodwin to Bryan, Jun 8, 1914.

CHAPTER THREE   *An Opportunity for the Exiles*

1. CO 295/490 M Costelloe (Detective Sub-Director) to Inspector General, Mar 2, 1914.

2. CO 295/495 Hartford to Grey, Apr 13, 1914.

3. AHMSGPRCP Oct 16–31, 1913, L. J. Calvani to Gómez, Oct 28, 1913.

4. Hernández, "El General Don José Manuel Hernández," *Heraldo Español,* San Juan, Sep 24, 1913, in Congreso de la República, *La Oposición a la Dictadura Gomecista,* vol. 2 (3), p. 266.

5. AHMSGPRCP Nov 1–15, 1913, Gil Fortoul to Gómez, Nov 15, 1913.

6. AHMSGPRCP Dec 1–16, 1913, Márquez Bustillos to Gómez, Dec 8, 1913.

7. CO 295/490 Minute Initialed GG, Feb 13, 1914, Governor of Trinidad to Secretary of State for the Colonies, Jan 12, 1914.

8. CO 295/490 Costelloe to Inspector General, Jan 20, 1914.

9. Ibid.

10. CO 295/495 W. Langley to Under Secretary of State for Colonies, Jan 31, 1914.

11. CO 295/491 Le Hunte to Lewis Harcourt, Mar 27, 1914.

12. CO 295/491 L. H. G. Andrews to Acting Inspector General, Mar 21, 1914.

13. Ibid.

14. CO 295/495 Hartford to Grey, Apr 3, 1914.

15. AHM Docs Jan–Dec 1914 Leyba to Gómez, Apr 6, 1914.

16. AHM Documentos Jan–Dec 1914 General Silverio González to Gómez, Apr 9, 1914.

17. "Proclama del General Hernández," Puerto España, AMLR vol. 9, no. 68, May 20, 1914, *El Universal,* May 22, 1914.

18. Ibid.

19. Ibid.

20. AHM Documents Jan–Dec 1914, Calvani to Gómez, Apr 29, 1914.

21. AHM Documents Jan–Dec 1914, Eleazar López Contreras to Gómez, May 22, 1914.

22. Ibid.

23. AHMCOP 238A Gómez to Manuel Sarmiento, Jun 22, 1914.

24. Gómez to Eutosquio Gómez, Apr 26, 1914, in Gómez, *Documentos para la historia,* p. 267.

25. AHMCOP 238A Gómez to Omaña, Jun 23, 1914.

26. AHMCOP 149 Márquez Bustillos to Gómez, Sep 7, 1915.

27. Arévalo Cedeño, *El Libro de Mis Luchas,* p. 38. According to Arévalo Cedeño, Horacio Ducharne, Pedro José Fernández Amparán, and Mocho Hernández were exceptions to this rule.

28. AHM Documents Jan–Dec 1914 Calvani to Gómez, Jul 12, 1914.

29. He was the first Venezuelan to graduate from the prestigious American military academy and was also married to an American citizen.

30. AHM Documents Jan–Dec 1914 Calvani to Gómez, Jul 12, 1914.

31. Ibid.

32. Ibid.

33. Ibid. Alcántara was also disappointed when Gil Fortoul was not appointed provisional president because he felt that together with Corao and others the latter could have overthrown Gómez.

34. Ds 831.00/687 McGoodwin to Bryan, Aug 3, 1914.

35. AJMH vol. 56, Rudi de Graaf, John J. Sullivan, William A. Rowan, and General José Manuel Hernández, "Agreement," Aug 31, 1914.

36. AHMSGPRCS Telegram Oct 15–26, 1914, Luis Eladio Contreras (*Jefe Civil*) to General Anzola, Oct 16, 1914.

37. DS 831.00/723 P McGoodwin to Bryan, Mar 1, 1915.

38. DS 831.00/710 McGoodwin to Bryan, Dec 7, 1914.

39. Cf. Cabrera, *Siniestro Recuento.*

40. DS 831.00/702 Santos Domínici to Bryan, Nov 28, 1914.

41. DS 831.00/707 Bryan to McGoodwin, Dec 18, 1914. In any case, the *Velocity* could not be used because it was subject to litigation.

42. AHMCOP 238A Gómez to Eustoquio Gómez, Jan 4, 1915.

43. Gómez to State Presidents, Jan 9, 1915, in Márquez Bustillos, *La Elección Presidencial,* p. 1.

44. Cf. Márquez Bustillos, *La Elección Presidencial.*

45. Venezuela, MinRelInt, *Memoria 1914* Exposición, p. xx.

46. AHMCOP 238A Gómez to Zumeta, Mar 13, 1916; Gómez, *Documentos para la historia,* p. 272; and Arias O., *Relieves Máximos,* p. 41.

47. ADM 137/1033 Ralph Paget to Secretary of the Admiralty, Nov 9, 1914.

48. ADM 137/1084 Hartford to Grey, Jan 2, 1915.

49. Ibid.

50. Ibid.; Sir Cecil Spring-Rice to Grey, Jan 15, 1915.

51. Cf. McGoodwin to Bryan, Jul 20, 1917, in Duffy, "Politics of Expediency"; FO 371/2502 Hartford to Foreign Office, May 6, 1915.

52. DS 831.001/8 McGoodwin to Bryan, Apr 3, 1915.

53. ADM 137/1033 Spring-Rice to Grey, Nov 27, 1914.

54. Ibid.

55. AHM Documents Jan–Dec 1914, Calvani to Gómez, Jul 7, 1914.

56. DS 831.00 Hernández to Robert Lansing, Jun 28, 1915.

57. DS 831.00/737 Santos Domínici, "Memorandum," Jul 8, 1915.

58. AJMH vol. 56, Joseph Montague Roberts and Hernández, "Agreement," Nov 17, 1915.

59. AHMSGPRCP Jul 15–31, 1917, Mateo Peraza Mujica to Gómez, Jul 24, 1917.

60. AJMH vol. 56, Joseph Montague Roberts and Hernández, "Agreement," Nov 17, 1915.

61. Ibid.

62. Ibid.

63. AJMH vol. 56, "Standard Venezuelan American Improvement Co.," undated.

64. Trino Baptista to Gabaldón, Apr 11, 1915, in Venezuela, Congreso de la República, *La Oposición a la Dictadura Gomecista*, Doc 36, Part 2, vol. 1 (3), pp. 311–14.

65. AHMSGPRCP Feb 1–14, 1916, Calvani to Gómez, Feb 13, 1916.

66. AHMSGPRCP Feb 1–14, 1916, Gómez to Calvani, Jan 2, 1916.

67. Trino Baptista to Gabaldón, Apr 11, 1915, in Venezuela, Congreso de la República, *La Oposición a la Dictadura Gomecista*, Doc 36, Part 2, vol. 1 (3), pp. 311–14.

68. Arévalo Cedeño, *El Libro de Mis Luchas*, p. 80.

69. Ibid., p. 80.

70. DS 831.00 Extracts of Letter, Carlos B. Figueredo to Rafael Mata, Jan 8, 1916.

71. Ibid. According to Luis E. Ferro, *jefe del cuerpo de aviación* of Guatemala, Mocho Hernández acquired twenty thousand rifles of the Grasse type from I. Luján, a former minister of war of Colombia (AHMSGPRCP Aug 15–31, 1916, P. R. Rincones to Santos Domínici, Aug 29, 1916).

72. This is an old-fashioned word for neurotic. Neurasthenia is described as excessive fatigue and weakness, both physical and mental.

73. AHMSGPRCP Sept 16–31, 1916, AKDT to Gómez, Sep 16, 1916.

74. AHMSGPRCP Mar 15–30, 1916, Anonymous La Mano Protectora, Mar 20, 1916.

75. AHMSGPRCP Mar 15–30, 1916, Hermán to Márquez Bustillos, Mar 27, 1916.

76. DS 831.00/780 P. McGoodwin to Robert Lansing, Sep 14, 1916.

77. FO 199/231 W. Langley to Beaumont, Jan 26, 1917.

78. AHMSGPRCP Aug 1–15, 1922, "El General Castro y los Demás Jefes Venezolanos reconocen Jefe para derrocar at Presidente Gómez," 1916 (misfiled). Ortega Martínez, whose properties in Venezuela were looked after by the Banco Mercantil Americano in Caracas, played a secondary role during Matos's Libertadora revolution and had supported Vice President Gómez's coup in 1908 against Castro and was rewarded with the post of public works minister in the 1909 cabinet.

79. Ibid.

80. Ibid.

81. AHMSGPRCP Jan 1–15, 1916, Zumeta to Gómez, Jan 9, 1916.

82. Venezuela, Congreso, Cámara del Senado, *Discurso Inaugural Pronunciado por el Senador Laureano Vallenilla Lanz,* p. 4.

83. Ibid.

84. Ibid., p. 5.

85. Ibid., p. 7–8.

86. FO 371/3074 Beaumont to A. J. Balfour, Apr 9, 1917.

87. CO 295/504. Hartford to Acting Governor, Trinidad, Jan 19, 1916.

88. CO 295/504 Hartford to Knaggs, Feb 25, 1916.

89. AHMCOP 161 Márquez Bustillos to Santos Domínici, May 13, 1917.

90. Ibid.

91. FO 199/258 Beaumont to Carlos and Eduardo Lopez, Jan 3, 1917.

92. Ibid.

93. FO 199/209 Lord Hardinge to Beaumont, May 5, 1917. On May 7, 1917 E. Lopez Rivas signed a receipt on His Majesty's paper for £100, which he promised to repay within six months or whenever the net profits of *El Fonógrafo* of Caracas exceeded $390 in any one month. He further agreed in order "to submit to His Majesty's Legation a monthly summary of receipts and expenditure within ten days of the conclusion of each month, and at the time allow a representative of the Legation to examine the books and accounts of the paper" (FO 199/209 "Agreement," May 7, 1917).

94. López Bustamante claimed later that he received some $6,000 from pro-Ally representatives in Maracaibo and La Guaira and a further $3,000 in Caracas to start the paper in the capital (DS 831.00 R C Bannerman to Leland Harrison, Jul 18, 1918).

95. FO 199/258 J. Robertson to Beaumont, Nov 12, 1917.

96. AHMCOP 177 Márquez Bustillos to García Velasco, Aug 24, 1917. A Swede by the name of Balk owned a large printing shop called "La Imprenta Moderna" and wanted to start publishing a pro-Allied newspaper in Maracaibo, which Robertson thought was a good idea.

97. FO 371/3074 Beaumont to Balfour, May 21, 1917.

98. FO 371/3074 Beaumont to Balfour, Aug 25, 1917.

99. AHMSGPRCP Mar 1–15, 1908, Márquez Bustillos to Gómez, Nov 13, 1917 (misfiled).

100. FO 371/3074 Beaumont to Balfour, Oct 27, 1917.

101. FO 199/209 Beaumont to J. Balfour, Aug 25, 1917.

102. AHMSGPRCP Aug 16–31, 1917, Andrade to Gómez, Aug 30, 1917.

103. Ibid.

104. FO 371/3074 Beaumont to Balfour, Jul 7, 1917.

105. DS 831.001/8 McGoodwin to Lansing, Apr 3, 1915.

106. Ibid.

107. FO 199/209 Arcaya to Beaumont, Aug 30, 1917.

108. AHMSGPRCP May 1–14, 1917, Leyba to Gómez, May 7, 1917.

109. CO 295/514 Beaumont to Balfour, Jun 21, 1917.

110. Ibid.

111. AHMSGPRCP May 1–14, 1917, Un Amigo Suyo to Gómez, May 12, 1917.

112. AHMCOP 161 Márquez Bustillos to Santos Domínici, May 13, 1917.

113. Ibid.

114. Ibid.

115. AHMSGPRCP Jun 1–16, 1917, Santos Domínici to Coronil, Jun 4, 1917.

116. DS 831.00/786 Fortoul-Hurtado to Lansing, Mar 7, 1917.

117. Ibid.

118. Ibid.

119. Arcaya, *Venezuela y su actual régimen*, p. 128.

120. AHMCOP 161 Márquez Bustillos to Gómez, May 3, 1917.

121. AHMCOP 161 Márquez Bustillos to Santos Domínici, May 13, 1917.

122. CO 295/414 Carabaño to A. Pam, Sep 29, 1917.

123. Ibid.

124. CO 295/414 Carabaño to Pam, Sep 29, 1917.

125. AHMSGPRCP Aug 1–15, 1917, Pedro César Domínici to Gómez, Aug 10, 1917.

126. FO 371/3433 "Memorandum Respecting the Venezuelan situation and the most efficacious means for ending the present intolerable condition," intercepted memorandum believed to have been written by P. Fortoul Hurtado and Ortega Martínez.

127. DS 831.00/791 Nicanor Bolet, P. Fortoul Hurtado, and J. López Rivero to Robert Lansing, May 31, 1917.

128. Ibid.

129. DS 831.00/800 Rivas Vásquez to President Wilson, Aug 25, 1917.

130. DS 831.00/947 Manuel Jové to Wilson, Jul 3, 1917.

131. DS 831.00/814 J. H. Stabler, Chief Bureau of Latin American Affairs, "Memorandum Re: Constitutionality of Present Government of Venezuela," Sep 26, 1917.

132. DS 831.00/817 Stabler, "Memorandum of an interview at the State Department on September 17, 1917 of Mr J M Ortega Martinez, A Prominent Venezuelan, with M.," Sep 17, 1917.

133. CO 295/513 Chancellor, "Note of Interview with General Colmenares y Pacheco [*sic*]," Oct 8, 1917.

134. CO 295/513 Chancellor to Colonial Office, Sep 29, 1917.

135. CO 295/513 Walter Long to Chancellor, Sep 29, 1917.

136. FO 371/3074 Beaumont to Balfour, Dec 31, 1917.

137. Arcaya, *Memorias,* p. 182.

138. AHMSGPRCP Nov 1–15, 1917, Calvani to Gómez, Nov 12, 1917.

139. AHMSGPRCP Oct 16–31, 1917, L Yépez to Gómez, Oct 17, 1917.

140. AHMSGPRCP Nov 16–30, 1917, M. Rodríguez Llamozas to Gómez, Nov 17, 1917.

141. Pedro María Morantes to Olivares, Dec 22, 1915, in Morantes, *Diario Intimo y Otros Temas,* pp. 525–26.

142. DS 831.00/816 William W. Russell "Memorandum," Nov 8, 1917.

143. Ibid.

144. Ibid.

145. "Acta de Instalación de la Sociedad Patriótica Joven Venezuela," in Venezuela, Congreso de la República, *La Oposición a la Dictadura Gomecista.,* Doc 43, Part 2, vol. 1 (3), pp. 365–78.

146. *La Joven Venezuela,* No. 1, New York, August 1918.

147. AHMSGPRCP Dec 1–15, 1917, Luis Yépez to Gómez, Dec 3, 1917.

148. AHMSGPRCP Nov 1–15, 1917, Manuel Sarmiento to Gómez, Nov 12, 1917.

149. DS 831.00/829 Emil Sauer (US Consul) to Lansing, Maracaibo, Mar 4, 1918.

150. FO 371/3074 Beaumont to Balfour Aug 31, 1917.

151. Ibid.

152. AHMSGPRCP Dec 1–15, 1917, Bernardino Mosquera to Gómez, Dec 10, 1917.

153. Ibid.

154. Ibid.

155. FO 199/209 Beaumont to Balfour, Aug 30, 1917.

156. Ibid.

157. FO 371/3074 Beaumont to Balfour, Aug 31, 1917.

158. Ibid.

159. FO 371/3074 Balfour to Spring-Rice Sep 3, 1917.

160. Ibid.

161. AHMSGPRCP Dec 1–15, 1917, Gómez to McGoodwin, Dec 10, 1917.

162. DS 831.00/813 Glenn Stewart "General Gomez's Legal Position," Jan 7, 1918. Stewart also stated that Gómez was an "Honourary officer of the German Army and takes great pride in being photographed in his German uniform." Moreover, according to Stewart, Gómez had $2 million deposited with the Disconto Bank of Berlin.

163. Ibid.

164. Ibid.

165. Ibid.

166. Ibid.

167. Ibid.

168. Ibid.

169. Ibid.

170. Ibid.

171. DS 831.00/834 W. W(ilson) to Robert Lansing, Feb 16, 1918.

172. Ibid.

173. Ibid.

174. DS 831.00/833a Lansing to Wilson, Jan 5, 1918.

175. CO 295/518 Victor Wellesly to Beaumont, Feb 7, 1918.

176. Munro, *Intervention and Dollar Diplomacy,* p. 426.

177. Ibid.

178. Ibid., p. 534.

179. FO 371/3433 Beaumont to Balfour, Feb 25, 1918.

180. FO 371/3433 Beaumont to Balfour, Mar 2, 1918.

181. FO 371/3433 Beaumont to Balfour, Feb 25, 1918.

182. Ibid.

183. FO 371/3433 Beaumont to Balfour, Feb 1, 1918.

184. Ibid.

185. FO 271/3433 Maurice de Bunsen to Beaumont, Feb 28, 1918.

186. FO 371/3433 Lord Reading to Balfour, Mar 6, 1918.

187. FO 371/3433 Beaumont to Balfour, Mar 9, 1918.

188. Ibid.

189. FO 371/3433 Lord Reading to Balfour, Mar 4, 1918.

190. According to Beaumont, Matos was jailed for five days for daring to offer advice (FO 371/3433 Beaumont to Balfour, Mar 9, 1918).

191. FO 199/250 Beaumont to Balfour, Mar 12, 1918.

192. DS 831.00/844 Carlos López Bustamante to W. Wilson, Jul 6, 1918.

193. DS 831.00 R. C. Bannerman to Leland Harrison, Jul 18, 1918.

194. AHMCOP 177 Márquez Bustillos to Gómez, May 24, 1918.

195. Ibid.

196. Ibid.

197. AHMSGPRCP Jul 1–30, 1920, McGoodwin to Gómez, Jul 6, 1920.

198. The shipping company dealt mainly with local coastal trading with the exception of the *Delta,* which went to Trinidad twice a month. The company leased the gunboat *Zamora* from the Venezuelan navy until the lease expired on October 4.

199. FO 371/3433 Beaumont to Balfour, Sep 18, 1918.

200. AHMSGPRCP Sep 1–15, 1918. Robert Lansing (Secretary of State) to Santos Domínici, Aug 21, 1918.

201. AHMSGPRCP Sep 16–30, 1918, Pérez Bustamante to McGoodwin, Sep 26, 1918.

202. FO 199/250 Beaumont to Balfour, Sep 28, 1918.

203. Ibid.

204. FO 371/3433 Beaumont to Balfour, Sep 18, 1918.

205. AHMSGPRCP Sep 1–15, 1918. McGoodwin to Mosquera, Sep 13, 1918.

206. Ibid.

207. Ibid.

208. Ibid.

209. Gómez to Eustoquio Gómez, Jun 26, 1918, in Gómez, *Documentos para la historia,* p. 278.

210. Ibid. The case illustrates Gómez's strong views on justice and acting within the law. He states to Eustoquio that:

> The Courts of Justice must be staffed with honest and competent men who guarantee the rights of the litigants, because without the good administration of justice, social peace is not possible, and the Executive should not interfere in its decisions, and in so doing keeping the independence of the Judicial Power, which is the best guarantee of maintaining its prestige, authority and success. . . .)
>
> Corrupt or ignorant judges are a plague that threaten the welfare of a people and they should be dealt with appropriately according to the law and swept away from the Public Administration as Jesus threw out the money lenders from the temple. (Ibid.)

211. DS 831.00/849 F. Mayer, "Memorandum: Revolutionary Activity in Venezuela," Sep 7, 1918.

212. AHMSGPRCP Oct 1–31, 1918, Diego Arcaya Smith to Gómez, Oct 14, 1918.

213. FO 199/232 Beaumont to Balfour, Dec 23, 1918.

214. Pedro César Gómez, Gómez's brother, also died of influenza the following day, on November 8, 1918.

215. Cf. Fernández, *Hombres y Sucesos de mi tierra.*

216. DS 831.00/865 McGoodwin to Lansing, Nov 15, 1918.

217. FO 371/4254 C Dormer to Foreign Office, Sep 24, 1919.

218. FO 199/232 Beaumont to Balfour, Dec 23, 1918.

219. FO 371/3433 "Memorandum respecting the Venezuelan situation and the most efficacious means for ending the present intolerable situation," intercepted message, undated.

220. Ibid.

221. FO 371/3433 Beaumont to Balfour, Sep 18, 1918.

222. FO 371/3433 C. Dormer to Balfour, Oct 24, 1919.

223. FO 199/250 Dormer to F. Sperling, Mar 11, 1920.

224. Ibid.

225. Duffy, "The Politics of Expediency," pp. 97–98.

226. Laureano Vallenilla Lanz later wrote to Gómez, "It was then that the enemies and traitors exploited the general dismay produced by the pandemic to

forge that horrible plot against you because they thought you were exhausted by the pain but you rose more energetically to the challenge to save Venezuela once again from anarchy and treachery" (AHM Unclassified Laureano Vallenilla Lanz to Gómez, Nov 6, 1924).

227. AHMSGPRCP Dec 1–31, 1918, Diego Arcay Smith to Gómez, Dec 30, 1918.

228. Dámaso Rojas, "Las 'Memorias' de Gustavo Machado," in Mariátegui et al., *Gustavo Machado,* vol. 1, pp. 207–24, 214.

229. Ibid., p. 215.

230. Ibid.

231. Pimentel, *Bajo la tiranía,* p. 24.

232. DS 831.00/890 P. McGoodwin to Lansing, Feb 11, 1919.

233. Pedro Elias Aristeguieta was warned by General Silverio González, President of Sucre State and a good friend of Aristeguieta's father, when Gómez found out about the plots, escaping from the country to settle in Costa Rica.

234. Dámaso Rojas, "Las 'Memorias' de Gustavo Machado," p. 216.

235. DS 831.00/887 McGoodwin to Lansing, Jan 27, 1919.

236. Venezuela, Ministerio de Hacienda, *Historical Sketch of the Fiscal Life of Venezuela.*

237. Cf. McBeth, *Juan Vicente Gómez.*

238. AHMSGPRCP Mar 21–31, 1928, Leonte Olivo to Jefe Civil del Distrito Maracaibo, Mar 28, 1928.

239. Cf. McBeth, *Royal Dutch Shell vs Venezuela.*

240. AJMH vol. 56, Rudi Graaf, John J. Sullivan, and William A. Rowan to Hernández, "Agreement," Aug 21, 1914.

241. AJMH vol. 56, Joseph Montague Roberts and J. M. Hernández, "Agreement," Nov 17, 1915.

242. Cf. Arévalo Cedeño, *El libro de mis luchas,* p. 195.

243. AAA File 2, Alberto Térega Fombona to Aranguren, Aug 14, 1934, and A. Térega Fombona to Santos Aníbal Domínici, Sep 2, 1934.

244. Interview with Gustavo Machado, Caracas; Arévalo Cedeño, *El Libro de mis luchas.*

245. AAA File 3, Telegram Gavila to Geólogo, Dec 8, 1924; AAA File 7, Reyes Belloso to Aranguren Dec 24, 1914; AAA File 1, J. R. Pocaterra to Aranguren, Nov 5, 1932; and, AAA File 2 S. McGill to Aranguren, Jul 22, 1934.

246. AAA File 2 S. McGill to Aranguren, Jul 6, 1936.

247. Cf. McBeth, *Gunboats, Corruption, and Claims,* p. 118.

CHAPTER FOUR *The* **Odin/Harrier** *Expedition*

1. "Estatutos de la Unión Patriótica Venezolana," in Venezuela, Congreso de la República, *La Oposición a la Dictadura Gomecista,* Doc 46, Part 2, vol. 1 (3), pp. 395–400.

2. José Heriberto López, Speech, Hotel Ansonia, New York, Aug 2, 1919, in Venezuela, Congreso de la República, *La Oposición a la Dictadura Gomecista,* Doc 53, Part 2, vol. 1 (3), pp. 449–51, 450.

3. Rivas Vásquez, "Labor Patriótica," in Venezuela, Congreso de la República, *La Oposición a la Dictadura Gomecista,* Doc 49, Part 2, vol. 1 (3), pp. 411–18.

4. Castillo, "Actitud de la "Unión Patriótica" Frente al Gobierno de Venezuela," in Venezuela, Congreso de la República, *La Oposición a la Dictadura Gomecista,* Doc 56, Part 2, vol. 1 (3), pp. 465–67.

5. Ibid., p. 465.

6. Ibid.

7. AJMH Vol. 93, Ortega Martínez, "Ideas en Estudio," 1919.

8. AHMSGPRCP Apr 1–30, 1919, Rosales to Gómez, Apr 18, 1919.

9. "Resumén del Programa del Partido Republicano, Fundado por Exiliados Venezolanos en Panamá (1919?)," in Venezuela, Congreso de la Republica, *La Oposición a la Dictadura Gomecista,* Doc 48, Part 2, vol. 2 (3), pp. 407–9, 407.

10. Ibid., p. 407.

11. AHMSGPRCP Apr 1–30, 1919, Rosales to Gómez, Apr 18, 1919.

12. AHMSGPRCS Apr–Jul 1920, Demetrio Losada Díaz to Antonio Gómez R., Apr 29, 1919.

13. Biamón was described as intelligent and a good medical doctor, but modesty was not one of his virtues. He was authoritarian and had been secretary to Roberto Vargas when the latter was president of Guárico. González Pacheco described Biamón, whom he met in Paris in 1916, as a person with "stentorian voice and a way of walking that was too mannered, the kind of walk taken in Bolivar Square during a night of an open air band concert" (AHMSGPRCP Jan 1–31, 1920, González Pacheco to Santos Domínici, Jan 10, 1920).

14. We do not know how Castro managed such a feat, as Chamorro Vargas was a fierce opponent of former president Zelayas, Castro's friend.

15. Pedro Elías Aristeguieta R., "Mi experiencia en la Revolución. Relato del Destierro, 1919–1929," in Venezuela, Congreso de la República, *La Oposición a la Dictadura Gomecista,* Doc 143, Part 2, vol. 2 (4), pp. 279–333, 283.

16. Ibid., p. 284.

17. AHMSGPRCP Aug 11–31, 1919, Henry Beaumont to General, Aug 24, 1919.

18. Villanueva to Alcántara, Sep 20, 1920, cited in "Un abuso de Confianza Diplomático: Descrédito de los Revolucionarios Venezolanos," *El Universal,* Sep 30, 1921.

19. AHMSGPRCP Feb 1–28, 1920, Leyba to Gómez, Feb 18, 1920.

20. AHMSGPRCP Mar 1–30, 1920, Leyba to Gómez, Mar 1, 1920.

21. DS 831.00/925 "Circular," Dec 16, 1919.

22. Cf. Aristeguieta R., "Mi experiencia en la Revolución. Relato del Destierro, 1919–1929," in Venezuela, Congreso de la República, *La Oposición a la Dictadura Gomecista.,* Doc 143, Part 2, vol. 2 (4), pp. 279–333.

23. FO 371/4623 Dormer to Lord Curzon, Mar 16, 1920. Moreover, Mc-Goodwin "probably realizes that an increasing disposition is being shown to encourage British capital and trade rather than American, and I regret to say that he could not be trusted to act with complete loyalty if a change occurred of scoring with the Government here at our expense" (ibid.).

24. Ibid.

25. Ibid.

26. AHMSGPRCP Mar 1–30, 1920, Miguel Bolívar (Presidente) Francisco González Blanco (Secretario) to J. H. Wall, Mar 1, 1920.

27. AHMSGPRCP Mar 1–30, 1920, Wall to Administrador de la Aduana La Guaira, Mar 10, 1920.

28. Ibid.

29. AHMSGPRCP Jan 1–31, 1920, L González Pacheco to Santos Domínici, Jan 10, 1920.

30. Ibid.

31. Ibid.

32. Ibid.

33. Ibid.

34. AHMSGPRCP May 1–30, 1920, Calvani to Gómez, May 31, 1920.

35. Georgetti's wealth stemmed mainly from sugar. He was the owner of the Plazuela Sugar Company of Barceloneta and together with his father-in-law the Sociedad Agrícola Industrial Balseiro y Georgetti.

36. AHMSGPRCP May 1–30, 1920, González Pacheco to Gómez, May 26, 1920.

37. Cf. Aristeguieta to Ortega Martínez hijo, Jul 12, 1920, in Pocaterra, *Archivo de José Rafael Pocaterra*, vol. 2, Doc 5, pp. 13–18. It should be noted that Aranguren's name is not mentioned. It was also thought that Félix Córdova Dávila, the resident commissioner of Puerto Rico in Washington, contributed funds to the *Odin* adventure.

38. AHMSGPRCP Jun 1–14, 1920, González Pacheco to Gómez, Jun 1, 1920.

39. DS 831.00/1160 Willis C. Cook to Charles Evans Hughes, Aug 16, 1922.

40. AHMSGPRCP May 1–30, 1920, González Pacheco to Gómez, May 26, 1920.

41. Ibid.

42. Ibid.

43. Ibid.

44. AHMSGPRCP Jun 1–14, 1920, González Pacheco to Gómez, Jun 2, 1920.

45. Ibid.

46. Ibid.

47. AHMSGPRCP May 1–31 1921 González Pacheco to Gómez, May 23, 1921.

48. DS 831.00/978 John C Wiley to Hughes, Nov 20, 1920.

49. AHMSGPRCP Sep 1–30, 1920, Pedro César Domínici to Gómez, Sep 9, 1920.

50. Ysaac Ain Bendelac was born on July 8, 1868, in Szechuan (China) of Dutch parents. In 1913 he moved to Paris and in 1921 had a flat in the *cité*, Trevise No. 1, and paid $150 in rent.

51. The *Odin* was the ex-*Paramariho*. In 1911–12 it was sold by the Dutch government to a man called Tideman in Holland for its break-up value, but the ship was repaired and then sold to Russia. The *Odin* had been engaged in trade in the Baltic, but was lying in Kiel when acquired by the Venezuelan exiles.

52. José Ignacio Cárdenas to Itriago Chacín, Nov 10, 1921, cited in "Los Proyectos Revolucionarios en Europa y una Polémica con Simón Barceló," *BAHM* 2, no. 10, pp. 109–35, 126–31, 127.

53. FO 371/5723 Sir Basil Thomson, "Report on W H B Quilliam," Feb 24, 1921.

54. FO 199/231 "Un abuso de confianza Diplomático," *El Universal,* Sep 30, 1921. The article was reprinted from *El Financiero* of Madrid.

55. FO 371/5723 Villanueva to Vickers Ltd., Oct 26, 1920.

56. cf. Aristeguieta to Ortega Martínez hijo, New York, Jul 12, 1922, in Pocaterra, *Archivo de José Rafael Pocaterra,* vol. 2, Doc 5, pp. 13–18.

57. AJMH Vol. 93, Ortega Martínez, Baptista, Carabaño, Biamón, F. H. Rivero, Villanueva, and Aristeguieta, "Convenio," 1921.

58. DS 831.00/978 Wiley to Hughes, Nov 20, 1920.

59. Ibid.

60. AJMH Vol. 93, Ortega Martínez et al., "Convenio."

61. Ibid.

62. AHMSGPRCS Jul 1922, Aristeguieta, "Carta Abierta," to Ortega Martínez, Jul 14, 1922 (flysheet).

63. Cf. Olivares to Rivero, Jan 18, 1921, in Venezuela, Congreso de la República, *La Oposición a la Dictadura Gomecista,* Doc 71, Part 2, vol. 1. (3), pp. 577–81.

64. AHMSGPRCP Oct 1–31, 1920, González Pacheco to Gómez, Oct 3, 1920.

65. AHMSGPRCP Dec 1–31, 1920, González Pacheco to Gómez, Dec 4, 1920.

66. AHMSGPRCP Jul 1–30, 1920, Luis F. Brandal to Gómez, Jul 26, 1920.

67. AHMSGPRCP Sep 1–30, 1920, J. M. Calderón to General Tobias Uribe, Aug 17, 1920 (misfiled).

68. *Junta Patriótica.*

69. FO 371/4623 Dormer to Lord Curzon, Oct 26, 1920.

70. FO 199/231 Dormer to Lord Curzon, Dec 31, 1920.

71. Ibid.

72. AHMSGPRCP Oct 1–31, 1920, González Pacheco to Gómez, Oct 3, 1920.

73. AHMSGPRCP Dec 1–31, 1920, Rafael Angel Ruiz to Gómez, Dec 29, 1920.

74. Ibid.

75. Ibid.

76. Ibid.

77. Arcaya, *Memorias*, p. 197.

78. AGT Correspondence Jul–Dec 1921, Simón Barceló to G. Torres, Jun 14, 1921.

79. Sturup was instrumental in using his close relations with the police in Hamburg and Kiel so that they were tipped off when the ship left for Amsterdam.

80. AHMSGPRCP Dec 16–31, 1922, José Ignacio Cárdenas to Gómez, Nov 9, 1922 (misfiled).

81. AHMSGPRCS Oct 1922, José Ignacio Cárdenas to Gómez, Aug 19, 1921.

82. AHMSGPRCP Sep 15–30, 1922, José Ignacio Cárdenas to Gómez, Sep 27, 1922.

83. Ibid. Cárdenas wrote to Gómez: "As you can see everything can be done with good friends! And it is very useful to maintain such good relationships that give us more than we give them. These are true friends. It is with great pleasure that I will hold a banquet in Karnebeek's honor to award him his well-deserved decoration" (AHMSGPRCP Sep 15–30, 1922, José Ignacio Cárdenas to Gómez, Sep 27, 1922).

84. FO 371/5723 Villanueva to W. H. B. Quilliam, Jan 20, 1921.

85. FO 371/5723 I. I. Bannon and J. McBrien, "Report," Apr 4, 1921.

86. FO 371/5723 Sir Basil Thomson, "Interrogation of Quilliam," Mar 14, 1921.

87. Cf. McBeth, *Royal Dutch Shell vs Venezuela*.

88. FO 371/5722 Beaumont to Foreign Office, Mar 4, 1921.

89. AHMSGPRCP Feb 1–28, 1921, González Pacheco to Gómez, Feb 23, 1921.

90. Cf. Tellería, *Mi Actuación en la Vida Pública*.

91. AHMSGPRCP Jan 1–15, 1921, Luis Francisco Aranda to Gómez, Jun 10, 1921.

92. DS 831.00/1007 McGoodwin to Hughes, Jul 26, 1921.

93. DS 831.00/P81 Félix Montes to Warren G. Harding, Apr 5, 1921.

94. AJMH Vol. 93, Ortega Martínez to Rolando, Oct 6, 1921. McGoodwin later returned to Venezuela in 1929 representing Pan American Airways (AHMSGPRCP Mar 1–11, 1929, McGoodwin to Gómez, May 2, 1929).

95. DS 831.00/1145 Willis C. Cook "Memorandum," State Dept., Aug 29, 1921.

96. Cf. McBeth, *Royal Dutch Shell vs Venezuela*.

97. AHMSGPRCP Dec 1–31, 1921, Nicolás Hernández, "Política Venezolana al Nacionalismo," Aug 30, 1921.

98. FO 371/5723 Beaumont to Foreign Office, Mar 19, 1921.

99. FO 371/5723 M. W. Gaisford to R. Sperling, Jun 23, 1921.

100. José Ignacio Cárdenas to Gómez, Jul 20, 1921, cited in "La diplomacia en Madrid, La Haya y Londres, 1920-1922," *BAHM*, vol. 16, nos. 79-82, (May–Dec 1974): pp. 235–66, 252.

101. According to José Ignacio Cárdenas up to April 1924 he had not received the condecorations for the chief of police and inspector of police and was quite annoyed about this (AHMSPRCP Apr 1–15, 1924, Cárdenas to Gómez, Apr 15, 1924).

102. FO 371/5723 Beaumont to Lord Curzon, Mar 19, 1921.

103. AHMSGPRCP Jul 1–31, 1921, José Ignacio Cárdenas to Gómez, Jul 20, 1921.

104. Ibid.

105. Cf. Richmond, *Venustiano Carranza's Nationalist Struggle;* Kamman, *In Search of Stability;* Salisbury, *Anti-Imperialism and International Competition;* and Buchenau, "Calles y el Movimiento Liberal en Nicaragua."

106. Salisbury, *Anti-Imperialism and International Competition,* p. 69.

107. Ibid.

108. Ibid.

109. Ibid.

110. Cf. Salisbury, "Mexico, the United States, and the 1926–1927 Nicaraguan Crisis," p. 322.

111. Cf. Buchenau, *In the Shadow of the Giant,* pp. 104–6.

112. The Carranza administration enacted the 1917 constitution, which Benjamin has described as the "most progressive charter in the world," providing the basic plan for rebuilding the country. The new political order, which included organized labor and peasants, would be used by the government to create a new social order (Benjamin, "Rebuilding the Nation," p. 471).

113. Richmond, *Venustiano Carranza's Nationalist Struggle,* p. 211.

114. Its most salient points were the denunciation of the Monroe Doctrine, a respect for Mexico's economic and territorial autonomy, the acceptance by foreign powers of nonintervention in Latin America, and a greater focus on forging alliances with European and Latin American countries that would offset the influence of the United States in the region. Cf. Schuler, "Mexico and the Outside World," pp. 503–41.

115. Salisbury, *Anti-Imperialism,* p. 71.

116. Ibid., p. 70.

117. Cf. Schuler, "Mexico and the Outside World," p. 510.

118. In 1922, Eduardo Ruiz, the Mexican minister in Managua, assessing the Nicaraguan political situation reported that "Nicaragua's state of slavery" under a "corrupt and traitorous government" could be relieved only through a program of support for "Nicaraguan patriots" (Salisbury, *Anti-Imperialism,* p. 71.) Such support could take the form of a Central American union led by Guatemala, El Salvador, and Costa Rica or even by Mexico itself (Eduardo Ruiz to Obregón, Aug 2, 1922, Expediente 429-S-4, Archivo General de la Nación, in Salisbury, *Anti-Imperialism,* p. 71). This did not progress further because of the Mexican-US negotiations on the renewal of diplomatic relations.

119. According to Schuler, Obregón "successfully maneuvered the anti-revolutionary Western diplomatic establishment into a position where it had to

grant recognition to a political regime in Latin America that had come to power neither through monarchic inheritance nor through the democratic ballot box" (Schuler, "Mexico and the Outside World," p. 513).

120. Benjamin, "Rebuilding the Nation," p. 475.

121. Schuler, "Mexico and the Outside World," p. 513.

122. Plutarco Elías Calles, "Speech in Victoria, Tamaulipas," *El Demócrata* [Mexico City], Apr 29, 1924, cited in Murray, *Mexico before the World*, pp. 49–50.

123. Schuler, "Mexico and the Outside World," p. 513.

124. Ibid.

125. Buchenau, "Calles y el Movimiento," p. 6.

126. Ibid.

127. Ibid., p. 10.

128. Salisbury, *Anti-Imperialism*, p. 78.

129. One expeditionary force, via the Pacific coast, was headed by General Escamilla Garza, and the other, on the Atlantic coast, was headed by general Julián Irías (cf. Buchenau, "Calles y el Movimiento Liberal").

130. Salisbury "Mexico, the United States, and the 1926–1927 Nicaraguan Crisis," p. 330.

131. Cf. Buchenau, *In the Shadow of the Giant*, p. 169.

132. Buchenau, "Calles y el Movimiento Liberal," p. 3.

133. Ibid., p. 15.

134. DS 831.00/963 US Chargé d'Affaires (México) to Bainbridge Colby, Oct 20, 1920.

135. AHMSGPRCP J.B. Pérez, Jan 1–31, 1931, Eudoro Urdaneta to J.B. Pérez, Jan 27, 1931.

136. Vasconcelos, *Memorias*, vol. 2, p. 28.

137. Ibid.

138. Ibid.

139. Ibid., p. 31.

140. Ibid.

141. AHMSGPRCP J.B. Pérez, Jan 1–31, 1931, Urdaneta to Pérez, Jan 27, 1931.

142. Ibid.

143. Vasconcelos, *Memorias*, vol. 2, p. 31.

144. Ibid., p. 119.

145. Ibid., p. 120. At the time, other Latin American rebels also arrived in Mexico. Haya de la Torre, who was deported from Peru on October 9, 1923, by the government of Augusto Bernardino Leguía y Salcedo (1919–1930), ended up in Mexico, where he was given a job as a teacher, and the Chilean writer Gabriela Mistral made her home in the country.

146. Rivas Vásquez's ostensible reason for traveling to Mexico was to relocate his *ponche crema* business to the country (*ponche crema* is an alcoholic drink similar to eggnog).

147. AHMSGPRCP Nov 1–30, 1921, McGoodwin to Gómez, Nov 19, 1921.

148. Ibid.

149. Ibid.

150. "El Partido Republicano de Venezuela: Frente a la Dictadura del General Gómez," Apr 20, 1927, in Venezuela, Congreso de la República, *La Oposición a la Dictadura Gomecista,* Doc 132, Part 2, vol. 2 (4), pp. 199–201.

151. Arévalo Cedeño, *El Libro de mis Luchas,* p. 220.

152. AHMSGPRCP Nov 1–12, 1922, Arcaya to Gómez, Nov 9, 1922.

153. Ibid.

154. AHMSGPRCS Oct 1924, "Draft of the Memorandum to the Government of Venezuela or to the Minister of Fomento by Managers of the American Oil Companies in That Country," Oct 18, 1924.

155. AHMCOP 243 Gómez to José Ignacio Cárdenas, Oct 25, 1924.

156. Ibid.

157. Zúñiga Cisneros, "Los Estudiantes del 21," p. 238.

158. Phelps et al. to Gómez, Apr 5, 1921, "Los Sucesos Estudiantiles de 1921," *BAHM,* vol. 2, no. 9 (Nov–Dec 1960): pp.101–5, 101–2.

159. Ibid., pp. 101–2.

160. AHMSGPRCP Nov–Dec 1921, P. R. Rincones to E. Urdaneta Maya, Dec 10, 1921.

161. DS 831.00/1169 Louis Sursdorff to Hughes, The Hague Sep 14, 1922.

162. Cárdenas to Gómez, Jul 9, 1922, "La Aventura del 'Odín' en 1922," *BAHM* vol. 2, no. 9 (Nov–Dec 1960): pp. 165–172, 166.

163. AHMSGPRCP Sep 1–31, 1921, José Ignacio Cárdenas to Gómez, Sep 8, 1921.

164. AHMSGPRCP Dec 16–31, 1922, José Ignacio Cárdenas to Gómez, Nov 9, 1922 (misfiled).

165. Cárdenas suggested to Gómez that the government purchased the cache of arms, which was worth $1.98 million but whose selling price was closer to $99,082 (ibid.).

166. AHMSGPRCP Sep 15–30, 1922, José Ignacio Cárdenas to Gómez, Sep 27, 1922. Cárdenas conferred the Orden del Libertador to Minister of State Dr. Herman Adriaan van Karnebeek in October 1922 because:

> the Government of Venezuela . . . has repeatedly received from the honorable and humanitarian government of your Majesty the Queen of the Netherlands valuable proof of its helpful and sincere friendship, awarding for the first time the Order of the Liberator, First Class, reserved previously to Heads of State, to the eminent Dutch Minister of State, His Excellency Mr. van Karnebeek. . . .
>
> The Venezuelan Minister at The Hague conferred the distinction that is so merited to the illustrious man of state, and with such a motive will offer a great banquet in the halls of the Venezuelan Legation. The respect, the gratitude, the true friendship

and the highest esteem are the feelings that inspire these diplomatic acts towards Holland, her graceful Sovereign, her honorable government and his eminent Minister of State. (AHMSGPRCP Oct 17–31, 1922, *El Mundo* (Spain) "Venezuela y los Países Bajos," Oct 26, 1922)

CHAPTER FIVE *The Angelita Expedition*

1. AHMSGPRCP Oct 1922, Cárdenas to Gómez, Dec 13, 1922.

2. Ibid.

3. Arévalo Cedeño, *El Libro de mis Luchas,* p. 88.

4. AHMSGPRCP Jun 16–30, 1922, J. M. Ortega Martínez hijo, *En defensa del ideal democrático, comentarios a la "Unión Revolucionara Venezolana* (pamphlet), New York, Jun 1922.

5. Ibid.

6. Ibid., cited in *El Venezolano,* Jun 1922, in Venezuela, Congreso de la República, *La Oposición a la Dictadura Gomecista,* Doc 80, Part 2, vol. 1. (3), pp. 625–29, 626.

7. Ibid.

8. Interview, Gustavo Machado, Caracas, Sep 1, 1976.

9. Venezuela, Congreso de la República, *La Oposición a la Dictadura Gomecista,* Part 2, vol. 1. (3), p. xxxviii.

10. Ortega Martínez hijo, *En defensa del ideal democrático,* p. 627.

11. AHMSGPRCP Jun 16–30, 1922, Ortega Martínez hijo, *En defensa del ideal democrático.*

12. Ibid.

13. Ibid.

14. Ibid.

15. Ibid.

16. AHMSGPRCP Aug 1–15, 1922, José Guerrero, *A Los Venezolanos,* New York, Jul 20, 1922 (misfiled).

17. AHMSGPRCP Jan 1–15, 1923, open letter from Nicolás Hernández to Francisco H. Rivero, Oct 28, 1922 (misfiled).

18. AHMSGPRCP Aug 1–15, 1922, Guerrero, *A Los Venezolanos.*

19. AHMSGPRCS Jun 1922, Alfredo to Nicanor, Jul 14, 1922.

20. AHMSGPRCS Jun 1922, Nicanor to Alfredo, Jun 23, 1922.

21. AHMSGPRCS Jun 1922, Alfredo to Nicanor, Jul 14, 1922.

22. AHMSGPRCP Jul 11–20, 1922, Leyba to Gómez, Jul 16, 1922.

23. AHMSGPRCS Sep 1922, Rincones to Urdaneta Maya, Sep 22, 1922.

24. Olivares to Ortega Martínez, Sep 21, 1922, in Venezuela, Congreso de la República, *La Oposición a la Dictadura Gomecista,* Doc 90, Part 2, vol. 1 (3) pp. 695–701, 700–701.

25. Ibid., 700–701.

26. Olivares to Ortega Martínez, Sep 14, 1922, in Venezuela, Congreso de la República, *La Oposición a la Dictadura Gomecista,* Doc 88, Part 2, vol. 1 (3), pp. 689–690, 690.

27. Cf. Ortega Martínez to Olivares, Sep 16, 1922, in Venezuela, Congreso de la República, *La Oposición a la Dictadura Gomecista,* Doc 89, Part 2, vol. 1 (3), pp. 691–93.

28. DS 831.00/1169 Louis Sursdorf to Hughes, Sep 14, 1922; and Duffy, "Politics of Expediency," p. 99.

29. AHMSGPRCP Oct 1922, Cárdenas to Gómez, Dec 13, 1922. In August, the *Odin* arrived in Malta on a provisional certificate of British registry that was cancelled when the vessel was registered on the island on August 16, 1923. The ship was detained indefinitely on the orders of the Lieutenant Governor of Malta (FO 371/9638 Sir C. Marlin to R. MacDonald, Aug 6, 1924).

30. AHMSGPRCP Oct 16–31, 1919, Eduardo J. Dagñino to Gómez, Sep 20, 1922 (misfiled).

31. AHMSGPRCS Apr–May 1922, Cárdenas to Gómez, Sep 24, 1922.

32. AHMSGPRCP Jan 16–31, 1922, Urdaneta B. to Gómez, Jan 24, 1922.

33. AHMSGPRCP Feb 1–28, 1922, Urdaneta B. to Gómez, Feb 2, 1922.

34. FO 199/275 Beaumont to Lord Curzon, Jan 18, 1923.

35. Ibid.

36. FO 371/7325 Beaumont to Lord Curzon, Jan 11, 1922.

37. DS 831.001/15 Cook to Hughes, Jun 27, 1922.

38. FO 371/7325 Beaumont to Lord Curzon, Jan 11, 1922.

39. Blanco Peñalver, *López Contreras ante la Historia,* p. 63.

40. FO 199/232 Beaumont to Lord Curzon, Mar 30, 1922.

41. Venezuela, *Compilación de Documentos de Adhesión al Acuerdo del Congreso del 22 de junio de 1921,* p. 3.

42. Ibid.

43. AHMSGPRCP Apr 1–30, 1921, Itriago Chacín to Gómez, Apr 20, 1921.

44. FO 371/5723 J. C. Clarke to FO, Feb 28, 1921. For further discussion see McBeth *Royal Dutch Shell vs Venezuela.*

45. FO 371/5723 J. C. Clarke to FO, Feb 28, 1921.

46. FO 371/5723 Sir Edward Howard to Foreign Office, Dec 1, 1921.

47. Ibid.

48. DS 831.00/1129 J. C. White to Hughes, Nov 28, 1921.

49. DS 831.001/11 Cook to Hughes, May 16, 1922.

50. *El Nuevo Diario,* "Decreto," Jul 4, 1922.

51. Gómez answered Domínici's July 15 letter of resignation in the following manner:

> Your tirade in your letter of July 15 has greatly surprised me, and I can see with great pain that you have lost your brains and you have launched yourself naked in the street without any consideration to your own decorum. . . .

> Your letter is a web of contradictions, which badly disguises your real motive for it: the purpose of taking sides in a political situation that will lead either now or later to the replacement of my government is that you can not wait another fourteen years of plenipotentiary life under the current regime. (AHMSGPRCS Jul 1922, Gómez to S. Domínici, Jul 19, 1922)

52. AHMSGPRCP Sep 1–14, 1922, Héctor Blanco Fombona to Carabaño, Sep 8, 1922. The rumor in Caracas was that the French legation had instigated such an action. We have been unable to discover any other reference to this abortive coup and must conclude that it is a total fabrication by Blanco Fombona's informant.

53. DS 831.00/1158 Cook to Hughes, Aug 7, 1922.

54. AHMSGPRCP Jun 14–30, 1920, González Pacheco to Gómez, Jun 24, 1920.

55. Ibid.

56. AHMSGPRCP Oct 17–31, 1922, José María Ontiveros to Gómez, Sep 28, 1922.

57. AHMSGPRCP Dec 16–31, 1922, Cárdenas to Gómez, Nov 29, 1922.

58. According to Pío Gil, Rafael Nogales Méndez was a small dark man, "with a face browned by the tropical sun," and was "nervous, restless, and loquacious." He dressed well, walking with his chest out, and in 1911 had invaded Venezuela by Táchira but had to return to Colombia because he ran out of arms and ammunition (cf. Morantes [Pío Gil], *Diario Intimo y otros temas,* p. 253).

59. Cf. Henríquez Vera, *Tejera, El Desterrado.*

60. AJMH Vol. 93, Carabaño, Biamón, Baptista, Olivares, "Convenio," Feb 6, 1923.

61. AHMSGPRCP Dec 17–31, 1913, Anonymous VVV to Gómez, undated (misfiled).

62. AHMSGPRCS Aug 1923, Rafael Angel Arraiz to Urdaneta Maya, Aug 3, 1923.

63. Aristeguieta R., "Mi experiencia en la Revolución: Relato del Destierro, 1919-1929," in Venezuela, Congreso de la República, *La Oposición a la Dictadura Gomecista,* Doc. 143, Part 2, vol. 2 (4), pp. 279-333, 293.

64. Ibid., p. 294.

65. AHMSGPRCP Dec 1–15, 1922, Arcaya to Gómez, Dec 5, 1922.

66. Ibid.

67. Arévalo Cedeño, *El Libro de Mis Luchas,* p. 188.

68. Their alternates were: Fernando Figueredo, Manuel María Chacín, Rafael Bruzual López, Jacinto López, Manuel Ayala, Nicolás Hernández, and José Rafael Pocaterra.

69. Hernández, "Partido Liberal Nacionalista Venezolano."

70. Cf. Arévalo Cedeño and León, "Reseña del Acto Patriótico Efectuado en el Salón de Recepciones del Hotel Ansonia," New York, Nov 12, 1922, in

Venezuela, Congreso de la República, *La Oposición a la Dictadura Gomecista,* Doc 91, Part 2, vol. 1 (3), pp. 703–11.

71. Arévalo Cedeño, *El Libro de Mis Luchas,* p. 194.

72. Ibid., p. 195.

73. Ibid.

74. Ibid.

75. AHMSGPRCP Apr 16–30, 1923, Nicolás Rolando to Gómez, Apr 28, 1923. Other people such as Henry Lord Boulton were also grateful for the small favors that Gómez would impart. Boulton, through his friend Julio F. Méndez, requested Gómez to allow him to bring into the country his wedding furniture free of import duties, something that Gómez readily allowed (AHMSGPRCP Jun 1–14, 1923, Henry Lord Boulton to Gómez, Jun 7, 1923).

76. Arévalo Cedeño, *El Libro de Mis Luchas,* p. 198.

77. "La grotesta alianza de los pseudo-redentores de Venezuela," *El Nuevo Diario,* Aug 7, 1923.

78. Married to Grace, Baptista's daughter.

79. AHMSGPRCS Jun 1923 Informe to Rincones, Jun 12, 1923.

80. Aristeguieta R., "Mi experiencia en la Revolución. Relato del Destierro, 1919-1929," in Venezuela, Congreso de la República, *La Oposición a la Dictadura Gomecistas,* Doc. 143, Part 2, vol. 2 (4), pp. 279–333, 299.

81. Ibid.

82. AHMSGPRS F. Veracochea Briceño to Urdaneta Maya, Sep 29, 1923.

83. Ibid.

84. Venezuela, Congreso de la República, *La Oposición a la Dictadura Gomecista,* Part 2, vol. 1 (3), p. xli–xlii.

85. AHMSGPRP Jun 1–9, 1924, Acción Radical Revolucionaria Venezolana, "Bases del Plan que sometemos a la consideración del venezolano del exilio y a todos los espíritus amantes de la libertad para derrocar la dictadura de Juan Vicente Gómez," undated.

86. AHMSGPRCS May 1924, Acción Radical Revolucionaria Venezolana, May 20, 1924.

87. Acción Radical Venezolana, signed by Alberto Ravell, F. Laguado Jayme, Gilberto Gil, Feliciano Montenegro, and Juan Montes to Néstor Luis Pérez, Jun 22, 1924, in Venezuela, Congreso de la República, *La Oposición a la Dictadura Gomecista,* Doc 111, Part 2, vol. 2 (4), pp. 115–118, 115.

88. Ibid., p. 116.

89. The writer refers to Néstor Luis Pérez.

90. Venezuela, Congreso de la República, *La Oposición a la Dictadura Gomecista,* Doc 111, Part 2, vol. 2 (2), pp. 115–118, 116.

91. Jose Heriberto López, "Discurso del Dr José Heriberto López al Pie del Monumento del Libertador en el Parque Central de Nueva York el 19 de abril de 1924" (handbill), Apr 19, 1924.

92. Baptista, *Venezuela, su historia y sus métodos de Gobierno,* p. 327.

93. Fernández, *Hombres y Sucesos de mi tierra,* p. 129.

94. A cousin of Barrientos.

95. Fernández, *Hombres y Sucesos de mi tierra,* p. 130.

96. Rangel, *Gómez el Amo del Poder,* p. 264–65.

97. Ibid., p. 265.

98. Ibid., p. 266.

99. Cf. Fuenmayor, *Historia de la Venezuela Política Contemporánea.*

100. Cf. Gallegos, *En el Puño de Juan Vicente Gómez.*

101. "Contestación del General J. V. Gómez a las Comisiones de las Cámaras Legislativas," *El Universal,* Jul 6, 1923.

102. Salazar Martínez, *Tiempo de Compadres,* p. 166.

103. Ibid..

104. See page 190.

105. "Contestación del General J. V. Gómez a las Comisiones de las Cámaras Legislativas," *El Universal,* Jul 6, 1923.

106. AHMCOP 225 Gómez to Eustoquio Gómez, Jul 24, 1923.

107. Ibid.

108. Ibid.

109. Ibid.

110. AHMCOP 225 Gómez to José Ignacio Cárdenas, Oct 25, 1923.

111. "Mensaje que Presenta el General Juan Vicente Gómez, Presidente Constitucional de los Estados Unidos de Venezuela al Congreso Nacional en sus Sesiones Ordinarias de 1924," Apr 26, 1924, in Venezuela, *Documentos para la historia,* pp. 110–17, 112.

112. Cf. McBeth, *Royal Dutch Shell vs Venezuela.*

113. AHMSGPRCP Oct 1–14, 1923, P.M. Arcaya to Gómez, Oct 4, 1923; and AAA File 7, R. Ernesto López and Reyes Belloso, "Informe presentado por el representante oficial de la revolucion en Nueva York," undated.

114. AHMSGPRCP Oct 1–14, 1923, Confidential to Arcaya, Oct 4, 1923. Arcaya years later informed Gómez that Biamón in 1924 "was negotiating with Dr. J. M. Ortega Martínez in order for Obregón to support the Revolution that he was organizing against you; but Obregón decided to support Baptista in the plan that failed because of the *Angelita*'s accident" (AHMSGPRCP Nov 1–10, 1931, Arcaya to Gómez, Nov 3, 1931).

115. AHMSPRCP Dec 17–31, 1923, Anonymous VVV to Gómez, undated.

116. AHMSPRCP Oct 15–31, 1923, Carlos B. Castillo to Gómez, Oct 17, 1923.

117. CO 295/548 H. D. Beaumont to Sperling, Nov 5, 1923.

118. AHMSPRCP Nov 16–31, 1923, (Illegible) to Gómez, Nov 11, 1923.

119. AHMSPRCP Dec 17–31, 1923, Pedro E. Betancourt Sucre to Gómez, Dec 26, 1923.

120. FO 371/8530 S I S Section to American Dept., Aug 24, 1923.

121. AHMSGPRP Oct 1–14, 1923, C. Aristimuño Coll to Gómez, Jun 16, 1923.

122. FO 371/8530 Diógenes Escalante to Foreign Office, Aug 18, 1923.

123. AHMSGPRP Sep 1–14, 1923, Aristimuño Coll to Escalante, Sep 17, 1923.

124. AHMSGPRCP Oct 1–14, 1923, A. F. Dupont, "Resumen Referente a las Investigaciones sobre el contrabando de armas," Oct 23, 1923.

125. The same route would be used a few years later in the *Falke* expedition.

126. AHMSGPRP Aug 16–31, 1923, F. Díaz Paúl to Gómez, Aug 20, 1923.

127. AHMSGPRS Oct 1923, Simón Barceló to Gómez, Oct 13, 1923.

128. AHMSPRCP Dec 1–16, 1913, Cárdenas to Gómez, Jun 26, 1924 (misfiled).

129. AHMSGPRP Sep 1–14, 1923, J. M. Betancourt Sucre to Gómez, Sep 5, 1923.

130. AHMSGPRS Oct 1923, Barceló to Gómez, Oct 13, 1923.

131. AHMSGPRCS Mar 1–31, 1923, Rincones to Urdaneta Maya, Mar 17, 1923.

132. AHMSGPRCP Nov 16–30, 1923, María Teresa Yanes to Gómez, Nov 19, 1923.

133. Arcaya, *Memorias,* p. 197.

134. AHMSGPRCP Mar 1–14, 1923, Carabaño to Maximiano Durán, Jan 11, 1924 (misfiled).

135. Ibid.

136. Arévalo Cedeño, "Carta Alocución—Al Pueblo de Venezuela: A mis compañeros de armas," Costas de Arauca (Edo Apure), Jan 1924, in Venezuela, Congreso de la República, *La Oposición a la Dictadura Gomecista,* Doc 101, Part 2, vol. 2 (4), pp. 63–66.

137. Arévalo Cedeño, *El Libro de Mis Luchas,* p. 220.

138. AHMSGPRCP Aug 21–31, 1924, R. A. Arraiz to Gómez, Aug 27, 1924.

139. Ibid.

140. Aristeguieta R., "Mi experiencia en la Revolución. Relato del Destierro, 1919-1929," in Venezuela, Congreso de la República, *La Oposición a la Dictadura Gomecista,* Doc. 143, Part 2, vol. 2 (4), pp. 279–333, 290.

141. Ibid., p. 290.

142. AHMSGPRCP Sep 1–12, 1928, Rivas Vásquez to Gómez, Sep 4, 1928.

143. AJMH Vol. 93, Ortega Martínez to Rolando, Jun 13, 1924.

144. AAA File 3, "Síntésis de lo que dice el Señor G. Confidencial," Sep 9, 1924.

145. Ibid.

146. Pulido Méndez, *Régulo Olivares y su época,* p. 90.

147. AHMSGPRCP Oct 1–10, 1924, Delfino to Gómez, Oct 7, 1924.

148. Ibid.

149. Sama de Atenero's first case was the *Angelita* yacht informing Rincones of all details, the cache of arms, and the date of departure. Yanes, the Venezuelan minister at Washington, did not trust Sama, but Pedro Rincones, the Venezuelan consul general in New York, wanted Gómez to give Sama $500 because of his invaluable help and information in the *Angelita* case. Yanes argued, however,

that he had obtained from the State Department all the information supplied by Sama with only a two-day delay. In the end, Sama de Atero traveled to Venezuela, where he met Gómez, who gave him $1,916 as a reward for his services rendered in 1924. Sama de Atenero also kept Rincones informed when Ortega Martínez and Baptista were negotiating with general Plutarco Elias Calles and the Mexican government (AHMSGPRCP Jan 1–20, 1935, M. Sama de Atero to Gómez, Jan 18, 1935).

150. Ibid.

151. AHMSGPRCP Oct 1–10, 1924, Delfino to Gómez, Oct 7, 1924.

152. Ibid.

153. Baptista, Carabaño, Tellería, Olivares, and Pérez, "Pacto Revolucionario Antigomecista del 'Angelita' (19 de Nov de 1924)," in Venezuela, Congreso de la República, *La Oposición a la Dictadura Gomecista,* Doc 118, Part 2, vol. 2 (4), pp. 135–36, 136.

154. Aristeguieta R., "Mi experiencia en la Revolución. Relato del Destierro, 1919-1929," in Venezuela, Congreso de la República, *La Oposición a la Dictadura Gomecista,* Doc. 143, Part 2, vol. 2 (4), pp. 279–333, 297.

155. AHMSGPRCS Dec 1924, Rincones to Urdaneta Maya, Nov 26, 1924 (misfiled).

156. AAA File 7, R. Ernesto López and Reyes Belloso, "Informe presentado por el representante oficial de la Revolución en Nueva York," undated.

157. AAA File 7, Aristeguieta to Ernesto López, undated.

158. AAA File 7, R. Ernesto López and Reyes Belloso, "Informe presentado por el representante oficial de la Revolución en Nueva York," undated.

159. Ibid.

160. AHMSGPRCP Oct 20–31, 1926, Pedro Ramírez to Gómez, Oct 28, 1928 (misfiled).

161. These were: Biamón, López Bello, Carabaño, Rivero, Dr. Juan M. Sanoja, Dr. Fernando Figueredo, Carlos Duarte, and M. Vallespolanco.

162. AHMCOP 252 Gómez to Arraiz, Jan 15, 1925.

163. AHMCOP 252 Gómez to Eustoquio Gómez, Jan 15, 1925.

164. DS 831.001C27/106 Cook "Memorandum" Jan 16, 1924. Note that the memo did not include the accent in "Gómez."

165. AHMCOP 252 Gómez to Zoila de Castro, Jan 15, 1925. Polanco states that Gómez sent Zoila Castro $1,000 monthly in Puerto Rico, debiting his own account. He does not give dates, but Castro settled in Puerto Rico in 1914, so that Gómez could have provided Zoila Castro with approximately $120,000 during her stay in Puerto Rico (cf. Polanco Alcántara, *Juan Vicente Gómez*).

166. AHMSGPRCP Jan 1–20, 1935, Sama de Atero to Gómez, Jan 18, 1935.

167. Rivas Vásquez together with Piñango Lara were now trying to introduce arms through Guanta using the *María Piñango,* which shipped Venezuelan cattle to Cuba.

168. AHMSGPRCP Mar 17–31, 1925, M. Miranda (Police Agent) to Jefe de la Policia Secreta Judicial Cubana, Apr 8, 1925.

CHAPTER SIX   *The Civil-Military Movements of 1928*

1. DS 831.00/1271 Cook to Frank B. Kellogg, May 16, 1925.

2. Ibid.

3. Ibid.

4. Ibid.

5. DS 831.001G58/5 Frederick C. Chabot to Kellogg, May 10, 1925.

6. DS 831.00/1274 Cook to Kellogg, Jul 17, 1925.

7. DS 831.00/1300 Alexander K. Sloan to Kellogg, Jun 9, 1926.

8. DS 831.00/1274 Cook to Kellogg, Jul 17, 1925.

9. AHMSGPRCS Mar 1924, Vicente Lecuna to Urdaneta Maya, Mar 6, 1924.

10. AHMSGPRCP May 1–10, 1924, R. J. M. Donald to Eustoquio Gómez, May 2, 1924.

11. AHMSGPRCP May 1–10, 1924, Donald to Eustoquio Gómez, Jul 23, 1924.

12. DS 831.00/1251 Gómez to General Martín Matos Arvelo, Jul 5, 1924.

13. DS 831.00/1282 Cook to Kellogg, Jan 6, 1926.

14. DS 831.00/1275 Cook to Kellogg, Aug 1, 1925.

15. Luis (Pimentel) to Chely (Pimentel), Oct 15, 1929, in Pimentel, *Bajo la Tiranía*, pp. 209–14.

16. Pocaterra describes the shocking state of Delgado Chalbaud when he first saw him in La Rotunda prison in 1919:

> All at once I caught sight of an extraordinary figure crossing the courtyard. Is it a lunatic or a man in fancy dress? He wears a bathrobe and his black curly hair falls to his waist. The bar of his shackle is so heavy that he drags them along on a little wagon, the wheels are made out of thread spools. He stops for a moment, bows pleasantly to the group of men warming themselves in the sun and raises his head. (*Gomez: The Shame of America*, p. 119)

17. See page 139.

18. FO 199/218 H. A. Hobson to A. Chamberlain, Jun 26, 1925.

19. This refers to July 21, 1903, when Gómez defeated Nicolás Rolando in Ciudad Bolívar and brought to an end the Matos Libertadora revolution. The day was declared a holiday by Castro, and Gómez was given the title of "El Pacificador de Venezuela" and "Salvador del Salvador" (cf. McBeth, *Gunboats, Corruption, and Claims*, p. 97).

20. AHMSGPRCP Jul 11–21, 1925, Velasco Bustamante to Gómez, Jul 11, 1925.

21. Ibid.

22. AHMSGPRCP Jul 11–21, 1925, Arcaya to Gómez, Jul 21, 1925.

23. García Ponce, *Memorias de un General de la Utopía*, p. 197.

24. Ibid. According to its statutes, the workers' union was established to "fight for the rights of man according to the doctrine of Marx and Engels" (G. Egea Mier, "La Tragedia de Cumaná," in Venezuela, Congreso de la República, *La Oposición a la Dictadura Gomecista,* Doc 1, Part 6, vol. 1 (12), pp. 3–4, 1).

25. AHMSGPRCS Aug–Sep 1925, Carlos Elias Villanueva to Baptista Galindo, Aug 13, 1925.

26. DS 831.00/1297 "Memorandum," Jun 2, 1926.

27. AAA File 4, Smith to Aranguren, Nov 21, 1925.

28. Arévalo Cedeño, *El Libro de Mis Luchas,* p. 220.

29. Cf. García Ponce, *Memorias de un General de la Utopía.*

30. AHMSGPRCP Aug 21–31 1924 R. A. Arraiz to Gómez, Aug 27, 1924.

31. AAA File 4, Smith to Aranguren, Nov 21, 1925.

32. The governor of Veracruz encouraged the formation of labor unions, agrarian leagues, and socialist parties. According to Benjamin, Tejeda "made alliances with the local Communist Party to establish the League of Agrarian Communities and Peasant Syndicates" (Benjamin, "Rebuilding the Nation," p. 474).

33. The program of the PRV included the following:

   1. Peasant emancipation.
   2. The creation of workers' unions.
   3. The incorporation of women into political life.
   4. State protection of children and their mothers.
   5. Strict control of foreign capital.
   6. Nationalization of public utilities.
   7. The creation of a central bank.
   8. Nationalization of all energy sources.
   9. Land deeds to be negotiable like money.
   10. The increase in state participation in all oil concessions granted.
   11. Industrial and rural education to be increased.
   12. The establishment of universities for the masses.
   13. The organization of a revolutionary army.
   14. Peculation to be punished.
   15. Union representation in Congress and legislative assemblies.
   16. The separation of the church from the state.

34. AHMSGPRCP Mar 1–16, 1925, González Pacheco to Gómez, Mar 2, 1925.

35. Ibid.

36. AHMSGPRCP Jun 1–15, 1925, González Pacheco to Gómez, Jun 8, 1925.

37. AHMSGPRCP Apr 17–30, 1925, Leyba to Gómez, Apr 25, 1925.

38. AHMSGPRCP Jun 1–15, 1925, Leyba to Gómez, Jun 10, 1925.

39. Córdoba, *Los Desterrados y Juan Vicente Gómez,* p. 172.

40. FO 199/276 Private and Confidential Letter from A. D. Butler to Dr. C. Mendoza, undated.

41. No specific Standard Oil is mentioned.

42. FO 371/11202 British Controlled Oilfields to C. Torr (Foreign Office), undated.

43. Ibid.

44. Ibid.

45. Lee, "The Rush for Oil in Venezuela."

46. DS 831.00/1290 Wainwright Abbott, Chargé d'Affaires, to Kellogg, Apr 3, 1926.

47. AAA File 2, E. Vivas Pérez to Aranguren, Jan 8, 1926.

48. Ibid.

49. Aristeguieta, "La Nueva Venezuela Revolucionaria: Memorias de Pedro Elias Aristeguieta," in Córdoba, *Los Desterrados y Juan Vicente Gómez*, pp. 149–94, 172. When Gómez heard that Aranguren was considering financing a further plot against him (something the latter denied), he wrote to him in September 1926, stating that "he need not worry in the knowledge that General Gómez is aware that Aranguren will not contribute anything to any revolutionary movement that will alter the peace in Venezuela" (AHMCOP 261 Gómez to Antonio Aranguren, Sep 30, 1926).

50. Tonopah was a gold-mining company operating in Nevada. Its major shareholder, the multimillionaire Charles M. Schwab, had made his fortune in steel, first as head of the United States Steel Company and then as president of the Bethlehem Steel Company.

51. DS 831.00 Revolution/6 Venezuelan Minister "Memorandum," May 26, 1928.

52. FO 199/276 Butler to Mendoza, undated.

53. Ibid.

54. Ibid.

55. Ibid.

56. FO 371/11202 H. A. Hobson to Sir Austen Chamberlain, Aug 17, 1926. A Foreign Office note about the affair states: "It is also remarkable as it is showing the lengths to which the oil interests of the world will go to attain their ends: Alcántara appears in fact to be mobilizing the oil 'outs' in order to displace the 'ins' through the removal of President Gómez" (FO 371/11202 "Notes made by Mr Craigie," Aug 20, 1926).

57. FO 371/11202 R. Vansittart to Escalante, Jul 2, 1926.

58. AHMSGPRCP Jul 12–22, 1926, Escalante to Gómez, Jul 14, 1926.

59. FO 371/11202 "Memorandum," Jul 15, 1926.

60. FO 371/11202 Escalante to R. Craigie, Jun 26, 1926.

61. FO 199/276 N. Byatt to HM Minister, Caracas, Jul 29, 1926, with enclosure, M. Costelloe, "Report by the Detective Inspector, Trinidad Constabulary," Jul 16, 1926.

62. FO 199/276 Hobson to Itriago Chacín, Sep 22, 1926.

63. AHMSGPRCP Oct 10–19, 1926, Juan Santaella to Gómez, Oct 17, 1926.

64. AHMSGPRCP Mar 1–10, 1927, Alejandro Fuenmayor to Gómez, Mar 6, 1927. Commander Armando Gil Pumarol, the chief of police, provided Fuenmayor with information on the revolutionaries (AHMSGPRCP Mar 20–31, 1927, A. Fuenmayor to Gómez, Mar 28, 1927).

65. AHMSGPRCP Sep 22–30, 1927, Rivas Vasquez to Gómez, Sep 24, 1927.

66. Aristeguieta, "La Nueva Venezuela Revolucionaria," in Córdoba, *Los Desterrados y Juan Vicente Gómez,* pp. 149–94, 179.

67. AHMSGPRCP Feb 14–28, 1927, Carlos B. Figueredo to Gómez, Feb 14, 1927.

68. Ibid.

69. AHMSGPRCS Jan–Mar 1928, "También se tramó una revolución en Venezuela," *Washington Herald,* Nov 14, 1927.

70. García Ponce, *Memorias de un General de la Utopía,* p. 73.

71. Ibid.

72. Ibid., p. 76.

73. The Universidad de Caracas was closed in 1913, and the Asociación de Estudiantes was closed the following year.

74. Gómez, "Alocución," Jan 1, 1928, in Venezuela, Presidencia, *Alocuciones Presidenciales de Año Nuevo,* pp. 52–53, 52.

75. The Rotunda jail was closed permanently making way for a storage warehouse for the Public Works Ministry.

76. AHMSGPRCP Apr 16–30, 1927, José E. Rios Hernández to Gómez, Apr 18, 1927.

77. AHMSGPRCP Apr 16–30, 1927, Luis F. Aranda to Gómez, Apr 23, 1927.

78. Gómez, "Alocución," p. 52.

79. G. Egea Mier, "La Tragedia de Cumaná," in Venezuela, Congreso de la República, *La Oposición a la Dictadura Gomecista,* Doc 182, Part 2, vol. 2 (2), pp. 3–7, 4.

80. Ibid., p. 4.

81. Delgado Chalbaud to Pocaterra, Jul 14, 1927, in Pocaterra, *La Oposición a Gómez,* vol. 1, pp. 141–42, 141.

82. AHMSGPRCP Aug 1–10, 1927, Barceló to Gómez, Aug 4, 1927.

83. Ibid.

84. AHMSGPRCP May 1–10, 1927, Zumeta to Gómez, May 3, 1927.

85. Arévalo Cedeño, *El Libro de Mis Luchas,* p. 250.

86. Ibid., p. 251.

87. While he was in Vichy, Arévalo Cedeño was careful to issue a "Carta Abierta" disassociating his plans from those of Salvador de la Plaza, Gustavo Machado, and the Cuban Julio Antonio Mella because they were communists and he was against "that terrible communism," although he did support the Unión Obrera Venezuelana (DS 831.00 E. Arévalo Cedeño, "Carta Abierta" Vichy [handbill], Jul 28, 1927). In the Miraflores archive there is a note that the Unión

Obrera Venezolana was an organization financed by the USSR and Mexico. In April 1927, Salvador de la Plaza represented Venezuela at the Congreso Internacional contra la Opresión Colonial at Brussels as a delegate of the Liga Anti-Imperialista Pan Americana.

88. Shared with Gustav Streseman of Germany.

89. Pocaterra to Baptista, May 21, 1927, in Pocaterra, *La Oposición a Gómez,* vol. 1, pp. 127–29, 128.

90. Ibid., p. 128.

91. Ibid.

92. Baptista to Pocaterra, May 18, 1927, in Pocaterra, *La Oposición a Gómez,* vol. 1, p. 125.

93. DS 831.00/1341 Cook to Kellogg, Dec 10, 1927.

94. Ibid.

95. Ibid.

96. AHMSGPRCP Dec 1–10, 1927, Figueredo to Gómez, Dec 5, 1927.

97. Delgado Chalbaud to Pocaterra, Dec 12, 1927, in Pocaterra, *La Oposición a Gómez,* vol. 1, pp. 164–65.

98. Cf. Luis F. Aranda to Gómez, Jan 8, 1928, and Aranda to Gómez, Jan 5, 1928, in Betancourt, *Archivo de Rómulo Betancourt,* vol. 1: 1917–1928, pp. 4–5, 5–6.

99. Cf. Delgado Chalbaud to Arévalo Cedeño, Nov 21, 1927, in Pocaterra, *La Oposición a Gómez,* vol. 1, pp. 162–63.

100. Gómez, "Alocución," p. 52.

101. Fuenmayor, *1928–1948,* p. 22.

102. Ibid.

103. Torrealba Fossi, *Los Años de la Ira,* p. 68.

104. Born in El Tocuyo, Lara.

105. This took place in 1925 during the government of Rodolfo Chiari. The tenants went on strike because the government increased property taxes by between 25 percent and 50 percent, which were immediately reflected in higher rents for the tenants. The strike threatened to get out of control, and the government requested assistance from the United States, which sent some six hundred marines stationed at the Panama Canal Zone and commanded by General William Lassiter (cf. García Ponce, *Memorias de un General de la Utopía*).

106. Mercedes Carrasquel, Liliana Iturbe, Carmelina Pérez, Olga Lange, Mercedes Ugueto, Alicia Dalke, Berta Bance, María Cristina Plaza, Mercedes Arreaza, Lulú Plaza, Caridad Irazabal, Eliza Matilde Todd, and Carmen Alicia Plaza were her ladies-in-waiting. Raúl Leoni, Manuel José Arreaza, Carlos Irazabal, Ramón Armando Leoni, José Tomás Jiménez Arráiz, José Antonio Marturet, Isaac Pardo, Miguel Otero Silva, Armando Zuloaga Blanco, Elias Benarroch, Juan Bautista Oropeza, Jóvito Villalba, Odoardo León Ponce, Angel Ugueto, and José Antonio Rodríguez Travieso were her gentlemen-in-waiting.

107. Agudo Freytes, *Pío Tamayo,* p. 170.

108. DS 831.00/1345 C. van H. Engert to Kellogg, Feb 25, 1928.

109. Fuenmayor, *1928–1948,* p. 24.

110. Part of the poem is as follows:

> Ah! I cannot continue, Queen Beatrice,
> I cannot continue!
> The Indian starts crying again with his sacred prophecy. . . .
> But no your Majesty,
> as I will bleed no longer.
> You, a smiling promise of fiery yearnings
> and the name of that bride looks like you:
> it is called Freedom.
> Tell your subjects,
> —so young that it is unknown to them—to start looking for it.

The original Spanish is as follows:

> Ah! no puedo más, reina Beatriz.
> No puedo!
> Vuelve a llorar el indio con su santo agorero. . . .
> Pero no, Majestad
> que he llagado hasta hoy.
> Vos, sonriente promesa de encendios anhelos,
> y el nombre de esa novia se me parece a vos:
> se llama Libertad.
> Decid a vuestros súbditos
> —tan jovenes que aún no pueden conocerla—
> que salgan a buscarla.

(Quintero, *El Petróleo y nuestra Sociedad,* p. 38)

111. Arcaya, *Memorias,* p. 138.

112. Ibid.

113. Gabaldón Márquez, *Memoria y cuento de la Generación del 28.*

114. Cf. Siso, *Castro y Gómez.*

115. Arcaya, *Memorias,* p. 138.

116. Ibid.

117. Ibid., p. 139.

118. Ibid.

119. López Contreras, *Páginas para la historia militar de Venezuela,* p. 151–52.

120. Arcaya, *Memorias,* p. 139.

121. Fernández, *Hombres y Sucesos,* p. 174.

122. López Contreras, *Páginas para la historia militar de Venezuela,* p. 152.

123. According to César González, who was a student at the time, the Dutch minister's wife was a nymphomaniac with many lovers among the detained students (interview with César González, Caracas, Sep 23, 1976).

124. DS 831.00/1350 Engert to Kellogg, Mar 7, 1928.

125. The conditions of the prisoners were by all accounts barbaric, unhygienic, and without adequate food and medical facilities. Gómez did send Dr. P. D. Rodríguez Rivero to operate on Pío Tamayo in April 1928, for which Pío Tamayo thanked Gómez effusively, writing: "This letter is prompted by the desire and obligation that I have with you to thank you effusively for your kind efforts in forwarding the medical report requested by my family in which the doctor states that there is an urgent need to have an operation. Today the operation took place successfully by your special envoy Dr. P. D. Rodríguez and having achieved such a successful outcome to my health, my first task is to thank you for it" (AHMSGPRCP Apr 13–19, 1928, Pío Tamayo to Gómez, Apr 5, 1928). Tamayo would suffer further. In November 1929 it was reported that "a tubercular fistula has developed and the doctor has stated that this in an advanced state of tuberculosis" (AHMSGPRCP Nov 1–14, 1929, A. P. Carrero R. to Gómez, Nov 12, 1929).

126. DS 831.00/1350 Engert to Kellogg, Mar 7, 1928.

127. Fernández, *Hombres y Sucesos,* p. 180.

128. DS 831.00/1350 Engert to Kellogg, Mar 7, 1928.

129. Fuenmayor, *1928–1948,* p. 32.

130. AAA File 2, McGill to Aranguren, May 23, 1936.

131. DS 831.00/1350 Engert to Kellogg, Mar 7, 1928.

132. Jiménez Arraíz, *Recuerdos,* p. 37.

133. Ibid.

134. Fuenmayor, *1928–1948,* p. 34n.

135. Ibid. They also stated that "imperialistic capitalism needs to support and maintain . . . Gómez in Venezuela as it sustains and maintains by force governments that, with brutal repression, drown all aspiration of improvement by the working classes."

136. AHM Varios 1921–1929, "Declaración de Irazabal," Mar 28, 1928.

137. He was Blanco Fombona's secretary when Blanco Fombona was governor of Amazonas Territory in 1904.

138. Fernández, *Hombres y Sucesos,* p. 186. See the section "Gabaldón on the Attack" in chapter 7 of this volume.

139. In 1930, Figueredo, the Venezuelan consul in New York, wrote to Gómez stating that Luis Bigott, owner of the cigarette factory Bandera Roja was an enemy of Gómez. Bigott lived in New York, was very rich, and "took part in the students' raid" (AHMSGPRCP Feb 21–28, 1930, Figueredo to Gómez, Mar 3, 1930), leaving the country after the disturbances. Ortega Martínez received monetary help from Bigott.

140. "Declaración de Enrique González Gorrondona, May 12, 1929," in Lisandro Alvarado, *El Archivo de la Rotunda,* pp. 95–97, 96.

141. AHM Varios 1921–1929, "Declaración de Joviano Sánchez," Mar 29, 1928.

142. Delgado Chalbaud to Pocaterra, Jun 9, 1928, in Pocaterra, *La Oposición a Gómez,* vol. 1, pp. 201–2.

143. Arévalo Cedeño to Dr Jugo, Jul 1, 1928, in Pocaterra, *La Oposición a Gómez,* vol. 1, p. 210.

144. CO 295/565 Governor of Trinidad to Lt. Col. L. S. Amery, Nov 21, 1928.

145. AHMSGPRCP Jan 11–20, 1927, F. Conde García to Gómez, Jan 13, 1928.

146. Castellanos, *La sublevación militar del 7 de abril de 1928,* p. 89.

147. Rangel, *Gómez el Amo del Poder,* p. 268.

148. He was the "link with the civilians" according to Barrios's wife. He came from Maturín and studied at the same Liceo Chávez in Caracas as Barrios (interview with Mrs. A. Sebal Benshimol de Barrios, Caracas, Nov 25, 1976).

149. Venezuela, MinRelInt, *Memoria 1928,* p. 111.

150. Rangel, *Gómez el amo del poder,* p. 269.

151. López Contreras, *Páginas para la historia,* p. 153.

152. Ibid.

153. Ibid., p. 154.

154. Ibid.

155. Ibid.

156. Ibid.

157. Ibid.

158. Ibid.

159. Ibid.

160. Ibid.

161. Ibid.

162. DS 831.00/1364 Engert to Kellogg, Apr 14, 1928.

163. AHMSGPRCP Apr 13–19, 1928, "Carta Abierta dirigida al pulcro señor General E. López Contreras, Apr 8, 1928.

164. DS 831.00/1545 Gómez, "Ciudadanos Senadores; Ciudadanos Diputados," Apr 23, 1928.

165. Matos to Gómez, Apr 30, 1928, cited in "La creación de los Bancos Agrícola y Pecuario y Obrero y el Ministro José Ignacio Cárdenas," *BAHM* vol. 2, no. 7 (Jul–Aug 1970): pp. 115–23, 122.

166. DS 831.00/1387 Willis C. Cook to Kellogg, Aug 23, 1928.

167. AHMSGPRCP Feb 1–9, 1928, Zumeta to Itriago Chacín, Oct 9, 1928 (misfiled).

168. AHMSGPRCS Nov–Dec 1928, "Pérez Soto trató de formar la República Zuliana arrebatándonos el Catatumbo," *El Tiempo* (Bogotá), Oct 14, 1928.

169. Díaz, *Por qué yo maté a Delgado Chalbaud,* p. 376.

170. Ibid.

171. Ibid., p. 376–77.

172. AHMSGPRCP Aug 10–19, 1928, Argenis Asuaje to Gómez, Jul 19, 1928 (misfiled).

173. Ibid.

174. AHMSGPRCP Oct 1–10, 1928, Leyba to Gómez, Oct 7, 1928.

175. AHMSGPRCP Oct 21–31, 1928, Leyba to Gómez, Oct 31, 1928.

176. Gabaldón Márquez, *Memoria y Cuenta*, p. 181.

177. AHMSGPRCP Oct 11–20, 1928, R. Cayama Martínez to Gómez, Oct 17, 1928.

178. D'Amico, "Una aproximación al desarrollo político y económico de Venezuela," p. 19.

179. Fuenmayor, *1928–1948*, p. 22.

CHAPTER SEVEN   *Renewed Hope for the Rebels*

1. V. León (Baptista) to Pocaterra, Jun 17, 1928, in Pocaterra, *La Oposición a Gómez*, vol. 1, pp. 205–6, 206.

2. Pocaterra to Baptista, Jun 18, 1928, in Pocaterra, *La Oposición a Gómez*, vol. 1, pp. 203–4, 203.

3. Atilano Carnevali to Pocaterra, Jun 26, 1928, in Pocaterra, *La Oposición a Gómez*, vol. 1, pp. 209–10.

4. Baptista to Pocaterra, May 18, 1927, in Pocaterra, *La Oposición a Gómez*, vol. 1, p. 125.

5. Simón Betancourt to Pocaterra, Jul 28, 1928, in Pocaterra, *La Oposición a Gómez*, vol. 1, pp. 225–26.

6. AHMSGPRCP Nov 11–20, 1928, Figueredo to Gómez, Nov 12, 1928.

7. Olivares to Pérez, Nov 17, 1928, in Pocaterra, *La Oposición a Gómez*, vol. 1, pp. 267–70, 267.

8. Ibid., p. 267.

9. Delgado Chalbaud to Pocaterra, Jul 28, 1928, in Pocaterra, *La Oposición a Gómez*, vol. 1, pp. 223–24, 223.

10. Santos Domínici, Smith, and Delgado Chalbaud to Pérez, Nov 2, 1928, in Pocaterra, *La Oposición a Gómez*, vol. 1, pp. 255–56, 255.

11. Ibid., p. 255.

12. Delgado Chalbaud to Pocaterra, Nov 5, 1928, in Pocaterra, *La Oposición a Gómez*, vol. 1, pp. 258–59, 258.

13. Delgado Chalbaud to Pocaterra, Oct 1, 1928, in Pocaterra, *La Oposición a Gómez*, vol. 1, pp. 240–41, 241.

14. Delgado Chalbaud to Pocaterra, Nov 5, 1928, in Pocaterra, *La Oposición a Gómez*, vol. 1, pp. 258–59, 258.

15. AHMSGPRCP Aug 1–15, 1926, Aranguren to Gómez, Sep 3, 1926.

16. AHMSGPRCP Mar 1–10, 1928, G. Torres to Gómez, Mar 5, 1928.

17. AHMSGPRCP Dec 23–31, 1928, Figueredo to Gómez, Dec 28, 1928.

18. AHMSGPRCP Dec 1–10, 1928, Zumeta to Gómez Dec 1, 1928.

19. AHMSGPRCP Aug 1–9, 1928, to Gómez, Aug 7, 1928.

20. DS 831.00/1394 Cook to Kellogg, Oct 29, 1928.

21. Delgado Chalbaud to Pocaterra, Jul 28, 1928, in Pocaterra, *La Oposición a Gómez*, vol. 1, pp. 223–24, 223.

22. Delgado Chalbaud to Pocaterra, Nov 5, 1928, in Pocaterra, *La Oposición a Gómez,* vol. 1, pp. 258–59, 259.

23. Blanco Peñalver, *López Contreras ante la historia,* p. 65.

24. Ibid.

25. Ibid., p. 66.

26. López Contreras, *Páginas para la Historia Militar,* p. 155.

27. Aranguren's son states that when the *Falke* expedition failed, Mrs. Delgado Chalbaud met with Aranguren to recover the family properties in Paris, but they had been written off by the oilman. This appears to be wrong, as the properties were mortgaged to Prenzlau (interview Antonio Aranguren Fonseca, Caracas, Sep 14, 1977).

28. Jacobs's father was British and his mother French.

29. John Jacobs, the son of Mrs. Pusch's brother, was born in Riga, Latvia, on January 23, 1863, and became a naturalized British subject on January 15, 1895.

30. FO 371/13557 A. Canning, "Venezuelan Armed Expedition," Mar 12, 1929.

31. FO 371/13557 Escalante to Foreign Office, Mar 8, 1929.

32. Ibid.

33. FO 371/13557 E. Bremond to Pusch, Mar 18, 1929.

34. Ibid.

35. AHMSGPRCP Apr 11–21, 1929, Escalante to Gómez, Apr 12, 1929.

36. Delgado Chalbaud to Pocaterra, Jan 10, 1928, in Pocaterra, *La Oposición a Gómez,* vol. 1, pp. 240–41, 241.

37. CO 295/565 Governor of Trinidad to Lt. Col. L. S. Amery, Nov 21, 1928.

38. Ibid.

39. Delgado Chalbaud to Pocaterra, Jul 28, 1928, in Pocaterra, *La Oposición a Gómez,* vol. 1, pp. 223–24, 223.

40. Arévalo Cedeño to Jugo Delgado, Nov 4, 1928, in Pocaterra, *La Oposición a Gómez,* vol. 1, pp. 256–57, 256.

41. AHMCOP 277 Gómez to Gabaldón Márquez, May 21, 1928.

42. Fernández, *Hombres y Sucesos,* p. 217.

43. Martín Fierro, "El Rebelde de Santo Cristo," *El Nacional,* Aug 3, 1952, in Fernández, *Hombres y Sucesos,* pp. 429–38, 433.

44. José R. Gabaldón, "Orígenes del Movimiento Revolucionario del General José Rafael Gabaldón en April de 1929," in Gabaldón Márquez, *Memoria y Cuenta,* pp. 204–12, 207.

45. AHMSGPRCP Jan 11–21, 1929, Figueredo to Gómez, Jan 14, 1929.

46. Gabaldón, "Origines del Movimiento Revolucionario," p. 208.

47. AHMSGPRCP Dec 1–10, 1928, Luis Alcalá Sucre to Gómez, Dec 7, 1928.

48. Ibid.

49. Delgado Chalbaud to Pocaterra, Nov 5, 1928, in Pocaterra, *La Oposición a Gómez,* vol. 1, pp. 259–60.

50. Delgado Chalbaud to Blanco Fombona, Dec 3, 1928, in Castellanos, *Rufino Blanco y sus Coterráneos,* p. 68.

51. Ibid.

52. Ibid.

53. DS 831.00/Revolution/146 Engert to Henry Lewis Stimson, Sep 11, 1929.

54. AHMSGPRCP Dec 1–10, 1928, Figueredo to Gómez, Dec 3, 1928.

55. AHMSGPRCP Jan 11–21, 1929, Escalante to Gómez, Jan 20, 1929.

56. AHMSGPRCP Dec 1–10, 1928, Escalante to Gómez, Dec 9, 1928.

57. AHMSGPRCP Feb 21–28, 1929, Zumeta to Gómez, Feb 28, 1929.

58. FO 371/13557 R. L. Craigie, "Memorandum," Feb 2, 1929.

59. Ibid.

60. FO 371/13557 Canning, "Armed Expedition to Venezuela," Mar 16, 1929.

61. AHMSGPRCP Feb 21–28, 1929, Arévalo Cedeño, "A Los Venezolanos," Feb 7, 1929.

62. AHMSGPRCP Feb 1–10, 1929, Arévalo Cedeño, "Carta Abierta," Feb 1929. He also issued a proclamation to the women of Venezuela to join his struggle.

63. Ibid.

64. AAA File 1, Aristeguieta to Aranguren, Apr 4, 1929.

65. Aristeguieta Rojas, *La Nueva Venezuela Revolucionaria,* p. 38.

66. AAA File 1, Aristeguieta to Aranguren, Apr 22, 1929.

67. FO 371/13557 Craigie to C.D.C. Robinson, Jun 11, 1929.

68. Ibid.

69. AHMSGPRCP Mar 1–11, 1929, Escalante to Itriago Chacín, Apr 20, 1929.

70. Cf. Fuenmayor, *1928–1948.*

71. Lisandro Alvarado, *Archivo de la Rotunda.*

72. Cf. Fuenmayor, *1928–1948,* p. 54.

73. Blanco Peñalver, *López Contreras ante la Historia,* p. 54. Severiano Giménez later committed suicide.

74. Gabaldón, "Orígenes del Movimiento Revolucionario," p. 210.

75. Cf. López Contreras, *Proceso Político Social 1928–36.*

76. Fernández, *Gómez el Rehabilitador,* p. 269.

77. Vallenilla Lanz (hijo), *Escrito de Memoria,* p. 127.

78. Ibid.

79. Ibid.

80. Ibid.

81. González, *Rubén González.*

82. Ibid., p. 73.

83. Gómez to President Congreso Nacional, May 3, 1929, in Venezuela, MinRelInt, *Memoria 1929,* Doc 48, pp. 72–73, 72.

84. Ibid., p. 72.

85. Ibid.

86. "La Palabra del Ilustre Hombre Público expone categorícamente los justificados y patrióticos motivos de su renuncia a la presidencía de la República," *El Universal,* May 16, 1929.

87. Gómez to Presidentes de Estado, May 14, 1929, in Venezuela, MinRelInt, *Memoria 1929,* Doc 85, pp. 107–8, 108.

88. Vallenilla Lanz, *Escrito de Memoria,* p. 127.

89. FO 371/13557 O'Reilly to Sir A. Chamberlain, May 18, 1929.

90. González, *Rubén González,* p. 74.

91. FO 371/13557 O'Reilly to Chamberlain, Apr 20, 1929.

92. Gómez to Presidentes de Estado, May 14, 1929, in Venezuela, MinRelInt, *Memoria 1929,* Doc 85, pp. 107–8.

CHAPTER EIGHT   *The* Falke *Expedition*

1. A Chinese warlord who controlled Manchuria from 1916 until 1928, when he was murdered by officers of the Japanese Guandong Army.

2. FO 371/13557 Metropolitan Police Special Branch to Bland, Aug 24, 1929, Appendix B: F. Prenzlau.

3. AAA File 2, McGill to Aranguren, Oct 10, 1937.

4. U.P. Cable, "Declaraciones del Capitán," Apr 9, 1930, in Pocaterra. *Archivo de José Rafael Pocaterra,* vol. 2, pp. 197–98.

5. AHMSGPRCP Aug 1–14, 1930, J. B. Pérez, Dagñino to Itriago Chacín, Aug 11, 1930.

6. Cf. U.P. Cable, "Segunda Audiencia en el Juicio," Apr 10, 1930, in Pocaterra, *Archivo de José Rafael Pocaterra,* pp. 198–201, 198–99.

7. *España Avanza,* Apr 19, 1930. Muhammad ibn Abd al-Karim al-Khattabi, a Moroccan nationalist, was accepted by the Berber Arabs of the Riff mountains as their resistance leader against both France and Spain. His troops defeated a Spanish army in July 1921, inflicting twelve thousand casualties.

8. Aristeguieta, *La Nueva Venezuela Revolucionaria,* p. 40.

9. Ibid.

10. Ibid., p. 41.

11. Ibid.

12. Córdoba, *Los Desterrados,* p. 189.

13. Ibid.

14. Aristeguieta, *La Nueva Venezuela Revolucionaria.,* p. 44.

15. According to McGill, Aranguren contributed between $24,000 and $40,000 (AAA File 2, S. McGill to Aranguren, Oct 10, 1937). In an earlier letter to Aranguren written on July 6, 1936, McGill stated that the Venezuelan oilman contributed $40,000 (AAA File 2, McGill to Aranguren, Jul 6, 1936).

16. Cf. Delgado Chalbaud to Blanco Fombona, Jun 4, 1929, in Castellanos, *Rufino Blanco y sus Coterráneos,* pp. 71–72.

17. AAA File 2, McGill to Aranguren, Oct 10, 1937.

18. AHMSGPRCP Aug 19–31, 1930, J. V. G. Felix Prenzlau and Company, "Orden para el Capitán del Vapor Falke," undated.

19. AHMSGPRCP May 1–31, 1930, Martin Esser to Presidente de Venezuela, May 20, 1930.

20. AHMSGPRCP Aug 19–31, 1930, J. V. G. Bulow to Dagñino, Jul 21, 1930 (misfiled).

21. Gómez was godfather to Román's heir.

22. Rufino Blanco Fombona, "Dos años y medio de Inquietud," in Rama, *Rufino Blanco Fombona Intimo,* pp. 255–325, 279.

23. Ibid., p. 279.

24. "Acta de la Asamblea General del Comité de la Liberación Venezolana," in Pocaterra, *La Oposición a Gómez,* vol. 1, pp. 317–18, 317.

25. Heredía A., *El Año 29,* p. 250.

26. Interview with Antonio Aranguren Fonseca, Caracas, Sep 14, 1977.

27. "Acta de la Asamblea General del Comité de la Liberación Venezolana," in Pocaterra, *La Oposición a Gómez,* vol. 1, pp. 317–18, 320.

28. "Manifiesto de la Junta Suprema de la Liberación de Venezuela," in Pocaterra, *La Oposición a Gómez,* vol. 1, pp. 334–36, 334.

29. Ibid., p. 334.

30. Blanco Fombona, "Dos años y medio de Inquietud," p. 279.

31. "Manifiesto de la Junta Suprema de la Liberación de Venezuela," in Pocaterra, *La Oposición a Gómez,* vol. 1, pp. 334–36, 334.

32. Aristeguieta, "Memorandum," undated, 1929, in Pocaterra, *La Oposición a Gómez,* vol. 1, Doc 33, pp. 313–16, 314.

33. Ibid., p. 314.

34. Baptista to Rodelchal, Jul 8, 1929, in Pocaterra, *La Oposición a Gómez,* vol. 1, pp. 324–27. It should be noted that the letter was written on July 8, with a note added on July 18. The letter was sent by Baptista with Rafael Dávila on July 18. Delgado Chalbaud was already on board the *Falke,* and Dávila gave back the letter on his return to New York.

35. Arévalo Cedeño, *El Libro de Mis Luchas,* p. 284.

36. Baptista to Rodelchal, Jul 8, 1929, in Pocaterra, *La Oposición a Gómez,* vol. 1, pp. 324–27, 325.

37. Ibid., p. 325.

38. Ibid.

39. Ibid.

40. Ibid.

41. Gil Borges to Santos Domínici, Jul 6, 1929, in Pocaterra, *La Oposición a Gómez,* vol. 1, pp. 323–24, 323.

42. Tácito (Atilano Carnevali) to Pocaterra, Jan 24, 1929, in Pocaterra, *La Oposición a Gómez,* vol. 1, pp. 289–90, 289.

43. Ibid.

44. Ibid.

45. AHMSGPRCP Mar 1–10, 1930, Santos Domínici et al., "Aclaratoria: Junta Suprema de la Liberación de Venezuela," Paris, Dec 23, 1929 (misfiled).

46. Olivares to Drs. S. Domínici and A. Smith, Mar 1, 1930, in Pocaterra, *Archivo de José Rafael Pocaterra,* vol. 2, pp. 180–82, 181.

47. *El Universal,* "Manifiesto de la Junta Suprema de la Liberación de Venezuela," Sep 10, 1929.

48. AHMSGPRCP Mar 1–10, 1930, Olivares, "Aclaración," Oct 4, 1929.

49. Ibid.

50. Ortega Martínez to Blanco Fombona, Mar 25, 1931, in Castellanos, *Rufino Blanco y sus Coterráneos,* pp. 209–11, 209.

51. Baptista to Rodelchal, Jul 8, 1929, in Pocaterra, *La Oposición a Gómez,* vol. 1, pp. 324–27, 325.

52. Cf. "Un Polémico Editorial de 'Libertad,'" in Pocaterra, *La Oposición a Gómez,* vol. 1, pp. 329–36.

53. Ibid.

54. Ibid.

55. Cf. Vandenbosch, "Dutch Problems in the West Indies."

56. AHMSGPRCP Jun 12–20, 1928, Asuaje to Gómez, Jul 3, 1928 (misfiled).

57. AHMSGPRCP Aug 9, 1928, Leyba to Gómez, Aug 7, 1928.

58. Edited by Francisco Laguado Jayme, Gustavo Machado, and Salvador de la Plaza and published in Cuba (cf. García Ponce, *Memorias de un General de la Utopía*).

59. AHMSGPRCP Sep 1–15, 1929, Itriago Chacín to J. M. Clemente, Sep 24, 1929.

60. AHMSGPRCP Mar 1–10, 1928, P. M. Reyes to Gómez, Mar 9, 1928.

61. AHMSGPRCP Aug 1–9, 1928, Acisclo Boscán, *A Mis Compatriotas: La Independencia del Zulia,* Baltimore, Jun 1928.

62. AHMSGPRCP Oct 1–10, 1928, Pérez Soto to Gómez, Oct 10, 1928. See also McBeth, *Juan Vicente Gómez and the Oil Companies,* pp. 150–51.

63. Montenegro was involved in Ducharne's 1914 invasion of Venezuela and was part of Sixto Gil's men that attacked Maturín jail. See pages 75–76.

64. Machado asserts that Gómez sent the assassin (cf. García Ponce, *Memorias de un General de la Utopía*).

65. Aurelio Fortoul Briceño, a Venezuelan who attended the International Communist League against Imperialism Congress in Frankfurt in September 1929, praised the support given by the Soviet Union in its "fight for freedom in Venezuela and in the city of Curazao" (AHMSGPRCP Sep 1–15, 1929, Clemente to Gómez, Sep 13, 1929).

66. Gustavo Machado, "El Asalto a Curazao," in Venezuela, Congreso de la República, *La Oposición a la Dictadura Gomecista,* Part 6, vol. 2 (13), Doc 87, pp. 43–143, 110.

67. García Ponce, *Memorias de un General de la Utopía,* p. 116.

68. Interview with Gustavo Machado, Caracas, Sep 1, 1976.

69. AHMSGPRCP Sep 1–15, 1929, Itriago Chacín to Clemente, Sep 24, 1929.

70. FO 371/13558 Gustavo Machado, Comité Ejecutivo Central del Partido Revolucionario Venezolano, "A Los Revolucionarios Venezolanos!!" Curacao, Jun 8, 1929.

71. Two British prisoners awaiting repatriation from Curacao were attacked by the rebels. G. Farrell of Barbados drowned trying to escape from the attackers

after he was beaten with a machete and his head was severely cut. F. E. Finlay of St. Kitts was more fortunate in that he was admitted to the hospital after receiving a severe injury to his head from a machete (FO 199/266 Outon-Powell to H. M. Minister at Caracas, Jun 20, 1929).

72. Urbina, *Victoria, Dolor y Tragedia*, p. 46.

73. FO 371/13558 Outon-Powell to Foreign Office, Jun 15, 1929.

74. FO 371/13558 "Summary of Statements made by the Netherlands Minister of the Colonies to the Press," R. Stevenson to Foreign Office, Jun 15, 1929.

75. FO 199/265 Odo Russell to A. Henderson, Jan 24, 1930.

76. FO 199/265 H. M. Consul Curacao to H. M. Minister Caracas, Nov 5, 1928.

77. AHMSGPRCP Sep 1–15, 1929, Itriago Chacín to Clemente, Sep 24, 1929.

78. Ibid.

79. FO 199/266 Outon-Powell to H. M. Minister at Caracas, Mar 25, 1930.

80. Baptista to Rodelchal, Jul 8, 1929, in Pocaterra, *La Oposición a Gómez,* vol. 1, p. 325.

81. Ibid.

82. Jugo Delgado to Santos Domínici, Oct 9, 1929, in Pocaterra, *La Oposición a Gómez,* vol. 1, pp. 339–41.

83. AHMSGPRCP Mar 12–21, 1931, R. Faria, "Información del Señor Rubén Faría," Mar 13, 1930 (misfiled).

84. AHMSGPRCP Aug 1–14, 1929, Consul to Gómez, Aug 1, 1929.

85. Román to Jugo Delgado, Jul–Aug 1929, in Pocaterra, *La Oposición a Gómez,* vol. 1, pp. 343–46.

86. He was involved in the 1915 Hodge case in Venezuela. See McBeth, *Royal Dutch Shell vs Venezuela.*

87. "Falke Filibuster," *Times* 14, no. 9, Aug 26, 1929.

88. AHMSGPRCP Nov 1–14, 1929, A. Zaleski to Zumeta, Oct 22, 1929.

89. The amount of arms carried by the Falke differs from author. According to Heinrich Kolling, first officer, the *Falke* took on board 1,186 cases of ammunition, fifty-four cases of rifles, and four cases of rifle straps, bayonets, daggers, revolvers, and machine guns. According to Fernández, the *Falke* had the following arms and ammunition:

> 2,000 Mausers, 8mm bore rifles
> 2 million rounds of ammunition
> 25 cavalry carbines
> 25 pistols
> 20,000 rounds of ammunition
> 25 swords
> 1000 ammunition belts
> 6 machine guns (cf. Fernández, *Hombres y Sucesos de mi tierra*)

According to Carlos Pérez Jurado, the *Falke* had the following arms and ammunition:

> 2,000 Mauser 8mm bore rifles
> 25 carbines
> 25 pistols
> 1000 ammunition belts
> 20 million rounds of ammunition for 4 machine guns (cf. Pérez Jurado, *Asalto a Cumaná*)

90. FO 199/266 "Enquiry into the Operations of SS Falke: Notes of Evidence Taken by Mr. J. E. Day, Shorthand Writer to the Legislative Council of Trinidad," in Dispatch Confidential, Sep 19, 1929, Enclosure 3, Franz Zucal, Second Witness.

91. FO 199/266 Horace Rumbold to Arthur Henderson, Oct 3, 1929.

92. DS 831.00 Revolution/159 "Adventure of the SS 'Falke,'" *Hamburger Fremdenblatt*, Oct 2, 1929.

93. The *Falke* took on 201 tons in Hamburg and a further 540 tons in Gdynia, leaving for Venezuela with approximately 760 tons for forty days' sailing at twelve miles per day (cf. E. Ziplitt, "Informe del Viaje del Vapor 'Falke,'" Sep 15, 1929, in Pocaterra, *Archivo de José Rafael Pocaterra*, vol. 2, pp. 69–72).

94. Román to Jugo Delgado, Jul–Aug 1929, in Pocaterra, *La Oposición a Gómez.*, vol. 1, pp. 343–46, 344.

95. Ibid., p. 344.

96. Danzig became a Prussian possession when Poland was partitioned in 1793. In 1807, after Napoleon defeated Prussia, Danzig became a free city controlled by the French and the Saxons. In 1815 at the Congress of Vienna the city was returned to Prussia. Following World War I, the Paris Peace Conference, at which the 1919 Treaty of Versailles was signed, established Danzig, with its half a million German citizens, as a Free City (a territory of 754 square miles) under the League of Nations rather than ceding it to Poland.

97. In 1924, Poland started building the new port of Gdynia, which was then only a small fishing village with a population of 1,500 people, in order to reduce its dependence on the German-dominated Danzig, which handled most of Poland's sea cargo.

98. Only seventeen men accompanied Delgado Chalbaud on the *Falke* from Gynia: Francisco Linares Alcántara, Doroteo Flores, Guillermo Egea Mier, Luis Rafael Pimentel, Rafael Angarita Arvelo, Carlos Mendoza, Luis López Méndez, Edmundo Urdaneta Auvert, Carlos Julio Rojas, Juan Colmenares Pacheco, Rafael Vegas, Armando Zuloaga Blanco, Carlos Delgado Chalbaud, Julio McGill Sarria, José Rafael Pocaterra, Raúl Castro Gómez, and Alejandro Russián.

99. DS 831.00 Revolution/159 "Adventure of the SS *Falke*," *Hamburger Fremdenblatt*, Oct 2, 1929.

100. AHMSGPRCP Aug 1–14, 1929, Zumeta to Itriago Chacín, Aug 13, 1929.

101. AHMSGPRCP Aug 15–31, 1929, Z.(umeta) to Itriago Chacín, Aug 27, 1929.

102. Ibid.

103. AHMSGPRCP Aug 1–14, 1929, Carlos J. Grisanti to Gómez, Aug 13, 1929.

104. Noguera Moreno admitted later paying Olga Varela $10 to write a letter to the authorities stating that Arévalo Cedeño was involved in a revolutionary plot. Varela was Moreno's lover, but she betrayed him, becoming Arévalo Cedeño's lover when he was last on the island (FO 199/276 W. E. Jackson to Lord Passfield, Jul 3, 1929). The incident also illustrates the manner in which these reports originated, with Jackson writing:

> Whatever view may be formed of the facts they seem to throw a good deal of light on the character of Dr Noguera Moreno, and on the manner in which reports of revolutionary activities in Trinidad may be expected to originate while he is in charge of Venezuelan interests here. If the suggestion that he has concocted the whole story be rejected as untenable it is difficult to escape the alternative conclusion that in accepting without the smallest attempt at verification the unofficial statements of a woman of this character he has shown a singular lack of sense of responsibility and a degree of credulity which must make him a some what dangerous representative of his Government. (FO 199/276 W. E. Jackson to Lord Passfield, Jul 3, 1929)

105. AHMSGPRCP Aug 1–14, 1929, Alejandro Fuenmayor to Foreign Affairs Minister, Aug 5, 1929. Moreover, Fuenmayor also sent a copy of the note to the foreign minister and to Dr. José Dolores Alfonseca, the vice president and interior and police minister: "It seems to me, that is if you agree, that the moment has come for making the alleged revolutionaries, who act with such rashness here, understand that in this country there is a serious government that should be respected" (AHMSGPRCP Aug 1–14, 1929, Alejandro Fuenmayor to Dr. José Dolores Alfonseca, Aug 5, 1929).

106. AHMSGPRCP Aug 1–14, 1929, Fuenmayor to Gómez, Aug 5, 1929.

107. FO 199/266 Horace Rumbold to Arthur Henderson, Oct 3, 1929, *Berliner Tageblatt*, "The Freight of the 'Falke,'" Oct 3, 1929.

108. Pimentel to Chely, Oct 15, 1929, in Pimentel, *Bajo la Tiranía*, pp. 209–14, 216.

109. Egea Mier, "La Tragedia de Cumaná," in Venezuela, Congreso de la República, *La Oposición a la Dictadura Gomecista*, Part 2, vol. 2 (2), Doc 182, pp. 3–7, 4.

110. AAA File 4, Egea Mier to Brito Salazar, Aug 26, 1929.

111. Russián, "Memorandum," Aug 21, 1929, in Pocaterra, *Archivo de José Rafael Pocaterra*, vol. 2, pp. 40–42.

112. AAA File 4, Delgado Chalbaud, "A los Pueblos Venezolanos," Aug 7, 1929.

113. AHMSGPRCP Aug 1–14, 1929, Aranda to Gómez, Aug 8, 1929.

114. AHM Unclassified Salvador de la Plaza to Rómulo A. Betancourt, May 29, 1929.

115. Cf. Tácito (Carnevali) to Pocaterra, Sep 9, 1929, in Pocaterra, *Archivo de José Rafael Pocaterra*, vol. 2, pp. 58–63.

116. Carnevali sought an explanation from Frontado, who had returned from his trip, for not honoring his commitment. Frontado explained that his ship was in bad shape, the prevailing winds were against him, he had no motor and no arms, and he did not want to lose his boat, as it was his only source of income.

117. Leoni to Pocaterra, Sep 17, 1929, in Pocaterra, *Archivo de José Rafael Pocaterra*, vol. 2, pp. 75–81.

118. According to Rodolfo Paradas, a Maracucho of Dominican parents, who had also taken part in Urbina's first attack on Curacao in 1928 together with Simón Betancourt, Vidal left on a schooner together with forty-eight Dominicans and a number of Venezuelan revolutionaries, with two hundred rifles, 130,000 rounds of ammunition, and six hundred grenades acquired with $2,000 from the Paris revolutionary committee sent by Aristeguieta from Barranquilla. A few miles out of port, the schooner "broke its rudder forcing them to return to their departure point and they unloaded the mentioned cache of arms that is still hidden there" (AHMSGPRCP Jan 15–31, 1930, General Consul to Gómez, Jan 31, 1930). I do not believe that this is an accurate portrayal of what happened.

119. AHMSGPRCP Aug 1–14, 1929, Fuenmayor to Alfredo Ricart Olines, Aug 2, 1929.

120. AHMSGPRCP Aug 1–14, 1929, Aranda to Gómez, Aug 8, 1929. This amount of money seems highly unlikely.

121. AHMSGPRCP Aug 1–14, 1929, Fuenmayor to Fonseca (Vice President and Interior Minister), Aug 5, 1929.

122. Fernández, *Hombres y Sucesos*, p. 322.

123. Ibid., p. 303–4.

124. Delgado Chalbaud to Pocaterra, Mar 2, 1930, in Pocaterra, *Archivo de José Rafael Pocaterra*, vol. 2, pp. 183–88, 184.

125. AAA File 4, Egea Mier to Salazar, Aug 26, 1929.

126. There is some dispute as to whether the arms were also thrown overboard. The captain of the *Ponemah* states that this was the case, whereas Pellicer is adamant that it did not happen. Piñerua in his report states that Pellicer, who was in charge of the schooner, gave the order to throw overboard the arms and ammunition against the better judgment of Egea Mier and David López (cf. Nicanor Piñerua R., "Informe," Aug 26, 1929, in Pocaterra, *Archivo de José Rafael Pocaterra*, vol. 2, .pp. 42–43. Pellicer, on the other hand, states that the arms were taken to Trinidad (Leopoldo Vicente Pellicer to Pocaterra, Feb 14, 1930, in Pocaterra, *Archivo de José Rafael Pocaterra*, vol. 2, pp. 173–74).

127. Venezuela, MinRelInt, *Memoria,1929*, p. 234.

128. Ibid., p. 239.

129. Fernández, *Gómez, el Rehabilitador,* p. 275.

130. Pocaterra, *Archivo de José Rafael Pocaterra,* vol. 1, p. 374.

131. Aristeguieta Rojas to M Flores Cabrera, Jan 1930, in Luciani, *La dictadura perpetua de Gómez y sus adversarios,* p. 97.

132. Ibid.

133. The name given to the local population.

134. Luis (Pimentel) to Chely (C Pimentel), Oct 15, 1929, in Pimentel, *Bajo la Tiranía,* pp. 209–14, 209.

135. Pocaterra, *Archivo de José Rafael Pocaterra,* vol. 1, pp. 380–81.

136. Ibid.

137. Fernández, *Hombres y Sucesos,* p. 315.

138. Ibid., p. 323.

139. Ibid.

140. Luciani, *La Dictatura perpetua de Gómez,* pp. 95–96.

141. Francisco de Paúla Aristeguieta to Manuel Flores Cabrera, Jan 1930, in Pocaterra, *Archivo de José Rafael Pocaterra,* vol. 2, pp. 155–58.

142. Pimentel to Chely, Oct 15, 1929, in Pimentel, *Bajo la Tiranía,* pp. 209–14, 210.

143. Heredía A., *El Año 29,* p. 261.

144. Fernández, *Hombres y Sucesos,* p. 326.

145. Ibid.

146. Ibid.

147. Flores to Pocaterra, Feb 14, 1930, in Pocaterra, *Archivo de José Rafael Pocaterra,* vol. 2, pp. 171–72.

148. Fernández, *Hombres y Sucesos,* p. 318.

149. Ibid., p. 318.

150. Flores to Pocaterra, Feb 14, 1930, in Pocaterra, *Archivo de José Rafael Pocaterra,* vol. 2, pp. 171–72.

151. Fernández, *Hombres y Sucesos,* p. 319.

152. In his memoirs Pocaterra refers to artillery shells shot at the *Falke,* but this is pure fantasy, as the fort's cannon was only used during official holidays to shoot blanks.

153. Fernández, *Hombres y Sucesos,* p. 336.

154. Ibid., pp. 333–34.

155. Flores to Pocaterra, Feb 14, 1930, in Pocaterra, *Archivo de José Rafael Pocaterra,* vol. 2, pp. 171–72.

156. His son Carlos states that he said "That's it!" ("*Ya esta!*"), but Velásquez dismisses this, since Carlos was on board the *Falke* and not an eyewitness. Fernández describes Delgado Chalbaud's death in the following manner: "When taking the flag of the fatherland from the hands of the wounded Angarita and after walking a little further, he falls for the last time, bathed in glory and covered by the folds of the flag" (Fernández, *Hombres y Sucesos,* p. 348).

157. Fernández's death was honored by the government, which declared five days of national mourning (J. B. Pérez, "Decreto," Aug 12, 1929, in MinRelInt, *Memoria 1929,* Doc 25, pp. 21–22).

158. Pocaterra to Santos Domínici et al., Aug 24, 1929, in Pocaterra, *Archivo de José Rafael Pocaterra,* vol. 2, Doc 9, pp. 17–40, 32.

159. Pocaterra, "Comunicado Oficial del ataque a la plaza de Cumaná," Paris, Oct 11, 1929, in Luciani, *La Dictadura Perpetua de Gómez y sus Adversarios,* pp. 82–84, 83.

160. Ibid., p. 83.

161. Pocaterra to Santos Domínici et al., Aug 24, 1929, in Pocaterra, *Archivo de José Rafael Pocaterra,* Doc 9, pp. 17–40, 31.

162. Delgado Chalbaud Gómez to José María Dávila, Sep 5, 1929, in Pocaterra. *Archivo de José Rafael Pocaterra,* vol. 2, pp. 45–48, 47.

163. Russián to Pocaterra, Sep 7, 1929, in Luciani, *La Dictadura Perpetua de Gómez,* pp. 81–82.

164. Pocaterra to Manuel Flores Cabrera, Sep 18, 1929, in Luciani, *La Dictadura Perpetua de Gómez,* pp. 89–90.

165. Russián to Pocaterra, Sep 7, 1929, in Luciani, *La Dictadura Perpetua de Gómez,* p. 82.

166. Luciani, *La Dictadura Perpetua de Gómez,* p. 108.

167. Luciani, *La Dictadura Perpetua de Gómez,* p. 109–11.

168. DS 831.00 Revolution Rafael Bruzual López, *¿La Revolución se acanalla?* New York, Sep 1929 (handbill).

169. Ibid.

170. Pimentel to Chely, Oct 15, 1929, in Pimentel, *Bajo la Tiranía,* pp. 209–14, 211.

171. Ibid., p. 211.

172. Pimentel, *Bajo la Tiranía,* p. 221.

173. FO 371/13557 G. Beard to A. Henderson, Aug 20, 1929.

174. Ibid.

175. González to Ministro del Relaciones Exteriores, Aug 20, 1929, in Venezuela, MinRelInt., *Memoria 1929,* Doc 96, p. 115.

176. This amount later increased tenfold, to between \$431,034 and \$574,713 (Pedro Pablo Montenegro to General Tobias Uribe, Oct 7, 1929, "Documentos sobre el ataque a Cumaná por el vapor Falke," *BAHM* 90, no. 17 (Apr 1976): pp. 129–73).

177. FO 199/266 S.M. Crier to Lord Passfield, Sep 18, 1929, Enclosure: Declaration of Witness 9.

178. AHMSGPRCP Jan 15–31, 1930, Max. Vásquez to Gómez, Jan 19, 1930.

179. Pocaterra to Baptista, Sep 25, 1929, in Pocaterra, *Archivo de José Rafael Pocaterra,* vol. 11, pp. 89–91, 90.

180. FO 199/266 Crier to Passfield, Sep 17, 1929, Enclosure 3.

181. AAA File 4, Russián, "Memo," Aug 21, 1929.

182. Pocaterra, "Comunicado Oficial del ataque a la plaza de Cumaná," Paris, Oct 11, 1929, in Luciani, *La Dictadura Perpetua de Gómez y sus Adversarios,* pp. 82–84, 83.

183. AAA File 4, Russián, "Memo," Aug 21, 1929.

184. Ibid.

185. Pocaterra, "Comunicado Oficial del ataque a la plaza de Cumaná," Paris, Oct 11, 1929, in Luciani, *La Dictadura Perpetua de Gómez y sus Adversarios,* pp. 82–84, 83.

186. Mateo Salazar, "Parte de las Declaraciones del Práctico del Falke," in Pocaterra, *Archivo de José Rafael Pocaterra,* vol. 2, p. 42.

187. Other accounts suggest that 1,000 rifles were dumped overboard with 1,500 boxes of ammunition.

188. Arévalo Cedeño, *El Libro de Mis Luchas,* p. 284.

189. Pocaterra to Santos Domínici et al., Aug 24, 1929, in Pocaterra, *Archivo de José Rafael Pocaterra. La Oposición a Gómez,* vol. 2, Doc 9, pp. 17–40.

190. Carlos Delgado Chalbaud to José María Dávila, Sep 5, 1929, in Pocaterra, *Archivo de José Rafael Pocaterra,* vol. 2, pp. 45–48, 48.

191. Ibid., p. 48.

192. FO 199/266 Crier to Lord Passfield, Sep 17, 1929, Enclosure 3.

193. AHMSGPRCP Mar 22–31, 1930, Rubén Faría, "Informaciones," Mar 13, 1930.

194. AHMSGPRCP Aug 1–14 1929, Grisanti to Gómez, Aug 13, 1929.

195. Ibid.

196. Ibid.

197. AHMSGPRCP Mar 22–31, 1930, Faría, "Informaciones," Mar 13, 1930.

198. Ibid.

199. AHMSGPRCP Aug 15–31, 1929, Escalante to Itriago Chacín, Aug 27, 1929.

200. DS 831.00 Revolution/137 "Mr. John J. O'Connell," Aug 30, 1929.

201. FO 199/266 S. M. Crier to Lord Passfield, Sep 18, 1929.

202. Ibid.

203. FO 199/266 Crier to Passfield, Sep 18, 1929, Enclosure 2.

204. AHMSGPRCP Sep 16–30, 1929, Dagñino to Gómez, Sep 23, 1929.

205. AHMSGPRCP Sep 16–30, 1929, Escalante to Gómez, Sep 28, 1929.

206. It was described in Spanish as "domestic legal piracy."

207. AHMSGPRCP Aug 19–31, 1930, JVG V. Bulow to Dagñino, Jul 21, 1930.

208. AHMSGPRCP Nov 14–30, 1929, Itriago Chacín to Dagñino, Nov 6, 1929.

209. Ibid.

210. Ibid.

211. AHMSGPRCP Feb 16–31, 1930, Dagñino to Juan Bautista Pérez, Jan 24, 1930 (misfiled).

212. AHMSGPRCP Aug 19–31, 1930, JVG Bulow to Dagñino, Jul 21, 1930 (misfiled).

213. Ibid.

214. AHMSGPRCP Aug 19–31, 1930, JVG Dagñino to Dr. Curtius, Jul 25, 1930.

215. AHMSGPRCP Aug 11–18, 1930, JVG H. Dalla Costa to Foreign Affairs Minister, Aug 1, 1930.

216. AHMSGPRCP Aug 1–14, 1930, J. B. Pérez, Dagñino to Pérez, Aug 8, 1930.

217. AHMSGPRCP Aug 11–18, 1930, JVG Dagñino to Gómez, Aug 11, 19030.

218. According to later reports the ship was then used to ferry arms between the United States and Cuba for the rebels on the island as well as revolutionaries to Gíbara (AHMSGPRCP Sep 19–30, 1931, H. C. Dalla Costa to Gómez, Sep 19, 1931, and López, *Veinte Años sin Patria,* p. 170n).

219. AHMSGPRCP Dec 1–10, 1930, JVG Itriago Chacín to Gómez, Dec 6, 1930.

220. AHMSGPRCP Feb 21–28, 1931, JVG Dagñino to J. Curtius, Jan 31, 1931 (misfiled).

221. Fernández, *Hombres y Sucesos,* p. 509.

222. Venezuela, Congreso de la República, *La Oposición a la Dictadura Gomecista,* vol. 2 (3), p. li.

CHAPTER NINE   *One Last Try*

1. DS 831.00/1449 Engert to Stimson, Dec 23, 1929.

2. A hundredweight is 100 pounds, which is equal to 45.4 kilograms.

3. FO 199/275 E. A. Keeling to Sir John Simon, Mar 3, 1934.

4. Ibid.

5. Ibid.

6. Ibid.

7. FO 199/275 Keeling to Simon, Mar 3, 1934.

8. AHMCOP 284 Gómez to Pérez, May 22, 1930. At the same time, Gómez wrote, "let me suggest the idea of inserting into the Budget that Congress will shortly approve the cancellation of the total foreign debt that is approximately some nineteen million bolívars."

9. AHMSGPRCP May 1–15, 1935, Arcaya to Gómez, May 11, 1935.

10. Gómez to Pérez Soto, Mar 24, 1931, in Zulia, *Memoria y Cuenta, 1932,* p. 54.

11. An *abasto* is a small food shop.

12. "Gomez Orders Cut in Prices of Food," *New York Times,* Jun 19, 1932.

13. Suárez Figueroa, *Programas Políticos Venezolanos,* vol. 1.

14. Fuenmayor, *1928–1948,* p. 74.

15. Ibid., p. 43.

16. Cf. García Ponce, *Memorias de un General de la Utopía.*

17. Fuenmayor, *1928–1948,* p. 80.

18. Cf. "Relación No. 1 de Andre Collins (Aurelio Fortoul) de Sección Latinoamericana de la Internacional Comunista," Apr 12, 1931, in Venezuela, Con-

greso de la República, *La Oposición a la Dictadura Gomecista*, Part 6, vol. 12, Doc 71, pp. 407–16.

19. Kornfeder trained at the Lenin School of Political Warfare in Moscow between 1927 and 1930.

20. Cf. "La Lucha Por El Pan y La Tierra," in Venezuela, Congreso de la República, *La Oposición a la Dictadura Gomecista*, Part 6, vol. 12, Doc 74, pp. 427–36.

21. The exiled Colombian communists were important for the nascent Venezuelan Communist Party.

22. Kornfeder later betrayed the Communist Party, becoming an FBI informer. Caballero postulates the idea that Kornfeder could have been used as an agent provocateur (cf. Caballero, *La Internacional Comunista y América Latina*).

23. AHMSGPRCP Sep 21–30, 1932, Arcaya to Gómez, Sep 23, 1932.

24. Cf. Caballero, *La Internacional Comunista y América Latina*.

25. Cf. Alexander, *Rómulo Betancourt*, p. 54. Most writers have wrongly attributed the managing of a greengrocer's shop to the students. Clemente Leoni, Raúl's father, and Emilio Calderón did own a greengrocer's shop in the city, and from that fact arose the mistaken belief that the students earned their meager existence from this source.

26. According to Alexander, both Betancourt and Haya de la Torre were aware of each other's work, but the "two men had little direct influence upon one another. Both men were in the process of building the political parties, which were to be the principal advocates of basic social, economic, and political reform in their respective countries" (Alexander, *Rómulo Betancourt*, p. 55).

27. AHMCOP 287 Gómez to Arcaya, Jan 20, 1931.

28. AHMSGPRCP Jul 20–31, 1931, Arcaya to Gómez, Jul 21, 1931.

29. AHMSGPRCP Oct 1–15, 1929, Figueredo to Gómez, Oct 8, 1929.

30. AHMSGPRCP Sep 16–30, 1929, Vicente to Gómez, Sep 20, 1929. José Vicente, while convalescing in Biarritz, saw Don Julián Sabal, who relayed the conversation he had with Aranguren in Paris to Gómez's son.

31. AHMSGPRCP Jan 15–31, 1930, A. Pulido Villafane to Gómez, Jan 28, 1930.

32. AHMSGPRCP Mar 1–10, 1930, Pérez Soto to Gómez, Apr 2, 1930 (misfiled).

33. Ibid.

34. AHMSGPRCP Jun 21–31, 1930, JVG Pérez Soto to Sixto Tovar, Jun 26, 1930.

35. "Perez Soto Is Seen As Gómez Successor," *New York Times*, Aug 11, 1930.

36. AHMSGPRCP Sep 10–18, 1931, Pérez Soto to Gómez, Sep 10, 1930 (misfiled).

37. AHMSGPRCP Sep 16–30, 1929, Vicente (José Vicente Gómez) to Gómez, Sep 20, 1929.

38. AHMSGPRCP Nov 1–14, 1929, Aristimuño Coll to Gómez, Nov 11, 1929.

39. AHMSGPRCP Feb 1–10, 1930, Figueredo to Gómez, Jan 28, 1930 (misfiled).

40. AHMSGPRCP Feb 1–10, 1930, Figueredo to Gómez, Feb 6, 1930.

41. AHM Documents 1900–1929, López Contreras to Gómez, Sep 25, 1929.

42. AHMSGPRCP Feb 1–10, 1930, Figueredo to Gómez, Feb 10, 1930.

43. AHMSGPRCP Feb 21–28, 1930, Figueredo to Gómez, Feb 24, 1930.

44. Rómulo Betancourt to Pocaterra, Jan 17, 1930, in Pocaterra, *Archivo de José Rafael Pocaterra*, vol. 2, p. 160.

45. AHMSGPRCP Aug 1–14, 1929, Carlos J. Grisanti to Gómez, Aug 13, 1929.

46. Ibid.

47. AHMSGPRCP Aug 1–14, 1929, Grisanti to Gómez, Aug 13, 1929.

48. AHMSGPRCP Aug 1–14, 1929, Consul General to Gómez, Aug 1, 1929.

49. AHMSGPRCP Jan 1–10, 1931, JVG Figuredo to Gómez, Jan 5, 1931.

50. AHMSGPRCP Jan 1–15, 1930, C. José Curiel to Gómez, Jan 6, 1930.

51. Ibid.

52. Ibid.

53. AHM Documents 1900–1929, Figueredo to Gómez, Sep 1, 1929.

54. AHMSGPRCP Nov 20–30, 1930, JVG Arcaya to Gómez, Nov 25, 1930.

55. AHMSGPRCP Feb 21–28, 1930, Figueredo to Gómez, Feb 24, 1930.

56. Ibid.

57. AHMSGPRCP Mar 12–21, 1931, Rubén Faría, "Información . . . ," Mar 13, 1930.

58. AHMSGPRCP Feb 21–28, 1930, Figueredo to Gómez, Mar 10, 1930 (misfiled).

59. Carlos Delgado Chalbaud to Pocaterra, Mar 30, 1930, in Pocaterra, *Archivo de José Rafael Pocaterra*, vol. 2, pp. 193–94.

60. AHMSGPRCP Apr 22–30, 1930, Figueredo to Gómez, Apr 28, 1930.

61. Ibid.

62. AHMSGPRCP Oct 21–31, 1930, JVG Pérez Soto to Gómez, Oct 25, 1930.

63. AHMSGPRCP Aug 11–18, 1930, JVG Pérez Soto to Gómez, Aug 13, 1930.

64. FO 199/274 Spencer M Dickson to A Henderson, Apr 13, 1931.

65. AHMSGPRCP Oct 21–31, 1930, JVG V. Sambrano to Gómez, Oct 27, 1930.

66. AHMSGPRCP Mar 20–31, 1932, Pérez Soto to Gómez, Mar 23, 1932.

67. Ibid.

68. AHMSGPRCP Nov 11–19, 1930, JVG Gabriel Picón Febres to Gómez, Nov 16, 1930.

69. AHMSGPRCP Dec 11–20, 1930, JVG Figueredo to Gómez, Dec 16, 1930.

70. AHMSGPRCP May 1–15, 1931, Jefatura de Policia del Distrito de Valencia, "Declaración de Leoncio Hilmond," May 12, 1931.

71. Ibid.

72. AHMSGPRCP Jun 1–10, 1931, JVG Escalante to Gómez, Jun 10, 1931.

73. AHMSGPRCP Sep 1–30, 1931, Tres Equis (XXX) to Gómez, Sep 4, 1931.

74. The same person who had taken La Vela de Coro in July 1928.

75. AHMSGPRCP Sep 19–30, 1931, Rafael Antonio Alamo, "Detalles completos de la espantosa muerte del General Juan Pablo Peñaloza. Un crimen atroz. Un Venezolano relata las torturas a que sometieron al anciano jefe revolucionario. El admirable valor del General," Leaflet, Girardot (Colombia), Aug 10, 1931 (misfiled).

76. Ibid. The tortol "is an instrument of torture made of hard wood, guayacán or macana; it is placed on the victim's head like a hat and two nuts are then slowly tightened" (ibid.).

77. Ibid.

78. Ibid.

79. AHMSGPRCP Sep 19–30, 1931, Telmo A. Arellano, "En Honor de la Verdad," Cúcuta, Sep 1, 1931.

80. See Pérez Soto on surveillance of the state, pages 138–39.

81. The same rebel who together with Roberto Fossi unsuccessfully attacked La Vela de Coro in 1928.

82. AHMSGPRCP Jan 1–10, 1931, JVG Radiogram, Jan 3, 1931 (unsigned).

83. AHMSGPRCP Jan 1–10, 1931, Gómez, Figueredo to Gómez, Jan 5, 1931.

84. FO 199/274 "Interview with Atilano Carnevali," *Washington Herald*, Jan 5, 1931.

85. Ibid.

86. AHMSGPRCP Feb 1–28, 1931, Figueredo to Gómez, Mar 30, 1931.

87. According to García Ponce and possibly stretching the point, the Mexican volunteers were "veteran officers of the army of Francisco 'Pancho' Villa" (García Ponce, *Memorias de un General,* p. 184).

88. Ibid.

89. AHMSGPRCP Sep 1–10, 1930, JVG P.M. Arcaya to Gómez, Sep 5, 1930.

90. Ibid.

91. Ibid.

92. On October 11, 1929, Pérez exiled Monsignor Salvador Montes de Oca, the bishop of Valencia, for asking the faithful to pray for the health and liberty of the political prisoners in Venezuela's jails. The Vatican retaliated by withdrawing the papal nuncio.

93. AHMSGPRCP Sep 1–10, 1930, JVG Arcaya to Gómez, Sep 5, 1930.

94. AHMSGPRCP Oct 1–9, 1930, JVG Aranda to Gómez, Oct 2, 1930.

95. AHMSGPRCP Sep 11–30, 1930, JVG Figueredo to Gómez, Sep 15, 1930.

96. AJM Unclassified, Aranda to Gómez, Jan 28, 1931.

97. AHMSGPRCP Oct 20–31, 1931, Arcaya to Gómez, Oct 27, 1931.

98. Ibid.

99. AHMSGPRCP Oct 1–10, 1931, Arcaya to Gómez, Oct 7, 1931.

100. AHMSGPRCP Apr 22–30, 1930, Figueredo to Gómez, Apr 28, 1930.

101. Urbina, *Victoria, dolor y tragedia,* p. 101.

102. AHMSGPRCP Aug 19–31, 1931, H. González to Gómez, Aug 21, 1931.

103. AHMSGPRCP Oct 1–10, 1931, Arcaya to Gómez, Oct 6, 1931.

104. MinRelInt, *Memoria 1931,* Itriago Chacín to P. Tinoco, Oct 30, 1931, Doc 41, pp. 64.

105. Urbina, *Victoria, dolor y tragedia,* p. 75.

106. FO 199/275 Keeling to Foreign Office, Apr 13, 1933.

107. AHMSGPRCP Oct 20–31, 1931, Arcaya to Gómez, Oct 27, 1931.

108. Urbina, *Victoria, dolor y tragedia,* p. 77.

109. Mieres, *Rafael Simón Urbina,* p. 9.

110. Córdoba, *Soñadores en el destierro,* p. 144.

111. Ibid.

112. AHMCOP 299 Requena to General Rafael Falcón, Dec 26, 1931. On January 6, 1932, the *Superior* with its crew of pardoned men arrived in Mexico. The *Superior* was carrying a large consignment of French linen valued at $59,524, and was insured by the London and Lancashire Insurance Company (MinRelInt, *Memoria 1931,* pp. 61–62).

113. AHMSGPRCP Dec 1–15, 1931, Arcaya to Gómez, Dec 21, 1931.

114. AHMSGPRCP Nov 11–20, 1931, Pérez Soto to Gómez, Nov 13, 1931.

115. AHMSGPRCP Dec 1–15, 1931, Arcaya to Gómez, Dec 5, 1931.

116. AHMSGPRCP Nov 1–10, 1931, Arcaya to Requena, Nov 10, 1931.

117. AHMSGPRCP Oct 1–10, 1931, Arcaya to Gómez, Oct 7, 1931.

118. Cf. Arévalo Cedeño to Jugo Delgado, Oct 31, 1931, in Pocaterra, *Archivo de José Rafael Pocaterra,* vol. 2, pp. 247–48.

119. Jugo Delgado, "Credencial," Nov 8, 1931, in Pocaterra, *Archivo de José Rafael Pocaterra,* vol. 2, p. 248.

120. AHMSGPRCP May 20–31, 1933, Andrés E. Rota to Gómez, May 24, 1933, Enclosure: Arévalo Cedeño, "Exposición Presentada al Dr Flores (Actual Ministro de Marina y Aviación)," undated.

121. AHMSGPRCP May 11–19, 1933, Rota to Gómez, Lima May 15, 1933.

122. Ibid.

123. Ibid.

124. AHMSGPRCP May 20–31, 1933, Rota to Gómez, May 26, 1933.

125. AHMSGPRCP Nov 11–20, 1931, Guillermo Abreu to Toribio Muñoz, Nov 3, 1931.

126. Ibid.

127. AHMSGPR J. B. Pérez Feb 1–28, 1931, Diego Córdoba, "Los Partidos Políticos Venezolanos en el Extranjero," *Pativilca,* vol. 1(1), Feb 1931.

128. Ibid.

129. Ibid.

130. Welch states that he thought his stay was sixty-eight days, but this is a mistake.

131. Arcaya, *The Venezuelan Courts and the Welch Case,* p. 2.

132. Ibid.

133. AHMSGPRCP Jul 16–31, 1930, J. B. Pérez Pérez Soto to Sixto Tovar, Jul 30, 1930.

134. Cf. Pocaterra, *Gómez: The Shame of America.*

135. US Congress, *Congressional Record: Proceedings and Debates,* 71 Cong 2 Sess. June 23–July 3, 1930, vol. 72, p. 11638.

136. Blendon, "Venezuela and the United States, 1928–1948," p. 91.

137. AHMSGPRCP Jun 10–19, 1930, JVG Figueredo to Gómez, Jun 16, 1930.

138. FO 199/274 The International Committee for Political Prisoners, *Venezuela.*

139. González, *Rubén González,* p. 89.

140. Ibid., p. 90.

141. Ibid.

142. Ibid.

143. Ibid.

144. Ibid.

145. Ibid., p. 91.

146. AHMSGPR JVG Jun 11–30, 1931, P. M. Arcaya to Gómez, Jun 14, 1931.

147. Senator Rómulo Gallegos of Apure later resigned on June 24 in protest at the way Congress acted in getting rid of Juan Bautista Pérez (AHMSGPRCS Aug 11–19, 1931, "El Gran Novelista Venezolano Rómulo Gallegos Renuncia la Senaduría Por Apure," undated).

148. AGT Correspondence Jan–Jun 1931, Congreso to Gómez, June 16, 1931.

149. Ibid.

150. AHMCOP 298 Gómez to Presidente del Congreso Nacional, Jul 11, 1932.

151. Ibid.

152. Some writers have interpreted the Pérez presidency as a way Gómez was able to shun the consequences of the Great Depression. In 1929, the seven-year constitutional period that started in 1922 was about to end, with Congress wanting to reelect Gómez. He refused, stating that he should be appointed head of the army instead and allowed to choose his successor. He looked around for a puppet candidate and found one in Pérez. The reason for such a volte-face, according to many writers, was that Gómez had always presented himself as the president of prosperity and did not want to head a government during the Great Depression. By 1931, when the crisis reached its most critical point, President Pérez was impeached, "accused of causing the economic crisis, of squandering the country's wealth, and the hunger, misery and unemployment of the Venezuelan working masses, as well as the bankruptcy of the rich classes; and to top it all, of not allowing the entry of communists ideas to Venezuela" (Fuenmayor,

1928–1948, p. 52). Gómez was once again elected president when he promised to restore prosperity.

153. AHMSGPRCP May 23–31, 1932, Cárdenas to Gómez, May 31, 1932. This strange combination lasted until 1950, when Urbina assassinated Carlos Delgado Chalbaud, who formed part of the ruling military triumvirate at the time, with Aranguren convicted of being the intellectual mastermind behind the plot.

154. AHMSGPRCP Jan 1–10, 1932, F. Figueredo to Gral Máximo Durán, Jan 7, 1932.

155. Urbina, *Victoria, dolor y tragedia*, p. 101.

156. AHMSGPRCP May 1–10, 1932, Cárdenas to Gómez, May 3, 1932.

157. AHMSGPRCP Jan 1–10, 1931, JVG M. Bustillos to Gómez, Jan 2, 1931.

158. AAA File 2, "Memorandum," undated, Aranguren annotation on document.

159. Interview with Antonio Aranguren Fonseca, Caracas, Sep 14, 1977. According to José Ignacio Cárdenas, "there is no doubt that Heyden-Altuna is connected with Urbina, with links that go back a long way and makes me think that said Heyden-Altuna played a revolutionary role in Caracas from the time of the students; but that he is an instrument of some other people, as when he was the Consul in London" (AHMSGPRCP May 1–10, 1932, José Ignacio Cárdenas to Gómez, May 3, 1932). Heyden Altuna's revolutionary connection was revealed to the Venezuelan government by an anonymous tip-off, prompting him to deny categorically to Gómez that he was involved with any revolutionary plots, as he was convalescing from an operation. He wrote to Rafael Requena, Gómez's secretary general, that whoever sent such information "must be mistaken or are obeying orders from our commercial enemies who want to harm us and who the informant has listened to without verifying the truth" (AHMSGPRCS Aug 15–31, 1932, Heyden Altuna to Rafael Requena, Jul 12, 1932 [misfiled]).

160. AAA File 4, Ortega Martínez to Aranguren, Aug 15, 1932.

161. AHMSGPRCP May 1–10, 1932, Cárdenas to Gómez, May 3, 1932.

162. AAA File 4, Ortega Martínez to Alberto Mascareñas, May 20, 1932.

163. AAA File 4, Ortega Martínez to Plutarco Elías Calles, May 20, 1932. In February 1932, Rafael Requena, secretary general, requested Rafael Falcón to pay close attention to the families Ravell and Carabaño in Puerto Cabello because they were used as messengers for clandestine letters. The students when first freed also received help from these families.

164. AHMSGPRCP Jan 11–19, 1932, A. B. Cárdenas to Gómez, Jan 13, 1932.

165. Pocaterra, *Archivo de José Rafael Pocaterra*, vol. 2, p. 292.

166. Ibid.

167. FO 199/259 Russell to Simon, Mar 24, 1932.

168. Ibid.

169. Pocaterra, *Archivo de José Rafael Pocaterra*, vol. 2, p. 293; emphasis in original.

170. Pocaterra to Blanco Fombona, Jul 8, 1932, in Castellanos, *Rufino Blanco y sus Coterráneos*, p. 255.

171. AAA File 4, Ortega Martínez to Aranguren, Sep 21, 1932.

172. Pocaterra to Blanco Fombona, Jul 8, 1932, in Castellanos, *Rufino Blanco y sus Coterráneos*, p. 255.

173. AAA File 7, Jorge Pocaterra to Aranguren, Sep 20, 1932.

174. AAA File 4, Ortega Martínez to Aranguren, Sep 21, 1932.

175. AAA File 1, Pocaterra to Smith and Aranguren, Nov 5, 1932.

176. AAA File 4, Ortega Martínez to Aranguren, Aug 1, 1932.

177. AAA File 4, Ortega Martínez to Aranguren, Aug 29, 1932.

178. AAA File 1, Aranguren to Pocaterra, Jan 27, 1933.

179. AAA File 4, Ortega Martínez to Aranguren, Nov 2, 1932.

180. AAA File 4, Mr. M. K. de Trairup to Dr. A. Smith, Sep 2, 1932.

181. AAA File 4, Ortega Martínez to AA, Apr 17, 1935.

182. AAA File 4, Ortega Martínez to Aranguren, Aug 15, 1932.

183. AAA File 4, Ortega Martínez to Aranguren, Apr 17, 1933.

184. M. Puig Casauranc to Calles, May 23, 1933, in Calles, *Correspondencia Personal (1919–1945)*, pp. 106-10, 109.

185. AHMSGPRCP Jul 11–20, 1932, Arcaya to Gómez, Jul 12, 1932.

186. Ibid.

187. AHMSGPRCP Jan 1–10, 1933, Cárdenas to Gómez, Jan 3, 1933.

188. AAA File 4, Ortega Martínez to Aranguren, Jan 29, 1933.

189. AHMSGPRCP Jan 1–10, 1933, Cárdenas to Gómez, Jan 3, 1933.

190. AAA File 4, Ortega Martínez to Aranguren, Feb 4, 1933.

191. AAA File 5, Ortega Martínez to Aranguren, Mar 13, 1933.

192. AAA File 4, Ortega Martínez to Aranguren, Apr 17, 1933.

193. AAA File 4, Ortega Martínez to Aranguren, Apr 24, 1933.

194. AAA File 1, Pocaterra to Aranguren, May 1, 1933.

195. Ibid.

196. Cf. Aranguren to Pocaterra, May 17, 1933, in Pocaterra, *Archivo de José Rafael Pocaterra*, vol. 2, pp. 299–300.

197. AAA File 4, Ortega Martínez to Aranguren, Nov 27, 1933.

198. AHMSGPRCP Aug 20–31, 1934, Rafael Seijas Cook to E. Urdaneta Carrillo, Aug 16, 1934 (misfiled), "Nómina de Familias Venezolanas Residentes en Barcelona de España."

199. The company was later taken over by Exxon.

200. AHMSGPRCP May 11–19, 1933, Rota to Gómez, Lima May 15, 1933.

201. Ibid.

202. Ibid.

203. AHMSGPRCP May 20–31, 1933, Rota to Gómez, May 19, 1933.

204. AHMSGPRCP Jan 1–10, 1934, Rota to Gómez, Jan 8, 1934.

205. AHMSGPRCP Jan 1–10, 1934, P. López Tejera to Itriago Chacín, Jan 9, 1934.

206. Ibid.

207. Ibid.

208. Ibid.

209. Ibid.
210. AHMSGPRCP Jan 1–10, 1934, López Tejera to Urdaneta Carrillo, Jan 22, 1934.
211. Ibid.
212. Ibid.
213. AAA File 6, Eduardo Héctor Machado to Aranguren, Jan 3, 1934. The ABC was a secret political organization formed by Joaquín Martínez Sáenz in September 1931 in retaliation for the government's brutal repression of the opposition. Its aim was to punish the most important members of the Gerardo Machado government. Its first victim was the assassination of Clemente Vásquez Bello, president of the Senate, in September 1931.
214. Ibid.
215. Ibid.
216. Ibid. The boat later on turned out to be an airplane that was in use with the army.
217. AAA File 6, Eduardo Machado to Aranguren, Jun 25, 1934.
218. AAA File 6, Eduardo Machado to Antonio Aranguren, Jul 4, 1934.
219. AHMSGPRCP Aug 20–31, 1934, Rincones to Gómez, Aug 27, 1934.
220. AHMSGPRCP Apr 1–20, 1935, Rincones to Gómez, Apr 17, 1935.
221. AHMSGPRCP Nov 15–31, 1935, M. A. Villarroel to Gómez, Nov 23, 1935.
222. AHMSGPRCP Apr 1–20, 1935, Rincones to Gómez, Apr 17, 1935.
223. Ibid.
224. Ibid.
225. AHMSGPRCP Apr 1–20, 1935, José Miguel Ferrer to Gómez, Apr 19, 1935.
226. Ibid.

CHAPTER TEN   *The Succession Is Resolved*

1. General J. V. Gómez, *Mensaje que el ciudadano General J. V. Gómez*, p. 3.
2. Ibid.
3. FO 199/275 Keeling to Simon, Mar 3, 1934.
4. Ibid.
5. AHMSGPRCP Jul 11–19, 1933, Arcaya to Gómez, Jul 15, 1933.
6. Delgado Chalbaud to Pocaterra, Jan 17, 1935, in Pocaterra, *Archivo de José Rafael Pocaterra*, vol. 2, pp. 306–7, 307.
7. AAA File 6, Eduardo Machado to Aranguren, May 1, 1933.
8. AHMSGPRCP Jun 1–10, 1935, E. Ramón París to Gómez, Jul 8, 1935.
9. Delgado Chalbaud to Pocaterra, Jan 17, 1935, in Pocaterra. *Archivo de José Rafael Pocaterra*, vol. 2, pp. 306–7, 307.
10. Parada, *De Ocumare a Miraflores*, p. 190.
11. Ibid.

12. FO 371/17619 John Simon, "Annual Report," Mar 3, 1934.

13. Parada, *De Ocumare a Miraflores*, p. 191.

14. Ibid.

15. FO 199/275 Keeling to Simon, Mar 3, 1934.

16. AAA File 4, Ortega Martínez to Aranguren, Apr 9, 1934.

17. Ibid.

18. FO 199/275 Keeling to Simon, Mar 3, 1934.

19. Ibid.

20. Ibid.

21. FO 371/18782 Keeling to Simon, Dec 24, 1934.

22. Arturo Uslar Pietri, Telex, Paris, Jun 17, 77, *Resumén* vol. 15, no. 190, Jun 26, 1977. Uslar Pietri would later deny as "absolutely false" (ibid.) that he had founded such a newspaper.

23. Velásquez, "Aspectos de la evolución política de Venezuela en su último medio siglo," pp. 3–385, 26.

24. Cova, *Entre barrotes*, p. 174.

25. Ibid.

26. López Contreras, "El 17 de diciembre de 1935," pp. 36–50, 45–46.

27. Ibid., p. 47.

28. Ibid., p. 46.

29. Cova, *Entre Barrotes*, p. 178.

30. Ibid., p. 177.

31. Ibid., p. 178.

32. López Contreras, "El 17 de diciembre de 1935," p. 46.

33. FO 371/19845 MacGregor to Eden, Dec 24, 1935.

34. Ibid.

35. Fernández, *Hombres y Sucesos*, p. 398.

36. Ibid., p. 401.

37. Cf. López Contreras, "El 17 de diciembre de 1935," p. 46.

38. Fernández, *Hombres y Sucesos*, p. 401.

39. Ibid.

40. Ibid.

41. Ibid., p. 402. According to Fernández, who was able to inspect the cadaver, it had "two wounds: one on the right part of the forehead, superficial; the other from behind to the height of the waist at point-blank range as indicated by the gunpowder trace had destroyed his liver. Both shots were made when he was disarmed and lead by his arms toward the private salon of the Governor" (ibid., p. 403).

42. This is defined as paralysis or weakness on one side of the body caused by damage or disease affecting the motor nerve tracts on the opposite side of the brain.

43. Besson, *Historia del Estado Zulia*, vol. 5, p. 366.

44. Ibid.

45. Cf. López Contreras, "Decreto," Dec 20, 1935, in Venezuela, MinRelInt, *Memoria 1935*, Doc 10, pp. 48–50.

46. AHMCOP 360, López Contreras, "Instrucciones para el Sr. Dr. Carmelo Paris, Consul General de Venezuela en Curazao," Feb 2, 1936.

47. AHMSGPRCP Dec 26–27, 1935, Aranguren to López Contreras, Dec 27, 1935.

Conclusion

1. Baptista, *Venezuela*, p. 262.
2. Ibid.
3. Ibid.
4. Arcaya, *Memorias*, p. 58.
5. Ibid.
6. AHMSGPRCP Cop 284 Gómez to Pérez, May 22, 1930.
7. Gil Fortoul, *El Hombre y la Historia*, p. 164.
8. Arcaya, *Memorias*, p. 89.
9. Roldán Oliarte, *El General Juan Vicente Gómez*, p. 105.
10. Ibid., p. 104.
11. Ibid.
12. AHMCOP 252 Telegram: Gómez to Arraiz, Jan 15, 1925.
13. AHMCOP 238A Gómez to Eustoquio Gómez, Jan 4, 1915.
14. Ibid.
15. Ibid.
16. FO 199/275 Keeling to Simon, Apr 3, 1933.
17. AAA File 4, Smith to Aranguren, Nov 21, 1924.
18. Cf. Blendon, "Venezuela and the United States."
19. Interview with Gustavo Machado, Caracas, Sep 1, 1976; Arévalo Cedeño, *El libro de mis luchas.*
20. AAA File 3, Telegram: Gávila to Geólogo, Dec 8, 1924; AAA File 7, Reyes Belloso to Aranguren, Dec 24, 1914; AAA File 1, Pocaterra to Aranguren, Nov 5, 1932; and, AAA File 2, S McGill to Aranguren, Jul 22, 1934.
21. AAA File 2, McGill to Aranguren, Jul 6, 1936.

BIBLIOGRAPHY

ARCHIVES

United Kingdom

Public Record Office
Admiralty
ADM 137   1914–18 War Histories

Colonial Office
CO 295   Trinidad Governor's Dispatches, 1905–35

Foreign Office
FO 368   General Correspondence, Commercial, 1908–19
FO 369   General Correspondence, Consular, 1908–33
FO 370   General Correspondence, Library, 1908–33
FO 371   General Correspondence, Political, 1908–36
FO 420   General Correspondence, Confidential Print, America, South and Central
FO 115   U.S. Embassy and Consular Archives
FO 199   Venezuela Embassy and Consular Archives, 1908–33

Science Museum Library (London)
S. Pearson and Sons, Ltd., Archives:
Box A 5–7
Box C-25, C-30

United States of America

Records of the Department of State relating to the Internal Affairs of Venezuela, 1910–29
National Film Archives Microcopy No. 366, Reels 24–28

Venezuela

Academia de la Historia
Archivo del General José Manuel Hernández
Archivo de Manuel Landaeta Rosales

Fundación John Boulton
Archivo del General Antonio Aranguren, Files 1–8

Palacio de Miraflores
Archivo Histórico de Miraflores
Presidential Copybooks, Nos. 100–362, 1908–36
Presidential and Secretary General's Correspondence, 985 file bundles, 1908–36

Private Archives
Archivo Particular del Dr Gumersindo Torres
Copybooks, 1917–22, 1928–31
Correspondence, 1917–22, 1928–31
Archivo del Dr. J. M. Capiola Torres
Various letters

CONTEMPORARY OFFICIAL PUBLICATIONS

United Kingdom

Board of Trade Journal and Commercial Gazette, 1908–36
Parliamentary Commons Debates (Hansard), 1908–36

United States of America

Congressional Record, Proceedings and Debates, 1908–35
Department of Commerce and Labor, Bureau of Manufacture, "Monthly Consular and Trade Reports—Venezuela," 1908–36
State Department, "Papers Relating to the Foreign Relations of the United States of America—Venezuela," 1908–36

Venezuela

Banco Agrícola y Pecuario, *Informes,* 1931
Banco Central de Venezuela, *Informe,* 1945
Consejo de Gobierno, *Memoria,* 1909–13
Consulate General of Venezuela (Liverpool), "The Venezuelan Commercial Review," 1933–35

Corte Federal y de Casación, *Memoria,* 1909–36
Diario de Debates de la Cámara de Diputados, 1918–36
Diario de Debates de la Cámara del Senado, 1909–19, 1922–36
Distrito Federal, Gobernación, *Exposición,* 1911–35
Gaceta Oficial, 1909–10, 1925
Ministerio de Fomento, "Anuario Estadístico de Venezuela," 1908–12, 1938
———, *Cuenta,* 1913–36
———, Dirección General de Estadística, *Estadística Mercantil y Marítima,* 1907–30
———, *Memoria,* 1908–36
Ministerio de Hacienda, *Memoria,* 1908–36
Ministerio de Obras Públicas, *Memoria,* 1908–36
Ministerio de Relaciones Exteriores, *Cuenta,* 1908–36
———, *Libro Amarillo,* 1908–36
Ministerio de Relaciones Interiores, Dirección de Sanidad Nacional, *Informe,* 1911–29
———, *Memoria,* 1908–36
Monagas (Estado), *Mensaje Presidencial,* 1910, 1912–14, 1917–18, 1922, 1925, 1927–28
———, Secretaría, *Exposición,* 1917–18, 1920–21, 1923, 1934
Recopilación de Leyes y Decretos de Venezuela, vols. 1–60
Zulia (Estado), *Memoria y Cuenta,* 1908, 1911, 1916–19, 1922–35
———. Presidencia, *Mensaje,* 1911–12, 1916–18, 1921–24, 1929, 1931, 1935

OTHER CONTEMPORARY SOURCES

El Agricultor Venezolano (Ministerio de Agricultura y Cría), nos. 31–48, 1938–42
Boletín de la Cámara de Comercio de Caracas, 1919–36
Boletín del Archivo Histórico de Miraflores, nos. 1–100
Boletín del Archivo Nacional, 1924–71
Boletín Comercial e Industrial (Ministerio de Relaciones Exteriores), 1920–24
Boletín del Ministerio de Fomento, 1909–35
Boletín del Ministerio de Relaciones Exteriores, vols. 1–10
Boletín del Ministerio de Relaciones Exteriores, Número Extraordinario, vols. 1, 3, 11
Boletín del Ministerio de Relaciones Exteriores. Suplemento Comercial e Industrial, nos. 1–4, 1930
Boletín del Petróleo (Caracas), nos. 1–37, Apr–Dec, 1925
Corporation of Foreign Bond-Holders (London), Newspaper Files, vols. 7–11
El Eco Alemán, 1916
España Avanza, 1930
Latin American World (London), 1925–32
Oil News (London), 1913–36
Revista del Instituto Nacional de Café (Caracas), vols. 1–3

Revista Mercantil (Maracaibo), 1924–32

Royal Bank of Canada, *Business Conditions in Latin America and the West Indies,* 1928–36

Royal Dutch Company, *Annual Reports,* 1907–36

The Shell Transport and Trading Company, *Annual Reports,* 1907–36

Skinner, Walter R., *The Oil and Petroleum Manual* (London), 1910–36

The South American Journal (London), 1900–1936

The Stock Exchange Yearbook, 1900–1914

Venezuela, Comercial, Social e Intelectual (Caracas), 1924–27

Venezuela Contemporánea (Caracas), 1916–17

Newspapers

El Constitucional (Caracas), 1908–1909

La Información (Maracaibo), 1921–22, 1926

El Nuevo Diario (Caracas), 1913, 1918–22, 1928–32

Panorama (Maracaibo), 1920–23, 1935

The Times (London), 1908–1909

El Universal (Caracas), 1918–22, 1928–32

Unpublished Sources

Blendon, Edith Myretta James. "Venezuela and the United States, 1928–1948: The Impact of Venezuelan Nationalism." PhD diss., University of Maryland, 1971.

Burggraaff, John Winfield, "Civil-Military Relations in Venezuela." PhD diss., University of New Mexico, 1967.

Carlisle, Douglas H. "The Organization for the Conduct of Foreign Relations in Venezuela, 1909–1935." PhD diss., University of North Carolina at Chapel Hill, 1951.

Carreras, Charles Edward. "U.S. Economic Penetration of Venezuela and Its Effects on Diplomacy, 1895–1906." PhD diss., University of North Carolina at Chapel Hill, 1971.

Cooke, Thomas M. "The Dynamics of Foreign Policy Decision in Venezuela." PhD diss., American University (Washington, DC), 1968.

Demetriou, George J., "A Consideration of Some Aspects of the Problem of Legitimacy in Venezuelan Politics, 1830–1953." PhD diss., University of Minnesota, 1954.

Duffy, Edward Gerald. "Politics of Expediency: Diplomatic Relations between the U.S. and Venezuela during the Juan Vicente Gómez Era." PhD diss., Pennsylvania State University, 1969.

Hendrickson, Julius Embert. "The New Venezuelan controversy: the relations of the U.S. and Venezuela, 1904–1914." PhD diss., University of Minnesota, 1964.

Knudson, David Lawrence Taylor. "Petroleum, Venezuela, and the United States: 1920–1941." PhD diss., Michigan State University, 1975.

McBeth, B. S. "Juan Vicente Gómez and the Oil Companies." D. Phil. thesis, Oxford University, 1980.

McMillan, Douglas Francis. "Venezuelan University Students as a Force in National Politics, 1928–1963." PhD diss., The University of New Mexico, 1971.

Muñoz, Arturo Guillermo. "The Táchira Frontier, 1881–1899: Regional Isolation and Integration in the Venezuelan Andes." PhD diss., Stanford University, 1977.

Rayburn, John C. "Some Aspects of the Impact of Anglo-Saxon Capital and Technology in Venezuela." PhD diss., American University, 1942.

Stann, E. Jeffrey. "Caracas, Venezuela 1891–1936: A Study of Urban Growth." PhD diss., Vanderbilt University, 1975.

INTERVIEWS

Dr. Antonio Aranguren Fonseca, Caracas, Sep 14, 1977

Sr. Alberto Barrios Sebal, Caracas, Nov 24, 1976

Dr. J. M. Capiola Torres, Caracas, Sep 27, 1977, and Sep 29, 1977

Sra. A. Sebal Benshimol de Barrios, Caracas, Nov 15, 1976

Sra. Carmen Carolina Torres de Lecuna, Caracas, Sep 27, 1977

Dr. Manuel R. Egaña, Caracas, Oct 13, 1976

Dr. César González, Caracas, Sep 23, 1976, and Jan 16, 1977

Dr. J. A. Giacopini Zárraga, Caracas, Apr 1, 1977, and Jul 25, 1977

Dr. Gustavo Machado, Caracas, Sep 1, 1976

Dr. Pedro José Muñoz, Caracas, Sep 7, 1976

Senator Dr. Ramón J. Velásquez, Caracas, Jan 9, 1977, Feb 5, 1977, Mar 20, 1977, Jul 9, 1977, and Aug 21, 1977

Dr. Guillermo Zuloaga, Caracas, Sep 28, 1977

Dr. Amenodoro Rangel Lamus, Caracas, Jul 2, 1977

OFFICIAL PUBLICATIONS

United Kingdom

Board of Trade—Department of Overseas Trade

Bancroft-Livingston, H. *Report on the Economic and Financial Conditions in Venezuela.* London, HMSO, 1927.

Kirwin, T. J. *Economic Conditions in Venezuela* London: HMSO, 1930.

———. *Economic Conditions in Venezuela* London: HMSO, 1932.

MacGregor, J. P. *Economic Conditions in Venezuela* London: HMSO, 1935.

Morris, T. J. *Report on the Economic and Financial Conditions in Venezuela.* London: HMSO, 1923.

Diplomatic and Consular Reports

Consul C.H. de Lemos, "Venezuela: Report for the Year 1905 on the Trade and Commerce of Ciudad Bolívar," *PP,* vol. 139 (1906): pp. 903–11.

Consul C.H. de Lemos, "Venezuela: Report for the Year 1908 on the Trade and Commerce of Ciudad Bolívar," *PP,* vol. 99 (1909): pp. 643–53.

Consul C.H. de Lemos, "Venezuela: Report for the Year 1910 on the Trade and Commerce of Ciudad Bolívar," *PP,* vol. 97 (1910): pp. 757–67.

Acting Vice Consul T. Ifor Rees, "Venezuela: Report for the Year 1913–14 on the Trade of Venezuela and the Consular District of Caracas," *PP,* vol. 75 (1915): pp. 849–81.

Vice Consul Guy Gilliat Smith, "Venezuela: Report for the Year 1909–10 on the Trade of Venezuela and the Consular District of Caracas," *PP,* vol. 97 (1911): pp. 767–807.

Vice Consul Guy Gilliat Smith, "Venezuela: Report for the Year 1910–11 on the Trade of Venezuela and the Consular District of Caracas," *PP,* vol. 101 (1912–13): pp. 575–607.

Vice Consul Guy Gilliat Smith, "Venezuela: Report for the Year 1911–12 on the Trade of Venezuela and the Consular District of Caracas," *PP,* vol. 73 (1913): pp. 693–727.

Acting Vice Consul N. van Stenis, "Venezuela: Report for the Year 1912–13 on the Trade of Venezuela and the Consular District of Caracas," *PP,* vol. 95 (1914): pp. 849–79.

Vice Consul H. Tom, "Venezuela: Report for the Year 1908–09 on the Trade of Venezuela and the Consular District of Caracas," *PP,* vol. 103 (1910): pp. 2207–49.

United States of America

Department of Trade, Bureau of Foreign and Domestic Commerce

Bell, P.L. *Venezuela: A Commercial and Industrial Handbook.* Special Agents Series, no. 212, 1922.

Brett, H. "Venezuela." *Supplement to Commerce Reports,* no. 48a, Jun 17, 1916.

———. "Venezuela." *Supplement to Commerce Reports,* no. 48a, Dec 31, 1917.

———. "Venezuela." *Supplement to Commerce Reports,* no. 51a, Jul 19, 1920.

Fletcher, S.J. "Venezuela." *Supplement to Commerce Reports,* no. 13, 1922.

Venezuela

Venezuela

Compilación de documentos de adhesión al acuerdo del 22 de junio de 1921. Caracas: Tip. Mercantil, 1921.

Conjuración contra la vida del General Juan Vicente Gómez, Presidente de Venezuela y sus consecuencias. Caracas: Imprenta Nacional, 1909.

Conjuración contra la vida del General Juan Vicente Gómez, Presidente Constitucional de la República. Caracas: Tip. Americana, 1911.

El General Gómez y los hombres de trabajo. Caracas: n.p., 1914.

General Juan Vicente Gómez Documentos para la historia de su Gobierno, comp. Luis Correa. Caracas: Lit. del Comercio, 1925.

Semblanza del General Juan Vicente Gómez. Caracas: n.p., 1919.

Banco Central de Venezuela

Ingreso Nacional de Venezuela en 1936. Monografías del Banco Central de Venezuela No. 1. Caracas: Editorial Relámpago, 1949.

Congreso

Contestación al Mensaje Presidencial. Caracas: Empresa El Cojo, 1909.

Contestación al Mensaje del Presidente Provisional de la República. Caracas: Imprenta Nacional, 1918.

Contestación al Mensaje del Presidente Provisional de la República. Caracas: Tip. Cosmos, 1919.

Contestación al Mensaje presentado por el Presidente Provisional de la República al Congreso Nacional en sus Sesiones Ordinarias de 1922. Caracas: Tip. Cosmos, 1922.

Contestación del Congreso Nacional al Mensaje del Presidente Provisional de los Estados Unidos de Venezuela, 1910. Caracas: Tip. Americana, 1910.

Contestación del Congreso Nacional Extraordinario al Mensaje Especial del General JV Gómez, Presidente de los Estados Unidos de Venezuela. Caracas: Tip. Americana, 1911.

Contestación del Congreso Nacional al Mensaje del General JV Gómez, Presidente de la República, 1924. Caracas: Tip. Mercantil, 1924.

Gómez, General J. V. *Mensaje que el ciudadano General J. V. Gómez, Presidente de los Estados Unidos de Venezuela presenta al Congreso Nacional en sus sesiones ordinarias de 1932.* Caracas: Litografía del Comercio, 1932.

La Oposición a la Dictadura Gomecista, Caracas, Ediciones Conmemorativas del Bicentenario del Natalicio del Libertador Simón Bolívar, 1983, vols. 2–4.

Congreso, Cámara de Diputados

Discurso pronunciado por el Presidente de la Cámara de Diputados, Doctor J L Arismendi al clausurar las sesiones del presente año de 1910. Caracas: Imprenta Nacional, 1910.

Discurso del Doctor Ezequiel A Vivas, Presidente de la Cámara de Diputados al inaugurar sus sesiones en el año de 1911. Caracas: Imprenta Nacional, 1911.

Discurso de clausura del Presidente Dr Rafael Garmendia Rodríguez. Caracas: Lit del Comercio, 1919.

Inocente de J. Quevedo. Discurso inaugural. Caracas: Tip. Cosmos, 1918.

Palabras del Diputado Simón Camejo al participar al Presidente de los Estados Unidos de Venezuela la clausura de las sesiones ordinarias de 1925. Caracas: Lit. del Comercio, 1925.

Congreso de Diputados Plenipotenciarios

Exposición que a las Asambleas de Diputados Plenipotenciarios de los Distritos de los Estados dirige el Presidente del Congreso de Diputados Plenipotenciarios de los Estados Unidos de Venezuela. Caracas: Imprenta Nacional, 1914.

Congreso, Cámara del Senado

Discurso inaugural pronunciado por el Doctor Pedro M. Arcaya, Presidente de esta Cámara, al instalarse en sus sesiones ordinarias de 1922. Caracas: Tip. Cosmos, 1922.

Discurso inaugural pronunciado por el Senador José Ignacio Lares al tomar posesión de la Presidencia de la Cámara en sus sesiones ordinarias de 1917. Caracas: Imprenta Nacional, 1917.

Discurso inaugural pronunciado por el Senador Laureano Vallenilla Lanz al tomar posesión de la Presidencia de la Cámara en sus sesiones ordinarias de 1916. Caracas: Imprenta Nacional, 1916.

Discurso inaugural pronunciado por el Senador Laureano Vallenilla Lanz al tomar posesión de la Presidencia de la Cámara en sus sesiones ordinarias de 1920. Caracas: Imprenta Nacional, 1920.

Discurso inaugural pronunciado por el Senador Laureano Vallenilla Lanz, al tomar posesión de la Presidencia de la Cámara, en sus sesiones ordinarias de 1923. Caracas: Imprenta Nacional, 1923.

Discurso pronunciado por el General Arístides Tellería, Presidente de la Cámara del Senado de los Estados Unidos de Venezuela al inaugurar las sesiones Constitucionales de 1909. Caracas: Tip. Americana, 1909.

Discurso pronunciado por el General P. Giuseppi Monagas al clausurar como Presidente las sesiones de la Cámara del Senado en su reunión extraordinaria de 1911. Caracas: Tip. Americana, 1911.

Discurso pronunciado por el Senador José A. Tagliaferro al tomar posesión de la Presidencia de la Cámara del Senado en su reunión extraordinaria de 1911. Caracas: Tip. Americana, 1911.

Discurso pronunciado por el Presidente Doctor José A Tagliaferro al clausurar las sesiones ordinarias de 1917. Caracas: Imprenta Nacional, 1917.

Discurso pronunciado por el Dr. J. de D. Méndez y Mendoza, Presidente del senado, en el Acto de Clausura de las sesiones ordinarias de la Cámara, en el año de 1918. Caracas: Imp. Bolívar, 1918.

Discurso de clausura del Presidente Dr. Carlos F. Grisanti. Caracas: Lit. del Comercio, 1919.

Discurso pronunciado por el Doctor D. A. Coronil, Presidente de la Cámara del Senado, al clausurar sus sesiones ordinarias de 1920. Caracas: Tip. Cosmos, 1920.

Discurso pronunciado por el Senador Rafael Viloria Cadenas en la Cámara del Senado el 20 de abril de 1921. Caracas: Tip. de la Editorial "Victoria," 1921.

Discurso pronunciado por el Doctor Rafael Requena, Presidente de la Cámara del Senado, al clausurar las sesiones ordinarias en el año de 1921. Caracas: Tip. Americana, 1921.

Discurso pronunciado por el Senador Dr José A Tagliaferro al tomar posesión de la Presidencia de la Cámara del Senado en sus sesiones ordinarias de 1924. Caracas: Tip. Mercantil, 1924.

Discurso pronunciado por el presidente de la Cámara (Pedro Emilio Coll) del Senado en la sesión de clausura el 17 de julio de 1926. Caracas: Lit. del Comercio, 1926.

Discurso pronunciado por el Señor Laureano Vallenilla Lanz, Presidente de la Cámara del Senado de los Estados Unidos de Venezuela, al inaugurar el 19 de abril las sesiones ordinarias de 1930. Caracas: Tip. El Universal, 1930.

Discurso pronunciado por el Senador Laureano Vallenilla Lanz, en su carácter de Presidente de la Cámara, al inaugurarse las sesiones ordinarias de 1931. Caracas: Tip. Universal, 1931.

Discurso pronunciado por el Senador Doctor Julio de Armas, en su carácter de Presidente de la Cámara, al clausurarse las sesiones ordinarias de 1932. Caracas: Tip. Americana, 1932.

Discurso pronunciado por el Doctor Federico Alvárez Feo, en su carácter de Presidente de la Cámara, al clausurarse las sesiones ordinarias de 1934. Caracas: Lit. y Tip. del Comercio, 1934.

Discurso pronunciado por el Senador César Zumeta, en su carácter de Presidente de la Cámara, al inaugurarse las sesiones de 1932. Caracas: Editorial Sur América, 1934.

Discurso pronunciado por el General Arístides Tellería, en su carácter de Presidente de la Cámara del Senado y del Congreso de los Estados Unidos de Venezuela en sus sesiones ordinarias de 1935. Caracas: Tip. Americana, 1936.

Consejo de Gobierno

Exposición documentada del Consejo de Gobierno de los Estados Unidos de Venezuela dirigida al Congreso Nacional en las Sesiones Ordinarias de 1911. Caracas: Imprenta Nacional, 1911.

Corte Federal y de Casación

Juicios seguidos por la señora Ella Robinson y por el señor Harry O Robinson contra la "Magnesite Mining and Manufacturing Company." Alegatos de la señora Robinson ante la Corte Federal y de Casación. Alegatos del señor Robinson y triunfo definitivo de éste por el voto unánime de los jueces del Distrito Federal y de los miembros de la Corte Federal y de Casación. Caracas: Empresa El Cojo, 1925.

Distrito Federal, Juzgado de Primera Instancia en lo Penal

Alegatos ante la Corte Superior del Distrito Federal en la causa seguida contra el general Eustoquio Gómez por homicidio. Caracas: Empresa El Cojo, 1909.

Estado Carabobo

La elección presidencial de 1931. Recopilación de documentos, Antecedentes y Noticias Oficiales, según Decreto de 11 de julio de 1931, del Presidente del Estado Carabobo, General Santos M Gómez. Caracas: Editorial Patria, 1931.

Estado Falcón, Secretaría
Por la paz y por el general Gómez. Coro: Imp. del Estado, 1910.

Estado Táchira, Asamblea Legislativa
Contestación de la Asamblea Legislativa del Estado Táchira al Mensaje Presentado en sus actuales sesiones por el Ciudadano General Eustoquio Gómez, Presidente Constitucional. San Cristóbal: Tip. Unión, Paz y Trabajo, 1922.

Estado Zulia
El voto del Zulia por la candidatura del General Juan Vicente Gómez para la presidencia Constitucional de la República de 1910 a 1914. Maracaibo: Tip "Los Ecos del Zulia," 1910.

Jurado de Responsabilidad Civil y Administrativa
Sentencias, 5 vols. Caracas: Imprenta Nacional, 1946.

Márquez Bustillos
La Elección Presidencial del General J. V. Gómez. Caracas: Imprenta Nacional, 1915.

Ministerio de Fomento, Dirección General de Estadística
Itinerarios de Venezuela. Caracas: Imprenta Bolívar, 1914.
Anuario comercial y estadístico de Venezuela. Caracas: Tip. Casa de Especialidades, 1924.
Resúmenes estadísticos de los Estados y del Distrito Federal. Caracas: Editorial Sur-América, 1924.
Quinto censo nacional de los Estados Unidos de Venezuela. 2 vols. Caracas: Tip. Nacional, 1962.
Censo comercial, Distrito Federal, 1936. Caracas: Tip. Garrido, 1937.
Números índices de precios al por mayor (1913–1937). Caracas: Lit. y Tip. Casa de Especialidades, 1937.
Resumén general de población del sexto censo nacional. Caracas: Tip. Garrido, 1938.
Estadística del petróleo para los años 1936, 1937, 1938. Caracas: 1940.

Ministerio de Fomento, Dirección de Estadística, Estado Zulia
Censo industrial, comercial y empresas que prestan servicios–1936. Caracas: Tip. Garrido, 1939.

Ministerio de Hacienda
Bosquejo histórico de la vida fiscal de Venezuela. Caracas: Tip. Vargas, 1924.
Crédito de la Nación: Ofrenda del Ministerio de Hacienda al Benemérito General Juan Vicente Gómez, Presidente Constitucional de los Estados Unidos de Venezuela. Caracas: Lit. y Tip. del Comercio, 1933.
Historical sketch of the fiscal life of Venezuela. Caracas Vargas Lit and Print Off. 1925.

Ministerio de Obras Públicas
Controversias entre el Ministerio de Obras Públicas y la Corporación del Puerto de la Guaira, con motivo del aumento de las tarifas de esta Compañía. Caracas: Lit. del Comercio, 1920.
Los Ferrocarriles de Venezuela. Caracas: Lit. del Comercio, 1920.

Ministerio de Relaciones Exteriores
Análisis del comercio exterior, 1913–1936. Caracas: Tip. Americana, 1938.

Ministerio de Salubridad y de Agricultura y Cría
La Sanidad en Venezuela, 1909–1930. Caracas: Editorial Elite, 1930.

Oficina Central de Sanidad Nacional
Informe que el Director de la Oficina de Sanidad Nacional presenta al ciudadano Ministro de Relaciones Interiores sobre las labores de la Oficina durante el año de 1917. Caracas: Tip. Cultura Venezolana, 1918.

Presidencia
150 años de vida republicana (1811–1961). Caracas: Ediciones de la Presidencia de la República, 1966.
Alocuciones Presidenciales de Año Nuevo (1901–1971). Caracas: Ediciones de la Presidencia de la República, 1971.

SECONDARY SOURCES

Books

Acosta, Héctor, et al. *Los Hombres del Benemérito: Epistolario Inédito.* Caracas: UCV, 1985.
Acosta Matute, Pedro Antonio. *Comercio internacional de Venezuela, 1830–1831, 1899–1900, 1913–1952.* Caracas: Mimeo, 1956.
Acosta Saignes, Miguel. *Latifundio.* México: Editorial Popular, 1936.
Adler, Selig. *The Uncertain Giant, 1921–1942: American Foreign Policy Between the Wars.* New York: Macmillan and Co., 1965.
Adriani, Alberto. *Labor venezolanista.* Caracas: Tip. La Nación, 1937.
Agudo Freytes, Raúl. *El albacea del Benemérito.* Caracas: Alfadil/Orinoco, 1990.
———. *Pío Tamayo, La Vanguardia y la Prensa de Caracas.* Caracas: UCV, 1968.
———. *La vida de un adelantado: Intento biográfico sobre José Pío Tamayo.* Caracas: Editorial Universitaria, 1948.
Alamo Ibarra, Roberto. *Datos comparativos, de producción agrícola, población y alimentación en los años 1936, 1950 y 1960.* Cagua: Ministerio de Agricultura y Cría, 1962.

————. *Orientaciones generales para el mejoramiento y progreso de la Agricultura Nacional*. Caracas: Editorial Elite (Cuadernos Verde No. 61), 1947.

————. *Resúmenes estadísticos del Comercio Exterior de los Estados Unidos de Venezuela correspondiente al lapso de 1908–1928 y el primer semestre de 1929*. Caracas: Lit. y Tip. Casa de Especialidades, 1930.

Alcántara, Francisco Segundo. *La Aclamación (1906), La Conjura (1907), La Reacción (1908)*. Caracas: Ediciones "Librería Europa," 1958.

Alexander, Robert J. *Rómulo Betancourt and the Transformation of Venezuela*. New Brunswick and London: Transaction Books, 1982.

Alta Comisión Internacional, Sección Venezolana. *Informe de la Sección Venezolana, 1916*. Caracas: Imprenta Bolívar, 1916.

————. *Informe de la Sección Venezolana, 1919*. Caracas: Empresa El Cojo, 1919.

Altuve Carrillo, Leonardo. *El Benemérito General Juan Vicente Gómez y el caso del destierro de Monseñor Salvador Montes de Oca, Obispo de Valencia*. Caracas: Ediciones Derrelieve, 1994.

Alvárez, Pedro J. *La higiene social en Venezuela (Contribución a un estudio)*. Caracas: Tip. Agencia Musical, 1943.

Amado, Anselmo. *Asi era la vida en San Cristóbal*. Caracas: BATT, 1960.

Amado Jiménez, Tulio. *Al margen de la Rehabilitación Nacional: La Ilustre personalidad del General J V Gómez*. Barinas: Tip. Barinas, 1932.

Angell, James W. *Financial Foreign Policy of the United States: A Report on the Second International Conference in the State and Economic Life, London May 29–June 2, 1933*. New York: The Council on Foreign Relations, 1933.

Anzola, Juvenal. *De Caracas a San Cristóbal*. Caracas: Tip. Empresa El Cojo, 1913.

————. *Discurso de clausura del Congreso de Diputados Plenipotenciarios de los Estados Unidos de Venezuela*. Caracas: Empresa El Cojo, 1914.

————. *Escenas Tropicales*. Caracas: Empresa El Cojo, 1917.

————. *Por la Patria y el Hogar*. Caracas: Empresa El Cojo, 1911.

Apolimar Uzcátegui, Juan. *Hojarasca*. 2nd ed. Maracaibo: Imp. El Propio Esfuerzo, 1932.

Araujo, Jesús. *Juan Vicente Gómez*. Caracas: n.p., 1990.

Arcaya, Pedro Manuel. *Address of the Minister of Venezuela, Dr. Pedro M. Arcaya, on the Conditions of His Country*. Washington, D.C.: n.p., 1930.

————. *Defensa del Doctor Pedro Manuel Arcaya en los juicios civiles que contra el y otros intentó el Doctor Juan José Abreu, Procurador General de la Nación*. Caracas: Lit. y Tip. del Comercio, 1939.

————. *Estudios de Sociología Venezolana*. Madrid: Editorial América, 1917.

————. *Estudios sobre personajes y hechos de la historia venezolana*. Caracas: Tip. Cosmos, 1911.

————. *Memorial sobre la inicua sentencia confiscatoria de sus bienes no hereditarios*. Caracas: n.p., 1947.

————. *Memorias del Doctor Pedro Manuel Arcaya*. Madrid: Talleres del Instituto Geográfico y Catastral, 1963.

————. *Nuevas orientaciones de Historia Política*. Washington, D.C.: n.p., 1924.

———. *Participación de las tierras de el Cardón en 1923. Sentencia que la ordenó y decreto que la aprobó.* Caracas: n.p., 1923.

———. *La protección internacional de los derechos humanos. (Los llamados juicios por peculado seguidos en Venezuela).* Bogotá: El Gráfico, 1948.

———. *Teratología Jurídica. Los Procesos Venezolanos por peculado y enriquecimiento indebido.* Caracas: Impresores Unidos, 1947.

———. *The Venezuelan Courts and the Welch Case; Los Tribunales Venezolanos y el caso Welch.* Washington, D.C.: n.p., 1930.

———. *Venezuela y su actual régimen.* Washington, D.C.: Press of the Sun Printing Office, 1934.

Arcila Faría, Eduardo. *MOP: Centenario del Ministerio de Obras Públicas: Influencia de éste Ministerio en el desarrollo, 1874–1974.* Caracas: Talleres Italgráfica, 1974.

Arellano, Angel María. *Mis Memorias: Vidas y Paisajes del Campo Tachirense.* Caracas: BATT, 1973.

Arellano Moreno, A. *Guía de Historia de Venezuela, 1492–1945.* Caracas: Ediciones Edime, 1955.

———. *Mirador de Historia Política de Venezuela.* Caracas: Imp. Nacional, 1967.

Arévalo Cedeño, Emilio. *Carta Abierta.* (Handbill.) Vichy, France. Jul 28, 1927.

———. *El libro de mis luchas.* Caracas: Tip. Americana, 1936.

Arévalo González, Rafael. *Apuntaciones históricas.* Caracas: n.p., 1936.

Arias O., Tobias. *Relieves máximos.* Caracas: n.p., 1930.

Aristeguieta Rojas, Pedro Elías. *La Nueva Venezuela Revolucionaria: Memorias de Pedro Elías Aristeguieta Rojas.* Mexico: n.p., 1929.

Arnold, Ralph, George A. MacGready, and Thomas W. Barrington. *The First Big Oil Hunt: Venezuela, 1911–1936.* New York: Vantage Press, 1960.

Arraiz, A. *Geografía económica de Venezuela.* Caracas: Cultural Venezolana, 1956.

———. *Puros hombres.* Caracas: Cooperativa de Artes Gráficas, 1960.

Arroyo Parejo, Francisco. *Juicio seguido por la Venezuelan Oil Concessions Limited contra Antonio Aranguren.* Caracas: n.p., 1917.

Avendaño, Astrid. *Arturo Uslar Pietri. Entre la razón y la acción.* Caracas: Oscar Todtmann Editores, 1996.

Baptista, Octavio. *Venezuela: Su historia y sus métodos de Gobierno.* Guadalajara, Mexico: Talleres Linotipográficos Gráfica, 1942.

Bates, Lindon. *The Path of the Conquistadores: Trinidad and Venezuela Guiana.* London: Methuen and Co. Ltd., 1912.

Beebe, Mary Blair, and Charles William Beebe. *Our Search for Wilderness.* London: Constable and Co. Ltd., 1910.

Bello Rodríguez, General Zoilo. *Archivo Político.* Caracas: Ediciones de la Secretaría de la Presidencia y del Ministerio de Defensa, 1979.

Benet, F. *Guía comercial de Venezuela.* 2 vols. Caracas: n.p., 1929.

Benítez, Cristóbal. *Los partidos políticos en Venezuela.* Caracas: Editorial "Patria," 1930.

———. *Sociología Política.* Caracas: Cooperativa de Artes Gráficas, 1938.

Besson, Juan. *Historia del Estado Zulia.* 5 vols. Maracaibo: Editorial Hermanos Belloso Rossell, 1951.

Betancourt, Rómulo. *Archivo de Rómulo Betancourt.* Vol. 1: 1917–1928. Caracas: Editorial Rómulo Betancourt, 1988.

———. *Archivo de Rómulo Betancourt.* Vol. 2: 1928–1930. Caracas: Editorial Rómulo Betancourt, 1990.

———. *En el ámbito del petróleo; en la entraña de Venezuela.* Caracas: Imprenta Nacional, 1960.

———. *Problemas venezolanos.* Santiago de Chile: Talleres Gráficos "San Vicente," 1940.

———. *Una República en Venta.* Caracas: Editorial Futuro, 1937.

———. *Rómulo Betancourt—Red Menace in America: Study of Communist Infiltration in Venezuela.* Caracas: Ed. Tamanaco, 1958.

———. *Semblanza de un político popular, 1928–1948.* Caracas: Ediciones Caribe, 1948.

———. *Venezuela: Política y Petróleo.* 2nd ed. Caracas: Editorial Senderos, 1967.

Betancourt Sosa, F. *Pueblo en rebeldía: Relato histórico de la sublevación militar del 7 de abril de 1928.* Caracas: Ediciones Garrido, 1959.

Bingham, Hiram. *The Journal of an Expedition across Venezuela and Colombia, 1906–1907.* New Haven: Yale Publishing Association, 1909.

Blanck S., Juan. *Los Desterrados.* Valencia: Imp. El Radical, 1909.

Blanco Fombona, R. *La Bella y la Fiera.* Madrid: Compañía Ibero-Americana de Publicaciones C.A. Renacimiento, 1931.

———. *Camino de Imperfección: Diario de mi vida, 1906–1914.* Madrid: Editorial Madrid, 1933.

———. *Diarios de mi vida.* Caracas: Monte Avila Editores, 1975.

———. *Judas Capitolino.* Paris: Chartres, 1912.

Blanco Peñalver, P. L. *El libro de la Paz. La Prensa de Venezuela y del Exterior juzga la obra y la personalidad del General Juan Vicente Gómez, Presidente de los Estados Unidos de Venezuela con motivo del "Día de la Paz."* Caracas: Tip. Garrido, 1929.

———. *López Contreras ante la historia.* Caracas: Tip. Garrido, 1957.

Borges, Carlos. *En la gesta de Gómez. Los trabajos de Hércules.* Caracas: Tip. del Comercio, 1925.

Boscán, Acisclo. *A Mis Compatriotas. La Independencia del Zulia.* Baltimore: n.p., 1928.

Botello, Oldman. *Mis 27 años junto al General Gómez (Las Memorias de Don Florencio Gómez).* Caracas: Voces del Presente / Planeta, 1993.

Boulton, Alfredo. *La Rotunda.* Caracas: n.p., 1936.

Bracale, Adolfo. *Mis Memorias.* Caracas: Editorial "Elite," 1931.

Bracamonte, Rafael. *El General Gómez y el XIX de Diciembre.* Caracas: Lit. y Tip. del Comercio, 1916.

Brachito, Montiel G. *Guachimanes.* Santiago de Chile: Ediciones "Seremos," 1954.

Brandt, Carlos. *La época del terror en el país de Gómez.* Caracas: Editorial Pentalfa, 1947.

Briceño Ayesterán, Carlos. *Memorias de su vida militar y política.* Caracas: Tip. América, 1948.

Briceño Romero, Gabriel. *Patobiografía del General Juan Vicente Gómez.* Caracas, n.p., 1983.

Brito Figueroa, Federico. *Venezuela Siglo XX.* La Habana: Casa de las Américas, 1967.

Bruzual López, Rafael. *¿La Revolución se acanalla?* Handbill. New York, Sep 1929.

Buchenau, Jürgen. *In the Shadow of the Giant: The Making of Mexico's Central American Policy, 1876–1930.* Tuscaloosa: University of Alabama Press, 1996.

Burgraaf, Winfield J. *The Venezuelan Armed Forces in Politics, 1935–1959.* Columbia: University of Missouri Press, 1972.

Caballero, Manuel. *Gómez el tirano liberal.* Caracas: Monte Avila Editores, 1993.

———. *La Internacional Comunista y América Latina: La Sección Venezolana.* Mexico: Cuadernos de Pasado y Presente, 1978.

Calatrava hijo, Alfonso. *El capital agrícola de Venezuela.* Caracas: Ministerio de Agricultura y Cría, 1963.

Calcaño Herrera, Julio. *Bosquejo Histórico de la Revolución Libertadora, 1902–1903.* Caracas: Lit. del Comercio, 1944.

Calles, Plutarco Elías. *Correspondencia Personal (1919–1945).* Mexico, Fondo de Cultura Económica, 1993.

Calvani, Luis F. *Nuestro máximo problema.* Caracas: Editorial Grafolit, 1947.

———. *Reminiscencias.* Caracas: Editorial Grafolit, 1947.

Camejo, Simón. *Voto razonado a la contestación al Mensaje del Presidente Constitucional de la República.* Caracas: Tip. Casa de Especialidades, 1924.

Campo, Juan. *Comercio exterior de Venezuela. Análisis estadístico y arancelario de importación y exportación. Diversos aspectos de la economía nacional.* Caracas: Editorial Elite, 1939.

Capo, José María. *La lección de Venezuela (Notas periodísticas de un viaje).* La Habana: Imprenta "La Prueba," 1930.

Cappelletti, Angel J. *Positivismo y evolucionismo en Venezuela.* Caracas: Monte Avila Editores, 1994.

Capriles Méndez, Ruth. *Los Negocios de Román Delgado Chalbaud.* Caracas, Biblioteca de la Academia Nacional de la Historia, No. 49, 1991.

Capriles, Miguel Angel. *Memorias de la inconformidad.* 3rd ed. La Victoria: Talleres de Grabados Nacionales C.A., 1973.

Capriles, Raúl. *Jira Patriótica: La Obra Progresista del General Gómez.* Caracas: Lit. del Comercio, 1916.

Carnevali, A. *Discurso inaugural de las sesiones de la Cámara del Senado.* Caracas: Imp. "Alma Venezolana," 1911.

Carreño Delgado, Francisco. *El Benemérito. Un bellaco admirable.* Caracas: Editorial Panapo, 1987.

Carreño, Eduardo. *Trayectoria de una vida ilustre.* Caracas: Ed. Elite, 1944.

Carrera Damas, Germán. *Consideraciones sobre los límites históricos del liberalismo en Venezuela.* Caracas: Imprenta Universitaria, 1959.

———. *Temas de Historia Social y de las Ideas*. Caracas: Ediciones de la Biblioteca, 1969.

———. *Tres temas de historia*. Caracas: UCV, 1961.

———, et al. *Sesenta años de cambio político en Venezuela*. Caracas: Cendes Mimeo, 1968.

Carrillo Batalla, Tomás Enrique. *Cuentas Nacionales de Venezuela, 1915–1935*. Caracas 33: Banco Central de Venezuela, 2003.

———. *Moneda, Crédito y Banca en Venezuela*. Caracas: Banco Central de Venezuela, 1964.

Casanova, Ramón Vicente. *Candelas en la Niebla*. Mérida: Talleres Gráficos Universitarios, 1972.

Castellanos, Rafael Ramón. *Rufino Blanco y sus Coterráneos*. Bogotá: n.p., 1970.

———. *La sublevación militar del 7 de abril de 1928*. Caracas: Italgráfica, 1974.

Castillo, Domingo B. *La cuestión monetaria en Venezuela*. Amberes: Tip van Rompaey and Co., 1912.

———. *Memorias de Mano Lobo: Sucesos y relatos de la época final de la influencia Guzmancista*. Caracas: Ed Garrido, 1956.

Castro, Cipriano. *La Verdad Histórica*. 2nd ed. Caracas, Tip Garrido, 1942.

Chacín Sánchez, Santos. *Horacio Ducharne. Un Romántico Iluso de la Libertad*. Caracas, Ediciones Oriente, 1965.

Ciliberto, José Angel. *Horacio Ducharne. Realida y Leyenda*. Caracas: Italgráfica S A , 1996.

Cordero Velásquez, Luis. *El General J V Gómez en Anécdotas*. Caracas: Urbina and Fuentes Editores Asociados, 1983.

Córdoba, Diego. *Los desterrados y Juan Vicente Gómez—Memorias de Pedro Elías Aristeguieta*. Caracas: n.p., 1968.

———. *Soñadores en el destierro (Episodios Venezolanos)*. Mexico: Editores e Impresos Beatriz de Silva, 1951.

———. *Venezuela Agonizante*. 3rd ed. Caracas: Cooperativa de Artes Gráficas, 1936.

Cova, J. A. *Entre barrotes*. Caracas: Ediciones Latorre, 1938.

Crespo Vivas, Raúl. *Conversaciones Parlamentarias*. Caracas: n.p., 1971.

Croce, Arturo. *Petróleo mi general*. Caracas: Monte Avila Editores, 1977.

Croes, Hemy. *El movimiento obrero venezolano, elementos para su historia*. Caracas: Ediciones Movimiento Obrero, 1973.

Dalton, Leonard V. *Venezuela*. 4th ed. London: T. Fisher Unwin Ltd., 1925.

D'Ascoli, Carlos. *Contribución al estudio del actual problema monetario venezolano*. Caracas: Publicaciones de la Sociedad de Estudios Económicos y Sociales, 1943.

Dávila, Antonio. *La dictadura venezolana*. Maracaibo: Tip. Criollo, 1954.

De Acevedo, Javier P. *Dos años en Venezuela bajo la dictadura de Gómez: Impresiones y Recuerdos*. La Habana: Molina Y Cia., 1940.

De la Plaza, Salvador. *El Petróleo en la vida venezolana*. Caracas: Pensamiento Vivo, 1962.

———. *El problema de la tierra.* 2 vols. Caracas: Fundación Salvador de la Plaza, 1974.

De Nogales Méndez, Rafael. *Memoirs of a Soldier of Fortune.* London: Wright and Brown, 1931.

———. *Verdades.* Caracas: n.p., 1909.

De Olivares, Celmira. *Juan Vicente Gómez en Maracay: De 1917 a 1935.* Caracas: Talleres Italgráfica, 1976.

De Sucre, María de Lourdes Acedo, and Carmen Margarita Nones Mendoza. *La Generación Venezolana del 1928: Estudio de una élite política.* Caracas: Editorial Ariel, 1976.

De Vivanco y Villegas, Aurelio. *Venezuela al día.* Caracas: Imprenta Bolívar, 1926.

Delgado Chalbaud, R. *Por mi jefe, por mi causa y por mi nombre.* Caracas: Empresa El Cojo, 1912.

Desconde, Alexander. *Herbert Hoover's Latin American Policy.* Stanford: Stanford University Press, 1951.

Días Mantilla, S. *Venezuela actual.* Caracas: Lit. y Tip. Taller Gráfico, 1926.

Díaz, Pedro Antonio. *Por qué yo maté a Delgado Chalbaud. Memorias de Pedro Antonio Díaz tal como se las contó a Oscar Yanes.* Caracas, Publicaciones Seleven, 1980.

Díaz Sánchez, Ramón. *Borburata.* Buenos Aires: Centro Editor de América Latina, 1967.

———. *Casandra.* Caracas: Ediciones Hortus, 1937.

———. *Transición.* Caracas: Ediciones "La Torre," 1937.

Diez del Cuervo, C. *Segunda conferencia por radio sobre agricultura y cría.* Caracas: Tip. Americana, 1931.

Domínici, Pedro César. *El mono trágico. (Réplica a un farsante).* Paris: L. Duc and Cie Imprimeurs, 1909.

Drago, Luis M. *La República de Argentina y el caso de Venezuela.* Caracas: OCI, 1976.

Dugdale, E.T.S. *German Diplomatic Documents, 1871–1914.* 3 vols. New York: Barnes and Noble, 1930.

El Nuevo Evangelio Liberal. Caracas: Tip. Americana, 1909.

El Pueblo del Táchira. *Homenaje de Justicia: El pueblo del Táchira en torno del Benemérito General Juan Vicente Gómez.* San Cristóbal: Imprenta del Estado, 1921.

Escobar Salom, Ramón. *Evolución política de Venezuela.* Caracas: Monte Avila Editores, 1975.

Ewell, Judith. *Venezuela: A Century of Change.* London: C. Hurst and Co., 1984.

Fergusson, Erna. *Venezuela.* New York: Alfred A. Knopf, 1939.

Fernández García, Alejandro. *Los buitres, los apaches, los falsos maestros.* Caracas: Tip. Universidad, 1929.

Fernández, Carlos Emilio. *Hombres y Sucesos de mi tierra, 1909–1935.* 2nd ed. Madrid: Talleres del Sagrado Corazón, 1969.

Fernández, Pablo Emilio. *Gómez el Rehabilitador.* Caracas: Jaime Villegas Editor, 1956.

———. *Rasgos biográficos del General Cipriano Castro.* Madrid: n.p., 1952.

Fernández Heres, Rafael. *Memoria de Cien Años: La Educación Venezolana, 1830–1980.* Caracas, Ediciones del Ministerio de Educación, 1981.

Ferrufino, Gerardo. *Venezuela y su desarrollo cultural.* Tegucigalpa: n.p., 1934.

Figueredo, Carlos Benito. *Presidenciales.* Madrid: Establecimiento Tip de El Liberal, 1908.

Finandes. *Juancho Gómez: Un drama de la realidad americana.* Caracas: Colección Libros Revista Bohemia, n.d.

Flores, Carlos M. *Gómez: Patriarca del Crimen. El Terror y el Trabajo en Venezuela.* Caracas: Editorial Ateneo de Caracas, 1980.

Flores Cabrera, M. *Siniestro Recuento. Prisiones y destierros bajo la dictadura del General Juan Vicente Gómez, Comandante en Jefe (nominal) del Ejercito Venezolano y Presidente (efectivo) de la República de Venezuela. Protesta que se hace por si sola. Perfidia, dolor, nepotismo, mercantilismo etc.* Santo Domingo: Imp. La Cuna de América—Vda de Roques y Cia., 1914.

Fossi-Barroeta, Luis. *Política en tono menor.* Caracas: BATT No.31, 1962.

Franco Quijano, Juan Francisco. *Letras al Dr R González Rincones.* Mérida: Tip. Los Andes, 1921.

Fuenmayor, Juan Bautista. *Historia de la Venezuela Política Contemporánea, 1899–1969.* 3 vols. Caracas: Talleres Tip. Miguel Angel García e hijos, 1975.

———. *1928–1948: Veinte Años de Política.* Madrid: Editorial Mediterráneo, 1968.

Fundación Eugenio Mendoza. *El campo venezolano.* Caracas: Fundación Eugenio Mendoza, 1972.

———. *Venezuela Moderna: Medio Siglo de Historia, 1926–1976.* Caracas: Fundación Eugenio Mendoza, 1976.

Fundación John Boulton. *Política y Economía en Venezuela, 1810–1976.* Caracas: Fundación John Boulton, 1976.

Fundación Polar. *Diccionario de Historia de Venezuela.* 3 vols. Caracas: Fundación Polar, 1988.

FUNRES. *Documentos Británicos Relacionados con el Bloqueo de las Costas Venezolanas.* Caracas, Funres, 1982.

Gabaldón Márquez, Joaquín. *Memoria y Cuenta de la Generación del 28: Con un apéndice documental y un epílogo.* Caracas: n.p., 1958.

Gallegos, Gerardo. *En el puño de Juan Vicente Gómez.* 2nd ed. Mexico: Editorial Diana, 1956.

Gallegos Ortiz, Rafael. *El cacharro Juan Vicente Gómez.* 2nd ed. Caracas: Editorial Fuentes, 1977.

———. *La historia política de Venezuela, de Cipriano Castro a Pérez Jiménez.* Caracas: Imp. Universitaria, 1960.

García Andrade, Numa. *Ensayo sobre costos de producción del café en Venezuela.* Caracas: Ministerio de Agricultura y Cría, 1949.

García Celis, Guillermo, and Félix Requena. *Editoriales políticos del "El Tesón."* Puerto Cabello: Imprenta Sanz, 1916.

García Dávila, Luis Manuel. *Memorias del General José María García, 1899–1954.* Caracas, n.p., 1992.

García Gil, Pedro. *Cuarenta y cinco años de uniforme: Memorias 1901–1945.* Caracas: Editorial Bolívar, 1947.

García Maldonado, J. *El sol de Venezuela desde 1909.* Caracas: Tip. Americana, 1933.

García Manfredi, Antonio. *Del solar venezolano. Impresiones.* Caracas: Tip. Americana, 1932.

———. *Venezuela: Síntesis de sus recursos económicos.* Caracas: Lit. y Tip. Vargas, 1929.

García Naranjo, Nemesio. *Venezuela and Its Ruler.* New York: Carranza and Co., 1927.

García Ponce, Guillermo. *Memorias de un General de la Utopía.* Caracas, Cotragraf, 1992.

García Villasmil, Martín. *Escuelas para formación de oficiales del ejército: Orden y evolución de la escuela militar.* Caracas: Oficina Técnica Mindefensa, 1964.

———. *40 años de evolución en las Fuerzas Armadas.* Caracas: n.p., 1965.

Garmendia, Hermán. *Eustoquio Gómez, un General de la Rehabilitación.* Mexico: Editorial Diana S.A., 1955.

Gerretson, F. C. *History of the Royal Dutch.* 4 vols. Leiden: E. J. Brill, 1957.

Gerstl, Otto. *Memorias e Historias.* Caracas: Fundación John Boulton, 1967.

Giacopini Zárraga, José A. *Hace 40 años . . . 1914–1954.* Caracas: Compañía Shell de Venezuela, 1954.

Gil Fortoul, José. *Historia Constitucional de Venezuela.* 5th ed. Caracas: Ediciones Sales, 1964.

———. *El Hombre y la Historia.* Paris: Librería de Garnier Hermanos, 1896.

———. *De hoy para mañana.* Caracas: Imprenta Nacional, 1916.

Gilmore, Robert. *Caudillism and Militarism in Venezuela, 1810–1910.* Athens: Ohio State University Press, 1964.

Giménez Santo, F. *A la luz de la razón. (De porque ha de considerarse el 19 de diciembre como una fecha verdaderamente clásica en los anales de la Patria y no meramente como una efemérides del partido político.)* Guanare: Tip. Oficial, 1913.

Gómez, Alejandro, comp. *Rómulo Betancourt 1928–1935. Contra la dictadura de Juan Vicente Gómez. Repertorio Americano, Costa Rica.* Caracas: Ediciones Centauro, 1982.

González, César. *Rubén González. Una vida al servicio de Venezuela.* Caracas: BATT No. 57, 1972.

———. *Vieja Gente del Táchira: Crónica Genealógica.* Caracas, n.p., 1975.

González, Fernando. *Mi compadre.* Barcelona: Ed. Juventud S.A., 1934.

González Baquero, R. *Análisis del proceso histórico de la Educación Urbana (1870–1932) y de la Educación Rural (1932–1957) en Venezuela.* Caracas: UCV, 1962.

González Berti, Luis. *Alberto Adriani. Ligeras anotaciones sobre sus ideas acerca de la agricultura y del petróleo.* Mérida: Universidad de los Andes No. 39, 1955.

González Bracho, Matías. *Verdad histórica de la Revolución acaudillada por el General José Rafael Gabaldón en Santo Cristo, año 1929.* Caracas: n.p., 1958.

González Escorihuela, Ramón. *Las Ideas Políticas en el Táchira de los años 70 del siglo XIX a la segunda década del siglo XX.* Caracas: BATT, 1994.

Gooch, G.P., and H. Temperley. *British Documents on the Origins of the War.* 2 vols. London: HMSO, 1928.

Grenville, John A. S., and George Berkely Young. *Politics, Strategy, and American Diplomacy – Studies in Foreign Policy, 1873–1917.* New Haven: Yale University Press, 1966.

Guerrero, F. *Para impedir tiranías.* Caracas: Editorial Venezuela, 1938.

Guzmán, Pedro. *Apuntaciones históricas del Estado Zulia.* Maracaibo: Ed. Universidad de L.U.Z., 1967.

Harwich, Nikita. *Arma y Coraza: Biografía Intelectual de Laureano Vallenilla Lanz.* Caracas, Universidad Santa María, 1984.

———. *Formación y crisis de un sistema financiero nacional: Banco y Estado en Venezuela (1830–1940).* Caracas: Fondo Editorial Buria, 1986.

Henríquez Vera, Rigoberto. *Tejera, El Desterrado: Un Quijote con dos Patrias: Venezuela y México.* Mérida: Talleres Gráficos Universitarios, 1972.

Heredía A., Cipriano. *El Año 29. Recuento de la Lucha Armada.* Caracas, Ediciones Centauro, 1974.

Hernández, Nicolás. *Partido Liberal Nacionalista Venezolano. Desnudeces de "El Republicano.* Habana, Dec 1922.

Herrera Luque, Francisco. *En la casa del pez que escupe agua.* 16th ed. Caracas: Pomaire, 1990.

Herwig, Holger H. *Germany's vision of Empire in Venezuela, 1871–1914.* Princeton, N.J.: Princeton University Press, 1986.

Hill, Howard C. *Roosevelt and the Caribbean.* Chicago: University of Chicago Press, 1927. .

Ibarra, Vicente. *De la Rotunda a la Calle Larga. La Odisea del "Falke."* 3rd ed. Caracas: Editorial Fuentes, 1977.

Iselin and Co. *A review of the financial and economic situation of Venezuela.* New York: n.p., 1930.

Jahn, Alfredo. *El desarrollo de las vías de comunicación en V⁻ 1ezuela.* Caracas: Lit. y Tip. Mercantil, 1926.

———. *El Estado Zulia. Esbozo Histórico-Geográfico.* Caracas: Lit. y Tip. Vargas, 1927.

Jiménez Arraiz, J. T. *Del vivac.* Cumaná: Imprenta Mila de la Roca, 1904.

———. *Recuerdos.* New York: Editorial Tierra Firme, 1961.

Junta Patriótica. San Antonio del Táchira: n.p., 1920.

Kamman, William A. *In Search of Stability: US Policy Towards Nicaragua, 1925–1933.* South Bend, Ind.: University of Notre Dame Press, 1967.

Labor Patriótica. *El Partido Progresista de Venezuela.* Barranquilla: Imp. El Siglo, 1912.

Laclé, Antonio. *Las guerras internas de Venezuela i como han perjudicado su población.* Caracas: Lit. y Tip. Taller Gráfico, 1932.

Landaeta Rosales, Manuel. *Conjuración contra la vida del General Juan Vicente Gómez*. Caracas: Imprenta Nacional, 1911.

———. *Maracay, 1697–1916*. Caracas: Empresa El Cojo, 1916.

———. *Rasgos biográficos del General Juan Vicente Gómez*. Caracas: Tip. Americana, 1909.

Lavin, John A. *A Halo for Gómez*. New York: Pageant Press, 1954.

León, Carlos. *Autonomías de los Nuevos Estados*. Caracas: Imprenta Federación, 1898.

———. *Autonomías: Narración histórica al Partido Liberal*. Caracas: n.p., 1900.

León, Ramón David. *De agro-pecuario a petróleo*. Caracas: n.p., 1944.

———. *El brujo de La Mulera*. Caracas: Editorial Fondo Común, 1976.

———. *Hombres y Sucesos de Venezuela (La República desde José Antonio Páez hasta Rómulo Gallegos)*. Caracas: Tip. Americana, 1952.

León Tapia, José. *Maisanta: El último hombre a caballo*. Caracas: Centro Editor, 1974.

Levine, Daniel H. *Conflict and Change in Venezuela*. Princeton, N.J.: Princeton University Press, 1973.

Lieuwen, Edwin. *Petroleum in Venezuela*. Berkeley: University of California Press, 1954.

———. *Venezuela*. London: Oxford University Press, 1965.

Linares, José Antonio. *El General Juan Vicente Gómez y las obras públicas en Venezuela, 19 de diciembre de 1908 – 4 de agosto de 1913*. Caracas: Lit. y Tip. del Comercio, 1916.

Lisandro Alvarado, Aníbal. *El Archivo de la Rotunda*. Caracas: Ediciones Garrido, 1954.

López, José Eliseo. *La expansión demográfica de Venezuela*. Mérida (Cuadernos Geográficos No. 2): Universidad de los Andes, 1963.

López, José Heriberto. *Cuentos de acero: Anecdotario satírico: Epoca del Gomezalato*. 2nd ed. Caracas: Cooperativas de Artes Gráficas, 1936.

———. *Discurso del Dr José Heriberto López al Pie del Monumento del Libertador en el Parque Central de Nueva York el 19 de abril de 1924*. Handbill. New York, Apr 19, 1924.

———. *Veinte años sin patria: Historia panfletaria de los Tirañuelos más feroces de la América Hispana: Juan Vicente Gómez y Gerardo Machado*. La Habana: Imp. P. Fernández y Cia., 1933.

López Contreras, Eleazar. *Cualidades militares del General Juan Vicente Gómez*. Caracas: Empresa El Cojo, 1917.

———. *Páginas para la historia militar de Venezuela*. Caracas: Editorial Las Novedades, 1945.

———. *El Presidente Cipriano Castro*. Caracas: n.p., 1983.

———. *Proceso político social, 1928–1936*. Caracas: Editorial Ancora, 1955.

López de Sagrado y Bru, José. *Gobernantes de Maracaibo, 1499–1952*. Maracaibo: Cámara de Comercio de Maracaibo, 1952.

López Rodríguez, B. *Memorias de mi vida de chofer*. Caracas: Tip. Universal, 1930.

Losada y Corrales, F. *En defensa del Jeneral* [sic] *León Jurado.* Sanare: Talleres "Sagitario," 1943.

Luciani, Jorge. *La dictadura perpetua de Gómez y sus adversarios.* Caracas: Cooperativa de Artes Gráficas, 1936.

Luzardo, Rodolfo. *Notas Históricas económicas, 1928–1963.* Caracas: Editorial Sucre, 1963.

Machado, Gustavo. *Manifiesto del Partido Revolucionario Venezolano.* Handbill. Mexico, Apr 1929.

———. *La prensa política venezolana del siglo XX.* 2 vols. Caracas: Colección Periodismo Político Siglo XX, 1967.

Maldonado, Gerónimo. *Cuestión Social.* Maracaibo: Imp. Americana, 1909.

———. *Patria.* Maracaibo: Imp. Americana, 1909.

Maldonado, Víctor V. *Estado Bolívar.* Caracas: Lit. del Comercio, 1918.

———. *Paz y trabajo.* Caracas: Empresa El Cojo, 1917.

Manzano, Lucas. *Caracas de mil y pico.* Caracas: Editora Cultura, 1946.

Mariátegui, Pocaterra, Otero Silva, Araujo, García Márquez et al. *Gustavo Machado: De Oligarca a Comunista, 1914–1971.* 2 vols. Caracas: Ediciones Centauro, 1975.

Mariñas Otero, Luis. *Las constituciones de Venezuela.* Madrid: Ediciones Cultura Hispánica, 1965.

Márquez Bustillos, V. *Dos campañas.* Caracas: Lit. y Tip. del Comercio, 1916.

———. *La reforma militar venezolana.* Caracas: Lit. y Tip. del Comercio, 1917.

———. *Semblanza del General Juan Vicente Gómez.* Caracas: Lit. y Tip. del Comercio, 1919.

Márquez Cairos, Fernando. *Vienen los Andinos.* Caracas: Ediciones Orinoco, 1956.

Martínez Sánchez, Antonio. *Nuestras contiendas civiles.* Caracas: Tip. Garrido, 1949.

Martínez, Carlos A. *Renacimiento.* San Juan de los Morros: n.p., 1909.

Matos Boscán, José V. *Necesidad de industrializar a Venezuela.* Caracas: Ed. Sur-América, 1932.

Matos, Manuel Antonio. *Recuerdos.* Caracas: Empresa El Cojo, 1927.

McBeth, Brian S. *British Oil Policy, 1919–1939.* London: Frank Cass and Co. Ltd., 1985.

———. *Gunboats, Corruption, and Claims: Foreign Intervention in Venezuela, 1899–1908.* Westport, CT: Greenwood Press, 2001.

———. *Juan Vicente Gómez and the Oil Companies in Venezuela, 1908–1935.* Cambridge: Cambridge University Press, 1983.

———. *Royal Dutch Shell vs Venezuela.* Oxford: Oxford Microfilm Publications, 1982.

McGill, Samuel. *Poliantea: Memorias del Coronel McGill.* Caracas: Ediciones de la Presidencia de la República, 1978.

Mendible, Luciano. *30 años de lucha: Documentos para la vida pública del Dr Luciano Mendible, 1908–1940.* Caracas: n.p., 1941.

Meyer Agráez, Angel. *Gómez de frente y de perfil: Ciento cincuenta anécdotas.* Madrid: Ediciones Edime, 1953.

Meyer, Michael C., and William H. Beezley, eds. *The Oxford History of Mexico.* Oxford: Oxford University Press, 2000.

Mieres, Teoboldo. *Rafael Simón Urbina y 137 mejicanos en Venezuela.* San Juan de los Morros: Tip. "El Lugareño," 1936.

Modesto Gallegos, Manuel. *Anales contemporáneo: Memorias del General Modesto Gallegos.* Caracas: Tip. Casa de Especialidades, 1926.

Montes, Félix. *Exposición Necesaria.* Flysheet. Curaçao, Oct 25, 1913.

Morantes, Pedro María (Pío Gil). *Amarillo, Azul y Rojo: Personalismo y verdades.* Caracas: Tip. Garrido, 1952.

———. *Cuatro años de mi carrera.* Caracas: Catalá-Centauro Editores, 1975.

———. *Diario íntimo y otros temas.* Caracas: Ediciones de la Presidencia de la República, 1975.

Moros, Eulogio. *Por Justicia.* La Asunción (Margarita): Tip. Popular-Modiano, 1909.

Muñoz, Pedro José. *La Noria de los Días.* Caracas: OCI, 1971.

Munro, Dana G. *Intervention and dollar diplomacy in the Caribbean, 1900–1921.* Princeton, N.J.: Princeton University Press, 1964.

———. *The Latin American Republics.* 3rd. ed. London: George G Harrap and Co. Ltd., 1961.

Murray, Robert Hammond, trans. and ed. *Mexico before the World: Public Documents and Addresses of Plutarco Elías Calles.* New York: Academy Press, 1927.

Navas, Juan Vicente. *Vida política y militar del Yaracuy, 1855–1945.* Caracas: Biblioteca de Autores y Temas Yaracuyanos, No. 1, 1962.

Núñez, Enrique Bernardo. *Bajo el Samán.* Caracas: Tip. Vargas, 1963.

Núñez, Hilarios, and Federico Restrepo. *Constitucionalidad ó dictadura.* Caracas: Tip. Americana, 1909.

Ochoa, Manuel. *El General Gómez y la Prensa Nacional.* Maracay: n.p., 1925.

Ojeda, José Melquíades. *Patria y Unión.* Caracas: Tip. Casa de Especialidades, 1910.

Ortega Martínez, José María. *A los Venezolanos.* New York, Jul 8, 1922.

———. *My Answer to a Defender of "General" Gomez's Despotism in Venezuela.* New York: Carranza and Co., 1924.

Otalora, Santiago. *Campañas al lado del General Gómez.* Caracas: Tip Garrido, 1951.

Otálvora, Edgar. *Eustoquio Gómez.* Caracas: Contexto Audiovisual 3/Pomaire, 1993.

Pacanins Acevedo, Feliciano. *Evolución bancaria de Venezuela.* 2nd ed. Caracas: Ediciones del Boletín de la Cámara de Comercio de Caracas, No. 6, 1971.

———. *51 años al servicio de Venezuela.* Caracas: Empresa El Cojo, 1970.

Pacheco, Emilio. *De Castro a López Contreras.* Caracas: Domingo/Fuentes, 1984.

Pacheco, Luis Eduardo. *Orígenes del Presidente Gómez.* Caracas: n.p., 1968.

Palacios, Inocente. *Urgencia de una economía dirigida.* Caracas: Lit. y Tip. Vargas, 1936.

Parada, Nemesio. *De Ocumare a Miraflores*. Caracas: BATT, No. 63, 1975.

Parodi, Gustavo. *Hombres de la Rehabilitación nacional, 1908 – 19 de diciembre 1919*. Caracas: Imp. Bolívar, 1919.

———. *La Obra del General Juan Vicente Gómez. Apuntes para la historia política y Administrativa de los EE.UU. de Venezuela*. Caracas: Tip. Americana, 1926.

Parra, Pedro María. *Venezuela oprimida. Cuadro político del Gobierno de Gómez*. Caracas: n.p., 1913.

Parra León, Miguel. *Problemas de transporte*. Caracas: Editorial Sur-América, 1930.

Parra Márquez, Héctor. *Presidentes de Venezuela*. Caracas: n.p., 1954.

Partido Liberal. *El Partido Liberal del Estado Yaracuy al General Juan Vicente Gómez, a quien proclama su candidato para presidir la República en el período constitucional de 1910 a 1914*. Caracas: Imprenta Bolívar, 1909.

Partido Liberal. *Pronunciamiento del pueblo Liberal del Estado Mérida por la candidatura del General Estebán Chalbaud Cardona para la Presidencia Constitucional del Estado en el período de 1910 a 1914*. Mérida: n.p., 1910.

Paúl, José de Jesús. *El doctor José de Jesús Paúl a sus compatriotas*. Paris: Imprenta de Lagny, 1909.

Penzini Hernández, Juan. *Vida y Obra de José Gil Fortoul (1861–1943)*. Caracas: Edición del Ministerio de Relaciones Exteriores, 1972.

Pereira H., Pedro N. *En la prisión (los estudiantes de 1928)*. Caracas: Editorial Avila Gráfica, 1952.

Pereja y Paz Roldán, J. *J.V. Gómez, un fenómeno telúrico*. 2nd ed. Caracas: Editorial Centauro, 1972.

Perera, Ambrosio. *Historia orgánica de Venezuela*. Caracas: Editorial Venezuela, 1943.

Pérez Díaz, José Antonio. *50 años de la aviación venezolana, 1920–1970*. Caracas: Ediciones del Congreso de la República, 1970.

Pérez Dupuy, H. *Algunas consideraciones sobre problemas económicos venezolanos*. Caracas: Lit. y Tip. del Comercio, 1939.

Pérez Jurado, Carlos. *Asalto a Cumaná: Historia de la Expedición del General Román Delgado Chalbaud, último intento para derrocar a Juan Vicente Gómez, Presidente de Venezuela*. Caracas: Mimeo, 1973.

———. *Gómez, Gomecismo y Ejército Nacional: Notas de Historia Venezolana*. Caracas: n.p., 1996.

Pérez Tenreiro, Tomás. *Comentario Militar a una carta de Juan Vicente Gómez sobre la defensa del Táchira*. San Cristóbal: Ministerio de Defensa, 1984.

———. *Juan Vicente Gómez (Ensayo de interpretación militar)*. Caracas: Tip. Vargas, 1960.

Pérez Vila, Manuel. *Fuentes para la historia de Venezuela en el siglo XX*. Caracas: Italgráfica, 1964.

Perkins, Bradford. *The Great Rapprochement: England and the United States, 1895–1914*. London: Victor Gollancz Ltd., 1969.

Perkins, Dexter. *The Evolution of American Foreign Policy*. New York: Oxford University Press, 1948.

————. *The Monroe Doctrine, 1867–1907.* Baltimore: Johns Hopkins University Press, 1937.

————. *The United States and the Caribbean.* Oxford: Oxford University Press, 1947.

Picón Salas, Mariano. *Venezuela independiente, 1810–1960.* Caracas: Fundación Eugenio Mendoza, 1962.

Pimentel, Cecilia. *Bajo la Tiranía, 1919–1935.* Caracas: Impreso Talleres Lit. y Tip. "La Bohemia" C.A., 1970.

Pino Iturrieta, Elías, ed. *Juan Vicente Gómez y su Epoca,* Caracas, Editorial Monte Avila, 1988.

Plaza, Elena. *José Gil Fortoul: Los Nuevos Caminos de la Razón: La Historia como Ciencia, 1861–1943.* Caracas, Ediciones del Congreso de la Republica, 1985.

————. *La tragedia de una amarga convicción: Historia y Política en el Pensamiento de Laureano Vallenilla Lanz (1870–1936).* Caracas: UCV, 1996.

Pocaterra, José Rafael. *Archivo de José Rafael Pocaterra: La Oposición a Gómez (1922–1935).* 2 vols. Caracas: Banco Industrial de Venezuela, 1973.

————. *Gómez: The Shame of America: Fragments from the Memoirs of a Citizen of the Republic of Venezuela in Her Days of Decadence.* Paris: Andre Delpeuch Editeur, 1929.

Polanco Alcántara, Tomás. *La huella de Pedro Emilio.* Caracas: Biblioteca Nacional de Historia, n.d.

————. *Juan Vicente Gómez: Aproximación a una biografía.* 2nd ed. Caracas: Academia Nacional de Historia, 1990.

Poletto, Santiago. *El hombre que mató a J.V. Gómez.* Caracas: Emp. Unidos, 1945.

Porras Bello, Eduardo. *La mazmorra caraqueña ó la Rotunda de Caracas y el régimen político de Gómez.* Caracas: Tip. Americana, 1937.

Prato, Luis F. *Mi Coronel.* Caracas: Ediciones Edime, 1953.

Pulido Méndez, Manuel A. *Régulo Olivares y su época.* Caracas: BATT No. 28, 1962.

Quintero, José Antonio. *Asi no fue.* Caracas: Cooperativa de Artes Gráficas, 1939.

Quintero, Rodolfo. *El Petróleo y nuestra Sociedad.* Caracas: UCV Ediciones de la Biblioteca, 1975.

————. *Sindicalismo y cambio social en Venezuela.* Caracas: UCV, 1965.

Rama, Angel. *Rufino Blanco Fombona Intimo.* Caracas, Monte Avila Editores, 1975.

Ramírez, Arturo. *Esbozo psiquiátrico del General Juan Vicente Gómez.* Caracas: Universidad de Carabobo, 1974.

Ramírez Medina, José. *Gómez en Sucre.* Caracas: Fondo Editorial Tropykos, 1994.

Rangel, Domingo Alberto. *Los Andinos en el poder.* Caracas: n.p., 1964.

————. *Capital y Desarrollo: El Rey Petróleo.* Vol. 2. Caracas: UCV, 1970.

————. *Gómez el amo del poder.* Valencia: Vadell Hnos., 1975.

————. *Junto al lecho del caudillo.* Caracas: Vadell Hnos. Editores, 1981.

Rescaniere, Alejandro. *Guerra de Guerrillas: Campaña del general Horacio Ducharne en Oriente.* Caracas, AvilaGráfica S A 1951.

Reyes, Vitelio. *Juan Vicente Gómez: Epítome Biográfico, 1857–1935.* Caracas, n.p., n.d.

Richmond, Douglas W. *Venustiano Carranza's Nationalist Struggle.* Lincoln: University of Nebraska Press, 1983.

Rios, Pompeyo. *Desarrollo económico de Venezuela: Desde 1830 hasta 1920.* Caracas: Imp. Universitaria, 1964.

Rivas Rivas, José. *Historia gráfica de Venezuela: de Gómez a Gallegos.* 2 vols. Caracas: Pensamiento Vivo C.A., 1963.

Rivas Vásquez, Alejandro, *Vibraciones democráticas venezolanas.* Caracas: Impresores Unidos, 1942.

Rodríguez, Irene, comp. *El Archivo de Salvador de la Plaza.* Vol. 1. Caracas, Centauro-Funres, 1992.

Rodríguez Jiménez, Carlos. *Venezuela, 1908–1933.* Tokyo: n.p., 1933.

Roldán Oliarte, Esteban. *Bolívar entre dos Américas, 1830–1930.* San José, Costa Rica: Editorial Bolívar, 1931.

———. *El General Juan Vicente Gómez. Venezuela de cerca.* Mexico: Imprenta Mundial, 1933.

———. *El libro de Venezuela.* San José, Costa Rica: Imprenta Linares, 1929.

———. *El sentido del Gobierno propio.* San José, Costa Rica: Imprenta Borrase Hnos., 1931.

———. *Venezuela adentro (Veinte años de política).* San José, Costa Rica: n.p., 1928.

———. *Venezuela ante el centenario del Bolívar.* San José, Costa Rica: n.p., 1930.

Romero, Aníbal et al. *Rómulo Betancourt. Antología Política. Vol 1 1928–1935.* Caracas: Editorial Fundación Rómulo Betancourt, 1990.

Roosevelt, Nicholas. *Venezuela's Place in the Sun: Modernizing a Pioneering Country.* New York: Round Table Press, 1940.

Salas, Federico. *El clamor de un pueblo. Estudios económicos.* 2 vols. Maracaibo: n.p., 1911.

Salazar Martínez, Francisco. *Tiempo de Compadres: De Cipriano Castro a Juan Vicente Gómez.* Caracas: Librería Piñango, 1972.

Salcedo Bastardo, J. L. *Historia Fundamental de Venezuela.* Caracas: UCV, 1970.

Salisbury, Richard V. *Anti-Imperialism and International Competition in Central America, 1920–1930.* Wilmington, Del.: Scholarly Resources, 1989.

Sánchez Pacheco, Ciro. *Los Andinos.* Caracas: Ediciones Garrido, 1968.

Schael, Guillermo José. *Apuntes para la historia. El automóvil en Venezuela.* Caracas: Gráficas Edición de Arte, 1969.

Segnini, Yolanda. *Las Luces del Gomecismo.* 2nd ed. Caracas: Alfadil, 1997.

Siso, Carlos. *Castro y Gómez. Importancia de la Hegemonía Andina.* Caracas: Editorial Arte, 1985.

———. *La formación del pueblo venezolano.* 2 vols. Madrid: Editorial García Enciso, 1953.

Siso Martínez, Carlos, Germán Carrera Damas, Rvdo. P. Martín Hurtado Lena, L. Hernández, Carmen Gómez, M. de L. Carbonell, Josefina Gávila, and Josefina Bernal. *El Concepto de la Historia de José Gil Fortoul.* Caracas UCV: Escuela de Historia, 1961.

Siso Martínez, Carlos, Germán Carrera Damas, Carlos Salazar, and Manuel Caballero. *El Concepto de la Historia en Laureano Vallenilla Lanz.* Caracas UCV: Facultad de Humanidades y Educación, Escuela de Historia, 1966.

Smith, Alberto. *Discurso pronunciado por el Dr Alberto Smith en el miting (sic) de protesta de la Asociación General de Estudiantes Latino-Americana "Agela" contra las iniquidades cometidas contra los estudiantes por J. V. Gómez.* Paris: Imp. Paul Dupont, 1928.

Smith, Robert Freeman. *The United States and Revolutionary Nationalism in Mexico, 1916–1932.* Chicago: University of Chicago Press, 1972.

Sosa A., Arturo, S.J. *La filosofía política del Gomecismo: Estudio del Pensamiento de Laureano Vallenilla Lanz.* Barquisimeto: Centro Gunilla, 1974.

Sosa, Arturo A., and Eloi Lengrand. *Del Garibaldismo Estudiantil a la Izquierda Criolla (Los origines marxistas del proyecto de A.D. (1928–1936).* Caracas: Ediciones Centauro, 1981.

Suárez Figueroa, Naudy, comp. *Programas Políticos Venezolanos de la Primera Mitad del Siglo XX.* Caracas: Editorial Arte, 1977.

Sullivan, William M., comp. *Dissertations and Theses on Venezuelan Topics, 1900–1985.* Metuchen, N.J.: Scarecrow Press, 1988.

Tejera, Humberto. *Cinco águilas blancas.* Mexico: n.p., 1932.

Tellería, Arístides. *Mi actuación en la vida pública.* La Habana: P. Hernández and Cia., 1950.

Tello Mendoza, R. *Ligeros rasgos biográficos del General Juan Vicente Gómez.* Caracas: Tip. Universal, 1904.

Texier-Unda, Gaston. *El general Gómez y su obra (Tres Lustro) (1908–1923).* Caracas: Tip. Americana, 1924.

The International Committee for Political Prisoners. *Venezuela: Land of Oil and Tyranny.* New York, 1931.

Torrealba Fossi, Mario. *Los Años de la Ira. (Una interpretación de los Sucesos del 28).* Caracas: Editorial Ateneo de Caracas, 1979.

Trujillo, Alejandro E. *La respuesta del destino (La Rotunda por dentro).* Caracas: BATT No. 1, 1962.

Urbaneja, Diego Bautista. *Pueblo y Petróleo en la Política Venezolana del Siglo XX.* Caracas: Ediciones Cepet, 1992.

Urbina, Rafael Simón. *Victoria, dolor y tragedia.* Caracas: Tip. Americana, 1936.

Urdaneta Auvert, Edmundo. *La revolución de Delgado Chalbaud 1929 y seis años largos bajo la férula Gomera.* Caracas: Cooperativa de Artes Gráficas, 1936.

Vallenilla Lanz, Laureano. *Cesarismo Democrático. Estudios sobre las bases sociológicas de la Constitución efectiva de Venezuela.* 3rd ed. Caracas: Tip. Garrido, 1952.

———. *Críticas de sinceridad y exactitud.* Caracas: Ediciones Garrido, 1956.

———. *Disgregación e Integración. Ensayo sobre la formación de la nacionalidad venezolana.* Caracas: Tip. Universal, 1930.

———. *Obras Completas.* Caracas: Universidad Santa María, 1983.

———. *La Rehabilitación de Venezuela: Campañas Políticas de "El Nuevo Diario" (1915–1926).* 2 vols. Caracas: Lit. y Tip. Vargas, 1926-28.

Vallenilla Lanz, Laureano (hijo). *Escrito de Memoria*. Caracas: Ediciones Garrido, 1957.

Vallenilla Marcano, José. *Carreteras de Venezuela: La obra máxima del General Juan Vicente Gómez*. Caracas: Lit. del Comercio, 1917.

Vandellós, José A. *Ensayo de demografía venezolana*. Caracas: Lit. y Tip. de Especialidades, 1938.

Varios. *Prisiones de Venezuela a la muerte de Juan Vicente Gómez, 1935*. Caracas: Ediciones Centauro, 1974.

Varios. *Verdades para el pueblo*. Caracas: n.p., 1911.

Vasconcelos, José. *Memorias*. Vol. 1: *El Desastre*. Vol. 2: *El Proconsulado*. 2nd ed. Mexico: Fondo de Cultura Económica, 1982.

Velásquez, Luis Cordero. *El General J V Gomes en Anécdotas*. 2nd ed. Caracas: Urbina y Fuentes Editores Asociados, 1983.

Velásquez, Ramón J. *La caída del Liberalismo Amarillo: Tiempo y drama de Antonio Paredes*. Caracas: Ediciones Venezuela, 1960.

————. *Confidencias imaginarias de Juan Vicente Gómez*. 7th ed. Caracas: Ediciones Centauro, 1980.

————. *Memorias de Venezuela. Vol. IV Cipriano Castro – Juan Vicente Gómez, 1899–1935*. Caracas, Ediciones Centauro, 1991.

————. *Los Pasos de los héroes*. 2nd ed. Caracas: Ediciones Centauro, 1981.

Veloz Goiticoa, N. *Maracay. Sus actividades dehesas y sus fundos de ganado: El Lactuario*. Caracas: n.p., 1916.

————. *Venezuela*. Caracas: Tip. Central, 1919.

————. *Venezuela, 1924*. Caracas: Tip. y Lit. Garrido, 1924.

Veloz, Ramón. *Economía y finanzas de Venezuela: Desde 1830 hasta 1944*. Caracas: Impresores Unidos, 1945.

Vetencourt, Roberto. *Tiempo de Caudillos*. Caracas: Italgráfica, 1994.

Villegas, Silvio. *La Política Exterior de Juan Vicente Góme.z* Mérida: Universidad de los Andes, 1993.

Wood, Bryce. *The Making of the Good Neighbor Policy*. New York: Columbia University Press, 1961.

Yarrington, Doug. *A Coffee Frontier. Land, Society, and Politics in Duaca, Venezuela, 1830–1936*. Pittsburgh: University of Pittsburgh Press, 1997.

Ziems, Angel. *El gomecismo y la formación del ejército nacional*. Caracas: Editorial Ateneo de Caracas,1979.

Zowain, José. *Como se vivía en Maracay cuando Gómez*. Maracay: n.p., 1986.

Articles

"La grotesta alianza de los pseudo-redentores de Venezuela." *El Nuevo Diario*, Aug 7, 1923.

Abreu, José Vicente. "Gustavo Machado: Una vida al servicio del pueblo." In Pocaterra Mariátegui, Otero Silva, Araujo, García Márquez, et al., *Gustavo Machado: De Oligarca a Comunista, 1914–1971*, vol. 1, pp. 129-43. Caracas: Ediciones Centauro, 1975.

Adler, Selig. "Bryan and Wilsonian Caribbean Penetration." *Hispanic American Historical Review* 20 (May 1940): pp. 198–226.

Adriani, Alberto. "La crisis, los cambios y nosotros." *Cultura Venezolana* 14, no. 112 (May–Jun 1931): pp. 87–112.

"Al Director de 'El Tiempo' de Bogota." *El Nuevo Diario* 8, no. 2817, Nov 4, 1920.

"Alemanes é Ingleses y el Petróleo Venezolano." *BAHM* 12, no. 68 (Jan–Jun 1971): pp. 131–75.

Altuve Carrillo, Leonardo. "Prólogo." In Carlos Siso, *Castro y Gómez y la importancia de la Hegemonía Andina,* pp. 5–57. Caracas, n.p., 1985.

Añéz, Julio R., et al. "Informe de la Comisión de Comerciantes del Estado Zulia." *Boletín de la Cámara de Comercio de Caracas (BCCC)* 11, no. 110 (Jan 3, 1922): pp. 1468–75.

Apulejo, Plinio. "Machado, de aristócrata a líder rojo." In Pocaterra Mariátegui, Otero Silva, Araujo, García Márquez, et al., *Gustavo Machado: De Oligarca a Comunista, 1914–1971,* pp. 145–74. Caracas: Ediciones Centauro, 1975.

Arellano Moreno, A. "Las siete reformas constitucionales de el General Juan Vicente Gómez.," *Política* 26 (Sep 1963): pp. 31–72.

Baldwin, R. "Terror Still Reigns in Venezuela," *Nation,* Mar 4, 1931.

"Baptista Galindo, Iturbe y Delgado Chalbaud (1926–1927)." *BAHM* 18, nos. 95–97 (Jan–Jun 1977): pp. 209–19.

Barberii, Efrain. "Entrevista con Efraín Barberii." *Resumén* 8, no. 91 (Aug 3, 1975): pp. 18–22.

Benjamin, Thomas. "Rebuilding the Nation." In Michael C. Meyer and William H. Beezley, *The Oxford History of Mexico,* pp. 467–502. Oxford: Oxford University Press, 2000.

Blanco Fombona, Rufino. "Dos años y medio de Inquietud." In Angel Rama, *Rufino Blanco Fombona Intimo,* pp. 255–325. Caracas, Monte Avila Editores, 1975.

Booth, W. H. "Venezuela: Its Resources and Opportunity as Seen by an Engineer." *Cassier's Magazine,* vol. 40, no. 3 (July 1911): pp. 226–43.

Brito Figueroa, Federico. "La Contribución de Laureano Vallenilla Lanz a la Comprensión Histórica de Venezuela." *Revista Universitaria de Historia* (Caracas), no. 3 (Sep–Dec 1982): pp. 62–94.

Buchenau, Jürgen. "Calles y el Movimiento Liberal en Nicaragua." *Boletín* (México, Fideicomiso Archivos Plutarco Elías Calles y Fernando Torreblanca), No. 9, Mar 1992.

Calvani, Arístides. "La política internacional de Venezuela en el último medio siglo." In Fundación Eugenio Mendoza, *Venezuela Moderna: Medio Siglo de Historia 1926–1976,* pp. 389–488. Caracas: Fundación Eugenio Mendoza, 1976.

Carrera Damas, Germán. "Consideraciones sobre los límites históricos del liberalismo en Venezuela." *Revista Paideia* 2, no. 2 (Jan–Mar 1959): pp. 107–8; (Aug 1975): pp. 22–29.

"Como se construía una carretera (La Gran Carretera Transandina)." *BAHM* 15, no. 77 (Jan–Feb. 1974): pp. 203–53.

"Contestación del General J. V. Gómez a las Comisiones de las Cámaras Legislativas." *El Universal,* 6.7.23.

Cooney, S. "Political Demand Channels in the Processes of American and British Imperial Expansion, 1870–1913." *World Politics* 27, no. 2 (Jan 1975).

Córdoba, Diego. "Los Partidos Políticos Venezolanos en el Extranjero." *Pativilca* 1, no. 1 (Feb 1931).

Crist, Raymond E. "Land tenure problems in Venezuela." *American Journal of Economics and Sociology* 1, no. 2 (Jan 1942): pp. 143–54.

D'Amico, Santiago Bonono. "Una aproximación al desarrollo político y económico de Venezuela: Desde la Generación del 28 hasta el gobierno Demócrata Cristiano." *América Latina* 13, no. 4 (Oct–Dec 1970): pp. 18–33.

Davis, Norman H. "Wanted: A Consistent Latin American Policy." *Foreign Affairs* 9, no. 4 (July 1931): pp. 547–68.

De Carrera, Pilar Molina. "Corrido del Mocho Hernández." *Archivo Venezolano Folklórico* 8 (1967): pp. 561–66.

De Sjostrand, María E. Castellanos. "La población de Venezuela – Migraciones internas y distribución espacial 1908–1935." *Semestre Histórico* 1, no. 1 (Jan–Jun 1975): pp. 5–62.

"Del Presidente Provisional al Presidente Electo 1919–1921–1922." *BAHM* 14, no. 74 (Sep–Dec 1972): pp. 271–315.

Dennis, William Cullem. "The Orinoco Steamship Company case before The Hague Tribunal." *The American Journal of International Law* 5, no. 1 (Jan 1911): pp. 32–64.

Dozer, Donald Marquand. "Roots of revolution in Latin America." *Foreign Affairs* 27, no. 2 (Jan 1949): pp. 274–88.

Dunn, W. E. "The Post-War Attitudes of Hispanic America towards the United States." *HAHR* 3, no. 2 (May 1920): pp. 177–84.

Dupuoy, Walter. "El petróleo y las tierras agro-pecuarias." *El Farol* 10, no. 111 (Aug 1948): pp. 2–9.

———. "Petróleo y Agricultura." *El Farol* 10, no. 112 (Sep 1948): pp. 2–9.

"El ex-Presidente de Venezuela." *Diario de Cádiz,* Dec 5, 1910.

"El Mocho Awaits Call." *Evening Post* (London), May 31, 1913.

"El motín de Maracaibo." *BAHM* 4, no. 19 (Jul–Dec 1962): pp. 243–67.

"El Zulia en 1926 y en 1929." *BAHM* 17, no. 90 (Mar–Apr, 1976): pp. 53–77.

"Executive Decree of Venezuela concerning Foreign Claims, Nov 13, 1912." *Supplement to the American Journal of International Law.* Official Documents, vol. 60, 8:1 (Jan 1914): pp. 174–75.

"Falke Filibuster." *The Times,* vol. 14, no. 9, Aug 26, 1929.

Fenton. P. F. "The Diplomatic relations of the United States and Venezuela, 1880–1915." *HAHR* 8, no. 3 (Aug 1928): pp. 330–57.

"Fontiveros y Pérez Soto en Trujillo (1923–24)." *BAHM* 18, no. 92–94 (Jul–Nov 1976): pp. 143–68.

Gabaldón, José R. "Orígenes del Movimiento Revolucionario del General José Rafael Gabaldón en April de 1929." In Joaquín Gabaldón Márquez, *Memo-*

ria y Cuenta de la Generación del 28: Con un Apéndice Documental y un Epílogo, pp. 204-12. Caracas, n.p., 1958.

Giacopini-Zárraga, J. A. "Juan Vicente Gómez Militar." *Resumén* 9, no. 100 (Oct 5, 1975): pp. 44-52.

Gilbert, Morris. "Venezuela's Rocking-Chair Czar." *North American Review* (Dec 1929): pp. 705-15.

Griffin, C.C. "Welles to Roosevelt: A Memorandum on Inter-American Relations, 1933." *HAHR* vol. 34, no. 2 (May 1954): pp. 190-92.

Griffin, Charles C. "Regionalism's Role in Venezuelan Politics." *The Inter-American Quarterly* III, no. 4 (October 1941): pp. 21-35.

Hanson, S.G. "The Economics of Dictatorship: Gómez of Venezuela." *World Affairs Interpreter* 8 (1939): pp. 114-32.

Haring, Clarence H. "Revolution in South America." *Foreign Affairs* 9, no. 2 (Jan 1931): pp. 277-96.

Hart, Albert Bushnell. "The United States and Latin American Dictatorships." *Current History* 31 (Jan 1930): pp. 744-46.

Harwich, Nikita. "'Arma y Coraza': Biografía Intelectual de Laureano Vallenilla Lanz." *Revista Universitaria de Historia* (Caracas) 3 (Sep–Dec 1982): pp. 37-61.

———. "Venezuelan Positivism and Modernity." *HAHR* 70, no. 2 (May 1990): pp. 327-44.

Herrera Luque, Francisco. "Juan Vicente Gómez visto por un psiquiatra." *Resumén* 9, no. 100 (Oct 5, 1975): 52-55.

Jahn, Alfredo. "Inmigraciones y colonización en Venezuela." *Boletín del Ministerio de Fomento* (Primera Epoca), 4, no. 8 (Feb 1913): pp. 596-607.

Jones, Chester Lloyd. "Gomez of Venezuela." *World Affairs* 99 (June 1936): pp. 89-93.

———. "War and Public Finance in South America." *Journal of Political Economy* 23, no. 7 (July 1915): pp. 791-806.

"La aventura del Odin en 1922." *BAHM* 2, no. 9 (Nov–Dec 1960): pp. 165-72.

"La diplomacia en Madrid, La Haya y Londres, 1920-1922." *BAHM* 16, nos. 79-82 (May–Dec 1974): pp. 235-66.

"La Federación de Estudiantes y los Tranvías (1921)." *BAHM* 16, nos. 79-82 (May–Dec 1974): pp. 281-303.

"La Segunda Parte de la Tragedia de Venezuela." *Carabobo* (Partido Republicano de Venezuela newspaper in Puerto Rico), vol. I, no. 8, Jul 1923.

Lee, Thomas E. "The Rush for Oil in Venezuela." *The World Today,* Dec 1925, pp. 355-68.

Leggitt, F.J. "Venezuela To-day." *The Contemporary Review,* 132:744 (Dec 1927): pp. 727-35.

"León Jurado y la Segunda Invasión de Castro." *BAHM* 15, no. 76 (Jul–Dec 1973): pp. 227-65.

Liscano, Juan. "Líneas de desarrollo de la cultura venezolana en los últimos cincuenta años." In Fundación Eugenio Mendoza, *Venezuela Moderna: Medio*

Siglo de Historia, 1926–1976, pp. 588–681. Caracas, Fundación Eugenio Mendoza, 1976.

López Contreras, Eleazar. "El 17 de diciembre de 1935. Fin de un régimen y comienzo de un nuevo tiempo." *Fuerzas Armadas* 265 (Oct–Dec 1976): pp. 36–50.

"Los Apuros del Canciller Matos (1911)." *BAHM* 31, nos. 133–35 (July 1990–June 1991): pp. 111–32.

"Los Memorables de Gumersindo Torres." *BAHM* 2, no. 9 (Nov–Dec 1960): pp. 157–65.

"Los negocios de Castro, Gómez y sus ministros, 1905." *BAHM* 17, no. 89 (Jan–Feb 1976): pp. 121–34.

"Los obreros petroleros venezolanos en Curazao, 1926." *BAHM* 13, no. 70 (Jan–Feb 1972): pp. 315–18.

"Los Presidentes de Estado y los sucesos del año 28." *BAHM* 2, no. 7 (Jul–Aug 1960): pp. 123–24.

"Los proyectos revolucionarios en Europa y una polémica con Simón Barceló." *BAHM* 2, no. 10 (Jan–Feb 1961): pp. 109–35.

"Los Sucesos Estudiantiles de 1921." *BAHM* 2, no. 9 (Nov–Dec 1960): pp. 101–5.

Lot, Leo B. "Executive power in Venezuela." *American Political Science Review* 13 (Summer 1956): pp. 422–41.

Machado, Gustavo. "El Asalto a Curazao." In Venezuela, Congreso de la República, *La Oposición a la Dictadura Gomecista: Liberales y Nacionalistas*, Part 6, vol. 2 (13), Doc 87, pp. 43–143. Caracas: Ediciones Conmemorativas del Bicentenario del Natalicio del Libertador Simón Bolívar, 1983.

"Manuel Díaz Rodríguez, Presidente de Estado (1926)." *BAHM* 18, nos. 92–94 (Jul–Nov 1976): pp. 169–87.

Márquez, Pompeyo. "A fortalecer la lucha contra Gómez contribuyó el 'Asalto a Curazao' hace 20 años." In Pocaterra Mariátegui, Otero Silva, et al., *Gustavo Machado: De Oligarca a Comunista, 1914–1971*, vol. 1, pp. 83–99. Caracas: Ediciones Centauro, 1975.

Martz, John D. "Venezuela's Generation of 28: The Genesis of Political Democracy." *Journal of Inter-American Studies* 6, no. 1 (Jan 1964): pp. 17–33.

"Mensaje que Presenta el General Juan Vicente Gómez, Presidente Constitucional de los Estados Unidos de Venezuela al Congreso Nacional en sus Sesiones Ordinarias de 1924," Apr 26, 1924, in Venezuela, *El General Juan Vicente Gómez: Documentos para la historia de su Gobierno*, pp. 110–17.

Mercado, Elis S. "Antecedentes del movimiento obrero venezolano." *Semestre Histórico* 1, no. 1 (Jan–Jun 1975): pp. 115–42.

Montilla, Pablo. "El asalto a Curazao o la primera ruptura con los caudillos." In Pocaterra Mariátegui, Otero Silva, et al., *Gustavo Machado: De Oligarca a Comunista, 1914–1971*, vol. 2, pp. 47–64. Caracas: Ediciones Centauro, 1975.

Moreno, Petra Josefina. "Venezuela 1928–1935." *Semestre Histórico* 1, no. 1 (Jan–Jun 1975): pp. 189–246.

Murillo, Horacio. "El Machado bueno." In Pocaterra Mariátegui, Otero Silva, et al., *Gustavo Machado: De Oligarca a Comunista, 1914–1971*, vol. 1, pp. 183–205.

Núñez, Angel María. "Los secretarios de Gómez." *Boletín del Centro de Historia Larense* (Barquisimeto), L-LI (Apr–Sep 1968): pp. 13–29.

Otero Silva, Miguel. "Apuntes sobre el asalto a Curazao." In Pocaterra Mariátegui, Otero Silva, et al., *Gustavo Machado: De Oligarca a Comunista, 1914–1971*, vol. 1, pp. 19–25. Caracas: Ediciones Centauro, 1975.

"Our Relations with South America." *The Nation* 88, no. 2277 (Feb 18, 1909): p. 157.

Páez, Gabriel José. "La última invasión del General Peñaloza." *Resumén* 9, no. 100 (Oct 5, 1975): pp. 56–60.

Párraga, Ramón. "Memorias." *BAHM* No. 3, pp. 84–94.

"Pérez Soto en Apure y en Bolívar (1919–1921)." *BAHM* 14, no. 74 (Sep–Dec 1972): pp. 191–46.

"Perez Soto Is Seen as Gomez Successor." *New York Times,* Aug 11, 1930.

"Pérez Soto y las Compañías petroleras, 1926." *BAHM* 13, no. 70 (Jan–Feb 1972): pp. 319–46.

Pierson, W. "Foreign influences on Venezuelan political thought, 1830–1930." *HAHR* 15, no. 1 (Feb 1935): pp. 3–43.

Platt, D.C.M. "British Diplomacy in Latin America Since the Emancipation." *Journal of Inter-American Affairs* 21, no. 3 (Winter 1967): pp. 21–43.

"Preocupaciones Nacionales de 1914." *BAHM* 5, nos. 28–29 (Jan–Apr 1964): pp. 307–47.

"Proyectos e Intrigas petroleras (1926)." *BAHM* 13, no. 70 (Jan–Feb 1972): pp. 353–65.

Quintero, Rodolfo. "Las bases económicas y sociales de una aristocracia obrera en Venezuela." *Economía y Ciencias Sociales* 5, no. 2 (Apr–Jun 1963): pp. 90–100.

Rangel Lamus, Amenodoro. "Eustoquio Gómez." In Anselmo Amado, comp., *Gente de Táchira (1900–1935),* vol. 2, pp. 447–55. Caracas: BATT No. 61, 1974.

"Reckless Propaganda." *Venezuelan Monthly Newsletter* (New York), Dec 15, 1925.

Rios, Pompeyo. "Desarrollo económico de Venezuela desde 1830 hasta 1920." *Revista de la Facultad de Agronomía* (Maracay), 3, no. 3 (Nov 1964): pp. 16–41.

Rippy, F. "British Investments in Latin America at Their Peak." *HAHR* 34, no. 1 (Feb 1954): pp. 94–103.

Rojas, Dámaso. "Las "Memorias" de Gustavo Machado." In Pocaterra Mariátegui, Otero Silva, et al., *Gustavo Machado: De Oligarca a Comunista, 1914–1971,* vol. 1, pp. 207–24. Caracas: Ediciones Centauro, 1975.

Saher, Alvarado. "La Hora trece o la vuelta a la patria de Gustavo Machado." In Pocaterra Mariátegui, Otero Silva, et al., *Gustavo Machado: De Oligarca a Comunista, 1914–1971,* vol. 1, pp. 225–38. Caracas: Ediciones Centauro, 1975.

Salcedo Bastardo, J.L. "Las autocracias venezolanas, 1830–1935." *Boletín Histórico* 8, no. 20 (Jan 1970): pp. 73–89.

Salisbury, Richard V. "Mexico, the United States, and the 1926–1927 Nicaraguan Crisis." *HAHR* 66, no. 2 (May 1986): pp. 319–39.

"Santos Matute Gómez y los obreros petroleros (1923)." *BAHM* 19, nos. 98–100 (Jul–Dec 1977): pp. 3–5.

Schuler, Friedrich E. "Mexico and the Outside World." In Michael C. Meyer and William H. Beezley, *The Oxford History of Mexico*, pp. 503–41. Oxford: Oxford University Press, 2000.

Silva, Carlos Rafael. "Bosquejo histórico del desenvolvimiento de la economía venezolana en el siglo XX." In Fundación Eugenio Mendoza, *Venezuela Moderna: Medio Siglo de Historia, 1926–1976*, pp. 491–587. Caracas, Fundación Eugenio Mendoza, 1976.

Sosa de León, Mireya. "La Ruptura de Relaciones Diplomáticas entre México y Venezuela: algo más que una cuestión teatral." *Tierra Firme* (Caracas, Venezuela), 1996. http://www.ecs.human.ucv.ve/docs/Jornadas/textos/Exiliados%20graterol-laboren.doc.

Stoddard, Lothorp. "Gomez Is Venezuela." *World's Work* 59 (Dec 1930): pp. 561–65.

Sullivan, William M. "Situación económica y política durante el período de Juan Vicente Gómez, 1908–1935." Fundación John Boulton, *Política y Economía de Venezuela, 1810–1976*, pp. 247–72. Caracas: Fundación John Boulton, 1976.

Trujillo, Alejandro E. "Un juicio sobre Gómez." *Revista Nacional de Cultura* 14, no. 95 (Nov–Dec 1952): pp. 154–61.

"Un Polémico Editorial de 'Libertad.'" In José Rafael Pocaterra, *Archivo de José Rafael Pocaterra: La Oposición a Gómez (1922–1935)*, vol. 1, pp. 329–36. Caracas: Banco Industrial de Venezuela, 1973.

"Una interview con Matos." In Venezuela, *Conjuracíon contra la vida del General Juan Vicente Gómez, Presidente de Venezuela y sus consecuencias*, pp. 417–20. Caracas: Imprenta Nacional, 1909.

Uslar Pietri, Arturo. Telex, Paris. Jun 17, 1977. *Resumen* 15, no. 190, Jun 26, 1977.

Vandenbosch, Amry. "Dutch Problems in the West Indies." *Foreign Affairs* 9, no. 2 (Jan 1931): pp. 350–52.

Velásquez, Ramón J. "Aspectos de la evolución política de Venezuela en su último medio siglo." In Fundación Eugenio Mendoza, *Venezuela Moderna: Medio Siglo de Historia, 1926–1976*, pp. 3–385. Caracas, Fundación Eugenio Mendoza, 1976.

———. "Los proyectos y los contratos de 1911. Gómez y Delgado Chalbaud." *Resumén* 9, no. 100 (Oct 5, 1975): pp. 65–79.

Veloz, Ramón. "El comercio exterior de Venezuela durante la primera y segunda guerra mundial." *BCCC* 31 (Sep 1942): pp. 8559–67.

"Venezuela en la Liga de las Naciones (1925)." *BAHM* 13, no. 70 (Jan–Feb 1972): pp. 207–39.

Yanqui. "La región zuliana y la cordillera." *BCCC* 12, no. 114 (May 1, 1923): pp. 1952–54.

Yarrington, Doug. "Cattle, Corruption, and State Formation in Venezuela during the Regime of Juan Vicente Gómez, 1908–35." *Latin American Research Review* 38, no. 2 (Jun 2003): pp. 11–33.

———. "The Vestey Cattle Enterprise and the Regime of Juan Vicente Gómez, 1908–1935." *Journal of Latin American Studies* 35, no. 1 (Feb 2003): pp. 89–115.

Zúñiga Cisneros, Miguel. "Los Estudiantes del 21." In R. Luzardo, *Notas Históricas Económicas 1928–1963*, Appendix B. Caracas: Editorial Sucre, 1963.

BRIAN S. MCBETH

is a Senior Common Room Member of St. Antony's College, Oxford.
He is the author of a number of books, including *Gunboats, Corruption,
and Claims: Foreign Intervention in Venezuela, 1899–1908.*